A PRACTICAL APPROACH

FAMILY LAW

EIGHTH EDITION

Jill Black DBE

Jane Bridge

Tina Bond

Liam Gribbin

OXFORD
UNIVERSITY PRESS

OXFORD
UNIVERSITY PRESS

Great Clarendon Street, Oxford OX2 6DP

Oxford University Press is a department of the University of Oxford.
It furthers the University's objective of excellence in research, scholarship,
and education by publishing worldwide in

Oxford New York

Auckland Cape Town Dar es Salaam Hong Kong Karachi
Kuala Lumpur Madrid Melbourne Mexico City Nairobi
New Delhi Shanghai Taipei Toronto

With offices in

Argentina Austria Brazil Chile Czech Republic France Greece
Guatemala Hungary Italy Japan Poland Portugal Singapore
South Korea Switzerland Thailand Turkey Ukraine Vietnam

Oxford is a registered trade mark of Oxford University Press
in the UK and in certain other countries

Published in the United States
by Oxford University Press Inc., New York

First Published Blackstone Press 1986; Eighth Edition 2007

British Library Cataloguing in Publication Data

Data available

Library of Congress Cataloging in Publication Data

Data available

Typeset by RefineCatch Limited, Bungay, Suffolk
Printed in Great Britain by Ashford Colour Press Limited,
Gosport, Hampshire

ISBN 978-0-19-921276-7

1 3 5 7 9 10 8 6 4 2

PREFACE

This eighth edition has been a shared effort between Jane Bridge, Tina Bond, and Liam Gribbin.

This edition includes new chapters on Your Practice, the Civil Partnership Act 2004, and the Gender Recognition Act 2004; both of which came into force in 2005.

In particular, we anticipate that practitioners will be involved in advising on the consequences of breakdown of civil partnership as time progresses and so, in addition to the specific chapter on this area, reference has been made to civil partnership in various chapters, for example, those dealing with financial provision and protection from domestic abuse.

Consideration is given to the significant case law developments in ancillary relief proceedings, with detailed discussion of *Miller* v *Miller, McFarlane* v *McFarlane* [2006] (see Chapter 19).

The book includes fully up-to-date information on the child support calculation.

The chapters relating to the public and private law in respect of children have been thoroughly revised with a detailed explanation of the new procedure introduced by the Family Proceedings (Amendment) Rules 2004, designed to identify those cases involving domestic abuse at an earlier stage in the court process.

In view of the increased use over the last few years of alternative dispute resolution as a method of resolving family issues, we have included a chapter on mediation in this edition (see Chapter 3). The chapter draws attention to and quotes from the Second Edition of the Family Law Protocol issued by the Law Society in March 2006 which places great emphasis on encouraging a constructive and conciliatory approach to resolving family disputes. It also gives an outline of the process of mediation and the way in which solicitors can best support their clients through the process. We are most grateful to the Law Society for their permission to refer extensively to the Protocol at appropriate points in the book. The Family Law Protocol includes and supplements the Pre-action Protocol for ancillary relief proceedings with which practitioners are already familiar.

We anticipate that, before the next edition, progress will have been made in reforming the law on opposite sex and same sex cohabitation and the present views of the Law Commission are set out, in summary, in Chapter 40.

We are, as ever, grateful to those who live with us and share the ups and downs of preparing a new edition for their support and patience. In addition, Tina would like to acknowledge the enormous help of Dr Edna Smith in deciphering Tina's handwriting and making sense of countless pages of material.

We also acknowledge with gratitude the help and support of Oxford University Press throughout the process of producing this book and liaising between authors who live at opposite ends of the country.

The various documents relating to the Community Legal Service scheme for public funding have been reproduced with the kind permission of the Legal Services Commission. Crown copyright is acknowledged in relation to the use of Divorce Form 6, Forms M4, D97, D104,

D109, FL 401, FL 402, FL 403, FL 404, FL 406, FL 407, FL 408, FL 415, FL 416, Form A, and Form E.

We have endeavoured to state the law as at 31 August 2006, although some chapters reflect changes to public funding, tax and benefit rates effective from April 2007.

Jane Bridge
Tina Bond
Liam Gribbin

CONTENTS SUMMARY

CONTENTS

PART I GENERAL MATTERS

1 THE FIRST INTERVIEW

2 COMMUNITY LEGAL SERVICE AND PUBLIC FUNDING FOR FAMILY PROCEEDINGS

3 MEDIATION AND COLLABORATIVE LAW

PART IV TAXATION

PART V ORDERS UNDER PART IV OF THE FAMILY LAW ACT 1996

PART VI GENERAL MATTERS CONCERNING THE HOME AND OTHER PROPERTY

26 THE HOME: PREVENTING A SALE OR MORTGAGE

27 KEEPING UP WITH THE MORTGAGE OR RENT

28 THE QUESTION OF WILLS

PART VII CHILDREN

29 THE CHILDREN ACT 1989: GENERAL PRINCIPLES, PARENTAL RESPONSIBILITY ORDERS IN FAMILY PROCEEDINGS, SECTION 8 ORDERS, GUARDIANSHIP ORDERS AND FAMILY PROCEEDINGS, FINANCIAL PROVISION AND PROPERTY ADJUSTMENT FOR CHILDREN

30 PROCEDURE FOR ORDERS UNDER THE CHILDREN ACT 1989

31 WARDSHIP AND THE INHERENT JURISDICTION

PART VIII FINANCIAL PROVISION AND PROPERTY DURING MARRIAGE

TABLE OF CASES

Note: Practice Directions are in chronological order

TABLE OF STATUTES

TABLE OF STATUTORY INSTRUMENTS

LIST OF ABBREVIATIONS

ACA 2002	Adoption and Children Act 2002
ADR	Alternative Dispute Resolution
AJA 1999	Access to Justice Act 1999
Allocation Order 1991	Children (Allocation of Proceedings) Order 1991
AVC	Additional voluntary contributions
CA 1989	Children Act 1989
CAA 1984	Child Abduction Act 1984
CAFCASS	Children and Family Court Advisory and Support Service
CASC	Children Act Sub-Committee
CCA 1980	Child Care Act 1980
CCP	Care Centre Plan
CCR	County Court Rules
CGT	Capital Gains Tax
CICA	Criminal Injuries Compensation Authority
CMC	Case Management Conference
CO	Care Order
CPA 2004	Civil Partnership Act 2004
CSA 1991	Child Support Act 1991
CSPASSA 2000	Child Support Pensions and Social Security Act 2000
CTC	Child Tax Credit
CTTA 1984	Capital Transfer Tax Act 1984
CYPA 1969	Children and Young Persons Act 1969
DPMCA 1978	Domestic Proceedings and Magistrates' Court Act 1978
DVMPA 1976	Domestic Violence and Matrimonial Proceedings Act 1976
DWP	Department for Work and Pensions
ECB	Economic Crime Branch (of NCIS)
EPO	Emergency Protection Order
FA 1988	Finance Act 1988
FDR	Financial Dispute Resolution
FLA 1986	Family Law Act 1986
FLA 1996	Family Law Act 1996
FLRA 1987	Family Law Reform Act 1987
FP(AJ)D 1999	Family Proceedings (Allocation to Judiciary) Directions 1999
FPC	Family Proceedings Court (FPCP=FPC Plan)
FPC(CA 1989)R 1991	Family Proceedings Courts (Children Act 1989) Rules 1991
FPC(MP etc.)R 1991	Family Proceedings Courts (Matrimonial Proceedings etc.) Rules 1991
FPR 1991	Family Proceeding Rules 1991
GMA 1971	Guardianship of Minors Act 1971
GRA 2004	Gender Recognition Act 2004
GRR	Gender Recognition Register

HFEA 1990	Human Fertilisation and Embryology Act 1990
HRA 1998	Human Rights Act 1998
IA 1975	Inheritance (Provision for Family and Dependants Act 1975
ICO	Interim Care Order
ICTA	Income and Corporation Taxes Act 1988
IHTA 1984	Inheritance Tax Act 1984
LA	Local Authority
LPA 1925	Law of Property Act 1925
MCA 1973	Matrimonial Causes Act 1973
MEA 1991	Maintenance Enforcement Act 1991
MHA 1983	Matrimonial Homes Act 1983
MLRO	Money laundering reporting officers
MWPA 1882	Married Women's Property Act 1882
NACCC	Network of Access and Child Contact Centres
NCIS	National Criminal Intelligence Service
PCA 2002	Proceeds of Crime Act 2002
PHR	Pre Hearing Review
RCJ	Royal Courts of Justice
RSC	Rules of the Supreme Court
SDF	Standard Directions Form
TCGA 1992	Taxation of Chargeable Gains Act 1992
UKCFM	United Kingdom College of Family Mediators
WTC	Working Tax Credit

PART I

GENERAL MATTERS

1

THE FIRST INTERVIEW

A PRELIMINARY POINTS

Family law practice is becoming increasingly complex, not only because of the sophisticated **1.01** requirements of clients, but because of the need to comply throughout with protocols and detailed rules of procedure. This chapter deals with the steps to be taken on first receiving instructions from a client in a family law case. Traditionally, a 'family law case' concerned the position of parties to a marriage only. More recently, it has encompassed parties who are cohabiting (whether in a heterosexual or same sex relationship) and, from 5 December 2005, it has been extended to cover civil partners whose relationship has been registered under the Civil Partnership Act 2004 ('CPA 2004'). The provisions of this Act are discussed in detail in

Chapter 14. As well as giving guidance on the information to be obtained from the client, the contents of the client care letter will be considered. Particular attention will also be paid to other tasks to be completed, for example, the registration of home rights where the client is a non-owning spouse or civil partner.

1.02 All practitioners need to be aware of the new edition of the Family Law Protocol published by the Law Society in 2006. This offers invaluable guidance because it contains details of relevant procedure needed to deal with commonly encountered family law problems together with good practical advice to avoid pitfalls. It also reproduces a range of specific guidance (for example Practice Directions, Practice Notes and Best Practice Guides) as Appendices and contains a helpful list of contacts and addresses including Relate and the UK College of Family Mediators.

1.03 Copies of the Protocol are available from Marston Book Services, tel 01235 465656 or fax 01235 465660 or e-mail law.society@marston.co.uk. Reference is made to the Protocol throughout this book and some of its guidance is quoted at length.

1.04 In considering these preliminary points it is important to recognize that the client may be a spouse, a heterosexual or same sex cohabitant, or civil partner following the coming into force of the CPA 2004 on 5 December 2005.

B   GENERAL POINTS

1.05 The first interview with any client is extremely important. Family cases are no exception. It is important to recognize that, as far as the interviewee or prospective client is concerned, the first interview may have two distinct purposes:

(a)   as a fact-finding exercise to obtain information from the solicitor as to the steps open to the interviewee to resolve the family problems he or she is experiencing. In addition, the interviewee will be assessing whether he or she feels comfortable with the solicitor and would have confidence in the solicitor if instructed to act on the interviewee's behalf;

or

(b)   to give formal instructions to act on the interviewee's behalf. This assumes that the interviewee already has a clear idea of the outcome he or she is seeking.

In any event, prior to the first interview, it is important to obtain sufficient information from the interviewee to check that there is no conflict of interest with an existing client.

1.06 In this regard, it is important to note that Chapters 15 and 16 of The Guide to the Professional Conduct of Solicitors 1999 have been withdrawn. The chapters are to be replaced with updated guidance yet to be brought into force. In the meantime, The Solicitors' Practice (Conflict) Amendment Rules 2004 came into force on 25 April 2006. Explanatory Notes to supplement the Rules are available on the Law Society's website at <www.lawsociety.org.uk/professional/conduct/guideonline.law>.

It is also necessary to give details in writing to the interviewee of the name and status of the **1.07** person who is to conduct the interview. Information should be given as to whether the interview is free or available at a fixed cost or that the cost of the interview is at a reduced cost of £X per hour pro rata. The interviewee should also be given details of who to contact if the interviewee has a complaint.

Interviewees should sign and date the document and both the interviewee and the solicitor **1.08** should keep a copy of the signed document.

After the interview, the solicitor should keep a note of the interview with the signed **1.09** document. This should be filed and kept for record purposes.

How should the solicitor approach the first interview?

The first interview provides the opportunity for the solicitor to gain the interviewee's **1.10** confidence and to equip himself with much information which he will need if he is to act for the interviewee in the future.

For example, the interviewee may have separated from her husband and not be receiving **1.11** maintenance. It is for the solicitor to ascertain the interviewee's views, not only on her immediate problem, but also on related matters so that he may advise her properly. Where the interviewee has a maintenance problem, for instance, there are a number of different ways in which she might secure a maintenance order against her husband, one involving the issue of a divorce petition. In order to decide on the appropriate course of action, the solicitor needs to know whether the interviewee envisages getting divorced and whether there is any basis on which she can file a petition.

It is important to recognize that the interviewee may be undecided about what she wants for **1.12** the future and, in most cases, there is no harm in putting the options to her, explaining the implications of those options and suggesting that she go away and think things over for a few days, arranging another interview for the following week.

Often the interviewee will be in a very distressed state at the first interview and care should **1.13** be taken not to pressure her into a particular course of action. It must be remembered that when a marriage gets into difficulties, divorce is not the only option!

C MATTERS TO BE COVERED WHEN TAKING INSTRUCTIONS

The basics

The guidance set out below assumes that the interviewee has decided to instruct you and will **1.14** now be referred to as the client.

At the outset, the solicitor must comply with the requirements of the Money Laundering **1.15** Regulations 2003 by asking the client to produce two forms of appropriate identification, one at least of which must confirm the client's home address. The client's passport and utility bills for the home address will usually suffice for these purposes.

Name, address, and telephone number

1.16   The client's full name and address must, of course, always be noted, as should her telephone number at home and at work so that she can be contacted urgently if necessary. It may also be necessary to note an address to which letters to a client may be sent, without the risk of the other party becoming aware of the contents.

1.17   Every firm has its own system for noting routine information of this sort, often on the file itself, on a printed label attached to it or on a computerised system. The client should be reminded to keep her solicitor up to date with any changes of address. If her address does change, the new address should be noted and the old address deleted from the file so that there is no danger of letters and documents being sent to the wrong address.

1.18   If the case is one where the client's address is to be kept secret from her spouse, cohabitant, or civil partner (for example, because it is feared that otherwise there will be violence), this should be noted clearly on the file with the address so that no member of the solicitor's firm inadvertently discloses the address.

1.19   Clear instructions should be taken from the client as to leaving messages on an answerphone. Detailed messages may be accessed by the other party to the marriage, putting the client at considerable risk—the same may apply to the use of e-mail.

The Community Legal Service scheme—Legal Help

1.20   The solicitor should find out whether the client is eligible for Legal Help. Before the client decides to accept Legal Help, the solicitor should clearly explain the Legal Service Commission's statutory charge (see Chapter 2). If the client decides to accept such advice, she must sign a form called Controlled Work 1.

1.21   The full details of the Community Legal Service scheme and the means of assessment are set out in Chapter 2. Note that there is an obligation on the solicitor to advise his client as to her eligibility for public funding generally whether or not his firm undertakes this work.

1.22   Where a client is financially eligible for public funding and certain types of work are contemplated, it may be necessary first to refer the client to mediation to determine whether the issue may be resolved by that process.

The Community Legal Service scheme: funding as the case progresses

1.23   The Legal Help scheme does not cover taking any steps in court proceedings (although, of course, it does cover the cost of the solicitor dealing with an undefended divorce case; see Chapter 2). It is therefore usually necessary at some stage to consider applying for a certificate for General Family Help or Legal Representation, depending on the circumstances.

1.24   Although the solicitor may be able to deal with the case initially on the basis of the Legal Help scheme, he should nevertheless consider at the outset whether a certificate is likely to become necessary later on. He should bear in mind that a certificate, in particular, can take some weeks to come through. This means that in an urgent case he may need to seek an emergency certificate. Full details of certificates for General Family Help, Legal Representation and Emergency Certificates are given in Chapter 2, paragraphs 2.21, 2.55, and 2.62 onwards.

Letter to client summarizing first interview

Once formal instructions are received, the solicitor should write two letters to the client: the **1.25** retainer letter and the client care letter. A common complaint made by clients against solicitors is that the solicitor fails to provide the client with relevant information at the appropriate stage in the conduct of the case. To address this, the solicitor is required to write a 'client care' letter once instructions have been received. The Guide to the Professional Conduct of Solicitors 1999 contains the revised Rule 15 of the Solicitors' Practice Rules 1990 and the Solicitors' Costs Information and Client Care Code 1999. The retainer letter and the client care letter may be incorporated into one letter or issued separately. If incorporated into one letter the following matters should be dealt with:

A. Contents of the retainer

(a) A summary of matters discussed.
(b) A summary of options considered.
(c) Confirmation of any specific instructions received from the client.
(d) Specific advice given to the client including a clear indication of how long the proposed steps will take. Be pessimistic as opposed to optimistic and risking unrealistic expectations on the part of the client.
(e) Clearly indicate what you will not be dealing with. For example, if tax is not your area of expertise, let the client know that you will not be dealing with any tax issues in the work you are undertaking but give help as to where reliable advice might be obtained. Where, for instance, an accountant has already been instructed by the client, it is sensible to have a copy of the accountant's retainer letter to ensure that all aspects of the client's case are being dealt with.
(f) You must warn the client of your duties under the Proceeds of Crime Act 2002 ('PCA 2002') and the Money Laundering Regulations 2003 and your duties of disclosure of your client's affairs or those of the other party (see paragraph 1.35 and onwards).
(g) Conclusion to the retainer. It is sensible, in this part of the letter, to summarize the matters discussed at the first interview, the advice given, the steps to be taken by you, together with the action to be taken by the client. For example, it may be necessary for the client to compile relevant documents (especially in relation to financial matters or to obtain details of the value of his or her pension from the employer or pension provider). Where appropriate, it should be emphasized that steps cannot be taken without further instructions or information from the client.

B. Client care matters

(a) Costs: In particular, unless there are good reasons for doing otherwise, the client must be informed about the likely overall cost, including a breakdown of fees, VAT, and disbursements. The hourly charging rate must be clearly stated. The client must be informed of the time likely to be spent in dealing with a matter, if time is a factor in the calculation of the fees.

Where it is not practicable to give a realistic estimate of the overall costs, an explanation of **1.26** why this is the case should be given to the client together with the best information possible as to the likely costs. This is especially relevant to a client involved in ancillary relief proceedings where it is generally impossible to predict at the outset whether the matter may be settled or dealt with only by a full court hearing at a later stage.

1.27   Of increasing importance is the requirement to discuss with the client at the outset whether the likely outcome will justify the expense or risk involved, including, if relevant, the risk of having to bear an opponent's costs. Costs must be proportionate to the value of the claim (*Piglowska* v *Piglowski* [1999] 1 WLR 1360).

1.28   Sources of funding should be considered including public funding and other sources, such as insurance schemes, or through a trade union or employer arrangement.

1.29   Rule 15, as amended, and referred to above, requires that specific additional information be given to the publicly funded and privately funded paying client, respectively.

1.30   In the case of the publicly funded client, the client must be informed of the statutory charge (see Chapter 2) and its likely amount, the obligation to pay any contribution assessed and the consequences of failing to do so.

1.31   Although the general principle is now that each party is to be responsible for his or her own costs with limited opportunities to recover costs from the other party (the significance of this is discussed more fully in Chapter 18), costs may nevertheless be awarded against one party and in favour of the other in cases of litigation misconduct. The client needs to understand, however, that such costs may in reality never be recovered from the payer.

1.32   In the case of the privately funded client, the solicitor should explain the client's potential liability for his or her own costs and those of the other party, including:

(i)   the fact that the client will be responsible for paying the solicitor's bill in full regardless of any order for costs made against an opponent;

(ii)   the fact that, if the opponent is publicly funded, the client may not recover costs, even if successful in demonstrating litigation misconduct.

The information on costs should be as complete and comprehensive as possible. It should be written in a language which the particular client is likely to understand, avoiding jargon and explaining terms such as 'disbursements'. Costs information should be updated at regular intervals and the client kept fully informed.

(b)   Who is dealing with the case? The name and status of the person dealing with the matter and the name of the principal responsible for the overall supervision of the case should be given to the client.

1.33   The need to indicate clearly the status of the person within the solicitor's firm who is to have the conduct of the case was highlighted by the Court of Appeal decision in *Pilbrow* v *Pearless de Rougement* [1999] 2 FLR 139. Here the court held that there was total non-performance of the contract, thus relieving the client of the obligation to pay the bill of costs, where the client had asked to see a solicitor to discuss some personal problems and after the conclusion of the case learnt that the person who had carried out the work on his behalf was not a solicitor.

(c)   Complaints handling: Part 7 of the Code requires firms to ensure that the client is told the name of the person to whom problems may be directed and to have in place a written complaints policy. A copy of the policy should be made available to the client on request.

(d) Other information: Other terms of business, for example, storage of documents and termination of instructions, should also be set out in the initial correspondence to the client.

The Law Society recommends that a copy of the terms of business should be signed and returned by the client to demonstrate acceptance of the terms. **1.34**

Money laundering

Introduction

The PCA 2002 has been the source of considerable uncertainty since it came into force in 2003. Fortunately, the Court of Appeal decision in *Bowman v Fells* [2005] EWCA Civ 226 sought to clarify many of these difficulties. **1.35**

The Act and the accompanying Regulations are complex and are largely beyond the scope of this book. What follows is intended to be a basic guide to those parts of PCA 2002 and the Regulations which are most likely to affect a lawyer working in family law. **1.36**

Becoming involved in 'an arrangement'—s. 328 PCA 2002

Bowman confirms that the criminal offence of 'becoming involved in an arrangement' involving money laundering under s. 328, PCA 2002 does not apply to the conducting of litigation in general or to the settling of a dispute in a litigious context. Legal advisers involved in such work therefore no longer need to make an 'authorized disclosure' under PCA 2002 to the National Criminal Intelligence Service (NCIS). **1.37**

The decision did not, however, consider 'transactional work' involving work outside a litigious setting such as conveyancing. Section 328 continues to apply to such work although, following *Bowman*, it is now clear that common law legal professional privilege has not been overridden by PCA 2002, as had previously been thought. Useful and detailed guidance provided by the Law Society in relation to transactional work and s. 328 in the light of *Bowman* can be found at: www. lawsociety.org.uk/documents/downloads-BowmanvFelsGuidance0905.pdf>. **1.38**

The duty to disclose in the 'regulated sector'—s. 330, PCA 2002

Section 330, PCA 2002 continues to apply to those working in the 'regulated sector' and makes it a criminal offence to fail to disclose where the 'professional legal adviser' has knowledge or a suspicion of money laundering or reasonable grounds for suspicion. The 'regulated sector' is defined in para. 2(2) of the Money Laundering Regulations (SI 2003/3075) and the generally accepted view is that divorce solicitors and legal executives do fall within this category. **1.39**

Section 330(6) provides a defence to a failure to disclose where the information came to the professional legal adviser in 'privileged circumstances'. It is improtant to note, however, that this exemption does not apply where the 'intention' behind the communication of the information is to 'further a criminal purpose' (s. 330(11)). The 'purpose' can be that of either the client or a third party. This can place the legal adviser in a difficult position in knowing **1.40** whether to protect the client's confidentiality and legal professional privilege or risk prosecution if the s. 330(6) is not available. A recent amendment to s. 330, PCA 2002 confirms that a legal adviser can speak openly with the firm's nominated money laundering officer without affecting the client's right to confidentiality. The Law Society guidance, referred to above, again provides a useful step-by-step guide in these circumstances. Guidance is also provided by the Law Society's Professional Ethics money laundering helpline (0870 606 2577).

Further general information

1.41 Having considered the Professional Conduct Matters above, the solicitor may find it helpful to use a checklist during the interview to ensure that all relevant matters are covered. The checklist below is merely a suggestion. No doubt the solicitor will need to add other matters which he regularly wishes to cover with clients.

Checklist: General information required from matrimonial clients

---

1. Name
2. Date of birth
3. National Insurance number
4. Current address (including e-mail address, if appropriate)
5. Correspondence address (if necessary)
6. Telephone   Home
7. Fax number   Work
8. Occupation
9. Eligible for public funding?
10. The Legal Services Commission's statutory charge explained?
11. Public funding applied for?
12. Arrangements made for referral to mediation? Role of mediation explained—willingness to participate in mediation?
13. Status; if married, date of marriage. If civil partnership, date of registration
14. Name, address, occupation, and date of birth of spouse/cohabitant/civil partner
15. Spouse/cohabitant or civil partner's solicitors, if any
16. Children (names, dates of birth, and status)
17. With whom do children live?
18. Previous proceedings   Nature
                                                                      Outcome
                                                                      Solicitors who acted
                                                                      Solicitors who acted for other
                                                                      spouse/cohabitant/civil partner
19. Nature of problem
20. Wants divorce/dissolution of civil partnership
21. Reconciliation discussed?
22. Any agreement with spouse/cohabitant/civil partner?
23. Conciliation service involved?
24. Schedule of basic financial details of client and spouse/cohabitant/civil partner
25. Advice given on need for a will or to change the terms of an existing will?

Reconciliation

The solicitor should always find out from the client whether there is any prospect of a **1.42** reconciliation. He should be alive to the possibility that the purpose of the visit to the solicitor may not actually be the stated purpose, for example, to obtain a divorce or dissolution of a civil partnership. The real claim may be, for instance, to encourage the other party to mend his or her ways by forcing upon him the realisation of what will happen if he or she does not.

The solicitor is not expected to offer practical assistance in bringing about a reconciliation, **1.43** nor is he qualified to do so. However, there are numerous agencies that do offer such assistance and the solicitor should be in a position to advise on some of the agencies available and how to contact them should the client be interested in pursuing the possibility of a reconciliation. The largest national organisation offering help with marital problems is:

> Relate
> National Marriage Guidance
> Herbert Gray College
> Little Church Street
> Rugby
> Warwickshire CV21 3AP
> Telephone 01788 573241
>
> <www.relate.org.uk>

Relate has local counselling centres, the addresses and telephone numbers of which appear in the telephone book. They do not only deal with reconciliation; they are also prepared to help people who are in the process of getting divorced come to terms with the divorce and make decisions about the future.

There are various religious organisations offering counselling, for example, the Jewish **1.44** Marriage Council and the Catholic Marriage Advisory Council. The local Citizens' Advice Bureau should have a file listing other organisations offering help and support, particularly those with branches in the area.

Conciliation

Reconciliation is concerned with helping the parties to overcome their difficulties and make **1.45** a fresh start together.

Conciliation, however, becomes important once it is accepted that the marriage or civil **1.46** partnership has finally broken down. The more bitter and protracted the aftermath of a broken marriage or civil partnership the more difficult it is likely to be for the spouses or civil partners and the children to put the relationship behind them and start to build a new life. Conciliation aims to make the breakdown of a marriage or civil partnership as painless as possible by assisting the parties to reach agreement over matters such as the family home and other property, finances, residence orders and contact orders, thus reducing the areas of conflict to a minimum.

1.47   The solicitor has a distinct role to play in conciliation. His own attitude to the case will, to some extent, condition that of his client. If he treats the case as a personal vendetta against the other spouse, cohabitant, or civil partner or his solicitor, this will encourage his own client to dig in her heels and refuse to negotiate or to reach agreement over contested matters unless her precise demands are met. On the other hand, if the solicitor remains objective about the matter, he can encourage his client to give careful consideration to any proposals made by the other spouse, cohabitant, or civil partner and it is much more likely that agreement will be reached.

1.48   In addition to the solicitor's own role in conciliation, there is an increasing number of local conciliation services being established to offer mediation and counselling. The exact nature of the facilities offered varies from service to service. The solicitor should be able to find out the addresses and telephone numbers of any services operating in his area through the local divorce court. If he feels that a conciliation service may be able to help he should encourage the client to contact them as soon as possible before 'battle lines' are drawn up.

1.49   As well as the independent conciliation services, many courts offer conciliation appointments as part of ancillary relief and/or Children Act 1989 ('CA 1989') proceedings at which the Children and Family Court Advisory and Support Service ('CAFCASS') officer will often be in attendance to assist.

Mediation services

1.50   Mediation is a refinement of the conciliation process. It is a form of alternative dispute resolution. There are a number of independent mediation services available. Both National Family Mediation and the Family Mediators Association have established centres nationwide and they operate under a common Code of Practice. These services provide a private and informal venue for separating couples to discuss issues relating to their children, property and the divorce itself in the presence of a trained mediator or mediators.

1.51   Increasing use is now being made of the mediation process and therefore it is important for the solicitor to understand how the process works and to be prepared to support it and recommend it where appropriate. In many instances it will now be necessary to refer a client to mediation and to establish the outcome of that process before a solicitor may make an application for public funding on his client's behalf. The detailed provisions relating to mediation and public funding are discussed in Chapter 2. How mediation works in practice is explained in Chapter 3.

Taking action on the client's behalf

Possible courses of action

1.52   The matters covered in the checklist on page 10 are fairly general. This general information should enable the solicitor to decide what course of action might be appropriate. The table below is designed as a reminder of the principal remedies available for most of the problems commonly encountered in family work.

Principal remedies available	
Client's problem	Remedies to be considered
Wants divorce	Divorce proceedings (though bear in mind that very occasionally, nullity proceedings may be more appropriate)
Wants dissolution of civil partnership	Dissolution order under CPA 2004 (see Chapter 14)
Maintenance problems—self (married client or civil partner)	Welfare benefits Maintenance pending suit and periodical payments under Magistrates' Courts Act 1973 ('MCA 1973') if intending to seek divorce/nullity If not intending to seek divorce/nullity, consider judicial separation (same ancillary relief as divorce) *or* application to family proceedings court (formerly magistrates' court) under ss. 2, 6 and 7, Domestic Proceedings and Magistrates' Courts Act 1978 ('DPMCA 1978') *or* s. 27, MCA 1973 (County Court) Please note that the DPMCA 1978 is not now included in this book because of its little use in practice. However, Chapter 33 of the sixth edition of this book (where it is discussed) is to be found on the OUP website at <www.oup.com/uk/booksites/law> Orders for civil partners under sch. 5, CPA 2004
Maintenance problems—self (unmarried client or same sex partnership where the partnership is not registered)	Welfare benefits. No court procedure for obtaining maintenance for self
Maintenance problems—children (married client)	Welfare benefits can include a sum in respect of children. Maintenance for child can be ordered in the course of divorce/nullity or judicial separation proceedings or under ss. 2, 6 and 7, DPMCA 1978 as it can for a spouse *alternatively* maintenance can be ordered in proceedings under the CA 1989, sch. 1 However, the effect of the Child Support Act 1991 ('CSA 1991') must be taken into account (see Chapter 20)
Maintenance problems—Children (unmarried client)	Welfare benefits. Maintenance orders can be made under sch. 1, CA 1989 but most child maintenance is likely to be dealt with under the CSA 1991
Dispute over property (married client or civil partner)	Ancillary relief under MCA 1973 if divorce/nullity being sought Section 17, Married Women's Property Act 1882 if divorce not intended Lump sums can be ordered under DPMCA 1978 and s. 27, MCA 1973 For civil partner, if dissolution or nullity being sought, financial relief available under sch. 5, CPA 2004. Schedule 6, CPA 2004 if dissolution or nullity not applied for

(Continued overleaf)

| *Principal remedies available* | |
Client's problem	*Remedies to be considered*
	Where children are involved, sch. 1, CA 1989 enables the court to make periodical payments (in limited circumstances), lump sum orders and property adjustment orders
Dispute over property (unmarried client or same sex partnership where the partnership is not registered)	Normal principles of contract, tort, trusts and property law apply, e.g., proceedings under ss. 14 and 15, Trusts of Land and Appointment of Trustees Act 1996 for order for sale of real property, proceedings for declaration of trusts, etc. Where children are involved, sch. 1, CA 1989 enables the court to make periodical payments (in limited circumstances), lump sum orders and property adjustment orders
Residence and contact (married client)	Can be resolved in course of proceedings for divorce/ nullity or judicial separation proceedings
	If financial order sought under DPMCA 1978, the court can exercise its powers under CA 1989 with respect to child *alternatively* CA 1989 *or* wardship (if unusual features, e.g., international element)
Residence and contact (civil partner) can be resolved in course of proceedings for dissolution, nullity or separation order	If financial order sought under DPMCA 1978, the court can exercise its powers under CA 1989 with respect to child *alternatively* CA 1989 *or* wardship (if unusual features, e.g., international element)
Residence and contact (unmarried client)	CA 1989 *or* wardship (if unusual features, e.g., international element)
Violence or molestation (married client or registered civil partner)	Non-molestation order under Part IV, Family Law Act 1996 ('FLA 1996')
Violence or molestation (unmarried client)	Non-molestation order under Part IV, FLA 1996
Difficulties over occupation of home (married client or civil partner)	Occupation order under Part IV, FLA 1996
Difficulties over occupation of home (unmarried client or same sex partnership not registered)	Occupation order under Part IV, FLA 1996

Note:

If there is agreement between the parties, the solicitor should not overlook the possibility of a separation/ maintenance agreement as an alternative to proceedings. There is no reason why an unmarried couple should not make a binding agreement on matters such as maintenance, property, etc. in just the same way as a married couple. (See Chapter 36.)

Preparing to commence proceedings

In some cases, the solicitor will have to commence proceedings without delay, for example, **1.53** where the client has been subjected to serious physical violence and requires a court order to prevent a repeat performance.

The solicitor should ensure that he takes down all the further information from the client **1.54** that he needs to start proceedings. One good way of ensuring that nothing is missed is for the solicitor to have in front of him at the interview a precedent of each of the documents required to commence proceedings. He then works through each document asking the client for the particulars required to draft each paragraph. So, for example, if divorce proceedings are to be commenced, the solicitor will work through a blank form of divorce petition and a blank statement of arrangements for children form with the client.

The solicitor should also bear in mind what additional documents he will need to file when **1.55** commencing proceedings so that he can ask the client for any required documents that may be in her possession. For example, in divorce cases the client must be asked for a copy of the marriage certificate.

Negotiating

Although it is sometimes necessary to issue proceedings without delay (for example, in a **1.56** domestic violence case), it will not always be desirable to launch proceedings straight away. It is often a good idea to attempt to negotiate a settlement of disputed matters without proceedings first. Obviously some remedies, such as divorce or a dissolution order, can only be obtained through the courts. With other matters, such as maintenance, the solicitor may be open to criticism if he embarks upon proceedings without first seeing whether agreement can be reached. In the first place, the proceedings may place added strain on relations between the parties concerned and reduce the chances of settling things amicably. Secondly, the party commencing proceedings may find herself responsible for extra costs (of her own and possibly of the other side) as a result of her precipitate action.

The solicitor is free to write to the other party, or to his solicitor if he is already represented, **1.57** asking whether he is willing to consent to a particular course (for example, to give his consent to a divorce decree based on two years' separation and consent) or to make his own proposals for settlement (for example, an offer of maintenance) or indeed, asking the other party to desist from a particular course of action (for example, from harassing the client).

However, if the other party is not represented, it is good practice to suggest in the letter that **1.58** he might like to seek independent legal advice, particularly if the issue is complex. A copy of the letter should be enclosed, to be passed on to any solicitor who is instructed.

The Family Law Protocol reminds solicitors of the need to show courtesy in writing such a **1.59** letter. The letter should be clear and free of jargon. Consideration should be given to the impact of any correspondence on its reader. It is sensible to send to the client a draft letter for checking before it goes to the other party. Indeed, copies of all but routine letters should be sent to the client for approval unless there is specific reason not to do so: see paras. 1.3.1, 1.3.2, 1.3.3, 1.3.4, and 1.3.6 of the Protocol.

Letter writing

1.60 Apart from writing to the other party or his solicitor, there may also be other letters to be written. For example, if the client is being pressed for payment of gas and electricity bills or of mortgage instalments it can be helpful for the solicitor to write a letter on her behalf explaining the family difficulties and asking for forbearance until matters are resolved. There may be witnesses to contact (for example, in support of an application for a non-molestation order) and reports to request (for example, a medical report in relation to a child of the family who is disabled, for the purposes of considering the arrangements for the children under s. 41, MCA 1973).

Advising the client

1.61 The client will no doubt be anxious about matters and have her own questions to ask. In particular she will want to know what is going to happen next. In addition to giving the client the information she requests, the solicitor should be alive to other matters of which the client will not be aware but of which she should be informed or warned. For example, a client seeking a divorce should be warned of the dangers of prolonged cohabitation in the run-up to the divorce (for example, more than six months' cohabitation after discovering the respondent's adultery will debar the petitioner from relying on the adultery).

1.62 The client will be understandably nervous at the first interview and may forget to ask all the questions that she had intended to raise with the solicitor. The solicitor should therefore be prepared to clarify matters and to respond to questions at the second and subsequent interviews when the client feels more at ease.

Miscellaneous other steps

1.63 Depending on the nature of the case, the solicitor will find there are a number of other jobs to do. For example:

    (a) If the family home is in the sole name of the other spouse or civil partner, he should register a Class F land charge or a notice to protect the client's home rights under Part IV, FLA 1996.

    (b) He should consider whether to serve a notice of severance of joint tenancy if the parties are joint owners of the family home.

    (c) He should consider the question of the client's will.

    (d) He should advise on the availability of welfare benefits.

All these topics are covered in later chapters.

1.64 The Family Law Protocol gives other examples of issues that may require consideration at an early stage (see the Protocol 1.1.18) including the need to consider whether there is a risk that a child may be removed from England and Wales without the knowledge or consent of the client and the need to limit access to credit cards.

1.65 Further it recommends that the solicitor should consider what leaflets may be helpful to the client. These could include leaflets on public funding (from the Legal Services Commission) and on court procedure (from the Department for Constitutional Affairs): the Protocol, para. 1.29.

Preparing a statement and proof of evidence

After the first interview with the client, it is customary to prepare a statement setting out all **1.66** the relevant information she has provided about the case in a readable manner for future reference.

Should it ever become necessary for the client to give oral evidence in court, it is good **1.67** practice to prepare a proof of evidence from the client's statement, setting out the matters that are relevant to the particular proceedings in a convenient order. The proof can then be used as an *aide-mémoire* when taking the client through her evidence in chief.

Keeping the client up to date

It may be a statement of the obvious but clients become frustrated if they are not kept up to **1.68** date; a short telephone call or letter setting out the up-to-date position may well avoid difficulties. Regular diary and file checks should ensure that cases do not get forgotten.

D KEY DOCUMENTS

'The Family Law Protocol' (2nd edition): published by The Law Society, 113 Chancery Lane, **1.69** London WC2A 1PL

2

COMMUNITY LEGAL SERVICE AND PUBLIC FUNDING FOR FAMILY PROCEEDINGS

A INTRODUCTION

General

2.01 This chapter explains the funding available through the Legal Services Commission (the LSC) to assist a client on a low income in meeting the costs of instructing a solicitor in family proceedings.

2.02 Such funding is now known as 'public funding' following major changes set out in the Access to Justice Act 1999 ('AJA 1999'). It was previously known as 'legal aid' and this is the term still used by many clients.

2.03 As will become apparent in the chapter, there are various forms of public funding available to the family law client—which is most appropriate will depend upon the client's instructions and the circumstances of the case. In any event, it is essential to remember that the client must be financially eligible for public funding and, in many circumstances, must convince the LSC that the case is worth pursuing.

2.04 In addition, as is explained at 2.93 and onwards, public funding is rarely free but should be seen as a loan to the client to be clawed back by the LSC from assets retained or won as a result of the proceedings.

This is a complex area but at the end of the chapter you should have an understanding of **2.05** the public funding scheme and, most importantly, be able to identify the circumstances in which the client would be eligible for such help.

Specific changes affecting family practitioners

In recent years there have been important developments of specific relevance to family **2.06** practitioners. For example, greater emphasis is now placed on the role of mediation as a means of resolving disputes. This means that as a precondition to obtaining various forms of public funding the client must take part in mediation and will only be eligible for such funding of services from a solicitor if mediation is found to be unsuitable or impractical.

Even where a solicitor does not undertake publicly funded family work, he must advise **2.07** clients of their rights to public funding (where appropriate). Where he persistently neglects to do this, he may find himself disciplined by the Law Society for professional mis-conduct. Furthermore, if a client suffers financially as a result of the solicitor's failure to advise him as to the availability of public funding (as may be the case, for example, where he has to meet legal fees from his own pocket that could have been met from the Com-munity Legal Service Fund) the solicitor may find himself sued successfully for negligence by the client.

Where to find guidance on the changes

The AJA 1999 establishes the framework for the changes in funding but detailed guidance on **2.08** the forms of funding available and the criteria for eligibility are to be found in regulations made under the Act and the Funding Code.

It should be noted that the regulations and Funding Code are amended from time to time **2.09** and a good source of up-to-date information is *Focus*, published by the Legal Services Commission twice or three times per year. For copies the Commission should be contacted on 020 7759 0000.

B   THE FUNDING CODE

The principal features of the Funding Code are as follows. The Code is divided into two Parts. **2.10** Part I explains the 'levels of service' available under the scheme and the criteria to be applied for deciding whether to fund or to continue to fund services. Each level of service has its own legal definition, criteria and procedures. In summary, the levels of service which are relevant to family practitioners are:

(a)   Legal Help (see paragraph 2.13 and onwards);
(b)   Approved Family Help (see paragraph 2.21 and onwards);
    (i)   General Family Help;
    (ii)   Help with Mediation;

(c) Family Mediation (see paragraph 2.43 and onwards);

(d) Legal Representation (see paragraph 2.55 and onwards);

(e) Emergency Representation (see paragraph 2.62 and onwards).

The levels of service are designed to provide funding for the different stages involved in dealing with family disputes. Initially a client may simply require advice but in more complex cases, court proceedings of some kind may be necessary and a different level of service and method of funding would then become available.

2.11 The Funding Code defines 'family proceedings' as proceedings which arise out of family relationships, including proceedings in which the welfare of the children is determined (other than judicial review proceedings). Family proceedings include all proceedings under any one or more of the following:

(a) the Matrimonial Causes Act 1973 ('MCA 1973');

(b) the Inheritance (Provision for Family and Dependants) Act 1975;

(c) the Adoption Act 1976;

(d) the Domestic Proceedings and Magistrates' Courts Act 1978;

(e) Part III of the Matrimonial and Family Proceedings Act 1984;

(f) Parts I, II and IV of the Children Act 1989 ('CA 1989');

(g) Part IV of the Family Law Act 1996 ('FLA 1996');

(h) the inherent jurisdiction of the High Court in relation to children (Section 2.2, the Funding Code); and

(i) the Civil Partnership Act 2004.

'Family dispute' is defined in the same section of the Funding Code as meaning 'a legal dispute arising out of a family relationship, including disputes concerning the welfare of children or which may give rise to family proceedings'.

2.12 Part II contains procedures for obtaining funding including granting, amending and withdrawing certificates.

C THE BASIC STRUCTURE OF THE SCHEME

Legal Help

Generally

2.13 Legal Help may be offered by a firm having a general civil contract from the Legal Services Commission with a licence to provide work in the family category. Legal Help does not cover the issue and conduct of court proceedings nor does it cover advocacy at court. It essentially covers (under s. 4(2), AJA 1999) 'advice and assistance' to the new client.

2.14 The following are examples of the type of work that can be handled under Legal Help:

(a) The solicitor can consider the client's problem and advise him on its legal implications and as to any practical steps that can be taken to sort it out.

Example The solicitor is consulted by a woman who complains that her husband is persistently violent towards her. Under the scheme, the solicitor advises her that she is entitled to the protection of an order from the family proceedings court under Part IV of the FLA 1996, that proceedings will have to commence in the family proceedings court and that meanwhile she is not obliged to continue to live with her husband if she would prefer not to do so. He might also suggest that she could take refuge temporarily in a hostel for victims of violence if there is one locally. He cannot commence the proceedings under the scheme. Before doing this he would have to make an application for a certificate to provide Legal Representation.

(b)   The solicitor can enter into correspondence on the client's behalf.

Example The solicitor is consulted by a woman who has got into difficulties with the mortgage instalments and other household bills relating to the family home since her husband left her. He advises her to write to the mortgage lender and other creditors explaining what has happened and asking them not to take any action yet as she will be seeking maintenance from her husband and therefore expects that her problems will be short-lived. He helps her with the terms of the letters. If necessary he could write the letters for her.

(c)   The solicitor can negotiate for the client.

Example The solicitor writes on behalf of the woman in the previous example to her husband asking what proposals he makes for her maintenance and that of the children. If the husband makes an offer he can advise the wife as to whether she should accept it, and in the event of the husband's proposals being unacceptable, he can negotiate with the husband (or his solicitor if he has one) to obtain a better offer. If an agreement is reached he can advise the wife as to the best method of putting it into practice. If no agreement is reached he can advise the wife as to her rights to take the matter to court but he cannot commence proceedings for her until he has obtained funding for representation on her behalf.

(d)   The solicitor can draft documents for the client.

Example The solicitor drafts a separation or maintenance agreement on behalf of the client where earlier negotiations have achieved a level of agreement between the parties.

(e)   The solicitor can make an application for further funding on the client's behalf if it is clear to him that he will need to take steps which are not covered by Legal Help.

Obtaining advice under Legal Help

To be eligible for Legal Help, the client must be financially eligible (see paragraph 2.17) and satisfy the sufficient benefit test. In essence, this means that Legal Help will not be provided where the client is seeking advice on a non-legal matter or where the claim is clearly hopeless from the outset.   **2.15**

Once the solicitor is satisfied that the client is financially eligible by completion of the Controlled Work 1 form, he may carry out up to £500 worth of work. However, the solicitor may exercise powers given to him under the terms of his contract with the Legal Services Commission to do additional work—the extent of the additional work will depend upon the upper financial limit set by the LSC.   **2.16**

Financial eligibility for Legal Help

2.17 A client is automatically entitled to Legal Help if in receipt of income support, income-based jobseeker's allowance, or of a disposable income not exceeding £672 per month (the client's gross monthly income must not exceed £2,435 per month unless he or she has more than four children). No contribution is payable. However, Legal Help is not available if the client's disposable capital exceeds £8,000: reg. 15, the Community Legal Service (Financial) (Amendment) Regulations 2007. It is disposable income and capital that matter and they are calculated as follows:

(a) To arrive at disposable capital and income the solicitor starts by ascertaining:
   (i)   all the client's capital resources at the date of assessment; *and*
   (ii) the total income from all sources which the client has received or may reasonably expect to receive in respect of the seven days up to and including the date of assessment.
   Note that the value of the subject matter of the claim in respect of which the client is seeking Legal Help is always left out of account.
(b) To these capital and income figures, the general rule is that the solicitor must add the capital and income resources of the client's partner. (Unmarried couples living together are to be treated for financial assessment purposes as spouses and civil partners.) However, this will not normally be necessary in the case of a client seeking advice about his family problems, because the regulations provide that the partner's resources shall be left out of account if the spouse has a contrary interest in the matter in respect of which advice and assistance is being sought.
(c) Various sums should be left out of account or deducted when calculating disposable capital and income as follows:

   Capital
   (i)   the value of the main or only dwelling-house where the client resides. However, since 1 June 1996, the capital value of a client's home, which had previously been exempt in every case, may be taken into account in certain circumstances, as follows:
      (aa) the capital value of the property (that is market value less any amount outstanding on any mortgage debt or charge) will be taken into account in so far as it exceeds £100,000;
      (bb) the capital amount allowed in respect of a mortgage debt or charge over the property cannot exceed £100,000;
      (cc) where a client has a number of properties, the total amount of mortgage debt to be allowed for all the client's properties cannot exceed £100,000.

   Example The applicant has a home worth £215,000. The mortgage is £200,000.

Value of home	£215,000
Deduct mortgage up to maximum allowable	£100,000
Deduct exemption allowance	£100,000
Amount to be taken into account in assessing financial eligibility	£15,000

   In this case the client would be ineligible for public funding unless the house formed the subject matter of the dispute because the capital to be taken into account exceeds the £8,000 limit.

(ii) the value of his household furniture and effects, personal clothing, and tools or implements of his trade;

(iii) the subject matter of the problem with regard to which the client seeks Legal Help;

(iv) clothes;

(v) household furniture and effects (unless of exceptional value).

Income

(i) income tax on the client's income;

(ii) national insurance contributions for the seven days up to and including the date of assessment;

(iii) a reasonable sum for maintenance payments for an 'adequate' period for a former partner, a child or a relative who is not a member of the client's household. It should be noted that the decisions as to the reasonable sum to be deducted for maintenance payments and the 'adequate period' are made by the 'assessing authority', that is, the Legal Services Commission, or otherwise the supplier (for the purposes of this chapter, the solicitor): regs. 2(1) and 21, Community Legal Service (Financial) Regulations 2000 as amended. The maintenance payments must be bona fide, and could include, for example, simply paying a former partner's household bills or mortgage;

(iv) if the client and his partner are living together (regardless of whether her resources are aggregated with his or left out of account) a fixed allowance is made to take account of the maintenance of the partner and any children living with the client. The allowances from 9 April 2007 are £146.62 per month for a partner and £206.75 per month for a child aged 15 or under. For a child aged 16 or over the allowance is similarly £206.75 per month.

(v) certain allowances can be made for rent or mortgage payments, including payments for any endowment policy linked to the mortgage arrangements. For a single applicant with no dependants, the maximum allowances for housing costs is £545 per month;

(vi) where the applicant and/or partner is receiving a wage or salary, there is a fixed allowance of £45 per month for *each* wage earner in the assessment to cover employment-related expenses such as travel costs. Actual child care costs can also be deducted.

A Keycard (No. 43) is to be found at the end of this chapter. It sets out the basic conditions as to financial eligibility.

Legal Help in proceedings for divorce or dissolution of a civil partnership

In view of the fact that a certificate for legal representation is not usually available for proceedings for divorce or dissolution of a civil partnership, Legal Help has a particular importance in undefended cases. Provided the client is financially eligible, the solicitor will be able to give the client considerable help with the decree proceedings under the scheme. The following are examples of the work that a solicitor may be expected to carry out under the scheme: **2.18**

(a) preliminary advice on the basis for divorce or dissolution of a civil partnership, the effects of a decree or dissolution order on status, the future arrangements for the children, the income and assets of the family and matters relating to housing and the family home;

(b) drafting the petition and the statement of the arrangements for the children and where necessary typing and writing the entries on the forms;

(c) advising on filing the documents at court and the consequential procedure, including service if no acknowledgement of service is filed;

(d) advising a client when the acknowledgement of service is received as to the procedure for applying for directions for trial, and typing or writing the entries on the form of affidavit of evidence;

(e) advising as to any attendance before the district judge to explain the arrangements for the children and advising on the court's powers under the CA 1989;

(f) advising on obtaining the decree absolute, in the case of divorce proceedings, or the final order where a civil partnership is to be dissolved.

2.19 It is important to remember that Legal Help cannot be used to cover the cost of attendance by the solicitor at court.

2.20 Boiled down to essentials, this means that the solicitor can give the client all the help he could reasonably expect in relation to his divorce or dissolution of a civil partnership except that he cannot accompany him to court on any children's appointment that might be requested by the district judge (pursuant to s. 41, MCA 1973) unless he agrees to do so as a favour without payment.

Approved Family Help

2.21 This may consist of General Family Help or Help with Mediation.

2.22 These levels of service under the Funding Code are designed to limit work undertaken by a solicitor in family cases to pre-proceedings work unless or until it becomes clear that the matter cannot be resolved through mediation or negotiation.

2.23 Both forms of Approved Family Help require an application to the LSC for a certificate before help can be provided: there is no provision for emergency applications.

General Family Help

2.24 **Introduction** This is defined as including 'help in relation to a family dispute including assistance in resolving that dispute through negotiation or otherwise. It may also include the issue of proceedings and representation in proceedings where necessary *to obtain disclosure of information from another party* (for example, in ancillary relief proceedings at the first appointment: see Chapter 18) or to obtain a consent order following settlement of part or all of the dispute as well as related conveyancing or other implementation work'. The certificate cannot be used to cover representation at a final contested hearing—in such circumstances an application will be necessary to amend the certificate to cover Legal Representation.

2.25 Application for authorization to give General Family Help is applied for by completion of Form CLS APP 3.

Scope of General Family Help   Certificates granted for General Family Help will be limited **2.26** both as to scope and costs. The standard costs limitation is £1,500. As well as being financially eligible, the client must demonstrate that there is sufficient benefit to him to justify the work being carried out. An emergency certificate is not available for General Family Help.

General Family Help is available for cases which are not required to be referred to mediation **2.27** or where the mediator has determined the case to be unsuitable or where Family Mediation has broken down. An example given in the Funding Code Guidance of where General Family Help would be appropriate is where the family case involves a history of violence and direct mediation between the parties may not be suitable but negotiations between lawyers may be an effective means of resolving issues relating to children and the family finances.

Financial eligibility for General Family Help   This is the same as for Legal Help **2.28** (see paragraph 2.17).

Other conditions to be fulfilled to obtain funding   As a general rule, General Family Help **2.29** and Legal Representation will be refused where the client fails to satisfy the 'private client test'. What this means in practice is that the benefits to be gained from representation for the client justify the costs such that 'a reasonable private paying client would be prepared to proceed in all the circumstances' (Funding Code Criteria).

Since October 2005, the Funding Code Criteria have been amended to add a new condition **2.30** to applications for Legal Representation in ancillary relief proceedings and to applications to extend a General Family Help Certificate to cover legal representation.

The Funding Code provides as follows: **2.31**

> Private funding.
>   Legal representation may be refused if it appears reasonable in all the circumstances for proceedings to be privately funded having regard to the financial circumstances of the client and the value of the assets in dispute.

What is intended here is that the client should use savings to pay legal costs or, alternatively, **2.32** and where able to do so, obtain a loan for this purpose.

The guidance makes is clear, however, that the client would not be expected to sell his/her **2.33** home to fund the proceedings.

Relationship with Help with Mediation   Help with Mediation is discussed at paragraph **2.34** 2.35. The Funding Code—Decision Making Guidance states that:

> A certificate for General Family Help should not be used for work covered by Help with Mediation. The reason for this is that Help with Mediation is exempt from the statutory charge, and hence must be done under a separate certificate in order to identify the costs separately.

The statutory charge will of course attach to work carried out under the terms of the certificate for General Family Help.

Help with Mediation

Generally   Help with Mediation is only available if a client is actually participating in **2.35** Family Mediation and enables a solicitor to assist the client, for example, by advising on the legal implications of a mediated settlement and taking steps to put the settlement into effect (by obtaining a court order by consent), thus generally supporting the process of Family Mediation.

2.36   **Applying for Help with Mediation**   Form CLSA APP 4 is completed to apply for a Help with Mediation certificate.

2.37   **Financial eligibility for Help with Mediation**   To be automatically eligible for Help with Mediation, for which no contribution is payable by the client, the client must be in receipt of income support, or income based jobseeker's allowance. The client will also be eligible if his gross monthly income does not exceed £2,435 and his monthly disposable income does not exceed £672. His capital must not exceed £8,000. The calculation of disposable income and capital is explained at paragraph 2.17.

2.38   **Limits on Help with Mediation**   Help with Mediation may not be used to conduct negotiations with the other side since this would interfere with the mediation process.

2.39   When the mediated settlement is to be put into effect (for example, by drafting and obtaining a consent order) this should not be used to reopen the settlement or endeavour to negotiate a new agreement. If the solicitor believes that the negotiated settlement is not acceptable and the client agrees, Help with Mediation will not extend to negotiating an alternative. However, the client may return to the mediator with the advice given by the solicitor and continue the mediation.

2.40   Inevitably Help with Mediation may only be provided where there is sufficient benefit to the client to justify the work being carried out. The Decision Making Guidance cites, as examples where Help with Mediation would not be granted, a dispute concerning handover arrangements for contact or a difference of opinion over contact times.

2.41   **Relationship with Legal Help**   Help with Mediation will be refused if it is more appropriate for the client to be assisted by way of Legal Help. This will arise, for example, where full agreement has been reached and all that is required is an exchange of open correspondence between solicitors to confirm the agreement.

2.42   However, it will be sensible for solicitors to obtain a certificate authorizing Help with Mediation where the client requires substantial legal advice in support of on-going mediation since work properly carried out under such a certificate is *exempt* from the statutory charge.

Family Mediation

Introduction

2.43   This is a separate level of service under the Funding Code, authorizing mediation of a family dispute and an assessment of whether mediation appears suitable to the dispute, the parties and all the circumstances.

2.44   In certain circumstances, a client must attend an assessment of suitability with a recognized mediator before an application can be made for General Family Help and for Legal Representation, where the following family proceedings are contemplated:

(a)   Matrimonial Causes Act 1973 (except s. 37 of the Act);

(b)   Domestic Proceedings and Magistrates' Courts Act 1978;

(c)   private law applications and financial relief proceedings under the CA 1989;

(d)   Civil Partnership Act 2004.

Exemptions from the requirement to participate in mediation

There are a number of occasions where it will not be necessary for the client to attend an **2.45** assessment appointment. These include, amongst other things, where Legal Representation should be granted as a matter of urgency, where the client has a reasonable fear of violence or abuse or significant harm from a partner or former partner, where, because of disability, the client is unable to travel to see a mediator, where a suitable mediator is not available within 10 days after an appointment is sought or where proceedings are already in existence and the client is the respondent who has been given a hearing date at court within the next three months. The solicitor must, however, contact all mediation services in his catchment area before the application may be exempted, permitting the application for General Family Help or Legal Representation to go ahead.

The referral process

The Commission recognizes that the client may arrange his own meeting with a mediator **2.46** but recommends that the solicitor takes responsibility for referring the client to a mediation service for a meeting with a mediator.

The mediation service is required to offer the client a meeting within 10 days, the period **2.47** beginning on the date that the solicitor or client makes contact with the mediation service. The service must inform the client that the meetings can take place either separately from or together with the other party. It is for the client to decide which type of meeting would be most appropriate for him.

Where both the client and the other party attend the same meeting with a mediator, the **2.48** mediator is required to carry out domestic abuse screening interviews separately with each party before the meeting takes place.

Determination of suitability

Where mediation is determined not to be suitable, the client will be informed that he may **2.49** consult his solicitor and that an application for General Family Help or Legal Representation may now be made. This will also be the position if mediation begins but subsequently breaks down with no prospect of progress being made.

Mediation may not be suitable because of the nature of the dispute, the parties and all the **2.50** circumstances. This assumes that the parties have attended a meeting with a mediator who has made such an assessment. However, mediation may not be possible because the other party does not respond or attend a meeting with a recognized family mediator or, having replied to an invitation to attend, refuses to participate in the process.

Financial eligibility for Family Mediation

To be financially eligible for Family Mediation the client must be in receipt of income **2.51** support, income based jobseeker's allowance or have a monthly disposable income not exceeding £672 nor a gross monthly income exceeding £2,435.

2.52   Where a client has capital exceeding £8,000, he will be ineligible for Family Mediation funding.

2.53   As with Help with Mediation, no contribution is payable for Family Mediation.

Family Mediation and the statutory charge

2.54   All work carried out under a certificate for Family Mediation is exempt from the statutory charge.

Legal Representation

Introduction

2.55   A certificate authorizing Legal Representation may be applied for in emergency situations, for example, in cases where protection from domestic abuse is required or where mediation and attempts to negotiate a settlement have proved to be unsuccessful and a contested hearing is inevitable. This will be necessary because a certificate for General Family Help cannot cover the cost of representation at a final contested hearing.

2.56   Where a certificate for General Family Help is already in existence, authority to provide Legal Representation may be obtained from the LSC by seeking an amendment to the existing certificate, otherwise a fresh certificate must be sought.

2.57   Application is made to the Commission by completion of form CLS APP3.

Financial eligibility for Legal Representation

2.58   The same conditions must be fulfilled as for a certificate for General Family Help (see paragraph 2.17). When public funding takes the form of a certificate for Legal Representation, in specified family proceedings a contribution may be payable for income and/or capital by the assisted person. 'Specified family proceedings' means family proceedings other than proceedings under Part IV, CA 1989 or Part IV, FLA 1996.

2.59   The contribution regime is as follows:

for Legal Representation an applicant with a disposable income of £290 or below per month and capital not exceeding £8,000 will not be required to pay any contributions. Where the applicant's monthly disposable income exceeds £290 but is less than £672, the contribution to be paid will be assessed as follows:

BAND	MONTHLY DISPOSABLE INCOME	MONTHLY CONTRIBUTION
A	£290 – £426	¼ of income in excess of £285
B	£427 – £565	£35.25 + ⅓ of income in excess of £426
C	£566 – £672	£81.60 + ½ of income in excess of £565

2.60   Further, the applicant must show that there are reasonable prospects of success and that the client will benefit from the institution of the proceedings. It will be necessary to demonstrate, for example, that assets exist, justifying an application for Legal Representation so that orders for ancillary relief may be made.

Funding for specific types of family proceedings

The Funding Code—Decision Making Guidance sets out fully the criteria to be fulfilled to **2.61** obtain funding for Legal Representation for specific types of family proceedings and also indicates the circumstances in which funding may be refused. Relevant guidance will be included when proceedings for orders for ancillary relief, for orders under Part IV of the FLA 1996 and for orders under the CA 1989 are considered in subsequent chapters. The certificate may be limited both as to scope and costs (usually £2,500) and it is essential to ensure that appropriate authority has been obtained from the Commission before certain steps are taken. A failure to do so will almost certainly result in the solicitor not being paid for the work undertaken.

D EMERGENCY REPRESENTATION

Introduction

Emergency Representation is only available as part of Legal Representation and does not **2.62** apply to any other level of service.

While a certificate for Emergency Representation should reduce the inevitable delay asso- **2.63** ciated with the grant of a certificate for Legal Representation, it will be necessary not only to satisfy the standard criteria for Legal Representation, as set out above, but also to demonstrate that the certificate should be granted as a matter of urgency because it appears to be in the interests of justice to do so.

'Urgency and interests of justice': an explanation

Chapter 12 of The Funding Code—Decision Making Guidance states that: **2.64**

The application may be urgent if any of the following circumstances apply and there is insufficient time for an application for a substantive certificate to be made and determined:

(a) Representation (or other urgent work for which Legal Representation would be needed) is justified in injunction or other emergency proceedings (for example for an injunction under s. 37, MCA 1973 or for an order under Part IV of the Family Law Act 1996);

(b) Representation (or other urgent work for which Legal Representation would be needed) is justified in relation to an imminent hearing in existing proceedings; or

(c) a limitation period is about to expire.

As far as 'in the interests of justice' is concerned, Emergency Representation is unlikely to be **2.65** granted unless 'the likely delay as a result of the failure to grant emergency representation will mean that either:

(a) there will be a risk to the life, liberty or physical safety of the client or his or her family or the roof over their heads; or

(b) the delay will cause a significant risk of miscarriage of justice, or unreasonable hardship to the client, or irretrievable problems in handling the case and, in either case, there are no other appropriate options to deal with the risk'.

The procedure to obtain Emergency Representation

Who may grant the application?

2.66   Emergency Representation may be granted by the LSC or by an Authorized Solicitor. This is a solicitor who has a full franchise in family law and devolved power to grant Emergency Representation. This power must be exercised reasonably and in accordance with any published guidance. Full records must be kept on the client's file of the circumstances of the case and the reasons for exercising the devolved powers in this way. An Authorized Solicitor must not grant any application which has previously been refused by the LSC unless there has been a clear and relevant change in circumstances to justify the grant. Further where there is doubt as to the client's financial eligibility, the application must be referred to the LSC for an urgent means assessment (or if an assessment is not possible in the time available, an urgent indication as to whether financial eligibility is likely to be established).

2.67   Where Emergency Representation has been granted by a solicitor, the Regional Director of the LSC must be notified as soon as possible and in any event not later than five working days after the decision to grant the emergency application.

2.68   In all other cases, it will be necessary to make the application to the Regional Office of the LSC.

The application

2.69   **By post**   The application will normally be by post and is made on form CLS APP3 indicating, by completion of the appropriate box, that this is an emergency application. This must be accompanied by a full application.

2.70   **By fax**   The Funding Code—Decision Making Guidance indicates that an application for Emergency Representation will only be accepted by fax if the urgency of the situation is such that a decision is required before a postal application could reasonably be made and processed. Such an application will generally only be justified when the work must be undertaken within a working day of the application (3 pm to 3 pm for this purpose).

2.71   In these circumstances the fax emergency application form (Form CLS APP6) and the fax means form (Form CLS APP6a) if appropriate, should be completed in full by the solicitor and faxed to the Regional Office.

2.72   Where the solicitor is unable to provide all the income or capital information necessary to complete the fax emergency means form in full, the solicitor will nevertheless have to demonstrate that the client is likely to be financially eligible, for example, because he has low capital or low earnings but is unable to provide details of the precise amount of outgoings.

2.73   A copy of the decision form confirming the description and limitation will be faxed back to the solicitor within a working day of receipt (3 pm to 3 pm for this purpose).

2.74   **By telephone**   Such application will only be permitted in exceptional circumstances where the Regional Office is satisfied that a decision is required before a faxed or written application could reasonably be processed or immediate work is required and the solicitor does not have immediate access to a fax machine.

The work to be covered must be undertaken within the next few hours, usually on the same **2.75** date the application is received. The Funding Code—Decision Making Guidance requires the solicitor to provide to the Regional Office adequate information relating to the means of the applicant and the merits of the case. In effect the solicitor must be able to give to the case worker the information required for completion of Form CLS APP6 (and CLS APP6a, if appropriate).

Where the Regional Office grants a telephone application the solicitor will be given details **2.76** of the scope of the work to be undertaken and any limitations under the certificate over the telephone and will be asked to agree to the conditions applied. The certificate will not be granted in the absence of agreement.

Steps to be taken following a fax or telephone application The solicitor is required to **2.77** send to the Regional Office the completed postal application forms within five working days of the grant of the certificate by fax or by telephone.

The information provided in the forms must be consistent with the information given in **2.78** the fax or telephone application.

If these conditions are not met the fax or telephone grant decision will not stand and **2.79** no emergency certificate will be granted.

The effect of the emergency certificate

An emergency certificate is very much a temporary measure. It tides the client over until **2.80** his application for Legal Representation has been considered at which stage, if emergency representation is granted, it will be replaced by a full certificate. The emergency certificate has cost and time limitations. All emergency certificates are subject to a time limitation which is normally a period of four weeks from the date of issue. If the emergency certificate looks likely to expire before all the work has been undertaken and before a full certificate is granted, the solicitor should make application to the Regional Director for an amendment to the emergency certificate.

Before application is made for an emergency certificate, the solicitor must make clear to **2.81** the client:

(a)   that, having sought an emergency certificate, he will be obliged (as and when required) to provide further information or documents or to attend for interview so that his means can be assessed and any contribution determined. If he fails to do so, he will not be granted a full certificate and his emergency certificate may be revoked;
(b)   that if he turns out to be financially ineligible once his means have been assessed, he will not be granted a full certificate and his emergency certificate may be revoked;
(c)   that if an offer of funding is made to the client, he will be told the basis on which he will be granted a full certificate (i.e., what his contribution must be) and given the opportunity to accept or reject the offer. If he wants to accept the offer, he must do so promptly. If he fails to accept the offer, not only will he not get a full certificate, his emergency certificate may also be revoked.

The client must not be left in any doubt as to the effect of revocation of the emergency certificate. The results of revocation are that the client will be deemed never to have been publicly funded at all and he will become liable to repay to the Commission all the costs paid out of the Fund on his behalf in connection with the work done under the emergency certificate. Furthermore, he will be liable to pay direct to his solicitor the difference between the costs the solicitor will be able to claim from the Fund and the costs he would have been entitled to charge had the client always been a private client.

E   THE ISSUE OF A CERTIFICATE FOR GENERAL FAMILY HELP AND/OR LEGAL REPRESENTATION

2.82   This is dealt with in Section 4 of Part 2 of The Funding Code.

Mechanics of issue where no contribution is payable

2.83   Where there is no contribution to be paid by the applicant or the application relates to special CA 1989 proceedings, a certificate will be issued forthwith. The actual certificate will be sent to the solicitor with a copy sent to the applicant.

Mechanics of issue where a contribution is payable

2.84   If the applicant is liable to pay a contribution, he will first be notified of the terms on which a certificate is offered to him (i.e., what his maximum and actual contributions would be, the terms for payment, etc.). If these terms are acceptable to the applicant, he must, within 14 days of being notified:

(a)   complete the acceptance form (and a form of undertaking to pay the contribution required) and return them as directed; *and*

(b)   if the contribution or any part of it is required to be paid before the certificate is issued (as is normally the case, for example, where a contribution from capital is required), make that payment accordingly.

When he has complied with these requirements, a certificate will be issued and sent to the solicitor and a copy will be sent to the applicant.

F   NOTIFICATION OF ISSUE OF A CERTIFICATE

2.85   If proceedings to which the client is a party have already been commenced by the time a certificate is granted, the solicitor should:

(a)   serve all other parties to the proceedings straight away with notice of the issue of the certificate: *and*

(b)   if any other person later becomes a party, serve him with a notice of issue also; *and*

(c)   send a copy of the certificate to the appropriate court office.

If the client is not yet a party to proceedings when he is granted the certificate, the solicitor's duty to notify other parties and to provide the court with a copy of the certificate arises as soon as his client does become a party to proceedings. It is not necessary (except in relation to appeals) to notify the other parties of any limitation on the certificate. The provisions as to notification and filing apply to both emergency and full certificates. The solicitor is also required to notify other parties of any amendment (other than financial) of the certificate, of the extension of an emergency certificate or its replacement with a full certificate and of the revocation or discharge of a certificate. In addition he must send a copy of the amendment, notice of discharge, etc. to the court.

G   THE EFFECT OF THE ISSUE OF A CERTIFICATE FOR GENERAL FAMILY HELP AND/OR LEGAL REPRESENTATION

Generally

Once a certificate is issued, the assisted person's legal expenses will be met from the Fund. **2.86** Generally speaking, this means that he can be represented by a solicitor (and, if necessary, counsel) and given all such assistance as is usually given by a solicitor or counsel in the steps preliminary and incidental to any proceedings or in arriving at or giving effect to a compromise to avoid or bring to an end any proceedings.

The exact nature of what can be done for the client under this particular certificate depends **2.87** on two things:

(a)   the terms of the certificate itself;
(b)   the provisions of the Funding Code which require special authorization to be obtained before certain steps are taken.

The terms of the particular certificate

The certificate will state what proceedings it covers and will set out any condition or **2.88** limitation imposed by the Regional Director.

The solicitor should always be careful to note the terms of the certificate and particularly so **2.89** in family cases where it is routine practice to impose quite a number of special restrictions on the scope of the certificate. Thus, for example, certificates issued in relation to *ancillary relief* in connection with divorce, nullity, judicial separation, or dissolution of a civil partnership are normally expressed to cover an application for all forms of ancillary relief except an order for the avoidance of a disposition or for variation. All ancillary relief certificates are limited, in the first instance, to the securing of one substantive order only. This means that the application for ancillary relief should be all-embracing and the order made should be as comprehensive as possible, since the wording of the certificate does not allow the client to have more than one 'bite at the cherry'.

The duty to act reasonably

The solicitor must remember that a certificate does not give him a free hand in relation to **2.90** his client's case. Apart from the need to obtain specific authority before taking certain steps:

(a) He must act with reasonable competence and expedition. If he wastes costs by not doing so, these costs may be reduced or even disallowed completely on assessment.

(b) He has an obligation to report to the Regional Director if he has reason to believe his client has required his case to be conducted unreasonably so as to incur unjustifiable expense to the Fund or has required unreasonably that the case be continued (for example, when he has been competently advised that the only proper course is to settle on the terms offered and he refuses to do so). The Regional Director has power to discharge the certificate in cases such as this.

Solicitor not to accept payment other than from Fund

2.91   Once a certificate has been granted, the solicitor must not take any payment from the client himself (or indeed from any other person) in respect of the client's legal costs. He must look only to the Fund for payment.

Costs in funded cases

2.92   The fact that one of the parties to the proceedings is publicly funded can affect the court's order for costs as follows:

(a) Order for costs *against* a funded party: the court can order a funded party to pay the costs of the proceedings. Because of provisions contained in Section 21 of the Practice Direction About Costs (Supplementary Parts 43–48 Civil Procedure Rules 1998), unsuccessful publicly funded family clients are subject to the same costs risks as privately paying family clients who become involved in litigation.

(b) Order for costs *in favour* of a funded party: the solicitor must not fall into the trap of thinking that, because his client is publicly funded there is no need to pursue an order for costs with any great enthusiasm. First, he has a duty to the Fund to apply for costs in the same situations as he would apply for costs on behalf of a private client. Secondly, he clearly has a duty to his client to seek costs in order to reduce the effect of the statutory charge (see below). The more of the client's costs that are paid by the other party to the proceedings, the less the deficit to the Fund that the client will have to make up from his own pocket.

H   REIMBURSEMENT OF THE COMMUNITY LEGAL SERVICE FUND AND THE STATUTORY CHARGE

Reimbursement of the Community Legal Service Fund

2.93   Where public funding has been granted, the Fund will assume responsibility for paying the legal costs of the funded person. The LSC will pay to the solicitor the costs approved following scrutiny of the solicitor's claim for costs by the court carrying out a detailed assessment. Where the solicitor's claim for costs does not exceed £2,500 the LSC carries out the assessment to check that the claim is reasonable. The LSC has a statutory duty to recoup for the Fund whatever this costs. It does so as follows:

(a) From any payment made in the funded person's favour under any order or agreement for costs with respect to the proceedings (s. 11(4), AJA 1999).

Example 1 Mr and Mrs Robinson are divorced. Mrs Robinson is granted a certificate to be heard in ancillary relief proceedings. It is agreed that Mr Robinson will transfer the house to Mrs Robinson and, in return, she will forgo all her remaining ancillary relief claims. Mr Robinson agrees to pay Mrs Robinson's legal costs in relation to ancillary matters. The agreement is embodied in a consent order.

Mr Robinson will pay an amount equal to his wife's legal costs to her solicitor who will pay it on to the LSC. The LSC will use it to reimburse the Fund partially or wholly for the cost of Mrs Robinson's public funding.

(b) If the costs recovered for the funded person are not enough to cover the cost of funding the case, the LSC will also put the funded person's contribution towards the costs.

Example 2 Mr Robinson pays £700 of his wife's costs by agreement. Her costs are in fact £1,000. The Fund therefore remains out of pocket in relation to Mrs Robinson's legal costs. Mrs Robinson has paid a contribution towards her funding. This contribution is retained by the LSC and put towards discharging the deficit.

Note that if the total contribution made by an assisted person to the Fund is more than is required to make up the deficit in the Fund the balance will be repaid to the funded person.

Example 3 Mrs Robinson's contribution towards her funding was £400. The deficit to the Fund after Mr Robinson has paid his share of her costs is only £300. She is entitled to have £100 repaid to her by the Legal Services Commission in respect of her unused contribution.

(c) If the deficit to the Fund has still not been made good, subject to certain exceptions, the LSC will look to any money or property recovered or preserved for the assisted person in the proceedings to which the certificate relates to recoup the balance (s. 10(7), AJA 1999). This is commonly called the LSC's statutory charge and is more fully described below.

Example 4 In ancillary relief proceedings after divorce, Mr Sidebottom is ordered to pay his wife the sum of £50,000. Mrs Sidebottom is funded with a nil contribution. No order for costs is obtained against Mr Sidebottom. At the end of the proceedings, therefore, the Fund is out of pocket to the tune of the entire cost of Mrs Sidebottom's public funding, £8,000. £8,000 of Mrs Sidebottom's lump sum will therefore be applied in discharging the cost of her funding.

If the total of (a), (b), and (c) above still does not make good the Fund's deficit, the Fund will bear the balance of the deficit. If there is no order for costs, no property recovered or preserved and no contribution paid by the assisted person, the Fund will, therefore, bear the entire costs of the proceedings.

I   SOLICITOR TO RECEIVE MONEYS DUE TO FUNDED PARTY

2.94   Regulation 18(1) of the Community Legal Service (Costs) Regulations 2000 (SI 2000/774) requires that all moneys payable to a funded party by virtue of any agreement or order made in connection with the action, cause or matter to which his certificate relates (whether made before or after proceedings were taken) must be paid to the funded party's solicitor. This includes sums due in respect of costs as well as sums due in settlement of the funded party's claim.

2.95   The solicitor is obliged forthwith:

(a)   to pay all moneys received by him by virtue of such an order or agreement to the LSC (though note the power of the Regional Director where the Fund would be sufficiently safeguarded by payment of a lesser sum to direct that only part of the moneys received by the solicitor should be paid to the LSC and the balance to the funded party himself); *and*

(b)   to inform the Regional Director of any property recovered or preserved for the funded party and to send him a copy of the court order or agreement (reg. 20(1)(a) and (b) *ibid.*).

The purpose of reg. 20 is, of course, to ensure that the question of reimbursement of the Fund can be dealt with before the funded party has a chance to spend any part of the money that may be required to reimburse the Fund.

J   THE STATUTORY CHARGE UNDER S. 10(7), ACCESS TO JUSTICE ACT 1999

Generally

2.96   As we saw in paragraph 2.93 above, the effect of s. 10(7), AJA 1999 is that if the amount of costs recovered for a funded party together with his own contribution towards his funding is not sufficient to cover the cost to the Fund of his legal expenses, the LSC can look to any property recovered or preserved for him in the proceedings to recoup the balance. Section 10(7) gives the LSC a first charge for the benefit of the Fund on any such property—this is commonly referred to as 'the statutory charge'.

2.97   Regulation 20 of the Community Legal Service (Costs) Regulations 2000 obliges the solicitor to notify the Regional Director of any property recovered or preserved (see paragraph 2.95 above) and it is the Regional Director who then decides whether or not a charge arises. In practice the question will normally arise in connection with ancillary relief proceedings following divorce, nullity, judicial separation, or proceedings to annul or dissolve a civil partnership and the remainder of Part J is therefore written with this in mind.

'Property' includes money

2.98   Although s. 10(7) refers only to property, this does include money. Therefore the statutory charge can attach, for example, to a lump sum received by the funded party just as it can to a house recovered or preserved for him.

Further, the wording of s. 10(7) makes it clear that the charge will arise whether the property **2.99** was recovered or preserved by the funded party for himself or any other person.

Has any property been recovered or preserved?

This can be a very vexed question. The leading case is *Hanlon* v *The Law Society* [1981] AC **2.100** 124, [1980] 2 All ER 199. In this case the House of Lords held that property is 'recovered or preserved' if it was *in issue* in the proceedings and either the funded party made a successful claim in respect of it (in which case the property is recovered for him or for any other person) or successfully defended a claim in respect of it (in which case the property is preserved for him or for any other person). The fact that the court has a general discretion over all property and money belonging to the parties in ancillary relief proceedings following a decree of divorce, nullity, judicial separation, or proceedings to annul or dissolve a civil partnership can be disregarded. What is important is whether the particular item that may be the subject of the charge has actually been in issue or not and this is a matter to be decided on the facts of each case by looking at the pleadings, the evidence and the court's judgment or order.

Example (The facts of the *Hanlon* case.) The husband and wife were married in 1957. In 1963 a family home was purchased in the husband's name with a mortgage. Both parties contributed equally in money and work to the family and the marriage. The wife got funding to petition for divorce (this was in 1971 when such funding was still generally available for divorce), to apply for the equivalent of occupation and non-molestation orders and to take proceedings under s. 17, Married Women's Property Act 1882. She made a small contribution towards her funding.

The wife was granted a divorce, given custody of the two children of the marriage and granted a property adjustment order requiring the husband to transfer the family home to the wife absolutely. The equity in the home was worth about £10,000.

The wife's costs were £8,025 (£925 for the divorce and applications for the occupation and non-molestation orders, £1,150 for the equivalent of residence and contact applications and £5,950 in respect of the property adjustment order). The husband was funded also and no order for costs was made against him. Clearly therefore the Fund was substantially out of pocket in relation to the wife's legal costs and the question arose as to whether the Law Society (now replaced by the Legal Services Commission) had a charge on the house in respect of the wife's costs.

The House of Lords held that the whole house had been in issue. It was pointed out that, if the husband had agreed at the outset that the wife had at least a half share in the house, then only the husband's half share would have been in issue (and therefore recovered by the wife and subject to the charge). However, in this case in the original pleadings each spouse was claiming the transfer of the other's interest in the house to themselves and this position was never altered by agreement or concession that the wife was entitled to at least part of the house. Thus the entire house was property recovered by the wife (the husband's interest) or preserved for her (her own interest) and therefore the whole house was subject to the charge.

The *Hanlon* case concerned an issue over *title* to property. The case of *Curling* v *Law Society* [1985] 1 All ER 705, carries the charge a stage further. In that case the family home was bought in joint names. The husband petitioned for divorce and sought a property adjustment order in respect of the home. The wife was publicly funded. She sought an order that the house be sold. The husband did not dispute the wife's entitlement to a half share in the property (so her title to half the house was never in issue). However, he did wish to remain in the house and negotiations led to an agreement whereby the husband would buy out the wife's interest in the house. The wife argued that as the title to the house had never been in issue in the proceedings, the sum she received for her interest in it could not be regarded as property recovered or preserved and therefore could not be the subject of the statutory charge. The Court of Appeal held that the ownership of the house could not be looked at in isolation when considering whether the wife had recovered or preserved property in the proceedings. The fact that a party recovers in the proceedings that to which he is already entitled in law does not by itself prevent the attachment of the statutory charge. The property has been in issue in the proceedings if the party's right to realise his share in the property is contested just as much as if his rights of ownership had been disputed. Thus, because the parties had been in dispute over whether the house should be sold forthwith enabling the wife to realise her share in it, her interest in the property had been in issue and the sum paid by the husband in respect of her interest was therefore property recovered by her and subject to the charge.

2.101 The statutory charge will apply to a property co-owned by two unmarried parents where an action has been compromised so that a sale of the property is postponed in order that the mother and child may live there, since the mother gains exclusive possession of the property over a long period of years and thus has the benefit of a 'property right' within the meaning of s. 10(7), AJA 1999 despite the fact that the parties' respective beneficial interests were never in issue (*Parkes* v *Legal Aid Board* [1997] 1 FLR 77).

2.102 In summary, and subject to paragraph 2.105 below the following propositions are put forward on the question of whether property has been recovered or preserved:

(a) Property can have been recovered or preserved only if it has been 'in issue' in the proceedings (*Hanlon*).

(b) Whether particular property has been in issue must be determined as a matter of fact from the statements, the evidence, the court's judgment/order (*Hanlon*), and, as in *Curling*, the correspondence.

(c) If there has been an argument over ownership of the property, the property has been in issue (*Hanlon*).

(d) However, it is necessary to look specifically to see whether the whole title to the property was in dispute or just part. If the person defending the claim conceded from the outset that part of the property belonged to the claimant as a matter of prior entitlement, the title to that part of the property was never in issue (*Hanlon*).

(e) The mere fact that a claim was made by the petitioner or applicant in the divorce, nullity, judicial separation petition, or petition to annul or dissolve a civil partnership (or presumably by the respondent in Form A or in his answer) in relation to particular property is not sufficient, by itself, to put that property in issue (*Curling* commenting on the case of *Jones* v *Law Society* (1983) 4 FLR 733).

(f) Although there has been no dispute over ownership of the property in question, that property can still have been in issue if there has been conflict over whether a party should be allowed to realize his share in the property within a certain time or not (*Curling*). Thus, if the parties agree that the matrimonial home is owned, say equally, but one party seeks a prompt sale and equal division of the proceeds (or a lump sum payment from the other party in respect of his interest) and the other seeks an order which provides for a postponement of the sale, the property has been in issue.

(g) Again, where there is no dispute over the beneficial entitlements in the property but a dispute over possession, the charge may apply if, as a result of the court order, one party preserves the right to remain in possession of the property and resists an application by the co-owner for an order for the immediate sale of the property (see *Parkes*, above).

Recovery or preservation for any other person

The wording of s. 10(7), AJA 1999 is wider than the previous provisions contained in s. 16, **2.103** Legal Aid Act 1988 and now the charge will arise whether the property is recovered or preserved for the funded party or *for any other person* (such as a child of the family).

Charge applicable to property recovered/preserved as a result of a compromise

Section 10(7) makes it quite clear that property recovered or preserved includes any property **2.104** paid to the funded party by way of a compromise arrived at to avoid or bring to an end the proceedings as well as property recovered or preserved as a result of a judgment or order of the court. Thus the funded party cannot avoid the charge by settling a claim out of court even if he does so before proceedings are commenced.

Exemptions from the charge

Regulation 44 of the Community Legal Service (Financial) Regulations 2000, as amended, **2.105** provides that certain property is exempt from the charge. The exemptions include:

(a) periodical payments of maintenance for a spouse or former spouse, civil partner or former civil partner or child;

(b) sums ordered to be paid under Part IV of the FLA 1996 (for example a compensating lump sum on transfer of a tenancy);

(c) pension sharing orders and the income (but not the capital element) of a pension attachment order;

(d) where the family home is recovered or preserved and the only funding received by the client has been Legal Help.

What costs form part of the charge?

It is the outstanding cost of 'the proceedings' that is the subject of the charge. This means **2.106** that the charge is not confined to the cost of the part of the proceedings which resulted in the recovery or preservation of the property in question. It extends to the cost of the whole cause, action or matter covered by the certificate (*Hanlon* v *The Law Society*; see above). The facts of the *Hanlon* case illustrate this principle. There, the wife's certificate covered the divorce suit and the ancillary relief proceedings arising out of it in relation to property adjustment and the equivalent of residence and contact orders in relation to the children. The charge on the family home therefore comprised not only the cost of the property adjustment proceedings themselves but also the cost of the divorce proceedings and the equivalent of residence and contact proceedings.

2.107   Where the client first receives Legal Help and then goes on to obtain a certificate for General Family Help and Legal Representation in relation to the same proceedings, the cost of the Legal Help will be added to the overall costs incurred by the funded party in determining the cost to the Fund of the case.

Example Mrs Wetherby petitions for divorce. Her solicitor advises her under the Legal Help scheme in relation to the divorce and drafts the petition. She then obtains a certificate for ancillary proceedings. She has a nil contribution. Her husband is ordered to pay her £70,000 in the ancillary relief proceedings but no order for costs is obtained against him in relation to ancillary relief or the divorce itself. The Commission will look to Mrs Wetherby's lump sum for payment of all the funding provided.

Settlement obtained through the mediation process

2.108   It is important to remember that where property is recovered or preserved by a settlement achieved through the use of mediation and funded by a certificate for Family Mediation the costs incurred are exempt from the statutory charge.

2.109   Similarly, costs incurred by a solicitor in putting the terms of a mediated settlement into effect, for example, by drafting and obtaining a consent order are also exempt from the statutory charge *provided* that such work is funded by a certificate for Help with Mediation (as distinct from a certificate for General Family Help).

Enforcement of the charge

2.110   The charge vests in the Commission which is entitled to enforce it in just the same way as anyone else entitled to a charge. If the charge affects land, it can be registered as a charge against the property (reg. 52, Community Legal Service (Financial) Regulations 2000). If both cash and a dwelling-house are recovered or preserved, the charge will first be enforced against the cash and the balance only against the property.

2.111   The Commission can agree to postpone the charge in appropriate cases. In practice this means that, if the charge relates to the funded party's home, the Commission will accept a registered charge over the property. Thus the funded party will not be forced to sell the property straight away to repay the Commission's charge. However, when he does decide to sell of his own accord he will be bound to repay the Commission out of the proceeds of the sale and the Commission may agree to transfer the charge to his next house. If the funded party wishes the charge to be transferred in this way, application should be made to the Commission.

2.112   Where the only property recovered or preserved is a sum of money which by order of the court or under the terms of the agreement reached is to be used for the purpose of purchasing a home for himself or his dependants, then the Commission may agree to defer enforcing its charge over the sum if:

(a)   the funded party wishes to purchase a home in accordance with the order or agreement, and agrees that the new home will itself be subject to a charge; *and*

(b)   the Regional Director is satisfied that the new property will provide adequate security for the amount in question.

Where the charge is postponed for any reason interest will accrue to be paid when the charge is redeemed. The calculation of interest is explained at paragraph 2.115.   **2.113**

In order to try to ensure that the Commission will agree to the postponement of the charge the order for ancillary relief should contain the following provision: **2.114**

> And it is certified for the purposes of reg. 52(1)(a) of the Community Legal Service (Financial) Regulations 2000 [that the lump sum of £x has been ordered to be paid to enable the petitioner/respondent to purchase a home for himself/herself (or his/her dependants)] [that the property (address) has been preserved/recovered for the petitioner/respondent for use as a home for himself/herself (or his/her dependants)].

Calculation of interest

Interest runs from the date on which the charge is registered and will continue until the outstanding costs are paid: reg. 53, Community Legal Services (Financial) Regulations 2000.   **2.115**

The annual interest rate is 8 per cent. Simple, not compound, interest will accrue.   **2.116**

Regulations 40, 42, and 43 of the Community Legal Services (Financial) Regulations 2000 change the method of valuing the statutory charge arising under the Access to Justice Act 1999.   **2.117**

The change affects cases where: **2.118**

(a)   at the end of the case, the property to which the charge attaches is worth less than the cost of the funded services; and

(b)   the Commission agrees to postpone enforcement by registering a charge on the assisted person's home.

Under the old Regulations, the amount to be recovered under the charge was fixed at the date of registration of the charge. Hence, if the net value of the property at the date of registration was £3,000 and the cost of the funded services giving rise to the deficit was £5,000, only the sum of £3,000 was ultimately recoverable under the statutory charge regime.   **2.119**

Under the 2000 Regulations, however, the fact that at the time of registration of the charge the property has a net value which is less than the deficit no longer limits the amount of the charge. Instead, the amount of the deficit capable of recovery by the Legal Services Commission is determined at the date on which the statutory charge is redeemed. If, since registration, the property has increased in value and exceeds the amount of the statutory charge, the full amount of the deficit will now by repayable to the Commission.   **2.120**

Waiver of the charge

In certain circumstances the charge may be waived. Where relevant property has been recovered or preserved under the Legal Help scheme, the Commission (or the solicitor who   **2.121** has devolved powers to do so) may waive the charge in part or in full if enforcement would cause to the funded party grave hardship or distress or would be unreasonably difficult (to enforce) because of the nature of the property.

2.122   In determining whether the funded party would suffer grave hardship the Commission will consider the personal and financial circumstances of that party compared to the value of the property recovered or preserved. Further the Commission will consider the nature of the property recovered or preserved. Where, for example, the funded party is in receipt of income support and the item of property recovered is an essential item, such as a cooker, the Commission may agree to waive the charge. Similarly where the item is of genuine senti-mental value (for example, a wedding ring) and enforcement would cause grave distress the Commission may agree to waive the charge.

2.123   As for the problem of enforcement, this may arise because the property is outside the juris-diction and leads to waiver of the charge. However where enforcement is likely to be inconvenient or slow this will not in itself justify waiver.

2.124   The Commission has no power to waive the charge arising from a certificate for representa-tion unless:

(a)   it funded Legal Representation in proceedings which it considered to have a significant wider public interest; and

(b)   it considered it to be cost-effective to fund Legal Representation for a specified claimant or claimants, but not for others who may benefit.

In effect these are 'public interest' cases and are unlikely in fact to apply to family proceedings.

K   THE DUTY TO MAKE THE CLIENT FULLY AWARE OF THE POTENTIAL IMPACT OF THE CHARGE

2.125   It is imperative that the client is made fully aware of the existence of the statutory charge and of its potential impact in his particular case. The client can hardly be reminded of the charge too frequently. It is suggested that, at minimum, the solicitor should explain it to him comprehensively:

(a)   in the client care letter;

(b)   when the client receives Legal Help; *and*

(c)   when application is made for a General Family Help certificate; *and*

(d)   when any settlement is being considered which would produce cash or property which might be affected by the charge; *and*

(e)   if the cost of proceedings is mounting particularly high for any reason.

Clients have a knack, as all solicitors are aware, of forgetting that unpalatable advice has ever been given. It is not unknown, therefore, for a client to turn round when, for example, a large part of his lump sum is eaten up by the statutory charge and say that he was never warned that this would happen. It is therefore suggested that, in addition to explaining the charge to the client orally and giving the short explanatory leaflet provided by the Commission, the solicitor should also write to the client giving a further brief explanation so there is a record of his advice. Such advice should be updated in writing as the case progresses and costs increase.

Solicitors should be aware that, in order for the client to appreciate properly how the charge **2.126** may affect him in practice, he must be given an estimate of the likely costs of the proceedings in just the same way as a privately paying client. For example, in ancillary relief proceedings the client must be informed of the costs estimates lodged at the court at each hearing (see Chapter 18).

L MINIMIZING THE EFFECTS OF THE CHARGE

The obvious way to *avoid* the impact of the charge completely is to achieve a settlement **2.127** through mediation, as explained above.

Failing that the most effective way to *minimize* the charge is to seek to recover the client's **2.128** costs from the other party to the proceedings. However, this is rarely possible in family cases.

As we have seen above, the charge will only attach to property that has been in issue. **2.129** Another way in which to minimize the charge is therefore for the issues involved in the proceedings to be narrowed down as far as possible *at the outset.*

Example Mrs Hill consults her solicitor with a view to a divorce. The family home is in joint names and Mrs Hill thinks that her husband accepts that she is entitled to half of it. She wishes to claim the entire house (in which there is an equity of about £40,000) in ancillary relief proceedings. She then proposes to sell the house and buy a smaller property. The solicitor writes to Mr Hill's solicitor asking him to confirm that Mr Hill accepts his wife's entitlement to half the house and that the dispute between the parties is only over the other half share. Mr Hill's solicitor confirms this. Mrs Hill files a divorce petition making a comprehensive claim for financial relief and property adjustment and, in particular, claiming the transfer of the house to her. She obtains funding for ancillary relief proceedings. The district judge ultimately orders that the house should be transferred to her.

Mrs Hill's half of the house was never in issue. The statutory charge in relation to her costs will only attach to the half share in the house which she has recovered from her husband in the proceedings. Mrs Hill does sell the house immediately after the proceedings are over. The Commission is not prepared to take a charge over her new house—it requires immediate repayment of its charge. Broadly speaking, her debt to the Commission will be as follows:

Equity in house	£40,000
Property recovered by Mrs Hill in the proceedings is therefore half this figure	£20,000
Property subject to the charge	£20,000

Mrs Hill's costs amounted to £8,000. She paid no contribution to her funding and no order for costs was obtained against Mr Hill. The Fund is therefore out of pocket by £8,000. Mrs Hill will be required to pay £8,000 to the Commission in respect of her costs.

Note that, had the whole of the house been in issue in the proceedings, Mrs Hill would have recovered half of it and preserved the remainder. Thus the entire equity of £40,000 would have been open to the charge.

If possible, not only the correspondence but also the statements and other documents filed should make clear what property is and what property is not in dispute.

M   OTHER METHODS OF FUNDING

2.130   There are occasions where a client is not eligible for public funding but has few resources, if any, to pay the solicitor on a private paying basis.

2.131   Since a solicitor is not allowed to enter a conditional fee agreement with a client in respect of family proceedings, other methods of funding have to be considered. These may include, for example,

(a)   an application to the court for an order for maintenance pending suit under s. 22 Matrimonial Causes Act 1973 (see Chapter 17);

(b)   A 'Sears Tooth' agreement. Held to be valid in *Sears Tooth (A Firm)* v *Payne Hicks Beach (A Firm) and Others* [1997] 2 FLR 116, this is an arrangement whereby solicitors can take a charge on any property recovered or preserved in the proceedings usually by an assignment of rights under an order dealing with property or capital (but no maintenance);

(c)   a personal loan from a bank or credit card company; or

(d)   a loan from relatives or friends—it is important in these circumstances to show that there is an enforceable contract for repayment of the loan, otherwise the court may not be prepared to take it into account when quantifying liabilities.

N   CHAPTER SUMMARY

2.132   1.   Where the client has limited financial resources, public funding may be available to enable the client to pay for legal advice and representation.

2.   There are various 'levels of service' which a publicly funded client may receive. These are:
    (i)   Legal Help;
    (ii)   General Family Help;
    (iii)   Help with mediation;
    (iv)   Legal Representation (which may be available in emergency situations).

3.   Except in public law children cases, the client will need to satisfy the means and merits tests to be eligible for public funding.

4.   Public funding is not free—a contribution may be payable as the case progresses.

5.   Public funding is often described as 'a loan not a gift' and will need to be repaid from property or capital 'recovered or preserved'. This is known as 'the statutory charge'.

6.   Where public funding is not available, other methods of funding should be considered.

Community Legal Service
KEYCARD NO 43 - Issued April 2007

General

This card is intended as a quick reference point only when assessing financial eligibility for those levels of service for which the supplier has responsibility: Legal Help; Help at Court; Legal Representation before the Asylum and Immigration Tribunal, and before the High Court in respect of an application under s. 103A of the Nationality, Immigration and Asylum Act 2002; Family Mediation; Help with Mediation, and Legal Representation in respect of Specified Family Proceedings before a Magistrates' Court (other than proceedings under the Children Act 1989 or Part IV of the Family Law Act 1996). Full guidance on the assessment of means is set out in Part F of Volume 2 of the Legal Services Commission Manual. References in this card to volume and section numbers e.g. volume 2F-section 1 are references to the relevant parts of that guidance. Suppliers should have regard to the general provisions set out in guidance volume 2F-section 2, particularly those set out in sub paragraphs 3-5 regarding the documentation required when assessing means. This keycard and the guidance are relevant to all applications for funding made on or after 9 April 2007.

Eligibility Limits

The summary of the main eligibility limits from 9 April 2007 are provided below:

Level of Service	Income Limit	Capital Limit
All Levels of Service*: o Legal Help; o Help at Court; o Family Mediation; o Help with Mediation, and o Legal Representation before the Asylum and Immigration Tribunal, and before the High Court in respect of an application under s. 103A of the Nationality, Immigration and Asylum Act 2002; o Legal Representation in respect of Specified Family Proceedings before a Magistrates' Court (other than proceedings under the Children Act 1989 or Part IV of the Family Law Act 1996).	Gross income not to exceed £2435** per month Disposable income not to exceed £672 per month. Passported if in receipt of Income Support, Income Based Job Seekers' Allowance or Guarantee State Pension Credit. [Also passported for Legal Help, Help at Court and Legal Reprecentation (asylum and immigration matters only), if in receipt of NASS Support].	Disposable Capital not to exceed £3000 (CLR immigration matters) £8000 (All other levels of service) Passported if in receipt of Income Support, Income Based Job Seekers' Allowance, or Guarantee State Pension Credit. [Also passported for Legal Help, Help at Court and Legal Representation (asylum and immigration matters only), if in receipt of NASS Support].

* May be subject to contribution from income and/or capital (see volume 2F-section 3.2 paras 1 to 5)
** A higher gross income cap applies to families with more than 4 dependant children. Add £205 to the base gross income cap shown above for the 5th and each subsequent dependant child.

Additional information regarding the financial eligibility criteria is also provided in guidance volume 2f-section 3

STEP BY STEP GUIDE TO ASSESSMENT

Step One Determine whether or not the client has a partner whose means should be aggregated for the purposes of the assessment (see guidance in volume 2F-section 4.2 paras 1-5).

Step Two Determine whether the client is directly or indirectly in receipt of either Income Support, Income Based Job Seekers' Allowance, Guarantee State Pension Credit or NASS support in order to determine whether the client automatically satisfies the relevant financial eligibility test as indicated by the 'passported' arrangements stated in the table on reverse.

Step Three For any cases which are not 'passported' determine the gross income of the client, including the income of any partner, (see guidance in volume 2F-section5). Where that gross income is assessed as being above £2,435 per month, then the client is ineligible for funding for all levels of service and the application should be refused without any further calculations being performed. Certain sources of income can be disregarded and a higher gross income cap applies to families with more than 4 dependant children.

Step Four For those clients whose gross income is not more than the gross income cap (see guidance in volume, 2f-section 3). Fixed allowances are made for dependants and employment expenses and these are set out in the table below. Other allowances can be made for: tax; national insurance; maintenance paid; housing costs and childminding. If the resulting disposable income is above the relevant limit then funding should be refused across all levels of service without any further calculations being necessary.

Fixed rate allowances (per month) from 9 April 2007	
Work related expenses for those receiving a wage or salary	£45

Dependants Allowances
        Partner
        Child aged 15 or under
        Child aged 16 or over
	£146.62
	£206.75
	£206.75

Housing cap for those without dependants	£545

Step Five Where a client's disposable income is below the relevant limit then it is necessary to calculate the client's disposable capital (see guidance in volume, 2F-section7). If the resulting capital is above the relevant limit, then the application should be refused (However in the case of Legal Representation in Specified Family Proceedings if the likely costs of the case are more than £5,000 then refer to LSC which may grant funding – see volume 2F-section 3.1 para 6).

Step Six For those clients whose disposable income and disposable capital have been assessed below the relevant limits then for all levels of service other than Legal Representation in Specified Family Proceedings, the client can be awarded funding.

Step Seven For Legal Representation in Specified Family Proceedings, it is necessary to determine whether any contributions from either income or capital (or both) should be paid by the client (see guidance in volume 2F-section 3.2 paras 1 to 5). For ease of reference the relevant income contribution table is reproduced below. Such contributions should be collected by the supplier (see guidance in volume 2F-section 3.2 para 4).

Band	Monthly disposable income	Monthly contribution
A	£290 to £426	1/4 of income in excess of £285
B	£427 to £565	£35.25 + 1/3 of income in excess of £426
C	£566 to £672	£81.60+ 1/2 of income in excess of £565

3

MEDIATION AND COLLABORATIVE LAW

A   MEANING OF MEDIATION

National Family Mediation, one of the main mediation bodies, has defined mediation   **3.01**
as follows:

> Family mediation is a process in which an impartial third person assists those involved in family
> breakdown, and in particular separating or divorced couples, to communicate better with one
> another and to reach their own agreed and informed decisions about some or all of the issues

relating to or arising from the separation, divorce, children, finance or property. Mediation is thus an alternative to decision-making by the courts. It is not part of the decision-making procedures of the court.

While the Family Law Act 1996 (one of the principal aims of which, though never implemented, was to bring in 'no fault' divorce) was being debated in Parliament, Sir Jim Lester MP encapsulated the nature of mediation and the tension that exists between mediation and legal representation as follows:

> Mediation is essentially a private and informed decision-making process, and that is its strength. However, because of that it does not include the safeguards of due legal process. Therefore, it requires high standards of training and practice to secure the participation of the two parties. Experience suggests that mediation is likely to be effective only when the couples involved feel that they are committed to the process. Success is unlikely if they do not feel that commitment, or if they feel that they have not entered the process by choice, with a willingness to adhere to the results. It is not suitable for everyone. (Hansard Standing Committee E, 14 May 1996, col. 248)

It is important to be clear about the real meaning of mediation so as not to confuse it with other concepts.

Mediation is not arbitration

3.02   Arbitration is 'the settlement of a question at issue by one to whom the parties agree to refer their claims in order to obtain an equitable decision' (*Oxford English Dictionary*). In mediation, solutions or settlement are not imposed on the parties. The mediator does not make findings of fact. The mediator's function is more limited. It is to assist the parties to come to a settlement themselves.

Mediation is not reconciliation

3.03   The process of reconciliation is 'to bring a person again into friendly relations with another after an estrangement' (*Oxford English Dictionary*). Mediation does not have as its prime object the aim of reconciling estranged parties. However, mediation may indirectly promote reconciliation because its process may well require the parties to address some of the issues which initially led to the breakdown of their marriage. A mediator must be aware throughout the process of mediation of the possibility of reconciliation between the couple concerned. Where there is such a possibility the mediator must ensure that the couple are given proper information about marriage counselling.

Mediation is not conciliation

3.04   Conciliation is 'to gain good will by acts which induce friendly feeling' (*Oxford English Dictionary*). Conciliation is just one of the tools used in mediation. For example, in the course of mediation one of the parties may make a concession over a particular issue in dispute. The other party may interpret that concession as a gesture of goodwill and therefore be encouraged to make further progress in the negotiation process. However, there are many other tools which may be used in the course of mediation. A mediator may work through a wide range of strategies before finding the one which fits the nature of the parties needing assistance.

Mediation organizations

The United Kingdom College of Family Mediators ('UKCFM') is the umbrella organization **3.05** under which the main mediation bodies are gathered. Two of the main bodies are National Family Mediation and the Family Mediators' Association. The address for the UKCFM is Alexander House, Telephone Avenue, Bristol BS1 4BS. The telephone number is 0117 904 7223 and the website is <www.ukcfm.co.uk>. The UKCFM has a code of practice to which its members must adhere. A directory of members and associates is available from the UKCFM on request for a modest cost.

B   PUBLIC FUNDING FOR MEDIATION

Public funding for family mediation is available for parties who come within the relevant **3.06** eligibility criteria. The Legal Services Commission administers the Community Legal Service Fund and greater emphasis is now placed on mediation as a means of resolving disputes generally. Chapter 2 deals comprehensively with the Community Legal Service scheme and therefore only a brief outline is given here to guide the practitioner to the appropriate sources. 'Family Mediation' is a separate level of service under the Funding Code, authorizing mediation of a family dispute and an assessment of whether mediation appears suitable to the dispute, the parties, and all the circumstances (see Chapter 2, paragraph 2.43). In certain circumstances a client must attend an assessment of suitability with a recognized mediator before an application can be made for General Family Help (see Chapter 2, paragraph 2.21) and for Legal Representation (see Chapter 2, paragraph 2.55) where the following family proceedings are contemplated:

(a)   Matrimonial Causes Act 1973 (except s. 37);
(b)   Domestic Proceedings and Magistrates' Courts Act 1978;
(c)   Private law applications and financial relief proceedings under the Children Act 1989.

There are a number of categories of proceedings for which it will not be necessary for the client to attend an appointment to be assessed for suitability for mediation (see Chapter 2, paragraph 2.45).

'Help with Mediation' is only available if a client is actually participating in Family **3.07** Mediation and it enables a solicitor to assist the client, for example by advising on the legal implications of a mediated settlement and taking steps to put the settlement into effect (for example, by obtaining a court order dealing with financial and property matters by consent): see Chapter 2, paragraph 2.35.

C FAMILY LAW PROTOCOL

Aims of the Protocol

3.08 The Law Society published the second edition of the Family Law Protocol in 2006 and this has already been discussed in Chapter 1, paragraph 1.02 and onwards. It covers best practice in all aspects of private family law disputes. It is worth repeating here that the Protocol places an emphasis upon the importance of mediation, family dispute resolution, and the interests of children in the family.

3.09 Part I, para. 1.1.15 of the Protocol requires that solicitors must:

(a) at an early stage, unless it is clearly inappropriate to do so, explain the mediation process or other appropriate forms of alternative dispute resolution (ADR) and advise clients on the benefits and/or limitations of mediation or ADR in their particular case, as well as the role of the solicitor in supporting the mediation or other process;

(b) keep the suitability of mediation and ADR under review throughout the case;

(c) encourage clients to go to mediation or ADR when and where appropriate.

Part 7, paras. 7.2 to 7.9 of the Protocol deal specifically with mediation and the solicitor's role in relation to it. It emphasizes that sometimes the dispute between a couple may involve a wider group of family members than just the couple. These may include step-parents, grandparents, aunts, uncles, children, and so forth. Any of these may participate in the mediation with the agreement of the couple and the mediator (although children do not usually participate directly and can only do so when the mediator is specifically trained to involve children): paras. 7.2.2 and 7.2.3 of the Protocol.

Screening for mediation (Part 7, para. 7.3)

3.10 The Protocol emphasizes that it is important that only suitable cases are referred to mediation. At an early stage solicitors must, unless it is clearly inappropriate to do so, explain the mediation process and advise clients on the benefits and/or limitations of mediation in their case, as well as the role of solicitors in supporting the mediation process (para. 7.3.2). Family mediation usually involves both parties meeting with the mediator at the same time. It can resolve or narrow issues in dispute. However, sometimes the issues may make mediation inappropriate, for example (para. 7.3.4):

(a) where there are child protection issues or a risk of child abduction;

(b) where clients do not have the capacity to mediate or their mental competence is in question;

(c) before emergency procedures which need to be taken have been concluded;

(d) where a particular issue can only be adjudicated upon by the court, for example, in paternity cases;

(e) in financial proceedings where either party is bankrupt;

(f) where bail conditions are in place restricting one party having contact with the other party;

Other examples of circumstances in which mediation may not be appropriate are (para. 7.3.5):

(a) where domestic abuse has occurred or is still occurring. If clients still wish to mediate, the solicitor should discuss the risks with them and decide whether any action can be taken to make them feel safe in the mediation, for example, by first obtaining a non-molestation order through the court;

(b) where the imbalance in power between the parties is likely to be beyond the capacity of the mediators to address;

(c) where relationship counselling or marital therapy may be more appropriate.

Selecting a mediator (Part 7, para. 7.4)

It is useful for solicitors to keep details of mediators who are trained and accredited with an established organization. Solicitors should advise publicly funded clients of the availability of publicly funded mediation and that the statutory charge (explained in Chapter 2, paragraph 2.96) does not apply to work done in respect of mediation. **3.11**

The benefits of mediation (Part 7, para. 7.5)

Solicitors should explain to their clients the benefits of mediation, which include: **3.12**

1. When parties divorce or separate, it is generally better if both parties can sort out together the practical arrangements for the future.
2. The aim of mediation is to help parties find a solution that meets the needs of all involved, especially the children, and that both parties feel is fair. At the end of mediation, those involved should feel that there has been no 'winner or loser' but that together they have arrived at sensible, workable arrangements.
3. Mediation can help to reduce tension, hostility, and misunderstandings and so improve communication between parties. This is especially important if children are involved, as parties may need to co-operate over their care and upbringing for some years to come.
4. Mediation can offer general costs savings as parties have only one professional assisting them. Clients who are able to agree will incur lower fee levels.
5. Mediation may have economic benefits because if a party is eligible for publicly funded mediation, he or she will not be required to make any contribution towards the cost of the mediation. If a party is eligible for mediation he or she will also be eligible for legal advice in respect of that mediation during and at the end of mediation and will not need to make a contribution to this.

The timing of the referral to mediation (Part 7, para. 7.6)

In publicly funded cases there is a requirement to consider mediation at the commencement of the matter and before a full certificate for representation or General Family Help can be obtained. Even if a case is unsuitable initially for mediation, the solicitor must keep under review the possibility of a referral to mediation later on as public funding might be available at that later stage. In private cases, the solicitor must give careful consideration to the timing of mediation. For example, it may be appropriate to refer contact disputes for mediation early on before parties' positions have become entrenched. In financial cases, it may sometimes be appropriate to deal with disclosure prior to a referral to mediation. **3.13**

Supporting clients in mediation (Part 7, para. 7.7)

3.14 Mediation usually works best when supported by independent legal advice. When a solicitor refers a client to mediation he should explain that:

(a) the mediation process should be supported by independent legal advice;

(b) public funding is available for mediation by way of 'Help with Mediation';

(c) no financial agreement is directly binding between the parties until it has been approved by the court as a consent order or made legally binding in some other manner;

(d) parties may consult their solicitors at any stage in mediation, but this is particularly important when financial disclosure and settlement proposals are being considered; and

(e) seeking advice from solicitors between mediation sessions can be positively helpful in seeing whether proposals are appropriate.

The role of solicitors during mediation (Part 7, para. 7.8)

3.15 The role of solicitors during the mediation process is very important. Solicitors should:

(a) assist clients to provide financial disclosure where necessary and assess the disclosure which takes place in mediation;

(b) give advice about settlement proposals as and when required, bearing in mind the long-term interests of clients and/or any children;

(c) give advice about other options;

(d) facilitate the obtaining of third-party input or information, for example, welfare benefits advice, expert valuation, or accountancy advice

(e) bear in mind the cost of mediation as opposed to the cost of negotiation through solicitors or resolution by way of court proceedings;

(f) give advice about any untenable position either clients or their partners may be adopting;

(g) assist clients to reach a decision and encourage clients to raise issues in mediation as appropriate.

The role of solicitors following mediation (Part 7, para. 7.9)

3.16 It is important that it is made clear to parties that proposals made in mediation are not legally binding between them and that each of them should have access to independent legal advice when proposals are made. Where mediation does not result in firm proposals between the parties the solicitor should:

(a) discuss with the client the reasons for the discontinuation of the mediation;

(b) note what has been achieved; and

(c) discuss the options with the client.

Where the parties have produced interim proposals, the solicitor should discuss the position and any potential difficulties, including the need to apply for any interim court orders. Where proposals for settlement have been made then solicitors should follow the guidance in the main protocol (which is discussed in Chapter 18, paragraph 18.128). Where it is appropriate to draft a consent order dealing with finances, the guidance on consent orders should be followed (see Part IV, paras. 16.1–16.6, which is discussed in Chapter 18, paragraph 18.137).

D   THE MEDIATION PROCESS

There is a range of different models of mediation, including co-mediation (two mediators), sole mediation (one mediator), and shuttle mediation (the mediator moves between the two parties, who remain in separate rooms). Sometimes children are directly involved in the mediation process where it is seen as an effective means of assisting the parents' negotiations. **3.17**

Mediation can address children's issues, property and financial issues, or all issues. It is for the clients to decide which areas they wish to be the subject of mediation. Sometimes clients will be asked to fill in a referral form prior to the first mediation appointment setting out basic details about the length of the marriage or cohabitation, the date of any separation, the names and ages of the parties and their children, the living arrangements, the stage of any legal proceedings, preliminary information about employment, housing, and an outline of their financial position. Each party will be invited to say on the form briefly what they hope to settle through mediation. The form often includes a question about the possibility of reconciliation. Finally, the form often includes questions about domestic abuse/imbalance of power between the parties so that the mediator can be alerted at the earliest opportunity to the possible existence of such issues. If there are any, the mediator will usually take steps to see each party separately at the first appointment to check out those issues with a view to deciding whether it would be appropriate for mediation to take place at all. In other cases, instead of using a referral form the mediator will gather the information verbally from the parties at the first appointment. **3.18**

The mediation process is divided into five major stages. These are discussed in turn. **3.19**

Establishing the arena

Once the mediator has gathered the preliminary information from the parties he will then establish from them whether or not they are willing to take part in mediation. The mediation process and its ground rules will be explained. The mediator will invite the parties to share any concerns they·may have about the process. If they wish to proceed then they will be asked to sign the Agreement to Mediate, confirming their commitment to the process. It is made clear at every stage that mediation is a voluntary process and that the parties are free to terminate it at any point. Likewise, the mediator has power to terminate mediation if it becomes inappropriate for any reason. **3.20**

Clarifying the issues

The next step is for the mediator to establish with the parties which issues they wish to discuss in mediation. The issues are defined and often the mediator will write them on a **3.21** flip-chart, explaining that others can be added if necessary as mediation proceeds. In this way the mediator helps the parties to set the agenda for mediation and to work out the order/priority in which they wish to tackle the issues. For example, the arrangements for children may need immediate discussion. In finance and property mediation and all issues mediation, the mediator explains to the parties how financial information is to be gathered. A substantial financial questionnaire, based on Form E used in ancillary relief proceedings, is distributed to the clients and they are asked to complete it before the next mediation session and to bring supporting documentation, with sufficient copies for each other and the mediator. By explaining the way in which the process works the mediator helps to establish the parties' trust in the process and in the mediator.

Exploring the issues

3.22   At the next mediation appointment, time will be allocated to cover the issues on the parties' agenda. If there are issues concerning the children the parties may wish to discuss them first. The mediator will enquire about the existing arrangements for the children and the parents' views and concerns about them. This will include exploring the parents' perception of each child's position, feelings, and point of view. There may be discussion about the sharing of parental responsibility and exploration of the options, taking account of the child's feelings and needs. The mediator will consider with the parties whether they will talk further to the children or whether the children themselves should be involved in the mediation. If so, then the parties will need to decide when and how this should take place. Interim arrangements may be agreed and tried out, while longer-term arrangements are considered.

3.23   Where financial information has been provided by both parties this is shared and discussed and is written up on the flip-chart to provide an overview. The mediator enquires about missing information, clarifies discrepancies, and gives information as required to help the parties to ensure that the whole financial picture has been given. If further information and supporting documentation is required, the mediator will help the parties to identify this and to establish a time frame for it to be supplied. The mediator will try to discover each party's self-interest in the dispute, increase the parties' motivation to solve their problems, develop trust, and establish motivation for them to build agreements between themselves where possible.

Developing options

3.24   The mediator will help the parties to identify, create, and develop various options for solving their problems. This is done by developing communication between the parties and seeking their respective ideas for possible solutions. The mediator will help them to look at the advantages and disadvantages of each option and test the consequences of their not reaching agreement. It is part of the mediator's job to understand the underlying needs and fears of the parties and to recommend that they seek independent legal and/or financial advice from solicitors, accountants, and other experts. The mediator may prepare an interim mediation summary to assist them in seeking advice. Further discussions about the children will take place if needed.

Securing agreement

The mediator will help the parties to clarify their proposals for settlement and the issues   **3.25**
that remain outstanding. He will seek detailed financial proposals and help the parties to
compare the proposals with their needs, budgets, and so forth. The mediator will help the
parties to quantify the differences between them to establish the size of any gap between
their respective positions and needs. He will explore the scope for reaching agreement and
invite further proposals from both parties. The mediator will encourage joint decision
making where possible and help the parties to fit together the different elements of their
proposals and reality-test them. The mediator helps the parties to record their proposals
and brings the process to a close.

Where the parties have reached proposals for settlement the mediator will usually draw   **3.26**
up a legally privileged document incorporating them. Where the proposals relate to
financial issues, the mediator will, in addition, draw up an 'open' statement of financial
information, summarizing the information disclosed during the process, which is not
legally privileged and which may be used in court if necessary. Different mediation bodies
have different precedents for these documents, but the basic content of each will be similar.
Both parties will be encouraged to seek legal advice on the proposals and any outstanding
issues. Further negotiations may take place between legal advisers over the drafting of formal
agreements or consent orders. If there are still substantial differences between the parties or
the parties need to review arrangements or deal with changed circumstances they may
return to mediation to work out further solutions.

E   COLLABORATIVE LAW

Collaborative family law is a process by which family lawyers and their clients agree in   **3.27**
writing to reach settlement in relation to the issues involved and agree not to go to court.
They agree to work together to resolve children and financial issues arising out of their
separation and/or divorce. They may enlist the help of experts, such as child specialists,
family therapists, financial specialists, and mediators, as part of the team. Collaborative
family lawyers use their skills in representation, negotiation, and problem-solving to help
their clients to shape agreements appropriate to their circumstances. Settlement is reached
by means of 'four way' face to face meetings involving the two clients and their respective lawyers. All information and disclosure is provided in the collaborative process.
Collaborative law has many benefits, in particular as regards the emotional management
of the parties to the dispute. However, the cost is unlikely to be very different from the
conventional process of settlement by inter-solicitor negotiation. The clients remain in
control of the process but have their lawyers present throughout for legal advice and
guidance. As with mediation, it will not be suitable for everyone, but is a useful process for
some clients and may help them to manage the breakdown of their relationship more easily.
However, if no settlement can be reached then the collaborative lawyers must withdraw
from acting for their clients and new lawyers must be instructed to take the matter forward
by way of court proceedings.

3.28 The Collaborative Family Law Group (<www.collabfamilylaw.org.uk>) has been established under the auspices of Resolution (formerly the Solicitors Family Law Association).

F KEY DOCUMENTS

3.29 'The Family Law Protocol' (2nd edition): published by The Law Society, 113 Chancery Lane, London WC2A 1PL

UK College of Family Mediators 'Code of Conduct': available from UKCFM, Alexander House, Telephone Avenue, Bristol BS1 4BS

Parenting plans: <www.dca.gov.uk/family/divleaf.htm> (from Department of Constitutional Affairs)

Websites
UK College of Family Mediators: <www.ukcfm.co.uk>]
Collaborative Family Law Group: <www.collabfamilylaw.org.uk>

PART II

DIVORCE, NULLITY, AND JUDICIAL SEPARATION: THE DECREE

PROCEEDINGS TO DISSOLVE A CIVIL PARTNERSHIP: THE DISSOLUTION

4

THE GROUND FOR DIVORCE AND THE FIVE FACTS

The present law of divorce is contained in the Matrimonial Causes Act 1973 ('MCA 1973').

A   THE GROUND FOR DIVORCE

4.01   There is only one ground for divorce, that is that the marriage has irretrievably broken down; s. 1(1), MCA 1973.

4.02   A decree absolute of divorce terminates the marriage and radically changes the status of the parties, especially in relation to eligibility for certain state benefits and pensions.

B   THE FIVE FACTS

4.03   The court cannot hold that the marriage has irretrievably broken down unless the petitioner satisfies the court of one or more of the five facts set out in s. 1(2), MCA 1973. These are:

(a)   that the respondent has committed adultery and the petitioner finds it intolerable to live with the respondent;

(b)   that the respondent has behaved in such a way that the petitioner cannot reasonably be expected to live with the respondent;

(c)   that the respondent has deserted the petitioner for a continuous period of at least two years immediately preceding the presentation of the petition;

(d)   that the parties to the marriage have lived apart for a continuous period of at least two years immediately preceding the presentation of the petition and the respondent consents to a decree being granted (two years' separation and consent);

(e) that the parties to the marriage have lived apart for a continuous period of at least five years immediately preceding the presentation of the petition (five years' separation).

Because of the requirement that one of the five facts should be proved, it is possible for a situation to arise where the marriage has undoubtedly broken down irretrievably but no divorce can yet be granted because neither party can establish any of the five facts.

Example A couple separate by mutual consent simply because they have found that they are incompatible. Neither has committed adultery or behaved in such a way that the other cannot reasonably be expected to live with them. Although the marriage has irretrievably broken down, they are not able to obtain a divorce during the first two years of their separation as none of the five facts can be established. When two years are up, assuming they both wish to be divorced, it will be possible to establish two years' separation and consent (s. 1(2)(d)) and one or other party will be able to seek a decree.

C IRRETRIEVABLE BREAKDOWN

No link necessary between s. 1(2) fact and irretrievable breakdown

It is not necessary for the petitioner to show that the irretrievable breakdown of the marriage **4.04** has been caused by the s. 1(2) fact on which she relies (*Stevens v Stevens* [1979] 1 WLR 885; *Buffery v Buffery* [1988] 2 FLR 365 (CA)).

Example (The facts of *Stevens v Stevens*.) The petitioner established that the respondent's behaviour was such that she could not reasonably be expected to live with him: s. 1(2)(b). The marriage had irretrievably broken down but in fact it was established that it was the petitioner's own behaviour that had caused the breakdown.

The petitioner was nevertheless entitled to a decree.

Proving irretrievable breakdown

Section 1(4), MCA 1973 provides that if the court is satisfied that one of the s. 1(2) facts **4.05** is proved, unless it is satisfied on all the evidence that the marriage has not broken down irretrievably it shall grant a decree of divorce (subject to the provisions of s. 5, MCA 1973, see Chapter 12). In other words, once one of the facts is established, a presumption of irretrievable breakdown is raised. In an undefended case, there is not normally any evidence to displace the presumption and the court therefore accepts the petitioner's statement in her petition that the marriage has irretrievably broken down without further enquiry.

However, it is open to the respondent to challenge the petitioner's assertion of irretrievable **4.06** breakdown by filing an answer denying that the marriage has irretrievably broken down. In this event, the suit will become defended and it will be up to the court to determine on the basis of all the evidence at the hearing whether or not the marriage has irretrievably broken down by that date (see *Ash v Ash* [1972] 1 All ER 582; *Pheasant v Pheasant* [1972] 1 All ER 587).

Adjournment with a view to reconciliation

4.07 If at any stage in the divorce proceedings the court feels that there is a reasonable possibility of a reconciliation between the parties, the court may adjourn the proceedings for whatever period it thinks fit to enable attempts at reconciliation to take place: s. 6(2), MCA 1973.

D ADULTERY: S. 1(2)(a)

Two separate elements to prove

4.08 There are two matters that the petitioner must prove:

(a) that the respondent has committed adultery; *and*

(b) that she finds it intolerable to live with him.

The adultery may be the reason why the petitioner finds it intolerable to live with the respondent but it is not necessary for there to be any link between the two matters (*Cleary* v *Cleary* [1974] 1 All ER 498, followed in *Carr* v *Carr* [1974] 1 All ER 1193).

Example (The facts of *Cleary* v *Cleary*.) The respondent wife committed adultery. The petitioner husband took her back afterwards but things did not work out because the wife corresponded with the other man, went out at night and then went to live at her mother's and did not return. The petitioner said that he could no longer live with the respondent because there was no future for the marriage. Although it was the respondent's conduct after the adultery and not the adultery itself that had made it intolerable for the petitioner to live with her, he had satisfied both limbs of s. 1(2)(a) and was entitled to a decree.

Meaning of adultery

4.09 Adultery is voluntary sexual intercourse between a man and woman who are not married to each other but one of whom at least is a married person (*Clarkson* v *Clarkson* (1930) 143 LT 775).

Proof of adultery

4.10 It would be quite extraordinary if the petitioner were able to produce a witness who had actually *seen* the respondent committing adultery. Proof is therefore normally indirect.

4.11 Examples of the type of evidence commonly used are set out in the following paragraphs.

Confessions and admissions

4.12 It used to be routine practice for a confession statement to be obtained from the respondent (and if possible the co-respondent as well) admitting adultery and setting out briefly the circumstances in which it took place.

4.13 Nowadays, the acknowledgement of service forms used by respondents and co-respondents in adultery cases ask the question 'Do you admit the adultery alleged in the petition?' If the respondent answers this question in the affirmative and signs the form, the court can accept this as sufficient evidence of adultery. Depending on the nature of the case and the practice of the particular court in which proceedings are pending, it may or may not still be necessary for the old style of confession statement or other evidence of adultery (see paragraphs 4.17 and 4.18 below) to be obtained as well.

In circumstances where there is some doubt as to whether the respondent will admit the adultery in his acknowledgement of service form, it is sensible to obtain a signed confession in any event before commencing divorce proceedings. To do otherwise may result in costs being incurred without any prospect of a divorce being obtained because the petitioner cannot prove the fact of adultery in any other way. **4.14**

If the respondent denies adultery and proceeds to file an answer, the case will be defended and the court will have to consider whether, on all the evidence available at the hearing, adultery is proved. **4.15**

If the respondent does not admit (or even denies) adultery in the acknowledgement of service but does not go so far as to file an answer, his lack of cooperation will not necessarily be fatal to the petitioner's case. She will simply have to attempt to prove adultery by other evidence. **4.16**

Circumstantial evidence

The following are examples of the type of evidence from which the court can be asked to infer adultery: **4.17**

(a) Evidence that the respondent and another woman are living together as man and wife. The petitioner may be able to state this from her own observations. Alternatively she may be able to produce an independent witness of her own to the fact (for example, the next-door neighbour of the respondent and his cohabitant). If necessary an enquiry agent can be instructed to watch the respondent and collect evidence of cohabitation.

(b) Evidence that the respondent and another woman had the inclination and the opportunity to commit adultery, for example that they had formed an intimate relationship (they may have been seen kissing or holding hands in public, for example, or the petitioner may have obtained copies of 'love letters' passing between them) and had spent the night together in the same bedroom or alone together in the same house. Again, the petitioner may be able to supply this evidence herself but if not, an enquiry agent may be able to help. Indeed in the case of evidence of the type set out in both (a) and (b), the court may *require* independent evidence before it is satisfied of adultery.

(c) Evidence that the wife has given birth to a child of which the husband is not the father. Normally it is presumed that a child born during the marriage is legitimate. However, this presumption can be displaced, for example, by evidence that the parties did not have any contact with each other during the time in which conception must have taken place (for example, where the husband has been working overseas continuously for a prolonged period). A birth certificate can be admitted as prima facie evidence of the facts required to be entered on it. This can be useful where the wife has registered the birth and named someone other than the husband as the father of the child.

Findings in other proceedings

4.18 Findings made by a court in other proceedings may be admissible as evidence of adultery by the party against whom the finding had been made, for example:

(a) where the husband has been found to be the father of a child in proceedings brought by the mother of the child under sch. 1, Children Act 1989, for a lump sum order or transfer of property order;

(b) where the husband has been found to be the father of a child in proceedings brought by the Child Support Agency for maintenance for the child;

(c) where a finding of adultery has been made against either party in family proceedings;

(d) where the husband had been convicted of rape;

(e) where the petitioner has already been granted a decree of judicial separation on the basis of the adultery on which she relies in the divorce proceedings, the court may treat the decree of judicial separation as sufficient proof of the adultery (s.4(2), MCA 1973): see Chapter 13.

The co-respondent

4.19 A person with whom it is alleged the respondent has committed adultery must be made a party to the suit unless he is not named in the petition or the court otherwise directs (see r. 2.7(1), Family Proceedings Rules 1991 ('FPR 1991')). As to whether it is necessary to name a co-respondent, see Chapter 8, paragraph 8.36.

4.20 Where a co-respondent is named, in most cases if there is no admission of adultery by the co-respondent, the co-respondent will be dismissed from the suit. This does not mean that the petitioner will be denied her decree of divorce. Provided that, by other evidence, she has proved to the satisfaction of the court that the respondent has committed adultery, the court can find adultery with a person against whom adultery has not been proved.

Intolerability

4.21 Normally, at least in an undefended case, the petitioner's statement in her petition that she finds it intolerable to live with the respondent will be accepted at face value.

4.22 However, further evidence may be required in support of her contention if either:

(a) the information supplied by the petitioner in the petition itself and in support of the petition raises doubts in the mind of the court (usually in the person of the district judge who considers the case under the special procedure) as to whether the petitioner finds it intolerable to live with the respondent: *or*

(b) the respondent files an answer challenging the petitioner's assertion, in which case the divorce will become defended and the court will hear evidence from both parties on the issue.

The test to be applied when an issue arises over whether the petitioner finds it intolerable to live with the respondent is a subjective one (*Goodrich* v *Goodrich* [1971] 2 All ER 1340), i.e., 'does *this petitioner* find it intolerable to live with the respondent' and not 'would *a reasonable petitioner* find it intolerable to live with the respondent?'

Living together

In some cases the petitioner can be prevented from relying on adultery because she has lived **4.23**
with the respondent after she discovered his adultery. This matter is dealt with at paragraph
4.57 below.

E BEHAVIOUR: S. 1(2)(b)

The test for behaviour

The test as to whether the respondent has behaved in such a way that the petitioner cannot **4.24**
reasonably be expected to live with him is a cross between a subjective and an objective test.
The formula used in the case of *Livingstone-Stallard* v *Livingstone-Stallard* [1974] Fam 47 seems
to have been accepted (see *Birch* v *Birch* [1992] 1 FLR 564) i.e.:

> Would any right-thinking person come to the conclusion that *this* husband has behaved in such
> a way that *this* wife cannot reasonably be expected to live with him, taking into account the
> whole of the circumstances and the characters and personalities of the parties?

Thus, not only must the court look at the respondent's behaviour but also at the petition- **4.25**
er's behaviour (asking, for example, whether she provoked the respondent deliberately or
simply by her own anti-social conduct). Consideration must also be given to what type
of people the petitioner and respondent are (asking, for example, whether the petitioner
is particularly sensitive and vulnerable) and to the whole history of the marriage. The
court must then evaluate all this evidence and decide objectively whether, in these
particular circumstances, it is reasonable to expect the petitioner to go on living with the
respondent.

Examples of behaviour

Violent behaviour

It is quite common for petitioners to rely on violent behaviour on the part of the respon- **4.26**
dent. One serious violent incident may entitle the petitioner to a decree (for example an
unprovoked attack upon the petitioner causing her an unpleasant injury for which she
required medical treatment). If the violence used is relatively minor (for example, the occasional push and shove), more than one incident will be required or it will be necessary for
the petitioner to show that there was other behaviour as well as the violence.

Other behaviour

The respondent's behaviour need not be violent to entitle the petitioner to a decree. All sorts **4.27**
of other anti-social behaviour can be sufficient as the following examples show. Incidents
which are relatively trivial in isolation can amount to sufficient behaviour when looked at as
a whole, particularly if the petitioner is especially sensitive to the respondent's behaviour for
some reason.

Example 1 (The facts of *Livingstone-Stallard* v *Livingstone-Stallard* above.) The husband was 56,
the wife 24. The marriage was unsatisfactory from the start. The wife's complaints about her

husband's behaviour included the following matters. The husband criticized the wife over petty things—her behaviour, her friends, her way of life, her cooking, her dancing—and was abusive to her, called her names and, on one occasion, spat at her. Once he tried to kick her out of bed. On one occasion he criticized her for leaving her underclothes soaking in the sink overnight (although he did the same himself) and said that it was indicative of the way she had been brought up. He made a fuss when she drank sherry with a photographer who had brought round their wedding photographs, forbidding her to give refreshment to 'trades-people' again (on the basis that if she drank sherry with a tradesman it might impair her faculties so that the tradesman might make an indecent approach to her). The wife left after the husband had bundled her out of the house on a cold evening and locked her out, throwing water over her when she tried to get back in. She suffered bruising and was in a very nervous state for six weeks, needing sedation.

Although many of these complaints were trivial themselves, the wife was entitled to a decree.

Example 2 (The facts of *Birch* v *Birch* above.) The parties had lived together for more than 27 years. The wife's main complaint against the husband was that he was very dog-matic and dictatorial with nationalistic, male chauvinistic characteristics, which she had resented for many years. The judge found that, in contrast, the wife was sensitive, taking a passive role and putting her own interests aside until the children had grown up and left home.

The wife was entitled to a decree.

Note that although Examples 1 and 2 are taken from the facts of decided cases they are not intended to be looked on as *precedents* of what is and is not sufficient behaviour; every case is different and must be decided on its own facts. The examples are only intended to show the sort of conduct which is relevant in establishing behaviour.

4.28   Other matters which can constitute behaviour include excessive drinking leading to unpleasant behaviour, unreasonably refusing to have sexual intercourse or making excessive sexual demands, having an intimate relationship (falling short of adultery) with another person, committing serious criminal offences, and keeping the other party unreasonably short of money.

Where the respondent is mentally ill

4.29   The fact that the respondent's behaviour is the result of his mental illness does not necessar-ily prevent it from being sufficient to entitle the petitioner to a decree. However, the fact that he is mentally ill will be a factor for the court to take into account in determining whether s. 1(2)(b) is satisfied (*Katz* v *Katz* [1972] 3 All ER 219 and see also *Richards* v *Richards* [1972] 3 All ER 695 and *Thurlow* v *Thurlow* [1975] 2 All ER 979).

Behaviour which is not sufficient

4.30   Section 1(2)(b) will not be satisfied if all that is proved is that the petitioner became disenchanted with the respondent or bored with marriage.

4.31   Simple desertion cannot amount to behaviour; the petitioner must wait for two years to elapse from the date of desertion and petition on the basis of s. 1(2)(c) (*Stringfellow* v *Stringfellow* [1976] 2 All ER 539).

The relevance of living together despite the behaviour

In some cases the petitioner may not be able to prove sufficient behaviour because she and the respondent have continued to live together, see paragraph 4.59 and onwards. **4.32**

F ESTABLISHING AS A MATTER OF FACT THAT THE PARTIES ARE LIVING APART

The facts set out in s. 1(2)(c) to (e) all require cohabitation to have ceased and the parties to have lived apart for a period of time. **4.33**

Living apart for the purposes of s. 1(2)(d) and (e)

'Living apart' is defined for the purposes of s. 1(2)(d) and (e) (the two-year and five-year separation facts) in s. 2(6), MCA 1973. This provides that a husband and wife shall be treated as living apart unless they are living with each other in the same household. **4.34**

It is usually possible to pinpoint a time at which the spouses began to live apart in the sense required by the Act. This is normally the time when one or the other moves out of the matrimonial home to live in his own accommodation elsewhere and the parties start to lead separate lives. However, difficulties can arise: **4.35**

(a) When the parties have been living separately in any event, not because the marriage has broken down but for some reason, for example because one spouse has gone to look after his or her invalid parents or because they are working in different cities or because one is working abroad. Although as a matter of fact they are living separately, this physical separation is not sufficient; they will not be counted as living apart within the meaning of the MCA 1973 until at least one of them has decided that the marriage is at an end (*Santos v Santos* [1972] 2 All ER 246). It is not necessary for that spouse to communicate this decision to the other spouse. Of course, it is easier to prove that the requisite state of mind did exist if something was said to the other spouse but in other cases, a decision that the marriage is at an end can be inferred from conduct, for example, where the party living away ceases to write or to telephone the other party or to return home for holidays or sets up home with someone else.

   Example 1 The husband is posted abroad. To begin with, he and his wife correspond frequently and he spends his periods of leave at home with her and the children. After he has been abroad for a year, contact between him and his wife ceases and he does not answer her letters. In April 2004 he writes to his mother saying that he does not see any future in the marriage and does not intend to come home when his posting is over. Two years later the wife wishes to petition for divorce; the husband consents to a decree. She can rely on s. 1(2)(d). It can be seen from the husband's conduct and his letter to his mother that he had decided in 2004 that the marriage was over. The two-year separation period therefore began to run from that date.

Example 2 The husband is sentenced to a period of six years' imprisonment. To begin with the wife intends to stand by him. However, after six months she meets another man whom she wishes, ultimately, to marry and with whom she starts to live. The parties will be treated as having separated at this point because it is then that the wife recognizes that the marriage has no future.

(b) When the parties continue to live under the same roof but contend that they are actually living there separately. Whether or not the court will accept in these circumstances that there has been a sufficient degree of separation will depend on the living arrangements. To establish that the parties have been living apart it must be shown that the normal relationship of husband and wife has ceased and that they have been leading separate existences. The position is best illustrated by an example.

Example (The facts of *Mouncer* v *Mouncer* [1972] 1 All ER 289.) The husband and wife slept in separate bedrooms in the matrimonial home. They shared the rest of the house. They continued to take meals (cooked by the wife) together and shared the cleaning of the house making no distinction between one part of the house or the other. The wife no longer did any washing for the husband. The only reason the husband went on living in the house was his wish to live with and help look after the children.

    The parties had not been living apart.

If the parties in *Mouncer* had lived in separate parts of the house, had not shared cleaning and had taken meals separately, no doubt the court would have found that they were not living in the same household, albeit that they were living under the same roof, and would have accepted therefore that they were living apart.

Living apart in desertion cases

4.36   Section 2(6) applies only to s. 1(2)(d) and (e). However, if a question were to arise in a desertion case as to whether cohabitation had ceased, there is no doubt that similar principles would be applied (see *Smith* v *Smith* [1940] P 49). In addition, recognition that the marriage is at an end must be communicated to the other party: *Beeken* v *Beeken* [1948] P 302 (CA).

G   DESERTION: S. 1(2)(c)

4.37   Under s. 1(2)(c), the petitioner must show not only that the respondent has deserted her but also that this state of affairs has gone on for a continuous period of at least two years immediately preceding the presentation of the petition.

Desertion rarely relied on

4.38   It is rare these days for a petitioner to rely on desertion. No doubt the reason for this is that if the respondent has seen fit to desert the petitioner, he is usually sufficiently disenchanted with the marriage to consent to a decree of divorce being granted. Thus the petitioner need not struggle with the technicalities of desertion but can base her petition much more conveniently on two years' separation and consent (s. 1(2)(d)). Furthermore, if the respondent has committed adultery, the petitioner need not even wait for two years' separation; she can petition immediately on the basis of the adultery.

It should never be necessary to rely on *constructive* desertion (i.e., behaviour by the respondent causing the petitioner to withdraw from cohabitation). In such cases, the petition should be based on behaviour under s. 1(2)(b). Apart from being more straightforward than desertion, the behaviour fact has the marked advantage that the petitioner need not wait for two years' separation to have elapsed before petitioning as she must with desertion. **4.39**

Desertion is thus only likely to be used where adultery and behaviour cannot be made out and where, despite having walked out in the first place, the respondent is not prepared to consent to a decree being granted or where he has simply disappeared and cannot therefore be asked to consent to a decree. **4.40**

What is desertion?

The law relating to desertion is detailed and rather technical. This book outlines the main provisions; it does not deal with the intricacies. A fuller picture of the law can be found in the standard practitioners' works on divorce. **4.41**

The essentials of desertion are as follows: **4.42**

(a) The respondent must have withdrawn from cohabitation with the intention of bringing cohabitation permanently to an end.

   (i) *Cessation of cohabitation*: it is vital that cohabitation should have ceased. The petitioner cannot say that the respondent has deserted her if he is, in fact, still living with her, even if he contributes virtually nothing to family life. See paragraph 4.33 and onwards as to when the parties will be taken to be living apart.

   (ii) *Intention*: the respondent must intend to bring cohabitation permanently to an end.

Example 1 As far as the wife is concerned, she and her husband have been living together in the matrimonial home perfectly happily. One day, the husband packs his suitcase and departs to live in his own flat, saying that the wife has done nothing wrong but that he needs his freedom and does not intend to live with her ever again. The husband has thus withdrawn from cohabitation with the intention of bringing it permanently to an end. He has, in fact, deserted the wife.

This example deals with a couple who are living in the same house at the time that the desertion occurs. While this is the normal situation, it is not always the case. It is quite possible for one party to desert the other at a time when they are living in different places anyway (*Pardy v Pardy* [1939] 3 All ER 779). It is not the actual packing up and leaving that is important. What is important is the change in the respondent's state of mind so that he no longer regards himself as a married man with all the normal obligations of married life (including, ultimately, returning to live with the petitioner), but decides that he will never resume cohabitation with the petitioner and therefore regards himself as a free agent.

Example 2 The husband and wife live together at 10 Acacia Avenue. The husband gets a job in Saudi Arabia and, with the wife's consent, he goes off for a year's contract. Just before he is due to come home, he decides that he is not going to return to live with the wife and he telephones to tell her so. The physical separation of the parties would, up to now, have had no consequence as far as divorce proceedings were concerned. At this point, however, the husband starts to be in desertion. If this state of affairs continues for two years, the wife will be able to petition for divorce on the basis of this desertion.

It does seem, however, that where the original separation was consensual, a party cannot be in desertion simply because he subsequently makes up his mind privately not to resume cohabitation at the end of the agreed period as originally planned. He will not be in desertion until he communicates this to the other party or until the agreed period of separation expires and he does not return (*Nutley* v *Nutley* [1970] 1 All ER 410).

In other cases, there is no need for an express statement by the respondent of his intentions. It can be inferred from his conduct that he intends to bring cohabitation permanently to an end. In Example 1, therefore, the husband would have been just as much in desertion if he had said nothing to the wife but had merely departed with all his belongings to live in his own flat, with no intention of resuming cohabitation.

Because the respondent's state of mind is the essence of desertion, he will not be in desertion if he is forced to live separately from his wife against his will, for example if he is imprisoned. However, if he is already in desertion when the involuntary separation supervenes (for example, he is sentenced to a period of imprisonment after he has deserted the wife), the desertion will be presumed to continue throughout the period of involuntary separation (*Williams* v *Williams* [1938] 4 All ER 445). The court may treat the respondent as having been in desertion during a period in which he was excluded from the matrimonial home by a court order (i.e., an occupation order made under Part IV of the Family Law Act 1996).

(b) The petitioner does not consent to the respondent's withdrawal from cohabitation. If the petitioner consented to the respondent's withdrawal from cohabitation, she cannot allege that he has deserted her. Consent can be expressed (for example, where a separation agreement is drawn up providing for immediate separation) or can be implied from what the petitioner says or does.

Example (The facts of *Spence* v *Spence* [1939] 1 All ER 52.) For a fortnight before she left home, the wife engaged in open preparations for her departure. Her husband was perfectly aware of her intentions and they discussed the division of their household goods. The husband did not make the smallest attempt to deter his wife from going or to delay her departure.

The husband was held tacitly to have consented to his wife's departure.

However, the mere fact that the petitioner breathes a sigh of relief when the respondent has gone does not mean that she has consented to his departure.

The following situations may arise:
(i) Consent can pre-date the respondent's departure, in which case desertion never begins.
(ii) On the other hand, the petitioner may decide to consent to the separation after the event, in which case her consent can bring the respondent's desertion to an end (*Pizey* v *Pizey* [1961] 2 All ER 658).

(iii) Consent may be to a limited period of separation (for example while the respondent works abroad). Such consent comes to an end when that period ends; thereafter, the respondent can be in desertion (*Shaw* v *Shaw* [1939] 2 All ER 381).

(iv) If consent is given to an unlimited period of separation, it can be withdrawn and either party can seek a resumption of cohabitation. If the other party, without just cause, refuses to resume cohabitation, he will be in desertion (*Fraser* v *Fraser* [1969] 3 All ER 654). Furthermore, if the parties originally separate contemplating that they will get back together eventually (even though no time may be fixed) and one of them then decides he will never go back to live with the other and communicates this to the other, he will be in desertion from that point unless, of course, the other spouse is agreeable to the permanent separation (*Nutley* v *Nutley*, above).

(c) The respondent must not have any reasonable cause to withdraw from cohabitation.

Normally, if the respondent has reasonable cause to leave, this will arise from the behaviour of the petitioner although there would seem to be no reason, in principle, why some cause unconnected with the petitioner should not be sufficient justification for the respondent going (for example, where it is shown that it is imperative for his health that he should leave the petitioner permanently). Where the petitioner's conduct is relied on, it must be shown to be 'grave and weighty' and not merely part of the ordinary wear and tear of married life (*Dyson* v *Dyson* [1953] 2 All ER 1511).

There are no recent authorities on the point but it would seem logical to suggest that the sort **4.43** of behaviour that would form the basis of a petition under s. 1 (2)(b) would also constitute reasonable cause in a desertion case. Furthermore, a reasonable belief that the petitioner has committed adultery will give the respondent reasonable cause to leave even though the adultery cannot be proved (*Glenister* v *Glenister* [1945] 1 All ER 513).

Termination of desertion

The ways in which desertion can be brought to an end include the following: **4.44**

(a) By the parties subsequently agreeing to live apart (*Pizey* v *Pizey* above).

(b) By the granting of a decree of judicial separation. Once a decree of judicial separation has been granted, neither party has any further obligation to live with the other and cannot therefore be in desertion by failing to do so. However, if the decree of judicial separation was based on two years' desertion, the petitioner can subsequently issue a divorce petition based on the same desertion (s. 4(1), MCA 1973). The desertion will be deemed to have taken place immediately prior to the issue of the divorce petition if the parties have not resumed cohabitation since the judicial separation decree was granted and the decree of judicial separation has continued in force since it was granted (s. 4(3)). Furthermore, the court may treat the decree as sufficient proof of desertion in the divorce proceedings: s. 4(2) (see further, Chapter 13, paragraph 13.12 and onwards).

(c) By the resumption of cohabitation for a prolonged period (certain periods of cohabitation are disregarded, however, in determining whether there has been a continuous period of desertion; see paragraph 4.61 and onwards).

(d) By the deserting spouse making a genuine offer to resume cohabitation which the deserted spouse unreasonably refuses (*Ware* v *Ware* [1942] 1 All ER 50).

(e) By the deserted spouse subsequently providing the deserter with reasonable cause to stay away, for example, where she commits adultery which comes to the notice of the deserter.

Living together during a period of desertion

4.45 In determining whether the period of desertion is continuous, certain periods of cohabitation can be ignored, see paragraph 4.61 and onwards.

H TWO YEARS' SEPARATION AND CONSENT: S. 1(2)(d)

Two separate matters to prove

4.46 There are two matters which the petitioner must prove:

(a) that she and the respondent have lived apart for a continuous period of at least two years immediately preceding the presentation of the petition; *and*

(b) that the respondent consents to a decree being granted.

Living apart

4.47 As to what is meant by living apart, see paragraph 4.33 and onwards. Certain periods of cohabitation can be disregarded in considering whether the parties have lived apart *continuously*, see paragraph 4.61 below.

Respondent's consent

4.48 The respondent normally signifies his consent to the court on the acknowledgement of service form (which must be signed by him personally and, if he is represented by a solicitor, his solicitor as well; see r. 2.10(1), FPR 1991), and see Chapter 9, paragraph 9.66 and onwards.

4.49 The respondent can make his consent conditional, for example, giving his consent provided that the petitioner does not seek an order for costs of the divorce (*Beales* v *Beales* [1972] 2 All ER 667).

4.50 Whether his consent is unqualified or conditional, the respondent can withdraw it at any stage before the decree is pronounced (*Beales* v *Beales* above). If s. 1(2)(d) is the only basis for the petition, the petition will then have to be stayed (r. 2.10(2), FPR 1991).

4.51 If decree nisi is granted solely on the basis of two years' separation and consent, the respondent can apply at any time before the decree is made absolute to have the decree rescinded if he has been misled by the petitioner (intentionally or unintentionally) about any matter which he took into account in deciding to give his consent (s. 10(1), MCA 1973).

Section 10(2), Matrimonial Causes Act 1973

Under s. 10(2), the respondent may seek to hold up decree absolute until his financial **4.52** position after the divorce has been considered by the court, see Chapter 12.

I   FIVE YEARS' SEPARATION: S. 1(2)(e)

Establishing the five years' separation

If the petitioner can establish that she and the respondent have been living apart for a **4.53** continuous period of at least five years immediately preceding the presentation of the petition, she is entitled to a decree whether or not the respondent consents to a divorce (subject only to the respondent's right to raise a defence under s. 5, MCA 1973 of grave financial or other hardship, see Chapter 12).

Cohabitation during the five-year period

Certain periods of cohabitation can be disregarded in determining whether the five-year **4.54** period is continuous, see paragraph 4.61 below.

Section 10(2), Matrimonial Causes Act 1973

As with section 1(2)(d), the respondent can seek to hold up decree absolute by an application **4.55** under s. 10(2) to have his financial position considered, see Chapter 12.

J   THE EFFECT OF LIVING TOGETHER IN RELATION TO THE FIVE FACTS: S. 2

Section 2 deals with the relevance of the parties having lived with each other when **4.56** considering whether any of the five facts have been made out. Section 2(6) provides that the parties are to be treated as living apart unless they are living together in the same household.

Cohabitation after adultery

Cohabitation exceeding six months is a total bar

Section 2(1) provides that the petitioner cannot rely for the purpose of s. 1(2)(a) on adultery **4.57** committed by the respondent if the parties have lived with each other for a period exceeding or periods together exceeding six months after the petitioner learnt that the respondent had committed adultery.

Example 1 Mr Brown commits adultery on one occasion only in June 2006. On 1 July 2006 Mrs Brown learns of this. She and her husband continue to live together as man and wife as before although they bicker constantly. In March 2007 Mrs Brown decides that the marriage is doomed and consults a solicitor with a view to petitioning for divorce on the basis of her husband's adultery. She cannot do so. She has cohabited for a period exceeding six months since she learnt of the adultery on 1 July 2006 and he has not committed further acts of adultery since then.

If the respondent commits adultery on more than one occasion, time will not begin to run until after the petitioner learns of the last act of adultery.

Example 2 Mr Green begins an affair with his secretary at the office party at Christmas 2005. He first commits adultery with her on 23 December 2005. The affair continues until April 2006. Mrs Green learns almost straight away of the adultery on 23 December 2005 but thinks that that is the only occasion on which adultery took place. She discovers the true facts about the continuing adultery on 1 August 2006. She continues to live with her husband until 1 September 2006 when she leaves him because relations have become so strained. Mrs Green will be able to petition for divorce on the basis of her husband's adultery. The last act of adultery was in April 2006, she learnt of it on 1 August 2006 and she only cohabited with her husband for one month thereafter.

Cohabitation of six months or under to be disregarded

4.58   Section 2(2) provides that where parties have lived together for a period or periods not exceeding six months in total after it became known to the petitioner that the respondent had committed adultery, the cohabitation is to be disregarded in determining whether the petitioner finds it intolerable to live with the respondent. Thus, in Example 2 above, it could not be said against Mrs Green that she did not find it intolerable to live with her husband because she had in fact lived with him for a month after finding out about his last act of adultery. This period of cohabitation would be disregarded in determining the question of intolerability.

Cohabitation and behaviour

Cohabitation of six months and under to be disregarded

4.59   Section 2(3) provides that the fact that the petitioner and the respondent have lived with each other for a period or periods not exceeding six months in total after the last incident of behaviour proved, is to be disregarded in determining whether the petitioner cannot reasonably be expected to live with the respondent.

Example 1 The last incident of behaviour proved by the petitioner was on 3 January 2006 when the respondent beat her over the head with a snow shovel. She did not leave the respondent until the middle of February 2006. The period of cohabitation from 3 January 2006 until mid-February 2006 will be disregarded.

The behaviour on which the petitioner relies may be continuous in which case time will only start to run against the petitioner if she cohabits with the respondent after the particular behaviour ceases.

Example 2 The petitioner makes several allegations of violence on the part of the respondent during 2006. She continues to live with the respondent until shortly before decree nisi is pronounced. No specific incidents are detailed in relation to the period after 2006. However, the petitioner alleges generally that the respondent continually criticizes and belittles her, keeps her short of money and prevents her from having any contact with her friends and family. Her cohabitation for more than six months since the last specific incidents in 2006 will not prejudice her entitlement to a divorce because the other behaviour of which she complains continued right up to the day when she left and time therefore never started to run against her.

Cohabitation of more than six months

If the petitioner continues to live with the respondent for a period or periods exceeding six   **4.60** months in total, the cohabitation will be taken into account in determining whether the petitioner can reasonably be expected to live with the respondent. The longer the petitioner goes on living with the respondent after the last incident of behaviour, the less likely the court is to find that it is not reasonable to expect her to live with the respondent unless she can give a convincing reason for her continued cohabitation. However, cohabitation for more than six months is not an absolute bar in a behaviour case as it is in a case of adultery (*Bradley* v *Bradley* [1973] 3 All ER 750).

Example (The facts of *Bradley* v *Bradley* above.) The wife petitioned on the basis of the husband's behaviour, alleging many incidents of violence. She was still living with the husband. The parties lived in a council house with four bedrooms with seven of their children. The wife said she had no alternative but to continue to sleep with the husband, cook his meals, etc. because she was too frightened of him to do anything else. She could not be rehoused by the council whilst she was still married. The wife was not prevented from relying on s. 1(2)(b) by reason of her continued cohabitation. She was entitled to have her case investigated on its merits and to call evidence to show that, although she was still living with her husband, she could not reasonably be expected to continue to do so.

Cohabitation and s. 1(2)(c) to (e)

Section 2(5) provides that in considering whether a period of desertion or living apart has   **4.61** been continuous, no account is to be taken of a period or periods not exceeding six months in total during which the parties resumed living with each other. However, no period or periods during which the parties lived with each other can be counted as part of the period of desertion or separation.

Example Husband and wife started living apart exactly two years ago. However, they have lived with each other for two periods of a month during this time. Neither can petition for a divorce therefore until two years and two months have elapsed since the initial separation.

It should be noted that s. 2(5) is dealing with the question of *continuity* of the period of separation. It does not say that the periods of cohabitation should be disregarded for other purposes. A short period of cohabitation (six months or less) may therefore be relevant in determining, for example, whether desertion has been terminated or whether, in the case of either separation ground, there has been the sort of decision required by *Santos* v *Santos* above, that the marriage is at an end.

Although the statute does not say so expressly, it must be the case that a period or periods   **4.62** of cohabitation in excess of six months *will* automatically break the continuity of the separation.

4.63   In drafting, the petition details of the date of separation must be specified in the particulars. Where there has been a period of resumed cohabitation, no matter how short, details of this should also be included.

The rationale behind the cohabitation rule

4.64   The provisions of s. 2 are designed to facilitate a reconciliation between the parties and to give them an opportunity to reflect on the state of their marriage without prejudicing proceedings for divorce if such proceedings become necessary at a later stage. It is vital that the solicitor understands the practical effect of the s. 2 provisions and warns the client from the outset about the rules which are relevant to the client's particular circumstances.

K   CHAPTER SUMMARY

4.65   1.   The only ground for divorce is that the marriage has broken down irretrievably.
   2.   The petitioner must prove one or more of the following 'facts' on the balance of probabilities:
   Fact A: respondent's adultery and the petitioner finding it intolerable to live with the respondent.
   Fact B: respondent's behaviour
   Fact C: respondent's desertion for a continuous period of at least two years.
   Fact D: petitioner and respondent have lived apart for a continuous period of at least 2 years and the respondent consents to the decree being granted.
   Fact E: the petitioner and the respondent have lived apart for a continuous period of at least 5 years.
   3.   Care is needed where the parties have resumed cohabitation as laid down in s. 2, MCA 1973.

L   KEY DOCUMENTS

4.66   Matrimonial Causes Act 1973

5

BAR ON PRESENTATION OF DIVORCE PETITIONS WITHIN ONE YEAR OF MARRIAGE

A   ABSOLUTE ONE-YEAR BAR

Proceedings for divorce cannot be commenced within the first year of marriage (s. 3(1), **5.01** Matrimonial Causes Act 1973 ('MCA 1973')).

This bar is absolute and means that no matter how difficult the circumstances the petitioner **5.02** must wait for at least one year before she may petition for divorce (*Butler* v *Butler, The Queen's Proctor Intervening* [1990] 1 FLR 114).

In many circumstances, alternative steps need to be taken to give the client immediate **5.03** assistance and these are listed below with reference to the relevant chapter where the provisions are described in greater detail.

In practice, the solicitor is most likely to be required to provide advice on protection from **5.04** domestic abuse and help in resolving disputes relating to children.

B   BAR NOT APPLICABLE TO NULLITY PETITIONS

It is important to remember that the one-year bar does not apply to nullity petitions. Indeed, **5.05** in the case of certain voidable marriages, far from there being a time bar which prevents the petitioner from presenting a petition too *soon* after the marriage, there is a bar which prevents her from petitioning if she leaves it too *long* after the marriage (in these cases, the petition must usually be presented within three years of marriage, see Chapter 16). If there are grounds on which the marriage is void or voidable (see Chapter 16) a petition for nullity can therefore be presented without delay, even within days of the wedding in an appropriate case.

C   ALTERNATIVE COURSES OF ACTION FOR THE FIRST YEAR OF MARRIAGE

5.06   The wish to remarry is of course one of the reasons why people seek divorces. Unless there are grounds for seeking a nullity decree, the absolute bar on divorce within the first year of marriage means that there is nothing the solicitor can do to enable a client to remarry during that period. However, even though divorce is temporarily out of the question, the chances are that something can be done to help a client. The main options are as follows:

(a)   The client can be advised that she is free to look for alternative accommodation if things are not working out—although she must remain married, no one can force her to cohabit with her spouse.

(b)   Judicial separation (see further at Chapter 13): there is no restriction on the presentation of petitions for judicial separation in the first year of marriage. However, now that the bar on divorce proceedings is so short it is questionable whether it is worth petitioning for judicial separation on behalf of a client who has made up her mind that she wants a divorce and is only prevented from seeking one by the one-year bar. Bearing in mind that it will take at least several weeks to obtain a decree of judicial separation, unless the solicitor is consulted only a short time after marriage, he may well find that no sooner has he obtained a decree of judicial separation than the one year is up and proceedings have to be commenced all over again to obtain the decree of divorce that the client really wants. Consideration should therefore be given to whether, whilst waiting for the year to elapse, time would be better spent in concentrating on alleviating the client's immediate problems by means of other proceedings in the family proceedings court or county court.

(c)   Section 27, MCA 1973 (see further at Chapter 35).

(d)   Domestic Proceedings and Magistrates' Courts Act 1978.

(e)   Children Act 1989 (see further at Chapters 29 and 30).

(f)   Wardship proceedings (see further at Chapter 31).

(g)   Proceedings under Part IV of the Family Law Act 1996 for an occupation order and/or a non-molestation order (see further at Chapter 25).

(h)   Section 17, Married Women's Property Act 1882 proceedings (see further at Chapter 37): it should be noted that under s. 17, the court only has power to declare existing property rights and not to vary them. Should a divorce subsequently take place it will be open to the court to override any declaration already made under s. 17 and adjust the parties' rights in the property under s. 24, Matrimonial Causes Act 1973. Therefore, in the case of a client who intends to petition for divorce as soon as she is allowed to do so, careful consideration should be given to whether a s. 17 application is worthwhile. It may well be better to advise the client to wait to have any property disputes determined in the aftermath of the divorce. It will usually be difficult to justify the costs involved in the two sets of proceedings in any event.

D WHEN THE FIRST YEAR IS UP

As soon as the first year of marriage is up it is open season for divorce. In practice, only **5.07** petitions based on adultery (s. 1(2)(a), MCA 1973) and behaviour (s. 1(2)(b), 1973 Act) will be feasible for at least another year as the other s. 1(2) facts depend on there having been at least two years' separation.

Even though the temptation is to shelve the question of divorce entirely until the first **5.08** year has elapsed, in fact there is no reason why the case should not be prepared (marriage certificate obtained, divorce petition drafted, etc.) before the end of the year so that the petition can be filed at the earliest possible opportunity.

Section 3(2), MCA 1973 makes it clear that a divorce petition may be based wholly or partly **5.09** on matters which occurred during the first year of marriage even though it cannot be presented during that year. Thus, for example, once the year is over a decree could be sought on the basis of adultery that occurred during the year and a period of separation upon which reliance is placed under s. 1(2)(c) to (e) can start to run during the first year.

E CHAPTER SUMMARY

1. Proceedings for divorce cannot begin until one year after the marriage takes place.   **5.10**
2. Proceedings for a decree of judicial separation or nullity can begin at any time after the date of the marriage.
3. Other courses of action for the first year of marriage are outlined in the chapter.

F KEY DOCUMENTS

Matrimonial Causes Act 1973   **5.11**

6

JURISDICTION IN DIVORCE, NULLITY, JUDICIAL SEPARATION, AND PROCEEDINGS TO DISSOLVE A CIVIL PARTNERSHIP

A INTRODUCTION

One important requirement in commencing proceedings for divorce is to be able to demon-   **6.01**
strate that the county court has jurisdiction to entertain a petition for divorce. Simply
because an individual is living in England does not give a court the power to deal with their
family difficulties.

The relevant law is found in s. 5, Domicile and Matrimonial Proceedings Act 1973 ('DMPA   **6.02**

1973'), as amended, and is now largely based on one or both spouses being habitually resident in England and Wales. Where 'habitual residence' cannot be demonstrated, it may be possible to base jurisdiction on one of the parties being domiciled in England and Wales.

6.03 The position may be unclear at times and it will be necessary to take careful instructions from the client to be sure that the court does in fact have jurisdiction. Hence, the characteristics of both 'habitual residence' and 'domicile' are explained in this chapter.

6.04 It should be noted that reference is made at paragraph 6.32 to the jurisdiction position where a civil partnership is to be dissolved.

B   JURISDICTION FOR DIVORCE: S. 5, DOMICILE AND MATRIMONIAL PROCEEDINGS ACT 1973

6.05 Council Regulation (EC) No 2201/2003 of 27 November 2003 now governs the jurisdiction conditions to be fulfilled to petition for a decree of divorce by amending s. 5(2), DMPA 1973. The 2003 Council Regulation repeals Council Regulation (EC) No 1347/2000 and is known as Brussels 11a. It came into force on 1 March 2005 (The Family Proceedings (Amendment) Rules 2005).

6.06 Section 5(2) now provides as follows:

The court shall have jurisdiction to entertain proceedings for divorce or judicial separation if (and only if):

(a)   the court has jurisdiction under the Council Regulation; or

(b)   no court of a Contracting State has jurisdiction under the Council Regulation and either of the parties to the marriage is domiciled in England and Wales on the date when the proceedings are begun.

6.07 The purpose of the Council Regulation, amongst other things, is to enact provisions to unify the rules of conflict of jurisdiction in family matters and provides that, in such matters, jurisdiction shall lie with the courts of the member state in whose territory:

(a)   (i)   the spouses are habitually resident, or

(ii)   the spouses were last habitually resident, insofar as one of them still resides there, or

(iii) the respondent is habitually resident, or

(iv) in the event of a joint application, either of the spouses is habitually resident, or

(v)   the applicant is habitually resident if he or she resides there for at least one year immediately before the application was made, or

(vi) the applicant is habitually resident if he or she resided there for at least six months immediately before the application was made and is either a national of the member state in question or, in the case of the United Kingdom and Ireland, has his 'domicile' there;

(b)   both spouses are nationals or, in the case of the United Kingdom and Ireland, it is the place of 'domicile' of both spouses.

The above list under the Council Regulation is designed to offer a multiple choice of jurisdictional factors to determine whether the court has authority to entertain the petition for divorce: the list is not intended to be hierarchical. Provided that one criterion is met, the court of the Contracting State has jurisdiction. It will be noted that it is based principally on the habitual residence of the parties as distinct from their domicile. 'Habitual residence' is discussed more fully in paragraph 6.10 and onwards.

Where no court of a Contracting State has jurisdiction under the Council Regulation, a petition for divorce may properly be lodged in a court in England and Wales where either party is domiciled in England and Wales on the date when the proceedings are begun. 'Domicile' is explained in paragraph 6.17 and onwards. **6.08**

How the amendments to s. 5, DMPA 1973 affect the drafting of the divorce petition and the completion of the acknowledgement of service is explained in Chapter 8. **6.09**

C HABITUAL RESIDENCE

Until 1985, habitual residence had not been defined for the purposes of s. 5, DMPA 1973. However, in the case of *Kapur* v *Kapur* [1985] 15 Fam Law 22, Bush J held that habitual residence is essentially the same as ordinary residence (a concept with which the courts are familiar in other areas of the law). He therefore held that habitual residence means voluntary residence with a degree of settled purpose; that a limited purpose such as education could be a settled purpose and the husband was held to have satisfied the requirement of 12 months' habitual residence. **6.10**

In *Ikimi* v *Ikimi* [2001] 2 FLR 1288, the Court of Appeal considered the term 'habitual residence'. Here Thorpe LJ held that to be 'habitually resident' meant the same as to be 'ordinarily resident'. Accordingly, it was possible to be habitually resident in England and Wales for the purpose of divorce proceedings even if residence in the country amounted to 161 days in the relevant year only and the petitioner had at the same time been habitually resident in Nigeria. More recently in *Armstrong* v *Armstrong* [2003] 2 FLR 375, however, the court held that living in England for 71 days per year with little evidence of a settled intention to remain did not amount to 'habitual residence'. The decree nisi was rescinded because the court did not have jurisdiction. **6.11**

On the other hand, in *Mark* v *Mark* [2004] 1 FLR 1069, the Court of Appeal held that the petitioner wife who had not obtained indefinite leave to remain in the United Kingdom at the time of the divorce proceedings (and, therefore, was categorized as an 'over stayer'), was nevertheless habitually resident and domiciled in England and Wales. Hence, the court had jurisdiction to entertain the petition for divorce. **6.12**

Thorpe LJ indicated that to deny the wife access to the court amounted to a breach of Art. 6 of the European Convention for the Protection of Human Rights and Fundamental Freedoms 1950. **6.13**

He also confirmed that the court had a margin of discretion in determining whether or not an element of illegality tainted the stay of the petitioner and thus precluded the acquisition of domicile of choice and the right to invoke the court's jurisdiction. **6.14**

6.15   This decision was subsequently confirmed by the House of Lords at [2005] UKHL 42.

6.16   It is suggested that, in summary, the practical position as to habitual residence is as follows:

(a)   There should not normally be any difficulty in establishing jurisdiction on the basis of 12 months' or six months' habitual residence if one or the other party has been living in England and Wales for, for example, business, education, family reasons, health, or even simply love of the country, throughout the whole year immediately preceding the presentation of the petition.

(b)   Temporary or occasional short absences, for example, on holiday abroad, will not prevent an individual from establishing habitual residence.

(c)   Even rather more prolonged absences will not necessarily disrupt an individual's habitual residence.

(d)   It is irrelevant that the individual's real home is outside England, or that he intends or expects to live outside England in the future.

(e)   The illegality of the stay may not necessarily mean that the court does not have jurisdiction.

D   DOMICILE

6.17   Determining a person's domicile can be very tricky. This book provides only a very broad outline of the law of domicile. Should a problem over domicile be encountered, reference should be made to the standard practitioners' works on family law and also to textbooks on private international law.

What is domicile?

6.18   Domicile is essentially a legal concept used to link an individual with a particular legal system. The concept of domicile is primarily used to determine which country's law should govern questions of an individual's personal status. Domicile and nationality are two quite separate matters; it is not possible to find out where a person is domiciled merely by finding out his nationality. Neither is it possible to ascertain a person's domicile simply by finding out where he lives; residence and domicile are not the same thing.

Key points

6.19   (a)   A person must be domiciled in a place which has only one legal system. This means that it is not possible to be domiciled in the British Isles—one is domiciled in England and Wales, or in Scotland or in Northern Ireland.

(b)   Every person has a domicile.

(c)   It is not possible to have more than one domicile at one time.

(d)   However, it is possible for an individual's place of domicile to change as his personal circumstances alter throughout his life.

Determining where a person is domiciled

There are three types of domicile: domicile of origin, domicile of dependence, and domicile **6.20** of choice.

Domicile of origin

The law attributes a domicile to every new-born baby. This is his domicile of origin. **6.21**

Normally a child of married parents will take as his domicile that of his father at the time of **6.22** his birth, whereas the child of the unmarried family will take that of his mother. Domicile of the relevant parent determines the domicile of the child, not the actual place of birth.

An individual must never be without a domicile. Therefore, he retains his domicile of origin **6.23** throughout his life. At times it may be overtaken by a different domicile of dependence or domicile of choice, but in the absence of any other domicile it will always revive.

Domicile of choice

Residence and intention   Once an individual reaches the age of 16, he will be able to **6.24** acquire a domicile of choice. An individual acquires a domicile of choice by living in a country other than the country of his domicile of origin with the intention of continuing to reside there permanently, or at least indefinitely.

(a) *Residence*
     For a domicile of choice to be acquired in a country, the individual must actually take up residence there. It is not enough for him to make up his mind in his freezing flat in North London that he will emigrate to Australia, or even for him to buy his airline ticket or board his plane. He must actually arrive in the country.

(b) *Intention*
     An individual cannot acquire a domicile of choice in a country until he decides to live there permanently, or at least indefinitely. Thus a domicile of choice will not be acquired in Saudi Arabia by someone simply posted there by his employers or spending some time there on holiday. See also *Cramer v Cramer* [1987] 1 FLR 116 where Stephen Brown LJ stated that the burden of establishing a change of domicile (from a domicile of origin to a domicile of choice) is '. . . a heavy one'.

This point was reinforced more recently in *R v R (Divorce: Jurisdiction: Domicile)* [2006] 1 FLR 389. In holding that the respondent wife in divorce proceedings had not acquired a domicile of choice in France, Philip Sapsford QC indicated that what would need to be demonstrated, on a standard of proof which went beyond a mere balance of probabilities, was a fixed and settled intention to abandon her English domicile of origin and to settle permanently in France. A change of domicile could not be established simply by making declarations to that effect nor by acquiring a home in a different country. In particular, the fact that the wife's driving licence, passport, nationality, bank accounts, credit cards, and medical insurance were all English undermined her argument that she had acquired a domicile of choice in France.

Examples of domicile of choice

Example 1 Mr Maynard has always lived in England as had his father before him. His domicile **6.25** of origin is English (taken from that of his father when he was born). He becomes a famous writer and decides to investigate the possibility of going to live in Switzerland. He goes to stay in Switzerland to look at property. At this stage, his domicile of origin is still operative as he has not yet made up his mind whether to live in Switzerland. He returns home and decides that he will move permanently to Switzerland. He has still not acquired a domicile of choice there as he has not taken up residence there. He sells his house and winds up his business in England and travels to Switzerland. He has now acquired a domicile of choice in Switzerland.

Example 2 Mr Connor, a man of 35, has always lived in the United States. He has a domicile of origin in Texas. He comes to England to work for an English company. He buys a house in England and moves his family over. However, he intends to return to the United States when he retires. He does not acquire a domicile of choice in England because he lacks the required intention to live here at least indefinitely.

6.26 **Loss of domicile of choice**   In contrast with the domicile of origin, a domicile of choice can be lost forever. Although there is a question mark over the exact nature of the intention required, it would seem that a domicile of choice will be lost if the individual gives up residence in the country in question and ceases to have the intention to reside there permanently or at least indefinitely. Both elements must be present. Intention to leave the country without actually leaving is not sufficient, neither is leaving without any change in the original intention to live there permanently or indefinitely.

6.27 An individual may acquire a new domicile of choice immediately the old one is abandoned. However, if he does not do so, for example, if he gives up his home in one country and then travels around whilst making up his mind where to settle for the future, his domicile of origin will revive to fill the gap.

6.28 **Proof of intention**   The individual concerned may not have formulated his intentions as to the future explicitly. His intention can, however, be inferred from all the circumstances of the case—what he did, what he said, etc.

Domicile of dependence

6.29 Until a child is 16 and can acquire an independent domicile of choice, he has a domicile of dependence on one or other of his parents. To begin with, this is the same as his domicile of origin, but if the domicile of his parent changes, so will the child's domicile of dependence.

6.30 Thus the domicile of a child of married parents will normally change with that of his father, or, if his father dies, with that of his mother. If however the child's parents are separated and he is living with his mother, his domicile will change with that of his mother: s. 4, DMPA 1973. A child of the unmarried family will have a domicile of dependence on his mother.

6.31 When the child becomes capable of acquiring an independent domicile at 16, he will retain his domicile of dependence until he acquires a domicile of choice.

Example Mr and Mrs Hall are happily married. Mrs Hall gives birth to a baby daughter, Sarah. Sarah takes her domicile of origin from her father who is domiciled in England at this time. Subsequently, Mr and Mrs Hall decide to go and live in France and take up residence there. They therefore acquire domiciles of choice in France and Sarah thus has a domicile of dependence in France. Mr and Mrs Hall then encounter marital problems and separate. Mrs Hall goes to live with her mother in Scotland, intending to stay there permanently and taking Sarah with her. Sarah's domicile is now dependent on her mother as her parents are living apart and she has her home with her mother. She is therefore domiciled in Scotland. This is still the case after her sixteenth birthday until, at the age of 23 she marries and goes to live permanently in Northern Ireland. She now has a domicile of choice in Northern Ireland.

E JURISDICTION FOR DISSOLUTION OF A CIVIL PARTNERSHIP

A combination of s. 219 Civil Partnership Act 2004 and Civil Partnership (Jurisdiction and Recognition of Judgments) Regulations 2005 (SI 2005/3334) makes it clear that jurisdiction for the termination of a civil partnership is as for divorce adopting the grounds prescribed in Brussels 11a. **6.32**

F RECOGNITION OF FOREIGN DECREES

Recognition of divorce and separation decrees

There are detailed statutory rules as to the recognition of foreign decrees of divorce and separation. These are set out in the Family Law Act 1986 ('FLA 1986'). **6.33**

A distinction is made between decrees granted under the law of any part of the British Isles and divorces and separations obtained overseas. A further distinction is made between an overseas divorce or separation obtained by means of proceedings on the one hand and one obtained otherwise than by means of proceedings on the other. The rules relating to recognition of a decree obtained otherwise than by means of proceedings are particularly stringent. The details are set out in s. 46, FLA 1986. Note that a decree of divorce or judicial separation granted under the law of any part of the British Isles must be recognized throughout the United Kingdom: s. 44(2), FLA 1986. **6.34**

Recognition of nullity decrees

The recognition of foreign nullity decrees is governed by the Family Law Act 1986, ss. 45 to 48. **6.35**

Entitlement to ancillary relief in English courts after foreign divorce, nullity, or legal separation

Part III of the Matrimonial and Family Proceedings Act 1984 gives the English courts jurisdiction to grant financial relief after an overseas divorce, annulment or legal separation obtained by *means of proceedings* and which is recognized in this country as valid. Such an application for ancillary relief can be made whether the decree in a foreign country was made before or after the 1984 Act came into force (*Chebaro* v *Chebaro* [1987] 2 FLR **6.36**

456). Permission of the court is required before such a financial relief application can be made. Recent case law includes *A v S (Financial Relief after Overseas US Divorce and Financial Proceedings)* [2003] 1 FLR 431 and *M v L (Financial Relief after Overseas Divorce)* [2003] 2 FLR 425.

G   CHAPTER SUMMARY

6.37   1.   The English court will only have jurisdiction to deal with petitions for divorce (or for application for dissolution of a civil partnership) if one of the grounds in Brussels 11a is satisfied.
2.   Jurisdiction is based on one party's habitual residence or domicile.

H   KEY DOCUMENTS

6.38   Domicile and Matrimonial Proceedings Act 1973
Family Law Act 1986
Part III Matrimonial and Family Proceedings Act 1984

7

PUBLIC FUNDING AND UNDEFENDED DIVORCES

A   GENERAL FAMILY HELP AND CERTIFICATE FOR LEGAL REPRESENTATION NOT GENERALLY AVAILABLE

Certificates to provide General Family Help or Legal Representation are not available for **7.01** undefended divorce and judicial separation proceedings, save in exceptional circumstances.

B   CERTIFICATE AVAILABLE FOR DEFENDED CASES

A certificate may be granted for defended divorce or judicial separation proceedings (either **7.02** to the respondent to defend the proceedings or to the petitioner to continue the proceedings after an answer has been filed).

C   CERTIFICATE EXCEPTIONALLY AVAILABLE FOR UNDEFENDED CASES

A certificate can be granted for an undefended case: **7.03**

(a) if the district judge directs that the petition shall be heard in open court (for example, where he is not satisfied that the petitioner has made out her case for a decree, see paragraph 9.76); *or*

(b) if by reason of physical or mental incapacity, it is impracticable for the applicant to proceed without a certificate.

In the case of (a) above, the circumstances of the case must justify representation and it must be demonstrated that there are sufficient prospects of obtaining the decree.

D   CERTIFICATES AVAILABLE FOR PROCEEDINGS IN CONNECTION WITH DIVORCE OR JUDICIAL SEPARATION OTHER THAN DECREE PROCEEDINGS

7.04   The restriction on certificates applies only to the proceedings for obtaining the decree itself. There is no restriction therefore on the granting of a certificate to make or oppose, for example:

(a) an application for an occupation or non-molestation order ancillary to the divorce or judicial separation proceedings;
(b) an application for ancillary relief;
(c) an application under the Children Act 1989, e.g., for residence or contact orders.

It should be remembered, however, that in many instances, the client will be referred first to mediation and a certificate will only be granted if mediation is not successful.

7.05   There is a residual power to grant a certificate for the purposes of making or opposing any other application or satisfying the court on any other matter which raises a substantial question for determination by the court. This provision covers, for example, applications under s. 10, Matrimonial Causes Act 1973 ('MCA 1973') (for consideration of the respondent's financial position after divorce, see Chapter 12).

7.06   However, there must be a substantial and practical benefit to be obtained from the order and it must be coupled with an application for ancillary relief.

E   LEGAL HELP AVAILABLE FOR DECREE PROCEEDINGS

7.07   In view of the fact that a certificate is not usually available for decree proceedings, Legal Help has assumed a particular importance in undefended divorce and judicial separation cases. Provided the client is financially eligible for Legal Help (see Chapter 2, paragraph 2.13 and onwards), the solicitor will be able to give her considerable assistance with the decree proceedings under the scheme. The following are examples of the work that a solicitor may be expected to carry out under the scheme:

(a) preliminary advice on the grounds for divorce or judicial separation, the effects of a decree on status, the future arrangements for the children, the income and assets of the family, and matters relating to housing and the matrimonial home;

(b) drafting the petition and the statement of the arrangements for the children and where necessary typing or writing the entries on the forms;

(c) advising on filing the documents at court and the consequential procedure, including service if no acknowledgement of service is filed;

(d) advising a client when the acknowledgement of service is received as to the procedure for applying for directions for trial, and typing or writing the entries on the form of affidavit of evidence;

(e) advising as to any attendance before the district judge to explain the arrangements for the children (this will be rare in practice) and as to what, if any, evidence will be required by the judge other than that of the petitioner, but not attending court;

(f) advising on obtaining decree absolute.

It is important to remember that Legal Help cannot be used to cover the cost of attendance by the solicitor at court.

The solicitor can also negotiate with the other party (for example, he can write to the proposed respondent asking him for his consent to a divorce on the basis of two years' separation: s. 1(2)(d), MCA 1973). **7.08**

Boiled down to essentials, this means that the solicitor can give the client all the help he could reasonably expect in relation to his divorce except that he cannot accompany him to court on any children's appointment that might be requested by the district judge (pursuant to s. 41, MCA 1973) unless he agrees to do so as a favour without payment. If the client is worried about the children's appointment, the solicitor should take care to explain fully to him what will happen. If necessary, the solicitor can write to the court or telephone in advance of the appointment, explaining any matters which are complex or may be of particular concern to the district judge. For further details as to the circumstances in which the district judge may decide to hold a children's appointment, see Chapter 9, paragraph 9.83 and onwards. **7.09**

The solicitor may just as easily find himself acting for a respondent under the Legal Help scheme. In such a case, he would be able to advise on the same matters as he would advise a petitioner on, help with filing documents and drafting (for example, with filling in the acknowledgement of service), advise on dealing with the court (for example, advising the respondent on returning the acknowledgement of service, how to obtain decree absolute if the petitioner has not done so, and negotiate with the petitioner's solicitor on liability for costs and the amount of costs to be paid etc.). **7.10**

Should it become necessary to exceed any limits on expenditure under the solicitor's contract with the Legal Services Commission in the case of a petitioner or a respondent (for example, if there are problems over service and it becomes necessary to instruct an enquiry agent to serve the petition), the solicitor should bear in mind the possibility of exercising his or her devolved powers to do additional work or to obtain an extension from the Regional Director (see Chapter 2). **7.11**

8

DRAFTING A DIVORCE PETITION

A   INTRODUCTION

Chapters 8 and 9 describe one of the most common tasks for the family law practitioner— **8.01** drafting the divorce petition and the procedure to be followed to obtain the decree absolute of divorce.

Before drafting the petition, it is helpful to check the following matters to ensure that your **8.02** client will obtain a decree of divorce.

1. Are the parties validly married? If not, the court has no jurisdiction to grant a decree of divorce but instead nullity proceedings may be appropriate.
2. Have the parties been married for at least one year? (see Chapter 5).
3. Does the court have jurisdiction to entertain a petition for divorce? (see Chapter 6).
4. Are you satisfied, following full discussions with the client, that the marriage has irretrievably broken down and hence the ground for divorce can be demonstrated?
5. Can you prove, on the balance of probabilities, the statutory fact to be relied on? For example, will the respondent admit to the adultery to be alleged or consent to a divorce based on the two years' separation? If you have any doubts, the potential difficulties should be resolved at this stage otherwise time and money will be wasted. Where it is known, for instance, that the respondent is unlikely to admit to the adultery to be alleged, consider whether the alternative fact of 'behaviour' might be appropriate as the basis for the divorce. The respondent's specific admission or consent will not be required.

The relevant rules of procedure governing the conduct of divorce proceedings are found in the Family Proceedings Rules 1991 (SI 1991/1247), as amended.

8.03 Every divorce suit is commenced by petition: r. 2.2(1)). The petition is the central document in the case. It is filed by the spouse seeking the divorce ('the petitioner') and served on the other spouse ('the respondent').

8.04 The petition informs the respondent and the court of the basis on which the petitioner claims to be entitled to a decree and of the other orders that she will be seeking as part of the divorce process, for example, in relation to periodical payments, property, and provision for the children.

8.05 The solicitor normally prepares the petition on behalf of the client. If the client is receiving Legal Help, the solicitor will be entitled to payment for doing this under the scheme. The private client must meet the cost personally. In some cases it may be possible to recover at least part of the cost of the proceedings from the respondent or co-respondent if there is one (see Chapter 9, paragraph 9.74).

B   THE CONTENTS OF THE PETITION

8.06 Rule 2.3 and Appendix 2 of the Family Proceedings Rules 1991 ('FPR 1991') stipulate what information shall be contained in the petition. Every petition for divorce shall contain:

(a) the names of the parties to the marriage and the date and place of the marriage;
(b) confirmation that neither the name of the petitioner nor the respondent has changed since the date of the marriage;
(c) the last address at which the parties to the marriage have lived together as man and wife;
(d) a statement of the grounds on which the court has jurisdiction under Art. 2(ii) of the Council Regulation (discussed in Chapter 6);
(e) the occupation and residence of the petitioner and the respondent;

(f) whether there are any living children of the family (see paragraph 8.22 below for a definition of 'child of the family') and, if so;

    (i) the number of such children and the full names (including surname) of each and his date of birth or (if it be the case) that he is over 18, and

    (ii) in the case of each minor child over the age of 16, whether he is receiving instruction at an educational establishment or undergoing training for a trade, profession or vocation;

(g) whether (to the knowledge of the petitioner in the case of a husband's petition) any other child now living has been born to the wife during the marriage and, if so, the full names (including surname) of the child and his date of birth or, if it be the case, that he is over 18;

(h) if it be the case, that there is a dispute as to whether a living child is a child of the family;

(i) whether or not there are or have been any other proceedings in any court in England and Wales or elsewhere with reference to the marriage or to any children of the family or between the petitioner and the respondent with reference to any property of either or both of them and, if so:

    (i) the nature of the proceedings,

    (ii) the date and effect of any decree or order, and

    (iii) in the case of proceedings with reference to the marriage, whether there has been any resumption of cohabitation since the making of the decree or order;

(j) whether there have been any applications under the Child Support Act 1991 ('CSA 1991') for a maintenance calculation in respect of any children of the family; give details of application and calculation made as appropriate;

(k) whether there are any proceedings continuing in any country outside England and Wales which relate to the marriage or are capable of affecting its validity or substance and, if so:

    (i) particulars of the proceedings, including the court in or tribunal or authority before which they were begun,

    (ii) the date when they were begun,

    (iii) the names of the parties,

    (iv) the date or expected date of any trial in the proceedings, and such other facts as may be relevant to the question whether the proceedings on the petition should be stayed under sch. 1 to the Domicile and Matrimonial Proceedings Act 1973 ('DMPA 1973');

and such proceedings shall include any which are not instituted in a court of law in that country, if they are instituted before a tribunal or other authority having power under the law having effect there to determine questions of status, and shall be treated as continuing if they have been begun and have not finally been disposed of;

(l) where the fact on which the petition is based is five years' separation, whether any, and if so what, agreement or arrangement has been made or is proposed to be made between the parties for the support of the respondent or, as the case may be, the petitioner or any child of the family;

(m) in the case of a petition for divorce, a statement that the marriage has broken down irretrievably;

(n) the fact alleged by the petitioner for the purposes of s. 1(2), Matrimonial Causes Act 1973 ('MCA 1973'). The statutory fact relied on should be set out verbatim from the wording in the Act. Brief particulars of the facts relied on should be given but not the evidence by which they are to be proved.

Every petition for divorce shall conclude with:

(a) a prayer setting out particulars of the relief claimed. The prayer should set out any claim for costs and any application for ancillary relief which it is intended to claim;

(b) the names and addresses of the persons who are to be served with the petition indicating if any of them is a person under a disability;

(c) the petitioner's address for service, which, where the petitioner sues by a solicitor, shall be the solicitor's name or firm and address. Where the petitioner, although suing in person, is receiving Legal Help from a solicitor, the solicitor's name or firm and address may be given as the address for service if he agrees. In any other case, the petitioner's address for service shall be the address of any place in England and Wales at or to which documents for the petitioner may be delivered or sent.

No form of petition is set out in the rules but printed forms of petition on which the relevant information can be typed or written can be obtained from law stationers or from the offices of divorce county courts. Not all printed petition forms are exactly the same; one of the forms commonly in use is reprinted at the end of this chapter.

8.07 A carefully drafted petition will go a long way towards ensuring that a decree of divorce is obtained swiftly and smoothly. The solicitor should therefore bear in mind the following notes when drafting the petition.

C   NOTES ON DRAFTING THE PETITION

8.08 These notes refer to the printed petition form reproduced at the end of this chapter. They should, however, be equally useful to the solicitor when he is using an alternative printed form or drafting a petition from scratch.

'In the county court'

8.09 The solicitor can decide in which divorce county court he will commence proceedings; alternatively he can commence proceedings in the Divorce Registry in London (see Chapter 9, paragraph 9.21). He should complete the divorce petition accordingly.

'No'

8.10 This refers to the number of the cause which is allocated by the divorce court office when the petition is filed. It will be inserted on the original of the petition and on the copy(ies) for service on the respondent (and co-respondent) by the court staff. The solicitor will be informed of the number and should take care to record it on his file copy of the petition as it must be quoted on all subsequent documents relating to the divorce and ancillary matters.

Paragraph 1

The details of the marriage should be taken exactly from the marriage certificate. The place **8.11**
of marriage should be fully stated, including the county in which it took place. The full
names of the parties should be given including their surnames. In the case of a wife there is
no need to give her maiden name as well as her married name, although this is commonly
stated for the sake of consistency together with her status at the time of the marriage.

Paragraphs (1a) and (1b)

In paragraph (1a) the petitioner is asked to confirm that his name has not changed since the **8.12**
date of the marriage. If the petitioner's name has changed, full details must be given.

In paragraph (1b) the petitioner is asked to state that he believes that the name of the **8.13**
respondent has not changed since the date of the marriage. If this is not the case, full details
of the change of name should be set out.

Paragraph 2

The full address of the place where the parties last lived together as husband and wife should **8.14**
be given, including the county.

Paragraph 3

This paragraph is concerned with the basis for the court's jurisdiction. The basis on which **8.15**
a court may have jurisdiction to entertain a petition for divorce is laid down in s. 5(2),
DMPA 1973, discussed in Chapter 6. Paragraph 3 now requires the petitioner to state on
what grounds the court has jurisdiction under the Council Regulation. This paragraph must
be correctly phrased to demonstrate clearly that the court has jurisdiction. The following
forms of words will all vest jurisdiction in the court:

(a)   the petitioner and the respondent are both habitually resident in England and Wales;
(b)   the petitioner and the respondent were last habitually resident in England and Wales
      and the [petitioner] [respondent] still resides there;
(c)   the respondent is habitually resident in England and Wales;
(d)   the petitioner is habitually resident in England and Wales and has resided there for at
      least one year immediately prior to the presentation of the petition (in this case the
      petitioner must give address(es) where he or she lived during that time and the length of
      time lived at each address);
(e)   the petitioner is domiciled and habitually resident in England and Wales and has res-
      ided there for at least six months immediately prior to the presentation of the petition
      (again, details of the address(es) and length of time at each address during that period
      must be specified);
(f)   the petitioner and the respondent are both domiciled in England and Wales.

If none of the above applies, the Notes for Guidance on completion of the petition require
you to cross out the standard wording of paragraph 3 and replace it with the following
paragraph (if it applies):

The court has jurisdiction other than under the Council Regulation on the basis that no other Contracting State has jurisdiction under the Council Regulation and [the petitioner] [the respondent] is domiciled in England and Wales on the date when this petition was issued.

Paragraph 4

8.16 Paragraph 4 also requires the present address of the petitioner and the respondent to be given. The addresses should be stated in full including the county but if either address is the same as that already stated in paragraph 2 (as it will be if either party has stayed in the family home), the address can be given in shorthand form by stating simply the first line followed by the word 'aforesaid' (for example, '10 Acacia Avenue aforesaid').

8.17 The occupation of both parties must also be given. It is acceptable to state that a wife who does not work by choice is a housewife by occupation but check how she wishes to be described. Where the party concerned is out of work involuntarily it would be more suitable to state that he is 'unemployed'.

Omitting the petitioner's address from the petition

8.18 In some cases the petitioner does not wish the respondent to know her address. Where the petitioner is receiving Legal Help (or where the solicitor is acting privately or on full public funding) the solicitor's address can be given for service but the rules still require a statement of the petitioner's address in the body of the petition. The district judge has a general power under r. 2.3 FPR 1991 to direct that information that would otherwise be required in the petition can be omitted and, where it is necessary for the protection of the petitioner, he can use this power to allow the petition to stand without the petitioner's address.

8.19 It must be stressed, however, that this is for the *protection* of the petitioner. Therefore, although it is understandable that the petitioner may want to start a new life with the security that the respondent does not know where she is living, this in itself will not be sufficient to justify the omission of the address. The district judge will normally look for evidence (often provided by the respondent's own past conduct) that if the address is given the petitioner will be in physical danger or will be subjected to serious molestation by the respondent. It should be borne in mind that an alternative method of dealing with problems of molestation is to apply for an order against the respondent.

8.20 Where the petitioner wishes to omit her address from the petition she must first seek permission to do so. Although r. 10.21, FPR 1991 generally allows a party not to reveal his private address during family proceedings, r. 2.3, FPR 1991 is specifically excluded from the general rule (r. 10.21(1)). In order to seek permission the petitioner must make an application, without notice to her spouse, to the district judge (r. 10.9) and must follow the procedure laid down in the *Practice Direction* [1975] 2 All ER 384, [1975] 1 WLR 787:

(a) The petition should be drafted and filed omitting the petitioner's address from the body of the petition and giving the solicitor's address as her address for service.

(b) An application without notice being given to the respondent should be made to the district judge before the petition is served for permission for the petition to stand notwithstanding the omission of the address. The application should be supported by an affidavit (or sworn statement) by the petitioner or her solicitor stating the reasons why the petitioner wishes to exclude her address. The affidavit should exhibit a copy of the petition with the petitioner's address left blank.

(c) If the district judge gives permission:

   (i) the petition and a copy of the district judge's order will be served on the respondent;

   (ii) the petitioner's solicitor should take care not to disclose her whereabouts directly or indirectly in other documents required for the divorce proceedings, for example, by the information given in the statement as to arrangements for the children about where the children are to live and about their schools or in sworn statements required later in the proceedings.

   If there is a danger that the statement as to arrangements will give away too much information, the information in question should be omitted and by way of explanation it should be stated that the petitioner has applied for permission for the petition to stand notwithstanding the omission of her address. It should still be possible for the petitioner to give sufficient information in the statement as to arrangements by simply stating the nature of the accommodation where the children will live and the type of school they attend, omitting any reference to names and addresses. Sworn statements (for example, in connection with ancillary relief) should omit any reference to the petitioner's address and commence with a statement that the petitioner has been given permission not to disclose her address in the petition. If there is any objection to the sworn statement in this form, permission for it to be accepted can be sought at the hearing for which it is intended;

   (iii) Form C8 will be completed. This is the confidential address form enabling the court to have details of the petitioner's address without disclosing it to the respondent.

(d) If the district judge does not grant permission, he will make an order that the petition be amended by inserting the petitioner's address.

Paragraph 5

This paragraph requires the details of all living children of the family to be given. **8.21**

'Child of the family' in relation to the parties to a marriage is defined in s. 52, MCA **8.22** 1973 as:

(a) a child of both of those parties; and

(b) any other child, not being a child who is placed with those parties as foster parents by a local authority or voluntary organization, who has been treated by both of those parties as a child of their family.

A child will qualify as a child of the family on the basis that he is a child of both parties to the marriage even if he was born to them before the marriage took place or after it broke down or was adopted by them rather than being their natural child.

A child can become a child of the family by virtue of the second limb of the definition even **8.23** though he is the child of only one party to the marriage or indeed where he is the child of neither of the parties. It is not always easy to determine whether a child has become a child of the family by virtue of treatment. It is a broad question of fact which must be decided by the court looking at all the circumstances of the case. The test is objective.

8.24 The following points should also be borne in mind:

(a) The exclusion of children boarded out with the parties automatically prevents children such as foster children becoming children of the family no matter how long the child has lived with the family.

(b) A child can only be treated as a child of the family once it is born so a generous attitude towards a forthcoming baby on the part of a husband during his wife's pregnancy by another man will not lead to the baby becoming a child of the family. It is only if he continues to treat the child as a child of the family once it is born that it will achieve the status of a child of the family (*A* v *A* (*Family: Unborn Child*) [1974] 1 All ER 755).

(c) The family can cease to exist before a divorce takes place if the parties to the marriage separate permanently. Where this happens and the wife gives birth to a child by another man after the separation, it is not possible for that child to be treated as a child of the family (*M* v *M* [1980] 2 FLR 39).

(d) If a child has been treated as a child of the family, the fact that the husband only behaved in this way towards the child because he believed, mistakenly as it turns out, that the child was his own will not prevent the child being classed as a child of the family (*W(RJ)* v *W(SJ)*) [1971] 3 All ER 303).

(e) The definition can include a child brought up by its grandparents in circumstances where the evidence suggests that the natural parents have handed over responsibility for the care of the child. Here, the child became 'a child of the family' to be considered in divorce proceedings following the breakdown of the marriage of the grandparents: *Re A* (*Child of the Family*) [1998] 1 FLR 346 (CA).

Example 1 Susan is the natural child of Mr and Mrs Smith born whilst they were living together before they got married. She is automatically a child of their family.

Example 2 Mr and Mrs Smith get divorced. Mrs Smith subsequently remarries. Susan lives with Mrs Smith and her new husband, Mr Jones. Mr Jones welcomes Susan as his own daughter and takes an interest in all that she does. For example, he regularly attends parents' evenings at Susan's school with Mrs Smith, he supports Mrs Smith in matters of discipline and he provides Susan with pocket money. Although Susan's natural father does pay £30 per week towards her maintenance, the housekeeping that Mr Jones gives to Mrs Smith is used to feed the family as a whole including Susan. Susan addresses Mr Jones as John. There is little doubt that Susan is a child of the family of Mrs Smith and Mr Jones.

Example 3 The wife has a child by her first marriage. The child goes to live with her grandparents when the first marriage breaks down. The wife remarries. The child visits the wife and her new husband to stay at weekends and for substantial periods during the school holidays (about 50/60 days a year in all). She has her own room at their house and the new husband buys her a pony which he expects her to groom and keep clean. He also reproves her if she does not keep her bedroom clean.

In the case of *A* v *A* (above), a child in this situation was held not to be a child of the family—her home was with her grandparents and the husband's behaviour towards her did not amount to treating her as a child of his and the mother's family.

Example 4 Mrs Brown remarries after the death of her first husband. Her son Sam is at boarding school. He spends the holidays living with Mrs Brown, her new husband and the new husband's two children by his previous marriage who live with their father permanently. He has his own room at their house and all three children are treated in exactly the same way by both Mrs Brown and her new husband. It is likely that all three children are children of the family.

The petition should state the full names (including surnames) of all living children whom the petitioner alleges are children of the family. If the child is not the natural or adopted child of both parents it is good practice to state his paternity and that he has been treated as a child of the family. It is open to the respondent subsequently to deny that a child is a child of the family. It may be necessary for him to do this, for example, in order that he should be excused from any financial liability for the child.

If the children are 18 or over this should be stated. The court has a duty under s. 41, MCA 1973 to look after the interests not only of minor children but also of those children over 18 who have special needs. (See Chapter 9.) Therefore if there is a child of the family who is over 18 but is still dependent on his parents and unable to look after his own interests, for example, because of learning disability, brief details should also be given of his circumstances to enable the court to decide whether it needs to look more closely at the arrangements for him in accordance with s. 41. **8.25**

If the children are not over 18, their dates of birth should be given. Where there are children of 16 and 17 the petition should state whether they are receiving instruction at an educational establishment (school, technical college, etc.) or training for a trade, profession, or vocation (e.g., an apprenticeship, day-release, etc.). There is no need to go into detail here; a simple statement that the child is receiving education/training will suffice. Further details will, however, be required for the statement as to arrangements for children (see Chapter 9, paragraph 9.08 and onwards). **8.26**

Paragraph 6

The full names and dates of birth (or a statement that the child is over 18 if that is the case) of any other children now living who have been born to the wife during the marriage should be given. If the husband is the petitioner, he may only be able to state the position to the best of his knowledge but this is quite sufficient. If there is a dispute as to whether a child mentioned is a child of the family, this should be stated. Therefore if, for example, the husband is the petitioner and he denies that one of the children that his wife has had during the marriage is a child of the family, that child's name will be omitted from the list of the children of the family in paragraph 5 and particulars of the child will be given instead in paragraph 6. Paragraph 6 will go on to state that the petitioner denies that the child is a child of the family and to state whom the petitioner alleges is the father. **8.27**

Paragraph 7

In this paragraph details must be given of *all* court proceedings in relation to the marriage or the children of the family or between the petitioner and respondent in relation to their property (see paragraph 8.06 above at (i) for exactly what details of the proceedings are required). This means that proceedings which were dismissed or adjourned must be included **8.28** as well as those in which an order was made. Applications to a court under Part IV of the Family Law Act 1996 for an occupation order and/or a non-molestation order, and s. 17, Married Women's Property Act 1882 proceedings must obviously be mentioned. Practitioners sometimes overlook the fact that if any of the children of the family have been adopted, details of the adoption proceedings must be given.

Paragraph 8

8.29 This paragraph requires the petitioner to give details of any applications made under the CSA 1991 for a maintenance calculation in respect of any child of the family, together with the details of any calculation made by the Child Support Agency under the Act.

Paragraph 9

8.30 It is less common for there to be any proceedings which are relevant to this paragraph. An example of the type of proceedings to which reference should be made would be foreign divorce proceedings. Full particulars of the proceedings should be given (see paragraph 8.06 above at (i)). The court would have to consider in the light of these particulars whether the English proceedings should be stayed under sch. 1, DMPA 1973.

8.31 It should be noted that the EU Council Regulation Concerning Jurisdiction and the Recognition and Enforcement of Judgments in Matrimonial Matters and the Matters of Parental Responsibility (EC No 2201/2003) provides that where a party issues proceedings in a jurisdiction of one of the contracting states (these are set out in Chapter 6), the court of the state in which proceedings are first issued shall have exclusive jurisdiction. Proceedings issued in another contracting state for the same remedy must be stayed. There is little scope for the exercise of discretion save for some limited exceptions including that a stay would be manifestly contrary to public policy.

8.32 What this means in practice is that if divorce proceedings are validly issued in (say) Spain, any divorce proceedings subsequently commenced in England must be stayed. Arguments as to fairness and convenience will carry no weight. The party to the marriage who commences the divorce proceedings first will be able to secure the jurisdiction of his or her choice.

Paragraph 10

8.33 It is only necessary for this paragraph to be included in a petition based on five years' separation. In all other cases it can be deleted and the subsequent paragraphs renumbered. If an agreement or arrangement has been made (for example, for the payment of periodical payments or the transfer of the matrimonial home), concise details should be given.

Paragraph 11

8.34 This paragraph can be left to stand just as it appears on the printed form.

Paragraph 12

The MCA 1973, s. 1(2) fact upon which the petition is based must be stated. The statement of **8.35** the s. 1(2) fact should follow the wording of the section. For example, in a s. 1(2)(b) case, the fact will be stated thus:

> The respondent has behaved in such a way that the petitioner cannot reasonably be expected to live with the respondent.

Paragraph 13

Brief particulars of the supporting facts relied on must be given in *Paragraph 13* but not the **8.36** evidence by which they are to be proved. It can be difficult to decide how much detail should be given. The standard practitioners' textbooks give precedents of petitions and the following guidelines should also help:

(a) Adultery cases: if possible, give the date(s) and place(s) of the adultery (or, where adultery has taken place frequently over a period of time, the dates between which it was committed). If the respondent and the other party to the adultery have been cohabiting, the dates and place of cohabitation should be given. If there has been a child as a result of the adultery, this should be stated. The FPR, r. 2.7(i) make it clear that it is no longer necessary for the co-respondent to be named in the petition even if his identity is known to the petitioner. However, if the petitioner seeks to make a claim for costs against that person it will be necessary to name the person and make him a party to the proceedings (i.e., as co-respondent) (see paragraph 8.45 and onwards).

(b) Behaviour cases: as a rule of thumb, where the petitioner's statement clearly discloses sufficient evidence of behaviour and there is no reason to believe that the petition will be defended, it should be sufficient to select about six allegations/incidents by way of particulars. Generally it is appropriate to include the first, the worst and the last incident of behaviour during the marriage. Incidents should be described in chronological order wherever possible. A long narrative is not required. The date of the incident should be given as precisely as possible together with sufficient information to identify the incident the petitioner has in mind and to see why it is alleged to constitute behaviour. The allegations should not be 'hopelessly general' (*Butterworth* v *Butterworth* [1997] 2 FLR 336). If the petitioner suffered an injury to health as a result of the incident or was otherwise affected, this should be stated. It is quite common to include a general paragraph summarizing the characteristics of the respondent's behaviour.

(c) Desertion cases: the date and circumstances of the respondent's departure should be given in sufficient detail to show that the respondent intended to bring cohabitation to an end permanently. The particulars should also state that the petitioner did not consent to the respondent's departure and gave him no cause to leave.

(d) Consensual separation cases: the date and brief circumstances of the separation should be given. Care must be taken in cases where the parties have continued to live in the same house to give sufficient information to establish that they did maintain separate households under the same roof.

(e) Five years' separation cases: particulars should be given as in consensual separation cases.

It should be made clear in all cases in the particulars whether the petitioner and respondent have ceased to cohabit and, if so, when. The provisions of s. 2, MCA 1973 as to cohabitation (see Chapter 4) should be borne in mind when drafting the particulars and any relevant periods of cohabitation should be referred to.

Example The petitioner and respondent separated on 4 May 2000. The petition alleges five years' separation. The parties have, in fact, resumed living together for two periods, from 1 August 2001 until 22 September 2001 and from 3 February 2002 until 8 April 2002. These periods do not together exceed six months, therefore they will be disregarded in determining whether the petitioner should get a decree. However, they should be referred to in the particulars of separation thus:

> The petitioner and the respondent have lived apart for a continuous period of at least 5 years immediately preceding the presentation of this petition, namely from 4 May 2000 when, after unhappy family difficulties, the petitioner left the respondent, save that the petitioner and the respondent have resumed living together for 2 periods not exceeding six months in all, namely from . . . In the premises, no account should be taken of the said periods.

The prayer

Prayer for dissolution of marriage

8.37 This is a standard prayer which takes the same form in all divorce petitions.

Prayer for costs

8.38 Careful consideration should be given to whether the costs of obtaining a decree should be claimed from the respondent or the co-respondent. A claim for costs will normally be included where the petitioner is receiving full public funding or is paying privately for the services of her solicitor. Whether costs will be ordered is a matter within the discretion of the court (see Chapter 9, paragraph 9.74). The general view is that costs should *not* normally be claimed where the petitioner is receiving Legal Help. There seem to be two reasons for this. First of all, the financial benefit of a claim for costs will inevitably be small as the petitioner will only be entitled to costs as a litigant in person in any event. Secondly, the prayer for costs can sometimes prove to be the last straw that decides the respondent not only to contest the issue of costs but also to oppose the granting of a divorce.

8.39 It must be said, however, that quite a number of practitioners do nevertheless claim costs in Legal Help cases and some district judges continue to grant costs although practice seems to vary around the country. It may be that the reason for solicitors continuing to claim costs is to reduce the potential impact of the statutory charge, or to save the trouble of amending the petition later to claim costs should the case be defended.

8.40 A sensible approach, therefore, is to word the prayer for costs to read as follows: 'That the respondent may be ordered to pay costs of this suit should the proceedings become defended or should the statutory charge apply'.

8.41 If a prayer for costs is included, it is open to the respondent/co-respondent to contest his liability to pay. He will do this initially by notifying the court of his objection on the acknowledgement of service form. For the subsequent procedure, see Chapter 9, paragraph 9.74

Prayer for ancillary relief

It will normally be advisable to include a prayer for all available forms of ancillary relief.　**8.42**
This is because the petitioner is obliged to make any claims that she wishes to make on her own behalf for maintenance pending suit, financial provision orders, property adjustment, and pension orders in the petition (r. 2.53(1), FPR 1991; Chapter 17, paragraph 17.68). If she fails to include all her claims in the petition at the outset, she will not be able to make them at all unless either:

(a) if the omission is discovered before a decree is granted, the petition is amended to include the appropriate claims. The petition can be amended without the court's permission before it is served but thereafter the permission of the court is required for amendments (r. 2.11(1), FPR 1991); as to amendment, see further Chapter 10, *or*

(b) if the omission is not discovered until after a decree has been granted, then the court's permission to make the application is necessary. The only exception to this is that if the parties are agreed as to the terms of the order, the petitioner can make an application for the agreed order without the court's permission (r. 2.53(2), FPR 1991).

If the omission is not discovered until after the petitioner has remarried, she will be debarred from making any claim at all (whereas a lump sum or property adjustment claim made *before* remarriage can be pursued after remarriage).

Example　Mr and Mrs Williams have been married for many years. They have always lived in a council house and, as far as Mrs Williams is aware, they have no savings. Mrs Williams leaves her husband and seeks a divorce. She obtains a flat from a housing association so she does not want a transfer of the council house nor does she want any of the contents of the house which have had their day. She does not even want maintenance because she has met someone she intends to marry. When her petition is filed, all the claims for ancillary relief are struck out of the prayer. After decree absolute comes through, Mrs Williams remarries. She then discovers that her husband had been saving a worthwhile sum from his earnings throughout the marriage without telling her. He has amassed savings of over £100,000 over the years. Mrs Williams consults her solicitor with a view to claiming a share. She cannot do so because no claim for a lump sum or property adjustment order was included in her petition and she is debarred from making one now by her remarriage. Had her petition included a comprehensive prayer for ancillary relief, she could have proceeded with a claim in relation to the savings despite her remarriage.

Although claims for ancillary relief for children can be made at any time, it will generally be convenient to include full claims on their behalf in the petition as well (remembering, of course, that the court's jurisdiction has been curtailed following the coming into force of the CSA 1991, see Chapter 20).

Signature

Where the petitioner is receiving advice under the Legal Help scheme, she should sign the　**8.43**
petition herself.

8.44 If the solicitor is acting for the petitioner in receipt of full public funding (that is, a certificate for legal representation) or on a private basis, the petition should be signed by the solicitor in his own or the firm's name (r. 2.5, FPR 1991).

When is there a co-respondent?

8.45 As explained at 8.36, r. 2.7(1), FPR 1991 states that where a petition alleges that the respondent has committed adultery, the person with whom the adultery is alleged to have been committed shall be made a co-respondent in the cause unless:

(a)　that person is not named in the petition; or

(b)　the court otherwise directs.

In practice, a third party is not named in the divorce petition, making him or her a co-respondent, unless the petitioner wishes to seek an order for costs against the co-respondent or has other specific reasons for naming the third party in this way.

8.46 If a person is made a co-respondent, that person is entitled to be served with a copy of the petition (and such of the accompanying documents as are appropriate) and to defend the allegations and/or any claim for costs made against him in the petition.

Addresses for service

8.47 The respondent's address for service (and that of the co-respondent if there is one) must be given. This will be the address of the last-known residence of the respondent (and co-respondent) unless the petitioner's solicitors have been notified that the respondent (or co-respondent) is represented by solicitors who will accept service of the petition on his behalf.

8.48 Where the petitioner is paying the solicitor privately or, very unusually, is in receipt of a certificate for full representation for the divorce proceedings, the petitioner's address for service will be that of her solicitors. However, where the petitioner is receiving advice under the Legal Help scheme, the solicitor must agree to give his own address as the petitioner's address for service and the fact of the petitioner acting in person will be indicated by the use of the words 'care of' before the name and address of the solicitor.

D　KEY DOCUMENTS

8.49 The Family Proceedings Rules 1991 (SI 1991/1247) as amended

Before completing this form, read carefully the **Notes for Guidance**

In the   County Court*

* Delete as appropriate

In the Principal Registry*   No.

Introduction

This petition is issued by   ("the Petitioner")

The other party to the marriage is   ("the Respondent")

(1)   On the   day of   [19   ][20   ]
                                                                  was lawfully married to

      at

(1a) Since the date of the marriage the name of the petitioner has [not] changed

(1b) The petitioner believes that since the date of the marriage the name of the respondent has [not] changed

(2)   The petitioner and respondent last lived together as husband and wife at

(3)   The court has jurisdiction under Article 3(1) of the Council Regulation on the following ground(s):

(4)   The petitioner is by occupation a   and resides at

      The respondent is by occupation a   and resides at

(5)   There are no children of the family now living *except*

(6)   No other child, now living, has been born to the petitioner/respondent during the marriage (so far as known to the petitioner) *except*

Delete any words in square brackets which do not apply

(7) There are or have been no other proceedings in any court in England and Wales or elsewhere with reference to the marriage (or to any child of the family) or between the petitioner and respondent with reference to any property of either or both of them *except*

(8) There are or have been no proceedings in the Child Support Agency with reference to the maintenance of any child of the family *except*

(9) There are no proceedings continuing in any country outside England or Wales which are in respect of the marriage or are capable of affecting its validity or subsistence *except*

(10) (This paragraph should be completed only if the petition is based on five years' separation.)
     No agreement or arrangement has been made or is proposed to be made between the parties for the support of the petitioner/respondent (and any child of the family) *except*

(11) The said marriage has broken down irretrievably.

(12)

CCD 8 Page 2

(13) **Particulars**

Prayer

The petitioner therefore prays

(1) The suit

That the said marriage be dissolved

(2) Costs

That the   may be ordered to pay the costs of this suit

(3) Ancillary relief

That the petitioner may be granted the following ancillary relief:

(a)   an order for maintenance pending suit

a periodical payments order

a secured provision order

a lump sum order

a property adjustment order

an order under section 24B, 25B or
25C of the Act of 1973
(Pension Sharing/Attachment Order)

(b)   **For the children**

a periodical payments order

a secured provision order

a lump sum order

a property adjustment order

Signed ....

The names and addresses of the persons to be served with the petition are:

Respondent:

Co-Respondent (adultery case only):

The Petitioner's address for service is:

Dated this   **day of**   **20**

Address all communications for the court to: The Court Manager, County Court,
The Court office at

is open from 10 a.m. to 4 p.m. (4.30 p.m. at the Principal Registry of the Family Division) on Mondays to Fridays.

CCD 8   Page 5

In the

County Court*

No.

In the Principal Registry*

Between

Petitioner

and

Respondent

Divorce Petition

Full name and address of the petitioner or of solicitors if
they are acting for the petitioner.

Divorce Petition - Notes for Guidance

Each of the notes below will help you to complete that paragraph in the divorce petition which has the same number as the note. You should not cross out any of the paragraphs numbered 1 to 13 unless the notes say that you should.

Introduction

After the words "This petition is issued by" you, the person making the petition, should state your current full name. You will be known as the Petitioner. Then after the words "The other party to the marriage is" give the current full name of your husband or wife. He or she will be known as the Respondent.

(1) You will find the information you need to complete the following paragraph on your marriage certificate

Please give:

- the date of your marriage,
- your full name at the time of the marriage.
- the full name of your husband or wife at the time of the marriage,
- the place of the marriage.

When giving the place of marriage you should write the words - both printed and hand-written - contained in the marriage certificate which come after the phrase "Marriage solemnised at", for example:

Where the marriage took place in a Register Office:
"The Register Office, in the District of ....
in the County of ...."

"Where the marriage took place in a church:
.......................Church, in the Parish of ....
in the County of ...."

1(a) If you have not changed your name(s) since the time of the marriage delete the words in square brackets.

If you have changed your name(s) since the marriage, delete the words "has not changed" and explain your change of name, for example by adding:

- by deed poll and I am now known as,
- I am now known as,
- I retained my maiden name at marriage and am known as

after the words in square brackets "has changed" and then stating the full name that you are now known by.

1(b) If you believe the respondent has not changed his or her name(s) since the date of the marriage delete the words in square brackets.

If you believe that the respondent has, since the marriage, changed his or her name(s), delete the words "has not changed" and explain how you believe he or she has changed their name, for example by adding:

- by deed poll and he/she is now known as,
- he/she is now known as,
- she retained her maiden name at marriage and is now known as

after the words in square brackets "has changed" and then stating the full name that you believe they are now known by.

(2) Please give the last address at which you have lived with the respondent as husband and wife.

(3) Please write in, exactly as set out below, the following paragraph (or paragraphs) upon which you intend to rely to prove that the court has jurisdiction under Article 3(1) of the Council Regulation and therefore may deal with your petition. If you are completing this form without a solicitor and need help deciding which paragraph(s) applies, a Citizens Advice Bureau will be able to help you.

(a) "The petitioner and respondent are both habitually resident in England and Wales."

(b) "The petitioner and respondant were last habitually resident in England and Wales and the *[petitioner][respondent] still resides there"
(*Delete as appropriate)

(c) "The respondent is habitually resident in England and Wales."

(d) "The petitioner is habitually resident in England and Wales and has resided there for at least a year immediately prior to the presentation of this petition." (You should give the address(es) where you lived during that time and the length of time lived at each address.)

(e) "The petitioner is domiciled and habitually resident in England and Wales and has resided there for at least six months immediately prior to the presentation of the petition." (You should give the address(es) where you lived during that time and the length of time lived at each address.)

(f) "The petitioner and the respondent are both domiciled in England and Wales."

If none of the above paragraphs apply to you but you believe that the court still has jurisdiction to deal with your petition, cross out the words "The court has jurisdiction under Article 3(1) of the Council Regulation on the following ground(s):" and add the following paragraph, if it applies:

"The court has jurisdiction other than under Council Regulation on the basis that no Contracting State has jurisdiction under the Council Regulation and the *[petitioner] [respondent] is domiciled in England and Wales on the date when this petition is issued."
(*Delete as appropriate)

(4) Please give your occupation and current address and those of the respondent.

(5) If there are no children of the family cross out the word "except". If there are any children of the family give:

- their full names (including surname),
- their date of birth, or if over 18 say so,
- if the child is over 16 but under 18, say if he or she is at school, or college,
  or is training for a trade, profession or vocation,
  or is working full time.

(6) If no other child has been born during the marriage you should cross out the word "except".

If you are the husband, cross out the word "petitioner" where it first appears in the paragraph, but do not cross out the words in brackets

If you are the wife, cross out the word "respondent", and cross out the words in brackets.

If there is a child give:

- the full name (including surname),
- the date of birth, or if over 18 say so.

If there is a dispute whether a living child is a child of the family please add a paragraph saying so.

(7) If there have not been any court proceedings in England and Wales or elsewhere concerning:

- your marriage,
- any child of the family,
- any property belonging to either you or the respondent

cross out the word "except".

If there have been proceedings please give:

- the name of the court in which they took place,
- details of the order(s) which were made,
- if the proceedings were about your marriage say if you and the respondent resumed living together as husband and wife after the order was made.

(8) If there have not been any proceedings in the Child Support Agency concerning the maintenance of any child of the family, cross out the word "except".

If there have been any proceedings please give:

- the date of any application to the Agency
- details of the calculation made.

(9) If there have been no proceedings in a court outside England and Wales which have affected the marriage, or may affect it, cross out the word "except".

If there are or have been any proceedings please give:

- the name of the country and the court in which they are taking/have taken place,
- the date the proceedings were begun and the names of the parties
- details of the order(s) made,
- if no order has yet been made, the date of any future hearing.

(10) If your petition is not based on five years separation, cross out this paragraph.

If your petition is based on five years separation but no agreement or arrangement has been made, cross out the word "except".

If your petition is based on five years' separation and an agreement or arrangement has been made with the respondent:

- about maintenance either for him or herself or for any child of the family,
- about the family property,

please give full details.

(11) If you are applying for a judicial separation or the annulment of your marriage please cross out this paragraph.

(12) Please write in, exactly as set out below, the paragraph (or paragraphs) upon which you intend to rely to prove that your marriage has irretrievably broken down.

(a) The respondent has committed adultery with a [man], [woman] and the petitioner finds it intolerable to live with the respondent.
   or
   The respondent has committed adultery [with (give the name) .... (called the co-respondent)] and the petitioner finds it intolerable to live with the respondent.

(b) The respondent has behaved in such a way that the petitioner cannot reasonably be expected to live with the respondent.

(c) The respondent has deserted the petitioner for a continuous period of at least two years immediately preceding the presentation of this petition.

(d) The parties to the marriage have lived apart for a continuous period of at least two years immediately preceding the presentation of the petition and the respondent consents to a decree being granted.

(e) The parties to the marriage have lived apart for a continuous period of at least five years immediately preceding the presentation of the petition.

Please note: You do not need to give the name of the person with whom the respondent has committed adultery unless you wish to claim costs against that person.

Particulars

(13) This space is provided for you to give details of the allegations which you are using to prove the facts given in paragraph 12. In most cases one or two sentences will do.

(a) If you have alleged adultery give;
- the date(s) and place(s) where the adultery took place.

(b) If you have alleged unreasonable behaviour give:
- details of particular incidents, including dates, but it should not be necessary to give more than about half a dozen examples of the more serious incidents, including the most recent.

(c) If you have alleged desertion give;
- the date of desertion,
- brief details of how the desertion came about.

(d) & (e) If you have alleged either two or five years separation give;
- the date of separation,
- brief details of how the separation came about.

CCD 8B

Prayer

The prayer of the petition is your request to the court. You should consider carefully the claims which you wish to make.

You should adapt the prayer to suit your claims.

(1) The suit

If you are asking for a judicial separation, cross out this paragraph and write in its place:

"That the petitioner may be judicially separated from the respondent".

(2) Costs

If you wish to claim that the respondent or co-respondent pay your costs you must do so in your petition.

It is not possible to make a claim after a decree has been granted.

If you do wish to claim costs write in respondent, or co-respondent, or both, as appropriate.

If you do not wish to claim costs, cross out this paragraph.

(3) Ancillary relief

If you wish to apply for any of these orders, complete paragraph 3 by deleting those orders you do not require.

You are advised to see a solicitor if you are unsure about which order(s) you require.

If you cross out this paragraph, or any part of it, and later change your mind, you will first have to ask the court's permission before any application can be made. Permission cannot be granted after re-marriage.

If you apply in the prayer for an order you must complete Form A when you are ready to proceed with your application.

If you are asking for a property adjustment order, give the address of the property concerned.

If you are asking for a pension sharing or attachment order, give details of the order you require.

You can apply to the court for ancillary relief for children if you are asking for one or more of the following:

- a lump sum payment,
- * settlement of property,
- * transfer of property,
- * secured periodical payments,
- financial provision for a stepchild or stepchildren of the respondent.

  * *These orders can only be made in the High Court or a county court.*

- periodical payments when either the child or, the person with care of the child, or the absent parent of the child is **not** habitually resident in the United Kingdom,
- periodical payments in addition to child support maintenance paid under a Child Support Agency calculation.
- periodical payments to meet expenses arising from a child's disability.
- periodical payments to meet expenses incurred by a child in being educated or training for work.

CCD 8B

If none of the above applies to you, you should make an application for child maintenance to the Child Support Agency; the court cannot make an order for child maintenance in your case. A leaflet about the Child Support Agency is available from any court office.

If you are not sure whether the court can hear your application please ask a member of the court staff. A leaflet 'I want to apply for a financial order' is also available

Finally, do not forget to

- sign and date the petition,
- give the name(s) and personal address(es) of the person(s) to be served with the petition,
- bring or send your marriage certificate and fee to the court,
- complete a Statement of Arrangements if there are children of the family.

Arrangements for Children

If you consider that the court will need to:

- determine where the child(ren) should live (a Residence Order),
- determine with whom the child(ren) should have contact (a Contact Order),
- make a Specific Issue Order,
- make a Prohibited Steps Order,

you must apply for the order form C2.

You may enclose the completed form with your petition or submit it later. If you wish to apply for any of these orders, or any other orders which may be available to you under part I or II of the Children Act 1989, you are advised to see a solicitor.

The Court will only make an order if it considers that an order will be better for the child(ren) than no order.

The Gender Recognition Act 2004

You should only read this section if you are applying to annul your marriage and the ground (or one of the grounds) on which the annulment is sought relates to the issue of an interim or full gender recognition certificate.

If the petition is brought on the ground that an interim gender recognition certificate has been issued to you or the respondent (under section 12(g), or paragraph 11(1)(e) of Schedule 1 to, the Matrimonial Causes Act 1973), you must when sending the petition to the court attach to it a copy of the interim gender recognition certificate issued to you or the respondent.

If the petition is brought on the ground that the gender of the respondent was the acquired gender at the time of the marriage under the Gender Recognition Act 2004 (under section 12(h) of the Matrimonial Causes Act 1973) and a full gender recognition certificate has been issued to him or her, you must when sending the petition to the court attach to it a copy of the full gender recognition certificate.

All forms and leaflets are available from your Court

9

UNDEFENDED DIVORCE: PROCEDURE FOR OBTAINING THE DECREE

A   DOCUMENTS REQUIRED

9.01 The following documents should be prepared/assembled for presentation to the court. A copy should be kept for the solicitor's own file of all documents that are to be filed at court.

The petition

9.02 For notes on drafting the petition, see Chapter 8. To assist you in understanding the procedure to obtain a divorce, a flow chart is to be found at the end of this chapter.

9.03 Every divorce suit is commenced by petition (r. 2.2, Family Proceedings Rules 1991 ('FPR 1991')). The court will require the petitioner to provide the original petition plus one copy for each party who is to be served. Therefore the solicitor must always have ready the original petition plus one copy for the respondent. Where there is a co-respondent, a further copy will be required. It is possible for there to be more than one co-respondent if the petition makes several allegations of adultery. In this event one further copy of the petition will be required for each additional co-respondent.

The marriage certificate

9.04 The marriage certificate must be filed with the petition (r. 2.6(2), FPR 1991). If the client does not have a marriage certificate one can be obtained by post or by personal attendance from the office of the Superintendent Registrar of Marriages for the district where the marriage took place. A standard fee is payable, presently £7.00. Alternatively a copy can be obtained by post from the General Register Office, Smedley Hydro, Southport, Merseyside, PR8 2HH, tel: 01704 569824. The fee varies depending on whether the applicant has the index reference (£8.50 with, or £11.50 without the index reference).

If the client is receiving Legal Help, the cost of obtaining the certificate can be met under **9.05** Legal Help. However, the financial limit on this advice is often little enough as it is and some solicitors request the client to obtain a copy of the certificate herself. If it is necessary for the solicitor to obtain the certificate for the client, the possibility of seeking or authorizing an extension of the Legal Help limit should be borne in mind if costs are nearing the normal limit.

Only one copy of the marriage certificate is required. It is kept on the court file and is **9.06** not usually returned to the petitioner if the divorce proceedings do not go ahead or are dismissed. An application for the return of the marriage certificate, granted at the court's discretion, is required where the parties subsequently become reconciled.

Where the marriage certificate is in a foreign language, the court will usually require a **9.07** certified translation of the certificate to be lodged as well.

The statement as to arrangements for children (Form M4)

Generally

Where there is a child of the family who is: **9.08**

(a)   under 16; or
(b)   over 16 but under 18 and receiving instruction at an educational establishment or undergoing training for a trade or profession,

then r. 2.2, FPR 1991 require the petitioner to file a Form M4 setting out the arrangements for those children. In 'exceptional circumstances' the district judge can direct that a decree not be made absolute until matters in respect of the children have been resolved (s. 41(2), Matrimonial Causes Act 1973 ('MCA 1973')).

Rule 2.2 requires that 'if practicable' the statement of arrangements for children be **9.09** agreed with the respondent (and provision is made for this in Part IV of the statement of arrangements Form M4). If this is not practicable, then it would appear that the petitioner cannot be compelled to comply with the requirement. If the respondent's agreement has not been, or cannot be obtained, then it would be good practice to provide a letter of explanation for the court when the Form M4 is filed (see also r. 2.38, FPR 1991 which deals with the respondent's statement in response to the petitioner's statement).

The statement of arrangements should be signed by the petitioner personally (even where **9.10** a solicitor is acting for her), giving background information about each child, for example, where he is to live after the divorce, details of his school, health etc. (r. 2.2(2), FPR 1991). This statement is the core of the information available to the district judge when he considers the arrangements for the children.

9.11 Form M4 can be obtained from the offices of divorce county courts, from law stationers, or on-line. Where there is more than one child to whom r. 2.2(2) applies, then details in relation to all the children can be given on one form. See paragraph 9.83 and onwards for a more detailed analysis of the way in which the procedures for s. 41, MCA 1973 operate.

Completing Form M4

9.12 Completing Form M4 is a relatively straightforward matter. The margin notes on the form indicate what information is required. A blank copy of Form M4 appears on pp. 122–9. The solicitor should take care to give as much information as possible on the form. The court will require the original statement as to arrangements plus one copy for service on the respondent, together with the original and a copy of any medical report that is attached to Form M4. The arrangements for the children are of no concern to the co-respondent and he is not provided with a copy of Form M4.

9.13 There are two particularly important features of the Statement of Arrangements for children:

(a) Where the petitioner intends to apply for an order under s. 8, Children Act 1989 ('CA 1989') (e.g., for a residence or contact order) in respect of a child of the family, this must be indicated in the Statement (Box 8(c) and 10(c)).

(b) The petitioner must indicate whether a maintenance calculation has been carried out by the Child Support Agency in respect of a child of the family as a result of which payments are being made for the benefit of the child (Box 7(c)); if not, then the petitioner must indicate whether or not she will make an application through the Child Support Agency (Box 7(e)).

Medical reports

9.14 If a child has a long-standing illness or suffers from a disability, this must be stated in Form M4. If there is an up-to-date medical report, it should be attached to Form M4. If there is not, consideration should be given as to whether a report or at least a letter should be obtained from the doctor responsible for the child. In a relatively straightforward case (for example, where a child was born with a disability, such as the lack of a finger on one hand, which does not need treatment and with which the child has learned to cope) no report or letter may be required. In more complex cases, for example, where the child is currently receiving regular treatment of more than a routine nature (as where the child is undergoing a series of surgical operations), a report will be necessary in order that the district judge is sufficiently well informed about the child to decide whether he can grant a s. 41 declaration.

9.15 If no report is provided and the district judge decides when giving directions for trial that a report is necessary, he can give a direction to that effect: see r. 2.39(3), FPR 1991 (see paragraph 9.89 below).

9.16 The cost of obtaining a medical report is covered by the Legal Help scheme. However, as this will increase the petitioner's costs of obtaining the divorce, the solicitor should bear in mind that it may become necessary to authorize or to apply for an extension at some stage.

Where children are not living with petitioner

9.17 Where the children are not living with the petitioner, she may not be able to give all the information required by Form M4. It would be good practice for the respondent in such a case to file a statement in Form M4 together with his acknowledgement without any prompting. However, this is not always done.

Where the petitioner is not able to give the necessary information and the respondent has **9.18** not supplied it voluntarily, it is likely that the court will ask the respondent to file a statement giving information about the children in the form of a letter or in Form M4 (see r. 2.38, FPR 1991). However, there does not appear to be any power to require the respondent to provide information and, if he fails to do so by the time the district judge considers the arrangements for the children, the proper course would appear to be for the district judge to direct that a report by an officer of the Children and Family Court Advisory and Support Service (CAFCASS) be prepared giving details of the respondent's arrangements for the children (see paragraph 9.83 below).

Certified copies of court orders

Where there have been previous proceedings relating to the parties to the marriage, or **9.19** children of the family, the court will usually expect the petitioner to lodge at the court certified copies of previous court orders so that the district judge may have as full a picture as possible of the history of the marriage.

Public funding

Public funding in its form of a certificate for Legal Representation is not normally granted for **9.20** the decree proceedings as opposed to proceedings in relation to ancillary matters such as applications made under the CA 1989 and property (see Chapter 7). If a certificate is granted, however, it must be filed with the court and a notice of issue served on the respondent and co-respondent, if applicable.

B   COMMENCEMENT OF PROCEEDINGS

Divorce proceedings are commenced by the presentation of the divorce petition and **9.21** supporting documents at court. The petition may be presented to any divorce county court (r. 2.6, FPR 1991), or to the Divorce Registry in London (the principal registry of the Family Division of the High Court which is treated in many respects as another divorce county court) (see r. 1.4, FPR 1991 and s. 42, Matrimonial and Family Proceedings Act 1984). Not all county courts are divorce county courts. They must be designated as such by the Secretary of State for Constitutional Affairs.

The solicitor will normally find it most convenient to commence the divorce proceedings in **9.22** his local divorce county court or the divorce county court nearest to where the petitioner lives. The petition and supporting documents listed in paragraph 9.01 and onwards must be filed at the court office of the chosen county court (or at the Divorce Registry). They can be handed in personally over the counter in the court office or sent by post.

Statement of Arrangements for Children
(Form M4, Appendix 1 FPR 1991)

FAMILY PROCEEDINGS RULES
Rule 2.2(2)

In the	County Court
Petitioner	
Respondent	
No. of Matter *(always quote this)*	

To the Petitioner

You must complete this form
if you or the respondent have any children ● under 16

or ● over 16 but under 18 if they are at school
or college or are training for a trade,
profession or vocation.

Please use black ink.

Please complete Parts I, II and III.

Before you issue a petition for divorce try to reach agreement with your husband/wife over the proposals for the children's future. There is space for him/her to sign at the end of this form if agreement is reached.

If your husband/wife does not agree with the proposals he/she will have the opportunity at a later stage to state why he/she does not agree and will be able to make his/her own proposals.

You should take or send the completed form, signed by you (and, if agreement is reached, by your husband/wife) together with a copy to the Court when you issue your petition.

Please refer to the explanatory notes issued regarding completion of the prayer of the petition if you are asking the Court to make any order regarding the children.

The Court will only make an order if it considers that an order will be better for the child(ren) than no order.

If you wish to apply for any of the orders which may be available to you under Part I or II of the Children Act 1989 you are advised to see a solicitor.

You should obtain legal advice from a solicitor or, alternatively, from an advice agency. Addresses of solicitors and advice agencies can be obtained from the Yellow Pages and the Solicitors Regional Directory which can be found at Citizens Advice Bureaux, Law Centres and any local library.

To the Respondent

The petitioner has completed Parts I, II and III of this form
which will be sent to the Court at the same time that the divorce petition is filed.

Please read all parts of the form carefully.

If you agree with the arrangements and proposals for the children you should sign Part IV of the form.

Please use black ink. You should return the form to the petitioner, or his/her solicitor.

If you do not agree with all or some of the arrangements or proposals you will be given the opportunity of saying so when the divorce petition is served on you.

1

Part I – Details of the children
Please read the instructions for boxes 1, 2 and 3 before you complete this section

1.	**Children of both parties**
	(Give details only of any children born to you and the Respondent or adopted by you both)

	Forenames	Surnames	Date of birth
(i)			
(ii)			
(iii)			
(iv)			
(v)			

2.	**Other children of the family**
	(Give details of any other children treated by both of you as children of the family: for example your own or the Respondent's)

	Forenames	Surname	Date of birth	Relationship to Yourself	Respondent
(i)					
(ii)					
(iii)					
(iv)					
(v)					

3.	**Other children who are not children of the family**
	(Give details of any children born to you or the Respondent that have not been treated as children of the family or adopted by you both)

	Forenames	Surnames	Date of birth
(i)			
(ii)			
(iii)			
(iv)			
(v)			

2

Part II – Arrangements for the children of the family

This part of the form must be completed. Give details for each child if arrangements are different.
If necessary, continue on another sheet and attach it to this form

4.	**Home details** *(Please tick the appropriate boxes)*	
	(a) The addresses at which the children now live	
	(b) Give details of the number of living rooms, bedrooms, etc. at the addresses in (a)	
	(c) Is the house rented or owned and by whom? Is the rent or any mortgage being regularly paid?	☐ No ☐ Yes
	(d) Give the names of all other persons living with the children including your husband/wife if he/she lives there. State their relationship to the children.	
	(e) Will there be any change in these arrangements?	☐ No ☐ Yes *(please give details)*

3

5.	**Education and training details** *(Please tick the appropriate boxes)*	
	(a) Give the names of the school, college or place of training attended by each child.	
	(b) Do the children have any special educational needs?	☐ No ☐ Yes *(please give details)*
	(c) Is the school, college or place of training, fee-paying?	☐ No ☐ Yes *(please give details of how much the fees are per term/year)*
	Are fees being regularly paid?	☐ No ☐ Yes *(please give details)*
	(d) Will there be any change in these arrangements?	☐ No ☐ Yes *(please give details)*

6.	**Childcare details** *(Please tick the appropriate boxes)*	
	(a) Which parent looks after the children from day to day? If responsibility is shared, please give details.	
	(b) Does that parent go out to work?	☐ No ☐ Yes *(please give details of his/her hours of work)*
	(c) Does someone look after the children when the parent is not there?	☐ No ☐ Yes *(please give details)*
	(d) Who looks after the children during school holidays?	
	(e) Will there be any change in these arrangements?	☐ No ☐ Yes *(please give details)*

7.	**Maintenance** *(Please tick the appropriate boxes)*	
	(a) Does your husband/wife pay towards the upkeep of the children? If there is another source of maintenance, please specify.	☐ No ☐ Yes *(please give details of how much)*
	(b) Is the payment made under a court order?	☐ No ☐ Yes *(please give details, including the name of the court and case number)*
	(c) Is the payment following an assessment by the Child Support Agency?	☐ No ☐ Yes *(please give details of how much)*
	(d) Has maintenance for the children been agreed?	☐ No ☐ Yes
	(e) If not, will you be applying for: ● a child maintenance order from the court ● child support maintenance through the Child Support Agency?	☐ No ☐ Yes ☐ No ☐ Yes

5

8.	**Details for contact with the children** *(Please tick the appropriate boxes)*	
(a) Do the children see your husband/wife?	☐ No	☐ Yes *(please give details of how often and where)*
(b) Do the children ever stay with your husband/wife?	☐ No	☐ Yes *(please give details of how much)*
(c) Will there be any change to these arrangements? Please give details of the proposed arrangements for contact and residence.	☐ No	☐ Yes *(please give details of how much)*

6

9.	**Details of health** *(Please tick the appropriate boxes)*	
(a)	Are the children generally in good health?	☐ Yes ☐ No *(please give details of any serious disability or chronic illness)*
(b)	Do the children have any special health needs?	☐ No ☐ Yes *(please give details of the care needed and how it is to be provided)*

10.	**Details of care and other court proceedings** *(Please tick the appropriate boxes)*	
(a)	Are the children in the care of a local authority, or under the supervision of a social worker or probation officer?	☐ No ☐ Yes *(please give details including any court proceedings)*
(b)	Are any of the children on the Child Protection Register?	☐ No ☐ Yes *(please give details of the local authority and the date of registration)*
(c)	Are there or have there been any proceedings in any Court involving the children, for example adoption, custody/residence, access/contact wardship, care, supervision or maintenance? (You need not include any Child Support Agency proceedings here).	☐ No ☐ Yes *(please give details and send a copy of any order to the Court)*

7

Part III — To the Petitioner

Conciliation

If you and your husband/wife do not agree about the arrangements for the child(ren), would you agree to discuss the matter with a Conciliator and your husband/wife?

☐ No ☐ Yes

Declaration

I declare that the information I have given is correct and complete to the best of my knowledge.

Signed   (Petitioner)

Date:

Part IV — To the Respondent

I agree with the arrangements and proposals contained in Part I and II of this form.

Signed   (Respondent)

Date:

8

OYEZ The Solicitors' Law Stationery Society Ltd, Oyez House, 7 Spa Road, London SE16 3QQ

1993 Edition
4.96 F31727
5046127
★ ★

Divorce 8

C   FEE

9.23   There is a court fee of £300 payable when the petition is filed. If the petitioner is in receipt of Legal Help or is receiving income support or otherwise on a low income (providing, in the latter two cases, that she is not also receiving full public funding), she is entitled to exemption from the fee. A form applying for exemption is obtainable from the court and should be completed on the petitioner's behalf. The fee will almost certainly be payable when the petitioner is paying privately for her solicitor's services. Where the petitioner (in exceptional circumstances) is publicly funded by certificate from the outset, a fee is payable when the petition is filed.

D   ADDITIONAL MATTERS WHERE THE SOLICITOR IS ACTING

When is the solicitor acting?

9.24   The solicitor *is not* acting in the divorce proceedings if his client is receiving only Legal Help in relation to them. Such a client is looked upon as a litigant in person for the purposes of the decree proceedings. This is unaffected by any certificate that may have been granted in the client's favour in relation to ancillary matters. The solicitor *is* acting in the divorce proceedings if his client is paying privately for his services or if a certificate has been granted in relation to these proceedings.

Additional duties

9.25   The solicitor must file a certificate in Form M3 (one copy only required) with the petition (r. 2.6(3), FPR 1991). This states whether or not he has discussed with the petitioner the possibility of a reconciliation and given her the names and addresses of persons qualified to help effect a reconciliation (see Chapter 1, paragraph 1.38 and onwards for further details of such persons). There is not, in fact, any requirement that the solicitor *must* discuss reconciliation with the client. However, the fact that he must file Form M3 ensures that he will at least turn his mind to the question and, unless it is clearly inappropriate in the client's particular circumstances, it will usually be good practice to discuss the possibility of reconciliation with the client. In any event, this would be necessary to establish that the marriage has in fact irretrievably broken down

E   ENTRY IN COURT BOOKS

9.26   When the court receives the petition, it enters the cause in the books of the court and a file number is allocated to it. The solicitor will be notified of the number. This is the official identity tag for the case and must be quoted on all correspondence with the court and used on all pleadings connected with the divorce and with ancillary matters.

F   SERVICE OF THE PETITION

Before the divorce can go any further the petition must be served on the respondent and any   **9.27**
co-respondent (rr. 2.9(1) and 2.24, FPR 1991) or, in exceptional circumstances, service may
be dispensed with (r. 2.9(11)).

Tracing a missing respondent

The petitioner may have lost touch with the respondent and be unable to provide an address   **9.28**
for him. Efforts will have to be made to trace him in order that the petition can be served
either by post or personally. Apart from the normal enquiries that can be made of the respondent's former employers, his relations and friends, his clubs and trade union, there are
various special ways of tracing a missing respondent. These are set out fully in *Practice
Direction* [1989] 1 All ER 765, [1989] 1 WLR 219. In summary, if the petition is filed by a wife
and includes a claim for maintenance for her or the children or there is an existing maintenance order in favour of the petitioner or children which the petitioner is seeking to enforce,
the court can request a search to be made on behalf of the petitioner for the respondent's
address from the records of the Department for Work and Pensions ('DWP') or, failing that,
of the Passport Office. Application should be made to the district judge for a search to be
requested. If the respondent is known to be serving or to have served recently in the Armed
Forces, the petitioner's solicitor can request an address for service on the respondent from
the appropriate service department.

It is also useful to know that if the petitioner is making or seeking to enforce a maintenance   **9.29**
claim, the DWP is often willing to provide the petitioner's solicitor with an address for the
respondent when requested to do so simply by a letter from the solicitor. This should be
tried before asking the district judge to request this information. The DWP will also forward
a letter to a party's last known address in all cases. The respondent's bank may well be
prepared to do the same.

Court normally responsible for service

Normally the court sees to the service of the petition and accompanying documents. The   **9.30**
administrative procedure followed by the court office is as follows:

1.   Each copy of the petition for service has annexed to it:
     (a)   a notice of proceedings (Form M5) which explains to the respondent that a petition
           for divorce has been presented and instructs him to complete the acknowledge-
           ment of service. It also contains notes on completing the acknowledgement of
           service;
     (b)   a form of acknowledgement of service (Form M6);
     (c)   if there is a certificate for Legal Representation, notice of issue of the certificate.
2.   The respondent's copy of the petition also has annexed to it a copy of the statement as
     to arrangements for the children if there is one plus a copy of any medical report
     attached to it.
3.   A copy of the petition and the documents annexed to it is served on the respondent by

the court. Normally service is effected by the court simply by posting the documents to the respondent at the address given for him by the petitioner at the foot of the petition (known as 'postal service').

4. If the acknowledgement of service is then completed and signed by the respondent (or his solicitor on his behalf if this is appropriate) and returned to the court, the petition is taken to have been duly served (r. 2.9(5), FPR 1991).

Alternatives to postal service by the court

General

9.31   Postal service through the court is not always successful or appropriate. All sorts of problems can arise over service, for example the petitioner may not be able to provide an address for service on the respondent or the respondent may fail to return the acknowledgement of service after the documents have been posted to him.

9.32   There are various alternatives to postal service by the court. What is appropriate depends on the nature of the problem that has arisen. The various methods of service are described in paragraph 9.34. Common problems and suggested solutions are dealt with in paragraph 9.49 and onwards.

9.33   Recent case law makes it clear that the FPR 1991 are designed to ensure that the respondent has direct personal knowledge of the change in status which the petitioner is seeking to achieve through divorce proceedings. Hence, in *Akhtar v Rafiq* [2006] 1 FLR 27 the decrees nisi and absolute of divorce were held to be void because there had been no proper service of the divorce papers on the respondent wife—the address given for service of the documents was not that of the wife and the husband had asserted that the thumb print on the acknowledgement of service was that of the wife without knowing it to be so. Bodey J indicated that it was not good enough to say after the event that, although the petition had not been duly served, the respondent in fact knew all about the proceedings.

Alternative methods of service

9.34   **Personal service by the court bailiff**   The district judge can direct bailiff service on the petitioner's request made in writing on the appropriate form. There is an extra fee payable for this service (currently £20) unless the petitioner is 'fees exempt'.

9.35   The petitioner must provide some means whereby the bailiff can identify the respondent, normally a photograph. Where the petitioner is represented by a solicitor it will be necessary to show why service by bailiff is requested instead of personal service by a process server. This does not, of course, apply in Legal Help cases.

9.36   Service is effected by the bailiff delivering a copy of the petition to the respondent personally. He will attempt to get the respondent to sign for the papers.

9.37   Once the bailiff has served the respondent personally he files a certificate to this effect, stating how he identified the respondent. If the respondent returns the acknowledgement of service to the court, this will prove service. Where the acknowledgement of service is not returned it will be necessary for the petitioner in her affidavit in support of the petition to identify the respondent's signature for the documents or to identify the respondent in the photograph used by the bailiff. Together with the bailiff's certificate, this will be sufficient proof of service.

Service through the petitioner The petitioner can request that service be carried out **9.38** through her (r. 2.9(2)(b), FPR 1991). The petitioner herself must never effect personal service of the documents (r. 2.9(3)) but her solicitor can serve the respondent or an enquiry agent can be instructed to do so. Some means of identification must be provided by the petitioner as with bailiff service, usually a photograph.

Personal service through the petitioner has an advantage over bailiff service in that the **9.39** bailiff cannot be expected to search for the respondent if the petitioner cannot supply a definite address or if the respondent is not at his address when the bailiff calls whereas an enquiry agent can be instructed to do so.

Where personal service through the petitioner is required, the solicitor will probably need to **9.40** obtain an extension of the Legal Help financial limit to cover the cost of service. Normally the solicitor will be able to extend the initial financial limit where it is reasonable and appropriate to do so in line with the contract under which the franchise has been granted. The sufficient benefit test should be re-applied before any extension is granted. The person serving the petition should attempt to get the respondent to sign for the documents. If no acknowledgement of service is returned to the court office, the server will be required to file an affidavit of service stating that he has served the petition and indicating how he identified the respondent (r. 2.9(7), FPR 1991). In her affidavit in support of the petition, the petitioner will then identify the respondent's signature for the documents or identify the photograph used by the server as a photograph of the respondent, as with bailiff service.

Deemed service Where the acknowledgement of service has not been returned to the **9.41** court but the district judge is nevertheless satisfied that the petition has been received by the respondent, he can direct that service is deemed to have been effected (r. 2.9(6), FPR 1991).

A letter should be sent to the district judge with the petitioner's request for directions for **9.42** trial (see paragraph 9.7 below) asking for service to be deemed. A fee of £40 is payable unless the petitioner is 'fees exempt'. The district judge will need some evidence that the respondent has received the petition; a sworn statement should therefore be filed from someone who can give evidence to this effect, exhibiting documentary evidence that the respondent has received the petition. The person who can give evidence that the respondent has received the petition is often the petitioner herself. However, to deem service effective on the basis of the petitioner's evidence alone does carry an obvious danger in that an unscrupulous petitioner could, by giving false evidence on this point, ensure that the respondent knew nothing of the divorce proceedings. Some district judges may therefore be reluctant to agree on the basis of the petitioner's uncorroborated evidence that service should be deemed.

Example 1 The petitioner and respondent continue to live in the same house even after divorce proceedings have been commenced. The petitioner is present when the respondent picks up the divorce papers which have arrived in the post, opens the envelope, glances at the contents and deposits them in the dustbin. The petitioner's sworn statement to this effect *may* be sufficient to satisfy the district judge that the respondent has received the documents.

Example 2 After receiving the petition the respondent consults a firm of solicitors who write an open letter to the petitioner's solicitors concerning the petition but the respondent then fails to return the acknowledgement of service, terminates his instructions to his solicitors and disappears into thin air. The district judge deems service to have been effected in view of the letter from his ex-solicitors.

Rule 2.9(6) has been amended by the insertion of r. 2.9(6A) which states that para. (6) shall not apply in cases where:

(a)   the petition alleges two years' separation coupled with the respondent's consent to the decree being granted; and

(b)   none of the other facts mentioned in s. 1(2) of the Matrimonial Causes Act 1973 is alleged, unless the petitioner produces to the court a written statement containing the respondent's consent to the grant of a decree: Family Proceedings (Amendment No 3) Rules 1997 (1997 No. 1893).

What this means in practice is that an order for deemed service will not be made in cases relying on s. 1(2)(d) unless some evidence can be produced to the court to demonstrate that the respondent previously consented to a decree of divorce being granted.

9.43   **Substituted service**   Where all the petitioner's efforts to trace the respondent have failed, the petitioner will have to ask either for an order for substituted service or for service to be dispensed with (see paragraph 9.46 below).

9.44   An order for substituted service directs that the petition be served in some way other than postal or personal service. It will only be permitted where the petitioner has made proper attempts to trace and serve the respondent by post or personally. The alternative method of service permitted will be clearly specified in the order.

Example The respondent is known to visit a relative regularly but efforts to effect personal service at that address have failed. Substituted service by posting the documents to that address could be authorized.

One method of substituted service is by advertisement. However, no order for service by advertisement will be given unless it appears to the district judge that there is a reasonable possibility that the advertisement will come to the knowledge of the person concerned (r. 2.9(9), FPR 1991). Indeed, in practice, the district judge is unlikely to permit any form of substituted service unless he is satisfied that it has a reasonable chance of bringing the proceedings to the knowledge of the person concerned. If service by advertisement is permitted, the district judge will settle the advertisement (r. 2.9(9)) and may well arrange himself for it to be inserted in the appropriate publication on payment of the required fees to him. If the court authorizes someone else to insert the advertisement, that person must file copies of the newspapers containing the advertisement at court (r. 10.5(3)).

9.45   Application for substituted services should be made to the district judge, without notice to the respondent, by lodging a sworn statement setting out the grounds on which the application is made (r. 2.9(9)).

9.46   **Dispensing with service**   If all else fails, the district judge may be asked to make an order dispensing with service of the petition. He will do this where in his opinion it is impracticable to serve the petition or for other reasons it is necessary or expedient to dispense with service (r. 2.9(11), FPR 1991).

Clearly it can be a serious matter for the district judge to dispense with service as it **9.47** means that the respondent may be divorced without even knowing that divorce proceedings have been commenced. The district judge will therefore have to be satisfied that exhaustive enquiries have been made to trace the respondent (see paragraph 9.28 above) and that substituted service would not be appropriate.

Example The petitioner has no idea where the respondent is. Enquiries of his relatives suggest that he has gone to work abroad but no one knows where. Enquiries of his past employers, past landlady, the DWP, the passport office, etc. draw a blank. The district judge may well be inclined to dispense with service.

The district judge can make an order dispensing with service altogether or dispensing with further service once one final method of service is tried.

An application for service to be dispensed with should be made, in the first place, without **9.48** notice to the other side by way of a sworn statement setting out the grounds of the application (the attempts made to serve the respondent, the enquiries made as to his whereabouts and so on) but the district judge can require the attendance of the petitioner to support the application (r. 2.9(11)).

Common problems and solutions

Problem 1 From the outset the petitioner is not able to give a definite address for service **9.49** for the respondent. The court cannot attempt to effect service.

Solution

(a) Check that enquiries of the nature outlined in paragraph 9.28 above have been made. **9.50** If they have not, they should be set in motion; they may produce an address at which postal service can be effected.

(b) If the petitioner is able to provide information as to where the respondent may be found (although she cannot provide an address as such), it may well be appropriate to request *personal service through the petitioner* so that an enquiry agent can be instructed to trace the respondent and serve him with the petition personally.

(c) If an address or information as to the respondent's whereabouts is still not forthcoming, apply for *substituted service* or for *service to be dispensed with*. Personal service by the court bailiff or through the petitioner will be impossible as the respondent cannot be traced. Deemed service is obviously inappropriate as the petitioner cannot even attempt to serve the petition on the respondent so he clearly cannot be deemed to have received it.

Problem 2 The petitioner thinks she knows where the respondent is and provides an **9.51** address for service. The acknowledgement of service is not returned.

Solution

(a) If the court office has not received the acknowledgement after seven days from the **9.52** date they posted the petition to the respondent they may automatically inform the petitioner's solicitor that the acknowledgement of service has not been returned and invite an application for bailiff service.

On the other hand some courts do not automatically inform the petitioner's solicitors of non-receipt of the acknowledgement, so the petitioner's solicitor should remember (he would be well advised to make a diary note to remind himself) to review the case after the respondent has had a reasonable period to return the acknowledgement (which will probably be not less than two weeks from the date of filing the petition). If at this stage no copy acknowledgement has been received from the court, the solicitor should confirm with the court office that nothing has been received by them and should then take the appropriate steps to deal with service.

(b)   If the petitioner still reasonably believes that the respondent is resident at the address given or can give another address, *bailiff service* should be requested.

(c)   If the petitioner is no longer confident about the respondent's address but still thinks she knows where he can be found (e.g., he regularly visits a certain public house), *personal service through the petitioner* should be requested.

(d)   If the petitioner no longer has any idea where the respondent is, an application should be made for *substituted service* or for *service to be dispensed with*.

(e)   Should the petitioner be able to provide evidence that despite his silence the respondent has received the petition, an application should be made for *service to be deemed* as an alternative to substituted service or dispensing with service.

9.53   Problem 3   Bailiff service is attempted and fails.

9.54   Solution   If the petitioner has any real idea of the whereabouts of the respondent and there is a prospect of him being traced by an enquiry agent, *personal service through the petitioner* should be requested. Otherwise, application should be made for *substituted service* or for *service to be dispensed with*. *Deemed service* is an alternative where appropriate as in Problem 2.

9.55   Problem 4   Personal service is attempted and fails.

9.56   Solution   Apply for *substituted service* or for *service to be dispensed with*. *Deemed service* is an alternative.

Service on a party under a disability

9.57   The court does not carry out service where the party to be served is under a disability, i.e., he is under 18 or a patient ('patient' for these purposes means a person who by reason of mental disorder within the meaning of the Mental Health Act 1983 is incapable of managing or administering his property or affairs) (r. 9.3, FPR 1991). Service must be through the petitioner (r. 2.9(2)(a)) and there are special rules as to the method of service and as to procedure generally (r. 9.2 and r. 9.3).

Service on a co-respondent

9.58   The procedure for serving a co-respondent with the petition is the same as for the respondent. The routine practice is for the court to attempt postal service. The copy of the petition for service has annexed to it a notice of proceedings in Form M5 and a form of acknowledgement of service in Form M6 and, if there is a funding certificate, a notice of issue of the certificate. The co-respondent does not, however, receive a copy of the statement as to arrangements for the children.

If postal service fails, bailiff service or personal service through the petitioner will normally **9.59** be tried. Application can be made for service to be deemed or dispensed with or substituted service ordered as in the case of service on the respondent. As the divorce will not affect the status of the co-respondent, it may be rather easier to persuade the court to dispense with service where difficulty is experienced than it is in relation to service on a respondent.

Service outside England and Wales

The FPR 1991, r. 10.6, allows any document in family proceedings (including a divorce **9.60** petition) to be served outside England and Wales *without* the court's prior permission either in accordance with the FPR 1991 (i.e., by prepaid first class post, or personally or by substituted service), or:

(a)   in a High Court case, in accordance with rr. 5 and 6, RSC Ord. 11; or
(b)   in a county court case, in accordance with rr. 8 to 10, CCR Ord. 8.

It should be noted that, except where indicated to the contrary elsewhere in this book, 'family proceedings' are not governed by the Civil Procedure Rules 1998 (r. 2.1) and hence, reference needs to be made to RSC and CCR.

G   RETURN OF THE ACKNOWLEDGEMENT OF SERVICE

Filling in the acknowledgement of service

The acknowledgement of service is straightforward. It is in question and answer form and **9.61** the respondent is given extra guidance as to how to fill it in in Form M5 (notice of proceedings).

The solicitor can sign the acknowledgement for the respondent unless either: **9.62**

(a)   in adultery cases, the acknowledgement contains an admission of adultery; *or*
(b)   in cases of two years' separation and consent, the acknowledgement is used to signify the respondent's consent to the decree (r. 2.10(1), FPR 1991).

In both these cases, the respondent must sign the acknowledgement personally. The solicitor will also sign the acknowledgement of service if he is representing the respondent (as opposed to advising and assisting him under the Legal Help scheme).

Note that the fact that the respondent states in the acknowledgement that he intends to **9.63** defend the divorce does not amount to a formal step towards defending. The respondent's statement merely ensures that the divorce will be held up to give him time to file an answer (see paragraph 9.66). However, if he fails to do so within the proper time, the case will proceed undefended as if he had never raised any objection.

Note also that what the respondent says about his intention when filling in the acknow- **9.64** ledgement of service in no way binds him. He may, for example, indicate that he intends to defend and then do nothing about it, or indicate that he has no intention of seeking a CA 1989 order in respect of the children and then change his mind and make an application.

9.65   In addition, the respondent is required to indicate whether there are any proceedings continuing in any country outside England and Wales which relate to the marriage or are capable of affecting its validity and substance, and to give details of any such proceedings. If such proceedings have already been commenced in another EU state, it is likely that subsequent proceedings issued in England and Wales will be automatically stayed, as discussed in Chapter 8, paragraph 8.31. Secondly, the respondent is now required to indicate in which country he is (i) habitually resident and (ii) domiciled. He must also state of which country he is a national. He must indicate whether he objects to paying the petitioner's costs, if claimed. Last, he must indicate whether he agrees with the statement of the petitioner as to the grounds of jurisdiction set out in the petition. If he does not agree, he must specify his reasons.

Returning the acknowledgement of service

9.66   The acknowledgement of service must be returned (normally by post) to reach the court within seven days after the respondent received the divorce papers (r. 10.8(2)(a), FPR 1991).

9.67   The respondent and co-respondent can normally be relied upon to return the acknowledgement of service at least with a little prompting from the court, who may well send a reminder and a new copy of the acknowledgement of service if the first one is not returned within a reasonable period.

9.68   If the acknowledgement of service is returned:

(a)   The court sends a photocopy of it to the petitioner's solicitor (r. 2.9(8)). This triggers the necessary steps to obtain the decree nisi of divorce (see paragraph 9.7).

(b)   If the respondent or co-respondent indicates in the acknowledgement of service that he or she intends to defend the case, matters will automatically be held up for a period of 28 days from the date he received the divorce petition to give him the opportunity to file an answer (r. 2.12(1)) (see Chapter 11 for further details concerning the filing of an answer). If neither the respondent nor the co-respondent files an answer within this period, the case will proceed as an undefended matter unless, at any time, the respondent or co-respondent gets permission of the court to file an answer out of time (see Chapter 11).

(c)   If, as is more likely, the respondent and co-respondent indicate that they do not intend to defend the case, the next step will usually be for the petitioner's solicitors to request the district judge to give directions for trial.

9.69   If the acknowledgement of service is not returned, the petitioner's solicitor will have to decide what further steps are to be taken in relation to service of the petition (see above).

H   WHEN DIRECTIONS FOR TRIAL CAN BE GIVEN

9.70   The district judge can give directions for trial if he is satisfied of the following matters:

(a)   *Due service*   The district judge must be satisfied that a copy of the petition has been duly served on every party required to be served (r. 2.24(1)(a), FPR 1991). Where there is a respondent and a co-respondent, service on both will be required. Where the acknow-ledgement of service has been returned by a respondent or co-respondent, this will be taken as proof of due service of the petition on that party provided:

(i) that it is signed by that party or by a solicitor on his behalf; *and*

(ii) where the form purports to be signed by the respondent, the signature is proved to be that of the respondent—this is usually proved by the petitioner identifying the signature as the respondent's in her Form M7(a) to (e) affidavit which she files in support of the petition when directions are applied for (see paragraph 9.71 below) (r. 2.9(5)). *And*

(b) *Case undefended* The district judge must be satisfied that the case can be classed as undefended, i.e., either:

(i) the respondent and co-respondent have informed the court (almost certainly in the acknowledgement of service) that they do not intend to defend the case; *or*

(ii) no notice of intention to defend has been given by either the respondent or any co-respondent and the time for giving such a notice has expired; *or*

(iii) if notice of intention to defend has been given by any party, the time allowed him for filing an answer has expired, i.e., 28 days from the date on which the respond-ent or co-respondent received the petition inclusive of the day of receipt (r. 2.12(1) and r. 2.24(1)). *And*

(c) *Consent given if s. 1 (2)(d) case* Where the petition is based on two years' separation and consent, the district judge must be satisfied that the respondent has given notice to the district judge that he consents to the decree being granted (r. 2.24(3)). This consent is normally given in the acknowledgement of service.

I APPLYING FOR DIRECTIONS FOR TRIAL

The district judge will not give directions for trial automatically. It is up to the petitioner's **9.71** solicitor to make a written application that he should do so (r. 2.24(1), FPR 1991). This is done by filing:

(a) A standard form of application for directions for trial signed personally by the petitioner (this form can be obtained from the court office if necessary). *And*

(b) An affidavit (the old terminology is still used here) from the petitioner in support of the petition. There is a standard printed form of affidavit suited to each of the s. 1(2), MCA 1973 facts (Form M7(a) to (e); Appendix 1, FPR 1991). These affidavits are in question and answer form and although use of the standard printed form is not obliga-tory, it is usually convenient. Even if for some reason the standard form is not used, the information required to answer the questions it contains must still be incorporated in the petitioner's affidavit as near as may be in the order set out in the printed affidavit form (r. 2.24(3)). Great care should be taken in completing the affidavit. The following points should be borne in mind:

(i) The affidavit requires the petitioner to swear that everything stated in the petition is true. If there are errors in the petition something must be done about them before the affidavit is sworn. If the corrections or amendments required are minor (for example, the date of birth of one of the children of the family is wrongly stated or, more commonly, the address of one party has changed since the petition was filed), they can be set out in the relevant paragraph of the affidavit. The district judge will then, in most cases, treat the petition as amended in these respects without any requirement that it should be re-served in its amended form on the respondent or co-respondent.

However, if the alterations required are more serious (for example, if the petitioner wishes to add an allegation of behaviour in a petition based on s. 1(2)(b), MCA 1973), the proper course will be to apply to the district judge for permission to amend the petition which will then have to be re-served on the respondent (and co-respondent if there is one) before the petitioner will be able to apply for directions and file her affidavit in support of the petition. See Chapter 10 for further details as to amendment of the petition.

(ii) It is this affidavit that provides the district judge with evidence of the fact relied on in the petition and of irretrievable breakdown of the marriage. It also replaces the need to attend court and to give oral evidence in front of the district judge. There are five different versions of Form M7 because each is tailored to one of the facts in s. 1(2) so that the petitioner is prompted to provide information relevant to the fact on which she relies. The solicitor has a great advantage over a petitioner filling in the affidavit without Legal Help because he knows the case law on the subject and he can therefore give an informed answer to each question ensuring that all the information that the petitioner can give in support of her case is given. It is most important for the solicitor to keep the substantive law as to divorce (set out in Chapter 4) in mind, so that this advantage is not thrown away.

(iii) Where the petitioner and respondent have lived in the same household since the matters complained of, care should be taken in stating the period(s) of this cohabitation and the reason why it occurred. Certain periods of cohabitation can be disregarded in considering whether the petitioner is entitled to a decree (see Chapter 4); cohabitation in excess of this may bar the petitioner from obtaining a decree unless she is able to give a good reason for it. If the petitioner and the respondent are still living together at the time the affidavit is completed, it would be prudent to give a reason for this in case it raises doubts in the district judge's mind as to whether the marriage has truly broken down.

(iv) Where the petitioner is relying on s. 1(2)(c) to (e) (all facts where a period of separation is required) and it is alleged that the parties have been living apart under the same roof, great pains should be taken to show that the parties were indeed maintaining two separate households (giving details of which rooms were used by which party, whether meals were shared, washing done by one for the other, etc.). *And*

(c) Any corroborative evidence on which the petitioner intends to rely (r. 2.24(3), FPR 1991). It is not always easy to decide when the district judge will be satisfied with the petitioner's evidence alone and when further independent evidence will be required. There are no rules about this; it depends on the standards of the district judge who considers the case and the best guide is therefore experience of the practice of the local district judges. However, the following points may be helpful:

(i) The object of the exercise is, of course, to satisfy the district judge that the petitioner is entitled to a decree. The district judge has a two-part decision to make when considering whether he is satisfied with the petitioner's case; first, he must decide whether the details contained in the petition, *if true*, would entitle the petitioner to a decree; and secondly, whether the details contained in the petition *are in fact true*. The first stage is a question of law and, if the district judge is not satisfied on the law no amount of evidence provided by the petitioner to corroborate what she says in the petition will change his mind—the case will have to be removed from the special procedure list (see paragraph 9.76 below). The second stage is a question of fact and corroborative evidence can help the district judge to be satisfied as to the truth of the petition.

(ii) The majority of the facts stated in the petition do not need any further support than the evidence of the petitioner in her Form M7 affidavit. However, corroboration may be required of the s. 1(2), Matrimonial Causes Act 1973 fact alleged and the particulars given in relation to it.

It should be emphasized that practice varies enormously from one county court to another and it is most important to check the particular requirements of the court where the petition has been lodged. In the authors' experience, specific corroboration will be required in adultery cases (usually provided by the respondent's personally signed acknowledgement of service admitting the adultery) and in behaviour cases (usually provided by a medical report or statement of a witness).

(d) Costs: it often happens that a petitioner claims costs against the respondent in her divorce petition without giving much thought as to whether she really wishes to pursue that claim. The respondent often files an acknowledgement of service objecting to the payment of costs, sometimes giving reasons and sometimes not. When the petitioner then goes on to file her M7 affidavit it will be of great assistance to the court if she makes it clear whether she still wishes to claim costs in spite of the respondent's objections. It will also assist if she can give any specific reasons to support her claim and to refute any of the objections made by the respondent. It may well save delay in the processing of the petition, since it will save the district judge from having to seek information from the parties as to whether or not they really wish to pursue the claim.

(e) It should be noted that Form M7 contains three additional clauses at the end which ask the petitioner whether she has read the Statement of Arrangements and whether she wishes to alter anything contained in that statement or in the petition itself. It also requires the petitioner to identify the signature at the bottom of Part IV of the Statement of Arrangements and to confirm that it is that of the respondent, assuming that this has been returned to the court by the respondent.

J DIRECTIONS FOR TRIAL

Entering the cause in the special procedure list

The district judge gives direction for trial first by entering the cause in the so-called 'special procedure' list (r. 2.24(3), FPR 1991). Despite its name suggesting otherwise, the special procedure is the usual way of obtaining a decree of divorce. **9.72**

Consideration by the district judge of the evidence (Family Proceedings Rules 1991, r. 2.36)

9.73 The entry of the cause on the special procedure list does not, of itself, entitle the petitioner to a decree. As soon as practicable after the cause is entered in the special procedure list, the district judge must consider the evidence filed by the petitioner (i.e., the petition, the petitioner's supporting affidavit and any corroborative evidence she has filed). In practice, the district judge will normally enter the cause on the special procedure list and consider the evidence at one and the same time. Only if he is satisfied on the evidence that the petitioner has sufficiently proved the contents of her petition and is entitled to a decree will the cause proceed to the pronouncement of a decree.

District judge satisfied

9.74 If the district judge is satisfied that the petitioner has sufficiently proved the contents of the petition and is entitled to a decree:

(a) He makes and files a certificate to that effect.

(b) A day is fixed for the district judge or the judge to pronounce decree nisi in open court (see r. 2.36(2), FPR 1991 which extends this power to district judges).

(c) Notice of the date and place fixed for pronouncement of decree nisi and a copy of the certificate are sent to each party.

(d) If the petitioner claims costs in her petition the district judge considers her claim and, if he is satisfied that she is entitled to the costs of obtaining the divorce, he includes in his certificate a statement to that effect. Whether costs are ordered is a matter within the discretion of the court. If there are any general rules, they are as follows:

 (i) behaviour and desertion cases—respondent pays the costs;

 (ii) adultery cases—respondent and/or co-respondent pay the costs unless they show that this would be unjust because the adultery took place after the breakdown of the marriage or was brought about by the petitioner's own conduct or, in the case of the co-respondent, because he/she did not know and could not have been expected to know that the respondent was married;

 (iii) consensual separation cases—petitioner and respondent pay half the costs each. However, it is open to the respondent to prevent this by refusing to give his consent to the decree unless the entire costs are borne by the petitioner;

 (iv) five years' separation cases—no order as to costs. This means that the respondent's solicitor's bill is likely to be noticeably less than that of the petitioner's solicitor.

 Costs can be awarded even though the petitioner is receiving only Legal Help and is therefore looked upon as a litigant in person: Litigants in Person (Costs and Expenses) Act 1975.

 The respondent and co-respondent are entitled to make representations on the question of costs (r. 2.37, FPR 1991). If they do not inform the court at any stage of any objection to paying the costs, many district judges will grant the petitioner costs without question. If, on the other hand, they do wish to object to a claim for costs, the appropriate place is normally in the acknowledgement of service. The district judge will then bear in mind their objections in deciding the question of costs. If the district judge does not feel that he has sufficient information as to why the respondent or co-respondent objects to paying the costs, he can require either of them to make a written statement setting out the reasons for the objection (r. 2.37(1)) in the hope that this will enable him to make his decision. A copy of the statement will be sent to the petitioner. She is free to withdraw her claim for costs at any stage, for example, because she reaches agreement with the respondent that he will not defend the case if she does not pursue her claim to costs or in the light of what the respondent says in his statement to the district judge. If she decides to withdraw her claim before she files her Form M7 affidavit, she can indicate this to the court in the affidavit. If she only decides after directions have been sought, she can withdraw her claim to costs simply by writing a letter to the court.

The district judge will not finally rule out the petitioner's claim for costs. If he is not satisfied that she is entitled to her costs, he will refer the question to the judge who is to pronounce decree nisi. Notice will be given to any party who objects to paying the costs that he must attend before the court on the date fixed for pronouncement of decree nisi to argue his case. If the party concerned fails to turn up on the day, it will be taken that he does not wish to proceed with his objection to paying the costs and an order will almost certainly be made in the petitioner's favour. The petitioner may attend to support her claim for costs to the judge or district judge but need not do so (see further at paragraph 9.79).

Where the respondent does not object to paying the petitioner's costs in principle, it is sensible to do one of the following:

(i) agree a figure for the costs with the solicitor advising the petitioner, such figure to include disbursements and VAT so that the extent of the respondent's liability is clear. It can be stated in the acknowledgement of service form that the respondent has agreed to pay costs in the amount specified;

(ii) ensure that the respondent indicates that he will be responsible for the costs if and only if the decree absolute is granted. Two benefits flow from this. First, the respondent knows that his liability for costs will only arise if the marriage is in fact dissolved. Secondly, he knows at what point his liability to pay arises.

(e) If the parties have reached agreement over finances, an order in relation to financial provision for the petitioner or respondent can be made by the judge or district judge when he pronounces decree nisi. The procedure laid down in r. 2.61, FPR 1991 should be observed (see Chapter 18, paragraph 18.137 and onwards), application being made at any time before the district judge gives directions for trial. The district judge will then include in his certificate a statement that the petitioner/respondent (whichever is appropriate) is entitled to an order as agreed. The draft order then becomes an order of the court on pronouncement of decree nisi by the judge or district judge in accordance with the district judge's certificate. However, the order itself will not become effective until the grant of the decree absolute. Alternatively, the parties' agreement as to financial provision can be made a rule of court; the district judge can give a direction to this effect.

Further details of the law and procedure in relation to financial matters are given in Part III of this book. **9.75**

District judge not satisfied

If the district judge is not satisfied that the petitioner is entitled to a decree he can do one of two things: **9.76**

(a) He can give the petitioner the opportunity to file further evidence: in this case, the petitioner will receive a notice from the court stating that the district judge is not satisfied and giving the reason for this. The district judge may tell the petitioner in the notice what further evidence he requires or he may leave it up to the petitioner to produce what further evidence she can. The district judge will direct the petitioner as to the way in which further evidence should be given. Normally this will be by way of further affidavits but the district judge has power to request the petitioner to attend to give oral evidence before him.

> **Example** The district judge reads the particulars of the petition setting out the allegations of the respondent's conduct where the petition is based on s. 1(2)(b) and considers the allegations to be insufficiently detailed. He may direct the petitioner to prepare and lodge an affidavit giving greater detail of the allegations made.

Once the petitioner has complied with the district judge's direction he will reconsider the case and decide whether to grant his certificate or to remove the case from the special procedure list with the result that a hearing before a judge in open court will be necessary (see (b) below).

(b) He can remove the case from the special procedure list: if the district judge does this he will normally refer the case for hearing by a judge in open court (see paragraph 9.80 below). If he does not fix a date for a hearing before a judge automatically, the petitioner can seek a hearing date in front of a judge by applying for directions for trial in the ordinary way.

It is important to realize that no order that the district judge makes can amount to a final refusal of a decree. It is only the judge who can finally dismiss the petition and in practice he will rarely find it necessary to do this.

K PRONOUNCEMENT OF DECREE NISI

9.77 If the district judge has certified that the petitioner is entitled to a decree, decree nisi will be pronounced by a judge or district judge in open court on the day fixed by the district judge.

9.78 The pronouncement of the decree is unexciting. It is quite likely that all that will happen is that the clerk of the court or the judge or district judge himself will read out a list of cases and ask if there are any applications in these cases (for example, objections as to costs or attempts by respondents to prevent the pronouncement of the decree by having the district judge's certificate set aside and seeking permission to file an answer). Once any applications are dealt with, the judge or district judge will then announce that decrees are pronounced in all the cases listed and that other relief is granted in accordance with the district judge's certificate. When the judge or district judge grants other relief in accordance with the district judge's certificate, this means that if the district judge has certified that the petitioner is entitled to costs or that the petitioner or respondent is entitled to agreed financial provision (see paragraph 9.74) an order of the court is automatically made to that effect. This saves the judge or district judge the trouble of going through all the cases on his list ordering costs here and financial provision there as appropriate.

Both parties can attend the pronouncement of the decree if they wish but it is not normally necessary for either to attend. However, if the respondent is making an objection to a claim by the petitioner for costs and the district judge has referred the question to the judge or district judge who is to pronounce decree nisi, it will be necessary for the respondent to attend the hearing to put his arguments on costs to the court if he wishes to pursue his objection to the bitter end (see paragraph 9.74). The petitioner will be aware that the question of costs has been referred to the judge or district judge from the notice she received from the court when the case was placed on the special procedure list and the district judge's certificate granted. She has no need to attend to argue her side of the costs question but she can do so if she wishes, for example, she may well wish to do so if the case was defended at some stage and her costs are therefore high. **9.79**

L   CASES REFERRED TO THE JUDGE

It can happen that the district judge is not satisfied with the petitioner's case and refers it for hearing in front of the judge (see paragraph 9.76 above). The hearing will take place in open court and the petitioner must attend as she will be required to give oral evidence on oath in support of her petition. A certificate for Legal Representation under the Community Legal Service scheme may be available for such hearings (see Chapter 7), so the petitioner will normally be represented by her solicitor or by counsel. Public funding will only be available if the circumstances of the particular case justify representation and there are sufficient prospects of obtaining the decree of divorce. **9.80**

The judge will consider the evidence and decide whether to grant the petitioner a decree nisi. If he decides to do so, decree nisi will be pronounced there and then and the judge will make whatever order as to costs he thinks fit. He will normally refer all ancillary matters to chambers for determination. Once decree nisi has been pronounced, the case will proceed in exactly the same way as a case dealt with under the special procedure. **9.81**

If the judge decides that the petitioner is not entitled to a decree (for example, in a s. 1(2)(b) case he may take the view that the behaviour of which the petitioner complains is not such that she cannot reasonably be expected to live with the respondent), he will dismiss her petition and will make whatever order as to costs he thinks fit. Apart from the possibility of an appeal against the judge's order, this is the end of the petition as far as the petitioner is concerned. **9.82**

M   CONSIDERATION OF ARRANGEMENTS FOR THE CHILDREN OF THE FAMILY

The FPR 1991, r. 2.39 place the main burden of 'considering' those arrangements upon the district judge. **9.83**

Section 41, MCA 1973 requires that in any proceedings for divorce, judicial separation, or nullity the court must *consider*, at the date on which the court considers the arrangements: **9.84**

(a) whether there is any child of the family who has not reached the age of 16; and

(b) whether there is a child who has reached 16 in respect of whom it should direct that s. 41 should apply.

In practice this duty will usually be carried out by the district judge in special procedure cases where there is no application for an order under the CA 1989 pending in respect of a child of the family.

Where there is no application for an order under the Children Act 1989 pending

9.85 The district judge will consider the arrangements that are proposed for the upbringing and welfare of the children immediately after making his certificate of entitlement to decree nisi under r. 2.36(1), FPR 1991. He will then consider whether he should exercise any of his powers under the CA 1989 with respect to any of the children of the family. He will do this by a close examination of the Form M4 which has been filed with the divorce petition. Usually it is the petitioner who has submitted it. The respondent is perfectly entitled to file a Form M4 if he wishes, but it is rare to find this in practice.

9.86 In examining the Form M4 the district judge will look for anything in the proposed arrangements which may be unsatisfactory so far as the children are concerned. He will look to see that there is, for example, adequate accommodation, education, health care and financial provision for the child.

9.87 If the district judge considers, pursuant to s. 41(2), MCA 1973, that:

(a) the exercise of his powers is, or is likely to be, necessary but the court is not in a position to exercise them without further consideration, *and*

(b) there are *exceptional* circumstances which make it desirable in the interests of the child to do so,

then he may direct that a decree of divorce or nullity be not made absolute, or a decree of judicial separation be not granted, until the court orders otherwise.

9.88 If, however, the court is satisfied, pursuant to r. 2.39(2), FPR 1991, that either:

(a) there are no children of the family to whom s. 41 applies, or

(b) there are such children, but that the court need not exercise its powers or make a direction under s. 41,

then the district judge will certify accordingly.

What happens if the district judge is not satisfied with the proposed arrangements?

9.89 If the district judge is not satisfied with the proposed arrangements for the children then he may give one of the following directions, pursuant to r. 2.39(3), FPR 1991:

(a) that the parties, or any of them, shall file further evidence as to the arrangements for the children (the exact nature of the information required may be specified, e.g., a medical report);

(b) that the parties, or any of them, shall attend before him. (Where a direction for attendance is made under r. 2.39(3)(c) it might well be prudent to seek a certificate for legal representation where the client is financially eligible and the circumstances of the case justify such funding.)

(c)   that a welfare report be prepared, although this would be a step of last resort.

Example 1   The Form M4 filed by Mrs Plum revealed that the three-year-old child of the family, Tracy, was living with Mrs Plum and was suffering from leukaemia. However, the form gave no information as to whether or not the child was still being treated for the illness. The district judge then asked the petitioner to file a medical report in relation to the child. The medical report showed that the child's treatment was being satisfactorily undertaken by the health authorities and that the parents were co-operating with the treatment programme. The district judge decided there was no need to look any further into the matter.

Example 2   The facts are as in Example 1 above but Mrs Plum failed to file any medical report. The district judge asked Mr and Mrs Plum to attend at court for an appointment with him so that he could find out from them the reasons for their failure to give the information requested. The parties failed to attend the appointment. The district judge decided to order a CAFCASS officer's report in respect of Tracy. He was reluctant to take this step unless it was absolutely necessary because he knew that generally it took two or three months for such a report to be compiled. However, there appeared to be no other way of obtaining proper information about Tracy.

Example 3   The facts are as in Example 2 above. The CAFCASS officer tried to make an appointment with Mr and Mrs Plum on many occasions but they refused to see her on any basis. The CAFCASS officer reported the difficulties to the court. The district judge applied the cumulative test in s. 41(2), MCA 1973 and found that the circumstances of the case might well require the court to exercise some of its powers under the CA 1989: s. 41(2)(a) (1973 Act) (e.g., to ask the local authority to investigate the case and to report to the court as to whether it wished to take any action in relation to the child: s. 37, CA 1989). Applying the next limb of the test (s. 41(2)(b) (1973 Act)), the district judge considered that he was not in a position to exercise that power without giving further consideration to the case. He wished to extend to the parties a final invitation to attend court for an appointment with him, along with a clear warning as to the consequences that might follow if they refused. He then applied the third, cumulative, part of the test in s. 41(2) and considered that there were 'exceptional circumstances' in this case which made it desirable in the interests of Tracy that he should direct that the decree was not to be made absolute until the outstanding problems had been resolved.

It seems clear from the wording of s. 41(2) that the intention of Parliament was that decree absolute should not be withheld lightly. The cumulative requirements of s. 41(2) make it clear that it should be a power used only in 'exceptional circumstances'. In practice many district judges recognize the limited resources available to CAFCASS or the local authority to assist and determine that there are 'exceptional circumstances' justifying refusal of the decree absolute. The onus is then placed on the parties to provide the court with the relevant information in order to satisfy the district judge about the arrangements and ultimately to obtain the decree absolute.

General examples of matters which might cause the district judge to consider whether the **9.90** court is, or is likely to be, required to exercise any of its powers under the CA 1989 are as follows:

9.91 **Accommodation** Where the parties are living in cramped accommodation (for example, three children with the petitioner and her parents and brother in a two-bedroomed flat), or in unsuitable accommodation (for example, a rented flat with no bathroom over a night-club), or where there is doubt as to the petitioner's security of tenure over the accommodation (for example, where she has been served with notice to quit). In such circumstances the district judge may want the CAFCASS officer to look at the accommodation, or he may require documentary evidence that the petitioner will soon be able to provide suitable accommodation, for example, a letter from the council promising her accommodation within a limited period of time. Sometimes the district judge will require an updated statement of arrangements to be filed at court once the petitioner has moved to suitable accommodation.

9.92 **Disputes over residence of and contact with the child** If it is clear that the parents are in dispute as to where the child should live and how much contact, if any, he should have with the parent with whom he is not residing, then it is likely that one or other of the parties will apply for a s. 8 order. If no application has yet been made for a s. 8 order by the time the district judge comes to consider the arrangements for the children then the district judge may well arrange an appointment for the parties to come to court and see him. He might well point out to them the relevant applications they might make to resolve the issue. If a s. 8 application is then made, the issue will automatically fall to be determined by the judge in any event, and the district judge need not consider the issue further.

9.93 If, however, the parties do not take any steps to seek a s. 8 order it is not clear to what extent the district judge will inquire further into the matter. If, in due course, the parents make it clear that neither of them wishes to make an application, and all of the other circumstances relating to the child appear satisfactory, then the authors would tentatively submit that the court is unlikely to take the view that it should interfere further. In that case, the court will certify under r. 2.39(2)(b), FPR 1991 that there is no need for the court to exercise any of its powers under the CA 1989 or to give any direction under s. 41(2), MCA 1973.

Where an application for an order under the Children Act 1989 is pending

9.94 Where an application for an order under the CA 1989 is pending then it will not be necessary for the district judge to consider the arrangements for the children because they will be fully considered in due course by the court which disposes of the application. The fact that an application, for example, for a residence or contact order, is merely contained in the prayer of the petition would not be sufficient to relieve the district judge of the duty to consider the arrangements for the children. There must be an actual notice of application before the district judge is no longer required to consider the arrangements.

9.95 Where an application for an order under the CA 1989 is pending in a family proceedings court prior to the commencement of the cause then the usual practice would be for the magistrates to transfer the application to a county court so that all matters could be heard together. In that case the district judge would not be required to consider the arrangements for the children, since they would be dealt with in the disposal of the application.

If an application were to be made to a family proceedings court *after* the commencement of **9.96** the cause then r. 2.40, FPR 1991 requires that the application be made within the cause.

N   DECREE ABSOLUTE

The need for decree absolute

The first decree granted to a petitioner is a decree nisi. This does not free the petitioner or **9.97** the respondent from the marriage. The marriage is only dissolved once decree absolute is obtained.

Application for decree absolute

A decree nisi normally may not be made absolute before the expiration of six weeks from the **9.98** date on which it is granted (s. 1(5), MCA 1973 as varied). There is power to expedite decree absolute but it is rarely used (see paragraph 9.108 and onwards).

As soon as the six-week period expires, the petitioner can apply for decree absolute by **9.99** lodging with the district judge a notice in Form M8 (r. 2.49(1) and Appendix 1, FPR 1991) together with the prescribed fee (currently £40.00) unless the petitioner is 'fees exempt'. There is no need to give the respondent notice of the application.

When he receives Form M8, the district judge searches the court records in relation to the **9.100** case. He has to satisfy himself on various matters which are set out in full in the Family Proceedings Rules 1991, r. 2.49(2). In a nutshell, he must be sure:

(a)   that the court has complied with the duty to consider the arrangements for the children under s. 41, MCA 1973 and has not given any direction under s. 41(2) that requires the decree not to be made absolute;

(b)   that no one is trying to upset the decree nisi by means of an appeal or an application for re-hearing;

(c)   that no intervention is pending by the Queen's Proctor or by any other person to show why the decree should not be made absolute;

(d)   that the provisions of s. 10(2) to (4), MCA 1973 (consideration of the respondent's financial position after the divorce) either do not apply or have been complied with.

If the district judge is satisfied as to the matters set out in r. 2.49(2), he will make the decree absolute.

Both the petitioner and the respondent will be sent a certificate in Form M9 (Family Proceed- **9.101** ings Rules 1991, Appendix 1) certifying that the decree nisi has been made absolute and giving the date on which this was done.

As soon as the decree is made absolute, the petitioner and respondent are both released from **9.102** the marriage and are free to remarry should they wish to do so.

Application by respondent

9.103   If the petitioner does not apply to have the decree made absolute, once three months have elapsed from the earliest date on which the petitioner could have applied for decree absolute, the respondent may make application for decree absolute (s. 9(2), MCA 1973). The earliest that the respondent can apply is therefore three months and six weeks after the pronouncement of decree nisi.

9.104   The respondent's application may be made to a judge or to a district judge. A fee of £80.00 is payable. Notice of the application must be served on the petitioner not less than four clear days before the day on which the application is heard (r. 2.50(2), FPR 1991). A short hearing usually takes place, affording the petitioner an opportunity to explain why she has not applied for the decree absolute. The usual reason for delay by the petitioner is because she wishes to have the security of orders for ancillary relief in place before forfeiting her right for example, to share in the respondent's pension arrangements. She would normally lose such a right following her change of status on the grant of the decree absolute. The decree absolute was refused for those reasons and because of the respondent husband's devious approach to ancillary relief proceedings in *Wickler* v *Wickler* [1998] 2 FLR 326.

9.105   Conversely, the respondent husband's application for the decree nisi to be made absolute will not be refused simply because ancillary relief proceedings are not yet concluded. To prevent the husband's application from succeeding, the wife must show not only significant non-disclosure of financial assets but also the probability that the husband will leave the jurisdiction and take no further part in the ancillary relief proceedings: *Re G (Decree Absolute: Prejudice)* [2003] 1 FLR 870.

District judge can require sworn statement

9.106   If application is not made to have the decree made absolute until after 12 months have elapsed after decree nisi was granted, the notice in Form M8 must be accompanied by a written explanation giving reasons for the delay, stating whether the parties have lived together since decree nisi and, if so, between what dates, and stating (if the wife is the applicant) whether the wife has given birth to any child since the decree or (if the husband is the applicant) whether the husband has reason to believe that the wife has given birth to such a child and, in either case, if so, stating the relevant facts and whether it is alleged that the child is or may be a child of the family.

9.107   The district judge may require the explanation to be verified by a sworn statement from the applicant and may make such order on the application as he thinks fit. In particular he must ensure that s. 41, MCA 1973 has been complied with where it appears that there is, or may be, a child of the family born since decree nisi (r. 2.49(2), FPR 1991).

Expediting decree absolute

9.108   If there is some urgency about obtaining decree absolute, it is possible to apply for a special order giving permission to expedite decree absolute. However, the normal six-week waiting period between decree nisi and decree absolute is so short that it should very rarely be necessary to do so (*Practice Direction* [1977] 2 All ER 714, [1977] 1 WLR 759).

It is suggested that, in urgent cases, rather than attacking the problem after decree nisi, the **9.109** solicitor should make efforts to speed things up at an earlier stage. Naturally this means him dealing with his own part of the case (drafting the petition, etc.) expeditiously. It is also suggested that the solicitor should write a letter to the court to accompany the petitioner's Form M7 affidavit explaining the urgency and asking the court to ensure that the district judge gives directions as soon as possible and fixes an early date for the pronouncement of decree nisi.

Declaration that the decree absolute is void

There are a number of circumstances where an application may be made for a declaration **9.110** that the decree absolute is void.

Such circumstances include: (a) where it emerges that the court does not have jurisdiction; **9.111** (b) where a fundamental irregularity undermines the entire proceedings; or (c) where there has been a failure to comply with the statutory requirements which are conditions precedent to the right to a decree. This latter situation was described as 'controversial' by Holman J in *Krenge* v *Krenge* [1999] 1 FLR 969 and did not cover the situation where the respondent had applied for the decree absolute to be set aside because the decree nisi and decree absolute had been sent to him in the same envelope. The judge's decision was based on the fact that the respondent had received the certificate of entitlement to a decree nisi on an earlier occasion and therefore was well aware of the stage the proceedings had reached.

O   PROCEDURE FOR DISSOLUTION OF A CIVIL PARTNERSHIP

The procedure described above, together with the guidance on drafting the petition in **9.112** Chapter 8, also applies where a civil partnership is to be dissolved.

As might be expected, the wording of the petition reflects the fact that a civil partnership has **9.113** been formed and requires details of the date and place.

Throughout the petition, reference is made to a civil partnership instead of a marriage: **9.114** Appendix 2 of the FPR 1991, as amended.

Orders for dissolution will be conditional in the first instance (the equivalent of the decree **9.115** nisi in divorce proceedings) and may not be made final (the equivalent of the decree absolute in divorce proceedings) until six weeks from the date of the conditional order.

P   KEY DOCUMENTS

The Family Proceedings Rules 1991 (SI 1991/1247). **9.116**

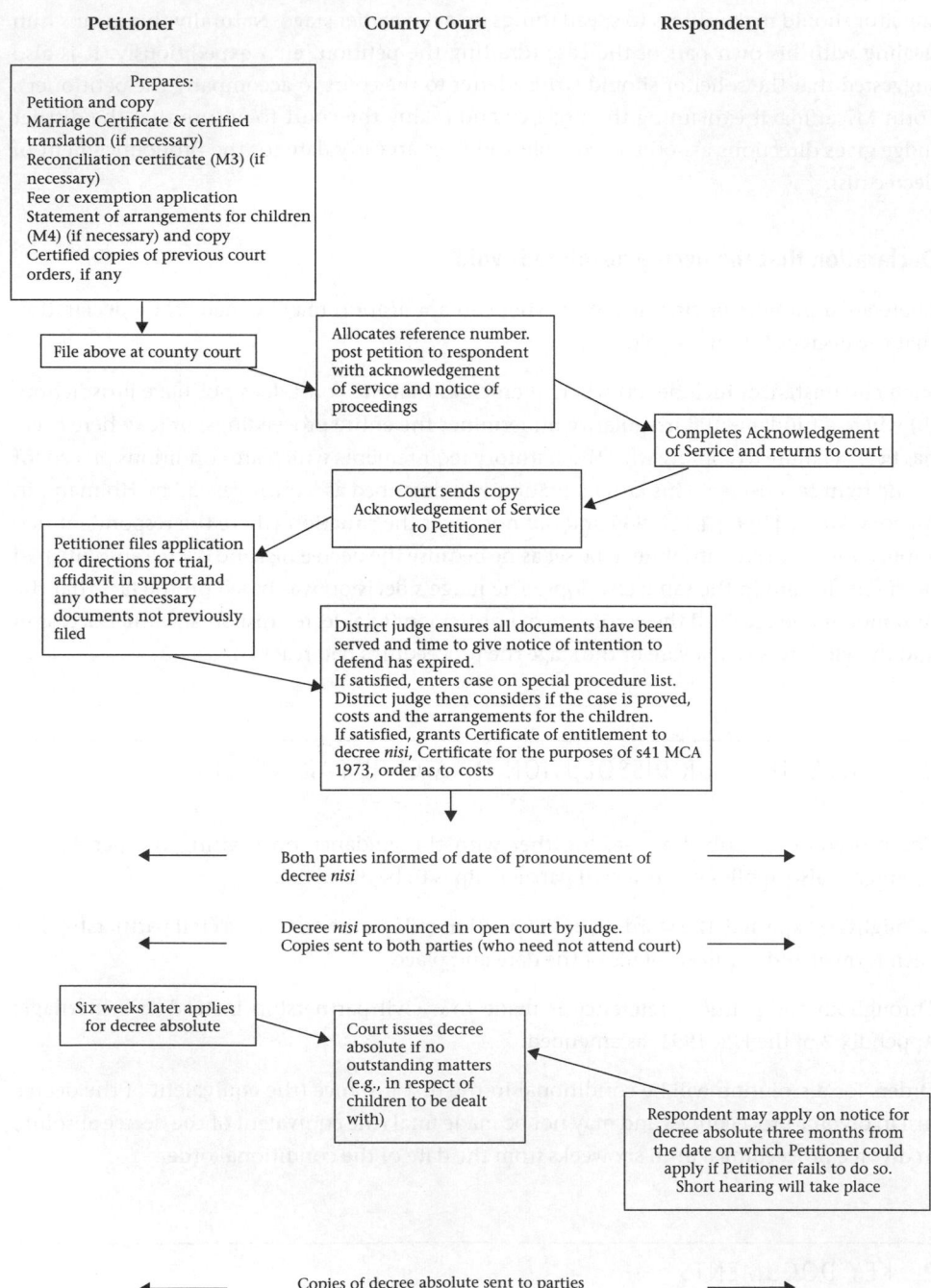

| **Petitioner** | **County Court** | **Respondent** |

Prepares:
Petition and copy
Marriage Certificate & certified translation (if necessary)
Reconciliation certificate (M3) (if necessary)
Fee or exemption application
Statement of arrangements for children (M4) (if necessary) and copy
Certified copies of previous court orders, if any

File above at county court

Allocates reference number. post petition to respondent with acknowledgement of service and notice of proceedings

Completes Acknowledgement of Service and returns to court

Court sends copy Acknowledgement of Service to Petitioner

Petitioner files application for directions for trial, affidavit in support and any other necessary documents not previously filed

District judge ensures all documents have been served and time to give notice of intention to defend has expired.
If satisfied, enters case on special procedure list.
District judge then considers if the case is proved, costs and the arrangements for the children.
If satisfied, grants Certificate of entitlement to decree *nisi*, Certificate for the purposes of s41 MCA 1973, order as to costs

Both parties informed of date of pronouncement of decree *nisi*

Decree *nisi* pronounced in open court by judge.
Copies sent to both parties (who need not attend court)

Six weeks later applies for decree absolute

Court issues decree absolute if no outstanding matters (e.g., in respect of children to be dealt with)

Respondent may apply on notice for decree absolute three months from the date on which Petitioner could apply if Petitioner fails to do so. Short hearing will take place

Copies of decree absolute sent to parties

10

AMENDED, SUPPLEMENTAL, AND NEW PETITIONS

A INTRODUCTION

On rare occasions the divorce petition will require amendment (for example, to give details **10.01** of previous family proceedings not recited in the original petition) or to be replaced by a new petition where the petitioner wishes to rely on a new s. 1(2) Matrimonial Causes Act 1973 ('MCA 1973') fact that has occurred only since the date of the original petition. This chapter briefly explains the relevant procedure.

B AMENDMENT, SUPPLEMENTAL PETITION, OR FRESH PETITION?

It is important to recognize which matters can be the subject of an amendment of the **10.02** petition and which necessitate the filing of a supplemental petition or of a completely fresh petition.

Addition of s. 1(2), Matrimonial Causes Act 1973 facts

10.03   (a)   Where the new facts arose *before* the date of the petition: if the petitioner wishes to add to the petition an additional s. 1(2) fact which arose before the date of the original petition, she may do so by means of a straightforward amendment.

Example 1 In October 2006 the wife discovers that her husband has committed adultery at Christmas. His behaviour towards her has been violent and unpleasant since the beginning of the marriage and this is the last straw. She leaves him immediately and files a petition based on his adultery. Contrary to expectations the respondent indicates that he intends to deny the allegation of adultery and the petitioner's solicitors decide that it would be prudent to add an allegation of behaviour under s. 1(2)(b). This can be done by amendment of the original petition because the behaviour alleged occurred before the date of the original petition.

   (b)   Where the new fact arose *after* the date of the petition: a petition cannot be amended to add new s. 1(2) facts that have arisen after the date of the original petition. This rules out not only straightforward amendments to the original petition but also the filing of a supplemental petition which (although a separate document) is, in effect, another means of amending the original petition. The petitioner wishing to add a s. 1(2) fact that has arisen (or, in the case of a separation fact, has been completed) since the date of the original petition must therefore file a fresh petition.

Example 2 In October 2004 the petitioner leaves the respondent and files a petition based on his adultery. The respondent defends the petition and the matter drags on into 2006. By this time the parties have been separated for two years and the respondent is prepared to consent to a decree. The petitioner now wishes to seek a decree on the basis of s. 1(2)(d) (two years' separation and consent). She cannot do this by amendment of the original petition because the two years' separation were not complete at the date of the original petition nor, for the same reason, can she file a supplemental petition. She must file a fresh petition based on s. 1(2)(d).

Addition or amendment other than the addition of new s. 1(2) facts

10.04   (a)   To take account of matters arising before the date of the petition: this can be done by means of a straightforward amendment to the original petition or, in the case of very minor corrections in special procedure cases, through the petitioner's Form M7 affidavit.

Example 1 The petitioner files a petition based on s. 1(2)(b) without first consulting a solicitor. She then seeks legal advice before obtaining decree nisi. It is clear to her solicitor that her petition is inadequate as it stands and that there are other allegations of behaviour on the part of the respondent before the date of the petition which should properly be added. This can be done by amendment of the petition.

Example 2 In the petition the date of birth of one of the children is given incorrectly as 1 June 1998. It should be 2 June 1998. This is a minor correction and can be dealt with by means of the petitioner's Form M7 affidavit.

   (b)   To take account of matters arising after the date of the petition: certain matters arising after the date of the petition can be dealt with by means of a straightforward amendment, for example, the petition can be amended to add details of a child born after the date of the petition.

However, if the petitioner wishes to add further allegations to the particulars of the s. 1(2) fact on which the petition is based in respect of incidents which arose after the date of the petition, she will have to file a supplemental petition.

Example In October 2005 the petitioner files a petition based on the respondent's behaviour (s. 1(2)(b)). The parties continue to live together after the petition is filed and nothing is done about the divorce. However, in July 2006 the petitioner leaves the respondent because of his unpleasant and violent behaviour which has continued since the date of the divorce petition. She wishes to proceed with the divorce. If the petitioner attempts to proceed on the basis of the petition as it stands she will find herself in difficulty in view of the long period of cohabitation that has followed the last incident of behaviour alleged (well in excess of the six-month period that s. 2(3) says should be disregarded). She cannot amend the petition to add further incidents of behaviour that have arisen between 2005 and 2006 as these post-date the petition. She will have to file a supplemental petition alleging further incidents of behaviour during this period.

C   PROCEDURE FOR AMENDMENT

In theory amendments can be made up until the date of decree absolute. In practice it will rarely be necessary or appropriate to make amendments after decree nisi. **10.05**

The standard procedure for amendment is set out in r. 2.11, Family Proceedings Rules 1991 ('FPR 1991'). The solicitor should prepare an amended petition with the amendments clearly shown in red: **10.06**

(a)   Where an answer has not yet been filed a petition may be amended without the court's permission (r. 2.11(1)(b), FPR 1991).

The amended petition should then be filed at court together with the appropriate number of copies for service (see Chapter 9, paragraph 9.03). It will be served on the respondent (and co-respondent) in the normal way.

(b)   Once an answer has been filed, permission is required and, whether an answer has been filed or not, once directions for trial have been given no pleading may be filed or amended without permission (r. 2.14, FPR 1991). A copy of the amended petition should first be sent to the respondent (and co-respondent if necessary) with a covering letter asking whether he would be prepared to consent to the proposed amendment. If he is prepared to consent in writing to the amendment an application to the district judge for permission should be made without notice to the other side. If either the respondent or the co-respondent is not prepared to consent to the amendment, an application for permission will have to be made on notice to the district judge. If the district judge grants permission the amended petition must be filed at the court office with a copy for re-service on the respondent (and co-respondent). The district judge will make any further directions that have become necessary as a result of permission being granted, for example, where the respondent (or co-respondent) has given notice that he wishes to defend he will need time to amend his answer if he has already filed one or to file an answer to the amended petition if not, so the district judge will fix the time within which he must do this.

Where only a minor amendment to the petition is required (for example, the date of birth of a child of the family has been wrongly stated), it is not likely to be necessary to go through the standard procedure for amendment. It will usually be acceptable if the amendment is detailed in the petitioner's Form M7 affidavit. The district judge will almost certainly give permission for the petition to stand corrected as outlined in the affidavit without the need for re-service on the respondent or co-respondent. He will then proceed to consider the case as if the petition had originally been filed as corrected.

D   SUPPLEMENTAL PETITIONS

10.07   A supplemental petition is a separate document filed at some stage after the petition itself. It is not a new petition; it is part of the original petition and is used to make amendments to this where it is inappropriate to do so by means of a straightforward amendment in red of the original document.

10.08   A supplemental petition may be filed without permission of the court at any time before an answer is filed, but thereafter only with the court's permission (r. 2.11(1)(a), FPR 1991).

E   FRESH PETITIONS

10.09   As we have seen at paragraph 10.01 above, where alterations required to the original petition cannot be accomplished by means of amendment or supplemental petition, a fresh petition will be required. The most frequent use of a fresh petition is probably where the petitioner wishes to rely on a new s. 1(2) fact that has only arisen since the date of the original petition.

10.10   The procedure for filing a fresh petition depends on whether the original petition is still extant.

10.11   If the original petition has been dismissed (either because it has been discontinued by the petitioner before service (r. 28, FPR 1991) or dismissed after service on the petitioner's application or after adjudication, or otherwise disposed of by final order, a fresh petition can be filed in the normal way without the court's permission.

10.12   It is quite likely, however, that the petitioner will not want to burn her boats by seeking to discontinue the first petition or to have it dismissed and will prefer to file a fresh petition whilst the original petition still stands. To do this she will require permission of the court (r. 2.6(4)). She will have to show good reason why two petitions should be on the go at the same time.

Example Reference should be made to Example 2 given in paragraph 10.03 above. The petitioner in that example may well wish to preserve the first adultery petition until after she has obtained decree nisi on the s. 1(2)(d) petition just in case the respondent should decide to withdraw his consent to the decree before decree nisi. If the s. 1(2)(d) decree is granted without difficulty, the first petition should be dismissed at the same time. However, should the respondent withdraw his consent, the petitioner could resurrect the adultery petition and go on to attempt to prove adultery and obtain a decree on that basis.

F   CHAPTER SUMMARY

1. Where the petitioner wishes to rely on a s. 1(2), MCA 1973, which arose *before* the   **10.13**
    petition was filed at court, the original petition may be amended
2. Where the petitioner wishes to rely on a s. 1(2), MCA 1973, which arose *after* the petition
    was filed, a fresh divorce petition will be required.
3. Where minor amendments are required, for example to rectify the spelling of a name or
    a date, this may be done by giving the correct information in the affidavit in support of
    the petition.

11

DEFENDED DIVORCES

A   GENERAL

Gone are the days of the sensational divorce suit reported in detail on the front page of the   **11.01**
national papers and attended by everyone who was anyone. Nowadays it is rare to see a
divorce contested to the bitter end at all.

Partly this is due to the shift in emphasis in family law from looking for a culprit when a   **11.02**
marriage breaks down to enabling the parties to extricate themselves from their unfortunate
situation with the minimum of distress. There is no doubt, however, that it is also due to
financial considerations (the cost of a defended suit can be enormous) and to the attitudes of
judges and district judges concerned with divorce cases who will encourage the parties time
and again to look for alternative ways of resolving their differences.

This book aims to deal with the routine family practice. Therefore, while the procedure for   **11.03**
an undefended divorce is described in great detail in Chapter 9, the procedure in relation to
defended divorce suits will be described in outline only in this chapter.

B   PUBLIC FUNDING FOR DEFENDED DIVORCES

For the respondent

The respondent who consults a solicitor wishing to contest a divorce petition will find that   **11.04**
the first hurdle he must overcome is the cost of the whole affair.

If the respondent is not financially eligible for public funding his decision on cost is simple—   **11.05**
can he afford to defend the case bearing in mind that he may not recover his costs, even if he
is successful in having the petition dismissed?

11.06 The fact that the respondent *is* financially eligible for public funding does not mean he can ignore the cost of the divorce:

(a) Despite the respondent's financial eligibility, public funding will only be granted to him to defend the case if he satisfies the Legal Services Commission that there is a substantial defence with sufficient prospects of success and there are substantial practical benefits to be gained by avoiding the decree.

(b) If he is granted public funding to defend, it will be limited to all steps up to and including disclosure of documents and thereafter obtaining counsel's opinion on the merits of the cause continuing as a contested cause. This means that he can only go so far on his initial certificate. If he wants to go on from disclosure of documents to a full contested hearing of the case, the papers will have to be sent to counsel for an opinion on the merits. Application will then have to be made to the Legal Services Commission to have the limitation on the certificate removed. The Commission is only likely to agree to this if counsel's opinion is favourable.

(c) Even if he is granted public funding to cover the entire proceedings, a large part of the ultimate bill is likely to be met by the respondent himself out of his share of the family property because of the Legal Services Commission's statutory charge.

For the petitioner

11.07 The petitioner will not have had public funding when she filed her petition; at most, she will have received Legal Help (see Chapter 7). If the respondent files an answer and the petitioner wishes to proceed with the petition, she will have to consider the cost of a defended suit just as the respondent must.

11.08 As soon as an answer is filed, the cause is looked upon as defended and public funding is, therefore, theoretically available. However, if the petitioner is to be granted public funding, she must satisfy the Legal Services Commission that it is reasonable for her to continue with the proceedings.

11.09 The statutory charge will also affect the petitioner. Thus if she loses (i.e., her petition is dismissed) or if she obtains a decree but fails to recover her costs, she too may find herself footing a large part of the public funding provided to her from her share in the family property.

Is it reasonable to defend/proceed with the case?

11.10 Whether the Legal Services Commission will be prepared to accept that it is reasonable for the respondent or the petitioner to defend the petition or to proceed with the petition after an answer has been filed will depend on the particular facts of the case. Public funding will not, however, be granted/continued if there is a suitable alternative way of proceeding with the case.

Example A petition is filed based on behaviour (s. 1(2)(b), Matrimonial Causes Act 1973 ('MCA 1973')). The petitioner is not publicly funded. The respondent is publicly funded. He obtains funding to file an answer denying the behaviour and cross-petition on the basis of the petitioner's adultery. The petitioner denies the adultery. Although it is clear that both parties want a divorce, the case drags on with both parties maintaining their positions.

Eventually two years elapse, during which the parties have lived apart. It would therefore be possible for one or the other party to obtain a decree on the non-contentious basis of two years' separation and consent. Both parties are willing to present a petition based on s. 1(2)(d) but neither party is willing to give consent to the other party obtaining the decree—each wants to obtain the decree *himself*. At this point, it is necessary for the respondent to seek counsel's opinion as disclosure of documents has taken place and he needs to have the limitation on his certificate lifted before he can go any further with the case. Counsel advises that the only reasonable course is for a decree to be obtained on the basis of s. 1(2)(d). In all probability, therefore, the respondent's certificate will be terminated and he will be forced, by financial considerations, to agree to a divorce on the basis of s. 1(2)(d).

Paragraph 54 of Chapter 20 of The Funding Code—Decision Making Guidance makes it clear that public funding, certainly in the form of a certificate for Legal Representation, will be refused unless, as previously indicated, there is a substantial defence with sufficient prospects of success. Funding will also be refused where the matter could be reasonably compromised by way of undefended cross-decrees or on the respondent's cross-petition or where the contents of the petition could be amended without prejudice to its prospects of success but so as to remove the contentious issues.

C   OUTLINE OF PROCEDURE IN A DEFENDED CAUSE

(a) Notice of intention to defend: the respondent/co-respondent returns the acknow- **11.11** ledgement of service giving notice of his intention to defend. The time for giving notice of intention to defend is seven days from service of the petition, inclusive of the day of service (r. 10.8(2)(a), FPR 1991).

(b) Filing an answer—the normal procedure: a respondent/co-respondent who wishes to defend the petition or dispute any of the facts alleged in it, or a respondent who wishes to make in the proceedings any charge against the petitioner in respect of which the respondent prays for relief, or to oppose the grant of a decree on the basis of s. 5(1), MCA 1973 (grave financial or other hardship), must file an answer within 21 days after the expiration of the time limit for giving notice of intention to defend, i.e., within 28 days after service of the petition inclusive of the day of service (r. 2.12(1), FPR 1991).

Note:

(i) An answer may be filed even though the party concerned has not given notice of his intention to defend (r. 2.12(2)).

(ii) No answer is necessary merely to contest the petitioner's claim for costs (for the procedure for contesting costs, see Chapter 9, paragraph 9.71), or to contest the petitioner's claim for an order under Part I or Part II of the Children Act 1989 or in relation to ancillary relief.

(c) Filing an answer—after directions for trial are given: it is not unknown for the respondent/co-respondent to make up his mind that he wants to defend only after directions for trial have been given. The case will normally have proceeded under the special procedure up to this point and the chances are that the district judge will therefore have granted his certificate that the petitioner is entitled to a decree (see Chapter 9, paragraph 9.71). The district judge's certificate is tantamount to decree nisi (*Day* v *Day* [1979] 2 All ER 187). To enable the respondent/co-respondent to defend, it will therefore be necessary for him to:

(i)   apply to the district judge before decree nisi is pronounced to have his certificate set aside; *and*

(ii) in accordance with r. 2.14, FPR 1991 seek permission from the district judge to file an answer out of time.

It may be an uphill battle to persuade the district judge to make the necessary orders to permit the respondent/co-respondent to defend.

Should the respondent/co-respondent only decide to defend immediately before decree nisi is pronounced, a last ditch attempt can be made to enable him to do so. The respondent/co-respondent should attend court for the pronouncement of decree nisi and should notify the court clerk before the day's list begins that he wishes to make an application in relation to the case. He should then ask the judge or district judge (see r. 2.36(2), FPR 1991) to adjourn the case for a limited period to enable him to make the necessary applications to the district judge. If there is time, the solicitor can contact the court himself by letter or telephone to explain the situation. If he is advising his client under the Legal Help scheme, he cannot, of course, attend court to deal with the matter for the client unless he does so without payment.

(d)   Transfer to High Court: when the answer is filed, the district judge may order that the cause be transferred to the High Court (s. 39, Matrimonial and Family Proceedings Act 1984). Transfer to the High Court is no longer mandatory.

(e)   Subsequent procedure: a reply by the original petitioner to the answer may be filed. Thereafter, once pleadings are closed, disclosure and inspection will take place, directions for trial will be given and the cause will proceed ultimately to a full hearing at which the judge will examine the evidence given by both parties and decide whether a decree should be granted. This gives the impression that a defended divorce will be resolved one way or the other speedily and clinically. The chances are, on the contrary, that the proceedings will be fraught with emotion and protracted over a long period of time.

There are now few reported cases dealing with a defended divorce. However, the case of *Butterworth* v *Butterworth* [1997] 2 FLR 336 is an example in which the Court of Appeal (Butler-Sloss LJ) made it clear that a defended divorce should be heard by a circuit judge and not a recorder. She also made it clear that the respondent should be made fully aware of the allegations made against him: 'hopelessly general' allegations were unacceptable.

12

PROTECTION OF RESPONDENTS IN SEPARATION CASES: SECTIONS 5 AND 10, MATRIMONIAL CAUSES ACT 1973

A INTRODUCTION

The Matrimonial Causes Act 1973 ('MCA 1973') provides two statutory protections for the **12.01**
respondent to a divorce petition.

First of all, s. 5 enables a respondent to defend a divorce based on the fact of five years' separ- **12.02**
ation. While rarely relied on now in practice, it may still be helpful in limited circumstances.

12.03 Secondly, s. 10 contains a procedure to enable the court to scrutinize the financial position of the respondent as it will be on dissolution of the marriage *before* the decree absolute is granted. The procedure applies where the petition is based on s. 1(2)(d) or s. 1(2)(e) and provides protection for the vulnerable respondent since the decree absolute will not usually be granted until satisfactory financial arrangements have been put in place for his or her benefit.

12.04 Solicitors often fail to recognize the tactical advantages in invoking s. 10—it can exert considerable pressure on a petitioner anxious to remarry.

12.05 Applications under ss. 5 and 10, MCA 1973 are normally made by wives. Therefore this chapter departs from the practice adopted in much of the rest of the book and assumes that the wife is the respondent.

B SECTION 5, MATRIMONIAL CAUSES ACT 1973—GRAVE FINANCIAL OR OTHER HARDSHIP

Provisions of s. 5(1)

12.06 Where a divorce petition is based on five years' separation (s. 1(2)(e), MCA 1973), the respondent may oppose the granting of a decree on the ground that the dissolution of the marriage will result in grave financial or other hardship to her and that it would in all the circumstances be wrong to dissolve the marriage (s. 5(1)).

Effect of s. 5 defence

12.07 Where the only fact on which the petitioner is entitled to rely is s. 1(2)(e), the court will have to dismiss the petition if it finds that the respondent's s. 5 defence is made out (s. 5(2)). There is no point, however, in the respondent raising a defence under s. 5 where the petitioner relies on and can establish alternative s. 1(2) facts as well. The s. 5 defence only operates in relation to s. 1(2)(e); therefore the petitioner would be able to go on to obtain a decree on the basis of one of the alternative facts despite the respondent's objection.

Hardship

Generally

12.08 Whether the respondent relies on financial hardship or some other form of hardship, she must show:

(a) that it would be grave: divorce almost inevitably causes a certain amount of hardship—the hardship must be very serious: *and*

(b) that it would result from the dissolution of the marriage: if the respondent's hardship arises, in fact, from the breakdown of the marriage rather than from the divorce, she will not be able to establish a s. 5 defence.

Section 5(3) specifically provides that hardship shall include the loss of the chance of acquiring any benefit which the respondent might acquire if the marriage were not dissolved (for example, widow's pension benefits).

Financial hardship

In deciding whether the respondent will suffer grave financial hardship, the court is entitled **12.09** to look not only at what the respondent will lose as a result of the divorce (for example, a substantial widow's pension because of her change in status following decree absolute) but also at what she will gain (for example, income support) (*Reiterbund* v *Reiterbund* [1974] 2 All ER 455, confirmed by Court of Appeal, [1975] 1 All ER 280 and *Jackson* v *Jackson* [1993] 2 FLR 848).

Where the respondent sets up a prima facie case of hardship, the petitioner will usually seek **12.10** to put forward proposals to alleviate the hardship and the court will then decide whether the proposals are sufficient. If the petitioner's best proposals are not sufficient to remove the hardship, the petition will be dismissed (see, for example, *Le Marchant* v *Le Marchant* [1977] 3 All ER 610).

Because of the availability of pension attachment and pension sharing orders (see Chapter **12.11** 17) the defence is less likely to succeed on the financial hardship ground than was the case in the past.

Other hardship

Most reported cases on 'other hardship' have concerned foreign wives who have claimed **12.12** hardship on social and religious grounds (see, for example, *Banik* v *Banik* [1973] 3 All ER 45). Their efforts to defend on this basis have generally met with failure.

Wrong in all the circumstances to dissolve the marriage

It is possible for the court to grant a decree despite the fact that the respondent has estab- **12.13** lished grave hardship. This is because the court will dismiss the petition only if it considers it would be wrong in all the circumstances to dissolve the marriage.

Section 5(2) provides that the circumstances the court must consider include the conduct of **12.14** the parties to the marriage and the interests of those parties and of any children or other persons concerned. The court can also consider any other relevant circumstances, for example, that the petitioner intends to remarry, and can consider the broader aspect of the case, i.e., whether a marriage which has hopelessly broken down long ago should be preserved or whether it is not right in the public interest to terminate it (see, for example, *Mathias* v *Mathias* [1972] 3 All ER 1, and *Brickell* v *Brickell* [1973] 3 All ER 508).

Procedure

If the respondent wishes to raise a s. 5 defence, she must do so by filing an answer setting out **12.15** her contentions.

She would be well advised to make a claim under s. 10(2), MCA 1973 (a less radical provision) **12.16** as an alternative (see paragraph 12.18 and onwards).

Indeed a failure to file an application under s. 10 could form the basis of an action for **12.17** breach of duty and negligence: *Griffiths* v *Dawson and Co.* [1993] 2 FLR 315. Here, Ewbank J held, amongst other things, that even if there had been no specific instructions to do so, it would have been negligent for the solicitor for the respondent wife not to have lodged an application under s. 10. The exception would be where the respondent understood the consequences of not making the application and gave clear instructions not to do so.

C SECTION 10, MATRIMONIAL CAUSES ACT 1973

Section 10(2): prevention of decree absolute pending consideration of respondent's financial position

When can s. 10(2) be used?

12.18 Where the petition is based on two years' separation and consent or on five years' separation, the respondent is entitled to apply to the court for consideration of her financial position after the divorce (s. 10(2)). The court will not consider the respondent's position under s. 10 where a finding has been made as to any other fact mentioned in s. 1(2), MCA 1973 (i.e., adultery, behaviour, or desertion) as well as a finding under s. 1(2)(d) or (e).

12.19 The time for consideration of the respondent's position is between decree nisi and decree absolute—the court has no power, if the case is proved, to refuse to grant the decree nisi.

Section 10(3) and (4)

12.20 Section 10(3) provides that, where the respondent makes an application under s. 10(2), the court shall not make the decree absolute unless it is satisfied:

(a) that the petitioner should not be required to make any financial provision for the respondent; *or*

(b) that the financial provision made by the petitioner for the respondent is reasonable and fair or the best that can be made in the circumstances.

Section 10(4) relaxes the provisions of s. 10(3) slightly by providing that the court can make the decree absolute notwithstanding the requirements of s. 10(3) if:

(a) it appears to the court that there are circumstances making it desirable that the decree should be made absolute without delay; *and*

(b) the court has obtained a satisfactory undertaking from the petitioner that he will make such financial provisions for the respondent as the court may approve.

Circumstances to be considered

12.21 The court hearing a s. 10(2) application must consider all the circumstances including the age, health, conduct, earning capacity, financial resources, and financial obligations of each of the parties and the financial position of the respondent as, having regard to the divorce, it is likely to be after the death of the petitioner, should the petitioner die first (s. 10(3)).

12.22 It is clear that the court is not restricted to looking only at the financial needs or obligations arising after the divorce, but can also refer to past obligations which have not been fulfilled.

Section 10(2)—a delaying tactic, not a defence

The respondent cannot prevent a divorce being granted by making an application under s. 10(2). What she can do is substantially delay the granting of decree absolute, thus, assuming that the petitioner is anxious to have the divorce made final as soon as possible (for example, so that he can remarry), putting pressure on the petitioner to make acceptable financial arrangements for her. **12.23**

Example The husband, who wishes to remarry, files a petition based on five years' separation. He is a wealthy man. The wife has very little in her own right. The parties are unable to reach any agreement over property and finance. The wife makes an application under s. 10(2) for consideration of her financial position after the divorce. Decree nisi is granted on the basis of five years' separation. The husband cannot obtain decree absolute until after the question of the wife's finances is sorted out. Therefore, in view of his wish to remarry, he is put under pressure to come up with a sensible offer of a settlement.

In a sense, of course, in a s. 1(2)(d) case (two years' separation and consent), s. 10(2) merely reinforces the bargaining power which the respondent already has in that she can withhold her consent until financial matters are sorted out to her satisfaction. In a s. 1(2)(e) case, however, the respondent has no bargaining power and s. 10(2) can be used to give her a valuable lever over the petitioner.

Procedure

A s. 10(2) application must be made by notice in Form B (Family Proceedings Rules 1991, r. 2.45(1), as amended). **12.24**

The considerations taken into account by the court are very similar to those listed in s. 25, MCA 1973 for consideration on ancillary relief applications. In practice, the respondent will usually make her s. 10(2) application together with a comprehensive application for ancillary relief under ss. 23, 24, 24B, 25B, and 25C, MCA 1973 and the two applications will normally be heard at the same time. It is convenient for one financial statement in Form E to be filed in support of both applications. **12.25**

It would seem that the same approach should be adopted in respect of both applications (see, for example, *Krystman* v *Krystman* [1973] 3 All ER 247). Thus it is likely that the hearing of the applications will be virtually indistinguishable from a normal ancillary relief hearing except that, as well as making ancillary relief orders, the court will be asked to make an order under s. 10(3) approving the financial provision so as to enable the petitioner to go on to obtain decree absolute. **12.26**

Section 10(1): rescission of decree nisi under s. 1(2)(D)

By virtue of s. 10(1), where the court has granted a decree nisi of divorce on the basis only of two years' separation and consent, the court may rescind the decree on the respondent's application if it is satisfied that the petitioner misled the respondent (whether intentionally or unintentionally) about any matter which the respondent took into account in deciding to give his consent. **12.27**

The respondent must apply before the decree is made absolute. **12.28**

Section 10A: divorce and dissolution of religious marriages

The background to the provisions

12.29 Section 10A was introduced into the MCA 1973 by the Divorce (Religious Marriages) Act 2002 and came into force on 24 February 2003. The provisions are similar in function to those set out above at paragraph 12.18 and onwards but operate in the circumstances described below.

12.30 The aim of the provisions is to remedy a disadvantage suffered by Jewish men and women who are prevented from remarrying because of the refusal of their former spouses to grant or accept a religious divorce, known as a 'get'.

12.31 In Jewish law, an individual cannot be married or divorced against his or her will. For a divorce obtained under the MCA 1973 to be recognized as effective in Jewish law, a 'get' must also be obtained. This is a divorce under Jewish law where the mutual co-operation of the parties is required. To obtain a 'get', the husband has to go before a Beth Din court to obtain the divorce, deliver it to his wife, and she is obliged to accept it. In the absence of this procedure, the wife is not permitted to remarry in Jewish law although the husband may be able to do so. Hence, a Jewish woman who remarries under the civil law but in the absence of a 'get' will be stigmatized in the Jewish community, being considered an adulteress and any children born as a result of the second marriage will be regarded as illegitimate in Jewish law.

The provisions of s. 10A, Matrimonial Causes Act 1973

12.32 The new provisions enable the county court to make an order refusing to grant the decree absolute of divorce until a declaration by both parties is produced to the court to the effect that they have taken such steps as are required to dissolve the marriage (in accordance with the usages of the Jews, or any other prescribed religious usages): s. 10A(2), MCA 1973.

12.33 The order preventing the grant of the decree absolute will only be made if the court is satisfied that, in all the circumstances of the case, it is just and reasonable to do so and the order may be revoked at any time: s. 10A(3)(a) and (b), MCA 1973.

12.34 In effect, the wife may use these provisions to exert pressure on the husband to obtain a 'get' thus enabling her to remarry free of stigma.

12.35 Incidentally, it should be noted that, while the Act is presently confined in its scope to the Jewish community, it empowers the Secretary of State for Constitutional Affairs to extend the provisions by order to other faiths so it could provide relief in similar cases in the Islamic community.

The procedure

12.36 The Family Proceedings (Amendment) Rules 2003 (SI 2003/184) which came into force on 24 February 2003 prescribe the procedure for seeking an order under s. 10A, MCA 1973 preventing the grant of the decree absolute and also set out the requirements for a valid declaration. The Amendment Rules amend the Family Proceedings Rules 1991.

12.37 Rule 2.45A(3) requires the application for the order to be supported by a sworn statement setting out the grounds for the application. A copy of the sworn statement is to be served with the notice on the other party or parties to the proceedings. The recipient is entitled to at least two days' notice of the hearing.

As for the declaration (to lift the bar on the grant of the decree absolute), r. 2.45B requires **12.38** that it:

(a) be made and signed by both parties;
(b) gives particulars of the proceedings in which the order under s. 10A(2) was obtained;
(c) confirms that steps as are required to dissolve the marriage in accordance with the religious usages, appropriate to the parties, have been taken;
(d) unless the court orders otherwise, be accompanied by a certificate from a relevant religious authority that all such steps have been taken; and
(e) be filed at the court before or together with the application to make the decree of divorce absolute.

Rule 2.49 is amended to provide that the court records must be checked to ensure that any order made in respect of a religious divorce has been complied with before the decree absolute of divorce is granted.

D RESCISSION OF THE DECREE NISI IN OTHER CIRCUMSTANCES

In rare circumstances, application may be made to the court for rescission of the decree nisi **12.39** of divorce under s. 9(2), MCA 1973. An example of such a case is *S v S* (*Rescission of Decree Nisi: Pension Sharing Provision*) [2002] 1 FLR 457 which demonstrated that the parties may, *by consent*, seek the rescission of a decree nisi granted before 1 December 2000, and never having been made absolute, in order then to lodge a new petition which would include an application for a pension sharing order (see Chapter 17). Singer J held that rescission of the decree was not contrary to public policy nor was it an attempt to outwit the intention of Parliament: it was a practical attempt to arrange family affairs to best advantage.

E PROTECTION FOR RESPONDENT CIVIL PARTNERS

Sections 47 and 48 Civil Partnership Act 2004 provide similar protection for civil partners to **12.40** that found in ss. 5 and 10, MCA 1973.

F CHAPTER SUMMARY

1. Section 5(1), MCA 1973 provides a defence to a divorce based on the parties having lived **12.41** apart for five years. The respondent must prove that the decree of divorce would result in the respondent suffering grave financial or other hardship and that it would be wrong to dissolve the marriage.
2. Section 10(2), MCA 1973 enables the respondent in divorce proceedings based on two

or five years' separation to ask the court to consider his or her financial position after the divorce—the decree absolute is delayed until the court is satisfied as to these matters.

G   KEY DOCUMENTS

12.42   Matrimonial Causes Act 1973
Divorce (Religious Marriages) Act 2002
Family Proceedings Rules 1991 (SI 1991/1247)
Family Proceedings (Amendment) Rules 2003 (SI 2003/184)

13

JUDICIAL SEPARATION

A WHAT IS A DECREE OF JUDICIAL SEPARATION?

In essence this decree relieves the parties to a marriage from the duty to cohabit and enables **13.01** either or both of them to apply to the court for orders for ancillary relief (discussed fully in Chapter 17).

B THE GROUNDS FOR JUDICIAL SEPARATION: S. 17, MATRIMONIAL CAUSES ACT 1973

13.02 A petition for judicial separation may be presented to the court by either party to a marriage on the ground that any of the facts mentioned in s. 1(2), Matrimonial Causes Act 1973 ('MCA 1973') exists (see Chapter 4 for a full discussion of the law concerning the s. 1(2) facts).

13.03 The provisions of s. 2, MCA 1973 concerning the effect of cohabitation in relation to the s. 1(2) facts apply as they do in the case of divorce (see Chapter 5).

C THE APPLICATION OF SS. 6 AND 7, MATRIMONIAL CAUSES ACT 1973 TO JUDICIAL SEPARATION

13.04 By virtue of s. 17(3), the provisions of s. 6, MCA 1973 apply as they do with divorce.

13.05 Section 6(1) provides that rules of court shall be made requiring a solicitor *acting* for a petitioner to file a certificate as to whether he has discussed the possibility of a reconciliation with the petitioner. The Family Proceedings Rules 1991, r. 2.6(3) provides that such a certificate shall be filed in Form M3 (see Chapter 9).

13.06 Section 6(2) enables the court to adjourn the proceedings at any stage for reconciliation attempts if there appears to be a reasonable possibility of a reconciliation.

D NO TIME RESTRICTION ON PETITION

13.07 Section 3, MCA 1973 (the one-year bar on divorce petitions) does not apply to judicial separation petitions. There is therefore no restriction on when a petition for judicial separation can be presented—if one of the s. 1(2) facts can be made out, a petition can be presented the day after the wedding.

E SECTION 5, MATRIMONIAL CAUSES ACT 1973 NOT APPLICABLE

13.08 Section 5 (see Chapter 12) does not apply to petitions for judicial separation. It is therefore not possible for the respondent to defend the proceedings on the basis that a decree would result in grave financial or other hardship to him. The best that he can do if he is worried about his financial position is to make an application for ancillary relief under ss. 23, 24, 25B, and 25C, MCA 1973.

F SECTION 10, MATRIMONIAL CAUSES ACT 1973 NOT APPLICABLE

Section 10 (see Chapter 12) does not apply either. The respondent cannot therefore seek to   **13.09**
have the judicial separation decree granted on the ground of s. 1(2)(d) (two years' separation
and consent) rescinded on the basis that the petitioner misled the respondent into giving his
consent. Nor can the respondent in a case based on s. 1(2)(d) or s. 1(2)(e) (five years' separation) hold up the granting of a decree, as he can in divorce proceedings, by applying to have
his financial position considered by the court.

G THE PROCEDURE FOR SEEKING A DECREE OF JUDICIAL SEPARATION

The procedure for seeking a decree of judicial separation is virtually the same as the pro-   **13.10**
cedure for seeking a decree of divorce: see Chapter 9. The following points should be noted,
however:

(a) There is only *one* decree of judicial separation as opposed to the two decrees (decree nisi
and decree absolute) in divorce proceedings. There is therefore no need to apply to have
the decree of judicial separation made absolute.
(b) The special procedure applies where appropriate. Doubtful cases can be referred for
hearing in open court in front of a judge as they can with divorce. Judicial separation
petitions can, of course, be defended in the same way as divorces but because a
judicial separation decree does not finally dissolve the marriage, the incentive to do
this may be rather weaker. If the petition is defended, the procedure for trial is the
same as with a divorce although, as we have seen, the court will only be looking
to see if the s. 1(2) fact is made out and will not be concerned with irretrievable
breakdown.
(c) Although the petition in a judicial separation case will look almost the same as a divorce
petition, irretrievable breakdown of the marriage will not be alleged and the prayer will
be for judicial separation instead of dissolution of the marriage. Other documents such
as the petitioner's Form M7 affidavit will also be amended accordingly.
(d) Whereas, with divorce, decree nisi will not be made absolute until the district judge
has considered the proposed arrangements for any relevant child of the family, in the
case of judicial separation no decree will be granted at all until the district judge has
considered the s. 41 arrangements.
(e) The funding position is the same as it is with divorce cases; see Chapter 7. Public funding is therefore only available in a limited class of judicial separation cases; the majority
of cases will be dealt with under the Legal Help scheme.

H THE EFFECT OF THE DECREE: S. 18, MATRIMONIAL CAUSES ACT 1973

Where a decree of judicial separation is granted it does not terminate the marriage but it does   **13.11**
have the following important consequences:

(a)   The petitioner is no longer bound to cohabit with the respondent (s. 18(1)). Of course, no one can force the petitioner to cohabit with the respondent even when there is no decree of judicial separation, so at first sight s. 18(1) seems to be stating the obvious. However, what it is designed to do is make it clear that neither the petitioner nor the respondent can be in desertion after the decree is granted by virtue of the fact that she or he declines thereafter to live with the other party.

(b)   If either party dies intestate whilst the decree is in force and the separation is continuing, his or her property devolves as if the other party to the marriage were dead (s. 18(2)). Note, however, that, in contrast with the position on divorce, wills are unaffected by a decree of judicial separation. If the client has made a will leaving property to her spouse, she should therefore be advised that he will benefit under the will despite the judicial separation. If she does not wish this to happen, a new will should be made.

(c)   The court can make ancillary orders as to finances and property under ss. 23, 24, 25B, and 25C, MCA 1973. Note that, as with divorce, the court can also make orders for maintenance pending suit in respect of the period between the filing of the petition and pronouncement of the decree. See Chapter 17 for full details of the court's powers in relation to these matters.

(d)   Orders under Part I and Part II of the Children Act 1989 can be made by the court, pursuant to s. 41, MCA 1973 (see Chapter 29).

I   SUBSEQUENT DIVORCE: S. 4, MATRIMONIAL CAUSES ACT 1973

Judicial separation no bar to divorce

13.12   The parties are free to petition for divorce even after they have been granted a decree of judicial separation (s. 4(1)).

Procedure for seeking subsequent divorce

13.13   The most convenient way in which a subsequent divorce can be sought is for the divorce petition to be presented by the spouse who petitioned for the decree of judicial separation on the basis of the same facts. The court may then treat the decree of judicial separation as sufficient proof of the fact by reference to which it was granted.

13.14   The petitioner will have to establish irretrievable breakdown of the marriage which would not, of course, have been established at the time of the judicial separation decree. In practice, however, irretrievable breakdown is normally presumed once a s. 1(2) fact is proved so this should not present a problem (see Chapter 4).

13.15   The petitioner must give evidence in support of her divorce petition in the normal way (usually in her Form M7 affidavit in support of her petition) even where the petition follows an earlier judicial separation (s. 4(2)).

13.16   One situation to watch out for is where the parties have resumed cohabitation since the date of the judicial separation decree. Where this has happened, the provisions of s. 2,

MCA 1973 must be borne in mind. Note that it will not necessarily be only the period(s) of cohabitation that has/have taken place since the date of the decree that will be relevant. Reference must be had to the terms of the section in order to ascertain which period of cohabitation is relevant in relation to which s. 1(2) fact.

In some cases it will not be possible or desirable for the divorce petition to be put on the same **13.17** basis as the judicial separation petition, for instance it may now be the other party who wishes to petition. In such situations the right approach is to examine the facts in the normal way to see whether any of the s. 1(2) facts can be made out independently of the judicial separation decree. The only bearing that the judicial separation decree has on this is that it prevents either party being in desertion after it has been granted.

Example In 2005 the wife obtains a decree of judicial separation on the basis of her husband's adultery. The reason why the husband had committed adultery was, in fact, that the marriage had broken down owing to the wife's thoroughly unpleasant behaviour. In 2006 the husband decides that he wishes to petition for divorce. He cannot petition on the basis of his own adultery but he can file a petition based on his wife's behaviour (s. 1(2)(b)).

J REASONS FOR SEEKING JUDICIAL SEPARATION

Although judicial separations are fairly rare these days, from time to time a case will arise in **13.18** which it is appropriate to seek a decree of judicial separation. Judicial separation does have the following advantages over divorce:

(a) There is no restriction as to when the petition can be presented. Judicial separation may therefore be useful during the first year of marriage when divorce is not permitted. If the client really wishes to be divorced and is contemplating judicial separation as second-best, it will often be better for her to wait patiently until the first year of marriage is up rather than devote several months of that year to obtaining a decree of judicial separation only to spend more time the next year having it converted into a decree of divorce.

(b) There are less likely to be religious objections on the part of either party to judicial separation than to divorce.

(c) Some people find it less traumatic to accept the half-way house of a judicial separation than to sever their ties with their spouse completely by a divorce. Judicial separation enables them to have their cake and eat it—the fact that judicial separation does not enable them to remarry is of no consequence to them because they are in no state of mind to do so anyway and they *are* able to take advantage of the same wide powers of the court in relation to ancillary relief as they could after a divorce.

(d) If the choice is between judicial separation and other methods of seeking financial relief during the marriage, for example, an application under s. 27, MCA 1973 (see Chapter 35), judicial separation has the advantage that the court's powers in relation to finances and property are more comprehensive. For example, the court can make orders for sale of the matrimonial home or transfer of specific assets from one party to the other after a judicial separation, whereas under s. 27, MCA 1973 the court can only grant periodical payments and lump sum orders.

However, for most clients seeking financial relief during the marriage, judicial separation will not fit the bill either because they are unable to make out any of the s. 1(2) facts and therefore cannot petition anyway, or because judicial separation seems too drastic a step.

Insoluble problems over property can be dealt with during the marriage by an application under s. 17, Married Women's Property Act 1882 (see Chapter 37), although in practice such applications are to be avoided where possible.

K   CHAPTER SUMMARY

13.19   1. A decree of judicial separation may be granted by establishing one of the five facts in s. 1(2), MCA 1973.

2. The decree relieves the parties from the duty to cohabit but does not terminate the marriage.

3. The court may make orders for ancillary relief (except pension sharing orders) in judicial separation proceedings.

14

CIVIL PARTNERSHIP ACT 2004

A INTRODUCTION

The Civil Partnership Act 2004 ('CPA 2004') is ground-breaking legislation which places **14.01**
same sex partners who register their partnership in virtually the same legal position as different sex partners who enter into marriage. It also brings the United Kingdom into step with
Art. 14 of the European Convention on Human Rights and Fundamental Freedoms 1950
(the prohibition of discrimination) and with a number of other European jurisdictions who
have enacted similar codes.

The Act is substantial and runs to eight parts and thirty schedules. It applies to all of the **14.02**
United Kingdom including Scotland and Northern Ireland. It amends a plethora of other
statutes by incorporating the mechanism and effect of civil partnership into each of those
earlier statutes.

For the family lawyer the principal areas of interest are those of formation, dissolution, and **14.03** termination of a civil partnership. The Act's application to children and domestic violence is also important.

B   FORMATION OF A CIVIL PARTNERSHIP

Eligibility

14.04   To be eligible to enter into a civil partnership the parties must be of the same sex, must not already be in a civil partnership or marriage, must be aged 16 or over and not within the prohibited degrees of relationship. The prohibited degrees of relationship are set out in Part 1 of sch. 1 of the Act and mirror those that apply in the case of marriage.

14.05   Where a prospective civil partner is aged 16 or 17 the consent of an 'appropriate person' must be obtained before the young person and the other person can register the civil partnership (s. 4(1)). 'Appropriate person' is defined in Part 1 of sch. 2 of the Act and includes any parent of the child with parental responsibility, special guardians, and, where the young person is in care, the relevant local authority or prospective adopters. Where consent is refused by an appropriate person the young person may then seek the court's consent (sch. 2 para. 4).

Registration

14.06   The Act contains three ways in which civil partnerships may be registered, namely the standard, modified, and special procedures.

14.07   Whichever procedure is followed, the prospective partners are regarded as having registered their civil partnership once each of them has signed the 'civil partnership schedule' in the presence of a civil partnership registrar and in the presence of each other and two witnesses (s. 2(1)). As in civil marriage, the place of registration must not be religious premises and no religious service is permitted to take place. In the case of the standard and modified procedures, the place of registration should be open to the public.

14.08   Both partners must have resided in England and Wales for at least seven days immediately before giving notice and must make a solemn declaration in writing that there is no impediment of kindred or affinity or other lawful hindrance to the formation of the civil partnership (s. 8(4)). Upon being given notice of the proposed civil partnership the 'registration authority' (a local council) publicizes the relevant information for a period of 15 days. Assuming no objections are made during this period, the registration authority then issues a Civil Partnership Schedule which must be signed within one year by the proposed civil partners and their witnesses. The signing of the Schedule creates and registers the civil partnership.

14.09   The modified procedure mirrors provisions in the Marriage Act 1983 enabling persons who are house-bound or detained to register their civil partnerships. The detailed requirements are set out in ss. 18 and 19.

14.10   The special procedure recreates the procedure of the Marriage (Registrar General's Licence)

Act 1970 and enables a prospective civil partner to register the partnership when he or she is seriously ill and not expected to recover. The procedure is set out in ss. 21 to 27.

In the case of all three procedures no form of words is prescribed for the registration itself and, strictly speaking, the process is one that is purely paper-based. Local authorities are therefore free to offer their own choice of words or ceremonies provided that they are non-religious in nature. **14.11**

Registration by a former spouse, one of whom has changed sex

Where a certificate under the Gender Recognition Act 2004 ('GRA 2004') has been issued to a spouse of a marriage which has been dissolved the former spouses can apply under a fast track procedure in sch. 3 of the Act for the registration of a civil partnership. In this instance there is no 15-day waiting period although the Civil Partnership Schedule must be signed by each spouse and their witnesses within one month or it will otherwise be void. **14.12**

C TERMINATION OF CIVIL PARTNERSHIPS

Dissolution orders

The Act mirrors the provision of the Matrimonial Causes Act 1973 ('MCA 1973') in that a civil partnership may not be dissolved for a period of 12 months following its creation. After this period it must be shown that the civil partnership has broken down irretrievably and that one of four 'facts' listed in s. 44(5) exists. The 'facts' are unreasonable behaviour, two years' separation with consent to a dissolution order, five years' separation without such consent, and desertion for a period of two years. The one difference is that while spouses may rely upon adultery to establish an irretrievable breakdown of their marriage, this option is not open to a civil partner. In this instance, such a person may seek to rely upon the adultery as 'behaviour' under s. 44(5)(a). **14.13**

As with divorce, dissolution orders are, in the first instance, conditional and are then made final after a period of six further weeks. **14.14**

Similarly, the case law that has developed in relation to divorce will apply to civil partnership dissolution orders. **14.15**

Nullity orders

Section 49 sets out the circumstances in which a civil partnership is void and these, in the main, relate to breaches of the various formal requirements, such as non-fulfilment of the eligibility criteria. In this instance the civil partnership will be void ab initio and treated as if it had never existed. **14.16**

Section 50 lists the grounds on which a civil partnership is voidable. These bear some similarities to the equivalent grounds in marriage, including there having been no valid consent (by way of duress, mistake, or unsoundness of mind), where at the date of its formation the respondent was pregnant by some person other than the applicant (presumably only **14.17** applicable in cases of gender change), and where an interim certificate has been issued under the GRA 2004. The Civil Partnership Act does not, however, render a partnership voidable on the basis of non-consummation or where one of the parties was suffering from venereal disease at the date of the civil partnership.

14.18   Nullity orders under s. 50 must be sought within three years of the date of formation except where the ground relied upon is an interim certificate issued under the GRA 2004. In this instance an application for nullity must be made within six months of the certificate.

Separation orders

14.19   Separation orders equate to judicial separation between spouses (see Chapter 13).

D   FINANCIAL RELIEF UPON TERMINATION

14.20   Schedule 5 of the Act is designed to mirror the provisions for spouses under the MCA 1973. Civil partners are therefore provided with the full range of financial relief that can be utilized by spouses including property adjustment orders, periodical payments orders, interim maintenance, sale of property orders, and pension sharing orders.

14.21   In considering any such application the court must have regard to the criteria contained in Part 5 of sch. 5 which are similar to ss. 25 and 25A, MCA 1973. For obvious reasons, therefore, the case law that has developed in respect of ancillary relief will apply to financial relief upon the termination of civil partnerships.

14.22   As with ancillary relief, entry into a subsequent civil partnership or marriage is a bar to any application for financial provision.

E   CHILDREN

14.23   The Civil Partnership Act amended s. 4 of the Children Act 1989 ('CA 1989') to enable a civil partner to obtain parental responsibility for a child in the same way that it is granted to a step-parent who marries a parent either by an order or by agreement.

14.24   A civil partner is also entitled to apply for contact, residence, prohibited steps, specific issue, and special guardianship orders without obtaining the leave of the court whether or not a civil partnership is currently subsisting.

14.25   Schedule 1 of the CA 1989 is also extended to enable civil partners to apply for financial provision for children.

F CIVIL PARTNERSHIP HOMES AND DOMESTIC VIOLENCE

Schedule 9 of the Act places civil partners in the same position as spouses as far as rights of **14.26** occupation of their shared home are concerned and in respect of remedies available to them under Part 4 of the Family Law Act 1996. 'Matrimonial home rights' are therefore now known as 'home rights'. Similarly, as far as applications for occupation orders are concerned, the status accorded to civil partners is the same as spouses and is therefore greater than the status of same sex couples who have not registered a civil partnership.

G KEY DOCUMENTS

<http://www.hmso.gov.uk> Full text of primary and secondary legislation including the   **14.27**
   Civil Partnership Act 2004
<http://www.lagla.org.uk> Association of gay and lesbian lawyers
<http://www.civilpartnership.com> On-line guide to civil partnership
Blackstone's Guide to the Civil Partnership Act (Nichola Gray and Dominic Brazil), OUP

15

GENDER RECOGNITION ACT 2004

A   INTRODUCTION

The Gender Recognition Act 2004 ('GRA 2004') came fully into force on 4 April 2005 and **15.01** provides for gender recognition certificates to be issued to enable transsexual people to be recognized, for legal purposes, in their acquired gender.

The legislation was prompted by the decision of the European Court of Human Rights in the **15.02** cases of *Goodwin* v *United Kingdom* and *I* v *United Kingdom* [2002] 2 FLR 487 which found that the United Kingdom government had breached Arts. 8 and 12 of the European Convention for the Protection of Human Rights and Fundamental Freedoms 1950 by denying transsexuals recognition of their acquired gender. It will be recalled that Art. 8 provides the right to respect for an individual's private and family life while Art. 12 establishes a right to marry and found a family. In addition, and in light of the ECHR decision, the House of Lords in *Bellinger* v *Bellinger* [2003] 1 FLR 1043 declared that the provisions of s. 11(c), Matrimonial Causes Act 1973 ('MCA 1973') (discussed fully in Chapter 16) were incompatible with both

Arts. 8 and 12, above, and the Human Rights Act 1998. Faced with such condemnation, reform became inevitable.

The recognition process

15.03   In order for a transsexual to obtain legal recognition of their acquired gender, an application for a full gender recognition certificate has to be made to a Gender Recognition Panel.

The Gender Recognition Panel

15.04   According to sch. 1 of the 2004 Act, those eligible to sit on the Panel fall into two categories—legal and medical members. Legal members must have a seven-year general qualification within the meaning of s. 71, Courts and Legal Services Act 1990. The medical member must be either a registered medical practitioner or a chartered psychologist (sch. 1, para. 1).

15.05   Except as discussed at 15.15, each Panel must include a legal member and at least one medical member. Each Panel has a presiding legal member who, where necessary, has a casting vote.

15.06   Schedule 1, para. 6 states that the Panel determines applications in private; no hearing takes place unless the Panel considers it to be necessary. Reasons for the decision must be communicated to the applicant.

Grounds for the application

15.07   Section 2(1) provides that a full gender recognition certificate must be granted if the Gender Recognition Panel is satisfied that the applicant (who must be aged at least 18 years: s. 1(1)(a)):

(a)   has or has had gender dysphoria;
(b)   has lived in the acquired gender throughout the period of two years ending with the date on which the application is made;
(c)   intends to continue to live in the acquired gender until death;
(d)   complies with the requirements imposed by and under s. 3.

The meaning of gender dysphoria

15.08   Section 25 provides that the term 'gender dysphoria' means the disorder 'variously referred to as gender dysphoria, gender identity disorder and transsexualism'. Arguably, this is not illuminating and Panels will rely, to a great extent, on the expert medical evidence to be submitted (see paragraph 15.11).

15.09   It is important to recognize, however, that there is no requirement for the applicant to have undergone gender reassignment surgery in order to succeed in the application. Clearly, careful scrutiny would be required by the Panel where no surgery had taken place but the House of Lords and House of Commons Joint Committee on Human Rights (Nineteenth Report of Session 2002–2003 HL 188–1, HC 1276–1(TSO, 2003)) concluded that the wide definition would 'avoid discriminating against people who for some medical reason unconnected with their gender, are unsuitable for particular kinds of surgical, hormonal or other treatment' (para. 28).

The evidence requirements

Section 3 deals with the evidence requirements in support of the application.   **15.10**

The application must be supported by: **15.11**

(a) a report by a registered medical practitioner or chartered psychologist practising in the field of gender dysphoria together with a report by another registered medical practitioner (who need not be such a specialist).
The report must include details of the diagnosis of the applicant's gender dysphoria from the specialist practitioner (s. 3(2)) and details of the treatment undergone, prescribed, or planned (s. 3(3));

(b) a statutory declaration by the applicant that he or she satisfies the requirements of s. 2(1)(b) and (c) (see paragraph 15.07). (It is suggested that the most difficult of these to establish will be that relating to the future intentions of the applicant);

(c) a statutory declaration as to whether or not the applicant is married (see paragraph 15.12 and onwards);

(d) any further information or evidence that the Secretary of State or Panel may require or that the applicant may wish to submit.

The issue of the certificate

Where the applicant is successful and is unmarried, the Panel must issue a full gender   **15.12**
recognition certificate: s. 4(2), GRA 2004. Conversely, where the applicant is already validly married, a successful application will lead to the grant of an interim recognition certificate which is of limited effect.

The interim gender recognition certificate

As will be seen in Chapter 16, the issue of an interim gender recognition certificate provides a   **15.13**
ground for nullity proceedings to be instituted under s. 12, MCA 1973. The proceedings must, however, be commenced within six months of the issue of the interim gender recognition certificate: s. 13(2A), MCA 1973.

Once the decree absolute of nullity is granted, the court granting the decree must issue a full   **15.14**
gender recognition certificate and send a copy to the Secretary of State (s. 5(1), GRA 2004).

Where the applicant's marriage is subsequently terminated by divorce or nullity proceedings   **15.15**
(on a ground other than the issue of an interim gender recognition certificate) within six months of the date of the issue of the interim certificate, the interim certificate may be converted to a full gender recognition certificate by application to the Panel: s. 5(2), GRA 2004. Such application must be made within six months of the termination of the marriage: s. 5(3), GRA 2004. The Panel in these circumstances will comprise one legal member.

Where the marriage is terminated by death within a period of six months from the date of   **15.16**
issue of the interim certificate, the interim certificate may be similarly converted to a full

certificate by application to the Panel within six months of the date of the death: s. 5(2) and (3), GRA 2004.

15.17   What is clear from these provisions is that a full gender recognition certificate will not be granted until any existing marriage to which the applicant is a party is terminated or annulled.

The Gender Recognition Register

15.18   Schedule 3 GRA 2004 requires the Registrar General to maintain a Gender Recognition Register ('GRR'). Once a full gender recognition certificate has been granted, the Secretary of State must send a copy to the Registrar General: s. 10(1), GRA 2004. On receipt, the Registrar is required to make an entry in the GRR, mark the birth register entry, and make a traceable connection between the entries. It is then possible to obtain certified copies of the entries in the GRR and short certificates of birth compiled from it. Neither must disclose that the entry or compilation is from the GRR: sch. 3, para. 3, GRA 2004.

15.19   The GRR is not available for public inspection and the applicant's confidentiality is protected throughout the application and registration process by provisions set out in detail in s. 22, GRA 2004.

Rejection of the application and appeal

15.20   Section 8, GRA 2004 deals with the position when the application is rejected. First of all, the applicant may appeal to the High Court on a point of law against the Panel's decision. The appeal must be heard in private if the applicant so requests. The High Court may allow the appeal and issue the certificate, allow the appeal and refer the matter back to the Panel or another Panel for reconsideration, or dismiss the appeal.

15.21   Where rejected, the applicant may not make a further application until a period of six months has elapsed from the date on which the application was rejected.

15.22   The procedure is laid down in r. 3.24, Family Proceedings Rules 1991. The application must be made by an originating summons issued out of the principal registry.

Referral to the High Court

15.23   Where a certificate is granted but the Secretary of State considers that the decision to grant the certificate was secured by fraud, he may refer the case to the High Court which must quash or confirm the decision: s. 8(6).

Application for recognition within two years of the Act coming into force

15.24   Special provisions apply where an application is made for a full gender recognition certificate within two years of 4 April 2005. The provisions are found in s. 27, GRA 2004.

15.25   Section 2(1)(a) has the following words added 'or has undergone surgical treatment for the purpose of modifying sexual characteristics'.

Where the application is based on such surgical treatment, the period during which the **15.26** applicant must have first lived in the acquired gender is increased from two to six years: s. 27(3), amending s. 2(1)(b), GRA 2004.

The rationale for this provision is to control the number of applications made to Panels in **15.27** the early days of the coming into force of the Act.

The consequences of the issue of a full gender recognition certificate

Section 9(1) provides that, once a full gender recognition certificate has been granted, 'the **15.28** person's gender becomes for all purposes the acquired gender'.

The subsection goes on to state 'if the acquired gender is the male gender, the person's sex **15.29** becomes that of a man and, if it is the female gender, the person's sex becomes that of a woman'.

Crucially, this means that where a full gender recognition certificate has been issued, the **15.30** recipient whose acquired gender is now that of a man, will be treated as a 'male' for the purposes of s. 11(c), MCA 1973 and will be able to contract a valid marriage with a woman, thus dealing with the longstanding difficulty highlighted by the case of *Corbett* v *Corbett* [1970] 2 WLR 1306, discussed in Chapter 16.

As with most other legislation, however, the provisions are not retrospective in effect and do **15.31** not, for example, validate the parties' marriage in *Bellinger* v *Bellinger* (paragraph 15.02). In that case, the House of Lords confirmed that the marriage was void by virtue of s. 11(c), MCA 1973 and following the coming into force of GRA 2004, Mrs Bellinger would be required to obtain a full gender recognition certificate and then marry Mr Bellinger in order to contract a marriage which would be recognized as valid under the terms of s. 11(c), MCA 1973.

Two further points need to be mentioned here. First of all, the Marriage Act 1949 is amended **15.32** to incorporate a conscientious objection clause. Section 5B states that 'a clergyman is not obliged to solemnize the marriage of a person if the clergyman reasonably believes that the person's gender has become the acquired gender under the Gender Recognition Act 2004'.

Secondly, as will be explained in Chapter 16, the grounds on which a marriage may be **15.33** voidable have been further extended by adding para. (h) to s. 12 MCA 1973. This makes a marriage voidable if, at the time of the marriage, the respondent is a person whose gender had become the acquired gender under the 2004 Act.

While outside the scope of this book, it should be noted that the 2004 Act makes consequen- **15.34** tial amendments in areas such as welfare benefits and pensions (sch. 5) and sex discrimin- ation (sch. 6).

What the acquired gender does not affect

There are certain areas of law and activity which remain unaffected by the fact that an **15.35** individual has an acquired gender. These include, for example, succession rights and the responsibilities of a personal representative (ss. 15, 16, and 17, GRA 2004), certain sports activities (s. 19, GRA 2004) and gender specific offences involving sexual activity (s. 20, GRA 2004).

15.36 Critically, however, for family lawyers, s. 12 GRA 2004 provides that the acquired gender does not affect the status of the person as the father or mother of a child.

Example Helen is unmarried at the time when she gives birth to her daughter, Octavia. She has parental responsibility for Octavia by virtue of s. 2(2)(a) Children Act 1989 ('CA 1989').

Helen is then granted a full gender recognition certificate and is to be treated as a man (s. 9 GRA 2004), becoming known as Paul. However, because Paul was a woman when Octavia was born, parental responsibility for the child is not lost on the issue of the full gender recognition certificate.

Paul then forms a relationship with Stacey but does not marry her. Paul and Stacey together receive treatment at a clinic licensed by the Human Fertilisation and Embryology Authority. Stacey is inseminated by donor sperm and subsequently gives birth to a child, William.

Stacey is William's mother (s. 27(1), Human Fertilisation and Embryology Act 1990 ('HFEA 1990')) and Paul is treated, by virtue of s. 28(3), HFEA 1990, as the child's father. Because the parties are unmarried, Paul will not automatically have parental responsibility for William (s. 2(2)(b), CA 1989) and will have to acquire it by one of the ways prescribed in s. 4, CA 1989.

Gender recognition and civil partners

15.37 Where an individual seeking a gender recognition certificate is a registered civil partner, the Panel may grant an interim gender recognition certificate (assuming that the grounds for the certificate are made out) only until the civil partnership is annulled or dissolved: s. 4(3), GRA 2004.

15.38 Provisions similar to those set out in paragraph 15.12 and onwards and found in s. 5A, GRA 2004 would then apply in order for the applicant to obtain a full gender recognition certificate.

15.39 Termination of a civil partnership is discussed in Chapter 14.

Guidance for clients

15.40 A Gender Recognition Helpline has been established and may be contacted on 01473 252749.

B   KEY DOCUMENTS

15.41 Gender Recognition Act 2004

16

NULLITY

A INTRODUCTION

In the eyes of the law some marriages suffer from impediments which lead to them being **16.01** either void or voidable. In relation to marriages celebrated after 31 July 1971 the grounds on which a marriage is void or voidable are contained in ss. 11 and 12, Matrimonial Causes Act 1973 ('MCA 1973'). The solicitor will rarely be called upon to deal with a marriage celebrated before this date.

B THE NEED FOR A NULLITY DECREE

Void marriages

16.02 A void marriage is void from the beginning and can, in theory, be treated by both parties as never having taken place without the need for a decree of nullity. However, it is almost always advisable to seek a decree even where the marriage clearly appears to be void. One reason for this is that most clients will wish to take advantage of the court's powers under the Matrimonial Causes Act 1973 ('MCA 1973') to grant ancillary relief in relation to finance, property, and pensions. These powers are only exercisable if a decree of nullity is sought. Another reason is that possession of a nullity decree puts the status of both parties beyond doubt (which is particularly important where one party does not agree that the marriage is void), thus avoiding complications that could arise, for example, when one party seeks to remarry.

Voidable marriages

16.03 Because a voidable marriage is valid unless and until a decree of nullity has been granted, a decree is essential.

C VOID MARRIAGES: S. 11

16.04 A marriage shall be void on the following grounds only:

(a) That it is not a valid marriage under the provisions of the Marriage Acts 1949, 1983, and 1994, i.e., where:
  (i) the parties are within the prohibited degrees of relationship (which can be relationship by blood or by marriage), for example, where they are father and daughter, brother and sister, son and step-mother; *or*
  (ii) either party is under the age of 16; *or*
  (iii) the parties have intermarried in disregard of certain requirements as to the formation of marriage, for example, where they marry according to the rites of the Church of England in a place which is not a church or other building in which banns may be published or without observing the requirements as to banns, licences, etc., both being aware of the irregularity at the time of the marriage.
  (Note that the Marriage Act 1994 permits civil ceremonies of marriage to take place on premises approved by local authorities, thus considerably increasing the number of venues available for marriage ceremonies.)

(b) That at the time of the marriage either of the parties was already lawfully married or a civil partner (amended by Civil Partnership Act 2004 ('CPA 2004'). The onus of proof, on the balance of probabilities, lies on the party asserting that the marriage is void: *Wicken* v *Wicken* [1999] 1 FLR 293. Here the husband's claim that the marriage was void because the wife was already lawfully married failed because documentary evidence of a divorce had been produced and the parties had gone through a marriage ceremony.

Further, both had asserted that the wife was free to marry. The parties had cohabited for a number of years during which they had held themselves out as validly married.

(c) That the parties are not respectively male and female. In *Bellinger* v *Bellinger (Validity of Marriage: Transsexual)* [2003] 1 FLR 1043, the House of Lords followed the decision in *Corbett* v *Corbett* [1970] 1 All ER 33 and dismissed the appeal of a male-to-female transsexual (Mrs Bellinger) against the refusal of the Court of Appeal to declare her marriage to a man to be valid and subsisting. The marriage was void on the grounds laid down in s. 11(c), MCA 1973 because the parties were not 'respectively male and female'. The court did not accept that, as a result of gender-reassignment treatment, Mrs Bellinger was 'female' at the time the marriage was celebrated.

In contrast with the trial judge and the Court of Appeal, however, the House of Lords went on to declare that s. 11(c), MCA 1973 was incompatible with Arts. 8 and 12 of the European Convention for the Protection of Human Rights and Fundamental Freedoms. The provisions of the subsequent Gender Recognition Act 2004 ('GRA 2004') are fully explained in Chapter 15.

(d) In the case of polygamous marriage entered into outside England and Wales, that either party was at the time of the marriage domiciled in England and Wales.

D   VOIDABLE MARRIAGES: S. 12

A marriage shall be voidable on the following grounds only: **16.05**

(a) that it has not been consummated owing to the incapacity of either party to consummate it;

(b) that it has not been consummated owing to the wilful refusal of the respondent to consummate it;

(c) that either party to the marriage did not validly consent to it whether in consequence of duress, mistake, unsoundness of mind, or otherwise;

(d) that at the time of the marriage either party, though capable of giving a valid consent, was suffering (whether continuously or intermittently) from mental disorder within the meaning of the Mental Health Act 1983 of such a kind or to such an extent as to be unfitted for marriage;

(e) that at the time of the marriage the respondent was suffering from venereal disease in a communicable form;

(f) that at the time of the marriage the respondent was pregnant by someone other than the petitioner;

(g) that an interim gender recognition certificate under the GRA 2004 has, after the marriage, been issued to either party to the marriage;

(h) that the respondent is a person whose gender at the time of the marriage had become the acquired gender under the GRA 2004.

Grounds (g) and (h) were inserted into s. 12, MCA 1973 by the GRA and their significance is explained in Chapter 15.

E   BARS TO RELIEF WHERE THE MARRIAGE IS VOIDABLE: S. 13, MATRIMONIAL CAUSES ACT 1973

Absolute bar applicable to all voidable marriages

16.06 The court shall not grant a nullity decree on the grounds that the marriage is voidable if the respondent satisfies the court:

(a)   that the petitioner, knowing that she could have the marriage annulled, so conducted herself in relation to the respondent as to lead the respondent reasonably to believe that she would not seek to do so; *and*

(b)   that it would be unjust to the respondent to grant the decree (s. 13(1)).

Bars applicable only to certain voidable marriages

Limitation period

16.07 There is a 'limitation period' for the institution of proceedings for a decree on the grounds set out in s. 12(c), (d), (e), (f), and (h) (see paragraph 16.05 above), i.e., lack of consent, mental disorder, venereal disease, pregnancy by someone else, and where, at the time of the marriage, the respondent is a person whose gender had become the acquired gender under GRA 2004. The court shall not grant a decree on any of these grounds unless it is satisfied that proceedings were instituted within three years from the date of the marriage (s. 13(2)). However, there is an exception to this rule: by virtue of s. 13(4), a judge may grant permission to institute proceedings on any of these grounds after the three-year period if:

(a)   he is satisfied that the petitioner has at some time during the three-year period suffered from a mental disorder within the meaning of the Mental Health Act 1983; *and*

(b)   he considers that in all the circumstances of the case it would be just to grant permission for the institution of proceedings.

An application for permission can be made even if the three-year period has already expired (s. 13(5)).

Knowledge of petitioner

16.08 The court shall not grant a decree on the grounds set out in s. 12(e), (f), or (h) (venereal disease, pregnancy, and acquisition of acquired gender) unless it is satisfied that at the time of the marriage the petitioner was ignorant of the fact alleged (s. 13(3)). This is an absolute bar.

F   PROCEDURE

16.09 (a)   The special procedure does not apply. The petition will therefore be heard in open court by a judge in the same way as a divorce that is removed from the special procedure list (see Chapter 9, paragraph 9.80). The procedure is laid down in rr. 2.1–2.51, Family Proceedings Rules 1991 ('FPR 1991'). It should be noted, however, that the FPR 1991 have been amended to reflect the changes introduced into s. 12 MCA 1973 by the GRA 2004 (notably s. 12(g) and (h)). The changes are found at rr. 2.6A, 2.6B, 2.9A, 2.12A, 2.12B, 2.13A, 2.51A, 3.24, 8.4, and 10.21B and include, for example:

- the requirement to file with the petition a copy of an interim gender recognition certificate issued to him or the respondent (as the case may be);
- the requirement to file with the petition a full gender recognition certificate issued to the respondent where s. 12(h), MCA 1973 is being relied on;
- a requirement that a respondent to proceedings brought under s. 12(g) or (h) MCA 1973 files an interim or full gender recognition certificate when returning the acknowledgement of service to the court;
- a requirement imposed on the court to keep such documents in a place of special security.

The President's Direction (Gender Recognition Act 2004: Procedure: (1) Title of the Cause, (2) Evidence at Trial of Cause) 5 April 2005 [2005] 2 FLR 122 sets out how the parties to proceedings for a decree of divorce, judicial separation or nullity should be described in any court list to reflect the changes brought about by the GRA 2004. In particular, titles (e.g. Mr, Mrs, Miss) should be omitted from court lists and documents.

Secondly, the Direction introduces an affidavit to be used in support of a petition based on the provisions of s. 12(g), MCA 1973 where the proceedings are undefended.

(b) Public funding is available for nullity proceedings. Paragraph 59 of Chapter 2 of The Funding Code—Decision Making Guidance indicates that a certificate for Legal Representation will be refused unless divorce is not appropriate, for example, because it is alleged that a marriage is void from the beginning.

(c) There are two decrees, decree nisi and decree absolute, as there are with divorce.

(d) Section 41 MCA 1973 (arrangements for children of the family) applies as it does in divorce cases (see Chapter 9, paragraph 9.83 and onwards).

G EFFECT OF A DECREE OF NULLITY

On status

Voidable marriages

A decree of nullity granted in respect of a voidable marriage operates to annul the marriage **16.10** only from after the date of decree absolute. The marriage is treated as if it had existed up to that time (s. 16, MCA 1973 and see *Ward* v *Secretary of State for Social Services* [1990] 1 FLR 119). Because the marriage existed until the decree, children of the union are automatically legitimate. Remarriage can take place after the decree absolute. Provision in a will by one spouse for the other will lapse (Wills Act 1837, s. 18A, added by the Administration of Justice Act 1982, s. 18(2)). Neither spouse will be able to claim on the other's intestacy.

Void marriages

A void marriage is a nullity from the very start and the nullity decree simply declares this **16.11** fact. Children of a void marriage are treated as legitimate by virtue of s. 1, Legitimacy Act 1976 if, at the time of conception or insemination (or the celebration of the marriage if this is later) both or either of the parents *reasonably* believed the marriage was valid and the father was domiciled in England and Wales at the time of the birth or, if he died before the birth, was so domiciled immediately before his death.

Other effects

16.12   The full range of ancillary relief orders under the MCA 1973 in relation to children, property, and finance are available in connection with a suit for nullity just as they are with a divorce.

H   NULLITY PROCEEDINGS AND CIVIL PARTNERSHIP

16.13   A nullity order is available for civil partnerships under ss. 49 and 50, CPA 2004. The position is explained fully in Chapter 14.

I   CHAPTER SUMMARY

16.14   1.   A decree of nullity is available where a marriage is void or voidable.
        2.   A void marriage is one that never existed despite the parties going through a ceremony of marriage. The grounds on which a marriage is void are set out in s. 11, MCA 1973.
        3.   A voidable marriage exists until steps are taken to set it aside. The grounds to do so are set out in s. 12, MCA 1973.
        4.   In certain circumstances, parties to a voidable marriage may be barred from obtaining a decree of nullity. The bars are set out in s. 13, MCA 1973.
        5.   The court may make orders for ancillary relief where a decree of nullity has been granted.

PART III

ANCILLARY RELIEF AFTER DIVORCE, NULLITY, AND JUDICIAL SEPARATION

Part III deals with ancillary relief after divorce, nullity, and judicial separation. The first three chapters deal with routine ancillary relief applications as follows:

Chapter 17 sets out the financial provision and property adjustment orders available in connection with divorce, nullity, and judicial separation.

Chapter 18 sets out the procedure for seeking ancillary relief orders.

Chapter 19 deals with the considerations that the court will bear in mind in deciding what orders to make and gives examples of the sort of orders that might be expected in particular circumstances.

Chapter 20 sets out the basic principles of the Child Support Act 1991, particularly in relation to the Act's impact on the law relating to ancillary relief.

Chapter 21 deals with a rather less routine matter—the preventing and setting aside of dispositions under s. 37, Matrimonial Causes Act 1973.

Chapter 22 covers collection and enforcement of ancillary relief orders.

Chapter 23 deals with variation of orders.

Reference should also be made to Chapter 24, which deals with taxation.

17

ANCILLARY RELIEF ORDERS AVAILABLE

A INTRODUCTION

17.01 An important task for a solicitor is to assist the parties in settling their financial and property affairs so that the family assets are fairly distributed following the dissolution of the marriage or civil partnership.

17.02 It is rare for the parties to have sorted out all such matters satisfactorily before separation. Subsequent negotiations may lead to an agreement to be embodied in a consent order as a record of the settlement—this can be extremely cost effective.

17.03 Where agreement cannot be reached, however, it will be necessary to commence proceedings for ancillary relief orders, that is, for orders dealing with income, property, and other capital assets and, most importantly today, pensions.

17.04 This chapter explains the forms of ancillary relief orders which are available in divorce proceedings and their principal characteristics.

17.05 The position on dissolution of a civil partnership is considered in Chapter 14 and summarized at the end of this chapter.

B MAINTENANCE PENDING SUIT: S. 22, MATRIMONIAL CAUSES ACT 1973

The nature of maintenance pending suit

17.06 An order for periodical payments in favour of a party to a marriage can only become effective once a final decree has been granted in the proceedings, be it proceedings for divorce, nullity, or judicial separation. However, it is quite likely that one or other spouse will be in financial difficulties as a result of the breakdown of the marriage and will not be able to wait for money until after a final decree has been granted. Maintenance pending suit exists therefore to bridge the gap between the commencement of the proceedings and final determination of the proceedings and is essentially a temporary measure. The order will be for the regular payment of a sum of money by one spouse to the other normally at weekly or monthly intervals.

17.07 An order can be made so that the applicant is able to pay legal fees, since these are 'recurring' expenses of an income nature and come within the meaning of 'maintenance': *A* v *A (Maintenance Pending Suit: Provision for Legal Fees)* [2001] 1 FLR 377 and confirmed in *G* v *G (Maintenance Pending Suit: Costs)* [2003] 2 FLR 71. Another example of the court awarding a significant sum (£33,000 per annum plus school fees) by way of maintenance pending suit is *M* v *M (Maintenance Pending Suit)* [2002] 2 FLR 123.

Who can apply?

17.08 Either party to the marriage can apply. It is immaterial whether they are the petitioner or the respondent in the proceedings.

17.09 Applications cannot be made by or on behalf of children. This is because they are not necessary—in contrast to the position in relation to periodical payments for the parties, periodical payments can be granted to or for a child of the family at any time after the petition is filed to become effective immediately, but it is now much more likely that financial support for children will be dealt with by a maintenance calculation carried out by the Child Support Agency, or by a maintenance agreement reached between the parties.

When available

The court can make an order for maintenance pending suit at any time after the petition has been filed until a final decree has been granted (i.e., decree absolute in divorce or nullity proceedings or the one and only decree in the case of judicial separation).   **17.10**

Duration of order

An order for maintenance pending suit can be made for such term as the court thinks reasonable beginning not earlier than the date of the presentation of the petition and ending with the determination of the suit (i.e., the decree of judicial separation or decree absolute of divorce or nullity or, in all cases, the dismissal of the suit). Orders for maintenance pending suit can therefore be back-dated from the date on which they are made as far as the date of presentation of the petition if the court thinks fit. Reference should be made to Chapter 18, paragraph 18.157 for the guidelines as to when the court will decide to back-date an order.   **17.11**

Maintenance pending suit distinguished from interim periodical payments

There is often confusion between maintenance pending suit and interim periodical payments. Whereas the former is ordered to tide a spouse over until such time as the court has power to make a periodical payments order and is only effective up to decree absolute, the latter is essentially a temporary periodical payments order in favour of a spouse or a child made at a time when the court *has* power to order periodical payments but is not yet in a position to make a final decision on the appropriate rate (for example, because the respondent's accounts are still in the course of preparation or the court does not have an appointment available for a full ancillary relief hearing). Interim periodical payments are dealt with more fully at paragraph 17.84 and onwards.   **17.12**

C   LONG-TERM ORDERS: SS. 23, 24, AND 24B, MATRIMONIAL CAUSES ACT 1973

Orders available

The following long-term ancillary relief orders are available: **17.13**

(a) financial provision orders (s. 23), i.e., periodical payments, secured periodical payments, and lump sums (including pension attachment orders under ss. 25B and 25C);
(b) property adjustment orders (s. 24), i.e., transfer of property, settlement of property, and variation of settlement;
(c) pension sharing orders under s. 24B.

In whose favour

Parties to the marriage

17.14 As a general rule the court can make any of the orders listed at paragraph 17.13 above in favour of a party to the marriage. However, pension sharing orders are not available in proceedings for a decree of judicial separation (s. 24B (1)).

Children of the family

17.15 Subject to certain age limits, the court may also make any of the orders listed at paragraph 17.13 in favour of a child of the family (defined in Chapter 8, paragraph 8.22). This does not necessarily mean that the child will receive money or property directly into his own hands. The court can order the payment of money or transfer of property to someone else for the benefit of the child.

17.16 A detailed account of the impact of the Child Support Act 1991 ('CSA 1991'), as amended, is set out in Chapter 20, but it should be noted at this stage that although the court retains power to make lump sum and property adjustment orders in favour of children of the family, generally speaking, the court no longer has power to make a periodical payments order in favour of such a child (see s. 8, CSA 1991). However, there are some exceptions to this, the most important being the power of the court to make a periodical payments order in favour of a child of the family who is not the natural child of the prospective payer. There are some other important exceptions fully set out in Chapter 20.

17.17 The age limits on orders for children are set out in s. 29, Matrimonial Causes Act 1973 ('MCA 1973'). The general rule is that no financial provision or transfer of property order shall be made in favour of a child who has attained the age of 18 (s. 29(1)). However, by virtue of s. 29(3) orders can be made for children who are 18 or over if either:

(a) The child is or will be (or if a financial provision order or transfer of property order were made would be) receiving instruction at an educational establishment or undergoing training for a trade, profession or vocation whether or not he is also (or will also be) in gainful employment.

> **Example** The parents of a child are divorced. At the age of 18 the child goes to university. A periodical payments order can be made in her favour as she is receiving instruction at an educational establishment.

(b) There are special circumstances justifying the making of an order.

> **Example** Bernard is a child of the family. He is 20 but he suffers from Down's syndrome and he has a mental age of about 6. He lives with his mother, the petitioner. The court can order the respondent to make financial provision for Bernard or to transfer property to him on the basis that there are special circumstances.

Note that there is no age limit on the making of orders requiring a settlement of property to be made for the benefit of a child or varying a settlement for the benefit of a child. Further, there appears to be no upper age limit on the payment of maintenance for the benefit of a child of the family provided that the conditions laid down in s. 29(3) are met.

The nature of the orders

Periodical payments (s. 23(1)(a) and (d), Matrimonial Causes Act 1973)

An order for periodical payments will be for the payment of a regular sum of money by one **17.18** spouse to the other or to or for a child of the family (where the court retains jurisdiction), normally at weekly or monthly intervals.

Secured periodical payments (s. 23(1)(b) and (e), Matrimonial Causes Act 1973)

Having decided that a spouse or a child of the family (where the court retains jurisdiction) is **17.19** entitled to periodical payments, the court may feel that it is necessary to take steps in advance to ensure that he will actually receive the sum ordered and will not be burdened with problems over enforcement. This can be done by means of a secured periodical payments order.

The way in which a secured order operates varies from case to case depending on the exact **17.20** terms of the order and the assets used as security. In some cases, the assets serving as security produce an income which is used to pay the periodical payments ordered. In other cases, assets which do not produce an income are used as security. The idea in cases of the second type is that the spouse against whom the order is made, let us say the husband, makes the periodical payments from his own income in the normal way, but if he defaults the assets stand charged with the amount of the unpaid periodical payments which the wife can therefore be sure of recovering by enforcing her charge.

Example 1 (income-producing assets). The court orders the husband to secure to the wife the annual sum of £5,000 upon his entire shareholding in three companies. The income by way of dividends from the shares is used to provide the wife with the annual sum of £5,000. If the husband paid the maintenance from other sources of income, the dividend income would continue to belong to him.

Example 2 (assets which do not produce income). The court orders the husband to secure to the wife the annual sum of £5,000 to be charged upon the freehold property Rose Cottage, Lake View, Gullswater (the husband's holiday cottage). As long as the husband pays the wife the annual sum of £5,000, the holiday property will be unaffected. Should he default at any stage, the amount of the arrears will form a charge over the property which the wife can seek to realize by forcing a sale of the property.

While the order for secured periodical payments is in force, the husband cannot dispose of the assets forming the security. Indeed, in a case such as Example 1, he may feel that the court might as well have ordered him to transfer the assets to the wife outright as he may be deprived of all the benefits of owning the property while the order is in force if the entire income is required for the payment of the secured order.

However, secured periodical payments do have the important advantage for the husband **17.21** that once the secured order comes to an end the assets revert to him to do with as he pleases.

In reality, secured periodical payments orders are rarely made, save in cases of consider- **17.22** able wealth or where there is evidence of persistent non-payment of maintenance in the past.

Lump sums (s. 23(1)(c) and (f), Matrimonial Causes Act 1973)

17.23 A lump sum order is, as its name suggests, an order for the payment of a specified sum of money. Payment of the whole sum at once may be required or the payment of the lump sum can be extended over a period of time as the court has the power to provide for payment by way of instalments (s. 23(3)(c)), as was demonstrated in *R* v *R (Lump Sum: Repayments)* [2004] 1 FLR 928 where the husband was ordered to make lump sum payments of £30,000 immediately together with 240 monthly instalments in a sum equivalent to the wife's obligations under a 20-year mortgage. Such an arrangement would survive any remarriage by the wife (because it related to the payment of a capital sum) and would be varied, if necessary, under s. 31(2)(d), MCA 1973.

17.24 The court can order that the payment of the instalments be secured to the satisfaction of the court (s. 23(3)(c)). Security will be provided in the same way as with secured periodical payments (see paragraph 17.19).

17.25 If the lump sum is not to be paid in full immediately (for example, where it is to be paid in instalments or where the payer is given a period of time to raise it), the court can order that the amount deferred or the instalments shall bear interest at a rate specified by the court and for a period specified by the court not commencing earlier than the date of the order (s. 23(6)). When obtaining an order for a lump sum payment within a specified time limit, consideration should be given to the inclusion of a clause requiring the payment of interest in the event of default, as provided for by s. 23(6). A claim for interest should not be pursued, however, where the value of benefits (maintenance and housing costs) received under the interim provisions of the order exceed the value of interest which would otherwise be payable until the lump sum payment is made: *H* v *H (Lump Sum: Interest Payable)* [2006] 1 FLR 327.

17.26 It should be noted, however, that a lump sum order (or an order for sale under s. 24A, MCA 1973 of assets to produce the lump sum) cannot be made on an interim basis at a time when the application for ancillary relief has not been set down for a substantive hearing. A better course of action in such circumstances is to apply for an order under s. 17, Married Women's Property Act 1882 for a declaration as to ownership of property with an order for sale being available by virtue of s. 7(7), Matrimonial Causes (Property and Maintenance) Act 1958; *Wicks* v *Wicks* [1998] 1 FLR 470 (CA) (see Chapter 37).

17.27 In practice, a lump sum order is a very useful and flexible form of provision. It can, for example, be used to compensate one party for the transfer to the other party of his interest in the matrimonial home, the house contents, savings, investments, or an endowment policy.

17.28 It can also be used to enable one party to meet liabilities or expenses reasonably incurred in maintaining that party or a child of the family: s. 23(3), MCA 1973. Although only one lump sum may be ordered, and therefore it is important to ensure that it is for the correct amount, it may be intended that the lump sum is to fulfil a number of different *purposes*. For example, in *Duxbury* v *Duxbury* [1987] 1 FLR 7, the wife received a large lump sum which was intended, amongst other things, to provide funds for new accommodation and to be invested to provide her with an income. Similarly in *Hobhouse* v *Hobhouse* [1999] 1 FLR 961, a multipurpose lump sum order was made.

17.29 Further, where there is evidence that a periodical payments order will be disregarded a lump sum order may be made in order to put an end to the expensive process of enforcement: *Fournier* v *Fournier* [1998] 2 FLR 990.

Transfer of property (s. 24(1)(a), Matrimonial Causes Act 1973)

The court can order one spouse to transfer to the other spouse or to or for the benefit of the children any property to which he is entitled either in possession or reversion. Transfer of property orders are most commonly used in relation to the title to the family home, for example, where the court orders the husband to transfer the house from his sole name into the wife's name or, where the house is in joint names, to transfer his share in it to the wife. However, there are all sorts of other property which can also be made the subject of an order, for example, a car, furniture, a holiday cottage, a tenancy, title to a building held by one spouse as an investment and presently let, shares, and choses in action, for example, copyright.   **17.30**

Settlement of property (s. 24(1)(b), Matrimonial Causes Act 1973)

The court can order one spouse to settle property to which he is entitled for the benefit of the other spouse or the children. One example of the use of this power is the making of a *Mesher* type of order ordering that the family home be held on a trust of land, the house not to be sold until the youngest child reaches 17.   **17.31**

The power could also be used, for example, to order one spouse to set up a trust fund out of capital perhaps to benefit the wife for life or until remarriage and thereafter for the children or alternatively for the wife for life and thereafter to revert to the husband.   **17.32**

Variation of settlement (s. 24(1)(c) and (d), Matrimonial Causes Act 1973)

The court can vary for the benefit of the parties or of the children of the family any ante-nuptial or post-nuptial settlement made on the parties to the marriage (including such settlement made by will or codicil). Where property is bought in contemplation of marriage during the parties' engagement and is subsequently used as the family home, it is likely to be regarded as being subject to an ante-nuptial settlement which will not be affected by an intervening tenancy: *N* v *N and F Trust* [2006] 1 FLR 856.   **17.33**

Variation of a post-nuptial settlement can include, for example, varying the terms of a trust to give the wife 30 per cent of the husband's shares in a company which formed the basis of the trust: *C* v *C (Variations of Post-nuptial Settlement: Company Shares)* [2003] 2 FLR 493.   **17.34**

Furthermore, the interest of either spouse in such a settlement can be extinguished or reduced.   **17.35**

Pensions in ancillary relief proceedings

Introduction   After the family home, the most valuable asset which a party to a marriage is likely to have is his or her pension.   **17.36**

Despite long recognition that the courts ought to be able to redistribute the pension asset in ancillary relief proceedings where a decree of divorce or nullity had been granted, until recently the courts have had few powers to do so. Until 1 August 1996 when s. 166, Pensions Act 1995 came into force, the judiciary had to resort to strategies such as the readjustment of the ownership of other family assets to compensate for pension loss (as happened in *B* v *B*   **17.37**

[1989] 1 FLR 119 where Lincoln J awarded the wife a lump sum payment of £225,000 to purchase a home and held that when she no longer needed a large property she could sell, investing the surplus proceeds of sale to provide an income in old age).

17.38 The courts now have extensive powers to deal with the pension asset in ancillary relief proceedings: pension attachment orders were introduced on 1 August 1996 and pension sharing orders on 1 December 2000 (under provisions contained in the Welfare Reform and Pensions Act 1999 ('WRPA 1999'), amending the MCA 1973).

17.39 **Section 166, Pensions Act 1995** Section 166 of the 1995 Act amended the MCA 1973 by the addition of ss. 25B, 25C, and 25D. The chief characteristics of ss. 25B, 25C, and 25D are as follows:

(a) *The importance of the pension asset*
     Section 25B(1) states that the matters to which the court is to have regard under s. 25(2) (discussed fully in Chapter 19) include:
     (i)   any benefits under a pension arrangement which a party to the marriage has or is likely to have, and
     (ii) any benefits under a pension arrangement which, by reason of the dissolution or annulment of the marriage, a party to the marriage will lose the chance of acquiring.
     Thus the court's duty to give full consideration to pension rights is reinforced.
        Further, s. 25B(1) goes on to state that, in considering benefits under a pension arrangement, there is no requirement to consider only those benefits which will be available 'in the forseeable future'. Hence the court is permitted to take account of such benefits irrespective of the length of time before the pension becomes payable.

(b) *Pension attachment orders*
     When the court is exercising its powers under s. 23, MCA 1973 in proceedings for divorce, nullity, or judicial separation, it may order that *once the pension becomes payable* the person responsible for the pension arrangement (that is, the trustees or managers of the fund) pay part of the pension income and/or lump sum available under the pension to the other party to the marriage in question: s. 25B(4), MCA 1973. This means that one party may benefit from the other's pension long after the marriage is dissolved.
        This arrangement is known as a 'pension attachment order' and is a method of securing periodical payments and/or lump sum orders against a pension—it is not a separate form of ancillary relief but payment of the benefits is deferred until the pension becomes payable.
        It should be noted that, unlike the position with 'normal' periodical payments, payments of income derived from the pension are taxable in the hands of the recipient: s. 347A(2), Income and Corporation Taxes Act 1988.
        Many occupational pension schemes in particular provide for benefits to be paid if an employee dies prematurely before retirement. These benefits are called 'death in service benefits' and may also be attached: s. 25C(1), MCA 1973, thus providing some financial security for the surviving former spouse. It should be noted, however, that children may not specifically benefit from this kind of order.
        Further, the court may require the person with pension rights to nominate the other

party to the marriage as the person to whom death-in-service benefits should be paid: s. 25C(2)(b), MCA 1973 (but see *T* v *T* [1998] 1 FLR 1078 below).

There are, however, limits on the powers of the court. For example, the court may not attach a widow's or dependant's pension whether payable on death-in-service or following retirement.

It is important to understand that MCA 1973 contains no guidance as to the circumstances in which an attachment order would be appropriate nor as to the amount of the pension income, lump sum, or death-in-service benefits to be attached: this is entirely a matter for the court's discretion. The only restriction is that the amount to be attached must be expressed as a percentage of the payment due to the person with pension rights: s. 25B(5). This requirement also applies where the pension is already in payment.

(c) *Availability of pension attachment orders*

Pension attachment orders are not available if the petition for divorce, nullity or judicial separation was filed at court before 1 July 1996.

Case law developments on pension attachment orders   The first reported case on pen-   **17.40**
sion attachment orders was *T* v *T* [1998] 1 FLR 1072. The judgment of Singer J in the Family Division of the High Court is important because it clarifies a number of points, as follows:

(a)   The MCA 1973 does not compel the court to compensate for pension loss. The court's obligations are limited to considering whether orders for periodical payments, secured provision, or lump sum are appropriate and then to examine how pension considerations should affect the terms of the orders to be made.

(b)   The pension attachment order (whether in respect of pension income or lump sum or both) may be varied by a subsequent court order: s. 31(2)(dd), MCA 1973.

(c)   The order attaching the pension income will cease to have effect on the death or remarriage of the recipient. (It would appear that the lump sum order may remain payable, despite the remarriage of the recipient, but it would be open to the pension holder to seek to have this aspect of the order varied under s. 31(2)(dd), MCA 1973 on the grounds of a change in circumstances (namely the remarriage of the recipient) since the order was originally made.)

In *T* v *T*, Singer J refused to make attachment orders in respect of the husband's pensions on the grounds, first, that the former wife was receiving a substantial lump sum at the time of the ancillary relief proceedings and, secondly, she was to receive significant periodical payments which could be varied in due course.

The judge recognized, however, that the former wife would be prejudiced in the event   **17.41**
of the husband's premature death before retirement because the periodical payments would terminate. He accepted that the death-in-service benefits may not form part of the husband's estate and therefore would not be susceptible to an application by the wife for support under the Inheritance (Provision for Family and Dependants) Act 1975. He also acknowledged that to require the husband to nominate his former wife as the beneficiary of death-in-service benefits might not be effective since the trustees had a discretion to disregard the nomination.

The judge, therefore, protected the income position of the former wife by making an   **17.42**
attachment order in respect of death-in-service benefits by requiring the trustees of the

pension fund to pay to the wife a lump sum equal to ten times the annual maintenance in the event of the husband's premature death.

17.43 By contrast, in *Burrow* v *Burrow* [1999] 1 FLR 508, Cazalet J upheld the attachment order relating to the lump sum to be derived from the pension arrangement while setting aside a similar order made by the district judge in respect of the pension income.

17.44 The judge considered that the lump sum order recognized past contributions made by the parties by ensuring an equal division of the capital assets. He held that the attachment order in respect of the pension income was unnecessary because the wife was to retain her entitlement to periodical payments in any event. Accordingly, once the pension became payable and the needs of the parties were known, the periodical payments order could then be varied, if required.

17.45 In this case, the judge went on to state that there was no need to provide for the attachment of death-in-service benefits because the wife retained an insurance scheme to protect her and, in addition, her potential claim against the husband's estate had also been preserved.

17.46 The drafting of pension attachment orders is complex and care needs to be taken to ensure that the recipient is as fully protected as possible. This is discussed fully in Chapter 18.

17.47 **The problems with pension attachment orders**   Pension attachment orders involve a number of practical difficulties, including, in particular:

(a) The arrangements undermine the principle of once and for all settlements embodied in clean break orders (because of the continuing commitment to make provision once the pension becomes payable).

(b) Attachment is necessarily a speculative exercise since it will usually be impossible to predict either the respective needs of the parties at the time the pension becomes payable, or the value of the asset to be divided, these difficulties being highlighted by Cazalet J in *Burrow* v *Burrow* (1999) discussed above.

(c) Where the attachment order relates to a private or money purchase pension scheme (where, for example, a self-employed individual is contributing to a scheme to provide a pension in retirement) the court has few, if any, powers to ensure that the individual continues to contribute to the scheme or retires by a specified age.

In practice, pension attachment orders have proved to be unpopular and will probably only be considered where the pension fund is of little value at the time of the ancillary relief proceedings but is expected to increase significantly in value by the date of retirement.

17.48 **The solution: pension sharing orders**   A better solution to dealing with the pension asset, is to enable the court to make an order sharing the pension asset *at the time* of the ancillary relief proceedings. Such arrangements are now contained in the WRPA 1999, which came into force on 1 December 2000 (Welfare Reform and Pensions Act 1999) (Commencement No. 8) Order 2000 (SI 2000/1116).

17.49 Section 19 of the 1999 Act states that sch. 3 amends the MCA 1973 to enable the court to make pension sharing orders. Further, sch. 4 to the 1999 Act amends the MCA 1973 in respect of attachment orders.

The definition of a pension sharing order is found in s. 21A(1), MCA 1973 which provides as   **17.50**
follows:

(1)   A pension sharing order is an order which:
    (a)   provides that one party's
        (i)   shareable rights under a specified pension arrangement, or
        (ii)   shareable state scheme rights
      be subject to pension sharing for the benefit of the other party, and
    (b)   specifies the percentage value to be transferred.

The principal features of the pension sharing order: s. 24B, MCA 1973   **17.51**

(a)   The order is not available retrospectively and is therefore only available where the petition for divorce or nullity is filed at court on or after 1 December 2000.

(b)   The order may not be made in proceedings for a decree of judicial separation: s. 24B(1), MCA 1973.

(c)   The order will not take effect before the grant of the decree absolute: s. 24B(2), MCA 1973.

(d)   The order may be varied but only *before* the decree absolute has been granted: s. 31(2)(g), MCA 1973. The order will not then take effect until the application to vary has been dealt with.

(e)   While pension sharing orders will be available in respect of occupational, personal, state earnings related pension schemes, and second state pension schemes (due to replace SERPS under the Child Support, Pensions and Social Security Act 2000) (all of which are 'pension arrangements' under s. 46(1), WRPA 1999), the basic state pension scheme may not be the subject of an order.

A pension sharing order may not be made in respect of a pension already subject to a pension sharing order in relation to the marriage in question (i.e. it is not possible for a pension sharing order to be made on two occasions to benefit the same party to the marriage); nor may a pension sharing order be made in any event where the pension is already subject to an attachment order: s. 24B(4) and (5), MCA 1973. To do otherwise would prejudice the party who is to benefit from the attachment order.

(f)   It is not possible for a party to a marriage to have both a pension sharing order and attachment order in respect of the *same* pension. Hence, where a party to a marriage obtains a pension sharing order, there can be no attachment of death-in-service benefits in respect of the same pension under s. 25C (as happened in *T* v *T*, discussed above). This fact may make it more sensible to seek a pension attachment order in certain circumstances, for example, where the dependant former spouse is caring for young children and death-in-service benefits would help to compensate for the loss of periodical payments on the premature death of the paying former spouse.

(g)   The question of whether to seek a pension sharing order is complex, and the involvement of an independent financial adviser will be crucial to determine the best solution in the circumstances. Such an adviser must have the G60 qualification in order to conduct pension transfer business. A suitable IFA may be found by contacting the Society of Financial Advisers (SOFA), 20 Aldermanbury, London EC2V 7HY (tel. 020 7417 4798).

The pension sharing order in practice   This book cannot discuss in detail the complexities   **17.52**

of pension sharing in practice and practitioners are referred to specialist texts such as *Pension Sharing in Practice* by David Salter, Family Law (2003). However, set out below is an introduction to the mechanics of the pension sharing order.

17.53 When the court decides to make a pension sharing order, the transferor's pension scheme will be debited with a specified amount and the transferee will be entitled to a credit of that amount. In essence, the transferor loses a percentage of his or her pension fund which is reduced in value and the transferee acquires a pension fund of his or her own.

17.54 As with any other form of ancillary relief, no obligation is placed on the court to make a pension sharing order nor is there any guidance in the MCA 1973, as amended, as to the circumstances in which the order will be made nor as to the percentage of the fund to be debited. These are matters for judicial discretion, bearing in mind the factors to be considered in s. 25, MCA 1973 which are discussed fully in Chapter 19.

17.55 The percentage of the fund to be debited is a percentage of the cash equivalent of the transferor's relevant benefits on the valuation date. The 'valuation date' is to be specified by the court, but the date must not be earlier than one year before the date of the petition nor later than the date on which the court is exercising its power: reg. 3(1)(a) and (b), Pensions on Divorce (Provision of Information) Regulations 2000 (SI 2000/1048).

17.56 When a pension sharing order is made the person responsible for pension arrangements (i.e. the trustees or managers of the scheme) are given a period of time in which to transfer the specified percentage of the fund. This is known as 'the implementation period' and is four months beginning on the date on which the order takes effect or on the day on which the trustee receives the order and prescribed information, whichever is the later. The prescribed information is contained in reg. 5 of the Pensions on Divorce (Provision of Information) Regulations 2000. The information includes names and addresses of the parties concerned, dates of birth, national insurance numbers etc.; all relevant information to enable the person responsible to carry out the necessary transfer.

17.57 The transferee receives a pension credit. The transferee cannot receive 'cash in hand' to spend as he or she pleases. The intention behind the legislation is to provide the transferee with some degree of security in old age.

17.58 Schedule 5, WRPA 1999 explains what may happen to the transferred fund. Essentially, where the pension arrangement is a *funded* occupational pension scheme or a personal pension scheme, the trustee for the scheme is required to offer to transfer the fund to a scheme of the transferee's choice. This scheme could be the one of which the transferee is already a member so that the effect of the transfer will be to boost the value of his or her fund. Alternatively, the transferee could become a member of the original scheme so that an internal transfer takes place. If the transferee fails to make a choice within a specified period, the trustee will decide on the destination of the pension credit.

17.59 Where the pension arrangement is unfunded (that is where the present contributors to the scheme are in effect paying the pensions of those retired from the scheme) and is a public service pension scheme, external transfer is not permitted for obvious reasons. However, where the scheme in question has been closed to new members, the transferee will be offered membership of an alternative public service scheme.

Where the pension arrangement is unfunded but is not a public service scheme, the person **17.60** responsible for the administration of the scheme has an absolute right to insist on an internal transfer: external transfer is available in limited circumstances laid down in the Pensions Sharing (Implementation and Discharge) Regulations 2000 (SI 2000/1053).

It would appear that there will be few opportunities for the transferor, who has suffered a **17.61** pension debit, to replenish his or her pension fund because of the limitations on pension contributions imposed by the Inland Revenue.

Where the pension sharing order relates to the state earnings related pension scheme, the **17.62** position is governed by s. 49(1), WRPA 1999. Put simply the transferor's entitlement is reduced by the amount of the debit and the transferee becomes entitled to an additional pension because of the pension credit which has been transferred to him or her.

The statutory charge and pension orders   Where either an attachment order or pension **17.63** sharing order is made, a lump sum may in effect be transferred from one party to the marriage to the other. The question then arises as to whether the statutory charge may attach to the lump sum. The basic position is as follows. An attachment order in respect of pension income will be exempt since it is regarded as a form of maintenance. However, an attachment order in respect of a lump sum is not exempt from the statutory charge which will apply assuming that the other conditions are fulfilled (e.g. that the assisted person has 'recovered' or 'preserved' the asset). However, interest will not accrue from the date of the order because the charge has not been postponed. The charge and interest will apply only once the lump sum has been received. Because the Legal Services Commission has nothing on which to secure the charge in the meantime, it is difficult for it to protect its position and therefore the Commission will look to satisfy the charge from other assets which may have been recovered or preserved. If the other assets are inadequate to meet the charge, notice in writing of the Commission's interest in the lump sum must be given to the person responsible for the pension arrangement.

By contrast, guidance issued by the Legal Services Commission, following advice from coun- **17.64** sel, makes it clear that a lump sum received by way of a pension sharing order is exempt from the statutory charge.

Offsetting   The amendments to MCA 1973, set out above, demonstrate the extensive **17.65** powers now available to the court in dealing with the pension asset.

Do not fall into the trap, however, of believing that in every case where there is a pension **17.66** asset in ancillary relief proceedings a pension order will be made. Often, the client with valuable pension rights will be anxious to preserve those rights intact and, where this is the case, will offer to the other party to the marriage other capital assets (e.g. the family home and/or other investments and savings) to compensate for the loss of a share of the pension— this is called an 'offsetting order' and is very common in practice. Care should be taken with orders of this kind, however. Where offsetting is planned, it must be remembered that the pension asset is very different from other capital assets in that the party with pension rights has little control over the final value of the pension fund or how it is invested to provide him or her with a lump sum or income in retirement (usually a significant part of the fund must be used to purchase an annuity).

17.67 Further, even with a final salary pension scheme (where benefits depend on length of service and the individual's salary at retirement) the pension fund may suffer a shortfall and be unable to produce the anticipated benefits. It is essential therefore to try, as far as possible, to ascertain the viability of the client's pension provision before embarking on an offsetting arrangement and to ensure that the pension asset is not valued unrealistically.

When are the orders for ancillary relief available?

In favour of a spouse

17.68 **The basic rules** All the orders set out in paragraph 17.13 above can be made in favour of a spouse on granting a decree nisi of divorce or nullity or a decree of judicial separation (except that an order under s. 24B, MCA 1973 cannot be made in proceedings for a decree of judicial separation) or at any time thereafter (s. 23(1) and s. 24(1)). Note that the fact that orders can be made at any time after granting a decree means that there are no time-limits on the making of an application for ancillary relief. Therefore a spouse could, at least in theory, make an application for ancillary relief out of the blue 10 years after the divorce or could suddenly decide to pursue an application made in the initial stages of the divorce which has been allowed to go to sleep for years. This is confirmed in *Twiname* v *Twiname* [1992] 1 FLR 29 (CA). In practice there are a number of reasons why this is unlikely to be profitable and may indeed be impossible:

(a) Rule 2.53(1), Family Proceedings Rules 1991, ('FPR 1991') dictates that all the petitioner's applications for ancillary relief must be made in her petition and all the respondent's applications in his answer if he files one (see Chapter 18, paragraph 18.41 and onwards). If an application is not made as required by r. 2.53(1), permission of the court will be needed before it can be made and the passage of time between the beginning of the suit and the application for permission will increasingly influence the court against granting permission.

(b) If the court first comes to consider an application for ancillary relief an unusually long time after the parties have been granted a final decree, it will be influenced adversely by the lapse of time in exercising its discretion as to what orders to make. The court will certainly want to know how the applicant has supported him or herself in the meantime and what has prompted the application at this time.

(c) Repeat applications for ancillary relief are not possible (see below).

Orders made on or after granting a decree nisi of divorce or nullity cannot take effect until the decree is made absolute (s. 23(5) and s. 24(3)). The gap between the commencement of the suit and the final decree is filled by maintenance pending suit (see paragraph 17.06 above). Orders made on or after granting a decree of judicial separation can become effective immediately.

17.69 **Repeat applications** Once the court has dealt with an application for ancillary relief on its merits (i.e., by making an order of the type sought or by dismissing the application), it has usually no future jurisdiction to entertain applications by that spouse for the same sort of ancillary relief. The most that the court can do is to vary or discharge the original order (if it is an order which is capable of variation—see, for example, *Minton* v *Minton* [1979] AC 591) but in doing so the court may now commute a periodical payments order by a single lump sum payment, a property adjustment order, and/or a pension sharing order: sch. 8, paras. 16(5)(a), (6)(b), and (7), Family Law Act 1996, brought into force with retrospective effect on 1 November 1998 by SI 1998/2572 and discussed more fully in Chapter 23.

Example 1 The petitioner makes a comprehensive prayer for ancillary relief in her petition. After the divorce the court orders that the family home should be transferred to her absolutely and that all her other claims to ancillary relief should be dismissed. The petitioner cannot come back to the court in two years' time when she has lost her job and is short of money asking for periodical payments or indeed for any other form of ancillary relief against the respondent. The court dealt with her application for all forms of ancillary relief on its merits after the divorce; she cannot revive the claims that were then dismissed and the one order that she was granted, being a transfer of property order, is not variable.

Example 2 The petitioner makes a comprehensive prayer for ancillary relief in her petition. After the divorce the court orders that the respondent should make periodical payments at the rate of £100 per week for the petitioner. As the respondent has no capital assets what-soever the petitioner's other claims for ancillary relief are dismissed. A year after the order the respondent has a substantial win on the lottery and the petitioner wishes to claim a share. She cannot do so as her claims for a lump sum and for property adjustment orders have been dismissed. The best she can do is to seek a variation of the periodical payments order under s. 31, MCA 1973 and invite the court, if appropriate, to terminate the periodical payments order and replace it with a lump sum, property adjustment order, and/or pension sharing order, if appropriate.

The fact that the court's original order was made by consent does not affect the principles governing repeat applications (see, for example, *Minton* v *Minton* above).

There are two ways round the rule about repeat applications: **17.70**

(a) If it appears that one spouse may come into a worthwhile sum of money (as yet of an uncertain amount) in the not-too-distant future, instead of the court pressing on to deal with the other spouse's application for ancillary relief immediately after the divorce, it would be possible (at her suggestion) for the court to adjourn some or all of her ancillary relief applications to be heard at a later date when the position is clearer. In the case of *M T* v *M T (Financial Provision: Lump Sum)* [1992] 1 FLR 362, the court considered the line of cases dealing with the adjournment of ancillary relief cases. It was held that on an application for a lump sum order in circumstances where there was a real possibility of capital from a specific source becoming available in the near future, and where an order for an adjournment was the only means whereby justice could be done to the parties, there was a discretionary jurisdiction to order an adjournment of the application. On the unusual facts of *M T* v *M T* (above) the wife's lump sum application was adjourned until the death of her then 83-year-old father-in-law since at that time the husband would have real prospects of inheriting substantial wealth (under German law, amount-ing to at least one-eighth of his father's estate), and otherwise the wife would be permanently without capital to buy even a modest property.

  More recently in *D* v *D (Lump Sum Order: Adjournment of Application)* [2001] 1 FLR 633, for example, the wife's application for a lump sum order to invest in a pension fund was adjourned until assets could be disposed of to produce the necessary capital. It is likely, however, that the court will only adjourn the ancillary relief proceedings for a limited period of time—in *Roberts* v *Roberts* [1986] 1 WLR 1437, Wood J indicated that the longest period a court should adjourn an application should be four to five years.

(b) Where one spouse, say the petitioner, seeks periodical payments against the other but a periodical payments order is not appropriate in the light of the parties' financial circumstances at the date of the hearing, instead of permanently debarring the petitioner from seeking periodical payments against the respondent by dismissing her claim, the court can preserve her entitlement to periodical payments in the future by making a nominal order for periodical payments against the respondent. This is an order for the payment of a nominal sum (5 pence/50 pence/£1 per annum) to the petitioner by way of periodical payments which the petitioner can seek to have varied under s. 31 to a worthwhile sum should circumstances change in the future.

Example When the petitioner's application for periodical payments is considered the respondent is out of work through no fault of his own. The petitioner is tied to the house with young children and cannot work. If the respondent were working, a periodical payments order would clearly be appropriate. The court can make an order for nominal periodical payments to the petitioner which she can seek to have increased when the respondent gets a job.

Nominal orders used to be made almost as a matter of course not only where the respondent was presently unable to make periodical payments because of his financial circumstances but also where the petitioner was not at the time in need of periodical payments because of her circumstances, for example, where she was working.

Further, where an attachment order is made in respect of pension income, it must be supported by a periodical payments order under s. 23, MCA 1973 even if the sum involved is nominal. It should be recognized, however, that in recent years courts have come to think more in terms of a clean break order between the parties where the parties can work. This approach is reinforced by the provisions of s. 25A, MCA 1973 (see Chapter 19). A clean break order is one where the parties' claims against each other are dealt with on a once and for all basis, in such a way that neither is allowed to return to the court in the future in an attempt to vary or revive an earlier claim.

In favour of a child of the family

17.71 (a) *Financial provision orders* These can be made in favour of a child of the family in certain circumstances at any stage after the commencement of the proceedings (s. 23(1) coupled with s. 23(2)(a)). Section 23(4) expressly provides that the power to make financial provision orders for a child can be exercised from time to time. Unlike the position with regard to spouses, therefore, an application for financial provision for a child can never be finally dismissed and repeat applications for financial provision orders can be made provided that the child concerned is still within the age limits for the order sought (see paragraph 17.17 above).

Even if the petition is dismissed, provided that this happens after the beginning of the trial, the court can make financial provision orders in relation to a child of the family on dismissing the petition or within a reasonable period after dismissal (s. 23(2)(b)). This is not possible in the case of an application for an order in favour of a spouse.

(b) *Property adjustment orders* These can be made for the benefit of a child of the family on granting a decree nisi of divorce or nullity or a decree of judicial separation or at any time thereafter. As there is no express power to make such orders from time to time, it would appear that the child is in the same position as a spouse in relation to repeat applications—once the child's application has been dealt with on its merits no further application for an order of the same type can be made.

Orders made on or after a decree of judicial separation become effective immediately. Orders made on or after granting a decree nisi of nullity or divorce do not take effect until the decree is made absolute (s. 24(3)).

Who can make the application

Parties to the marriage

Either party to the marriage can apply for any of the orders listed in paragraph 17.13 above **17.72** on behalf of himself or herself or on behalf of a child of the family.

Children of the family

Where he has been given permission to intervene in the cause for the purpose of applying **17.73** for ancillary relief, the child himself can apply for any of the orders listed in paragraph 17.13 (r. 2.54(1)(f), FPR 1991).

Others on behalf of a child

Apart from the parties to the marriage and the child himself, there are various other people **17.74** empowered by r. 2.54(1), FPR 1991 to apply for ancillary relief in respect of a child of the family, for example, the child's guardian or any person in whose favour a residence order has been made with respect to a child of the family.

Duration of periodical payments and secured periodical payments order (ss. 28 and 29, Matrimonial Causes Act 1973)

In favour of a spouse

Subject to s. 25A(2) (duty of court to consider making order for fixed term only, see below in **17.75** this paragraph and also Chapter 19, paragraph 19.20 and onwards), an order for periodical payments or secured periodical payments for a spouse can last for whatever period the court thinks fit with these limitations:

(a) Commencement of the term: the term shall not begin earlier than the date of the making of an application for the order (s. 28(1)(a)). This provision enables the court, if it sees fit, to back-date its order for periodical payments or secured periodical payments to the date of the making of the application (see Chapter 18, paragraph 18.157 for guidelines in relation to back-dating of orders). A petitioner's application will normally have been made in her petition and the court therefore has the power to back-date an order in her favour to the date of the presentation of the petition.

If the respondent files an answer he will normally make his claim for periodical payments in his answer. The FPR 1991 do not lay down rules as to when a respondent who does not file an answer should make his application for ancillary relief (see Chapter 18, paragraph 18.46 and onwards). His application will be made at whatever stage in the proceedings his solicitor sees fit by filing a notice of application in Form A and an order for periodical payments or secured periodical payments can be back-dated to the date on which this notice was filed.

(b) End of the term: the court cannot make an order for a term defined so as to extend beyond:

    (i) The remarriage of the party in whose favour the order is made (this provision applies only, of course, to cases of divorce and nullity as remarriage is clearly out of the question in a case of judicial separation). Note that remarriage of the paying spouse will not have any direct effect on the periodical payments or secured periodical payments order. However, where the paying spouse remarries this may constitute a change in his circumstances that would justify his making an application for a reduction in the rate of the order (see Chapter 23 with regard to variation). *Or*

    (ii) In the case of an unsecured periodical payments order, the death of either of the parties to the marriage, or, in the case of a secured periodical payments order, the death of the spouse in whose favour the order is made. (Note that in contrast to a straightforward order for periodical payments, a secured order can continue beyond the death of the paying spouse.)

Subject to these limitations the court can leave the periodical payments order open-ended if it thinks fit. On the other hand, the court can make the order for a limited period of time. The court has always been able to do this but s. 25A, MCA 1973 draws particular attention to this power by directing the court, when exercising its power to make periodical payments orders in favour of a spouse, to consider whether it would be appropriate to make the order only for a limited period such as would be sufficient to enable the payee to adjust to being self-supporting.

17.76   Where the court makes such an order in favour of a party to the marriage, it may direct that that party shall not be entitled to apply under s. 31 for the order to be varied by extending the term (s. 28(1A)).

Example ('Open-ended' order.) 'It is ordered that the respondent do make periodical payments to the petitioner for herself during their joint lives until she shall remarry or until further order at the rate of £x per week payable weekly in advance.'

Example ('Fixed term' order.) 'It is ordered that the respondent do make periodical payments to the petitioner for herself at the rate of £x per month payable monthly in advance for a period of one year from the date of this order or during their joint lives or until the petitioner shall remarry or until further order whichever period shall be the shortest. And it is directed that the petitioner's right to make any further application in relation to the marriage of the petitioner and the respondent for an order under s. 23(1)(a) and (b) of the MCA 1973, shall stand dismissed'.

The case of *Richardson* v *Richardson* [1993] 4 All ER 673 is a warning to all practitioners to ensure that where the periodical payments order is intended to be of limited duration, the order contains a clause expressly prohibiting the payee from seeking to extend the term. Failure to include such a clause will mean that the court retains jurisdiction to vary the order, although it may impose a time limit on the extended order: *Richardson* v *Richardson (No. 2)* [1996] 2 FLR 617 (CA).

17.77   In practice, however, recent case law suggests that the court will be unlikely to extend an order where the payer has a legitimate expectation that his obligation to make periodical payments will end by a specified date unless the circumstances are exceptional: *Fleming v Fleming* [2004] 1 FLR 667.

Special provisions with regard to children

Section 29(2) provides that the term specified in a periodical payments or secured periodical **17.78** payments order in favour of a child (in cases where the court retains jurisdiction despite the CSA 1991) may begin with the date of the making of the application or at any later date (so back-dating is possible), but:

(a) shall not extend, in the first instance, beyond the child's next birthday after he attains school-leaving age unless the court considers that in the circumstances of the case the welfare of the child requires that it should extend to a later date. As the present school-leaving age is 16 this means that when first granted most periodical payments orders will be expressed to be 'until the said child shall attain the age of 17 years or further order'. If it is clear that the child will not be leaving education at the first possible opportunity, for example, where it is certain that the children will be staying on at school to do A-levels, the court should be asked specifically to grant the order to last until the child is 18 instead. *And*

(b) shall not in any event extend beyond the date of the child's eighteenth birthday unless s. 29(3) applies. Reference should be made to paragraph 17.17 above for the full provisions of s. 29(3). Basically it enables the court to make orders in favour of children who are over 18 if they are being educated or there are special circumstances.

The death of the paying spouse will bring a periodical payments order in favour of a child to **17.79** an end unless it is secured (s. 29(4)). Remarriage of either spouse will not affect orders in favour of a child.

D ORDERS FOR SALE: S. 24A, MATRIMONIAL CAUSES ACT 1973

The power to order sale

Where the court makes: (a) a secured periodical payments order; (b) a lump sum order; (c) a **17.80** property adjustment order, on making the order or at any time thereafter the court may make a further order for the sale of property in which or in the proceeds of sale of which either or both of the parties to the marriage has or have a beneficial interest either in possession or reversion.

Consequential and supplementary provisions

The sale order may contain whatever consequential or supplementary provisions the court **17.81** thinks fit (s. 24A(2)). Two forms of consequential or supplementary provision are specially mentioned in the subsection:

(a) A requirement that a payment be made out of the proceeds of sale (s. 24A(2)(a)) (for an example of this, see Example 2 at paragraph 17.83 below); *and*

(b) A requirement that the property be offered for sale to a particular person or class of persons specified in the order (s. 24A(2)(b)).

Directions as to the conduct of the sale (for example, as to whose solicitor should be in charge of the conveyancing and how the sale price is to be fixed) can be given under the s. 24A(2) power and will usually be necessary.

When effective

17.82 (a) Not before decree absolute: if an order for sale is made before decree absolute, it will not become effective until after the decree is made absolute (s. 24A(3)).
   (b) Suspended orders: the court can specifically direct that the order (or a particular provision of it) shall not take effect until a particular event has occurred or a specified period has elapsed.

Examples

17.83 (a) Order for sale enabling capital provision to be made: the order for sale may be made at the same time as the secured periodical payments, lump sum or property adjustment order, timed to take effect before it as an enabling measure.

Example 1 The court orders that the matrimonial home which is in the respondent's name be sold (the s. 24A(1) order) and a sum equal to half the net proceeds of sale be paid by the respondent to the petitioner (a lump sum order).

   (b) Order for sale as an enforcement measure: alternatively the spouse in whose favour a secured periodical payments, lump sum or property adjustment order has been made already may need to return to court for an order for sale as a means of enforcement if the original order has not been complied with.

Example 2 The court orders the respondent to pay to the petitioner a lump sum of £10,000 within three months of the date of the order. The respondent fails to comply within the three-month period. The petitioner applies for an order for sale of certain of the respondent's assets and payment of £10,000 from the proceeds to her.

   (c) Not available as a means of varying a property adjustment order: the power to order a sale cannot, however, be used to vary a property adjustment order (*Norman* v *Norman* [1983] 1 All ER 486).

Example 3 (The facts of *Norman* v *Norman*.) In 1979 in ancillary relief proceedings after a divorce, the registrar (now district judge) made a property adjustment order under s. 24(1)(b) settling the matrimonial home on trust for sale (now on a trust of land) on the husband and wife equally, the sale to be postponed until the youngest child ceased to receive full-time education or training, whereupon the property would be sold and the proceeds divided equally between the husband and wife. In 1982, when one child still remained in full-time education, the husband applied for an order for immediate sale of the house so that he could buy himself a mobile home. The court held that there was no jurisdiction under s. 24A(1) to grant the order for sale which would in effect vary the original property adjustment order by substituting an earlier sale date.

E   INTERIM ORDERS

Pending the final determination of an ancillary relief application and subject to r. 2.69F,   **17.84**
FPR 1991 (which lays down the procedure to be followed and is described in Chapter 18),
the district judge has power to make an interim order upon such terms as he thinks just
(r. 2.64(2), FPR 1991) (but see *Wicks* v *Wicks* [1998] 1 FLR 470).

By far the most common form of interim order is an interim periodical payments order: **17.85**

(a) Interim periodical payments for children: while the court does have power to make a
     final order for periodical payments for children in certain circumstances it is likely that
     only interim periodical payments will be ordered until the full hearing of the ancillary
     relief application takes place. This leaves the way open for the court to adjust the rate of
     payments in the light of the provision made for the spouses without the need for a
     variation application to be made in respect of the children.
(b) Interim periodical payments for a spouse: interim periodical payments for a spouse can
     be ordered in divorce and nullity cases at any time on or after granting decree nisi to
     become effective after decree absolute (in judicial separation, interim periodical pay-
     ments can be ordered and become effective as soon as the single decree is granted). An
     interim order should be sought when ancillary relief matters cannot be finally resolved
     until some time after decree absolute. The gap between commencement of the proceed-
     ings and decree of judicial separation/decree absolute can be filled by maintenance
     pending suit.
         Occasionally, however, an interim lump sum order will be made as happened in
     Askew-Page v *Page* [2001] Fam Law 794 to meet expenses and liabilities incurred by a
     mother on behalf of her children.

F   FINANCIAL PROVISION AND CIVIL PARTNERSHIP

Where a civil partnership is dissolved or annulled, or a separation order is made, either party   **17.86**
may apply to the court for orders for financial provision: Chapters 3 and 4 and schs. 5, 6, and
7, Civil Partnership Act 2004 ('CPA 2004').

Section 72(1), CPA 2004 states that sch. 5 'corresponds to provision made for financial relief   **17.87**
in connection with marriages by Part 2 of the Matrimonial Causes Act 1973'.

In practice, the court may therefore make any of the orders discussed in this chapter except a   **17.88**
pension attachment order. Where, however, one partner's pension scheme provides for the
payment of a lump sum in the event of that partner's death, the court may direct the person
responsible for the pension arrangement to pay the whole or part of that sum, when it
becomes due, to the other civil partner: sch. 5, Part 4, para. 26, CPA 2004.

As with ancillary relief proceedings in relation to spouses, the orders do not take effect until   **17.89**
the dissolution or nullity order has been made final or the separation order granted.

17.90 Further pension sharing orders are not available in proceedings for a separation order, mirroring the position for spouses.

G CHAPTER SUMMARY

17.91 1. Part II, MCA 1973 provides a regime for dealing with financial and property matters in proceedings for a decree of divorce, nullity, or judicial separation.

2. Unsecured or secured periodical payments orders are designed to provide a regular income for a spouse or child of the family (where the Child Support Agency has no jurisdiction).

3. A lump sum order can be made to distribute capital assets such as savings and the like. Its other important use is in an off-setting arrangement where one party to the marriage 'buys out' the interest of the other in the family home or pension asset by making a lump sum payment.

4. Property adjustment orders are available to deal with the future of the family home and other real or personal property owned by the parties.

5. Pension assets may be redistributed through pension sharing or attachment orders.

6. The above orders do not take effect in relation to spouses until a decree of judicial separation or a decree absolute of divorce or nullity has been granted.

7. Virtually the same orders are available to civil partners with similar principles applying as to when the orders may be applied for and take effect.

18

PROCEDURE FOR ANCILLARY RELIEF APPLICATIONS

A INTRODUCTION

18.01 The procedure for making application to court for an ancillary relief order is contained in the Family Proceedings Rules 1991 ('FPR 1991'), as substantially amended.

18.02 This chapter explains the procedure for making the application and the pre-action protocol to be observed. It emphasizes the need for the exchange of information about each spouse's financial circumstances to be on a full and frank basis and explains the procedure where such disclosure is not forthcoming.

18.03 Many parties resolve the distribution of the assets by negotiation and agreement with the settlement embodied in a consent order. The procedure for this arrangement is discussed.

18.04 Responsibility for drafting a consent order lies with the solicitor. Considerable care is needed if pitfalls are to be avoided. Guidance on drafting such orders is included in the chapter. Appeals and methods of challenging orders are discussed.

18.05 The procedure for making claims for financial provision for civil partners is briefly explained. At p. 289 you will find a flow chart to guide you through the complex procedure.

18.06 Throughout this chapter, reference will be made to the recent and very important case of

K v K (Financial Relief: Management of Difficult Cases) [2005] 2 FLR 1137 where Baron J offered trenchant and valuable guidance on case management.

B   THE COST OF THE APPLICATION

Public funding

The solicitor will no doubt have assessed whether his client is eligible for Legal Help   **18.07** when first consulted by his client in relation to the divorce. He can give preliminary advice on ancillary matters under the scheme. However, it will be necessary for him to make an application on his client's behalf for a certificate to cover ancillary relief proceedings (see Chapter 2, especially on the likely reference to mediation under Family Mediation as a pre-condition to a solicitor obtaining a certificate for public funding to represent his client and the need to consider whether the client could fund the proceedings by way of a loan from other sources). Funding to take the application to court, assuming that mediation is unsuccessful, will be by a certificate for General Family Help in the first instance. Such a certificate extends to all steps up to and including the financial dispute resolution hearing, and any interim financial application dealt with before or at that hearing.

The solicitor should also remind the client of the potential impact of the Legal Services   **18.08** Commission's statutory charge when making the application.

Private cases

If the client is not eligible for public funding, the solicitor is required to give him some   **18.09** estimate of the potential cost of the ancillary relief proceedings, or, if this is not possible, he should at least warn the client that they may be very expensive. He should consider whether he needs to take a payment on account to cover the cost of preliminary work and disbursements. Whether he insists on this will depend on the normal practice of the firm and his knowledge of the individual client. Certainly, the client would be expected to provide money for the payment of disbursements as the case progresses (see Chapter 1).

It is important not to rule out mediation where the client is paying privately: in *Al-Khatib* v   **18.10** *Masry* [2004] 3 FCR 573, Thorpe LJ emphasized that there was no case, however complex and contentious, which was not potentially open to successful mediation, although judicial supervision of the mediation process might be necessary in difficult cases.

C   PROTECTING THE APPLICANT PENDING THE MAKING OF AN ORDER

One of the first matters that the solicitor should consider is whether the client's interests are   **18.11** adequately protected pending the making of an ancillary relief order. Could the other spouse sell the matrimonial home over his client's head, for instance? Will his client's assets pass by will or on intestacy to the respondent if she dies before everything is sorted out? Where the solicitor does not feel his client's interests are sufficiently secure, he should consider steps such as severing the joint tenancy or registering a charge or notice under the Family Law Act 1996 or a pending land action. Reference should be made to Chapter 26 where these matters are dealt with more fully.

D   THE ANCILLARY RELIEF PROCEDURE

Introduction

18.12   The rules governing ancillary relief procedure are contained in the Family Proceedings (Amendment No. 2) Rules 1999 (SI 1999/3491). They amend the Family Proceedings Rules 1991.

18.13   There are a number of further points to note. First, *Practice Direction (Ancillary Relief Procedure)* [2000] WLR 1480 offers guidance on the practical application of the new Rules and introduces a Pre-action Protocol outlining the steps that the parties should take to seek and provide information from and to each other prior to the commencement of the proceedings. Compliance with the Protocol is expected and non-compliance may be reflected in costs penalties. The Protocol forms part of the Family Law Protocol discussed in Chapter 1.

18.14   Secondly, the Family Proceedings (Amendment) Rules 2000 (SI 2000/2267) came into force on 1 December 2000 with a new procedure for making applications for pension sharing and attachment orders.

18.15   Thirdly, the Rules have been further amended by the Family Proceedings (Amendment) Rules 2003 (SI 2003/184), the Family Proceedings (Amendment No. 2) Rules 2003 (SI 2003/2839), the Family Proceedings (Amendment) (No. 5) Rules 2005 (SI 2005/2922), and the Family Proceedings (Amendment) Rules 2006 (SI 2006/352).

E   THE PRE-ACTION PROTOCOL

Introduction

18.16   The aim of the Protocol is 'to build on and increase the benefits of early but well-informed settlement which genuinely satisfy both parties to the dispute'. The Protocol sets down the pre-action procedure to be followed. The court will be entitled to decide, if ancillary relief proceedings are subsequently begun, whether there has been non-compliance with the Protocol and whether, in the event of non-compliance, costs consequences should follow.

The scope of the Protocol

18.17   The Protocol is intended to cover all claims for ancillary relief. Practitioners are reminded that, in considering the options of pre-application disclosure and negotiation, there may in fact be an advantage in having a court timetable and court managed process. There is a warning to the profession that exercising the option of pre-application disclosure and negotiation can carry risks of excessive and uncontrolled expenditure and delay (para. 2.2, Notes for Guidance). Pre-application disclosure and negotiation should be encouraged only where both parties agree to follow this route and disclosure is not likely to be an issue, or has been adequately dealt with in mediation or otherwise.

Practitioners are also urged to keep under review whether it would be appropriate to suggest **18.18** mediation as an alternative to solicitor negotiation or court-based litigation (this is discussed above at Chapter 3).

Further, making an application to court should not be regarded as a hostile step or last **18.19** resort but 'rather as a way of starting the court timetable, controlling disclosure, and endeavouring to avoid the costly final hearing and the preparation for it' (para. 2.4). However, such an application should only be made where there is no reasonable prospect of a settlement, for example, where protracted negotiations by correspondence have been inconclusive.

The first letter

While recognizing that it is difficult to prescribe a specimen first letter since the circum- **18.20** stances of the parties to an application for ancillary relief will be so different, the tone of the first letter is very important: therefore the guidance in para. 3.7 of the Protocol must be followed. This states that consideration must be given to the impact of any correspondence on the reader and, in particular, the parties. Irrelevant issues should be avoided, as should contents which cause the recipient of the letter to adopt an entrenched or hostile position.

The client should approve the first letter in advance. Solicitors writing to an unrepresented **18.21** party should always recommend that he seeks independent legal advice and enclose a second copy to be passed to any solicitor instructed. A reasonable time limit for a response should be included—usually 14 days.

All correspondence should focus on the clarification of claims—protracted correspondence **18.22** should be avoided (para. 3.6).

Disclosure

The Protocol emphasizes that disclosure of all material facts, documents, and other relevant **18.23** information must be full and frank. This is regarded as being fundamental if the parties are to seek to clarify and identify the issues between them. Practitioners are required to explain to clients in clear terms the nature of the duty and the possible consequences of breach of that duty. It is important to remember that the duty is on-going and therefore details of material changes after initial disclosure must be given to the other party.

The Protocol indicates that if parties carry out voluntary disclosure before the issue **18.24** of proceedings, the parties should provide the information and documents using Form E (see para. 18.60) as a guide to the format of the disclosure. Hence, documents should be disclosed only to the extent that they are required by Form E. Excessive and disproportionate costs should not be incurred.

Are there any circumstances in which it is safe not to insist on full and frank disclosure? **18.25**

The answer is 'no'—to avoid the risk of later difficulties. However, where the parties are communicating fully, co-operating well, and a realistic and sensible offer has been made, the entire procedure set out above may not be insisted upon. Such an approach would only be appropriate where the client was satisfied that he or she had a good knowledge of the financial position of the other party and considered that rigorous insistence on further disclosure of minor matters might be counter-productive, leading to undesirable delay and excessive costs.

Expert evidence

18.26   The Protocol indicates that 'expert valuation evidence is only necessary where the parties cannot agree or do not know the value of some significant asset. The cost of valuation should be proportionate to the sums in dispute' (para. 3.8). Parties are urged, wherever possible, to obtain a valuation from a single expert (this principle being reinforced by Baron J in *P v P (Financial Relief: Illiquid Assets)* [2005] 1 FLR 548 who commented that it would have been much better (and significantly cheaper) if one expert had been instructed to report on an unbiased basis to the court. In this case, each party had instructed an accountant who had valued one of the principal assets, a series of family companies, from different perspectives so that their evidence to the court was inevitably coloured).

18.27   Where one party wishes to instruct a valuer, he is required to give to the other party a list of names of one or more experts in the relevant speciality whom he considers suitable to instruct. Within 14 days the other party may indicate any objection and, if so, supply a list of experts whom he considers to be more suitable.

18.28   If no agreement is reached as to the identity of a suitable expert, the parties must consider the costs implications of instructing their own expert. Where the costs implications are significant, it may be better for the court to decide the issue in the context of an application for ancillary relief: para. 3.10.

18.29   In any event, where each party instructs an expert, the parties should be encouraged to agree that the reports will be disclosed so that areas of agreement and disagreement may be identified as early as possible.

18.30   In the event of a single expert being jointly instructed, the following requirements must be complied with:

   (a)   the parties should agree a joint letter of instruction;
   (b)   the parties are required to disclose whether they have already consulted that expert about the assets in issue: paras. 3.9 and 3.13.

18.31   Irrespective of there being single or joint valuations, it must be established that the expert is prepared to answer reasonable questions raised by either party: para. 3.11.

18.32   All of the above is reinforced in a Best Practice Guide for Instructing a Single Joint Expert issued by the President of the Family Division's Ancillary Relief Advisory Group. The Guide is reproduced in full at [2003] 1 FLR 573. It confirms the need for the use of a single joint expert wherever possible, gives guidance on the matters to be established with the expert before formal instructions are given (e.g., that there is no conflict of interest and that the matter is within the range of expertise of the expert) and on the contents of the joint instructions to reflect the proportionality principle and to include, among other things, basic relevant information and the specific questions to be answered.

The Guide recommends that all communication by the single joint expert should be 18.33 addressed to both parties, all meetings and conferences should be attended by both parties and/or their advisers, and the report should be served simultaneously on both parties. It concludes with guidance on the resolution of disputes or other difficulties.

In *K* v *K* [2005] 2 FLR 1137, Baron J confirmed that the general practice in the Family 18.34 Division should be that only joint valuations are acceptable, echoing the principles set out above. Further, she indicated that, if an updated valuation or additional information was required, this should not be sought unilaterally from the valuer. Where there was lack of co-operation from one side, an application to the court should be made for directions to be given.

F THE PROCEDURE IN DETAIL

The overriding objective

This replicates the provisions in r. 1.1, Civil Procedure Rules 1998 and is contained in 18.35 r. 2.51D, FPR 1991, as amended. The overriding objective is stated to be that of 'enabling the court to deal with cases justly'.

Rule 2.51D(2) explains the meaning of 'to deal with a case justly', including as far as 18.36 practicable:

(a) ensuring that the parties are on an equal footing;
(b) saving expense;
(c) dealing with the case in ways which are proportionate—
   (i)   to the amount of money involved,
   (ii) to the importance of the case,
   (iii) to the complexity of the issues, and
   (iv) to the financial position of each party;
(d) ensuring that it is dealt with expeditiously and fairly; and
(e) allotting to it an appropriate share of the court's resources, while taking into account the need to allot resources to other cases.

The court is required to seek to give effect to the overriding objective when it:

(a) exercises any power given to it in the ancillary relief rules; or
(b) interprets any rule: r. 2.51D(3).

The court is also obliged to further the overriding objective by 'actively managing cases' (r. 2.51D(5)), and this is stated to include:

(a) encouraging the parties to co-operate with each other in the conduct of the proceedings;
(b) encouraging the parties to settle their disputes through mediation, where appropriate;
(c) identifying the issues at an early date;

(d)　regulating the extent of disclosure of documents and expert evidence so that they are proportionate to the issues in question;

(e)　helping the parties to settle the whole or part of the case;

(f)　fixing timetables or otherwise controlling the progress of the case;

(g)　making use of technology; and

(h)　giving directions to ensure that the trial of a case proceeds quickly and efficiently: r. 2.51D(6).

The parties to the proceedings are under a corresponding duty to help the court to further the overriding objective (r. 2.51D(4)), and therefore compliance with timetables and willingness to negotiate a settlement will be expected.

18.37　Ancillary relief case law had already highlighted the need for cases to be conducted in such a way that the costs involved are proportionate to the value of the assets in dispute (e.g. see *Piglowska* v *Piglowski* [1999] 1WLR 1360).

18.38　As to the principle of proportionality, the Protocol requires the principle to be borne in mind at all times. It states that 'it is unacceptable for the costs of any case to be disproportionate to the financial value of the subject matter of the dispute': para. 3.2.

18.39　The court has considerable discretion as to how it applies the other principles. For example, the phrases 'the importance of the case' and 'the complexity of the issues' indicate that not all cases turn on the value of the assets alone but on how such assets as there are should be distributed between the parties.

18.40　Under the general principles of the Protocol, already referred to, para. 3.1 requires the parties to bear in mind the overriding objective and 'to try to ensure that all claims should be resolved and a just outcome achieved as speedily as possible without costs being unreasonably incurred'. Further, the paragraph states that:

> The needs of children should be addressed and safeguarded. The procedures which it is appropriate to follow should be conducted with minimum distress to the parties and in a manner designed to promote as good a continuing relationship between the parties and any children affected as is possible in the circumstances.

Making the application

Section 26, Matrimonial Causes Act 1973

18.41　Section 26 provides that where a petition for divorce, nullity, or judicial separation has been filed, then, proceedings for orders for ancillary relief may be begun at any time after the filing of the petition.

18.42　However, with the exception of an order for maintenance pending suit, no other order for the benefit of the other party to the marriage takes effect until the grant of the decree absolute in proceedings for divorce or nullity or the decree of judicial separation: ss. 23(5) and 24(3), Matrimonial Causes Act 1973 ('MCA 1973').

Petitioner's application

18.43　Rule 2.53(1) of the FPR 1991 provides that any application by a petitioner for:

(a) an order for maintenance pending suit;
(b) a financial provision order;
(c) a property adjustment order;
(d) a pension attachment or pension sharing order.

(i.e., all the main forms of ancillary relief except an order for sale under s. 24A, MCA 1973) must be made in the petition. The application will then be 'activated' by filing Form A at the court. A copy of Form A is found at the end of this chapter.

The importance of making a comprehensive claim for ancillary relief

It is usually advisable to make the fullest possible claim for ancillary relief in the petition/ **18.44** answer or Form A (despite the fact that it may seem inappropriate at the time to claim, e.g., periodical payments from a spouse who is unemployed or a lump sum from a spouse with no capital assets) for the following reasons:

(a) Circumstances can change between the initiation of the application and the hearing, and the spouse who was impecunious when ancillary relief was originally claimed in the petition may, by the date of the hearing, have obtained a lucrative job or won the lottery. It is obviously in the interests of all concerned that the court should have the fullest possible powers to resolve the case at the hearing.
(b) The client must be prevented from falling into the remarriage trap. Section 28(3) provides that if a party to a marriage remarries after a decree of divorce or nullity, that party shall not be entitled *to apply* for a financial provision order or for a property adjustment order in his or her favour against the other party to the former marriage.

A party who may want to remarry can, however, preserve her claim for lump sum and property adjustment orders by making them before remarriage, in which case he or she will be able to pursue the claims after remarriage. (This is confirmed in *Re G (Financial Provision: Liberty to Restore Application for Lump Sum)* [2004] 1 FLR 994.) Nothing can be done, of course, to preserve a claim for periodical payments, which will always cease on remarriage in any event (s. 28(1) and (2), MCA 1973).
(c) The petitioner/respondent who later wishes to make a claim for ancillary relief that should have been made in her petition/answer in accordance with r. 2.53 will, in most cases, need permission of the court to make the claim.

Respondent's application

Respondent filing an answer Rule 2.53(1) also applies to a respondent who files an **18.45** answer, save that, of course, it is in his answer that he must make his ancillary relief claims.

Respondent not filing an answer A respondent who does not file an answer (and this will **18.46** apply in the majority of cases) may make his application for ancillary relief by notice in Form A (r. 2.53(3)). There are no particular requirements as to when Form A should be filed. In theory, therefore, a respondent can file Form A months or years after the decree has been granted.

However, delay in filing Form A can prejudice a respondent's ancillary relief claims—in **18.47** particular the client may fall into the remarriage trap (see paragraph 18.44), or may find the court reluctant to grant relief if the lapse of time has led the petitioner to believe that no claim will be made. It is therefore suggested that the solicitor should make it his practice to file a notice in Form A claiming the full range of ancillary relief as a matter of course in the early stages of the main proceedings, and certainly before decree absolute.

18.48   Note that indicating in the acknowledgement of service that the respondent intends to apply for ancillary relief does not count as making a formal ancillary relief claim: *Hargood* v *Jenkins* [1978] 3 All ER 1001.

Making the application where no claim has been made in the prayer in the petition or answer

18.49   Where no claim has been made in the prayer to the petition or in the answer to the petition then an application may be made subsequently by permission of the court by notice in Form A or at the trial; or if the parties have agreed the terms of the proposed order, permission of the court is not required and the application proceeds by notice in Form A: r. 2.53(2).

Proceeding with the application made in the prayer in the petition or answer

18.50   Rules 2.61A to 2.61F govern the procedure where the application for ancillary relief is made comprehensively in the prayer to the petition or in the answer to the petition.

18.51   **The application form**   Rule 2.61A provides that the notice of intention to proceed with the application for ancillary relief is made by notice in Form A, the notice being filed in a county court or registry of the High Court in which the petition was filed.

18.52   **The contents of Form A**   Rule 2.59(2) requires that where there is an application for a property adjustment order relating to land, the notice in Form A must identify the land and state whether it is registered or unregistered and, if registered, the Land Registry title number, giving particulars, so far as is known to the applicant, of any mortgage of the land or any interest in it.

18.53   Rule 2.61A(3) requires that where an application is made for a pension sharing order under s. 24B or a pension attachment order under s. 25B or 25C, MCA 1973, the terms of the order requested must be specified in the notice in Form A. However, it has to be recognized that this is not always possible where important information has not been made available.

18.54   **Other documents to be filed**   In addition to Form A (and a copy for service on the respondent), the following documents should be taken to the court (normally the divorce county court where the proceedings were commenced) to be issued/filed:

(a)   Where the client is publicly funded:
       (i)   a copy of the certificate for General Family Help or representation;
       (ii) a notice of issue of the certificate.
(b)   Notice of acting if the solicitor is not already on the court record (if the divorce proceedings have been handled under the Legal Help scheme so far, the solicitor will not be on the court record).
(c)   A fee (currently £210).
(d)   A copy of any family proceedings court maintenance order currently in force in respect of a spouse or child.

Further, if the applicant is seeking periodical payments or secured periodical payments for **18.55** children, Form A must state whether the petitioner/respondent is applying for payment:

(a)   for a step-child or children;
(b)   for top-up maintenance over and above that payable under a Child Support Mainten-ance Calculation (see Chapter 20);
(c)   to meet expenses arising from a child's disability;
(d)   to meet educational or training expenses for a child;
(e)   to cover a situation where the Child Support Act 1991 ('CSA 1991') does not apply because the carer parent, the non-resident parent, or the child in question is not habitually resident in the United Kingdom;
(f)   for any other reason (for example, to reflect a written agreement under s. 8(5), CSA 1991).

Steps to be taken by the court

Once Form A has been filed at the court, the court is required to: **18.56**

(a)   fix a first appointment not less than 12 weeks and not more than 16 weeks after the date of filing Form A and to give notice of the date to the applicant;
(b)   serve a copy of the notice on the respondent within four days of the filing of Form A: r. 2.61A(4).

A notice in Form C is sent by the court to both parties and advises them of the date of the first appointment and lays down a timetable of the steps to be taken before the first appointment. Form C was amended in 2003 to direct the parties to contact each other to agree when exchange of Form E (the financial statement) is to take place.

In line with the principle of active case management, no court appointment may be can- **18.57** celled except with the court's permission and, if cancelled, the court must immediately fix a new date: r. 2.61A(5).

The applicant must serve on the respondent a notice of issue of public funding and a notice **18.58** of acting, where appropriate.

In the weeks before the first appointment, a considerable amount of work has to be under- **18.59** taken by the solicitor both in terms of collating information and of assessing the conduct of the case in future.

The preparation of the financial statement in Form E

The layout of Form E

Rule 2.61B(1) requires that both parties to the application, at the same time, exchange with **18.60** each other and file at the court a financial statement in Form E. (A copy of the Form is to be found at the end of this chapter.) This is a complex form running to some 27 pages requiring a comprehensive account of the financial circumstances of the party making the statement. The statement requires details, amongst other things, of the personal and family history, the financial resources, liabilities and needs of the maker of the statement, together with details of future marriage plans, and an indication of the nature of the orders applied for or sought.

The documents to be annexed to Form E

18.61   The form must have attached to it the documents specified in the statement, but no others (r. 2.61B(3) and (4)). Documents include, for example, the last three payslips and a form P60, a mortgage statement, a property valuation, bank and building society statements for the last 12 months, the surrender value of any endowment policy. The Schedule of Documents to Accompany Form E (see the end of this chapter) is a reminder in tick box form of the documents to be attached with an opportunity to indicate if the documents are attached, not applicable, or are to follow.

18.62   Rule 2.70(1) applies where an application is made in Form A and the applicant or respondent is likely to have any benefits under a pension arrangement.

18.63   Within seven days of receiving details of the date of the first appointment, a party with pension rights must normally request the person responsible for each pension arrangement to furnish details of the arrangement. The information to be provided includes a valuation of the pension rights, details of whether the person responsible for the pension arrangement offers membership to a person entitled to a pension credit, the types of benefit which would be available under such membership and the position on charges (Pensions on Divorce etc. (Provision of Information) Regulations 2000 (SI 2000/1048): r. 2.70(2)).

18.64   The reason for this rule is to ensure that pension details are sought from the person responsible for the pension arrangement as early as possible in the ancillary relief process: some pension providers (for example, the NHS and the Teachers' Pension Agency) can take anything up to three months to provide the relevant information.

18.65   A copy of the above information together with the name and address of the person responsible for each pension arrangement must be sent to the other party to the marriage by the person with pension rights within seven days of receipt: r. 2.70(3).

18.66   The above steps are not required where the person with pension rights has already obtained or requested a recent valuation, provided that the valuation in question is less than 12 months old, calculated from the date of the first appointment: r. 2.70(4) and (5).

18.67   If the required documents, indicated above, cannot be attached to Form E, they must be served on the other party at the earliest opportunity and copies of the documents must be filed at the court with a statement explaining the failure to send the documents with Form E: r. 2.61B(5). The parties are not permitted disclosure or inspection of any other documents before the first appointment.

18.68   Clearly, it is sensible to begin the collection of information and documents required in the statement before filing Form A in order to be as well prepared as possible. This is especially the case where the solicitor anticipates that he will be acting for the respondent in the proceedings and therefore has little control over when the application is to be made. A period of, at most, 11 weeks to collect and collate information may be insufficient especially when documents must be obtained from a variety of sources.

18.69   The reason for the requirement that certain documents be attached to Form E is so that, if possible, the first appointment may be used as a Financial Dispute Resolution appointment and this would not be possible in the absence of vital documents.

Completing Form E

For the main part, completion of Form E is relatively straightforward. It is a matter of **18.70** completing those Parts which are relevant to the client's case. It is inevitable that a number of Parts of the Form will not be completed at all. For example, where the client is an employee and has no self-employed earnings, Part 2, paras. 2.11 and 2.16 may be safely ignored.

In para. 3.1.1, the client must give details of his or her expenditure from income. In some **18.71** so-called 'big money' cases, full details have been omitted on the grounds that the client is sufficiently wealthy to be able to afford any periodical payments order which the court is likely to make, making detailed disclosure unnecessary. Such an approach was heavily criticized in *McFarlane* v *McFarlane, Parlour* v *Parlour* [2004] 2 FLR 893, Thorpe LJ indicating that the court is entitled to have a full picture both of the client's income and expenditure in order properly to deal with the application for ancillary relief.

Guidance on the proper completion of Form E was given by Nicholas Mostyn QC in *W* **18.72** v *W (Financial Provision: Form E)* [2004] 1 FLR 494. A number of points emerge from the judgment but of particular importance are the following:

(a) a contingent liability (for example, monies set aside to meet the cost of potential damages in litigation unconnected with the ancillary relief proceedings) should be mentioned in the calculations at para. 3.2.1 if, on the balance of probabilities, the maker of the statement and his legal advisers are satisfied that the liability will arise;

(b) where a spouse has remarried, his or her assets should not be treated as assets jointly owned with the new spouse: to do otherwise would be to reduce the assets available for distribution in relation to the first marriage.

It is suggested that particular care is needed, however, with the completion of paras. 4.3, 4.4, **18.73** and 5.1. Since the House of Lords' decision in *White* v *White* [2000] 3 WLR 1571 (discussed fully in Chapter 19), contributions of both a financial and non-financial kind (e.g., domestic contributions such as running the home and caring for the children) have achieved a greater significance and it is sensible in completing para. 4.3 to highlight these. Furthermore, one party may seek to argue that his or her contribution has been so significant (e.g., by making a major contribution to the family wealth) that greater weight should be given to this contribution. An indication of this argument can be set out in para. 4.3.

As for para. 4.4, dealing with issues of conduct, the guidance in Form E makes it clear that **18.74** conduct will only be taken into account in exceptional circumstances. This is in line with case law discussed in Chapter 19. Nevertheless, it is possible to indicate at para. 4.4 that conduct will be raised in ancillary relief proceedings, the nature of that conduct and the effect it might reasonably have on the outcome of those proceedings. For example, if it is alleged that the husband disposed of significant savings and investments without the knowledge or consent of the wife, it may be possible to argue on her behalf that the family home, as the remaining family asset, should be transferred to her sole name (but see *K* v *K (Financial Relief: Management of Difficult Cases)* referred to above).

In the writer's view, particular caution is needed in completing para. 5.1. The paragraph **18.75** seeks an indication of the type of ancillary relief order(s) sought. It may be difficult to be specific at this stage in the absence of the financial statement of the other spouse. It may be sensible, therefore, to be non-committal unless the identity and value of all assets are already known or the client has a clear view as to an appropriate settlement. In essence, do not sell the client short!

18.76 Once completed, Form E must be signed by the maker of the statement and sworn to be true: r. 2.61B(1).

Mutual exchange of Form E

18.77 In order for the application to be dealt with as expeditiously as possible, Form E must be exchanged and filed not less than 35 days before first appointment.

18.78 The requirement for simultaneous exchange of Form E is to prevent either side from trying to gain an advantage over the other. However, the Rules are silent as to the steps to be taken if one party fails to co-operate.

18.79 It is suggested that the party whose statement has been prepared within the prescribed time limit should file Form E at court in any event, in a sealed envelope marked 'Not to be opened until the Respondent's Form E is filed', but not serve the document on the other side. An application should then be made to the district judge, without notice to the other side, for an order that the respondent file and exchange his Form E within a prescribed period of time. A penal notice should be attached to the order and costs should be applied for (see paragraph 18.103). The order should be served personally on the recalcitrant party.

18.80 If the order is not complied with, it becomes impossible to prepare for the first appointment (see paragraph 18.90) and it will be necessary to seek an adjournment of the first appointment usually at the first appointment itself. The court should be asked to assess the wasted costs and require the respondent to pay these within a short, prescribed period.

18.81 Where Form E is served by the respondent without the required documents, this may be dealt with in the questionnaire (see paragraph 18.94 and onwards) and reflected in an order for costs against the respondent at the first appointment (see paragraph 18.103).

Service of Form A and Form E on other parties

18.82 Where the application is made for a variation of an ante-nuptial or post-nuptial settlement, r. 2.59(3) requires a copy of Form A and Form E, completed by the applicant, to be served on the trustees of the settlement.

18.83 Where the property in the proceedings is subject to a mortgage, a copy of Form A must be served on any mortgagee mentioned in the application and the mortgagee may apply to the court for a copy of the applicant's financial statement in Form E. The mortgagee may file a statement in answer to the application within 14 days after service or receipt of the statement but will rarely do so in practice.

18.84 Similarly, where the notice in Form A seeks a pension sharing order under s. 24B or a pension attachment order under ss. 25B and/or 25C, MCA 1973, the applicant must serve a copy of the notice in Form A on the person responsible for the pension arrangement: r. 2.70(6) and (7).

Where the application is for a *pension attachment order*, additional information laid down in **18.85** r. 2.70(7) must be sent to the person responsible for the pension arrangement. This includes, among other things, an address for service, and an address of a bank, building society, or other place to which payment is to be sent.

In these circumstances, the person responsible for the pension arrangement may, within **18.86** 21 days after service, require the applicant to provide him with a copy of para. 2.13 of the applicant's Form E. The applicant must then provide the document not less than 35 days before the date of the first appointment, or within 21 days of being required to do so, whichever is the later: r. 2.70(8).

Paragraph 2.13 of Form E deals with the pension position of the applicant. The person **18.87** responsible for the pension arrangement is not entitled to see details of the applicant's other financial circumstances.

Under r. 2.70(9) the person responsible for the pension arrangement may then send to the **18.88** court, the applicant, and the respondent a statement in answer. This step must be taken within 21 days of receipt of a copy of para. 2.13 of Form E.

Further, the applicant is required to file at the court and serve on the respondent, at least **18.89** 14 days before the date of the first appointment, confirmation of the names of all persons served in accordance with r. 2.59(3) and (4) and that there are no other persons who must be served: r. 2.61B(9).

Preparation for the first appointment

Rule 2.61B(7) requires that at least 14 days before the first appointment, each party must file **18.90** with the court and serve on the other party:

(a)   a concise statement of the issues between the parties;
(b)   a chronology (as to the history of the marriage and the divorce proceedings);
(c)   a questionnaire setting out by reference to the concise statement of issues any further information and documents requested from the other party, or a statement that no information or documents are required;
(d)   a notice in Form G stating whether that party will be in a position at the first appointment to proceed on that occasion to a Financial Dispute Resolution ('FDR') giving reasons. The purpose and structure of the Financial Dispute Resolution is explained at paragraph 8 below.

Although the Rules do not require it, it is suggested that a summary of the income, assets, and liabilities of each party is exchanged and a copy filed at court—this is certainly a requirement routinely imposed by the court in preparation for the FDR hearing.

The concise statement of issues

This is an important document and its principal purpose is to identify the issues in **18.91** the case. Since Form E concludes with an opportunity for each party to indicate the terms of the order sought by them, it should be possible to establish the issues without difficulty.

18.92   The document should be concise and avoid unnecessary details.

18.93   An example of a matter which should be highlighted in the statement of issues is when the respondent husband is arguing that he should not be required to make periodical payments for his wife and the wife is contending that maintenance is essential.

The questionnaire

18.94   In line with the principle of active case management, the parties are not permitted to ask for information or documents on an informal basis once the application for ancillary relief has been filed. Hence the questionnaire is important and, having received the other party's Form E, time will be spent deciding what information or documents should be requested, if any, and drafting the questionnaire.

18.95   At the risk of stating the obvious, the starting point will be to check that the other spouse has provided all the relevant documents. If not, these should be requested. Remember to concentrate on *relevant* documents—requesting receipts for expenditure from several years ago is unlikely to be very productive!

18.96   What is made clear by Baron J in *K v K (Financial Relief: Management of Difficult Cases)*, referred to above, is that, if the solicitor considers that insufficient relevant information has been given, enquiries must be pursued rigorously in the questionnaire (and if necessary, at the next court hearing). It is not acceptable 'simply (to) wait to use the absence of information as a forensic ambush at trial'.

18.97   Following the approach of Coleridge J in *OS v DS (Oral Disclosure: Preliminary Hearing)* [2005] 1 FLR 675, Baron J acknowledged that 'In some cases continual orders for disclosure can be counter-productive and it is better to have an oral hearing . . .' (the purpose being for the oral examination of the recalcitrant party on matters where disclosure has not been forthcoming).

Compliance with *Practice Direction (Family Proceedings: Court Bundles)* [2006] 2 FLR 1999

18.98   This Practice Direction came into force on 2 October 2006 and applies to all hearings in family proceedings except for Family Proceedings Courts. It is explained in detail at paragraph 18.122.

G   THE FIRST APPOINTMENT

18.99   Rule 2.61D of the FPR 1991, as amended, governs the conduct of the first appointment which has the objective of 'defining issues and saving costs'. Both parties must personally attend the first appointment unless the court orders otherwise: r. 2.61D(5), as amended. Further, the person responsible for the pension arrangement is entitled to be represented at the first appointment where he has filed a statement in answer. To facilitate this, although it is rare in practice, the court must give that person notice of the date of the first appointment within four days of receipt of the statement in answer: r. 2.70(10).

18.100   The district judge will have read the documents filed and has a number of duties at the first appointment laid down in r. 2.61D(2), as amended:

(a) He must determine the extent to which any questions seeking information or docu-ments requested in r. 2.61B must be answered or produced, giving directions for the production of such further documents as may be necessary. It is helpful to the court in producing replies to the other party's questionnaire to reproduce the original question and then add the reply so that a comprehensive document is created. This saves the court having to locate the question in one document and the reply in another.

In determining, for example, the additional information required, the district judge may, by virtue of r. 2.62(4) order the attendance of any person (including the applicant or the respondent: *OS v DS (Oral Disclosure: Preliminary Hearing)* [2005] 1 FLR 675), for the purpose of being examined or cross-examined, and order the disclosure and inspection of any document or require further statements. In addition, he may, on the application of either party, order that any person attend an appointment (now known as an 'inspection appointment') before the court and produce documents to be specified or prescribed in the order: r. 2.62(7). A person attending an inspection appointment may be legally represented: r. 2.62(9).

Great care should be taken before seeking an inspection appointment if case law prior to the new ancillary relief procedure is anything to go by. In *Frary v Frary* [1993] 2 FLR 696, the judge at first instance ordered the mistress to produce a range of documents, including credit card statements, tax returns, and the like. On appeal, the Court of Appeal discharged the order on the grounds that there was no evidence that the former husband and his mistress were mixing funds and, in consequence, the information sought was totally irrelevant to the dispute between the former spouses. The mistress was awarded costs on an indemnity basis.

However, in *D v D (Production Appointment)* [1995] 2 FLR 497, the Family Division indicated that it was prepared to order an inspection appointment despite pleas of professional and client privilege by the accountant of one of the parties. The court considered the inspection appointment to be necessary in order to ensure that the duty to give full and frank disclosure was complied with. In looking at the issue of evidence, the question of relevance, will always be an important consideration for the court.

Nevertheless, if the court pays heed to the overriding objective, previously discussed, it is likely that of even greater importance will be the question of proportionality. The court may therefore refuse disclosure on the grounds that while, strictly speaking, the documents are relevant to the case, the cost of disclosure is not proportionate to the complexity of the issues or the value of the assets in dispute.

(b) The district judge may also require a valuation of a pension arrangement, if the appli-cant seeks a pension sharing or an attachment order: r. 2.61D(2)(f). Information as to the value of pensions should in fact be dealt with in Form E but may have been omitted.

Where either party is seeking an order in respect of the other's pension, the district judge may direct any party with pension rights to file and serve a Pension Inquiry Form (Form P) (this is not reproduced). This provides full information about the pension and is to be signed by the pension provider: r. 2.61D(f)(iii). The completed Form must be available for the Financial Dispute Resolution appointment.

For a detailed commentary on the practicalities of completion of Form P, see D. Salter, 'The New Pensions Procedure' [2005] *Family Law* 977.

It should be noted that after the first appointment, a party is not entitled to the production of any further documents except as already directed by the district judge or with the later permission of the court: r. 2.61D(3). Therefore, informal questionnaires or letters seeking clarification of issues will not be permitted. To this end, r. 2.61D(4) permits a party at any stage in the proceedings to apply for further directions or a Financial Dispute Resolution appointment.

(c) The district judge must give directions about the valuation of assets (including, where appropriate, the joint instruction of a single joint expert), the obtaining and exchanging of expert evidence, if required, and the evidence to be adduced by each party including, where appropriate, further chronologies or schedules to be filed by each party.

In addition to the guidance set out in the Best Practice Guide (discussed above at paragraph 18.32 and onwards), the following principal points should be noted:

(i) The expert has a duty to help the court on the matters within his expertise. This overrides any obligation to the person from whom he has received instructions or by whom he is paid.

(ii) The report, which will usually be in writing, unless the court directs otherwise, must be addressed to the court rather than to the party who instructed the expert: para. 3.12 of the Protocol requires experts instructed pre-application to be aware of this.

(iii) Where the expert has been instructed by one party, other parties may put written questions to the expert once only and within 28 days of service of the report.

(iv) The expert may at any time ask the court for directions without notice to the parties (thus reinforcing the independence of the expert witness from those instructing him).

(v) While expert evidence may be called only with the permission of the court, no guidance is offered as to how the discretion should be exercised. However, the court will be concerned to ensure that any imbalance in availability of expert evidence should be corrected by the court. This is consistent with the overriding objective 'that the parties are on an equal footing'.

The parties must be able, therefore, at the first appointment, or when the matter comes to be considered by the court, to provide the court with a list of suitable experts or to make submissions as to the method by which the expert is to be chosen.

(d) Where the parties are not able to reach an agreement on financial and property matters, the district judge must also direct that the case be referred to a Financial Dispute Resolution appointment unless he concludes that a referral is not appropriate in all the circumstances. This may arise, for example, where the parties are in dispute on a point of principle and need a formal determination of the issue from a district judge. The question of the extent to which an inheritance should be available for distribution is an example of such a dispute. Where this is the case, he must direct one or more of the following:

(i) that a further directions appointment be fixed;

(ii) that an appointment be fixed for the making of an interim order;

(iii) that the case be fixed for a final hearing and, where that direction is given, the district judge must determine the judicial level at which the case must be heard;

(iv) that the case be adjourned for out-of-court mediation or private negotiation or, in exceptional circumstances, generally: r. 2.61D(2)(d), as amended by the Family Proceedings (Amendment) Rules 2003 (SI 2003/184).

(e) Further, he may make an interim order where an application was made for such an order to be dealt with at the first appointment.

(f) Where the case is referred to a FDR appointment, the district judge may require the parties to file and serve skeleton arguments and/or schedules of assets prior to the FDR.

(g) He must consider whether to make a costs order in respect of the hearing under r. 2.71(4), having regard to all the circumstances and the extent to which each party has complied with the Rules, especially in respect of the requirement to send documents with Form E.

H   A NOTE ON COSTS

In order to comply with certain aspects of the overriding objective, in particular, those of saving expense and dealing with the case in a way proportionate to the amount of money involved, etc., it is necessary for the parties involved to understand throughout the extent of the costs incurred both to date and in respect of particular applications to the court.   **18.101**

Hence, by r. 2.61F(1), FPR 1991, as amended, at *every* court hearing or appointment each party must produce to the court an estimate in Form H of the costs and disbursements incurred by him up to the date of that hearing or appointment. This means that the court and the party will be aware of the 'running total' of costs incurred. This document is also disclosed to the other party.   **18.102**

Where a party wishes to claim the costs of the hearing or appointment from the other side he must, at least 24 hours in advance of the hearing, prepare, file, and serve a written statement of costs in Form N260. It must state that the costs estimated do not exceed the costs which the solicitor's own client is liable to pay and must be signed by the party's solicitor. Failure to do so may affect entitlement to costs. (Please also see paragraph 18.128 and onwards for the additional procedural requirements in these circumstances, as set out in *President's Direction (Ancillary Relief: Costs)* [2006] 1 FLR 865).   **18.103**

Guidance was offered in the case of *MacDonald* v *Taree Holdings Ltd, The Times*, 28 December 2000. Here, Neuberger J held that failure to serve a costs schedule in time need not be fatal to an application for costs. The court must first consider the prejudice to the paying party, and it should do so on the following bases: **18.104**

(a) Should there be a short adjournment on the day of the hearing for the paying party to consider the proposed receiving party's statement of costs?

(b) Should there be a full detailed assessment of costs, with the result that the assessment of the amount of costs would be put back in the usual way?

(c) Should summary assessment take place on another date?

The fact of initial failure to comply with the Rules could then be reflected in a slight reduction in the amount of costs ultimately awarded against the paying party.

I INTERIM ORDERS

18.105 Rule 2.69F of the FPR 1991, as amended, deals with interim orders. It is recognized that the long delay before the date of the first appointment may cause hardship where the applicant needs immediate financial support in the form of periodical payments. Rule 2.69F(1) therefore permits *either* party to apply at *any stage of the proceedings* for an order for maintenance pending suit, interim periodical payments or an interim variation order.

18.106 The wording of r. 2.69F(1) indicates that the proceedings of ancillary relief must have begun and therefore one of the parties will have filed Form A.

18.107 To make an application for an interim order, a notice of application is filed at the court and the date fixed for the hearing must not be less than 14 days after the date of issue of the application: r. 2.69F(2) (unless the court abridges the time under Ord. 13, r. 4, CCR 1981). A copy of the notice of application must be served forthwith on the respondent: r. 2.69F(3).

18.108 It is likely, of course, that at this stage neither party will have filed Form E. The applicant is therefore required to file with the application and serve on the other party a draft of the order requested and a short sworn statement explaining why the order is necessary and giving the necessary information about his means: r. 2.69F(4).

18.109 Not less than seven days before the hearing, the other party must file with the court and serve on the other party a short sworn statement about his means unless he has already filed Form E: r. 2.69F(5).

18.110 To determine the application the court will adopt normal principles using the factors under s. 25, MCA 1973 (see Chapter 19).

J THE FINANCIAL DISPUTE RESOLUTION APPOINTMENT

18.111 The FDR appointment is a major innovation, dealt with in r. 2.61E, FPR 1991, as amended.

18.112 The FDR appointment will normally take place when all the evidence has been exchanged and the court and the parties are able to identify the issues. At the first appointment and any FDR appointment, legal representatives attending are expected to have full knowledge of the case so that effective use may be made of the appointment: para. 3.4 of the Protocol.

18.113 The purpose of the FDR appointment is for discussion and negotiation, r. 2.61E(1). The process is seen as reducing the tension which inevitably arises in a family dispute and facilitating settlement of those disputes. The parties must personally attend the FDR appointment unless the court orders otherwise (r. 2.61E(9)) and must use their best endeavours to reach agreement on the matters in issue between them (r. 2.61E(6)). The FDR appointment gives the parties an opportunity to put their fundamental positions to the district judge and for him to make such comments as may be helpful to assist in arriving at a settlement.

18.114 In addition to complying with any direction given at the first appointment, not later than seven days before the FDR appointment, the applicant must file with the court details of all offers and proposals and responses to them: r. 2.61E(3).

The appointment is then conducted on a privileged basis so that the parties have the **18.115** reassurance that nothing can be repeated at a later date, for example, at a final hearing if no settlement is reached.

Although the Rules are not explicit on the point, it is clearly the function of the district judge **18.116** to help the parties to settle their dispute by eliminating unrealistic expectations and giving a general indication of how the court would be likely to approach the particular circumstances of the case.

If a settlement cannot be achieved, the district judge or judge hearing the FDR appointment **18.117** is not permitted to have any further involvement with the application, other than to direct a further FDR appointment, make a consent order or a further directions order: r. 2.61E(2).

Where there is no agreement, all offers, proposals and responses to them must, at the request **18.118** of the party who filed them, be returned to him and not retained on the court file: r. 2.61E(5).

The FDR appointment may be adjourned from time to time and, at its conclusion, the court **18.119** may make an appropriate consent order. If that is not appropriate because a settlement has not been reached, the court must give directions for the future conduct of the proceedings including, for example, the filing of evidence and fixing a final hearing date: r. 2.61E(7) and (8).

Where agreement has been reached but a consent order cannot be obtained at court that **18.120** day, the following is suggested:

(a) do not leave the court building without, at the very least, 'heads of agreement' containing all relevant terms and undertakings, signed by the parties, their legal representatives and initialled as approved by the judge. This is known as a 'Rose agreement', following *Rose* v *Rose* [2002] 1 FLR 978. This will be an unperfected order;

(b) the heads of agreement must by detailed—not simply broad terms. In particular, care must be taken with the terms of any undertakings (see paragraph 18.151 and onwards) which may be vital to the working of the order but which the court cannot compel a party to give;

(c) if the final order is not drafted and approved at the FDR, ensure that a date is fixed within about 28 days for a five-minute appointment at which the order can be approved or any *Rose* style problems explored. The hearing should be listed as an adjourned FDR.

K PREPARATION FOR THE FINAL HEARING

In preparing for the final hearing, which will be necessary if the FDR appointment has not **18.121** succeeded and there is little prospect of a consent order, attention must be paid to the 1991 Rules and a number of Practice Directions. A fair degree of common sense is also required.

It is suggested that the following matters should be covered: **18.122**

(a) In addition to complying with directions made at the FDR, the solicitor should spend some time isolating the issues in the case and ensuring that he can prove any disputed factual matters that may have a bearing on the district judge's decision.

(b) Preparation of the bundle of documents. Preparation of the bundle of documents is now governed by *Practice Direction (Family Proceedings: Court Bundles) (Universal Practice to be Applied in All Courts Other Than the Family Proceedings Court)* [2006] 2 FLR 199 which came into force on 2 October 2006.

This Practice Direction has to be complied with in High Court proceedings, proceedings in the Principal Registry of the Family Division and at all hearings in family proceedings except for family proceedings courts.

The term 'hearing' is defined as 'all appearances before a judge or district judge whether with or without notice to other parties and whether for directions or for substantive relief': para. 2(2). The scope of the Practice Direction is therefore much wider than previous Practice Directions dealing with court bundles. Further, the Practice Direction applies whether the bundle is being lodged for the first time or being re-lodged for a further hearing.

However, the Practice Direction does not apply in the following circumstances:

(i)   cases listed for an hour or less in the Principal Registry or a county court;

(ii) the hearing of an urgent application if and to the extent that it is impossible to comply with it (para. 2.4).

The following is a summary only of the Practice Direction.

Responsibility for preparation of the bundle lies with the applicant or, where the applicant is a litigant in person, by the first respondent who is not a litigant in person: para. 3.1.

If possible, the contents of the bundle should be agreed by all parties and in any event the bundle should be paginated and indexed: para. 3.2.

The bundle should be contained in one or more A4 size ring binders or lever arch files. Each is to be clearly marked on the front and spine to identify the case, the court, the hearing date and time and, if known, the name of the judge hearing the case: paras. 5.1 and 5.2.

As for the contents of the bundle, the documents must be in chronological order from the front of the bundle, paginated, and indexed and divided into separate sections as follows:

(i)   preliminary documents and any other case management documents required by any other practice direction;

(ii) applications and orders;

(iii) statements and affidavits (which must be dated in the top right hand corner of the front page);

(iv) care plans (where appropriate);

(v)   experts' reports and other reports;

(vi) other documents, divided into further sections, as may be appropriate: para. 4.1.

At the commencement of the bundle there must be inserted the following documents (these are known as the preliminary documents):

(i)   an up-to-date summary of the background to the hearing limited, if possible, to one A4 page;

(ii) a statement of the issue or issues to be determined (1) at the hearing and (2) at the final hearing;

(iii) a position statement of each party including a summary of the order or directions sought (1) at the hearing and (2) at the final hearing;

(iv) a chronology, if it is the final hearing;

(v) skeleton arguments, if appropriate, with copies of all authorities relied on;

(vi) a list of essential reading for that hearing: para. 4.2.

Paragraphs 4.3, 4.4, and 4.5 set out additional requirements for the preparation of the preliminary documents including, for example, giving the date of preparation of the document and the date of the hearing for which it was intended, comprehensive cross-referencing of the documents which should be agreed by all parties. Where that is not possible, the fact of disagreement and their differing contentions should be set out at appropriate places in the document.

Further, para. 10.1 requires an agreed time estimate to be inserted at the front of the bundle which separately specifies:

(i) the time estimated to be required for judicial pre-reading;

(ii) the time required for hearing all evidence and submissions;

(iii) the time estimated to be required for preparing and delivering judgment.

The time estimate is to be prepared on the basis that before they give evidence, all witnesses will have read all relevant filed statements and reports.

Paragraph 10.2 sets out the procedure if there is a change in the time estimate once the case is listed for hearing while para. 11 deals with the situation where a case is to be taken out of the list.

According to para. 6.1, the party preparing the bundle shall provide a paginated index to all parties not less than four working days before the hearing, irrespective of whether the bundle has been agreed. Counsel is to receive a paginated bundle by those instructing him or her not less than three working days before the hearing (para. 6.2) and the bundle (with the exception of the preliminary documents if and insofar as they are not then available) is to be lodged at the court not less than two working days before the hearing or at such other time as may be specified by the judge (para. 6.3).

Paragraph 6.4 provides that the preliminary documents are to be lodged no later than 11.00am on the day before the hearing and, where the hearing is before a High Court judge whose identity is known, the documents should also be sent by e-mail to the judge's clerk.

Paragraph 7 sets out in detail how and where the bundle is to be lodged at court with specific additional requirements, set out in para. 8, to be followed for cases being heard in the Principal Registry of the Family Division at First Avenue House or at the Royal Courts of Justice.

What is clear, at para. 12, is that, where there is a failure to comply with any part of the Practice Direction, the judge is authorized to remove the case from the list or put the case further back and he may also make a 'wasted' costs order against the party at fault.

It will be apparent from the above that now a trial bundle is to be lodged and then re-lodged as the case progresses. Paragraphs 9.1 and 9.2 deal with this by requiring the person responsible for the bundle to retrieve it immediately on completion of the hearing. If that is not practicable, the bundle must be collected from the court within five working days, otherwise it may be destroyed.

Before the bundle is re-lodged in readiness for the next hearing, it must be updated and all superseded documents (for example, outdated summaries and chronologies) are to be removed (para. 4.7).

(c) A calculation of both parties' tax positions should be prepared with copies for the other side and the district judge. This is likely to be limited now to an indication of any capital gains tax liability which a party may incur in carrying out the order.

(d) It is suggested that, where there are children of the family in respect of whom the Child Support Agency is likely to carry out a maintenance calculation, the solicitor should make the calculation to establish his client's future liability since this will have an impact on the outcome of the ancillary relief application.

(e) It is of enormous help to the court if the solicitor prepares a schedule summarizing the income and outgoings, together with the assets and liabilities of his client as they stand at the date of the hearing. This enables the district judge, at a glance, to see the basic parameters of the financial information. It is becoming common practice for the schedule of assets to be divided into two parts, namely total assets without pension and a separate statement of the pension CETVs. The pension figures should be divided to show the sum which may be taken as a lump sum and the date on which that could happen, and the balance which would provide an income stream.

Example

Mrs A:	age 42
Mr A:	age 45
Samantha:	age 12 (resides with Mrs A)
Tom:	age 10 (resides with Mrs A)

SCHEDULE OF INCOME AND ASSETS

Mrs A: Income and Outgoings

Mrs A's income (net of tax and national insurance)	£20,000 pa
Mrs A's outgoings (itemized on separate sheet)	£25,000 pa

Mr A: Income and Outgoings

Mr A's income (net of tax and national insurance)	£35,000 pa
Mr A's outgoings (itemized on separate sheet)	£20,000 pa

Capital Assets (joint)

House: Value: £250,000 [Mortgage: £30,000]	Equity: £220,000
Endowment Policy	Surrender value: £25,000
Shares × 100 (£50 each)	Value: £5,000
Building Society account	£450
	TOTAL: £250,450

Capital Assets (Mrs A)

Jewellery	£10,000
Premium Bonds	£750
Bank account (fluctuating balance)	£1,000
Pension:	£35,000
	TOTAL: £46,750

Capital Assets (Mr A)

Sailing boat	£15,000
Painting (original oil)	£3,000
Bank account (fluctuating balance)	£1,200
Pension (CETV)	£85,000

TOTAL: £104,200

Debts (joint)

Bank loan	[outstanding] [£6,000]
Credit card debts	[outstanding] [£3,000]

TOTAL OUTSTANDING: £9,000
Summary of assets
TOTAL ASSETS: £401,400
TOTAL LIABILITIES: £9,000

BALANCE: £392,400

(f) The division of chattels should not be overlooked. In *K v K* (above), Baron J recommended that the division of chattels should be accomplished before the final hearing, with a clear schedule indicating who is to receive what. Where this is not possible, a *Scott* schedule should be drawn up with the items marked as agreed or remaining in dispute. The schedule should set out in very short form the reasons why any particular item is sought.

(g) As indicated in paragraph 18.117, where the FDR appointment does not lead to a settlement and costs order, the district judge may give appropriate directions for the future conduct of the proceedings. This may include filing further evidence about the finances of the parties or specific outstanding issues. In the majority of cases such further evidence should be unnecessary because of the nature of the information in Form E and the replies to questionnaires. Nevertheless, in *W v W (Ancillary Relief: Practice)* [2000] Fam Law 473, Wilson J indicated that in cases of greater wealth it would be helpful for the evidence to be broadened by narrative sworn statements.

(h) Rule 2.61F now requires (unless the court directs otherwise) each party 14 days before the final hearing to file with the court and serve on the other party a statement in Form H1 (not reproduced) giving full details of all costs in respect of the proceedings incurred or expected to be incurred. This is to enable the court to take account of the parties' liabilities for costs when deciding what order (if any) to make for ancillary relief.

Form H1 is a far more comprehensive document than Form H. It requires the solicitor over three pages to detail the costs incurred at each stage of the case. Since it takes time to complete and may be a disproportionate exercise, consideration should be given to asking the district judge to dispense with this requirement. This should be done at the conclusion of the FDR hearing and, if the request is granted, Form H (discussed in paragraph 18.102) would be completed instead.

(i) The procedure in preparation for a final hearing also requires some specific steps to be taken prior to the hearing.

Where a date is fixed for the final hearing, the applicant is required to file with the court and serve on the respondent an open statement which sets out concise details, including the amounts involved, of the orders he proposes to ask the court to make.

This must be done not less than 14 days before the date fixed for the final hearing: r. 2.69E(1).

This is known as 'an open proposal'. The respondent is then required to file with the court and serve on the applicant an open statement which sets out concise details, including the amounts involved, of the orders he proposes to ask the court to make. This step must be taken not more than seven days after the service of the applicant's statement: r. 2.69E(2).

These steps are designed to promote a settlement even where this has not been achieved by the FDR appointment.

The steps also serve to concentrate the minds of the parties on the question of the liability for costs set out in paragraph 18.128 and onwards.

(j)   At the risk of stating the obvious, it must be stressed that the practitioner should think out *in advance* what matters are covered adequately in his client's financial statement and what further evidence he will need to elicit from her at the hearing. Similarly, thought must be given to cross-examination—the art is putting telling questions pleasantly and in knowing what not to ask and when to stop. This is easier if a brief list has been made in advance of the points that need to be put to the witness.

(k)   In the average case, accommodation for the parties is the principal concern. It is useful, therefore, to obtain details from estate agents to demonstrate the cost of suitable accommodation, letters from the council setting out details of waiting lists and, perhaps most importantly, an indication from the present mortgagee as to its willingness to rearrange the mortgage or to lend additional amounts and so on.

(l)   Negotiations should be carried on right up to the last minute. The client may be saved a substantial sum in costs if a contested hearing can be averted.

L   THE HEARING

The hearing itself

18.123   The hearing will almost always be before a district judge (though the district judge does have power to refer the application to a judge; r. 2.65, 1991 Rules). It will be held in the district judge's chambers and will be private. In theory, the procedure should follow the normal pattern (applicant opens the case and calls evidence, respondent calls evidence, respondent addresses the district judge, applicant addresses the district judge). Many district judges do require proceedings to be run in this traditional manner. Others are prepared/prefer to adopt a much more informal approach. It is not unknown for the district judge to start off the proceedings by letting the parties know what he has in mind having read their financial statements and open proposals and inviting comment and discussion before going on to hear evidence and argument. Sometimes this produces agreement between parties without a fully contested hearing. Even if it does not, it is often valuable to the advocate in giving him an idea as to how the district judge's mind is working—it helps to know what aspects of the client's case do not appeal to the district judge and what points are particularly troubling him.

18.124   The important thing to remember is to cover all relevant points concisely. Often evidence is one of the least important parts of the case as the district judge knows much of what he needs to know already from Form E and any sworn statement filed. Some points should, however, be made here on addressing the district judge, which may be a good deal more important.

The applicant's advocate must be prepared to open the case formally, outlining to the dis- **18.125** trict judge the history of the matter (although often he will have gleaned this from his preliminary reading of the papers) and explaining what order it is that his client wants. It is a help to get matters clear in one's own mind before the hearing by preparing a timetable of the case so far (date of marriage, birth of children, separation, petition, etc.).

When it comes to addressing the district judge in closing the case, it is not often useful to **18.126** indulge in a review of the evidence that the district judge has just heard, although important points can be brought out if necessary. It can, however, be a great help to put to the district judge the types of orders that the advocate submits may be appropriate, outlining how his suggestions (and any suggestions made by the other side) would work in practice, for example, what effect they would have on the parties' tax positions, on income support entitlement, and on the statutory charge. Where maintenance is concerned, it is also helpful to draw to the district judge's attention how the proposed order would (or would not) enable both parties to meet their reasonable outgoings. From time to time it may be necessary to cite authorities on a legal point, but on the whole ancillary relief cases depend upon their own facts and authorities are not therefore particularly useful.

The district judge may make a bald announcement of his decision or he may give a short **18.127** judgment. A careful note should be taken of what he says as it can be important if an appeal is made against his order or if an application is made for a variation of the order at a later stage.

M   ORDERS FOR COSTS

The Family Proceedings (Amendments) Rules 2006 (SI 2006/352) came into force on 3 April **18.128** 2006. They are accompanied by an explanatory *President's Direction (Ancillary Relief: Costs)* [2006] 1 FLR 865. The Rules fundamentally change the position on costs in ancillary relief proceedings. Set out below is a summary of the principal provisions. Detailed guidance may be found in David Burrows, *The New Ancillary Relief Costs Regime* (*Family Law*, Jordans, 2006).

The main features of new scheme

These are as follows: **18.129**

(a) The new Rules, which amend the 1991 Rules, apply to ancillary relief proceedings only. It follows, therefore, that rr. 44.3(1)–(5) Civil Procedure Rules 1998 do not apply to ancillary relief proceedings. The principles do not apply therefore to divorce proceedings in themselves with the consequence that it may still be legitimate to seek an order for costs against the respondent in the main suit.

(b) The Rules are not retrospective in effect. They apply to an application for ancillary relief contained in a petition or answer filed on or after 3 April 2006 or to such an application which has not been made in a petition or answer but is made in Form A on or after that date. The Rules also apply, it should be noted, to an application under s. 10(2), MCA 1973 (see Chapter 12) or under s. 48(2), Civil Partnership Act 2004 ('CPA 2004') (see Chapter 14) made in Form B on or after that date.

(c)   As a general rule, there should now be no order for costs in ancillary relief proceedings: r. 2.71 (4)(a). The fundamental principle is that each party should be responsible for his or her own costs. Although not explicitly stated in the Rules (to avoid interfering with the exercise of judicial discretion), it is intended that these costs should be treated as part of reasonable financial needs of the parties to be paid for from the family 'pot of assets' before the court distributes the remainder between them: thus, crucially, '*Calderbank* offers' are no longer relevant.

18.130   This approach, however, is not without difficulty. Supposing one party runs up unnecessary costs pursuing a claim that assets had been concealed which proved to be unfounded or incurs costs of a high-charging city solicitor on a straightforward matter?

18.131   These matters would have to be raised during the course of the hearing and the judge invited to take them into account in fulfilling his duty to have regard (under s. 25(1), MCA 1973) to all the circumstances of the case and in his consideration of the appropriate terms of the order. It may be that the judge finds that certain costs are excessive and should be funded by the party incurring them.

In what circumstances will a costs order still be made?

18.132   The court retains a discretion to make a costs order at any stage of the proceedings where it considers it appropriate to do so because of the conduct of a party in relation to the proceedings: r. 2.71 (4).

18.133   In practical terms, this means that an order might be made in the following circumstances:

(a)   where there has been non-compliance with the Rules or a direction or order of the court (see, for example, the Practice Direction on Court Bundles [2006] discussed at 18.122, above);

(b)   where there has been disproportionate pursuit of an issue which turns out to be irrelevant;

(c)   where there has been unjustifiable delay in giving full disclosure.

18.134   To assist the court in deciding whether an order for costs should be made, r. 2.71(5) requires the court to have regard to the following:

(a)   any failure by a party to comply with the Rules, any order of the court, or any practice direction which the court considers relevant;

(b)   any open offer to settle made by a party;

(c)   whether it was reasonable for a party to raise, pursue, or contest a particular allegation or issue;

(d)   the manner in which a party has pursued or responded to the application or a particular allegation or issue;

(e)   any other aspect of a party's conduct in relation to the proceedings which the court considers relevant; and

(f)   the financial effect on the parties of any costs orders.

The President's Direction makes it clear that where a party is seeking an order for costs **18.135** against the other this should be made plain in open correspondence or in skeleton arguments before the date of the hearing—these requirements are in addition to the need to file and serve a statement of costs in Form N260.

Maintenance pending suit to pay legal fees

The President's Direction confirms that where an order for maintenance pending suit **18.136** is made which includes an element to allow a party to deal with legal fees (as in *A* v *A (Maintenance Pending Suit: Provision for Legal Fees)* [2001] 1 FLR 377), the order is not a 'costs order' within the meaning of r. 2.71, FPR 1991, as amended.

N CONSENT ORDERS

The importance of attempting to settle ancillary relief disputes without incurring the costs of **18.137** a contested hearing cannot be stressed too heavily. There is no point in fighting over £750 if a costs bill of £1,000 is run up in the process. Furthermore, a continuing battle over ancillary relief does nothing to help the parties get over the breakdown of their marriage and resolve other difficulties, for example, over children.

Just as each party has a duty to make full disclosure of all material facts to the court hearing **18.138** an ancillary relief application, each party has a duty to make full and frank disclosure of all material facts to the other party during negotiations which may lead to a consent order (see the case of *Livesey* v *Jenkins* [1985] 2 WLR 47).

The solicitor should not be frightened therefore to seek from the other party all the informa- **18.139** tion that he considers to be necessary in order to advise his client whether a proposed settlement is acceptable.

Rule 2.61 of the FPR 1991 should go some way to ensuring that relevant facts are disclosed. **18.140** This rule deals with the procedure for seeking a consent order for financial relief. The procedure where agreement is reached before the hearing date of the ancillary relief applications should now therefore be as follows:

(a) If agreement is reached before either party has filed a notice in Form A, application should be made by one or the other party in Form A for an order in the agreed terms and, in accordance with r. 2.61(1), there should be lodged with the application two copies (although many courts require three) of a draft of the order, one of which must be endorsed with a statement signed by the respondent signifying his agreement. Presumably, if agreement is reached after Form A has been filed, the applicant should simply lodge the endorsed draft order with the court requesting that the district judge should make an order in these terms. It is essential to check with the client that the draft order reflects the terms of settlement to prevent errors.

(b) Section 33A, MCA 1973 provides that, on an application for a consent order for financial relief, the court may, unless it has reason to think that there are other circumstances into which it ought to inquire, make an order in the terms agreed on the basis only of the prescribed information furnished with the application.

Rule 2.61 prescribes the information that must be furnished. It requires that there shall be lodged with the application a statement of information in Form M1 relied on in support of the application.

18.141 Matters that must normally be incorporated include details of the duration of the marriage (or civil partnership) ages of the parties and any children of the family; an estimate in summary form of the approximate amount or value of the capital, income resources and value of any benefits under a pension arrangement which either party has or is likely to have, including the most recent valuation provided by the pension arrangement (Family Proceedings (Amendment) Rules 1997 (SI 1997/637), taking into account the Pensions Act 1995), and, where relevant, of any minor child of the family; details of what is intended with regard to the occupation or disposal of the matrimonial home and what is intended with regard to accommodation of both parties and minor children; whether either party has remarried, or presently intends to remarry or cohabit (or form a civil partnership) confirmation that, where appropriate, the mortgagee of the property and/or the person responsible for the pension arrangement has been served with notice of the application and has not objected within 14 days (in the case of the mortgagee) or 21 days in the case of the pension provider (see r. 2.61(1)). Where the person responsible for the pension arrangement does object, the court must consider their objections. In doing so, the court may make such directions as it thinks fit for the person responsible to attend before it or to furnish written details of their objections: r. 2.70(8). The form concludes with the opportunity to set out other especially significant circumstances and this may be used to explain the rationale of the order.

18.142 It should be noted that the rules as to notification of the person responsible for the pension arrangement are slightly more onerous where the consent order includes provision for pension attachment.

18.143 Here, r. 2.70(11) requires that the person responsible for the pension arrangement must be served with

(a)   a notice of application for a consent order under r. 2.61(1);
(b)   a draft of the proposed order; and
(c)   the detailed information as to addresses for service and payment as laid down in r. 2.70(7).

18.144 Rule 2.70(12) goes on to state that a consent order will not be made in these circumstances unless the person responsible for the pension arrangement has not made any objection within 21 days after the notice was served on him or the court has considered any such objection.

18.145 The statement of information can be provided in more than one document. No doubt where Form E has already been filed in relation to the application this will be sufficient to provide the court with some of the information required but practice varies from court to court.

18.146 The client needs to be warned that the court retains a discretion to refuse to make the order in the proposed terms, especially if it takes the view that the provision for the other spouse is inadequate. It is sensible therefore to explain the reasons for the particular terms of the order under 'any other especially significant circumstances' rather than leaving the court to guess and raise concerns.

Where agreement is reached only at the door of the court, r. 2.61(3) enables the court **18.147** to dispense with the lodging of the draft of the order and a statement of information and to give directions for the order to be drawn and the information that would otherwise be required in the statement of information to be given in such manner as it sees fit.

It is incumbent upon the solicitor to make sure that the order is carefully drafted so as to **18.148** embody what the parties have agreed upon comprehensively, leaving no room for future doubt (*Sandford* v *Sandford* [1986] 1 FLR 412; *Dinch* v *Dinch* [1987] 1 WLR 252).

O SOME POINTS ON DRAFTING ANCILLARY RELIEF ORDERS

Introduction

There are a number of reasons for becoming familiar with the requirements of a well-drafted **18.149** order dealing with ancillary relief matters. First of all, many claims for ancillary relief are eventually agreed. It is the responsibility of the solicitor to incorporate the terms of the settlement in a consent order to be submitted to the court for approval and sealing before its terms can be implemented. Secondly, often the solicitor is asked to approve a draft order submitted by the other party's solicitor and it is important to know how the document should be drawn up so that any amendments can be made. Thirdly, it is not uncommon for a district judge, at the conclusion of his judgment, to outline the terms of the order and require the solicitors or counsel to draft the order for his approval.

The form of the order

Most ancillary relief orders are made up of two elements: **18.150**

(a) the preamble, and
(b) the body of the order.

The preamble

The main purpose of the preamble is to record essential elements in the financial settle- **18.151** ment which the court has no power to order because of the restrictive wording of the MCA 1973.

The preamble may indicate the basis upon which certain provision is to be made (e.g., that **18.152** periodical payments are to be made on the basis that the recipient uses them to pay specified outgoings). In addition the preamble may contain a number of undertakings.

An undertaking is a promise to the court to do certain things. Breach of an undertaking is a **18.153** contempt of court and may be enforced like an order.

An undertaking may be used to deal with matters which the court cannot expressly order. It **18.154** is important to distinguish between an undertaking to do something and an undertaking to use best endeavours to achieve a particular outcome. The latter form of undertaking is used where the co-operation or consent of a third party is required, for example, the petitioner may give an undertaking to use her best endeavours to secure the release of the respondent from his covenants under the mortgage. Obviously this arrangement requires the consent of the mortgage lender over whom the petitioner has no control. By contrast, the performance of other undertakings will be well within the power of the person giving them. Such undertakings include, for example:

(a)   to make mortgage payments;
(b)   to pay contributions in respect of a personal pension;
(c)   to pay other debts or outgoings.

An example of such an undertaking is set out below:

> And upon the Petitioner undertaking as from the date of the order:
>
> (a)   To pay or cause to be paid the mortgage to the Wessex Building Society and all other liabilities relating to the property known as 28 Acacia Avenue, Ambridge, Wessex.
>
> (b)   To use her best endeavours to procure the release of the Respondent from any liability under the mortgage in favour of the Wessex Building Society and in any event to indemnify the Respondent against all such liability.

In order to ensure that an undertaking is enforceable as far as possible the following additional steps are recommended:

- The parties and their solicitors should sign one copy of the order and the solicitor for a party giving an undertaking should declare that he has explained the meaning of the undertaking to his client and the consequences of failing to comply with it.
- The order should contain a statement by the giver of the undertaking 'I understand the undertaking(s) that I have given and that if I break any of my promises to the court I may be sent to prison for contempt of court'—and be endorsed with a penal notice: 'You may be sent to prison if you break the promises you have given to the court'.

(from District Judge Adam Taylor, 'Promises, Promises',
Law Society Gazette, 13 March 2003.)

- A copy of the document recording the undertaking should be served personally upon the party giving the undertaking as soon as practicable.

18.155   The preamble can also be used to set out the history of the division of the family assets which has already taken place. For example, it may record that the family home has already been sold and the net proceeds of sale divided equally between the parties. Further, the preamble may explain the rationale of aspects of the order. For example, it may record that one party is taking responsibility for discharging outstanding family debts (and that is why he or she is to receive an enhanced lump sum payment).

The body of the order

18.156   This will deal with those aspects of the financial settlement which the court has power to order.

Periodical payments

18.157   (i)   The order must indicate the following:

(a) to whom and by whom is the payment to be made;

(b) the amount of the payment;

(c) whether the payment is to be made weekly, monthly, or annually;

(d) whether the payment is to be made in advance or in arrears;

(e) the date on which payment is to begin;

(f) the events which will bring payment to an end.

(ii) *Back-dating an order for periodical payments*: there is power to back-date periodical payments orders to the date of the making of the application (see Chapter 17). If an order is back-dated, the payer is instantly in arrears in respect of the payments due prior to the hearing. For this reason, the court will be reluctant to back-date unless the payer has actually been making voluntary periodical payments in the run-up to the hearing which can be offset against the arrears. Care must be taken therefore to ensure that the payer is given credit for any payments he may have made between the date to which the order is back-dated and the date on which the order is made. Where such credit is given, it has the effect of reducing the arrears (or even extinguishing them).

(iii) *Registration of periodical payments order in family proceedings court*: this means that the order will be paid and enforced through the family proceedings court and that any application for a variation will have to be made to that court. It also means that the diversion procedure can be used with regard to social security benefits (see Chapter 38). An application for registration should certainly be considered where it appears that payment under the order may be erratic.

Lump sums

In addition to the order specifying the details of the amount to be paid and the date of payment, it is important to specify the rate of interest to be paid should default occur. **18.158**

The clause would read as follows: **18.159**

> The Respondent do within 28 days of the date of this order pay or cause to be paid to the Petitioner a lump sum of £10,000, interest to accrue at the rate of per cent per annum calculated on a daily basis in the event of default.

Property adjustment orders

Such orders normally deal with the future of the family home but can also determine the disposal of personal property, for example, house contents, cars, and investments and savings. The precise terms of the property adjustment order will depend on how the assets are to be disposed of but set out below is a non-exhaustive list of matters to be considered with the more usual types of order. **18.160**

(a) *Outright transfer of the family home*   The order must include provision for the transfer of the legal and equitable interest in the property and a date or event for transfer. This is essential to determine whether default has occurred.

(b) *Deferred trust*   Here the property will remain in joint names or be transferred into the joint names of the parties to hold the legal estate as trustees and the order will then include provisions to regulate the trust.

The following matters must be dealt with:

(i) a statement as to who is to have the exclusive right to occupy the property until sale;

(ii) identifying the 'triggering' events for the sale to occur, for example, of the youngest child of the family attaining the age of 17 years, or on the death or remarriage of the occupying party (whichever occurs first);

(iii) provision as to how the net proceeds of sale are to be calculated and an indication of the division of the net proceeds between the parties;

(iv) determining who is to be responsible for the cost of repairing and insuring the property in the meantime;

(v) who is to pay for any costs associated with implementing the terms of the order (e.g., the cost, if any, of preparation of the transfer documents).

(c) *Deferred charge*

(i) if necessary the order will require the transfer of the legal estate into the sole name of the occupying party, the transfer to be completed by a specified date.

(ii) the occupying party will also be required to execute a charge in favour of the non-occupier to ensure that he receives payment of a sum representing a specified proportion of the net value of the property.

The legal charge is a comprehensive document which not only regulates the occupation of the property (e.g., preventing the occupying party from remortgaging the property without the consent of the other party), but specifies the triggering events for the statutory power of sale to arise.

Orders for sale

18.161 Where there is to be an immediate sale of assets the order must of course specify the division of the net proceeds of sale and indicate which party is to have responsibility for the conduct of the sale (this is particularly important where one party is likely to be unco-operative) and which estate agent is to be instructed.

18.162 For a fuller discussion on orders in relation to the family home, see Chapter 19.

Pension attachment orders

18.163 These orders, made under ss. 25B and 25C, MCA 1973 and described in Chapter 17, require careful drafting.

18.164 The following points should be noted:

(a) The attachment order may relate to a personal, as distinct from an occupational, pension. Here responsibility for payment of the pension contributions lies with the pension-holder. The court has no power to order that payments be made to increase the value of the pension fund. The pension-holder should therefore be required to give an undertaking to the court, recorded in the preamble to the order, to continue to make such payments (and, arguably, to increase them on an annual basis in line with inflation or by a specified percentage).

(b) The order cannot take effect until the pension becomes payable. The court is unable to order that the pension-holder retire by a specified date, and therefore it is imperative that the preamble to the order contains an undertaking from the pension-holder to retire by a certain date or take the benefits under a personal pension arrangement by a specified date.

(c) For a lump sum to be payable on maturity of the pension, a proportion of the pension fund must be commuted (i.e., pension benefits are exchanged for a tax-free single lump sum payment). Under s. 25B(7), MCA 1973, the court may order the pension-holder to commute a proportion of the pension fund to provide a lump sum for the benefit of the receiving party. What the court is not able to do is to order the pension-holder *not* to commute the pension fund, and yet such action will reduce the pension income otherwise payable and, in consequence, the benefit of any order attaching the pension income. The solution is to incorporate an undertaking into the preamble in which the pension-holder agrees to commute a specified proportion of the pension benefits only.

(d) While the order attaching the pension income will end on the remarriage of the receiving party, this is not the case with the payment of a lump sum which has been attached. The pension-holder may consider this to be unjust, and unless it can be demonstrated that payment of a lump sum at the time of the maturity of the pension is simply part of the process of the redistribution of capital assets, as happened in *Burrow* v *Burrow* [1999] 1 FLR 508, it is sensible to include a provision in the order allowing the lump sum payment to lapse on the remarriage of the receiving party;

(e) the order attaching the pension income is seen as a form of periodical payments order made under s. 23, MCA 1973. In consequence it is essential that the body of the order contains a periodical payments order (for a nominal amount). This will enable the receiving party, if appropriate, to seek a prospective variation of the attachment order, to become effective on the retirement of the pension-holder.

The terms of a pension sharing or pension attachment order

Rule 2.70(13) requires that where such an order is to be made, the body of the order must contain a statement that there is to be provision by way of pension sharing or pension attachment in accordance with the annex to the order and be accompanied by an annex containing information which will be determined by whether a pension sharing or pension attachment order is made. Where provision is made in relation to more than one pension arrangement there must be an annex for each pension arrangement. **18.165**

The information in the annex (Form P1)—pension sharing order

The detailed information is set out in the annex and includes, among other things, details of the court making the order and of the transferor and transferee, details sufficient to identify the pension arrangement concerned, the specified percentage required to create the pension debit and pension credit, details as to who is to pay the costs of implementing the order, the date on which the order takes effect, and whether there is to be an internal or external transfer etc. **18.166**

Most importantly, the annex indicates that, before making the pension sharing order, the court must be satisfied that the person responsible for the pension arrangement has provided the information required by the Pension on Divorce, etc. (Provision of Information) Regulations 2000 (SI 2000/1048), reg. 4 and that in consequence there is a power to make a pension sharing order. **18.167**

The information in the annex (Form P2)—pension attachment order

The detailed information is similar to that contained in Form P1. The annex enables the parties to set out the precise terms of the order (for example, the percentage of the pension **18.168** income to be paid to the recipient). In addition, however, the annex must also prescribe what the person responsible for the pension arrangement is required to do and details of addresses where payment is to be made.

Clean break orders

18.169 Where the parties have agreed that there should be a clean break order (see Chapter 19, paragraphs 19.20 and onwards), the order should be drafted in such a way that the arrangement works on a mutual and comprehensive basis, as demonstrated in the clause set out below:

> Upon compliance with paragraphs 1 and 2 of this order and upon compliance by the Respondent with his undertaking herein the Petitioner's and the Respondent's claims for financial provision and property adjustment orders do stand dismissed, and it is directed that neither party shall be entitled to apply to the court thereafter for an order under s. 23(1)(a), (b) or (c), s. 24, s. 24A, s. 24B or ss. 25B and C of the Matrimonial Causes Act 1973 as amended or substituted nor under the Married Women's Property Act 1882.
>
> Pursuant to the Inheritance (Provision for Family and Dependants) Act 1975, s. 15, the court considering it just so to order, neither the Petitioner nor the Respondent shall be entitled on the death of the other to apply for an order under s. 2 of that Act.

18.170 It should be noted that where the order contains provision for pension sharing, claims should not be dismissed until the pension sharing order takes effect so that the non-member party is left with a claim against the member's estate under the 1975 Act, if the member dies during the implementation process.

Costs

18.171 These have been discussed at paragraph 18.128 and onwards. However it may be necessary to ask the court to direct that a detailed assessment of costs is carried out.

18.172 Where a client is publicly funded, such a direction should be requested to enable costs to be recovered from the Community Legal Service Fund.

18.173 The detailed assessment must be carried out within three months of the date of the order otherwise costs penalties are imposed by the Commission.

18.174 Sometimes it is not possible to implement the terms of the order within such a time limit, especially where delays occur in completing the conveyancing work to be undertaken because, for example, one party refuses to sign the transfer documents. In order to avoid the costs penalties, it is suggested that the following clause is included in the order: 'The time for commencement for the detailed assessment of costs under r. 4(1) of the Matrimonial Causes (Costs) Rules 1988 shall not commence until the date of completion of the relevant conveyancing and working out of this order'.

18.175 Remember the need to try to ensure that the Legal Services Commission will agree to the postponement of the charge where property has been recovered or preserved for the publicly funded client (see Chapter 2).

Liberty to apply

18.176 This provision should be included to enable either party to seek guidance from the court in respect of the interpretation and/or implementation of the order if difficulties subsequently arise. However, note that this provision does not enable the parties to return to court for a variation of some of the substantive parts of the order.

The liberty to apply provision is essential in orders relating to property. For example, **18.177** it enables the matter to be referred back to the district judge for execution of the transfer, or for an order for possession if one party refuses to co-operate. Similarly, it can be relied on if one party fails to sign an assignment of a life policy, or refuses to sell when the triggering event occurs in respect of property held on a trust of land (see Chapter 22).

P APPEAL

Where an order is made after a contested hearing in front of the district judge, either party **18.178** may appeal, if dissatisfied, to a judge in chambers. Note that the appeal period is 14 days from the date of the district judge's order (see r. 8.1(4), FPR 1991). Furthermore, the appellant must now set out his grounds of appeal in his notice of appeal. The manner in which the circuit judge should approach the appeal was determined by the Court of Appeal in *Cordle* v *Cordle* [2001] EWCA Civ 1791 and confirmed in amended wording to r. 8.1(3) introduced by the Family Proceedings (Amendment) Rules 2003 (as to (ii) and (iii) below), as follows:

(i)   The decision of the district judge should be interfered with only if the decision was clearly incorrect (e.g., because the district judge had taken into account irrelevant matters or ignored relevant matters) or in the event of a procedural error having been made (*Cordle* v *Cordle*, above) and confirmed in *V* v *V* (*Financial Relief*) [2005] 3 FLR 697.
(ii) The appeal is to be limited to a review of the decision or order of the district judge unless the judge considers that, in the circumstances of the case, it would be in the interests of justice to hold a rehearing: r. 8.1(3)(a).
(iii) Oral evidence or evidence which was not before the district judge may be admitted if in all the circumstances of the case it would be in the interests of justice to do so, irrespective of whether the appeal be by way of review or rehearing: r. 8.1(3)(b).

As to (ii) above, a rehearing is likely to be ordered if there were inadequate findings of fact at **18.179** first instance or if the decision of the district judge was considered to be unjust because of some procedural or other irregularity.

As to (iii) above, oral evidence or fresh evidence will not be admitted on appeal unless either **18.180** it was not available at the trial to the party seeking to rely on it, or that reasonable diligence would not have made it available and that it would have formed a determining factor in, or an important influence on, the outcome of the case.

Appeal is normally to a circuit judge, except in the Principal Registry of the Family Division **18.181** where the appeal is heard by a judge of the Family Division. Appeals which involve issues of complexity or gravity (for example, allegations of deception or fraud or material non-disclosure, etc.) should be dealt with in the High Court.

Q   CHALLENGING ANCILLARY RELIEF CONSENT ORDERS

Procedure

18.182   As the case of *Livesey* v *Jenkins* (see paragraph 18.138) illustrates, a consent order can also be set aside. The court would be justified in so doing if it could be shown that the parties' agreement was reached on the basis of a serious mistake by one of the parties, or as a result of fraud or serious misrepresentation, or in circumstances where one party had not disclosed all the material facts to the other and this had led the court to make an order substantially different from that which it would otherwise have made (e.g., see *T* v *T* (*Consent Order: Procedure to Set Aside*) [1997] 1 FCR 282, and, for a case where the Court of Appeal refused to set aside, stating that the policy of the law is to encourage a clean break, *Harris* v *Manahan* [1997] 1 FLR 205).

18.183   The correct procedure for challenging an ancillary relief consent order is to apply for a rehearing if the order was made in a county court, or for the order to be set aside if made in the High Court. The only practical route is to apply to set aside under CCR 1981, Ord. 37, r. 1. This is confirmed in *T* v *T* (above). Under this provision the judge has power on an application made within 14 days (or later with permission) to order a rehearing where no error of the court at the hearing is alleged. The rehearing will be on the basis of a consideration of the documents only. In the High Court where the application would be to set aside the original order, there is no specific time limit for the application to set aside to be made, but two weeks would normally be regarded as the time for application.

Appeal out of time

18.184   Events may occur shortly after the order is made which have the effect of undermining the basis on which the order was made. In these circumstances it would be inappropriate to apply for a rehearing (in the case of a county court order) or to have the order set aside (in the case of a High Court order) since the event in question occurred *after* the order was made. Nor could there be a conventional appeal, since it would be impossible to argue that the judge had made an error on the facts before him.

18.185   The solution is to apply to the court for permission to appeal out of time.

18.186   The criteria to be met are set out in *Barder* v *Barder* (*Caluori intervening*) [1988] AC 20, as follows:

(a)   that new events have occurred since the making of the order which invalidate the basis, or fundamental assumption, upon which the order was made so that, if permission to appeal out of time were given, the appeal would be certain, or very likely, to succeed;

(b)   that the new events have occurred within a relatively short time of the order having been made;

(c)   the application for permission to appeal should be made reasonably promptly in the circumstances of the case;

(d)   granting of permission to appeal out of time should not prejudice third parties who have acquired, in good faith and for valuable consideration, interests in the property which is the subject matter of the relevant order.

The first two conditions above were demonstrated in *Reid* v *Reid* [2004] 1 FLR 736 where the **18.187** wife died two months after a consent order had been made. Her early death justified permission to appeal out of time and enabled the court to make a more generous order in favour of the husband while ensuring that the wife's estate retained some capital.

The fact that there had been a delay of three months between the death of the wife and the **18.188** making of the application did not fall foul of the requirement to act promptly. However, an application for permission to appeal out of time will fail where there is an unjustified delay in making the application (for example, a period of approximately four years in *Burns* v *Burns* [2004] 3 FCR 263).

Recent guidance on the application of the above principles in practice has been offered by **18.189** the Court of Appeal in *Williams* v *Lindley* [2005] 2 FLR 710. In particular, where it is found that a supervening event (in this case, the wife's remarriage) has invalidated the original order, then reassessment by appeal out of time would be appropriate. The reassessment would include a full consideration of all the factors in s. 25, MCA 1973 and not simply a consideration of what assets the parties had at the time of the hearing and what their current value is.

Hence, practitioners need to ensure that in drafting the application to appeal out of time: **18.190**

(i)   the application should clearly identify the supervening event;
(ii) explain why the event would produce a fundamentally different result had it been anticipated at the time of the original order; and
(iii) clearly indicate the effect the supervening event has (a) on the original order and (b) on what happens subsequently.

R   ANCILLARY RELIEF PROCEDURE AND CIVIL PARTNERSHIP

The procedure described above also applies to ancillary relief proceedings brought where a **18.191** civil partnership is to be annulled or dissolved or where a separation order is applied for: r. 2.51B, FPR 1991, as amended.

S   FLOWCHART

This is to be found on page 289. **18.192**

T   KEY DOCUMENTS

The Family Proceedings Rules 1991 (SI 1991/1247), as amended **18.193**

Notice of [intention to proceed with] an Application for Ancillary Relief

Respondents (Solicitor(s))
name and address

In the	
	[County Court]
	[Principal Registry of the Family Division]
Case No. *Always quote this*	
Applicant's Solicitor's reference	
Respondent's Solicitor's reference	

(* delete as appropriate)

Postcode

Between   (petitioner)

and   (respondent)

Take Notice that

the Applicant intends   ***to apply** to the Court for

*delete as   ***to proceed** with the application in the [petition] [answer] for
appropriate
                             *to apply to vary:

☐ an order for maintenance pending suit or   ☐ a periodical payments order
   outcome of proceedings
                                                    ☐ a lump sum order
☐ a secured provision order
                                                    ☐ a pension sharing order or a pension
☐ a property adjustment order *(please provide address)*   attachment order

If an application is made for any periodical payments or secured periodical payments for children:

- and there is a written agreement made before 5 April 1993 about maintenance for the benefit of children,
  tick this box ☐

- and there is a written agreement made on or after 5 April 1993 about maintenance for the benefit of children,
  tick this box ☐

- but there is no agreement, tick any of the boxes below to show if you are applying for payment:

  ☐ for a stepchild or stepchildren
  ☐ in addition to child support maintenance already paid under a Child Support Agency assessment
  ☐ to meet expenses arising from a child's disability
  ☐ to meet expenses incurred by a child in being educated or training for work
  ☐ when either the child **or** the person with care of the child **or** the absent parent of the child
     is not habitually resident in the United Kingdom
  ☐ Other *(please state)*

Signed: _____   Dated:
[Applicant][Solicitor for the Applicant]

The court office at

is open between 10 am and 4 pm (4.30 pm at the Principal Registry of the Family Division) Monday to Friday. When corresponding with the court, please address forms or
letters to the Court Manager and quote the case number. If you do not do so, your correspondence may be returned.

Cat.No. **FP-A**   QFU 27802 (1.4)
                                                                                     12/2005

FINANCIAL STATEMENT

OF

*Husband/*Wife/*Civil partner

In the	
	*[High/County Court] *[Principal Registry of the Family Division]
Case No. *Always quote this*	
Petitioner's Solicitor's reference	
Respondent's Solicitor's reference	

*(*delete as appropriate)*

Between

and

Who is the *husband/*wife/*civil partner
 *Petitioner/*Respondent in the
 *divorce/*dissolution suit

Applicant in this matter

Who is the *husband/*wife/*civil partner
 *Petitioner/*Respondent in the
 *divorce/*dissolution suit

Respondent in this matter

Please fill in this form fully and accurately. Where any box is not applicable, write 'N/A'.

You have a duty to the court to give a full, frank and clear disclosure of all your financial and other relevant circumstances.

A failure to give full and accurate disclosure may result in any order the court makes being set aside.

If you are found to have been deliberately untruthful, criminal proceedings for perjury may be taken against you.

You must attach documents to the form where they are specifically sought and you may attach other documents where it is necessary to explain or clarify any of the information that you give.

Essential documents that must accompany this statement are detailed in the form.

If there is not enough room on the form for any particular piece of information, you may continue on an attached sheet of paper.

If you are in doubt about how to complete any part of this form you should seek legal advice.

This Statement must be sworn before a solicitor, a commissioner for oaths or an Officer of the Court or, if abroad, a notary or duly authorised official, before it is filed with the Court or sent to the other party (see last page).

This statement is filed by

Name and address of solicitor

1 General Information

1.1 Full name

1.2 Date of birth	Date	Month	Year	1.3 Date of the marriage/ civil partnership	Date	Month	Year

1.4 Occupation

1.5 Date of the separation	Date	Month	Year	Tick here if not applicable ☐

1.6 Date of the

	Petition			Decree nisi/Decree of judicial separation Conditional order/ Separation order			Decree absolute/ Final order (if applicable)		
	Date	Month	Year	Date	Month	Year	Date	Month	Year

1.7 If you have subsequently married or formed a civil partnership, or will do so, state the date

Date	Month	Year

1.8 Are you co-habiting?   Yes ☐   No ☐

1.9 Do you intend to co-habit within the next six months?   Yes ☐   No ☐

1.10 Details of any children of the family

Full names	Date of birth			With whom does the child live?
	Date	Month	Year	

1.11 Details of the state of health of yourself and the children if you think this should be taken into account

Yourself	Children

1.12 Details of the present and proposed future educational arrangements for the children.

Present arrangements	Future arrangements

1.13 Details of any child support maintenance calculation or any maintenance order or agreement made in respect of any children of the family. If no calculation, order or agreement has been made, give an estimate of the liability of the non-resident parent in respect of the children of the family under the Child Support Act 1991.

1.14 If this application is to vary an order, attach a copy of the order and give details of the part that is to be varied and the changes sought. You may need to continue on a separate sheet.

1.15 Details of any other court cases between you and your spouse/civil partner, whether in relation to money, property, children or anything else.

Case No.	Court

1.16 Your present residence and the occupants of it and on what terms you occupy it (e.g. tenant, owner-occupier).

Address	Occupants	Terms of occupation

2 Financial Details *Part 1 Real Property and Personal Assets*

2.1 Complete this section in respect of the family home (the last family home occupied by you and your spouse/civil partner) if it remains unsold.

Documentation required for attachment to this section:

a) A copy of any valuation of the property obtained within the last six months. If you cannot provide this document, please give your own realistic estimate of the current market value

b) A recent mortgage statement confirming the sum outstanding on **each** mortgage

Property name and address	
Land Registry title number	
Mortgage company name(s) and address(es) and account number(s)	
Type of mortgage	
Details of who owns the property and the extent of your legal and beneficial interest in it (i.e. state if it is owned by you solely or jointly owned) with your spouse/civil partner or with others) **If you consider that the legal ownership as recorded at the Land Registry does not reflect the true position, state why**	
Current market value of the property	
Balance outstanding on any mortgage(s)	
If a sale at this stage would result in penalties payable under the mortgage, state amount	
Estimate the costs of sale of the property	
Total equity in the property (i.e. market value less outstanding mortgage(s), penalties if any and the costs of sale)	

TOTAL value of your interest in the family home: TOTAL A £

2.2 Details of your interest in any other property, land or buildings. Complete one page for each property you have an interest in.

Documentation required for attachment to this section:

a) A copy of any valuation of the property obtained within the last six months. If you cannot provide this document, please give your own realistic estimate of the current market value

b) A recent mortgage statement confirming the sum outstanding on **each** mortgage

Property name and address	
Land Registry title number	
Mortgage company name(s) and address(es) and account number(s)	
Type of mortgage	
Details of who owns the property and the extent of your legal and beneficial interest in it (i.e. state if it is owned by you solely or jointly owned with your spouse/civil partner or with others) **If you consider that the legal ownership as recorded at the Land Registry does not reflect the true position, state why**	
Current market value of the property	
Balance outstanding on any mortgage(s)	
If a sale at this stage would result in penalties payable under the mortgage, state amount	
Estimate costs of sale of the property	
Total equity in the property (i.e. market value less outstanding mortgage(s), penalties if any and the costs of sale)	
Total value of your interest in this property	

TOTAL value of your interest in ALL other property: TOTAL B £

2.3 Details of all personal bank, building society and National Savings Accounts that you hold or have held at any time in the last twelve months and which are or were either in your own name or in which you have or have had any interest. This applies whether any such account is in credit or in debit. For joint accounts give your interest and the name of the other account holder. If the account is overdrawn, show a minus figure.

Documentation required for attachment to this section:

For each account listed, all statements covering the last 12 months.

Name of bank or building society, including branch name	Type of account *(e.g. current)*	Account number	Name of other account holder *(if applicable)*	Balance at the date of this statement	Total current value of your interest

TOTAL value of your interest in ALL accounts: (C1) £

2.4 Details of all investments, including shares, PEPs, ISAs, TESSAs, National Savings Investments (other than already shown above), bonds, stocks, unit trusts, investment trusts, gilts and other quoted securities that you hold or have an interest in. (Do not include dividend income as this will be dealt with separately later on).

Documentation required for attachment to this section:

Latest statement or dividend counterfoil relating to each investment.

Name	Type of investment	Size of holding	Current value	Name of any other account holder *(if applicable)*	Total current value of your interest

TOTAL value of your interest in ALL your holdings: (C2) £

2.5 Details of all life insurance policies including endowment policies that you hold or have an interest in. Include those that do not have a surrender value. Complete one page for each policy.

Documentation required for attachment to this section:

A surrender valuation of each policy that has a surrender value.

Name of company			
Policy type			
Policy number			
If policy is assigned, state in whose favour and amount of charge			
Name of any other owner and the extent of your interest in the policy			
Maturity date *(If applicable)*	Date	Month	Year
Current surrender value (if applicable)			
If policy includes life insurance, the amount of the insurance and the name of the person whose life is insured			
Total current surrender value of your interest in the policy			

TOTAL value of your interest in ALL policies: (C3) £

2.6 Details of all monies that are OWED TO YOU. Do not include sums owed in director's or partnership accounts which should be included in section 2.11.

Brief description of money owed and by whom	Balance outstanding	Total current value of your interest

TOTAL value of your interest in ALL debts owed to you: (C4) £

2.7 Details of all cash sums held in excess of £500. You must state where it is held and the currency it is held in.

Where held	Amount	Currency	Total current value of your interest

TOTAL value of your interest in ALL cash sums: (C5)   £ _____

2.8 Details of personal belongings individually worth more than £500.

INCLUDE:
- **Cars (gross value)**
- **Collections, pictures and jewellery**
- **Furniture and house contents**

Brief description of item	Total current value of your interest

TOTAL value of your interest in ALL personal belongings: (C6)   £ _____

Add together all the figures in boxes C1 to C6 to give the TOTAL current value of your interest in personal assets: TOTAL C   £ _____

2 Financial Details   *Part 2 Capital: Liabilities and Capital Gains Tax*

2.9 Details of any liabilities you have.

EXCLUDE liabilities already shown such as:

- Mortgages
- Any overdrawn bank, building society or National Savings accounts

INCLUDE:

- Money owed on credit cards and store cards
- Bank loans
- Hire purchase agreements

List all credit and store cards held including those with a nil or positive balance. Where the liability is not solely your own, give the name(s) of the other account holder(s) and the amount of your share of the liability.

Liability	Name(s) of other account holder(s) *(if applicable)*	Total liability	Total current value of your interest in the liability

TOTAL value of your interest in ALL liabilities: (D1)	£

2.10 If any Capital Gains Tax would be payable on the disposal now of any of your real property or personal assets, give your estimate of the tax liability.

Asset	Total Capital Gains Tax liability

TOTAL value of ALL your potential Capital Gains Tax liabilities: (D2)	£
Add together D1 and D2 to give the TOTAL value of your liabilities: TOTAL D	£

2 Financial Details   *Part 3 Capital: Business assets and directorships*

2.11 Details of all your business interests. Complete one page for each business you have an interest in.

Documentation required for attachment to this section:

a) Copies of the business accounts for the last two financial years

b) Any documentation, if available at this stage, upon which you have based your estimate of the current value of your interest in this business, for example a letter from an accountant or a formal valuation. It is not essential to obtain a formal valuation at this stage.

Name of the business	
Briefly describe the nature of the business	
Are you *(Please delete all those that are not applicable)*	a) Sole trader b) Partner in a partnership with others c) Shareholder in a limited company
If you are a partner or a shareholder, state the extent of your interest in the business (i.e. partnership share or extent of your shareholding compared to the overall shares issued).	
State when your next set of accounts will be available.	
If any of the figures in the last accounts are not an accurate reflection of the current position, state why. **For example, if there has been a material change since the last accounts, or if the valuations of the assets are not a true reflection of their value (e.g. because property or other assets have not been revalued in recent years or because they are shown at a book value).**	
Total amount of any sums owed to you by the business by way of a director's loan account, partnership capital or current accounts or the like. Identify where these appear in the business accounts.	
Your estimate of the current value of your business interest. Explain briefly the basis upon which you have reached that figure.	
Your estimate of any Capital Gains Tax that would be payable if you were to dispose of your business now.	
Net value of your interest in this business after any Capital Gains Tax liability.	

TOTAL value of ALL your interests in business assets: TOTAL E | £

2.12 List any directorships you hold or have held in the last 12 months (other than those already disclosed in Section 2.11)

2   Financial Details   *Part 4   Capital: Pensions*

2.13 Give details of your pension rights. Complete a separate page for each pension.

EXCLUDE:
- Basic State Pension

INCLUDE (complete a separate page for each one):
- Additional State Pension (SERPS and State Second Pension (S2P))
- Free Standing Additional Voluntary Contribution Schemes (FSAVC) separate from the scheme of your employer
- Membership of ALL pension plans or schemes

Documentation required for attachment to this section:

a) A recent statement showing the cash equivalent transfer value (CETV) provided by the trustees or managers of each pension arrangement (or, in the case of the additional state pension, a valuation of these rights).

b) If any valuation is not available, give the estimated date when it will be available and attach a copy of your letter to the pension company or administrators from whom the information was sought and/or state the date on which an application for a valuation of a State Earnings Related Pension Scheme was submitted to the Department of Work and Pensions.

Name and address of pension arrangement	
Your National Insurance Number	
Number of pension arrangement or reference number	
Type of scheme e.g. occupational or personal, final salary, money purchase, additional state pension or other (if other, please give details)	
Date the CETV was calculated	
Is the pension in payment or drawdown or deferment? *(Please answer Yes or No)*	
State the cash equivalent transfer value (CETV) quotation, or in the additional state pension, the valuation of those rights	
If the arrangement is an occupational pension arrangement that is payinng reduced CETVs, please quote what the CETV would have been if not reduced. If this is not possible, please indicate if the CETV quoted is a reduced CETV.	

TOTAL value of ALL your pension assets: TOTAL F   £

2 Financial Details *Part 5 Capital: Other assets*

2.14 Give details of any other assets not listed in Parts 1 to 4 above.

INCLUDE (the following list is not exhaustive):

- Any personal or business assets not yet disclosed
- Unrealisable assets
- Share option schemes, stating the estimated net sale proceeds of the shares if the options were capable of exercise now, and whether Capital Gains Tax or Income Tax would be payable
- Business expansion schemes
- Futures
- Commodities
- Trust interests (including interests under a discretionary trust), stating your estimate of the value of the interest and when it is likely to become realisable. If you say it will never be realisable, or has no value, give your reasons
- Any asset that is likely to be received in the foreseeable future
- Any asset held on your behalf by a third party
- Any asset not disclosed elsewhere on this form even if held outside England and Wales

You are reminded of your obligation to disclose all your financial assets and interests of ANY nature.

Type of asset	Value	Total NET value of your interest
	TOTAL value of ALL your other assets: TOTAL G	£

2   Financial Details   *Part 6 Income: Earned income from employment*

2.15 Details of earned income from employment. Complete one page for each employment.

Documentation required for attachment to this section:
a)   P60 for the last financial year (you should have received this from your employer shortly after the last 5th April)
b)   Your last three payslips
c)   Your last Form P11D if you have been issued with one

Name and address of your employer	
Job title and brief details of the type of work you do	
Hours worked per week in this employment	
How long have you been with this employer?	
Explain the basis of your income i.e. state whether it is based on an annual salary or an hourly rate of pay and whether it includes commissions or bonuses	
Gross income for the last financial year as shown on your P60	
Net income for the last financial year i.e. gross income less income tax and national insurance	
Average net income for the last three months i.e. total income less income tax and national insurance divided by three	
Briefly explain any other entries on the attached payslips other than basic income, income tax and national insurance	
If the payslips attached for the last three months are not an accurate reflection of your normal income briefly explain why	
Details and value of any bonuses or other occasional payments that you receive from this employment not otherwise already shown, including the basis upon which they are paid	
Details and value of any benefits in kind, perks or other remuneration received from this employer in the last year (e.g. provision of a car, payment of travel, accommodation, meal expenses, etc.)	
Your estimate of your net income from this employment for the next 12 months. If this differs significantly from your current income explain why in box 4.1.2	

Estimated TOTAL of ALL net earned income from employment for the next 12 months:
TOTAL H   £

2 Financial Details *Part 7 Income: Income from self-employment or partnership*

2.16 You will have already given details of your business and provided the last two years accounts at section 2.11. Complete this section giving details of your income from your business. Complete one page for each business

Documentation required for attachment to this section:

a) A copy of your last tax assessment or, if that is not available, a letter from your accountant confirming your tax liability

b) If net income from the last financial year and estimated net income for the next 12 months is significantly different, a copy of management accounts for the period since your last account

Name of the business	
Date to which your last accounts were completed	
Your share of gross business profit from the last completed accounts	
Income tax and national insurance payable on your share of gross business profit above	
Net income for that year (using the two figures directly above, gross business profit less income tax and national insurance payable)	
Details and value of any benefits in kind, perks or other remuneration received from this business in the last year e.g. provision of a car, payment of travel, accommodation, meal expenses etc.	
Amount of any regular monthly or other drawings that you take from this business	
If the estimated figure directly below is different from the net income as at the end date of the last completed accounts, briefly explain the reason(s)	
Your estimate of your net annual income for the next 12 months	

Estimated TOTAL of ALL net income from self-employment or partnership for the next 12 months: TOTAL I £ _____

2 Financial Details   *Part 8 Income: Income from investments*
 e.g. dividends, interest or rental income

2.17 Details of income received in the last financial year (the year ended last 5th April), and your estimate of your income for the current financial year. Indicate whether the income was paid gross or net of income tax. You are not required to calculate any tax payable that may arise.

Nature of income and the asset from which it derived	Paid gross or net	Income received in the last financial year	Estimated income for the next 12 months

Estimated TOTAL investment income for the next 12 months: TOTAL J   £

2 Financial Details   *Part 9 Income: Income from state benefits (including state pension and child benefit)*

2.18 Details of all state benefits that you are currently receiving.

Name of benefit	Amount paid	Frequency of payment	Estimated income for the next 12 months

Estimated TOTAL benefit income for the next 12 months: TOTAL K	£

2 Financial Details   *Part 10 Income: Any other income*

2.19 Details of any other income not disclosed above.

    INCLUDE:
- Any source from which income has not been received during the last 12 months (even if it has now ceased)
- Any source from which income is likely to be received during the next 12 months

You are reminded of your obligation to give full disclosure of your financial circumstances.

Name of income	Paid gross or net	Income received in the last financial year	Estimated income for the next 12 months

Estimated TOTAL other income for the next 12 months: TOTAL L £

2 Financial Details *Summaries*

2.20 Summary of your capital (Parts 1 to 5).

Description	Reference of the section on this statement	Value
Current value of your interest in the family home	A	
Current value of your interest in all other property	B	
Current value of your interest in personal assets	C	
Current value of your liabilities	D	
Current value of your interest in business assets	E	
Current value of your pension assets	F	
Current value of all your other assets	G	

TOTAL value of your assets (Totals A to G less D): £

2.21 Summary of your estimated income for the next 12 months (Parts 6 to 10)

Description	Reference of the section on this statement	Value
Estimated net total of income from employment	H	
Estimated net total of income from self-employment or partnership	I	
Estimated net total of investment income	J	
Estimated state benefit receipts	K	
Estimated net total of all other income	L	

Estimated TOTAL income for the next 12 months (Totals H to L): £

3　Financial Requirements　*Part 1　Income needs*

3.1　Income needs for yourself and for any children living with you or provided for by you. ALL figures should be annual, monthly or weekly (state which). You *must not* use a combination of these periods. State your current income needs and, if these are likely to change in the near future, explain the anticipated change and give an estimate of the future cost

The income needs below are:　　　　Weekly　　　　Monthly　　　　Annual
(delete those not applicable)

I anticipate my income needs are going to change because

3.1.1　Income needs for yourself.

INCLUDE:

* All income needs for yourself
* Income needs for any children living with you or provided for by you only if these form part of your total income needs (e.g. housing, fuel, car expenses, holidays etc.)

Item	Current cost	Estimated future cost

SUB-TOTAL your income needs:	£

3.1.2　Income needs for children living with you or provided for by you.

INCLUDE:

* Only those income needs that are different from those of your household shown above

Item	Current cost	Estimated future cost

SUB-TOTAL children's income needs:	£

TOTAL of ALL income needs:	£

3 Financial Requirements *Part 2 Capital Needs*

3.2 Set out below the reasonable future capital needs for yourself and for any children living with you or provided by you.

3.2.1 Capital needs for yourself

INCLUDE:
- All capital needs for yourself
- Capital needs for children living with you or provided for by you only if these form part of your total capital needs (e.g. housing, car, etc.)

Item	Cost
SUB-TOTAL your capital needs:	£

3.2.2 Capital needs for your children living with you or provided for by you.

INCLUDE:
- Only those capital needs that are different from those of your household shown above

Item	Cost
SUB-TOTAL your children's capital needs:	£
TOTAL of ALL capital needs:	£

4 Other Information

4.1 Details of any significant changes in your assets or income.

At both sections 4.1.1 and 4.1.2, INCLUDE:

- ALL assets held both within and outside England and Wales
- The disposal of any asset.

4.1.1 Significant changes in assets or income during the LAST 12 months.

4.1.2 Significant changes in assets or income likely to occur during the NEXT 12 months.

4.2 Brief details of the standard of living enjoyed by you and your spouse/civil partner during the marriage/ civil partnership.

4.3 Are there any particular contributions to the family property and assets or outgoings, or to family life, or the welfare of the family that have been made by you, your partner or anyone else that you think should be taken into account? If there are any such items, briefly describe the contribution and state the amount, when it was made and by whom.

INCLUDE:
- Contributions already made
- Contributions that will be made in the foreseeable future.

4.4 Bad behaviour or conduct by the other party will only be taken into account in very exceptional circumstances when deciding how assets should be shared after divorce/dissolution. If you feel it should be taken into account in your case, identify the nature of the behaviour or conduct below.

4.5 Give details of any other circumstances that you consider could significantly affect the extent of the financial provision to be made by or for you or any child of the family.

INCLUDE (the following list is not exhaustive):
- Earning capacity
- Disability
- Inheritance prospects
- Redundancy
- Retirement
- Any plans to marry, form a civil partnership or cohabit
- Any contingent liabilities

4.6 If you have subsequently married or formed a civil partnership (or intend to) or are living with another person (or intend to), give brief details, so far as they are known to you, of his or her income, assets and liabilities.

Annual Income		Assets and Liabilities	
Nature of income	Value (if known, state whether gross or net)	Item	Value (if known)
Total income　£		**Total assets/liabilities**　£	

5 Order Sought

5.1 If you are able at this stage, specify what kind of orders you are asking the court to make.
Even if you cannot be specific at this stage, if you are able to do so, indicate:

a) If the family home is still owned, whether you are asking for it to be transferred to yourself or your
spouse/civil partner or whether you are saying it should be sold

b) Whether you consider this case for continuing spousal maintenance/maintenance for your civil partner
or whether you see the case as being appropriate for a 'clean break'. *(A 'clean break' means a settlement
or order which provides amongst other things, that neither you nor your spouse/civil partner will have any
further claim against the income or capital of the other party. A 'clean break' does not terminate the
responsibility of a parent to a child.)*

c) Whether you are seeking a pension sharing or pension attachment order

d) If you are seeking a transfer or settlement of any property or assets, identify the property or assets
in question

5.2 If you are seeking a variation of an ante-nuptial or post-nuptial settlement or a relevant settlement
made during, or in anticipation of, a civil partnership, identify the settlement, by whom it was made,
its trustees and beneficiaries and state why you allege it is a settlement which the court can vary.

5.3 If you are seeking an avoidance of disposition order, or if you have already applied for such an order,
identify the property to which the disposition relates and the person or body in whose favour the
disposition is alleged to have been made.

Sworn confirmation of the information

I _____ *(the above-named Applicant/Respondent)*

of _____

MAKE OATH and confirm that the information given above is a full, frank, clear and accurate disclosure of my financial and other relevant circumstances

Sworn by the above named

at   )
)
)
)
this   day of   20   )

Before me, _____

A solicitor, commissioner for oaths, an Officer of the Court appointed by the Judge to take affidavits, a notary or duly authorised official.

Address all communications to the Court Manager of the Court and quote the case number. If you do not quote this number, your correspondence may be returned.

SCHEDULE OF DOCUMENTS TO ACCOMPANY FORM E

The following list shows the documents you must attach to your Form E if applicable. You may attach other documents where it is necessary to explain or clarify any of the information that you give in the Form E.

Form E paragraph	Document	Attached	Not applicable	To follow
			Please tick	
1.14	**Application to vary an order:** if applicable, attach a copy of the relevant order.	☐	☐	☐
2.1	**Matrimonial home valuation:** a copy of any valuation relating to the matrimonial home that has been obtained in the last six months.	☐	☐	☐
2.1	**Matrimonial home mortgage(s):** a recent mortgage statement in respect of each mortgage on the matrimonial home confirming the amount outstanding.	☐	☐	☐
2.2	**Any other property:** a copy of any valuation relating to each other property disclosed that has been obtained in the last six months.	☐	☐	☐
2.2	**Any other property:** a recent mortgage statement in respect of each mortgage on each other property disclosed confirming the amount outstanding.	☐	☐	☐
2.3	**Personal bank, building society and National Savings accounts:** copies of statements for the last 12 months for each account that has been held in the last twelve months, either in your own name or in which you have or have had any interest.	☐	☐	☐
2.4	**Other investments:** the latest statement or dividend counterfoil relating to each investment as disclosed in paragraph 2.4.	☐	☐	☐
2.5	**Life insurance (including endowment) policies:** a surrender valuation for each policy that has a surrender value as disclosed under paragraph 2.5.	☐	☐	☐
2.11	**Business interests:** a copy of the business accounts for the last two financial years for each business interest disclosed.	☐	☐	☐
2.11	**Business interests:** any documentation that is available to confirm the estimate of the current value of the business, for example, a letter from an accountant or formal valuation if that has been obtained.	☐	☐	☐
2.13	**Pension rights:** a recent statement showing the cash equivalent transfer value (CETV) provided by the trustees or managers of each pension arrangement that you have disclosed (or, in the case of the additional state pension, a valuation of these rights). If not yet available, attach a copy of the letter sent to the pension company or administrators requesting the information.	☐	☐	☐
2.15	**Employment income:** your P60 for the last financial year in respect of each employment that you have.	☐	☐	☐
2.15	**Employment income:** your last three payslips in respect of each employment that you have.	☐	☐	☐
2.15	**Employment income:** your last P11D if you have been issued with one.	☐	☐	☐
2.16	**Self-employment or partnership income:** a copy of your last tax assessment or if that is not available, a letter from your accountant confirming your tax liability.	☐	☐	☐
2.16	**Self-employment or partnership income:** if net income from the last financial year and the estimated income for the next twelve months is significantly different, a copy of the management accounts for the period since your last accounts.	☐	☐	☐
State relevant Form E paragraph	Description of other documents attached:	☐	☐	☐
		☐	☐	☐
		☐	☐	☐

FP-E

* Delete as appropriate

Case No.

In the

*[High/County Court]
*[Principal Registry of the Family Division]

In the Marriage/Civil Partnership between

who is the husband/wife/civil partner

and

who is the husband/wife/civil partner

_____

Financial Statement
on behalf of

who is the husband/wife/civil partner
and the Petitioner/Respondent in the
divorce/dissolution suit

_____

This statement is filed by:

who are solicitors for the husband/wife/civil partner.

FP-E (Form E - Financial Statement (12.05))

In the

[County Court]*
[Principal Registry of the Family Division]*

Delete as appropriate or amend if the proceedings are pending in the High Court

No. of matter

Between

and

Petitioner	*Solicitor's ref*
Respondent	*Solicitor's ref*

Statement of information for a consent order

Duration of Marriage or Civil Partnership

In the case of a marriage: Give the date of your marriage and the date of the decree absolute (if pronounced).
In the case of a civil partnership: Give the date of the formation of the civil partnership and the date of the final order (if made).

Ages of parties

Give the age of any minor (i.e. under the age of 18) or dependant child(ren) of the family.

Petitioner   Respondent

Child(ren)

Summary of means

Give, as at the date this statement is signed on page 2:

(1) the approximate amount or value of **capital resources**. If there is a property give its net equity and details of the proposed distribution of the equity.

(2) the **net income** of the petitioner and respondent and, where relevant, of minor or dependant child(ren) of the family.

(3) the value of any benefits under **a pension arrangement** which you have or are likely to have, including the most recent valuation (if any) provided by the pension scheme.

Note: If the application is only made for an order for interim periodical payments, or for variation of an order for periodical payments, you only need to give details of 'net income'.

	(1) Capital Resources *(less any unpaid mortgage or charge)*	(2) Net Income	(3) Pension
Petitioner			
Respondent			
Children			

Where the parties and the children will live

Give details of the arrangements which are intended for the accommodation of each of the parties and any minor or dependant child(ren) of the family

Future plans

Please tick a box and, if appropriate, give the date of the marriage or formation of the civil partnership, if you know it.

	No intention to marry, form a civil partnership, or cohabit at present	Has remarried or formed a civil partnership	Intends to marry or form a civil partnership	Intends to cohabit with another person
Petitioner	☐	☐ Date of marriage or formation of civil partnership:	☐ Date of marriage or formation of civil partnership:	☐
Respondent	☐	☐ Date of marriage or formation of civil partnership:	☐ Date of marriage or formation of civil partnership:	☐

Notice to Mortgagee

These questions are to be answered by the applicant where the terms of the order provide for a transfer of property.

Has every mortgagee (if any) of the property been served with notice of the application?   Yes ☐   No ☐

Has any objection to a transfer of property been made by any mortgagee, within **14** days from the date when the notice of the application was served?   Yes ☐   No ☐

Notice to Pension Arrangement

These questions are to be answered by the applicant where the terms of an order include provision for a pension attachment order.

Has every person responsible for any pension arrangement been served with notice of the application and notice under Rule 2.70 (7)(a) to (d) of the Family Proceedings Rules 1991?   Yes ☐   No ☐

Has any objection to an order under -

(i)   section 23 of the Matrimonial Causes Act 1973 which includes provision by virtue of section 25B and section 25C of that Act; or

(ii) Part 1 of Schedule 5 to the Civil Partnership Act 2004 which includes provision by virtue of paragraphs 25 and 26 of Schedule 5 to that Act

- (as the case may be) been made by a Trustee or Manager within **21** days from the date when the notice of the application was served?   Yes ☐   No ☐

Pension Sharing on Divorce or Dissolution

These questions are to be answered by the applicant where the terms of an order include provision for a pension sharing order.

Has the Pension Arrangement furnished the information required by Regulation 4 of the Pensions on Divorce etc. (Provisions of Information) Regulations 2000?   Yes ☐   No ☐

Does it appear from that information that there is power to make an order including provision under section 24B of the Matrimonial Causes Act 1973 or under paragraph 15 of Schedule 5 to the Civil Partnership Act 2004 (Pension Sharing)?   Yes ☐   No ☐

Other information

Give details of any other especially significant matters.

Signed

| [Solicitor for] Petitioner | [Solicitor for] Respondent |
| Date | Date |

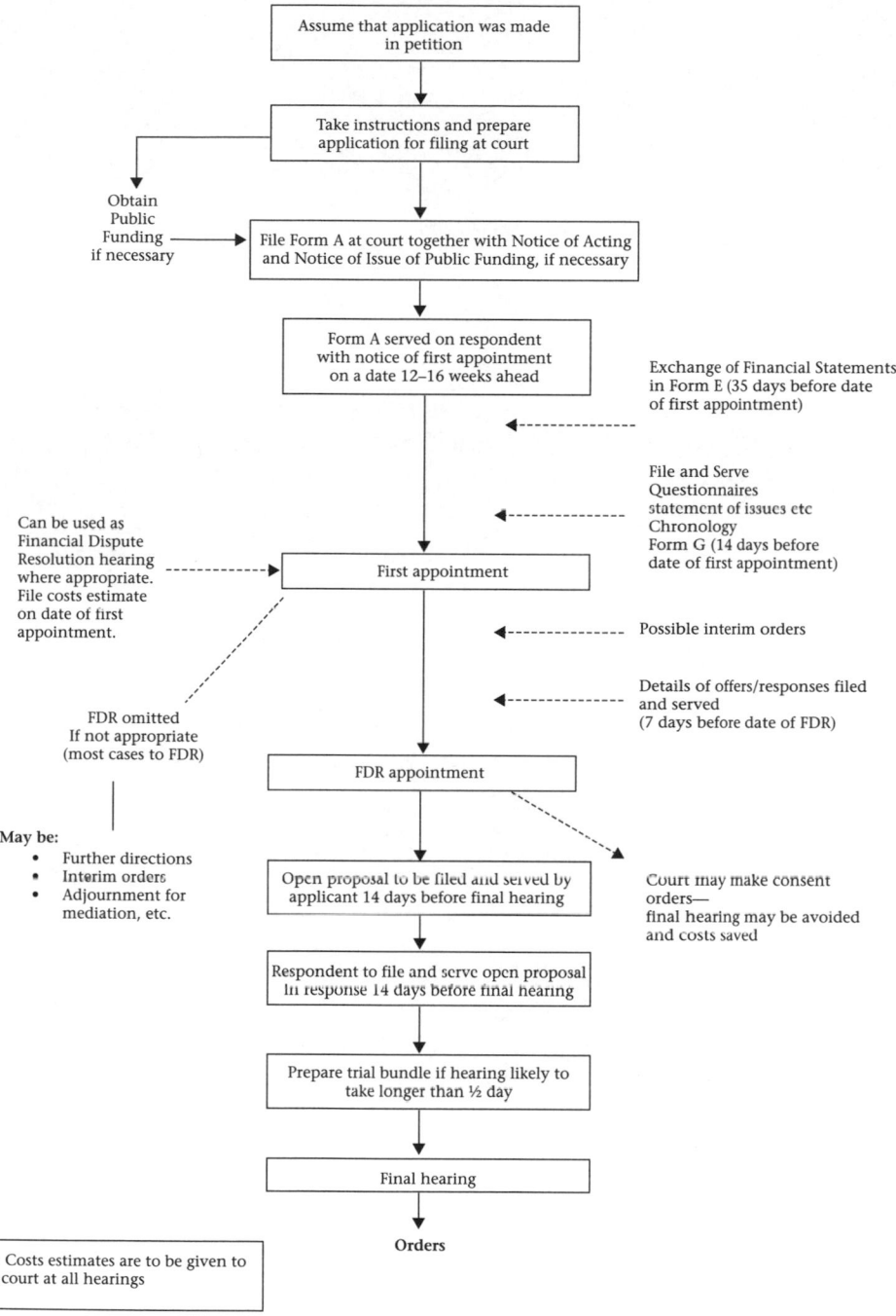

```
                    ┌─────────────────────────────┐
                    │  Assume that application     │
                    │  was made in petition        │
                    └─────────────────────────────┘
                                 │
                    ┌─────────────────────────────┐
                    │  Take instructions and       │
                    │  prepare application for     │
                    │  filing at court             │
                    └─────────────────────────────┘
```

Obtain Public Funding if necessary

File Form A at court together with Notice of Acting and Notice of Issue of Public Funding, if necessary

Form A served on respondent with notice of first appointment on a date 12–16 weeks ahead

Exchange of Financial Statements in Form E (35 days before date of first appointment)

File and Serve Questionnaires statement of issues etc Chronology Form G (14 days before date of first appointment)

Can be used as Financial Dispute Resolution hearing where appropriate. File costs estimate on date of first appointment.

First appointment

Possible interim orders

Details of offers/responses filed and served (7 days before date of FDR)

FDR omitted If not appropriate (most cases to FDR)

FDR appointment

May be:
• Further directions
• Interim orders
• Adjournment for mediation, etc.

Open proposal to be filed and served by applicant 14 days before final hearing

Court may make consent orders—final hearing may be avoided and costs saved

Respondent to file and serve open proposal In response 14 days before final hearing

Prepare trial bundle if hearing likely to take longer than ½ day

Final hearing

Orders

NB: Costs estimates are to be given to the court at all hearings

19

FACTORS TO BE CONSIDERED ON ANCILLARY RELIEF APPLICATIONS

A   INTRODUCTION

19.01   The court has a very wide discretion as to what orders to make on an application for ancillary relief. Section 25 of the Matrimonial Causes Act 1973 ('MCA 1973') directs that all the circumstances of the case should be taken into account and it has been stressed by the courts that every case has to be dealt with individually on its own facts.

19.02   This chapter sets out the s. 25, MCA 1973 considerations that must be taken into account and explains a number of principles derived from case law, that provide guidance in ancillary relief claims. It should be appreciated at the outset that the MCA 1973 does not indicate what type of ancillary relief order should be made in particular circumstances nor does it give guidance on how an award for ancillary relief should be quantified.

19.03   This is a matter for the judge to decide, bearing in mind:

(i)   the forms of ancillary relief order available;
(ii) the s. 25, MCA 1973 factors;
(iii) the relevant case law; and
(iv) the facts of the particular case.

19.04   This area of family law requires patience and attention to detail. It is important to remember that there is usually more than one possible outcome in an application for ancillary relief orders: learn to develop arguments to justify the settlement you are seeking.

19.05   In practice, knowledge of the likely approach of the local county court(s) is invaluable.

19.06   Many of the reported cases discussed below involve 'big money' where the courts have to determine the destination of surplus assets. While the judges in these cases emphasize that the general principles laid down in such cases are of general application, it is important to remember that, in many cases, the assets for distribution will be so limited that the courts will be hard-pressed to ensure that even the basic needs of the parties (for accommodation and the like) will be met. Priority will inevitably be given in these circumstances to the needs of the party who has the care of any minor children of the family.

19.07   Nevertheless, it is worth identifying the general principles which underpin the approach of the judiciary at the outset and which were laid down by Nicholls LJ in *White* v *White* [2000] 2 FLR 981 and confirmed by him in *Miller* v *Miller; McFarlane* v *McFarlane* [2006] UKHL 24.

19.08   These are:

(i)   treating the welfare of a minor child of the family as the court's first consideration;
(ii) the need to achieve a fair outcome in which discrimination plays no part;

(iii) the need to encourage the parties to become self-sufficient; and

(iv) the need to apply to any proposed award the yardstick of equality (discussed at 19.81) to assess whether a fair outcome will be achieved.

B   THE S. 25 FACTORS

General duty

The court's general duty on all ancillary relief applications is set out in s. 25(1) as follows: **19.09**

> It shall be the duty of the court in deciding whether to exercise its powers under section 23, 24, 24A or 24B above and, if so, in what manner, to have regard to all the circumstances of the case, first consideration being given to the welfare while a minor of any child of the family who has not attained the age of eighteen.

In *Suter* v *Suter* [1987] 2 FLR 232, the Court of Appeal underlined that the welfare of the children was to be given first consideration but was not the overriding consideration. Thus the task for the court was to consider all the circumstances, always bearing in mind the important first consideration of the welfare of the children, and then to try to attain a financial result that was just between husband and wife.

Ensuring that a child was suitably accommodated in reasonable travelling distance to his   **19.10** school amounted to giving the child's needs first but not paramount consideration so that the statutory duty was properly carried out: *Akintola* v *Akintola* [2002] 1 FLR 701.

It should be noted that the duty is limited to the child of the family: it does not extend to   **19.11** other children who might be affected by the outcome of the ancillary relief proceedings such as children from new relationships entered into by either spouse.

The provision 'all the circumstances' can include the existence of a pre-nuptial agreement, as   **19.12** happened in *M* v *M (Pre-nuptial Agreement)* [2002] 1 FLR 654. Here, Connell J held that the court was not bound by the terms of the pre-nuptial agreement. The court should look at it and decide in the circumstances what weight should be attached to the agreement.

Similarly in *K* v *K (Ancillary Relief: Pre-nuptial Agreement)* [2003] 1 FLR 120 Hayward Smith QC   **19.13** held that the fact of the pre-nuptial agreement was 'one of the circumstances' to be taken into account by the court. In this case, the agreement dictated the capital but not the income settlement on the breakdown of the short-lived marriage. Factors which influenced the judge in reaching this decision included the wife having understood the terms of the agreement, her being properly advised, and willingly signing the document—this amounted to 'conduct' under s. 25(2)(g), MCA 1973 which it would be impossible to disregard. (Conduct is discussed more fully at paragraph 19.71 and onwards.)

It is likely therefore that even greater weight will be attached by the court to a separation   **19.14** agreement made following the breakdown of the marriage and before divorce proceedings are instituted, provided that each party has had the opportunity to receive independent legal advice and there has been full and frank disclosure of assets. (An example of a case taking into account the terms of a separation agreement and giving appropriate weight to it is *G* v *G (Financial Provision: Separation Agreement)* [2004] 1 FLR 1011.)

Specific matters to consider on application for provision for a spouse

19.15   Section 25(2) directs the court in particular to have regard to the following matters when dealing with an application for ancillary relief for a party to the marriage:

(a)   the income, earning capacity, property, and other financial resources which each of the parties to the marriage has or is likely to have in the foreseeable future, including in the case of earning capacity any increase in that capacity which it would in the opinion of the court be reasonable to expect a party to the marriage to take steps to acquire;

(b)   the financial needs, obligations, and responsibilities which each of the parties to the marriage has or is likely to have in the foreseeable future;

(c)   the standard of living enjoyed by the family before the breakdown of the marriage;

(d)   the age of each party to the marriage and the duration of the marriage;

(e)   any physical or mental disability of either of the parties to the marriage;

(f)   the contributions which each of the parties has made or is likely in the foreseeable future to make to the welfare of the family including any contribution by looking after the home or caring for the family;

(g)   the conduct of each of the parties, if that conduct is such that it would in the opinion of the court be inequitable to disregard it;

(h)   in the case of proceedings for divorce or nullity of marriage, the value to each of the parties to the marriage of any benefit which, by reason of the dissolution or annulment of the marriage, that party will lose the chance of acquiring.

19.16   In *Piglowska* v *Piglowski* [1999] 2 FLR 763 the House of Lords indicated, amongst other things, that with the exception of the consideration of the children of the family there was no hierarchical order to the factors: each is of equal value and must be considered in turn.

Impact of Pensions Act 1995

19.17   Section 25B, inserted into the 1973 Act by s. 166 of the Pensions Act 1995 provides as follows:

> 25B.—(1)The matters to which the court is required to have regard under section 25(2) above include—
>
> (a)   in the case of paragraph (a), any benefits under a pension arrangement which a party to the marriage has or is likely to have, and
>
> (b)   in the case of paragraph (h), any benefits under a pension arrangement which, by reason of dissolution or annulment of the marriage, a party to the marriage will lose the chance of acquiring and, accordingly, in relation to benefits under a pension arrangement, section 25(2)(a) above shall have effect as if '*in the foreseeable future*' were omitted. [emphasis added]

The effect of this amendment is to enable the court to take into account any pension benefits which a party to a marriage has accrued irrespective of the length of time before the pension becomes payable.

Specific matters to consider on application for provision for a child

19.18   Section 25(3) directs the court to have regard in particular to the following matters when dealing with an application for ancillary relief for a child of the family:

(a) the financial needs of the child;

(b) the income, earning capacity (if any), property, and other financial resources of the child;

(c) any physical or mental disability of the child;

(d) the manner in which he was being and in which the parties to the marriage expected him to be educated or trained;

(e) the considerations mentioned in relation to the parties to the marriage in paragraphs (a), (b), (c), and (e) of subsection (2) above.

These factors are now less relevant because of the introduction of the Child Support Act 1991 ('CSA 1991'), but will still be considered where the application relates to a lump sum or property adjustment order. They must, of course, be considered where provision is sought for a child who is not the natural child of the prospective payer, or in the other categories of cases where the court still retains jurisdiction to make orders for the maintenance of children (see Chapter 20 for further details).

Furthermore, where the application relates to a child of the family who is not the child of the **19.19** party against whom an order is sought, the court must also have regard:

(a) to whether that party assumed any responsibility for the child's maintenance, and, if so, to the extent to which, and the basis upon which, that party assumed such responsibility and to the length of time for which that party discharged such responsibility;

(b) to whether in assuming and discharging such responsibility that party did so knowing that the child was not his or her own;

(c) to the liability of any other person to maintain the child (s. 25(4)).

The clean break approach

Section 25A, MCA 1973 deals with the concept of clean break orders. A clean break order is **19.20** one that achieves a once and for all settlement between the parties to the marriage by dismissing any outstanding claims for orders for ancillary relief at the time of making the order and preventing them reviving such claims in the future.

What s. 25A has done is to oblige the courts to give thought to achieving a clean break **19.21** between the parties in every case of divorce or nullity whether the parties suggest it or not, and to give the court the power to dictate a clean break by dismissing a party's application for periodical payments without his or her consent if appropriate.

It is not possible to achieve a completely clean break where there are children as applications **19.22** in relation to the children cannot be finally dismissed. However, there is no reason why the dependence of the *wife* on the husband (or vice versa of course) should not be ended in such a case if she can be expected to be self-supporting despite the children.

Section 25A(1) obliges the court, when exercising its ancillary relief powers in relation to a **19.23** spouse on or after divorce or nullity, to consider whether it would be appropriate to exercise those powers so as to achieve a clean break between the parties as soon after the decree as the court thinks just and reasonable.

Section 25A(2) applies to cases where the court decides to make a periodical payments or **19.24** secured periodical payments order in favour of a spouse on or after divorce or nullity. It obliges the court to consider, in particular, whether it would be appropriate to make an order for a fixed term only of sufficient length to enable the spouse in whose favour the order is made to adjust without undue hardship to being financially independent of the other party. This may be appropriate where, for example, there are young children but the wife is trained or experienced, or plans to acquire a skill and can be expected to go back to work when the children are old enough, or where a wife who has been working part-time through choice needs time to arrange to work full-time and adjust to the prospect. This may, of course, be a highly speculative exercise and the court must look carefully at the particular circumstances of the case. In *Waterman* v *Waterman* [1989] 1 FLR 380, for example, the Court of Appeal held that it was appropriate to impose a time limit of five years on the maintenance order for the wife. However, the court went on to remove the prohibition, which had been included in the original order, preventing the wife from seeking an extension of the term. The child of the family would only be 10 years old at the time that the order was scheduled to come to an end and it would be impossible to predict what the needs of the former wife might be at that stage. The prohibition was described as 'draconian'.

19.25   Further, in *McFarlane* v *McFarlane* (above), the House of Lords upheld the wife's appeal and removed the five-year time limit imposed by the Court of Appeal on the periodical payments order made in her favour, stating that the five-year term was 'most unlikely to be sufficient to achieve a fair outcome and indicating that the onus should be on the payer, rather than the payee, to seek a variation as future circumstances changed'.

19.26   Nevertheless, s. 25A(3) enables the court to impose a clean break between the parties when it considers that no continuing obligation to make or secure periodical payments should be imposed on either spouse in favour of the other. In such a case, the court can dismiss an application for periodical payments or secured periodical payments without the consent of the applicant and, to put the matter beyond doubt, direct that the applicant shall not be entitled to make any further application in relation to that marriage for a periodical payments or secured periodical payments order.

19.27   The Court of Appeal has over the years given guidance as to the circumstances in which a clean break order will be appropriate or inappropriate, stating that it is not usually appropriate to provide for the termination of periodical payments in the case of a woman in her mid-forties. Such orders would usually be justified only where the wife had her own substantial capital and a significant earning capacity: *Flavell* v *Flavell* [1997] 1 FLR 353. This approach has been confirmed by the Court of Appeal in *SRJ* v *DWJ* [1999] 2 FLR 176.

19.28   Similarly, a clean break order may not be appropriate where there is insufficient capital available (because of the illiquidity of certain assets) to compensate the wife for the loss of periodical payments. In these circumstances, the wife is denied access to capital and hence it is proper that the husband should pay maintenance to the wife from the profits from the capital tied up, for example, in a family company: *F* v *F* *(Clean Break: Balance of Fairness)* [2003] 1 FLR 847. This approach was followed in *Parlour* v *Parlour* [2004] 2 FLR 893 where the wife was awarded periodical payments at a level which exceeded her income needs but were designed to enable her to build a capital fund to ensure her financial independence in the future.

Note that if there is to be a clean break between the parties, it will usually be appropriate to ask the court to direct that neither party shall have any right to apply for provision out of the other's estate under the Inheritance (Provision for Family and Dependants) Act 1975 (at s. 15). **19.29**

What is clear, however, is that 'a clean break is not to be achieved at the expense of a fair result': per Baroness Hale in *McFarlane* v *McFarlane* (above). **19.30**

C   THE S. 25 FACTORS IN MORE DETAIL

Certain of the s. 25 factors need no further commentary. Those that do require further explanation are dealt with below. **19.31**

Income and earning capacity

Income and earning capacity can be relevant not only in deciding whether periodical payments should be ordered and if so at what rate but also in deciding on lump sum and property adjustment orders. **19.32**

For example, a lump sum may be ordered not only where a party has capital from which to pay but also where his income is sufficient to meet the repayments on a loan raised for that purpose. Furthermore, in deciding what is to happen to the family home, it is crucial to know whether there is sufficient income available to pay the mortgage and outgoings—if not, the only realistic course is to order a sale. When it comes to sharing out the equity, again income and earning capacity are important; for instance, a wife may need less from the proceeds of sale if she has an earning capacity and can obtain a mortgage than if she has no income of her own and needs to buy accommodation outright. **19.33**

Where a spouse is in work, there is normally evidence of his earnings in the form of wage slips or accounts. Benefits in kind such as the use of a company car and free meals must be taken into account as well as cash payments. The court will look at earnings before deduction of tax but normally giving credit for the expenses of working such as travelling to work, union dues, national insurance, superannuation and pension contributions. **19.34**

The court can take into account not only what a spouse actually *is* earning but also what he or she could reasonably be expected to earn. Thus it is possible for a periodical payments order to be made against a man who is unemployed on the basis that there is work that he could do if he tried. However, in areas of high unemployment, district judges will normally be reluctant to make such an order unless there is very clear evidence that the spouse concerned is shirking. The court can be asked to proceed on the basis that a spouse who is already earning could be earning more, for instance, because he is not working full-time when he could be. **19.35**

A wife who is not working, for example, because she gave up work on marriage or to look after children, may be expected to get a job. However, the court is unlikely to take the view that she should be working unless any children are, at the very least, of school age and unless there appears to be work available that she could do. If there is evidence that, **19.36** at the date of the hearing, there is work available to her that would fit in with her domestic commitments, the court can reduce her maintenance, or (if it appears that she can be expected to be self-sufficient in the long term) dismiss her claim entirely. If the evidence is only that she should be able to go back to work in the future (for instance, when the children are rather older or when she has re-trained), the court may consider making a fixed term periodical payments order allowing her a period to adjust to her financial independence or may make a normal open-ended order leaving the onus on the husband to seek a variation when the wife gets a job or when he feels she should be making efforts to seek employment.

Property and other financial resources

19.37   Assets of all sorts can be taken into account, and not only assets that each spouse has at the date of the hearing (which should be valued at that date, rather than the date of separation: *Cowan* v *Cowan* [2001] 2 FLR 192), but also assets which he or she is likely to have in the foreseeable future.

19.38   Thus, for example, money or property that a spouse is likely to inherit under a will may be taken into account (see *M T* v *M T (Financial Provision: Lump Sum)* [1992] 1 FLR 362 where the wife's application for a lump sum was adjourned until the death of her father-in-law because the husband had real prospects under German law of inheriting substantial wealth from his father and there was no other source of capital available to meet the wife's needs). Obviously, wills can be changed right up to death and this element of uncertainty is borne in mind in assessing how valuable the spouse's prospects really are, with the result that the courts tend to be very reluctant to set much store by possible inheritances. One further difficulty is in obtaining evidence of what the inheritance is likely to be.

19.39   Where monies have been inherited by the time of the ancillary relief proceedings, the court's approach to that asset very much depends on the circumstances of the case. In *H* v *H (Financial Provision: Special Contribution)* [2002] 2 FLR 1021 the Family Division judge held that the husband's inheritance from his father, which has always been kept separate from the family's assets, should not be taken into account in the ancillary relief proceedings. Conversely, the inheritance will go into the pot for distribution if this is the only way to meet the reasonable needs of the parties: per Lord Nicholls in *White* v *White* [2000] 2 FLR 981.

19.40   The debate as to which assets should be subject to division in ancillary relief proceedings continues. At the outset, it should be emphasized that, in the majority of ancillary relief cases this exercise is academic for reasons highlighted in the introduction. However, where the assets exceed needs, the matter has to be explored. In the leading speeches of Nicholls and Hale LJJ in *Miller* v *Miller, McFarlane* v *McFarlane* (above), both judges agreed that the source of an asset is a relevant issue in determining how it should be allocated or shared. They differed, however, on what forms of asset might be distinguished.

19.41   While Lord Nicholls viewed non-matrimonial property as all property which the parties brought into the marriage or acquired by inheritance or gift during the marriage and matrimonial property as all other property, Baroness Hale categorized the assets rather differently. She readily accepted that family businesses and joint ventures could be regarded as matrimonial or 'family assets', considering, however, that non-family assets included not only property brought into the marriage but also business or investment assets generated solely or mainly by the efforts of one party during the marriage.

Since Lords Mance and Hoffman agreed with the approach taken by Baroness Hale, this appears to be the preferred approach. **19.42**

For practitioners, it highlights the need for pre-nuptial agreements, at the very least to identify the nature and value of assets brought by each party into the marriage. **19.43**

Entitlements under an insurance policy that could be surrendered or is likely to mature anyway in the foreseeable future can be taken into account. Pension and lump sum entitlement on retirement can be considered irrespective of the length of time which must elapse before the pension becomes payable (see paragraph 19.17 above). **19.44**

The court will pay attention to the fact that not all assets are readily realizable. A businessman, for example, may not be able to draw substantial capital sums out of his business without affecting its liquidity, indeed, he may not even be able to withdraw his entire income entitlement each year as profits may need to be ploughed back as working capital. The court would not make an order that would cause a spouse to lose his livelihood, for example, by forcing him to sell his business. If the other spouse's contribution to a business should be recognized, this will have to be done in some other way, for example, by giving her a greater share in the family's other assets such as the family home or by ordering a lump sum payment to her to be made by instalments, the instalments being at such a level that the husband can afford to pay them from income without prejudicing his business interests. **19.45**

Account may be taken of property and income of a cohabitant or new spouse (see paragraph 19.53 and onwards) and property acquired after separation if it is necessary to do so to achieve a fair outcome: *A v B (Financial Relief: Agreements)* [2005] 2 FLR 730. **19.46**

Note that where there is doubt as to a party's future prospects, it may be worth considering seeking an adjournment until such time as the position becomes clearer if it appears that this will not delay matters unduly or prejudice either side, as happened in *D v D (Lump Sum: Adjournment of Application)* [2001] 1 FLR 633. However, courts do prefer to achieve certainty at the time of the hearing, if possible, and it has been held that it would be wrong to adjourn an application for a lump sum payment for more than four or five years (*Roberts v Roberts* [1986] 2 All ER 483). **19.47**

How is the pension to be treated in considering the assets of the parties? **19.48**

At the present time, there is little consistency of approach amongst the judiciary. In *White v White* (above), for example, Lord Nicholls added the cash equivalent transfer values of the pensions of the husband and the wife to the other assets before determining an appropriate division. **19.49**

However, the pension asset is different from the other capital assets: it is not a cash fund over which the parties may have complete control but, according to Thorpe LJ in *Cowan v Cowan* (above), a pension fund 'is no more and no less than a whole life fixed rate income stream'. Hence, in *Maskell v Maskell* [2003] 1 FLR 1138, Thorpe LJ criticized the circuit judge **19.50** for aggregating the value of the pension fund with the other assets since only 25 per cent of the husband's fund could be taken as capital, the balance having to be taken as an income stream. Thorpe LJ commented 'He simply failed to compare like with like'.

19.51   Where a pension is already in payment, as in *Martin-Dye* v *Martin-Dye* [2006] EWCA Civ 681, it should not be treated as capital but, according to Thorpe LJ, as 'another financial resource' sitting comfortably neither in the category of 'property' nor 'income'.

19.52   There will be occasions, and the case of *TL* v *ML and Others (Ancillary Relief: Claim Against Assets of Extended Family)* [2006] 1 FLR 1263 is an example of this, where one party to the marriage claims that the other is the beneficial owner of property legally owned by a member of the extended family. Here, Mostyn QC, sitting as a deputy High Court judge, indicated that the task of determining a dispute as to ownership between a spouse and a third party is completely different in nature from the discretionary exercise undertaken in determining an ancillary dispute between spouses. The dispute with the third party should be approached as if it were to be determined in the Chancery Division. As to the appropriate procedure, he stated that the third party should be joined as a party to the proceedings at the earliest opportunity; directions should be given for the issue to be fully pleaded by points of claim and points of defence; separate witness statements should be directed in relation to the dispute and the dispute should be heard separately as a preliminary issue before the Financial Dispute Resolution appointment.

Needs, obligations, and responsibilities

19.53   Needs and obligations vary from household to household. Invariably, however, both spouses will need a roof over their heads and the spouse who has the care of the children will have a particularly pressing need for a home for the family. This factor is likely to be of great importance in the court's decision. The court will also look at each party's regular outgoings (fuel bills, rent, council tax, water rates, mortgage, food, hire-purchase debts, payments following a maintenance calculation under the CSA 1991, etc.) and take into account such as are reasonable for a person in his circumstances. What is reasonable will obviously vary from case to case—someone travelling a mile to work each day may be expected to use a bicycle or walk if money for the family is tight whereas a person who travels many miles in the course of his job can fairly expect to do so in a relatively comfortable car. The court's approach to each party's regular expenditure will have to be realistic—it may be wholly unreasonable for one party to be purchasing a video recorder on hire-purchase where the other party does not even have enough money for food, but, once the party has entered into the commitment, there is very little that can be done about it and the continuing obligation to pay will have to be taken into account.

19.54   Although the abstract prospect of remarriage is not relevant, where one or the other party has actually remarried or formed a new relationship, this will have to be taken into account as it will obviously have an effect on his needs and obligations and possibly also on his resources. He may be in a better position than if he had remained single (for example, where the new partner has substantial means), or the new relationship may burden him with more responsibilities, particularly if there is a child of the new family. Where the new partner is earning or has resources, the proper course is to take these into account not as a figure to add to the spouse's own income and resources but on the basis that the partner's resources release the spouse from obligations he would otherwise have had towards her (and in some cases also from expenditure on himself) and therefore free a greater part of his income or property for distribution by way of ancillary relief. Douglas Brown J in *B v B (Periodical Payments: Transitional Provisions)* [1995] 1 WLR 440, held that while it was quite legitimate to take account of the new wife's earnings, it was wrong to make an order which had the effect of casting the burden of maintaining the first family on to her. Here, the husband was unemployed and the order was varied to a nominal amount. Where the new partner is a liability (for instance, where she is a widow with young children who is not working), the needs for the second family have to be taken into account in assessing financial relief for the first family, as happened, for example, in *S v S (Financial Provision: Departing from Equality)* [2001] 2 FLR 246, where the need to accommodate the husband's new family led to an unequal division of the capital assets.

'Needs' may include a costs allowance to be paid in the form of a periodical payments order **19.55** to enable a 'poor spouse' to obtain legal services in connection with ancillary relief proceedings between the parties. The court must be satisfied, however, that the 'poor spouse' could not fund legal services in any other way (that is, by public funding or obtaining a loan): *Currey* v *Currey* [2006] EWCA Civ 1338.

A new form of 'need' was identified by Nicholls LJ in *Miller v Miller, McFarlane v McFarlane* **19.56** (above). The judge described this as 'compensation' and explained, 'This is aimed at redressing any significant prospective disparity between the parties arising from the way they conducted their marriage. For instance, the parties may have arranged their affairs in a way which has greatly advantaged the husband in terms of his earning capacity but left the wife severely handicapped so far as her own earning capacity is concerned. Then the wife suffers a double loss: a diminution in her earning capacity and the loss of a share in her husband's enhanced income . . . When this is so, fairness requires that this feature should be taken into account by the court when exercising its statutory powers.' In *McFarlane* v *McFarlane*, the need to compensate was reflected in the significant long-term periodical payments to the wife.

The concept of 'need' has also been extended by the new costs rules discussed in Chapter 18, **19.57** paragraph 18.130 since the litigation costs of the parties will be taken into account before the division of the remaining assets.

The standard of living enjoyed by the parties

Briefly, two points are to be made here. First of all, the court is no longer under a duty to **19.58** apply the minimal loss principle and to endeavour to place the parties in the position in which they would have been if the marriage had not broken down.

Secondly, while courts are to recognize the standard of living enjoyed by the parties **19.59** during the marriage, Nicholls LJ in *Miller v Miller* (above) deprecated any attempt to extend the scope of this to include the concept of 'legitimate expectations' stating that 'Both hopes and expectations, as such, are not an appropriate basis to assess financial needs.'

Age of parties and duration of marriage

19.60   Age can have an important bearing on the court's decision. Where the parties are young when the marriage breaks down, it may well be reasonable to impose a clean break between them immediately if there are no children, or to expect the wife to make her way on her own within a period of time (granting her a periodical payments order for a fixed term, for instance) where she is looking after children. Furthermore, young spouses are likely to have a greater capacity to borrow money than those in their fifties or over. This can be taken into account when deciding what is to be done about lump sum and transfer of property orders. Thus where the parties are young it may be possible, for instance, to transfer the matrimonial home to the wife who is looking after young children and to expect the husband to raise capital on mortgage to purchase alternative accommodation for himself; in contrast, the older husband with no prospect of obtaining a mortgage will need some capital to rehouse himself.

19.61   The court is less likely to expect a wife in her late forties or fifties to go out and get a job (particularly if she has not worked since getting married or having children) than a younger wife brought up in the tradition of working wives and mothers. It can also be taken into consideration that parties who are nearing retirement are likely to need to preserve their capital for when they stop work and will therefore be less able to transfer assets or make lump sum payments than younger people who have time to build up provision for their retirement over the course of their working lives.

19.62   The length of the marriage is also an important factor—the longer the marriage, the more each party is likely to have contributed to it and the harder it will be for them to achieve independence again when it breaks down. Where there is a very short marriage with no children, as a general rule each party can expect to withdraw from the marriage only what he or she put into it in terms of money and effort; property rights may be expected to play a larger part than normal and periodical payments may well be inappropriate (see, for example, *Foster* v *Foster* [2003] 2 FLR 299, where the Court of Appeal restored the order of the district judge in ancillary relief proceedings giving the wife 61 per cent and the husband 39 per cent of the total assets).

19.63   In *Foster*, Court of Appeal had to determine the proper approach to the parties' respective contributions in a short childless marriage where both were working in light of the decision in *White* v *White* (above) and later decisions of the Court of Appeal.

19.64   The court held that there were no special principles applicable to assessing contributions made by parties in such circumstances. In looking at financial contributions the court was not limited to considering merely the amounts contributed but could take into account such factors as the part each party played in acquiring and realizing assets in the name of one or other of the parties, and the fact that each party contributed what he or she could from his or her financial resources.

19.65   The district judge had sought to give the parties back what they had brought into the marriage at the value it held at that date but had divided equally between them the profits made on property during the marriage. (The Court of Appeal concluded that his approach was, on the facts, fair to both parties.)

19.66   In essence, the decision in *Foster* turns its back on older cases which had focused on awards that enabled a wife to get back on her feet at the end of a short marriage. This approach found favour with Nicholls LJ in *Miller* v *Miller* (above). As he put it 'A short marriage is no less a partnership of equals than a long marriage'. He did acknowledge, however, that there was a perception that parties have less of a claim against each other after a short marriage and it might be fair if any award is not on an equal basis. This was the outcome in *Miller* where the wife received £5 million which represented less than one-third of the increase in the value of shares accrued by the husband during the marriage and less than one-sixth of his total wealth.

In any event, where there are children of a short marriage, the shortness of the marriage may **19.67** well be less significant than the fact that the children will almost certainly hamper the parent with whom they are living in achieving financial independence. In such a case, the shortness of the marriage may make little difference to the outcome of the case. Cases confirming this proposition are *C* v *C (Financial Relief: Short Marriage)* [1997] 2 FLR 26 (CA) and, more recently, *B* v *B (Mesher Order)* [2003] 2 FLR 285.

Courts have also had to determine what weight, if any, should be attached to extensive pre- **19.68** marital cohabitation. Since s. 25(2)(d) MCA 1973 refers to 'the duration of the marriage', the plain words of the statute are ignored if account is taken of pre-marital cohabitation at this point in the exercise. On the other hand, fairness demands that, on occasions, due weight is given to pre-marital cohabitation especially where that cohabitation moves seamlessly to marriage. It is suggested that a better approach is to consider pre-marital cohabitation either as part of 'all of the circumstances of the case' under s. 25(1) MCA 1973 or as an aspect of 'contribution' or (positive) conduct under s. 25(2)(f) and (g) MCA 1973, respectively. Certainly, in *CO* v *CO (Ancillary Relief: Pre-marriage Cohabitation)* [2004] 1 FLR 1095, Coleridge J held that, to ignore a committed, settled period of cohabitation would fly in the face of the duty of the court to have regard to all the circumstances of the case.

Contributions

In *White* v *White* (above), Nicholls LJ emphasized that, especially in a long marriage **19.69** (that is taken now to mean marriages of ten years or longer), both parties make different and significant contributions. He held that it was wholly wrong to discriminate against the party to the marriage who has remained at home caring for the children and household while the other party may have been the principal breadwinner. (It should be noted that it has been subsequently held to be wrong to discriminate between spouses on the basis of differences in income: *Foster* v *Foster* (above).)

It is important to note that that wording of s. 25(2)(f) also refers to contributions likely to be **19.70** made in the foreseeable future to the welfare of the family. Hence, even where the duration of the marriage is relatively short, the ancillary relief award can be calculated to include that future important contribution.

Conduct

Conduct is a vexed question in ancillary relief applications. **19.71**

In practice, however, the courts appear to treat the issues of conduct as they have always **19.72** done so that it will be taken into account only if it is 'obvious and gross' (a phrase derived from *Wachtel* v *Wachtel* [1973] 1 All ER 829, and interpreted in *West* v *West*, see Example (b) below, as meaning 'of the greatest importance'). Thus in the majority of cases the court will continue to take the view that a certain amount of unpleasant behaviour can be anticipated on both sides when a marriage is breaking down, including a certain amount of violence, and that such matters should not affect the outcome of ancillary relief applications.

19.73   From time to time the conduct of one or the other party will stand out in some way and demand consideration. Examples of conduct which has been thought relevant in past cases are given below. Standards change, however, and the facts of cases are always different, so examples should be used simply to get a feel of the attitude of the courts, not as precedents dictating what is and is not relevant conduct.

19.74   At the risk of stating the obvious, the task for the court when dealing with allegations of conduct is twofold:

(a)   Is the conduct of a kind which it would be inequitable for the court to ignore? *and*

(b)   What effect should the conduct, if taken into account, have on the outcome of the application?

Examples

(a)   *Jones* v *Jones*, [1975] 2 All ER 12: wife seriously attacked by husband after decree absolute with a razor causing continuing disability rendering her virtually unemployable; whole house transferred to her from joint names.

(b)   *West* v *West*, [1977] 2 All ER 705: short marriage, wife refused to join husband in the home he had provided and lived at her parents' home instead. Wife's conduct found obvious and gross and, despite the fact there were two children of the marriage living with her, her financial provision was substantially reduced.

(c)   *Kyte* v *Kyte* [1987] 3 All ER 1041: husband was a manic depressive and wife connived at his suicide attempts with a view to gaining as much of the husband's assets as possible. Wife's conduct found to be gross and obvious so that it would be inequitable to ignore it, and accordingly her financial provision was reduced but not extinguished.

The point is often taken by a husband that it is unreasonable to expect him to make provision for his wife when she has committed adultery or formed a continuing relationship with another man. Unless it takes place in particularly aggravated circumstances (for example, having an affair with the husband's father, see *Bailey* v *Tolliday* (1982) 4 FLR 542), the simple fact that the wife has committed adultery will not generally affect her entitlement to ancillary relief. However, if the wife forms a continuing relationship with another man and starts to cohabit with him or derives financial support from him, this *will* affect her entitlement to ancillary relief. Periodical payments do not automatically cease in this situation as they do on remarriage, but if the wife's boyfriend is or should be expected to contribute towards her maintenance, this will clearly reduce the obligations of the husband towards her, often to nil. Whether the court will see fit to dismiss the wife's periodical payments claim in such a case, thus debarring her from claiming maintenance from her husband for all time, will depend on all the circumstances of the case. The alternative is, of course, for the court to reduce her periodical payments to a small or nominal amount leaving her with the right to seek a variation should her relationship come to an end. Capital provision for the wife may or may not be affected by her new relationship/cohabitation depending on all the circumstances of the case.

An example of the relevance of conduct is to be found in the case of *B* v *B* (*Financial Provision:* **19.75**
Welfare of Child and Conduct) [2002] 1 FLR 555 where Connell J ordered that the family home
be transferred into the sole name of the wife. He recognized that such an award reflected the
wife's on-going contribution to the care of the child but the principal reason for the order
was the husband's conduct which the judge considered would be inequitable to disregard.
The conduct included the husband's failure to disclose that he had removed monies from
the jurisdiction, the effect being to prevent the court from having a meaningful say in the
disposal of the monies, and his abduction of the child which had led to a conviction for
child abduction and a sentence of 18 months' imprisonment.

More recently, in *H* v *H* (*Financial Relief: Attempted Murder As Conduct*) [2006] 1 FLR 990, **19.76**
Coleridge J had to consider what impact on the ancillary relief order the conduct of the
husband should have where that conduct comprised a conviction for the attempted murder
of the wife, and a refusal either to consent to the sale or letting of the family home.
The wife had been compelled to leave the property because she was unable to cope with the
memories which the property evoked.

In awarding the wife the family home and the bulk of the assets, Coleridge J held that **19.77**
the conduct was not simply of a kind which it would be inequitable to disregard but it was at
the very top end of the scale. The conduct here was not merely a backdrop to the s. 25 MCA
1973 exercise: it had seriously affected her mental health, had almost destroyed her earning
capacity, and had deprived her of financial and parenting support from the husband.

The fact of non-disclosure of financial matters will often entitle the court to draw adverse **19.78**
inferences and reflect its displeasure in both the ancillary relief award and the order as to
costs: *Al-Khatib* v *Masry* [2002] 1 FLR 1053. In this case, the award also reflected the fact that
the husband had abducted the children to Saudi Arabia. In addition to a significant lump
sum payment, the wife received a further £2.5 million to fund her litigation costs to secure
the return of the children.

It is important to emphasize, however, that conduct will only be taken into account where it **19.79**
is (to use well-established terminology) 'gross and obvious'.

The principle was reaffirmed in the House of Lords' decision in *Miller* v *Miller* (above) with **19.80**
Lord Nicholls rejecting the approach taken both by Singer J and the Court of Appeal in that
case. To make the position clear, Nicholls LJ stated 'In most cases, fairness does not require
consideration of the parties' conduct. This is because in most cases misconduct is not relevant to the bases on which ancillary relief is ordered today. Where, exceptionally, the position is otherwise, so that it would be inequitable to disregard one party's conduct, the
statute permits that conduct to be taken into account.'

The importance of the yardstick of equality

In *White* v *White* (above), Nicholls LJ offered guidance on how a capital award should be **19.81**
quantified. While ruling out a 'presumption of equal division', he indicated that the court
should measure any proposed award against 'the yardstick of equality'. Departure from the
yardstick should only be for very good reason, which the court should clearly set out.
Nicholls LJ saw this approach as an essential element in the need to achieve a fair outcome.

19.82 Subsequent cases made it clear that the application of the yardstick of equality was to apply even where a clean break order was not possible and where the assets for distribution were limited, as in *Elliott* v *Elliott* [2001] 1 FLR 477.

19.83 In the months following the *White* decision, there were a number of cases which suggested a reluctance on the part of the judiciary to countenance an equal division of assets and a willingness to sanction a departure from the yardstick of equality.

19.84 For example, in *Cowan* v *Cowan* (above) and *Dharamshi* [2001] 1 FLR 736, the court recognized that the husband by his special skill and effort had accumulated wealth surplus to that needed to enable both parties to be housed and continue to live in a manner to which they were accustomed. Hence, in *Cowan* the husband's contribution, described as 'stellar' by the Court of Appeal, justified a departure from the yardstick of equality with the wife receiving 38 per cent of the assets and the House of Lords dismissing her petition for leave to appeal.

19.85 Inevitably, what is a fair outcome depends upon the particular facts of the case. However, in many cases there is unlikely to be a departure from the yardstick of equality since this is often consistent with the objective of achieving a fair outcome. Departure from the yardstick is likely to leave one party with a sense of grievance that his or her efforts have been under-valued by the court. This was recognized by Coleridge J in *H-J* v *H-J* [2002] 1 FLR 415, the first reported case after *White* of an equal division in a 'big money' case. Here, the value of the assets amounted to £2.7 million and were divided equally between the parties, the judge having found nothing exceptional or special about the husband's contribution.

19.86 This case marked a shift in thinking among the judiciary and was followed in other cases, notably in *Lambert* v *Lambert* [2003] 1 FLR 139.

19.87 Here the Court of Appeal held (in reference to 'contributions' under s. 25(2)(f), MCA 1973) 'the subsection certainly does not suggest any bias in favour of the breadwinner. There must be an end to the sterile assertion that the breadwinner's contribution weighs heavier than the homemaker's'.

19.88 While Thorpe LJ went on to acknowledge that 'stellar' or 'special contributions' remained a legitimate possibility in some exceptional cases, the present case was not one of these. He indicated that a good idea, initiative, entrepreneurial skill, and extensive hard work were insufficient to establish a 'special' contribution (which might lead to a division of the assets other than on an equal basis). In particular, he rejected as an argument for 'stellar' or 'special contribution' that the standard of living enjoyed by the parties by the time of the breakdown of the marriage had far exceeded the expectations of the parties at the time of the marriage.

19.89 However, Thorpe LJ would not be drawn into setting out an exhaustive list of what consti-tutes a 'stellar' or 'special' contribution, saying, 'It would be futile and dangerous to even attempt to speculate on the boundaries of exceptional . . . All that seems to me to be more safely left to future case by case exploration'.

19.90 It is clear that the task for the court is to achieve a *fair outcome on the particular facts* and Thorpe LJ acknowledged in *Lambert* that, in some cases, an equal division would not guarantee that the parties would depart without a sense of grievance.

19.91 This is an area of law which is still developing.

The principle was reaffirmed by the House of Lords in *Miller* v *Miller, McFarlane* v *McFarlane*   **19.92**
(above), the court stating that to regard 'contribution' as a factor pointing away from
equality of division is only appropriate where it would be inequitable to do otherwise.

Recent examples of departure from the yardstick of equality include *Sorrell* v *Sorrell* [2006] 1   **19.93**
FLR 497 where Bennett J held that a fair outcome was to award to the wife 40 per cent of the
assets: the unequal division was justified by the husband's special contribution to the marriage in the form of an exceptional business talent amounting to genius. Similarly, in *Charman* v *Charman* (The Times, 27 July 2006), Coleridge J sanctioned a departure from the
yardstick of equality (awarding the wife 37 per cent of the assets) first, because of the husband's wealth-creating abilities and, secondly, because of the fact that the wife was to receive
cash whereas the husband would continue to operate high-risk assets. This case has subsequently been considered by the Court of Appeal. A decision is awaited.

Calculating the lump sum in capitalized maintenance cases

As mentioned in Chapter 17, paragraph 17.28, the case of *Duxbury* v *Duxbury* [1987] 1 FLR 7 is   **19.94**
an example of a case where a multi-purpose lump sum order was made. While the purpose of
part of the lump sum payment was to enable the former wife to purchase a home and furnish
it, a large proportion of the lump sum was intended to be invested to provide her with an
income for life. Her claim for a periodical payments order was dismissed. To calculate the
fund needed to provide the former wife with a reasonable standard of living the court took
the advice of accountants and actuaries and had to consider such matters as the age of the
recipient, tax bands, the likely effect of inflation and so on.

Calculating the periodical payments order

What remains unclear is the approach to be adopted by the courts in determining applica-   **19.95**
tions for periodical payments for the benefit of one of the parties to the marriage.

So what should be the proper approach to determining the level of periodical payments to be   **19.96**
made by one party for the benefit of the other party to the marriage?

There is no alternative but to consider s. 25 with first consideration being given to the   **19.97**
applicant's reasonable needs. In determining those needs, regard will be had to other s. 25
factors such as the length of the marriage and the standard of living enjoyed by the parties.
Clearly, the income of the applicant must be taken into account, together with his or her
capacity to increase that income either by exploiting earning capacity or claiming relevant
benefits.

Against this should be measured the other party's ability to meet those needs out of net   **19.98**
income—usually the courts will not prescribe a level of payment which would reduce the
payer's income to below subsistence level (that is the amount which the Department for
Work and Pensions would find that the payer needed for the normal, additional, and housing
requirements of his family unit if he were on income support together with whatever he
would receive by way of housing benefit (see Chapter 38)).

The court must assess the overall fairness of the proposed order and to do this must consider   **19.99**
'the net effect' of the order on both parties. (For example, in *V* v *V (Financial Relief)* [2005]

2 FLR 698, Coleridge J held that it was not fair that the judge had left the husband with double the wife's disposable income when there was to be no clean break. He directed that the wife should receive 40 per cent of the available income to recognize more fully her contribution over the length of the marriage.) This will require the preparation of 'a net effect schedule' to demonstrate to the court the practical consequences of the proposed order on the financial positions of both parties. For example, the effect of the order may be to disqualify one party from claiming welfare benefits and, if so, the court may wish to reconsider the terms.

19.100   What appears to be clear from the decision of the Court of Appeal in *McFarlane* v *McFarlane, Parlour* v *Parlour* [2004] 2 FLR 893 is that the yardstick of equality is not the appropriate method of quantification. In *McFarlane*, for example, the wife received periodical payments equal to one-third of the husband's net income.

D   OTHER CIRCUMSTANCES NOT SPECIFICALLY REFERRED TO IN S. 25

19.101   Section 25 is not an exhaustive catalogue of the circumstances that are to be taken into account on an ancillary relief application. This paragraph lists additional matters which, among others, may be relevant.

Agreements as to ancillary relief

19.102   It can happen that, on or after the breakdown of the marriage, the parties reach an agreement on property and finance and make it a term of the agreement that no claims will be made thereafter for any further or different ancillary provision.

Example Soon after separating, husband and wife agree that the wife will be allowed to remain in the family home until the children are grown up and that it will thereafter be sold and the proceeds divided equally between them. The wife agrees never to make any claim for periodical payments for herself and the husband agrees to maintain the children at the rate of £60 per week per child, the figure to be increased periodically to keep pace with inflation.

The wife changes her mind about the agreement and wants to seek a transfer of the house into her name and/or periodical payments for herself after decree nisi of divorce is granted.

19.103   While a party cannot be bound by a promise not to apply to the court (see Chapter 36), the court *can* take into account the making of the agreement as part of the conduct of the parties under s. 25 (see *Edgar* v *Edgar* [1980] 3 All ER 887). As the Court of Appeal pointed out in *Edgar*, the district judge will decide what weight to give to the agreement by considering the circumstances surrounding the making of it (for example, was there undue pressure on one side, bad legal advice, inadequate knowledge?), the conduct of both parties in consequence of it and any important change of circumstances unforeseen or overlooked at the time of making the agreement. These principles were reconfirmed in *Xydhias* v *Xydhias* [1999] 1 FLR 683 and followed in *A* v *B (Financial Relief: Agreements)* [2005] 2 FLR 730. However, in *Xydhias* the Court of Appeal also stated that the existence of a financial agreement between the parties to a marriage does not avoid the need for the court to exercise its discretion under s. 25 to explore the circumstances leading to the agreement and to determine whether it should stand.

More recently, Munby J reviewed the whole line of authorities in *X* v *X (Y and Z intervening)* **19.104** [2002] 1 FLR 508 in deciding whether a wife could resile from an agreement under which in consideration for various concessions in relation to divorce proceedings, the husband was to receive a lump sum payment of £500,000. The husband had complied with his obligations under the agreement and applied to the court for the wife to show cause why the terms of the agreement should not be converted into an order of the court. Munby J concluded that the agreement should be upheld: the wife had not been disadvantaged and had received 'the most expert legal advice'. Munby J held that s. 25, MCA 1973 required the court to ensure that a fair outcome had been achieved between the parties. The fact that the parties had reached an agreement was an important factor and where the agreement was formally drawn up following competent legal advice, the agreement should be upheld by the court unless there were 'good and substantial grounds' for concluding that an injustice might otherwise be done to one of the parties. As in so many recent cases, Munby J concluded by indicating that, so far as it is consistent with its obligations under s. 25, MCA 1973, the court should aim to achieve finality between the parties.

The tax implications of orders

The tax implications of a proposed order may be important. For example, the court will need **19.105** to know if the husband will have to bear a considerable amount of capital gains tax in selling assets to raise a lump sum—it may reduce the lump sum payable to take account of this or choose to make a different order with less severe tax consequences.

The availability of state benefits

The court is not generally entitled to take into account the fact that the applicant for **19.106** ancillary relief is on income support and that she is therefore unlikely to derive any real advantage from the order that can be made in her favour (see, for example, *Peacock* v *Peacock* [1984] 1 All ER 1069), except where the available financial resources are very limited and an order would result in the husband being left with a sum that would be inadequate to meet his own financial commitments (see, for example, *Delaney* v *Delaney* [1990] 2 FLR 457).

E SPECIAL CONSIDERATIONS WITH REGARD TO PARTICULAR TYPES OF ORDER

Orders in relation to the family home

Family home owned by one or both parties

Common orders The home is often one of the most substantial assets that the parties have **19.107** and is therefore generally the focus of ancillary relief disputes. Although the court has the power to resolve the question of the home in whatever manner it thinks appropriate, in practice there are several types of order which frequently crop up:

(a)   immediate sale and division of the net proceeds of sale;

(b)   transfer of the house into the sole name of one spouse, with or without a charge in favour of the other spouse or an immediate payment of a lump sum in his favour in respect of his interest;

(c)   sale of house postponed, proceeds to be divided between the spouses on eventual sale.

19.108   Importance of securing homes for all concerned   What will normally be at the forefront of the district judge's mind is the question of homes for both parties and particularly for the children. This consideration is likely to override all others and in particular will undoubtedly take precedence over strict property rights. For example in *M v B (Ancillary Proceedings: Lump Sum)* [1998] 1 FLR 53 the Court of Appeal stated that every effort should be made to deal with the need to provide a home for minor children of the family. This approach is confirmed in *B v B (Financial Provision: Welfare of the Child and Conduct)* [2002] 1 FLR 555 where Connell J ordered the outright transfer of the former family home in order to meet the need of the child of the family to be housed to a reasonable standard. In essence, therefore, the principal carer requires a home from the resources available and ideally the parent having regular contact with the children should be allocated sufficient monies to acquire accommodation where contact may be enjoyed.

19.109   When will immediate sale be appropriate?   The following are illustrations of the sorts of situation in which the court may be prepared to order immediate sale of the family home:

(a)   Where the equity in the family home is sufficiently large to be divided between the parties and to enable them both to buy somewhere new, not necessarily of the same size and standard as the family home but with adequate accommodation for their needs. In working out what the equity is and whether it is sufficient, account must be taken not only of any outstanding mortgage on the property, but also of the estate agent's and conveyancing fees that will arise on a sale and new purchase and of removal costs. Furthermore, in the case of a publicly funded client, the effect of the Legal Services Commission's statutory charge must be borne in mind (see Chapter 2); if the Legal Services Commission has (or will have when the proceedings are over) a charge over a party's house, that charge *may* have to be redeemed and repaid on sale of the property thus reducing the sum available to that party.

    On the plus side, the court will take into account the availability of loans and mortgages to assist the parties in their new purchases.

    Example 1 Husband and wife live in a five-bedroomed house which they bought 20 years ago in their joint names. The children have all grown up and left home. The wife is living in the property on her own whilst the husband is in rented accommodation. The house is worth £200,000 and there is an outstanding mortgage of £10,000. The equity in the property is therefore £190,000 less the costs of sale. To be on the safe side, these are estimated at £5,000 and the available equity is taken to be £185,000. The court takes the view that this would be sufficient to enable both parties to purchase suitable accommodation for one person with enough room for the children and their families to come to stay and in the same locality as the family home. The sale of the family home is ordered, with equal division of the net proceeds.

Example 2 Husband and wife are both in their thirties. There are two children. The husband is a businessman with a healthy income. The wife works part-time as a receptionist to fit in with the children. The family home is in joint names. It is worth £400,000 but there is a substantial mortgage of £100,000. The wife is to have a residence order in respect of the children. The equity in the house will be in the region of £300,000 after repayment of the mortgage and payment of expenses. The Legal Services Commission will have a statutory charge over the wife's share in the property for her publicly funded costs of £8,000 but it is anticipated that they would agree to the charge being transferred to another house. The wife is unable to obtain a mortgage. Equal division of the equity would give her only £150,000 and, as she shows to the court by bringing estate agents' particulars to the hearing, this would not be enough to enable her to buy a three-bedroomed property in the area where the children go to school. She estimates that she requires £200,000 to buy a suitable property. The husband, on the other hand, can obtain a mortgage of up to £200,000. The court therefore orders that the house should be sold and that the husband should receive one-fifth of the proceeds (£60,000, which should be enough, together with a mortgage, to enable him to purchase a house for himself) and the wife four-fifths £240,000). Because the wife is doing rather well out of the house, the level of her maintenance payments is reduced considerably from what she would otherwise have been granted. The court may conclude that there should be no maintenance payments to her. This is possible because she can buy a property outright and will therefore have no mortgage or rent.

(b) Where one party has already got suitable alternative accommodation and the house can be sold and the proceeds divided enabling her to realize some capital from it but leaving the other spouse with sufficient to purchase accommodation.

Example After the breakdown of the marriage the wife goes to live with another man in his four-bedroomed detached house taking with her the two children of the family. The husband has continued to reside in the family home; sale would free approximately £20,000. The wife would like the property to be sold so that she can buy furniture and furnishings for her new home which her cohabitant has allowed to run to seed since his wife died. The court orders that the family home be sold and the proceeds divided equally. The wife's share of £10,000 would not be enough to enable her to purchase alternative accommodation but she has, of course, no need to do so because she looks upon her cohabitation as a long-term venture. £10,000 is enough to enable the husband to pay a deposit on a new house for himself. He can raise the balance of the purchase price on mortgage. The wife's claim to periodical payments for herself is dismissed in view of her cohabitation with the other man who is in a good job.

(c) Where there is not enough money to pay for the mortgage and other outgoings on the family home. In this situation, there is no choice but to sell the home even if this means one or the other party seeking housing association or other rented accommodation when they have been accustomed to owning their own home.

Example Both husband and wife are working, taking home about £250 per week each. The husband is living with his parents, while the wife has continued to live in the family home since the separation but she cannot afford to run it or to make the mortgage repayments on it—neither could the husband. There is very little equity in the house (only about £4,500 before the expenses of sale, etc. are deducted). There is no alternative to a sale of the house which will produce hardly anything for division between the parties. What this means in practice is that the husband will have to go on living with his parents and the wife will have to move into rented accommodation.

Note that where one party wants a sale and the other does not, the party who wants to stay can attempt to raise capital to buy the other spouse out. The court can make an order to this effect by requiring the house to be transferred into the sole name of one spouse in return for the payment of a lump sum, amount stipulated, to the other spouse (see paragraph 19.110 below). This will only be possible, of course, where the spouse has borrowing power or can lay his hands on realizable assets.

19.110   **Transfer into name of one spouse**   There are infinite variations of the orders of this type that can be made. What is usually involved is that the house is transferred into the name of the spouse who is living there either:

(a)   on immediate payment of a lump sum to the other spouse as compensation for losing his interest; *or*

(b)   on the other spouse being given a charge over the property for a proportion of the proceeds of sale realizable when the owner chooses to sell the property (while a charge for a fixed sum of money is normally undesirable as it will be whittled away by inflation, it is possible for the charge to be for a fixed amount but index-linked by reference to the property prices index for the area in which the property is situated—this is seen by some commentators as fairer to both parties);

(c)   outright with no charge or lump sum (although in such cases, it is usual for the transferring spouse to be compensated in some other way for the loss of his interest, for example, by his maintenance liability for his spouse being wiped out).

Whether an immediate lump sum can be ordered depends on the ability of the spouse who will be staying on to raise the necessary capital. Whether a charge is feasible depends on whether the transferor can afford to wait to realize his capital interest in the home (does he, for instance, need money now to buy somewhere to live or has he already obtained alternative accommodation?) and also, whether, after the charge is ultimately paid off, the transferee will still have enough to buy a new home. It is possible for the charge to be made realizable not only on the sale of the home but also on the happening of other events such as the remarriage of the transferee or her cohabitation for more than six months. Where this is done, the order will operate very much like a *Mesher* order (described in paragraph 19.112 below).

19.111   Outright transfer with no capital compensation may seem harsh but the idea of, for example, shaking off continuing liability for maintaining a spouse in return for a transfer can appeal, particularly where the transferring spouse has already secured accommodation for himself or has sufficient capital from other sources or borrowing power to buy somewhere else. In particular circumstances, it may even be appropriate to deprive one spouse of his interest in the family home with little or no reduction in maintenance payments or other compensation—it is really a question of who needs what. Furthermore, any mortgage will be transferred into the sole name of the transferee (provided that the mortgage lender which has provided the mortgage agrees to this step). This releases the transferor from his covenants under the mortgage and enables him more easily to obtain a mortgage for the purchase of alternative accommodation.

Example 1 Husband is living with his new girlfriend in her house. Wife and the two young children continue to live in the family home, a two-bedroomed bungalow with an equity of approximately £30,000. The mortgage repayments on the bungalow are £200 per month. The wife works part-time but does not earn much. The court orders that the bungalow should be transferred into the sole name of the wife. The husband is ordered to pay the wife maintenance for herself fixed at a rate sufficient to cover the mortgage repayments and water rates on the family home.

In all probability the level of financial support to be provided by the husband for the two children will be determined by a maintenance calculation carried out by the Child Support Agency.

Example 2 Husband goes to live temporarily with his parents. Wife continues to live in the family home which is subject to a very small mortgage. Both parties are earning but the wife earns considerably less than the husband. The mortgage lender is happy for the wife to take over the existing mortgage repayments and for the husband to be released from his covenants in relation to the mortgage. They are also prepared to lend the wife a further £5,000. The court orders that the home should be transferred to the wife and that she should pay the husband £5,000 in respect of his interest therein (in fact, £5,000 representing about one-quarter of the equity in the property). This will provide the husband with a deposit and he can obtain a mortgage for the balance of the purchase price of another property. The wife's claim to periodical payments is dismissed.

Mesher type order An order preserving both parties' interests in the family home but postponing sale until certain specified events, has come to be called a '*Mesher* order' after the case of *Mesher* v *Mesher and Hall* decided in 1973 but reported at [1980] 1 All ER 126.   **19.112**

The beauty of the *Mesher* order is that it enables the court to escape from a difficult situation— it does not force the wife and children (if there are any) on to the street immediately nor does it totally deprive the husband of his capital asset. It is a particularly useful arrangement where the lender refuses to release a party from his covenants under the mortgage deed. Because of this it was seized upon as the ideal answer and such orders were widespread in the mid-1970s.   **19.113**

In 1978, however (see for instance *Martin* v *Martin* [1977] 3 All ER 762, and *Hanlon* v *Hanlon* [1978] 1 WLR 592), the Court of Appeal voiced disapproval of the universal use of *Mesher* orders. It was pointed out that this type of order simply stores up trouble for the future. Families do not, of course, split up when the youngest child leaves school and a family home is often needed for considerably longer. Even when the children have grown up, the wife will need somewhere to live. What the *Mesher* order does in putting off the evil day is to force the wife into the property market to look for another house when she is least able, probably in her forties with poor employment prospects (particularly if she has not worked for some time), and possibly vulnerable emotionally because her children are growing up and need her less.   **19.114**

19.115   In *Clutton* v *Clutton* [1991] 1 All ER 340, the Court of Appeal (Lloyd LJ) decreed that where there is doubt as to the wife's ability to rehouse herself, on the statutory charge taking effect, then a *Mesher* order should not be made. However, such an order did provide the best solution:

> where the family assets are amply sufficient to provide both parties with a roof over their heads if the family home were sold, but nevertheless the interests of the children require that they remain in the matrimonial home. In such a case it may be just and sensible to postpone the sale until the children have left home, since, *ex hypothesi*, the proceeds of sale will then be sufficient to enable the wife to rehouse herself. In such a case the wife is relatively secure.

19.116   Where the non-occupier retains an interest in the equity of the former family home (whether by charge or continuing joint ownership), it has become common practice for the division of the proceeds of sale to be on an equal basis—this seems appropriate in the light of the high level of financial support likely to be required of the non-resident parent following a maintenance calculation by the Child Support Agency and the yardstick of equality approach.

Rented homes

19.117   **Transfer under s. 24**   Most tenancies are 'property' for the purposes of s. 24, MCA 1973 and the court can therefore make an order that one spouse should transfer the tenancy to the other (*Hale* v *Hale* [1975] 1 WLR 931 (private sector tenancy); *Thompson* v *Thompson* [1975] 2 All ER 208 (council tenancy)). It does not matter whether the tenancy is for a fixed term or periodic (for example, weekly). The court may also make an order transferring a housing association tenancy: *Akintola* v *Akintola* [2002] 1 FLR 701. Transfer of an assured, protected or secure tenancy can be ordered and, whereas normally assignment of a secure tenancy would cause it to cease to be a secure tenancy, assignment pursuant to an order under s. 24 does not have this effect (s. 91, Housing Act 1985).

19.118   The court is only likely to order a transfer of a tenancy under s. 24 if there is no prohibition against assignment or the landlord agrees to the transfer.

19.119   Statutory tenancies (i.e., under the Rent Act 1977) are *not* property within s. 24 and no order can therefore be made for such a tenancy to be transferred. However, statutory tenancies are covered by sch. 7, Family Law Act 1996 (see paragraph 19.120 below).

19.120   **Transfer under sch. 7, Family Law Act 1996**   Quite apart from the power under s. 24 to order the transfer of tenancies, sch. 7, para. 2 empowers the court, on granting a decree of divorce, nullity or judicial separation or at any time thereafter, to order the transfer of a protected, statutory, secure or assured tenancy (under the Housing Act 1988) from one spouse to the other (or from joint names into one spouse's sole name) and to order that a statutory tenant shall cease to be entitled to occupy and the other spouse shall be deemed to be the statutory tenant. The landlord must be given the opportunity to be heard before the court makes an order under the schedule (sch. 7, para. 14(1)).

19.121   The court may make the order only if the dwelling-house is or was the family home (sch. 7, para. 4).

19.122   In deciding whether to make the order the court must have regard to all the circumstances of the case, including:

(a) the circumstances in which the tenancy was granted to either or both spouses, or the circumstances in which either or both became a tenant;
(b) the matters set out in s. 33(6)(a)–(c) of the Act (see Chapter 25);
(c) (not relevant to spouses—see Chapter 40 for details in respect of cohabitants);
(d) the suitability of the parties as tenants: sch. 7, para. 5.

On making such an order (known as a Part II order) the court may direct that the transferee **19.123** make a payment to the transferor. It must have regard under sch. 7, para. 10(4) to all the circumstances of the case, including:

(a) the financial loss which would otherwise be suffered by the transferor as a result of the order;
(b) the financial needs and financial resources of the parties;
(c) the financial obligations which the parties have or are likely to have in the foreseeable future, including financial obligations to each other and to any relevant child.

Where the court considers a payment to be appropriate, it may direct that the payment be deferred (wholly or partly) until a specified date or the occurrence of a specified event, or that the payment be made by instalments: sch. 7, para. 10(2). It should be noted that any payment received in this way is exempt from the statutory charge: reg. 44(1)(c), Community Legal Service (Financial) Regulations 2000.

Provision for children

Periodical payments

Following the coming into force of the CSA 1991, there are fewer occasions when the court **19.124** will have jurisdiction to make a periodical payments order for the benefit of a child of the family. The court retains jurisdiction where the child to be supported is not the natural child of the prospective payer but has been treated by the prospective payer as a child of the family. It is clear now that courts apply a formula similar to that used by the Child Support Agency to determine the level of periodical payments to be made. The effect of this is that orders are likely to be for greater amounts than has been the case in the past. (See for example, *E v C (Calculation of Child Maintenance)* [1996] 1 FLR 472.)

The court also retains jurisdiction to make a periodical payments order for the benefit **19.125** of a child who has specific needs, for example, a disability (as happened, for example in *C v F (Disabled Child: Maintenance Order)* [1998] 2 FLR 1), or a need to be educated in a certain way. It is expected that the level of payments to be ordered in such cases will be linked to the needs of the child, balanced against the resources of the payer to meet those needs.

Other provision for children

It is not common for orders other than periodical payments orders to be made for chil- **19.126** dren (for instance, transfers of property to them or lump sums). No doubt the reason for this is that there is enough difficulty sharing the parties' capital between the two of them without trying to cut the cake into even smaller slices for the children as well. Nevertheless, where there is money to spare, or the children have special needs, it may be appropriate for the court to make a lump sum order or property adjustment order in their favour.

Payment of expenses

19.127   It must be noted that the court does not have power in ancillary relief proceedings to order a spouse to make payments to third parties (except for the benefit of the children). However, it is usually possible to find a way round this. For example, the court cannot order a husband to make the mortgage repayments on the former matrimonial home but it can step up the maintenance that he has to pay for the wife to include an element to cover the mortgage repayments. Nor can the court order a husband or wife to take out an insurance policy to make provision for the other spouse in the event of his or her death but it could, for example, order him or her to provide a lump sum that the spouse could use to make his or her own provision. Nor can the court order a spouse to pay the parties' joint debts or repay a loan from the other spouse's parents but it could order him to pay a lump sum to the other spouse to cover the parties' debts so that she can pay off the debts herself if he is not to be trusted to do so voluntarily.

19.128   As explained in Chapter 18, paragraph 18.155, an alternative method of ensuring that the other spouse will pay money to third parties is to accept an undertaking from him to that effect if he is prepared to give it. The undertaking is set out as a preamble to the order. If the spouse breaches the undertaking, the ultimate sanction is committal to prison. A further alternative is that the order recites that it is made on the basis that the party will be responsible for certain debts. If he fails to pay it is not possible to seek to enforce the payment of the debts but variation of the original order can be sought and his non-payment will be clear evidence of a change in circumstances since it was made.

F   MAINTENANCE PENDING SUIT

19.129   The court is not directed to take the s. 25 factors into account on an application for maintenance pending suit, simply to make such order as it thinks reasonable (s. 22, MCA 1973). The court's calculation will, of necessity, be rather rough and ready. The district judge will not normally have the advantage of a very full hearing nor will all the income and outgoings of each party necessarily be ascertained by that stage. What the district judge has to do therefore is to take into account the income, outgoings, and needs of each party as they appear at the time and make an order that will tide the applicant over until the final hearing without causing undue hardship to the respondent. It is quite likely that the sum ordered as maintenance pending suit will be rather less than the applicant can ultimately expect by way of a full periodical payments order.

G   CIVIL PARTNERSHIPS AND ORDERS FOR FINANCIAL PROVISION

19.130   Provisions found in sch. 5, para. 21 of the Civil Partnership Act 2004 ('CPA 2004') largely replicate those found in s. 25, MCA 1973 in setting out the factors to be considered by the court in determining an application for financial orders.

19.131   It remains to be seen, however, how the above provisions will be interpreted in practice, although it can be anticipated that, at least initially, the present case law will be applied to civil partnerships.

The duration of the civil partnership is likely to mean that the case law on seamless cohabit- **19.132** ation will be highly relevant.

Further, sch. 5, para. 23, CPA 2004 retains the clean break philosophy which has been **19.133** incorporated wholesale into civil partnership.

As for pre-partnership agreements, these are unenforceable if they seek to restrict or oust the **19.134** jurisdiction of the court so that the weight to be attached to the terms of the agreement will depend on all the circumstances of the case. It is important to remember, however, that there is no concept of a lifelong arrangement in civil partnership, as there is in marriage, and hence arguably greater justification in the parties seeking to organize their financial affairs before forming a civil partnership.

H CHAPTER SUMMARY

1. The court is required to consider the factors in s. 25, MCA 1973 and the clean break **19.135** philosophy in s. 25A, MCA 1973.
2. The court retains a considerable discretion as to the precise terms of the order made, especially as MCA 1973 offers no guidance as to how the award should be quantified.
3. The principal objective of the court is to achieve a fair outcome between the parties.
4. All proposed orders are to be measured against the yardstick of equality which should be departed from only with good reason.

I KEY DOCUMENTS

Matrimonial Causes Act 1973, as amended **19.136**
Family Law Act 1996
Civil Partnership Act 2004

20

CHILD SUPPORT

A   INTRODUCTION

20.01   The Child Support Act 1991 ('CSA 1991') came into force in April 1993. It is largely in the form of a framework: the detailed provision is contained in numerous regulations, some of which have been significantly amended. This chapter is designed to explain the basic principles of the Act, but throughout the book reference has been made to the Act and the implications of its provisions have been indicated. For further detail the practitioner is advised to consult a specialist textbook on the subject (for example, Roger Bird, *Child Support. The New Law* (5th edn, Family Law, 2002)). In particular, the Act's impact on the law relating to ancillary relief, and the position of cohabitants is discussed.

20.02   The 1991 Act has been significantly amended by the Child Support Pensions and Social Security Act 2000 (CSPASSA 2000) which provides a new formula for the calculation of child support. The amendments came into force on 3 March 2003.

20.03   Despite the 2003 reforms, the child support regime and the Child Support Agency, which has responsibility for the administration of the regime, remain subject to considerable scrutiny and criticism. In February 2006, Sir David Henshaw was asked by the Secretary of State for Work and Pensions to redesign the system of child support. Sir David's report (Recovering child support: routes to responsibility (CM 6894)) was published in July 2006, followed by the government's response (A fresh start: child support redesign—the Government's response to Sir David Henshaw (CM 6895)) in the same month. In essence, the proposals for reform advocate giving greater autonomy to parents to make their own arrangements for child support (even where the carer parent is claiming state benefits of some kind), and strengthening enforcement powers where the parents cannot agree on the level of child support or where default in providing adequate child support occurs. This would be coupled with provisions to ensure that the carer parent in receipt of state benefits can retain a greater proportion of the maintenance paid.

20.04   The government's response takes the form of a Consultation Paper but it is made clear that the government's ambition is to see aspects of the new system in place from 2008.

20.05   In the meantime, the regime described in this chapter remains in force and is applicable to all cases arising since 3 March 2003.

20.06   Cases arising before that date are dealt with under the original child support regime which is discussed fully in specialist practitioner texts (see above). Although it was initially intended that pre-March 2003 cases would be brought into the new scheme (a process described as 'migration'), on 9 February 2006 the Secretary of State announced an indefinite postponement of migration.

B   THE PURPOSE OF THE 1991 ACT

20.07   The aim of the 1991 Act is to establish a regime to ensure that non-resident parents (whether or not married) make a significant contribution to the financial support of their natural children.

It is important to note the following:
20.08

(a) The provisions of s. 23, Matrimonial Causes Act 1973 ('MCA 1973') still remain available for the financial support of a child by a step-parent who has treated the child as a child of the family.

(b) In *any* case where an order for a lump sum, property adjustment, or transfer or settlement of property for the benefit of a child is required, application must be made to the court in the usual way (see MCA 1973, and sch. 1, Children Act 1989 ('CA 1989')).

C SOME BASIC DEFINITIONS

The 'qualifying child'

The natural child is described in the Act as a 'qualifying child', and the term is defined in   **20.09**
s. 3(1) of the 1991 Act so that a child is a 'qualifying child' if: '(a) one of his parents is, in relation to him, a non-resident parent; *or* (b) both of his parents are, in relation to him, non-resident parents'. The term includes an adopted child and a child born to a married couple by artificial insemination by donor, unless it is proved that the husband did not consent to the treatment (s. 28(2), Human Fertilisation and Embryology Act 1990).

The provisions of the CSA 1991 apply to a child who is under the age of 16, or under the age   **20.10**
of 19 and receiving full-time, non-advanced education (i.e., education at school). The Act does not apply if the child is or has been married or is a civil partner; s. 55(2), CSA 1991, amended by the Civil Partnership Act 2004 ('CPA 2004').

The 'non-resident parent'

This term is defined in s. 3(2), CSA 1991 as follows:
20.11

The parent of any child is a 'non-resident parent', in relation to him, if:

(a) that parent is not living in the same household with the child; and

(b) the child has his home with a person who is, in relation to him, a person with care.

The 'person with care'

This term is defined in s. 3(3) as follows:
20.12

a person:

(a) with whom the child has his home;

(b) who usually provides day to day care for the child (whether exclusively or in conjunction with any other person); and

(c) who does not fall within a prescribed category of person.

Parents, guardians, or a person in whose favour a residence order has been made in respect of the child can never come within 'a prescribed category of person': s. 3(4).

For the purposes of the 1991 Act a local authority is not normally a person with care   **20.13**
(reg. 21(1) of the Child Support (Maintenance Calculation Procedure) Regulations 2000

(SI 2001/157)) and a procedure to enable a local authority to recover the cost of caring for a child is contained in the CA 1989. For the purpose of this chapter it will be assumed that the person with care is the other parent of the child, who will be referred to as the 'carer parent'.

D   THE DUTY TO MAINTAIN

20.14   This is laid down in s. 1(1), CSA 1991 in the statement 'each parent of a qualifying child is responsible for maintaining him'.

20.15   Further, in s. 1(3) it is provided that 'where a maintenance calculation made under this Act requires the making of periodical payments, it shall be the duty of the non-resident parent with respect to whom the calculation was made to make those payments'.

20.16   In order to give effect to this statutory duty a Child Support Agency was established, and it has extensive powers to trace non-resident parents, to investigate their means and to calculate, collect, and enforce child maintenance payments.

20.17   Because of amendments to s. 44 of the 1991 Act the Agency's jurisdiction to carry out maintenance calculations is extended to cover non-resident parents who are not habitually resident in the United Kingdom but are in certain classes of occupation including, for example, the diplomatic service, overseas civil service, and HM forces, or who are employed by employers described in the Child Support (Information, Evidence and Disclosure and Maintenance Arrangements and Jurisdiction) (Amendment) Regulations 2000 (SI 2001/161). Essentially, this covers employees who work outside the United Kingdom, but whose payment arrangements are made by their employers in the United Kingdom.

E   THE CALCULATION OF CHILD MAINTENANCE

20.18   The CSPASSA 2000 amends substantially Part I of sch. 1 to the CSA 1991 in prescribing the calculation of child maintenance.

The calculation

20.19   The level of child maintenance is to be determined by calculating the income of the non-resident parent. No account is taken of the income or other resources of the carer parent even where there is a significant disparity in earning capacity. There is no longer any attempt to determine the level of maintenance based on the specific needs of the qualifying child.

The calculation process

20.20   The level of maintenance to be paid depends upon which rate of payment is applicable given the financial circumstances of the non-resident parent.

20.21   In calculating the level of child maintenance to be provided by the non-resident parent, the following questions must be asked:

(a)   Which rate is to apply (i.e., basic, reduced, flat, or nil rates)?

(b)   When the basic or reduced rate applies, what sum is payable?

(c)   How is the flat rate calculated?

(d)   In what circumstances does the nil rate apply?

(e)   Should there be apportionment of the figure in (b) above?

(f)   Is care shared? If so, should it lead to a reduction in the level of maintenance to be paid by the non-resident parent?

The application and calculation of the basic rate

The basic rate will be the one applicable to most families when the non-resident parent   **20.22**
is working. The basic rate is a specified percentage of the net income of the non-resident parent, dependent upon the number of qualifying children to be maintained, namely:

- 15 per cent where the non-resident parent has one qualifying child;
- 20 per cent where he has two qualifying children;
- 25 per cent where he has three or more qualifying children: sch. 1, Part 1, para. 2(1), CSA 1991.

On the face of it, therefore, the calculation of maintenance is simple. If the non-resident parent earns £400 per week net, he will pay £60 for one child and £100 for three or more children, irrespective of the ages or individual needs of the children concerned. Net weekly income is defined in Part 1 of the Schedule to the Child Support (Maintenance Calculations and Special Cases) Regulations 2000 (SI 2001/155) as any remuneration (including overtime and bonuses) or profit derived from employment, together with working tax credit, if paid to the non-resident parent, less income tax, Class 1 or Class 2 and Class 4 national insurance contributions and any contributions to an occupational or personal pension scheme, except where the scheme is intended to provide a capital sum to discharge a mortgage secured on a non-resident parent's home in which case 75 per cent of the contribution may be deducted.

While investment income is ignored, an income derived from a pension is included.   **20.23**

Recently, by a majority decision, the House of Lords held that, in calculating a self-employed   **20.24**
trader's income for child support purposes, no deduction for capital allowances should be made: *Smith v Secretary of State for Work and Pensions and another* [2006] UKHL 35. The decision had a significant impact on the non-resident parent's income to be subject to the child support calculation. The non-resident parent had, during the period 1 April 2000–31 March 2001, made a taxable profit (before capital allowances) of £169,520, reduced by capital allowances of £148,628 to the sum of £20,892 on which he was charged income tax. Disregarding the capital allowances enhanced the non-resident parent's net income for CSA purposes and substantially increased the level of child support payable to the carer parent.

The ceiling on net weekly income   Although initially it was the view of the government   **20.25**
that there should be no limit on the income, a percentage of which could be taken in child maintenance, it did not oppose an amendment to the legislation proposed in the House of Lords which now has the effect of ignoring any net income of the non-resident parent which exceeds £2,000 per week (sch. 1, Part 1, para. 10(3), CSA 1991). Thus, very high earners have some measure of protection under the CSA regime.

20.26 **Position where the non-resident parent has a child at home with him**   The CSA 1991, sch. 1, Part 1, para. 2(2) deals with the situation where the non-resident parent has a child at home with him (e.g., a child of a new relationship, or the child of a new partner) for whom he or his partner receives child benefit. Schedule 1, Part 1, para. 10C(4) defines the term 'partner' as follows:

(a) if they are a couple, the other member of that couple (this is further defined in para. 10C(5) to mean a man and a woman who are married to each other and members of the same household, or who are not married to each other but are living together as husband and wife or two people of the same sex who are civil partners of each other and are members of the same household or two people of the same sex who are not civil partners of each other but are living together as if they were civil partners (amended by Part 1, sch. 24, CPA 2004)).

(b) if the person is a husband or wife by virtue of a valid polygamous marriage, another party to the marriage who is of the opposite sex and is a member of the same household.

In such circumstances, allowance is made for 'any other relevant children' in calculating the level of maintenance for the qualifying child. No account is taken of any income of the new partner or of the 'relevant children'.

20.27 The allowance which is made is by way of a percentage deduction from the net weekly income of the non-resident parent before the basic rate is calculated. The percentages are:

- 15 per cent, where he has one relevant other child;
- 20 per cent, where he has two relevant other children;
- 25 per cent, where he has three or more relevant other children.

If, therefore, the non-resident parent has a net weekly income of £400 and one relevant other child, 15 per cent is first deducted from his net weekly income, leaving £340 available to support the qualifying child. Hence, the qualifying child receives maintenance at the rate of £51.00 per week, not £60.00, which would have been payable if there had been no relevant other child.

20.28 This reform recognizes the variety of domestic relationships which exist today while giving some preference to the first family.

The application and calculation of the reduced rate

20.29 The reduced rate is designed to recognize that low wage earners need a disproportionate percentage of their income to meet their basic living expenses. Such a rate is payable where neither the flat rate nor the nil rate applies and the non-resident parent's net weekly income is less than £200 but more than £100.

20.30 According to reg. 3 of the Child Support (Maintenance Calculations and Special Cases) Regulations 2000, the reduced rate is an amount calculated as follows:

$$F + (A \times T)$$

where F is the flat rate liability applicable to the non-resident parent (i.e., £5.00) (see paragraph 20.31); A is the amount of the non-resident parent's net weekly income above £100 but not exceeding £200; and T is the percentage determined in accordance with Table 20.1.

Table 20.1 Determining the percentage '*T*'

	1 qualifying child of the non-resident parent				2 qualifying children of the non-resident parent				3+ qualifying children of the non-resident parent			
Number of relevant other children of the non-resident parent	0	1	2	3+	0	1	2	3+	0	1	2	3+
T(%)	25	20.5	19	17.5	35	29	27	25	45	37.5	35	32.5

Example Assume that the flat rate liability applicable to John, the non-resident parent, is £5.00 and that his net weekly income is £130. He has one qualifying child to support and no relevant other children.

The amount payable is:

5 + (£30 (being the amount by which his net income exceeds £100) × 25 per cent) =
5 + (£7.50) =
£12.50

The application and calculation of the flat rate

This is dealt with in sch. 1, Part 1, para. 4(1) and (2), CSA 1991, and the Child Support **20.31** (Maintenance Calculations and Special Cases) Regulations 2000.

The flat rate operates where the nil rate does not and where the non-resident parent's net **20.32** weekly income is less than £100 or he is in receipt of certain benefits.

There are two possible flat rates: **20.33**

(a) a flat rate of £5 is payable if the nil rate does not apply and:
  (i) the non-resident parent's net weekly income is £100 or less, or
  (ii) the non-resident parent receives any prescribed benefit (e.g., incapacity benefit), pension, or allowance, or
  (iii) his partner receives any prescribed benefit (e.g., income support or income-based jobseeker's allowance);
(b) a flat rate of a 'prescribed amount' is payable if the nil rate does not apply and:
  (i) the non-resident parent has a partner who is also a non-resident parent;
  (ii) the partner is a person with respect to whom a maintenance calculation is in force, and
  (iii) the non-resident parent or his partner receives benefit in the form of income support or income-based jobseeker's allowance.

The 'prescribed amount' of the flat rate is laid down in reg. 4(3) as follows:

(a) if the non-resident parent has a partner, the amount payable by the non-resident parent is one-half of the flat rate (i.e., £2.50);
(b) if the non-resident parent has more than one partner, the amount payable by the non-resident parent is the result of apportioning the flat rate (i.e., £5) equally among him and his partners.

The application and calculation of the nil rate

20.34 Under reg. 5 of the Child Support (Maintenance Calculations and Special Cases) Regulations 2000, there is no liability to pay child support in a number of circumstances, including where the non-resident parent has a weekly income of less than £5 or is:

(a) a student;

(b) a child, as defined by s. 55(1) of the 1991 Act;

(c) a prisoner;

(d) a person who is 16 or 17 years old and is in receipt of income support or income-based jobseeker's allowance, or is a member of a couple whose partner is in receipt of income support or income-based jobseeker's allowance;

(e) a person receiving an allowance in respect of work-based training for young people;

(f) a person in a residential care home or nursing home who:
   (i) is in receipt of a specified pension, benefit, or allowance, or
   (ii) has the whole or part of his accommodation met by a local authority;

(g) a patient in hospital who is in receipt of income support and is a patient for more than six weeks;

(h) a person whose benefit has been reduced after 52 weeks in hospital.

F   APPORTIONMENT OF THE CHILD SUPPORT LIABILITY

20.35 If the non-resident parent has two or more qualifying children living with different people, the rate of maintenance liability is divided by the number of qualifying children and shared among the persons with care according to the number of qualifying children living with that person.

20.36 For example, if a non-resident parent has a net income of £500 per week and two qualifying children, one of whom lives with X and one with Y, then the starting point of his maintenance liability would be £100 (20 per cent of £500). X and Y would each receive £50 per week by way of child support.

G   THE POSITION WHERE CARE IS SHARED

20.37 As with previous legislation, sch. 1, Part 1, para. 7, CSA 1991 recognizes that where the care of the qualifying child is shared, it is proper that there should be some reduction in the level of child support paid by the non-resident parent. The decrease applies only if the rate of child support maintenance payable is the basic or reduced rate and the non-resident parent from time to time has the care of the child overnight.

20.38 Under reg. 7(1), Child Support (Maintenance Calculations and Special Cases) Regulations 2000, a night will count for the purposes of shared care where the non-resident parent:

(a) has the care of the qualifying child overnight; and

(b) the qualifying child stays at the same address as the non-resident parent.

The amount of the decrease for *one* child is set out in Table 20.2.

Table 20.2 Reduction in maintenance where care shared

Number of nights contact takes place	Reduction in maintenance
52–103	One-seventh
104–55	Two-sevenths
156–74	Three-sevenths
175 nights or more	One-half

If the non-resident parent is caring for more than one qualifying child, the applicable **20.39** decrease is the sum of the appropriate fractions in Table 20.2 divided by the number of such qualifying children.

Where the qualifying child stays with the non-resident parent for more than 175 nights per **20.40** annum, the applicable fraction is one-half in relation to any qualifying child. In these circumstances the total sum payable to the person with care is then further decreased by £7 for each such child. Presumably this is designed to recognize the substantial level of care provided by the non-resident parent.

However, staying contact cannot reduce the flat rate or reduced rate maintenance to **20.41** less than £5. If the flat rate is payable because the non-resident parent or his or her partner is on benefits then, if there is shared care for at least 52 nights, the sum payable by way of child support is nil: sch. 1, Part 1, paras. 7(5), (6), (7), and 8(1) and 8(2), CSA 1991.

Example X and Y have two children, W and Z. The children live with X but have overnight contact with Y for a different number of nights. W spends 70 nights per annum with Y; Z stays 140 nights.

The fractions to be aggregated are therefore one-seventh and two-sevenths. The result is three-sevenths. That fraction is then divided by the number of children (two) so that the reduction is 1.5/7.

If the non-resident parent had a net income of £300 per week, the initial maintenance liability would be £60. This would now be reduced by 1.5/7, resulting in a net figure of £47.15 to be paid by way of child support.

It remains to be seen whether these provisions will lead to an increase in applications for contact orders under the CA 1989 as the non-resident parent seeks to take advantage of this 'discount'.

H THE ROLE OF THE COURTS

The position is governed by s. 8(1) and (3), CSA 1991. Generally speaking, a court has no **20.42** power to make, vary, or revive any maintenance order in relation to the child and the non-resident parent concerned. However, the court retains power to revoke a maintenance order (s. 8(4)). Further, the court retains jurisdiction in the following circumstances to make a maintenance order for the benefit of a child:

(a) in respect of children of wealthy parents where 'top-up' provision would be appropriate because the non-resident parent's net weekly income exceeds £2,000 and the court is satisfied that the circumstances make it appropriate for the non-resident parent to make periodic payments under the terms of a maintenance order in addition to child support maintenance payable by him. In these circumstances the income of both parents will be taken into account under s. 25(3), MCA 1973. 'Top-up' orders are rare in practice;

(b) in respect of children aged 16 years or over who are in receipt of advanced education or who are training for a trade, profession, or vocation;

(c) in respect of school fees for children (see, for example, *L v L (School Fees: Maintenance Enforcement)* [1997] 2 FLR 252);

(d) in respect of the additional needs of disabled children (s. 8(6), (7), and (8)).

In addition, by s. 8(5) of the 1991 Act, the court may make a child maintenance order, provided that a written maintenance agreement exists and the order is in exactly the same terms as the agreement. The written agreement should be formally recorded as a recital in the preamble to the order (see Chapter 18, paragraph 18.149 and onwards). Such an order may be subsequently varied and enforced by the court under s. 8(3A), CSA 1991, as amended.

20.43 Care must be taken with the use of s. 8(5), however. In *Dorney-Kingdom* v *Dorney-Kingdom* [2002] 2 FLR 855, the Court of Appeal confirmed that a court has no power to make a period-ical payments order for the benefit of the natural child of the payer in the absence of the agreement of the parties to the marriage as to the level of maintenance. Wilson J held similarly in *V v V (Child Maintenance)* [2001] 2 FLR 799, while reminding the parties that, in any event, the court retained its power to make lump sum orders for the benefit of the children.

20.44 Further, where a court order is made on or after 6 April 2002, the jurisdiction of the Child Support Agency cannot be ousted on a permanent basis. Under s. 4(10)(aa), CSA 1991, the court may still make the maintenance order (by consent) but the order will only oust the jurisdiction of the Child Support Agency for one year. Thereafter, either party may apply to the Child Support Agency for a maintenance calculation and will no doubt do so if dissatisfied with the way in which the maintenance order has operated.

20.45 It should be noted, however, that this arrangement is not available if the carer parent is on benefit.

I THE BENEFIT CASE

20.46 Where the carer parent is in receipt of income support or income-based jobseeker's allow-ance, the provisions of s. 6, CSA 1991 apply. In effect, such a parent is deemed to have made an application to the Child Support Agency for a maintenance calculation to be carried out against the non-resident parent in respect of qualifying children: s. 6(3)(a). Further, the Secretary of State may take action to recover from the non-resident parent, on the parent's behalf, the child support maintenance so calculated: s. 6(3)(b).

Under s. 6(5) the carer parent may request the Child Support Agency (acting on behalf of the **20.47** Secretary of State) not to act under s. 6(3). In these circumstances, or if the carer parent refuses to provide information to enable the non-resident parent to be identified and traced with a view to carrying out a maintenance calculation (as she is required to do under s. 6(7)), the carer parent may find that her benefit is reduced under provisions contained in s. 46 of the 1991 Act.

The carer parent will be given an opportunity to give reasons for her request or failure to **20.48** supply relevant information: s. 46(2). The reasons will be considered; the Child Support Agency, on behalf of the Secretary of State, having to decide whether there are reasonable grounds for believing that co-operation would result in a risk to the carer parent, or to any children living with her, of undue harm or distress: s. 46(3).

Neither the Act nor the regulations indicate what may amount to 'harm or undue distress', **20.49** but it is suggested that the circumstances in which the Secretary of State may decide not to proceed include where:

(a) the carer parent has been a victim of rape leading to the birth of the qualifying child;
(b) the child was conceived as a result of incest;
(c) the non-resident parent has sexually assaulted a child living in the household of the carer parent.

Conversely, the fact that the non-resident parent is seeking contact or is married to someone else will not be reasons to justify no further action.

If the Agency considers that the carer parent's reasons are valid, no further action will be **20.50** taken and the carer parent will be notified in writing: s. 46(4).

It should be noted that this is one of the few areas of the Act where considerable discretion **20.51** is vested in the Child Support Agency, and that in exercising such discretion the Agency 'shall have regard to the welfare of any child likely to be affected by [its] decision': s. 2, CSA 1991.

Where no reasonable grounds for the initial request or for the failure to co-operate are **20.52** established, the benefit will be reduced: s. 46(5).

This is called a reduced benefit decision. The period and rate of reduction are pre- **20.53** scribed in regulations. The reduction lasts for a period of three years, but may be sus- pended on subsequent co-operation. The maximum reduction is 40 per cent of the single adult income support allowance. Only one reduced benefit decision may be in force at any one time. Where a parent subject to a reduced benefit decision ceases to claim benefit, the reduced benefit decision is suspended for 52 weeks and then ceases to have effect.

However, the reduced benefit decision may not be given in 'prescribed circumstances' which **20.54** include where the carer parent is in receipt of income support or other prescribed benefits and the applicable amount paid to the claimant includes a higher pension premium, or disability premium or a disabled child premium.

J   THE NON-BENEFIT CASE

20.55   Where the carer parent is not in receipt of income support or other prescribed benefits, there is a choice at the present time so far as claiming maintenance for a child is concerned. She may:

(a)   apply to the Child Support Agency for a maintenance calculation to be carried out;
(b)   enter into a maintenance agreement with the non-resident parent; or
(c)   rely on s. 8(5), CSA 1991.

It should be noted that if (b) or (c) is relied on, the carer parent is still at liberty to request the Child Support Agency to carry out a maintenance calculation in the future, and any attempt to restrict this will be void (s. 9(4), CSA 1991).

K   REVISIONS

20.56   Under s. 16, CSA 1991, the Child Support Agency, acting on behalf of the Secretary of State, may revise (formerly the wording was 'review') any of the decisions which fall within the section. In practice, this means that certain decisions may be changed or modified. The Agency may carry out the revision on its own initiative, or on the application of anyone entitled to apply. Decisions capable of revision include maintenance calculations and a decision to reduce benefits. The effect of the revision is backdated to the date of the original decision.

20.57   Where the non-resident parent considers that the maintenance calculation is wrong for some reason, he should make a request in writing for revision of the decision by a child support officer. This must be done within one month of receipt of the notice of the maintenance calculation.

L   APPEALS FROM THE MAINTENANCE CALCULATION

20.58   If a revision is refused, or the outcome is unsatisfactory for the non-resident parent, then an appeal to the Child Support Appeal Tribunal would be appropriate. The procedure is laid down in the Social Security and Child Support (Decisions and Appeals) Regulations 1999 (SI 1999/991) as amended by the Child Support (Decisions and Appeals) (Amendment) Regulations 2000 (SI 2000/3185). It should be noted that generally the notice of appeal must be lodged within one month of the date when notification was given or sent to the appellant. Public funding is not available for tribunal hearings.

20.59   Thereafter, appeal on a question of law will be to the Child Support Commissioner and then, with permission, on a point of law to the Court of Appeal and to the House of Lords.

M COLLECTION AND ENFORCEMENT

The 1991 Act and the regulations contain detailed provisions to ensure compliance with the maintenance calculation. **20.60**

A method of payment may be prescribed by the Agency, including payment by standing order, by cheque, or in cash. **20.61**

Methods of enforcement include: **20.62**

(a) deduction from earnings order (this is an administrative procedure: no court order is needed);

(b) liability orders (available in the magistrates' court: this is not a means of enforcement in itself but a requisite for other forms of enforcement). It should be noted that the House of Lords held in *Farley* v *Child Support Agency and another* [2006] UKHL 31 that, in proceedings brought in the magistrates' court for a liability order, the court's jurisdiction was confined to checking that the maintenance calculation related to the defendant and that payments which had become due had not been made. The magistrates' court was not authorized to determine whether the maintenance calculation had been lawfully made in the first place;

(c) enforcement by distress;

(d) warrant of committal to prison for a maximum of six weeks;

(e) disqualification from driving. This method of enforcement came into effect in January 2001 and is contained in s. 39A(2)(b), CSA 1991, introduced by the CSPASSA 2000. The application is made to the magistrates' court. The court may disqualify for a maximum period of two years, or suspend disqualification on condition that the non-resident parent pays both the existing maintenance calculation and a sum to discharge the arrears: s. 40B(1)(a) and (b). Before deciding to disqualify or to suspend disqualification the court must enquire as to the following matters:

   (i) whether the non-resident parent needs his licence to earn a living;

   (ii) his means; and

   (iii) whether he has not paid because of 'wilful refusal or culpable neglect' on his part.

It should be noted that under s. 41 of the 1991 Act, as amended by CSPASSA 2000, penalty payments may now be required by the Child Support Agency where the Agency is authorized to recover child support maintenance and the non-resident parent has failed to make one or more payments due. These arrangements replace the former provisions for interest on arrears.

The amount of the penalty payment may not exceed 25 per cent of the amount of the child support maintenance payable for that week. Payment of the penalty does not relieve the non-resident parent from the obligation to continue to pay the child support maintenance. Any monies collected do not go to the carer parent but to the Consolidated Fund. **20.63**

Once the Child Support Agency has carried out a maintenance calculation, it alone is responsible for enforcement rather than the carer parent: *R (on the application of Kehoe)* v **20.64**

Secretary of State for Work and Pensions [2005] UKHL 48. The House of Lords, in confirming the above principle, held that, since Mrs Kehoe had no rights under the CSA 1991 which she could exercise against the non-resident parent entitling her to take part in the calculation or enforcement process, there had been no breach of her right to access to the court under Art. 6 ECHR.

N   CHILD SUPPORT ACT 1995 AND VARIATIONS UNDER THE CHILD SUPPORT PENSIONS AND SOCIAL SECURITY ACT 2000

20.65   The CSA 1991 was amended by the Child Support Act 1995, which resulted from the government White Paper *Improving Child Support* (Cm 2745, 1995). The White Paper recognized the validity of a number of previously ignored complaints about the child support regime.

20.66   The 1995 Act did not affect the general characteristics of the 1991 Act. The duty to maintain continued, the obligation lying principally on the non-resident parent in respect of the qualifying child. What the 1995 Act sought to do was to incorporate greater flexibility into the scheme by a series of 'departure directions' designed to modify the operation of the scheme in specific circumstances. This was achieved by the addition to the 1991 Act of new ss. 28A–28I and schs. 4A and 4B. The CSPASSA 2000 preserves the scheme in a somewhat modified form, departure directions becoming known as 'variations'.

20.67   By s. 28F, a child support officer, on behalf of the Secretary of State, may agree to a variation if two conditions are fulfilled:

(a)   the case falls within one or more of the cases set out in Part 1 of sch. 4B or in accompanying regulations; *and*

(b)   it is his opinion that, in all the circumstances of the case, it would be just and equitable to agree to the variation.

The overall effect of a variation is to permit the Child Support Agency to take account of certain circumstances such as additional expenses borne by the non-resident parent, or the fact that the non-resident parent has transferred property to the carer parent.

20.68   The additional or 'special' expenses are prescribed by the Child Support (Variations) Regulations 2000 (SI 2000/156) and include:

(a)   costs (e.g., travel expenses) incurred by a non-resident parent in maintaining contact with the child in respect of whom he is liable to pay child support under a current calculation;

(b)   debts incurred, before the non-resident parent became a non-resident parent, in relation to a child with respect to whom the current calculation was made. 'Debts' are not defined, but certain debts are excluded (e.g., debts taken out for a trade or business, gambling debts, and amounts due after use of a credit card);

(c)   costs attributable to a long-term illness or disability of a relevant other child (within the meaning of para. 10c(2) of sch. 1);

(d)   certain boarding school fees for a child in relation to whom the application for a maintenance calculation has been made;

(e)   the cost to the non-resident parent of making payments in relation to a mortgage and other expenses (e.g., insurance) on the home that he and the carer parent shared, if he no longer has an interest in it, and if she and the child in relation to whom the application for a maintenance calculation has been made still live there.

As might be anticipated, each 'special' expense is subject to a number of rigorous conditions before it will qualify for consideration for a variation. In addition to the requirement to demonstrate one of the circumstances outlined above, a variation will be permitted only where the child support officer forms the opinion that it would be *just and equitable* to allow it. There is a range of matters to be considered in dealing with this, including:

(a)   all the circumstances of the case;

(b)   any factors prescribed in regulations; and

(c)   the welfare of any child likely to be affected by the variation.

This gives the Secretary of State considerable discretion, but the Variations Regulations 2000 go on to prescribe other matters which he must consider, including whether the variation would result in a relevant person ceasing paid employment. Curiously there are also matters which are not to be taken into account. These include the fact that the conception of the child in question was not planned, the responsibility for the breakdown of the relationship, and the existence of a new relationship.

The procedure for an application for a variation is set out in s. 28A, CSA 1991. Essentially, the application must be made where a maintenance calculation is in force, or at any time before the Child Support Agency has made a decision on the calculation application, and may be made by the non-resident parent, the carer parent, or the child. The application need not be in writing, but it must state the grounds on which it is made.   **20.69**

O   CHAPTER SUMMARY

1.   The Child Support Agency will calculate the level of child support to be paid by the non-resident parent where the qualifying child is: **20.70**

    (a)   below the age of 16;

    (b)   between the ages of 16 and 19 and in full-time, non-advanced education.

2.   The calculation of child support is based on a percentage of the non-resident parent's net income determined by the number of qualifying children.

3.   Shared care, the fact of other children living with the non-resident parent or certain prescribed circumstances (called 'variations') may alter the level of child support to be paid.

4.   The court may make a maintenance order for the benefit of a child where:

    (a)   the child is a step-child of the non-resident parent;

    (b)   the child is above the age of 16 and in advanced education;

    (c)   where the parents agree the level of maintenance to be paid provided that the carer parent is not in receipt of state benefits;

  (d) to provide top-up maintenance;

  (e) to cover education or disability expenses.

P KEY DOCUMENTS

20.71 Child Support Act 1991, as amended by Child Support Pensions and Social Security Act 2000

21

PREVENTING AND SETTING ASIDE DISPOSITIONS UNDER SECTION 37, MATRIMONIAL CAUSES ACT 1973

A   INTRODUCTION

The powers of the court under the Matrimonial Causes Act 1973 ('MCA 1973') to make orders   **21.01**
in favour of a spouse in relation to finance and property would be seriously diminished if it
were open to the other spouse to wriggle out of his obligations by simply divesting himself of
property and income to a suitable accomplice or by transferring it out of the country beyond
the reach of the courts before an order was made or before the order could be enforced.

Therefore, under s. 37 the court has power where financial relief proceedings are brought by   **21.02**
one spouse to prevent the other spouse from making a disposition or to order him to set
aside a disposition that he has made.

21.03   In this chapter the spouse or civil partner making the application for financial relief is referred to as the applicant and the other spouse or civil partner as the respondent.

B   REQUIREMENT OF FINANCIAL RELIEF PROCEEDINGS

21.04   In order to qualify for an order under s. 37 the applicant must have brought proceedings for financial relief against the respondent.

21.05   The following applications are classed as financial relief proceedings:

(a)   for maintenance pending suit;

(b)   for any financial provision order for a spouse or a child of the family;

(c)   for any property adjustment order for a spouse or a child of the family;

(d)   for a pension-sharing order for a spouse;

(e)   for a pension attachment order;

(f)   for an order under s. 27, MCA 1973 (failure to provide reasonable maintenance) for a spouse or a child of the family;

(g)   for most forms of variation of financial orders under s. 31, MCA 1973;

(h)   for alteration of a maintenance agreement under s. 35, MCA 1973.

C   ORDERS THAT CAN BE MADE

Preventing a disposition

21.06   If the court is satisfied that the respondent is about to make any disposition or to transfer out of the jurisdiction or otherwise deal with any property with the intention of defeating a claim for financial relief, it may make such order as it thinks fit to restrain him from so doing or otherwise for protecting the claim: s. 37(2)(a).

Example Mrs Watson has petitioned for divorce. Her petition includes a comprehensive prayer for ancillary relief. She learns that her husband intends to transfer all the funds that he has in his bank account with Lloyds Bank in Grimsby to a bank account in his new girlfriend's name in Switzerland. Mrs Watson may apply for an order freezing her husband's bank account.

Setting aside a disposition

Disposition to defeat claim

21.07   If the court is satisfied:

(a)   that the respondent has made a reviewable disposition with the intention of defeating the claim for financial relief; *and*

(b)   that if the disposition were set aside financial relief or different financial relief would be granted to the applicant, it may make an order setting aside the disposition: s. 37(2)(b):

Example Before the ancillary relief hearing, Mrs Watson also discovers that her husband has transferred his valuable shareholdings in two companies to his girlfriend. She can apply to have the transfer set aside if she can show that this will make a difference to her ancillary relief claim.

Disposition to prevent enforcement

Section 37(2)(b) deals with the situation where the respondent has disposed of assets *before* the applicant's application for financial relief is dealt with. Even if the respondent waits until *after* the court has made a financial relief order before attempting to put his assets out of reach, he will find himself caught. By virtue of s. 37(2)(c), in a case where a financial relief order has already been made against the respondent, if the court is satisfied that he has made a reviewable disposition with the intention of defeating the order, that disposition may be set aside. **21.08**

An example of this in practice is *Trowbridge* v *Trowbridge* [2003] 2 FLR 231. Here the former wife had been awarded a lump sum payment in ancillary relief proceedings which had not been paid. In the meantime, the former husband had invested moneys in a house vested in the sole name of his new wife. The Chancery Division held that the former husband had intended to impede enforcement of the lump sum order and hence the payments in respect of his new wife's property could be set aside. The judge went on to declare that the former husband had acquired a beneficial interest in his second wife's home by way of a constructive trust. The former wife was then permitted to register a charge on the former husband's share of the property for the amounts still owed to her under the terms of the lump sum order. **21.09**

Consequential directions

Unscrambling a disposition that has already been made is rarely straightforward so the court is given power by s. 37(3) to make such consequential directions as it thinks fit in conjunction with an order under s. 37(2)(b) or (c). **21.10**

Example The court makes an order setting aside a conveyance of 10, Acacia Avenue, made by the respondent to his brother who was fully aware of the applicant's claims and of the respondent's intention to prevent the applicant from obtaining any share in the family home by the sale. The brother paid £10,000 for the property. The court can direct that this sum should be repaid to him.

D DEFINITIONS

Various terms used in s. 37 require further definition. **21.11**

'Defeating' the applicant's claim

Any reference in s. 37 to 'defeating' a person's claim for financial relief is a reference to: **21.12**

(a)   preventing financial relief from being granted to that person or to that person for the benefit of a child of the family; *or*

(b)   reducing the amount of any financial relief which might be granted; *or*

(c)   frustrating or impeding the enforcement of any order which might be or has been made by way of financial relief: s. 37(1).

Presumption of intention

21.13   Section 37 is concerned with respondents who *intend* to defeat financial relief claims and orders. Clearly it is not always easy to prove the intention behind a disposition or intended disposition. Section 37(5) therefore provides that in certain circumstances, the respondent will be presumed to intend to defeat the applicant's claim for ancillary relief. Thus where:

(a)   the disposition or other dealing in question:
   (i)   is about to take place; *or*
   (ii)   took place less than three years before the date of the application under s. 37; *and*

(b)   the court is satisfied that the disposition would have the consequence or has had the consequence of defeating the applicant's claim;

it is presumed that the respondent has made or is about to make the disposition with the intention of defeating the applicant's claim for financial relief.

21.14   If the presumption arises it is then up to the respondent to show that he did *not* intend to defeat the applicant's claim. If the presumption does not arise, the burden of proving intention will be on the applicant.

'Disposition'

21.15   Section 37(6) provides that the term 'disposition' includes any conveyance, assurance, or gift of property of any description by instrument or otherwise except any provision contained in a will or codicil. Examples would include selling or mortgaging a house, giving away assets, and squandering money. The meaning of 'property' is not defined but it is not restricted to property in England and Wales; it also includes real and personal property situated abroad (*Hamlin v Hamlin* [1986] Fam Law 11, [1986] 1 FLR 61). However, the surrender of a tenancy is not a disposition and therefore once it has been made it cannot be set aside under s. 37(2)(b) or (c). If it appears that a tenancy or joint tenancy is about to be surrendered, then in the absence of an undertaking by the person about to surrender that he will not do so, the person seeking to prevent the surrender should make an application to restrain the surrender under s. 37(2)(a). Any such undertaking or order should be served on the landlord: *Bater v Greenwich London Borough Council* [1999] 2 FLR 993.

'Reviewable disposition'

21.16   A disposition that has already been made will only be set aside if it is a reviewable disposition. 'Reviewable disposition' is defined in s. 37(4) to comprise *any* disposition made by the respondent *unless* it was made:

(a)   for valuable consideration other than marriage; *and*

(b) to a person who, at the time of the disposition, acted in relation to it in good faith and without notice of any intention on the part of the respondent to defeat the applicant's claim for financial relief.

Thus a sale to a purchaser who paid good money and had no idea of the respondent's intention to defeat his wife's claim could not be set aside.

Procedure

In order to restrain an anticipated disposal under s. 37(2)(a) the applicant should file notice of his application, supported by a sworn statement in accordance with r. 2.68, Family Proceedings Rules 1991. In order to set aside a disposition that has already taken place, an application in Form A should be filed and the procedure in rr. 2.51A to 2.69D of the 1991 Rules should be followed. **21.17**

A copy of Form A and the financial statement in Form E should be served on the person in whose favour it is alleged that the disposition has been made and on such other persons as the district judge may direct. **21.18**

The date on the Form A will be important for calculating the three-year period to determine whether the presumption of intention to defeat a claim under s. 37(5) MCA 1973 can be relied on. **21.19**

If there is any doubt as to the applicant's ability to demonstrate the grounds under s. 37(2)(a), the application should not be issued before a district judge but before a High Court judge or circuit judge (with a s. 9 ticket) (authority to exercise certain powers), who has power to make the order under the court's inherent jurisdiction. **21.20**

E   PREVENTING AND SETTING ASIDE DISPOSITIONS AND CIVIL PARTNERSHIP

Provisions virtually identical to those set out above are found in sch. 5, paras. 74(2), (3), and (4), and 75(3) Civil Partnership Act 2004 to protect one civil partner from transactions planned or entered into by the other for the purposes of defeating a claim for financial relief. **21.21**

F   CHAPTER SUMMARY

1. An injunction may be obtained under s. 37, MCA 1973 to protect against one party to a marriage or civil partnership from disposing of assets or property to thwart the other party's claims in ancillary relief or financial relief proceedings. **21.22**

22

COLLECTION AND ENFORCEMENT OF ANCILLARY RELIEF ORDERS

A   INTRODUCTION

This chapter deals in outline only with the means of enforcing ancillary relief orders. The **22.01** practitioner is referred to standard textbooks for further details. It is assumed throughout the chapter that it is the wife who seeks to enforce an order against the husband, but the principles would be no different were the roles reversed.

B   ENFORCING ORDERS FOR THE PAYMENT OF MONEY

There are the following considerations where the wife seeks to enforce an order for the **22.02** payment of money (usually an order for periodical payments or for the payment of a lump sum):

(a) Payments made direct between the parties: unless the court directs that the periodical payments order should be registered in the family proceedings court, maintenance payments under the order will be made direct between the parties and not through the court. Lump sums will also be paid between the parties direct. It is therefore up to both parties to keep a record of payments made/received in case there are problems in the future. One of the most convenient ways of ensuring that there is a record of payment and guarding against default is for the payments to be made through the bank by cheque in the case of a lump sum and by standing order in the case of periodical payments.

(b) Affidavit required by r. 7.1(1): before any process is issued to enforce an order made in family proceedings for the payments of money, it is necessary to file an affidavit or a sworn statement verifying the amount due under the order (i.e., the arrears in the case of periodical payments or the unpaid portion of the lump sum) and showing how that amount is calculated: r. 7.1(1), Family Proceedings Rules 1991 ('FPR 1991').

(c) Permission of the court is required to enforce arrears more than 12 months old: where a party wishes to enforce arrears that are more than 12 months old, permission to enforce the arrears must be sought: s. 32, Matrimonial Causes Act 1973 ('MCA 1973').

(d) Application for oral examination: where there is uncertainty about the husband's financial position (and therefore how to approach the question of the outstanding money), an application can be made for him to be orally examined as to his means. If the district judge agrees to the application he will order him to produce documents to verify or support his evidence. The aim of the examination is to find out exactly what assets and income the husband has and what his liabilities are. Once the true picture is available, it will be possible for the wife's solicitor to decide what is the best way of enforcing payment of the arrears/outstanding lump sum.

(e) Methods of enforcement available: the methods of enforcement available include the following:

(i) Judgment summons (r. 7.4, FPR 1991)—the wife applies for a judgment summons which requires the husband to attend before a judge to be examined as to his means. At the hearing the judge will make such order as he thinks fit in relation to the arrears/outstanding lump sum. There is power to commit the husband to prison for non-payment, but any committal order made will normally be suspended on condition that the husband pays the amount due by a specified date or by specified instalments.

The application in Form N17 is supported by an affidavit or sworn statement confirming the amount said to be owed, with a breakdown of how the sums claimed are calculated (r. 7.1, FPR 1991). Unlike the other methods of enforcement mentioned already, if there are arrears of over 12 months, the application to enforce those arrears must be included in the same application. A copy of the order to be enforced should be exhibited, if the application is not being made to the court which made the original application (r. 7.1(5)(b), r. 7.4(3), as amended by the Family Proceedings (Amendment) Rules 2003 (SI 2003/184)). The judgment summons must be served on the debtor at least 14 days before the hearing. Personal service of a number of documents must be effected on the debtor including an affidavit in support of the creditor's application and copies of written evidence to be relied on.

Further, Form M17 (the judgment summons) has been amended by the 2003 Amendment Rules to make it clear that the creditor must prove:

- the amount ordered to be paid has not been paid;
- the debtor has (or, since the date of the order, has had) the means to pay it; and

- the debtor is refusing or neglecting (or has refused or neglected) to pay the amount ordered.

The summons will require the debtor to attend court and it is for the claimant to prove that the debtor has 'had the means to pay the debt but has wilfully refused to do so'. The debtor is not now compelled to give evidence against himself since this is contrary to Art. 6 European Convention on Human Rights: per *Mubarak* v *Mubarak* and others [2001] 1 FLR 698.

(ii) While a bankruptcy order is not generally made as a means of enforcing a lump sum order in family proceedings, such an order will be made in exceptional circumstances (see, for example, *Levy* v *Legal Services Commission* [2001] 1 FLR 435). It should be noted that r. 12.3 Insolvency Rules 1986 (SI 1986/1925) was amended by Insolvency (Amendment) Rules 2005 (SI 2005/527), effective from 1 April 2005, so that lump sum orders and costs orders are now provable debts in bankruptcy proceedings. This means that the debt owed to the wife will take its place among the other debts in the bankruptcy and she will receive a proportion of the proceeds of the bankruptcy in the settlement of the debt.

(iii) Section 24A sale order—if she is seeking to enforce a lump sum order, the wife can consider seeking an order for sale of property under s. 24A, MCA 1973 (with a consequential direction that the proceeds of sale or part of them should be paid to her).

(iv) The usual enforcement methods, such as warrant of execution, attachment of earnings, charging order, and third party debt order.

C THE MAINTENANCE ENFORCEMENT ACT 1991

The Maintenance Enforcement Act 1991 improves the method of collecting and enforcing maintenance payments for spouses and children. The Act provides for the High Court or county court to specify that payments of maintenance be made by standing order or some other method, or by attachment of earnings. However, unlike the position in the family proceedings court, the direction as to the method of payment in the county court may only be given on a later occasion on an application by the interested party or on the court's own motion. **22.03**

The Act provides that in the family proceedings court the court must specify that payments be made direct from the debtor to the creditor, through the court, by standing order or similar method, or by attachment of earnings. **22.04**

The Act was an interim measure to improve the mechanics of maintenance collection and enforcement pending the coming into force fully of the Child Support Act 1991 ('CSA 1991'). However, it will continue to be used even though the CSA 1991 is now in force because it deals with *all* maintenance payments and not simply child maintenance payments. **22.05**

D   REGISTRATION OF A PERIODICAL PAYMENTS ORDER IN THE FAMILY PROCEEDINGS COURT

22.06   On or at any time after making a periodical payments order, the High Court or county court may direct that it shall be registered in a family proceedings court with the result that it will be paid and enforced through that court (see further, Chapter 18, paragraph 18.157).

E   ENFORCEMENT OF PROPERTY ADJUSTMENT ORDERS

22.07   Property adjustment orders are most commonly made in relation to the family home. Let us take as an example, an order that the husband should transfer the family home (which is in his name) to the wife. In order that the necessary conveyance or transfer can be effected, the husband's co-operation will be required. What if he refuses to execute the required documents? The answer is simple. The wife can apply to the court for an order that unless he does so within a specified time, the document be executed by a district judge of the court instead: s. 39, Supreme Court Act 1981 in the High Court and s. 38, County Courts Act 1984 in the county court.

22.08   If it is anticipated that there may be a problem over the drafting of the necessary documents (rather than over execution of them), the court can direct that the matter be referred to one of the conveyancing counsel of the court for him to settle the proper instrument to be executed by all necessary parties. Where the order is made in proceedings for divorce, nullity, or judicial separation, the court may also, if it thinks fit, defer the grant of the decree in question until the instrument has been duly executed: s. 30, MCA 1973.

22.09   Where the court has ordered a sale of property under s. 24A, MCA 1973, and one party refuses to co-operate with the sale process by, for example, refusing to give vacant possession of the property, it is possible to make an application to the court requiring the recalcitrant party to give up possession so that the sale will proceed: r. 2.64, FPR 1991. (See Chapter 18, paragraph 18.176 for the importance of the 'liberty to apply' provision.)

F   ENFORCEMENT AND CIVIL PARTNERS

22.10   The above methods of enforcement are available to civil partners where the court has made a financial provision order of some kind.

G   CHAPTER SUMMARY

22.11   1.   An ancillary relief order may be enforced in the county court or the family proceedings court.

2. The order is usually enforced by the court that made the order in the first place. Sometimes, however, it is sensible to register a county court order (for example, relating to maintenance) in the family proceedings court and enforce it there.

3. The following methods of enforcement are available in the county court:

    (a) judgment summons;

    (b) s. 24A, MCA 1973 (order for sale);

    (c) warrant of execution;

    (d) third party debt order;

    (e) charging order;

    (f) attachment of earnings.

4. The following methods of enforcement are available in the county court:

    (a) attachment of earnings;

    (b) committal to prison.

5. The county court may sign documents to transfer property (including the assignment of insurance policies) where the respondent fails to do so.

23

VARIATION OF ANCILLARY RELIEF ORDERS

A   THE SCOPE OF S. 31

Orders that can be varied

By virtue of s. 31(2), s. 31 applies to the following orders: **23.01**

(a) any order for maintenance pending suit or interim maintenance;
(b) any periodical payments or secured periodical payments order (though see paragraph 23.03 and onwards with regard to fixed term orders);
(c) any order providing for the payment of a lump sum by instalments;
(d) any order for a settlement of property or for a variation of settlement which was made on or after a decree of judicial separation (such an order can, however, only be varied where application is made in proceedings for the rescission of a decree of judicial separation or in subsequent divorce proceedings: s. 31(4));
(e) any deferred order made by virtue of s. 23(1)(c) (lump sums) which includes provision made by virtue of:
    (i) s. 25B(4); or
    (ii) s. 25C (settlement or provision in respect of pension rights (inserted by s. 166, Pensions Act 1995));
(f) any order for settlement or sale of property made under s. 24(1)(b) and s. 24A(1), Matrimonial Causes Act 1973 ('MCA 1973') respectively;
(g) a pension-sharing order under r. 24B which is made at a time before the decree has been made absolute (inserted into s. 31(2) by sch. 3, Welfare Reform and Pensions Act 1999 ('WRPA 1999')).

Note that it makes no difference to the court's powers of variation that the original order was made by consent.

23.02   Although this chapter deals with the variation of orders made in ancillary relief proceedings, an order made on a s. 27, MCA 1973 application (failure to provide reasonable
maintenance; see Chapter 35) for periodical payments or for interim maintenance or for
the payment of a lump sum by instalments is equally variable. The case of *Burrow v Burrow*
[1999] 1 FLR 508 clarifies the point that an order 'earmarking' pension provision is an order
under s. 23, MCA 1973 and is therefore capable of variation under s. 31, MCA 1973 (see
s. 31(b), (e)).

Orders that cannot be varied

23.03   There is no power to vary an order for the transfer of property made under s. 24(1)(a),
MCA 1973, nor, except in limited circumstances where the order has been made on judicial
separation, an order under s. 24(1)(b), (c), or (d) for the settlement of property or varying an
ante-nuptial or post-nuptial settlement or extinguishing the interest of either party to the
marriage in such a settlement.

23.04   There is no power to vary the amount of a lump sum payment (made under s. 27 or
s. 23). The most that the court can do is to adjust the arrangements for paying the
lump sum if it has been ordered to be paid by instalments or has been deferred for a period
of time.

23.05   Where the court has, in connection with divorce or nullity, granted periodical payments
for a fixed term in favour of a party to the marriage, it may specify that that party shall not
be entitled to apply under s. 31 for an extension of the fixed term: s. 28(1A), MCA 1973 as
added by the Matrimonial and Family Proceedings Act 1984 ('MFPA 1984'). *Jones* v *Jones*
[2000] 2 FLR 307 confirmed that the application to vary a fixed-term periodical payment
order must be issued during the life of the order. It did not matter that the hearing took place
once the order had expired.

23.06   The reason for preventing the variation of such orders is the need of the parties to know
where they stand. The court has a limited power to set aside such orders in appropriate cases:
Cornick v *Cornick* [1994] 2 FLR 530.

B   WHAT CAN THE COURT DO ON A VARIATION APPLICATION?

23.07   On a variation application the court has power to vary or discharge the order concerned or
to suspend any provision of the order temporarily and to revive any provision so suspended:
s. 31(1). The most common applications for variation are by the recipients of periodical
payments who seek to have their payments increased and by payers who seek to have their
payments reduced.

23.08   Where the court has made an order for maintenance of some kind (maintenance pending
suit, interim maintenance, and periodical payments, secured or unsecured), it has power to
remit arrears due under the order in whole or in part: s. 31(2A).

23.09   Provisions contained in sch. 8, Family Law Act 1996 ('FLA 1996') amended s. 31, MCA 1973
so as to introduce new powers in s. 31(7B) of the MCA 1973 to enable the court, in dealing

with variation proceedings, to make a 'compensating' lump sum or property adjustment order so that a 'clean break' may be achieved at that stage.

As a general rule, the court has no power to make a property adjustment order or a lump **23.10** sum order on an application for variation of a periodical payments order or secured periodical payments order in favour of a spouse: s. 31(5), MCA 1973. However, the 'clean break' provisions give the court further powers after the dissolution of a marriage in cases where:

(a) it discharges a periodical payments order or secured periodical payments order made in favour of a party to the marriage (s. 31(1)); or

(b) it varies such an order so that the payments under the order are required to be made or secured only for such further period as is determined by the court: s. 31(7A).

By virtue of its powers in s. 31(7B) the court may substitute one of the following orders **23.11** when it discharges a periodical payments order:

(a) an order for the payment of a lump sum in favour of a party to the marriage;

(b) one or more property adjustment orders in favour of a party to the marriage (provided that each falls within different subsections of s. 21(2)(a) to (d): see s. 31(7E));

(c) one or more pension sharing orders, although with the limitation that the petition must have been filed on or after 1 December 2000: WRPA 1999, s. 85;

(d) a direction that the party in whose favour the original order discharged or varied was made is not entitled to make any further application for:

(i) a periodical payments order, secured periodical payments; or

(ii) an extension of the period to which the original order is limited by any variation made by the court.

Any lump sum order so made can be ordered to be paid by instalments, deferred, or secured and to carry interest at the discretionary rate under s. 22A(7) and (8): see s. 31(7C) and (7D). The power to capitalize periodical payments orders with lump sum or property adjustment orders applies to all petitions including those filed before 1 November 1998: *Harris v Harris* [2002] 1 FLR 248.

It is not therefore possible to have a 'clean break' as to capital while an order for periodical **23.12** payments is in existence. Clients will have to be warned that, while an order for periodical payments is in force, it will always be possible for a court to make an order requiring the paying party to make capital provision for the receiving party as compensation for the termination or variation of periodical payments. The court has power to make such an order 'of its own motion' regardless of whether one or other of the parties has made an application for such an order.

C FACTORS TO BE TAKEN INTO ACCOUNT ON A VARIATION APPLICATION

23.13 In exercising its powers to vary, etc. under s. 31, the court is directed by s. 31(7) (as amended by the MFPA 1984 and sch. 8 to the FLA 1996) to have regard to all the circumstances of the case, the first consideration being given to the welfare while a minor of any child of the family is under 18. The circumstances of the case include any change in any of the matters to which the court was required to have regard when making the order to which the application relates (i.e., the s. 25, MCA 1973 factors; see Chapter 19) and, in a case where the party against whom the order was made has died (a situation that normally only arises on an application for variation of secured periodical payments), the circumstances of the case shall also include the changed circumstances resulting from his or her death. As well as having power to bring periodical payments to an end immediately, the court has power, on a variation application, to limit the future term of the periodical payments or secured periodical payments order to such term as will be sufficient to enable the payee to adjust to the termination of the payments without undue hardship and must always give consideration to exercising this power in all variation applications concerning periodical payment orders (secured and unsecured) made on or after a decree of divorce or nullity. It is particularly important to realize that, as a result of the amendments to s. 37 made by sch. 8 to the FLA 1996, the court, when considering the application, may look to capital accumulated by the parties after the divorce, since it is entitled in variation proceedings to take a fresh look at the evidence of the parties' means as they stand at the date of the variation application. It is not restricted to the evidence of the parties' means as they stood at the date of the original order: s. 31(7), (7B).

23.14 The factors to be taken into account on a variation application were considered by the Court of Appeal in *Pearce* v *Pearce* [2003] 2 FLR 1144 who emphasized that:

(a) On dismissing an entitlement to future periodical payments, the court's function is not to reopen the capital claims of the parties but to substitute for the periodical payments order such other order or orders as will both fairly compensate the payee and, at the same time, complete the clean break. The Court of Appeal disapproved the approach of Charles J in *Cornick* v *Cornick (No. 3)* [2001] 2 FLR 1240 in which he sought to say that the court is not tied to such capitalization. In rejecting Charles J's approach Thorpe LJ explained (at [39]):

> that this discipline is necessary as a safeguard against the temptation to further adjust the capital division between the parties to reflect the factors which were not foreseen or which did not pertain at the date of the original division.

(b) In surveying what substitute order or orders should be made, consideration should first be given to the option of carving out of the payer's pension funds a pension for the payee that is equivalent to the discharged periodical payments order. This would require a pension-sharing order, under s. 31(7B)(ba) (which is only available for orders made in divorce proceedings commenced on or after 1 December 2000).

23.15 In summary, the court must:

(a) determine the application for variation, applying s. 31(7) and the relevant authorities culminating in *Cornick* v *Cornick (No. 2)* [1995] 2 FLR 490. Depending on the facts of each case this exercise may require an upward or downward variation of periodical payments;

(b)   fix the date from which the varied order is to commence;

(c)   calculate the capital payment (which may include a pension-sharing order in appropriate cases) to be made in lieu of an order for periodical payments, using the *Duxbury* tables to achieve the appropriate sum.

PART IV

TAXATION

24

TAX CONSIDERATIONS

A INTRODUCTION

Solicitors and barristers tend, all too often, to look upon taxation as solely the province **24.01** of the accountant. This tendency is particularly dangerous when the solicitor is being consulted in connection with the breakdown of a marriage. It is not possible to advise a client properly on arrangements in relation to property and finance on separation or divorce without considering how tax is likely to affect him or her.

24.02 An understanding of the principles of taxation will enable the practitioner to see to it that the family's affairs are arranged in the most tax-efficient way. As we shall see, this may simply improve one party's cash flow situation or it may actually produce a saving of tax so that there is more money to go round. Furthermore, should the court have to consider the question of finance and property, it will expect the parties' legal advisers to have worked out the tax effects of the proposals that they are urging on the court so that the actual results for the parties can be clearly seen and the court can make an informed decision. In a complicated case, the solicitor should consider seeking the expert assistance of an accountant or tax consultant in working out the best solution.

24.03 A certain number of the ground rules on taxation are set out in this chapter but, on the whole, it has been assumed that the reader already has a working knowledge of taxation and attention has therefore been directed specifically to the implications of taxation on the family. For a more detailed analysis of taxation, the reader is referred to specialist textbooks such as *Butterworths UK Tax Guide* for the relevant year. When dealing with the tax consequences of separation and divorce, the chapter works on the basis that any payments of money or transfers of property are being made by the husband to the wife or children. The same principles would, however, apply if the wife were to be the provider. As of 5 December 2005, the statutory provisions apply equally to registered civil partnerships. Therefore all references to spouses made below also now include registered partners.

24.04 Note that the figures used in the examples are chosen to produce convenient tax calculations. They do not necessarily give any indication of the appropriate maintenance or other payments in a particular case.

PART I   INCOME TAX

24.05 The Income and Corporation Taxes Act 1988 is referred to throughout as ICTA 1988. The Finance Act 1988 is referred to as FA 1988.

B   GENERAL RULES

24.06 Husbands and wives are taxed separately on their earned and investment income. Each has their own allowance and independent rates of taxation.

Present rates and bands of tax

24.07 For the tax year 2007/2008 the rates and bands of tax are as follows:

	£
Lower rate band (10% tax)	£2,230
Basic rate band (22% tax)	£2,230–£34,600
Higher rate band (40% tax)	Over £34,600

Personal allowances

Everyone (including a married woman) is entitled to a personal allowance which can be set **24.08** against all types of income (s. 257, ICTA 1988). The personal allowance is increased if the individual (or one of a married couple) is over 65, and further increased at the age of 75. The amount of the personal allowance for 2007/2008 is £5,225.

Year of marriage; year of separation; year of divorce

When couples separate each of them will continue to be entitled to the personal allowance **24.09** throughout the year of marriage, the year of separation, and the year of divorce.

Married Couple's Allowance (ICTA 1988, s. 257A)

This relief was abolished with effect from 6 April 2000, though it exists for married couples **24.10** where either spouse was born before 6 April 1935.

Child Tax Credit

From 6 April 2003 the Child Tax Credit consolidated various tax credits. It is a payment to **24.11** support families with children. It can be claimed by a person who is responsible for one or more children. The claimant does not have to be working in order to make a claim. It will be paid in addition to Child Benefit and any Working Tax Credit. Awards are dependent on joint income and paid to the main carer. Families are entitled to the family element of £545 per year and a baby addition of £545 per year in the first year of a child's life. This is tapered where joint annual income exceeds £50,000. The child element of £1,845 per year applies for each child in families with joint income up to £14,495 per year. Maintenance payments are ignored.

To qualify for Child Tax Credit: **24.12**

(a) the claimant must be over 16 years old and responsible for at least one child;
(b) the child must be either under 16 years of age or under 19 years of age and still in full-time education, up to and inclusive of A-levels or their equivalent;
(c) the upper limit before all tax credits are lost is a joint gross income of £58,000. This rises to £66,000 where a child was born in the year of the claim.

Working Tax Credit

Working Tax Credit is a payment to top up the earnings of working people on low incomes, **24.13** including those who do not have children. There are extra amounts for working households in which someone has a disability. It is available to employees and self-employed people, and includes support for the costs of qualifying child care. It is paid in addition to any Child Tax Credit to which the claimant may be entitled. As with Child Tax Credit, maintenance payments are ignored.

To qualify for Working Tax Credit: **24.14**

(a) the claimant must be a lone parent, or a couple with at least one child, where the claimant is over 16 years of age and works at least 16 hours per week on average;

(b) if the claimant has no children, then he/she must be over 25 years of age and work at least 30 hours per week on average;

(c) if the claimant is disabled, then he/she must be over 16 years of age and work at least 16 hours per week on average;

(d) the threshold for the Working Tax Credit is a joint income of £14,495. No credit is due for income in excess of this level.

24.15 A qualifying individual may also claim up to 70 per cent of eligible childcare costs subject to a maximum eligible weekly cost of £300 for those with two or more children or £175 in the case of one child.

C TAX ON MAINTENANCE ORDERS

24.16 There are four ways in which a husband can find himself paying maintenance to his wife or children:

(a) He can do so voluntarily.

(b) He can enter into a binding agreement to pay maintenance.

(c) He can be obliged to pay maintenance by a court order.

(d) He can be obliged to pay under a maintenance assessment determined by the Child Support Agency.

Voluntary maintenance for a spouse or child

24.17 Maintenance is paid voluntarily if it is not paid under any legally binding agreement or under a court order. Voluntary maintenance payments have never attracted income tax relief.

Maintenance paid under a binding agreement or court order

24.18 The availability of tax relief on maintenance payments was finally abolished as from 5 April 2000 (save to a very limited extent for maintenance orders and agreements made before 15 March 1988 where one or both parties to the marriage are aged 65 or over on 6 April 2000).

Maintenance assessment by the Child Support Agency

24.19 No tax relief is available to a payer required to make payments following a child support maintenance assessment.

PART 2   INHERITANCE TAX AND CAPITAL GAINS TAX

24.20 As a general rule, transfers of assets between husband and wife during their marriage do not give rise to any liability for inheritance tax or capital gains tax ('CGT'). If the spouses separate or divorce, however, the incidence of these two taxes must be considered when deciding what is to be done with their assets. It is on this aspect of inheritance tax and CGT that this chapter concentrates. The two main statutes to be considered are the Inheritance Tax Act 1984 ('IHTA 1984') and the Taxation of Chargeable Gains Act 1992 ('TCGA 1992').

D   INHERITANCE TAX

During the marriage

Transfers of value between spouses during the marriage are exempt from inheritance tax **24.21** (s. 18, IHTA 1984). This exemption continues right up to decree absolute of divorce or nullity regardless of whether the spouses separate before the decree comes through.

After divorce or nullity

It is often not possible to sort out finances and property before decree absolute. In particular, **24.22** if it is necessary to refer matters to the court for resolution under ss. 23, 24, and 24B, Matrimonial Causes Act 1973 ('MCA 1973'), the court's order does not become effective until after decree absolute. Nevertheless, transfers made after decree absolute will usually continue to escape inheritance tax. The reason for this is twofold:

(a)   The transfer will normally be covered by s. 10, IHTA 1984. This provides that a disposition is not a transfer of value (and therefore has no consequence for inheritance tax) if it is shown:

  (i)   that the transfer was either made in a transaction at arm's length between persons not connected with each other or if made between connected persons, was such as might be expected to be made in a transaction at arm's length between persons not connected with each other; *and*

  (ii) that the transfer was not intended to confer gratuitous benefit on any person.

  Husband and wife are no longer connected persons after divorce: s. 270, IHTA 1984 and s. 286, TCGA 1992. Transfers between them pursuant to an order of the court in consequence of a decree of divorce or nullity will generally be regarded as transactions at arm's length not intended to confer any gratuitous benefit (see the statement issued by the Senior Registrar of the Family Division in 1975 with the agreement of the Revenue (1975) 119 SJ 596) and therefore within s. 10. It would appear that transfers to children pursuant to a court order will also normally escape inheritance tax on this basis as will periodical payments made under a court order. It is recognized, however, that exceptionally a transfer made pursuant to a court order will not simply be made in order to fulfil legal obligations to provide for wife and children but will be intended to confer gratuitous benefit on them. In such circumstances, s. 10 will not apply and inheritance tax may be payable.

  Although the Registrar's statement does not refer specifically to transfers of money or property made pursuant to an agreement or voluntarily rather than under a court order, there would seem to be no reason why such payments should not be covered by s. 10 provided they are along the same lines as the order a court could have been expected to make.

(b)   Even if s. 10 does not assist, s. 11, IHTA 1984 may. This provides that a disposition is not a transfer of value if made by one party to a marriage in favour of the other party or of a child of either party for the maintenance of the party to the marriage or the maintenance, education, or training of the child whilst he is under 18 or in full-time education or training. A disposition made on the occasion of the dissolution or annulment of a marriage in favour of the former spouse is within s. 11: s. 11(6). Although it is not easy to interpret how s. 11 applies on marriage breakdown, it does seem that it will ensure that no inheritance tax arises by virtue of periodical payments to a spouse or infant children after divorce or, indeed, to an infant child during the marriage (provided the amount is not so excessive that it cannot be said to be for maintenance, education, etc.) or presumably by virtue of any lump sum which can be described as maintenance (for example, capitalized periodical payments). Transfers of some assets may also be said to be for maintenance and covered by the section (arguably, for instance, a transfer of the matrimonial home). Dispositions *varying* provision made on the occasion of divorce or nullity are covered by s. 11: s. 11(6).

In the rare cases where the transfer is not protected by ss. 10 and 11, IHTA 1984, the normal inheritance tax rules still provide further opportunities for exemption from charge, for example, the transfer may be covered by the transferor's annual exemption (currently £3,000 for 2007/8; s. 19, IHTA 1984), or by the exemption for small gifts (£250 per person per year: s. 20, IHTA 1984) or as normal expenditure out of income (s. 21, IHTA 1984) or it may, if a gift, qualify as a potentially exempt transfer (s. 3A, IHTA 1984).

There will be no inheritance tax liability if the disposition falls within the transferor's nil band, which is currently £300,000. This is not a one-off limit but is available every seven years (s. 7(1)(a), IHTA 1984). Each gift drops out of account after seven years and it works on a gift-by-gift basis, so that one looks back from the date of the proposed transfer to see if gifts totalling £300,000 have been made in the past seven years.

E   CAPITAL GAINS TAX

During the marriage

24.23   As the law stands at present a husband and wife living together are basically treated as one person for CGT purposes even though both spouses are separately taxable upon their own gains and have their own allowances (£9,200 for 2007/8). Any disposal of a chargeable asset by one to the other is treated as if the consideration were such that neither a gain nor a loss would accrue to the disponor: s. 58, TCGA 1992. Broadly speaking this means that the disponee (let us say the wife) steps into the disponor's shoes (so that, for example, when the asset is finally disposed of outside the marriage, the chargeable gain or loss will be traced back to the time when the asset was first acquired by the husband). Where this rule applies, no CGT can arise on the disposal between the spouses.

After separation

24.24   It is separation, not divorce, that is important for CGT purposes. If the spouses are no longer living together on a permanent basis they start to be treated as separate individuals for CGT.

Thus, for example, each has an annual exemption for gains (currently £9,200 for 2007/8) and the inter-spouse disposal rule ceases to operate (although, in practice, it seems that the Revenue regard the inter-spouse rule as continuing to apply until the end of the tax year in which separation occurs).

Potential charge to CGT after separation

What the rules mean in the context of marriage breakdown is that transfers of assets from **24.25** one spouse to the other after the year of separation can give rise to CGT. Furthermore, although there is no CGT on a disposal of cash and therefore lump sum payments (and, of course, periodical payments) have no CGT implications, it must be borne in mind that if the payer has to dispose of assets to raise the lump sum, there may be CGT to pay on that disposal if he makes a chargeable gain.

Before jumping to the conclusion that there has been a disposal of an asset between spouses **24.26** and that CGT may arise, the position as to ownership of the asset in question must be checked. If a spouse already owns an asset or a share in a particular asset, there cannot be a disposal of that asset/share to her.

Example Husband and wife purchase a painting from their joint savings. They own the painting in equal shares. The painting is now valuable and, after divorce, it is decided that the wife will keep it. This arrangement amounts to a disposal by the husband of his half share in the painting. There is no disposal of the wife's half share—she simply keeps what she already owns. Only half the gain on the painting is potentially liable to CGT.

It follows that orders of the court under s. 17, Married Women's Property Act 1882 can never give rise to any CGT as the court's only power under that Act is to declare existing property rights. Under s. 24, MCA 1973 the court has a wide discretion to redistribute property between the parties. As the court rarely makes any finding as to what the parties' property rights were before the s. 24 order, the CGT implications of the order will depend on whether it is possible to persuade the Revenue that all or part of the asset made the subject of the order already belonged to the transferee. The same is true of arrangements made by the parties in relation to property without a court order.

Lines of defence against CGT

Non-chargeable assets, exemptions, etc.

Certain disposals cannot give rise to a CGT liability. These include disposals of cars, of **24.27** tangible movable property which is a wasting asset (i.e., predictable useful life of 50 years or less), of chattels where the consideration/deemed consideration of the disposal is £6,000 or less (marginal relief is given where tangible movable property is disposed of for more than £6,000), and of the individual's principal private residence (see paragraph 24.28 below). Most disposals on the occasion of marriage breakdown should be covered by these provisions and there should therefore be no question of CGT liability. If, however, a chargeable gain arises, it may be covered by the annual exemption of the spouse concerned. Failing that, it may be possible to hold over the gain.

Particular points on the matrimonial home

24.28 Often the parties' only major capital asset is the matrimonial home. Is there any CGT liability on a transfer of one spouse's interest in the home to the other spouse or on a sale of the property on the open market? In dealing with this question in this paragraph it is assumed that the wife stays on in the home and the husband leaves and that any transfer between them is from husband to wife.

Most disposals covered by private residence exemption Most disposals of the matrimonial home following marriage breakdown (whether between spouses or on the open market) are covered by the private residence exemption.

24.29 Any gain accruing to an individual on a disposal of a dwelling-house which is or has at any time in his period of ownership been his only or main residence will be wholly or partially exempt from CGT by virtue of the private residence exemption provided by ss. 222 and 223, TCGA 1992. Where the individual has occupied the house as his home throughout the whole of his period of ownership, the whole of the gain will be exempt. Where the house has only been his home for part of his period of ownership, the gain will be apportioned and the part attributable to the time when he was not in residence will be chargeable to CGT. Note, however, that the individual will be treated as having been in residence during the final 36 months of his ownership whether he actually was or not. How this operates in practice can best be shown by examples of common situations.

Example 1 Husband and wife own the matrimonial home jointly. When the marriage breaks down, the husband moves out leaving the wife to occupy the home on her own. After divorce, the husband agrees to transfer his half share in the house to the wife. Provided he does so within three years of having left home, any gain he is taken to have made on the disposal will be exempt from CGT under the private residence exemption.

Example 2 The facts are as in Example 1 but the court orders that the house should be sold. Provided the sale takes place within three years of the husband moving out, his gain is exempt as before. The wife's gain is exempt, also on the basis of the private residence exemption, as she is actually resident right up to the time of sale.

24.30 **Extra-statutory concession (Statement of Practice D4)** Suppose that by that time the husband transfers his share in the matrimonial home, he has been out of occupation for more than three years. Does this mean he will have to pay capital gains tax on the gain that has accrued during the excess period?

24.31 If Statement of Practice D4 applies, the answer is 'no'. Concession D4 provides that if one spouse transfers an interest in the matrimonial home to the other spouse as part of a financial settlement on divorce or separation, *and*

(a) the other spouse continues to occupy the home as her only or main residence, *and*

(b) the transferring spouse has not elected to treat any other property as his only or main residence,

the transferring spouse is deemed to continue in occupation of the home until the date of the transfer, however long it is since he actually left.

Example The facts are as in Example 1 above save that the husband does not transfer his interest in the home to the wife until he has been away for over five years. Up to this point the husband has been living in rented accommodation so he has not elected to treat any other property as his only main residence; the wife has lived in the home throughout. The transfer takes place as part of a settlement following the parties' divorce on the basis of five years' separation. Concession D4 applies.

Cases of absence for more than three years where concession D4 does not apply   Where   **24.32** the husband has been absent from the home for more than three years before he transfers or sells his interest in it and where concession D4 does not apply (for instance, where the husband has bought another house and elected to have that as his main residence or where the disposal in question is not a transfer to the wife but a sale on the open market), capital gains tax will, prima facie, be payable not on the gain made whilst he was living in the house or during the three years immediately thereafter, but on any gain accruing to him after the three-year period elapsed. There are a number of reasons why this may not be as bad as it seems:

(a)   It is not the gain for the whole period of ownership that is being taxed, only for the period while the husband has been out of occupation less three years.
(b)   Indexation may reduce the amount of the gain so that the husband is not paying tax on gains arising purely by virtue of inflation (at least, that is, inflation since March 1982).
(c)   Any gain that there is may be covered by the husband's annual exemption.
(d)   It may be possible to hold over any gain under s. 79, Finance Act 1980 so that tax is not immediately payable.

Settlements and postponed sales of the matrimonial home

The reader should be aware that certain court orders may create settlements for CGT pur-   **24.33** poses (for example, where there is an order that the house be held on trust for the wife for life or until remarriage or until she ceases to reside there and thereafter for husband and wife in equal shares). There are special rules governing the incidence of CGT on the creation of, during, and at the end of a settlement. They are fairly detailed and the reader is referred to a specialist book on matrimonial taxation such as *Butterworths UK Tax Guide* for the provisions. *Mesher* orders (see Chapter 19, paragraph 19.112 and onwards) do not appear to create a CGT settlement but also require special consideration.

Calculating the gain

Where it is necessary to calculate the chargeable gain, this is done by deducting the acquisi-   **24.34** tion cost of the asset from the consideration received or deemed to be received on the disposal. Where an asset is sold on the open market, the consideration will normally be the price actually received. When one spouse transfers an asset or a share in an asset to the other, the Revenue will usually deem the consideration for the transfer to have been market value on the basis that it is made between connected persons (spouses are connected until decree absolute) or that the disposal is made otherwise than by way of a bargain at arm's length or for a consideration that cannot be valued: s. 17, TCGA 1992.

However, as a result of s. 35, provision is made for 'rebasing' the cost of a disposal for the   **24.35** purposes of calculating a chargeable gain for capital gains tax. The general rule is that where assets were held at 31 March 1982, it is to be assumed that they were sold on that date and immediately reacquired at their market value at that time. Further rules apply to the disposal of assets which were held at 6 April 1965. This means that all of the gains accrued before that date are now wiped out.

F STAMP DUTY

24.36 When a property is purchased stamp duty land tax is paid by the purchaser on the 'effective date', which is normally on completion. This is something which the family lawyer should take into account if acting for a client who is to buy a new home following divorce.

24.37 The current rates of stamp duty are as follows:

Consideration	Rate
Up to £125,000	Nil
£125,001 to £250,000	1%
£250,001 to £500,000	3%
£500,001+	4%

24.38 Where a property is transferred under the terms of a court order on divorce (or under a separation agreement), the transfer or conveyance effecting the transfer is exempt from stamp duty: s. 83, Finance Act 1985 and Stamp Duty (Exempt Instruments) Regulations 1987 (SI 1987/516).

PART V

ORDERS UNDER PART IV OF THE FAMILY LAW ACT 1996

(The authors are indebted to Paul Mallender and Jane Rayson in the preparation of this chapter.)

25

OCCUPATION ORDERS AND NON-MOLESTATION ORDERS

A   INTRODUCTION

Part IV of the 1996 Act has been in force since 1 October 1997. It provides a simple and **25.01** unified system designed to offer protection from domestic violence. Protection is provided to those who fall within the class of 'associated persons' and includes provision for powers of arrest to be attached to orders, the granting of orders on a 'without notice' basis and considerable flexibility over how the family home is to be occupied.

B   THE ORDERS AVAILABLE

Two forms of order are available in all courts having jurisdiction in family matters because **25.02** s. 57 generally provides for a unified jurisdiction between the High Court, county courts, and magistrates' courts. The orders are 'occupation orders' and 'non-molestation orders'.

An occupation order

25.03 This is defined in s. 39 as meaning an order made under ss. 33, 35, 36, 37, or 38 of the 1996 Act. Such an order may be applied for in other family proceedings or without any other family proceedings being instituted (i.e., a free-standing application is possible).

25.04 Section 39(4) emphasizes that the fact that a person has applied for an occupation order under ss. 35 to 38 shall not affect the right of any person to claim a legal or equitable interest in any property in any subsequent proceedings.

A non-molestation order

25.05 A non-molestation order means an order containing either or both of the following provisions:

(a) a provision prohibiting the respondent from molesting another person who is associated with the respondent;

(b) a provision prohibiting the respondent from molesting a relevant child (s. 42(1)).

The term 'molestation' is not defined in the 1996 Act. It has been held that 'molestation' includes any conduct which can properly be regarded as such a degree of harassment as to call for the intervention of the court: *Horner* v *Horner* [1982] Fam 90. In colloquial terms, it means 'pestering': *Vaughan* v *Vaughan* [1973] 3 All ER 449.

25.06 In *C* v *C* [2001] EWCA Civ 1625 it was stressed that the judge must be satisfied on the balance of probabilities that judicial intervention is required to control the behaviour which is the subject matter of the complaint before the court. The form that that behaviour takes is also an important consideration.

25.07 The case of *C* v *C* [1998] 1 FLR 554 confirms that a non-molestation order should only be made where there was some conduct which harassed and affected the applicant. It was not appropriate to seek a non-molestation order to prevent an invasion of the applicant's privacy by the publication of an article which related to the marriage and relationship between the applicant and his former wife and which he feared might damage his reputation. In *Banks* v *Banks* [1999] 1 FLR 726 the court held that it would be wrong to make the wife subject to a non-molestation order where the abuse to which the wife had subjected the husband was a symptom of her mental condition and was something over which she had no control. A non-molestation order would serve no practical purpose in such circumstances, even if the wife were capable of understanding it.

C ASSOCIATED PERSONS AND RELEVANT CHILD

25.08 The concept of 'associated persons' is used in applications under s. 33. Further, as will be seen later, in determining whether a client will be able to obtain a non-molestation order the first matter to be ascertained is whether the applicant or respondent are associated or where it is a child who is to be protected, whether the child is a 'relevant' child.

Associated persons

The list of 'associated persons' appears in s. 62(4) and (5) of the 1996 Act. **25.09**

The definition

Persons are 'associated' with each other if: **25.10**

(a) They are married: s. 62(3)(a).

(b) They are or have been civil partners of each other: s. 62(3)(aa).

(c) They have been married: s. 62(3)(a).

(d) They are cohabitants or former cohabitants (i.e., two persons who, although not married to each other, are or were living together as husband and wife or (if the same sex) in an equivalent relationship): ss. 62(1)(a) and 62(3)(b), which should be interpreted generously so as not to exclude borderline cases: *G v F (Non-molestation Order: Jurisdiction)* [2000] Fam Law 519.

(e) They live in the same household or have lived in the same household: (s. 62(3)(c)) otherwise than by reason of one of them being the other's employee, tenant, lodger, or boarder.

(f) They are relatives: s. 62(3)(d). 'Relative' is defined by s. 63, the interpretation section, of the Act to include the following:

father	stepson
mother	stepdaughter
stepfather	grandmother
stepmother	grandfather
son	grandson
daughter	granddaughter

of a person *or* of that person's spouse or former spouse, civil partner or former civil partner; and

brother	aunt
sister	niece
uncle	nephew

(whether of the full blood or of the half blood or by affinity) of a person *or* of that person's spouse or former spouse, civil partner or former civil partner.

It should be noted that cohabitants and former cohabitants are treated as though they were married to each other or in a civil partnership, for the purpose of the above definition.

(g) They have agreed to marry one another (whether or not that agreement has been terminated): s. 62(3)(e).

(h) They have entered into a civil partnership agreement (as defined by s. 73 of the Civil Partnership Act 2004 ('CPA 2004') (whether or not that agreement has been terminated): s. 62(3)(eza).

(i) They are parents of the same child: s. 62(3)(f).

(j) They have or have had parental responsibility for the same child: (s. 62(3)(f)) (unless one of those persons is a body corporate—s. 62(6)). The most obvious example of a body corporate in this context would be a local authority which would of course acquire parental responsibility for a child upon the making of a care order: Children Act 1989 ('CA 1989'), s. 33(3)(a).

(k)   They are parties to the same family proceedings (other than proceedings under the Act): s. 62(3)(g). The exception to this is where one of the parties is a body corporate, e.g., a local authority: s. 62(6).

25.11   At the time of writing, s. 4 of the Domestic Violence, Crime and Victims Act 2004 ('DVCVA 2004') is yet to be brought into force. When it is brought into force a further category of relationship will be added to the definition of 'associated persons', namely where they have or have had an intimate personal relationship with each other which is or was of significant duration. This important amendment will therefore extend the definition to couples or former couples (either opposite sex or same sex) who have never cohabited.

Same sex couples

25.12   By virtue of the CPA 2004 and the DVCVA 2004 the protection afforded to members of same sex couples (whether in a civil partnership or not) now mirrors that which was available to either married, cohabiting, or formerly cohabiting couples of the opposite sex.

Associated persons in adoption

25.13   In recognition of the fact that strong feelings (and hence the need for injunctive relief) may arise in connection with adoption proceedings, the Act provides that a child who is adopted or who has been freed for adoption, the relatives of such a child, and the child's new adoptive carers shall be 'associated persons' for the purposes of the Act: s. 62(5).

Relatives

25.14   The mere fact that an applicant seeks protection from a relative is not, in itself, necessarily enough to engage the 1996 Act. The nature of the dispute must be of a 'domestic' type.

25.15   In *Chechi* v *Bashier* [1999] 2 FLR 489 the applicant was subjected to violence at the hands of his brother and nephew following a dispute concerning land in Pakistan. It was held that the family relationship was merely incidental and therefore fell outside the intended ambit of the 1996 Act. Civil proceedings were the appropriate means of resolving the dispute.

25.16   In *Rafiq* v *Muse* [2000] 1 FLR 820 a mother obtained non-molestation injunctions against her son and after successive breaches of the injunctions he was imprisoned for six months.

Relevant child

25.17   By s. 62(2) of the Act a 'relevant child' in relation to any proceedings under the Act means:

(a)   any child who is living with either party to the proceedings;

(b)   any child who might reasonably be expected to live with either party to the proceedings;

(c)   any child in relation to whom an order under the Adoption Act 1976 is in question in the proceedings;

(d)   any child in relation to whom an order under the CA 1989 is in question in the proceedings;

(e)   any other child whose interests the court considers relevant.

Engaged couples or same sex couples who have entered into a civil partnership agreement

Where proceedings are based on the fact that the parties have entered into an agreement **25.18** to marry or become civil partners, no application for an occupation order or a non-molestation order may be made if a period exceeding three years has expired since the date of termination of the agreement: ss. 33(2) and 42(4).

This is one of the few examples in this Part of the Act of the right to make an application **25.19** being time-limited.

Section 44 prescribes what constitutes an agreement to marry or form a civil partnership. **25.20** The agreement must be evidence in writing or evidenced by the gift of an engagement ring or other gift in contemplation of marriage or civil partnership or by a ceremony entered into by the parties in the presence of one or more witnesses assembled for the purpose of witnessing the ceremony.

The agreement to marry or form a civil partnership need not itself be in writing, but there **25.21** needs to be some evidence in writing of an agreement to marry—for example, a press announcement or wedding/civil partnership invitations.

D　OCCUPATION ORDERS—THE MENU

There are various occupation orders available. Entitlement to apply for the order depends **25.22** not only on the status and circumstances of the applicant, but also on those of the respondent. While the occupation order is basically the same no matter under which of the five sections of the Act the application has been made, differences do arise principally in relation to the duration of the order and its precise scope.

The Act favours couples who are either married or have registered their civil partnership and **25.23** property owners by offering a greater level of protection to them.

The basic format is as follows: **25.24**

(a) If the applicant is entitled to occupy—whether or not the respondent is also entitled—apply under s. 33.
(b) If the applicant is not entitled to occupy—*but the respondent is entitled*—and:
    (i)　the parties are *former spouses or civil partners* apply under s. 35; or
    (ii)　the parties are *cohabitants or former cohabitants*, apply under s. 36.
(c) If *neither* the applicant *nor* the respondent is *entitled* and:
    (i)　the parties are *spouses/civil partners or former spouses/civil partners*, apply under s. 37; or
    (ii)　the parties are *cohabitants or former cohabitants*, apply under s. 38. [emphasis supplied]

E POSITION WHERE THE APPLICANT IS ENTITLED TO OCCUPY

25.25 An applicant is an entitled applicant if he or she is entitled to occupy a dwelling-house by virtue of:

    (a) a beneficial estate or interest; or

    (b) a contract; or

    (c) any enactment giving him or her the right to remain in occupation; or

    (d) rights in relation to the dwelling-house: s. 33(1)(a)(i)(ii).

Conditions

25.26 The court has jurisdiction to grant an occupation order under s. 33 provided that the dwelling-house:

    (a) is the home of the applicant and of another person with whom he or she is associated (see paragraph 25.10 above);

    (b) *has been* the home of the applicant and of another person with whom he or she is associated; or

    (c) was at any time *intended* by the applicant and a person with whom she is associated to be their home.

At the risk of stating the obvious, it is important to note, first, the wide range of potential applicants for an order under s. 33; and, secondly, the fact that the dwelling-house need not be presently occupied by the applicant as a pre-condition to seeking the order.

Example Mary is a single parent and the tenant of a council flat. She agrees to let her brother stay with her following the breakdown of his marriage. Initially, things go well and Mary appreciates having the extra cash provided by the board and lodging he pays. However, following service on him of his wife's divorce petition, his behaviour becomes increasingly unpredictable culminating in a violent attack on Mary, witnessed by her young daughter. Mary asks him to leave, but he refuses to do so, saying that he has nowhere else to go. Mary could seek an occupation order under s. 33 because:

    (a) she is entitled to occupy the property;

    (b) the property has been the home of her and her brother (albeit for a short period of time, but no time scale is prescribed under the Act); and

    (c) the respondent is someone with whom she is associated (they are relatives (s. 62(2)).

At the very least, Mary would be advised to seek a regulatory order requiring her brother to leave the property and to stay away from the area in which the flat is situated.

What a s. 33 order may contain

25.27 A s. 33 order may contain any of the following provisions:

    (a) enforcing the applicant's entitlement to remain in occupation as against the respondent;

    (b) requiring the respondent to permit the applicant to enter and remain in the dwelling-house;

(c) requiring the respondent to permit the applicant to enter and remain in part of the dwelling-house;

(d) regulating the occupation of the dwelling-house by either or both parties;

(e) prohibiting, suspending, or restricting the exercise by the respondent of his right (whether by virtue of a beneficial estate or interest, contract, or enactment) to occupy the dwelling-house;

(f) restricting or terminating the respondent's home rights;

(g) requiring the respondent to leave the dwelling-house;

(h) requiring the respondent to leave part of the dwelling-house;

(i) excluding the respondent from a defined area in which the dwelling-house is included: s. 33(3).

Because orders containing any of the above provisions effectively *regulate* the occupation of the home, they are sometimes referred to as *regulatory* orders, as opposed to *declaratory* orders which declare or extend existing rights and grant rights.

The test for regulatory orders

Section 33(6) of the Act provides that in deciding whether or not to make any of the above **25.28** regulatory orders under s. 33(3) the court shall have regard to all the circumstances including:

(a) the housing needs and housing resources of each of the parties and of any relevant child;

(b) the financial resources of each of the parties;

(c) the likely effect of any order, or of any decision by the court not to exercise its powers under s. 33(3), *on the health, safety, or well-being* of the parties and of any relevant child;

(d) *the conduct of the parties* in relation to each other and otherwise: s. 33(6)(a), (b), (c), (d).

In accordance with s. 33(7), the court *must* make an order if it appears that the applicant or any relevant child is likely to suffer *significant harm* attributable to conduct of the respondent if an order is *not* made, *unless* it appears that:

(a) the respondent or any relevant child is likely to suffer significant harm if the order is made, and

(b) the harm likely to be suffered by the respondent or the child in that event *is as great as, or greater than*, the harm attributable to conduct of the respondent which is likely to be suffered by the applicant or child if the order is not made.

This is known as 'the balance of harm test'.

The test explained

In cases where the question of significant harm does not arise, the court has *power* to make **25.29** an order taking into account the four factors considered above (i.e., *housing needs and housing resources, financial resources, health, safety or well-being*, and *conduct*). However, in cases where there is a likelihood of significant harm, the power becomes a *duty* (the section says 'shall', so it is mandatory) and the court must make an order after balancing the degree of harm likely to be suffered by both parties and by any children concerned. If both parties are able to establish significant harm, but neither is able to show *greater* harm, then the court still has the *power to* make an appropriate order, but is not under *a duty* to do so.

25.30   It is very likely that in cases where it can be established that there is a risk of significant harm to a child, the child's interests will become in effect the paramount consideration since it is that factor which will have imposed a duty on the court to make an order.

25.31   The reported cases provide some guidance as to how the new provisions will be applied in practice. In *Chalmers* v *Johns* [1999] 1 FLR 392 there had been assaults by the mother on the father and the father on the mother. The mother left the family home, taking their seven-year-old daughter with her. The mother applied for an occupation order. The court at first instance made the order, but it was subsequently set aside by the Court of Appeal. In allowing the appeal, the court held that in deciding whether to make an order under s. 33 the court had first to consider whether, if the order were not made, the applicant or any relevant child would be likely to suffer significant harm attributable to the conduct of the respondent. If the answer was 'yes', then, under s. 33(7), the court had to make the order unless the harm to the respondent or the child if the order were made was likely to be as great or greater. If the answer was 'no', then the court had a discretion based on the s. 33(6) factors. On the facts of this case, neither the mother nor the child were likely to suffer 'significant harm' attributable to the conduct of the father if the order were not made and therefore the case was one for the exercise of the s. 33(6) discretion. The court must first consider s. 33(7) and then, if the precondition of significant harm is satisfied, it must move on to consider s. 33(6). Under s. 33(7), significant harm must be attributable to the respondent's conduct. The court should concentrate on the effect of the conduct of the respondent, rather than on his or her intention. The 'balance of harm' test is a comparison of the harm which would be suffered by the applicant and any relevant child if the order were not made with that which would be suffered by the respondent and any relevant child if the order were made. The discretionary exercise under s. 33(6) is precise and is governed by the factors specified in the checklist.

25.32   In the case of *B* v *B* [1999] 1 FLR 715 the court refused to make an occupation order in favour of the applicant wife where the wife had left the matrimonial home as a result of the husband's violence towards her, taking their baby daughter with her. The husband remained in the property with his six-year-old son from a previous marriage. The court applied the 'balance of harm' test and held that the husband's child would suffer more harm if an order were made than the wife and baby if it were not.

25.33   In *Banks* v *Banks* (above) the court held that it would be wrong to make an order excluding the 79-year-old wife from the home she shared with her 75-year-old husband even though the wife's behaviour towards the husband had been verbally and physically aggressive. The wife suffered from manic depression and dementia, had been hospitalized and was ready to return home. The husband sought to exclude her. The court found that her behaviour did not significantly threaten the husband's health and that the strain of her continuing to live in the same house as him would not cause him significant harm. It held that the harm caused to the wife if the order was made would be significantly greater than the harm caused to the husband if it was not made.

25.34   In *Re Y (Child)* (Court of Appeal, 18 April 2000, unreported) the Court stated that occupation orders were not to be used to resolve deadlock in ancillary relief proceedings, particularly in a case where the parties could be accommodated in separate quarters within the home and cross-undertakings given by each party not to molest the other seemed to be effective.

'Harm', etc. defined

'Harm' is defined in s. 63 of the Act. In relation to a person who is 18 or older, 'harm' means **25.35** 'ill-treatment or the impairment of health' and in relation to a child it means 'ill-treatment or the impairment of health or development'.

'Ill-treatment' includes forms of ill-treatment which are not physical. In the case of a child, **25.36** the phrase includes sexual abuse.

'Health' includes physical and mental health. **25.37**

'Development' means physical, intellectual, emotional, social, or behavioural development. **25.38**

Preparation of the case

Clearly, it will be of assistance to the court if the applicant's sworn statement deals with each **25.39** of the matters listed in s. 33(6) separately following a paragraph on the general background to the case.

In particular, as far as the applicant is concerned, a paragraph setting out what is alleged to **25.40** constitute significant harm will be extremely helpful since, assuming that the court is satisfied that significant harm has arisen and there is no attempt on the part of the respondent to rebut this, an occupation order must be made.

By contrast, if acting for the respondent in a case where significant harm is alleged by the **25.41** applicant, it would be sensible to deal with this specifically in the respondent's statement, in particular seeking to demonstrate any significant harm suffered by the respondent or a relevant child and the effect on the respondent or child should an order be made.

Mental capacity for submission to the jurisdiction

It is important to establish the degree to which the respondent to proceedings under **25.42** Part IV of the 1996 Act understands the nature of the court's jurisdiction and the concept of contempt. In *P v P (Contempt of Court: Mental Capacity)* [1999] 2 FLR 897 the husband was deaf and dumb, had limited vision and an average IQ, but was not suffering from mental illness or impairment. On 29 occasions he breached an injunction with a power of arrest attached prohibiting him from returning to the former matrimonial home where the wife lived. The husband applied for a discharge of the order. The wife applied for the husband's committal to prison for his breaches of the order. The Court of Appeal held that a comprehension of the nature of the court's jurisdiction and of the concept of contempt was not a prerequisite for contempt nor for the making of an order. It was sufficient for the contemnor to understand that an order had been made forbidding him to do certain things and that if he did them he would be punished. The court made no order on the committal but the injunction was extended for six months with a power of arrest attached.

Duration of the order

25.43 Section 33(10) provides that orders under s. 33 may be for a specified period, until the occurrence of a specified event or until further order. There is therefore no maximum duration of the order.

25.44 If the applicant has family home rights and the respondent is the other spouse or civil partner, an order under this section made during the marriage may provide that those rights are not to be brought to an end by:

(a) the death of the other spouse/civil partner; or

(b) the termination (otherwise than by death) of the marriage/civil partnership

provided that the court considers that in all the circumstances it is just and reasonable to make the direction: s. 33(5) and (8).

Declaratory orders

25.45 Section 33(4) of the 1996 Act provides that an occupation order may *declare* that the applicant is *entitled to occupy a dwelling-house* by virtue of a beneficial estate or interest or contract, or by virtue of an enactment giving him or her the right to remain in occupation, or declare that the applicant *has family home rights*. This power to make declaratory orders is unlikely to be invoked frequently as an entitled applicant already has, by definition, the right to occupy the dwelling-house and has no need for those rights to be declared by the court. However, one circumstance which may cause the court to use this power is where there is an initial dispute between the parties about whether the applicant is in fact an entitled applicant.

F   OCCUPATION ORDER WHERE APPLICANT IS A FORMER SPOUSE/CIVIL PARTNER WITH NO EXISTING RIGHT TO OCCUPY

25.46 Section 35 sets out the powers of the court to make an occupation order where the applicant is a former spouse/civil partner and is not entitled to occupy the dwelling-house but the respondent is so entitled. The dwelling-house must have been or at any time intended to be the matrimonial home or civil partnership home: s. 35(1).

The nature of the order

25.47 The section empowers the court to grant occupation rights to the applicant. The order may include certain regulatory provisions, for example, exclusion of the respondent from the area in which the dwelling-house is situated.

25.48 The order must include, in the case of an applicant who is already in occupation of the dwelling-house, a provision giving the applicant the right not to be evicted or excluded from the dwelling-house or any part of it by the respondent for the period specified in the order, together with a provision prohibiting the respondent from evicting the applicant during that period: s. 35(3).

In the case of an applicant who is not in occupation, the occupation order must contain a **25.49** provision giving the applicant the right to enter into and occupy the dwelling-house for the period specified in the order and requiring the respondent to permit the exercise of that right: s. 35(4).

The court's power to confer these rights in an appropriate case is necessary because the **25.50** applicant under s. 35 is by definition 'non-entitled'.

Practitioners should be aware of the effect of *Sanctuary Housing Association* v *Campbell* **25.51** [1999] 3 ALL ER 460, in which the Court of Appeal gave an important judgment which limits the effectiveness of rights of occupation under the Matrimonial Homes Act 1983 (now known as 'family home rights' by virtue of s. 30, Family Law Act 1996 ('FLA 1996') in relation to third parties). As a general rule, where one spouse or civil partner is a tenant of a matrimonial home and the other is not, the other may rely on his or her family home rights so that, for example, his payment of rent to the landlord has the same effect as if it were paid by the tenant: s. 30(3). This would work in a case where the tenant deserts the spouse/civil partner and simply does not notify the landlord that he or she is leaving the property. However if, as in this case, the tenant actually surrenders the tenancy when she leaves, then the remaining spouse/civil partner will lose his or her family home rights unless he has already registered them under s. 31, FLA 1996. On that basis, the remaining spouse/civil partner would appear to have no defence to possession proceedings instituted by the landlord.

The test for an occupation order

In deciding whether to make an occupation order and the terms of it, the court shall **25.52** have regard to all the circumstances including the matters laid down in s. 33(6) (see paragraph 25.28 above). The following additional matters will also be taken into account:

(a) the length of time that has elapsed since the parties ceased to live together;
(b) the length of time that has elapsed since the marriage/civil partnership was dissolved or annulled;
(c) whether there are any proceedings pending between them for financial provision, or relating to the legal or beneficial ownership of the dwelling-house: s. 35(6).

Mental capacity

The court will need to consider whether or not the respondent has sufficient mental capacity **25.53** to submit to the jurisdiction of the court (see paragraph 25.42 above).

Regulatory orders

It has already been noted that if the court decides to make an order under s. 35 of the Act, it **25.54** *must* include a provision dealing with occupation rights. In addition the court *may* grant an order containing any of the following provisions:

(a) *regulating the occupation* of the dwelling-house by either or both parties;
(b) *prohibiting, suspending, or restricting* the exercise by the respondent of his right (whether

by virtue of a beneficial estate or interest, contract, or enactment) to occupy the dwelling-house;

(c) requiring the respondent to *leave* the dwelling-house;

(d) requiring the respondent to *leave part* of the dwelling-house;

(e) excluding the respondent *from a defined area* in which the dwelling-house is included: s. 35(5).

The test for regulatory orders

25.55 When the parties are former spouses/civil partners, in deciding whether to make a regulatory order under s. 35(5) the court must have regard to all the circumstances including:

(a) the *housing needs and housing resources* of each of the parties and of any relevant child;

(b) the *financial resources* of each of the parties;

(c) the likely *effect* of any order, or of any decision by the court not to exercise its powers under the subsection, on *the health, safety, or well-being* of the parties and of any relevant child;

(d) the *conduct of the parties* in relation to each other and otherwise;

(e) the length of time that has elapsed since the parties ceased to live together: s. 35(6) and (7).

But again, as with regulatory orders granted under s. 33(3) to entitled applicants, the court *must* make a regulatory order if it appears likely that the applicant or any relevant child will suffer *significant harm* attributable to conduct of the respondent if an order is *not* made, *unless* the harm caused to the respondent or to any relevant child will be *as great as or greater than* the harm attributable to conduct of the respondent which is likely to be suffered by the applicant or any relevant child if the order is not made: s. 35(8). See paragraph 25.31 above for case law concerning the 'balance of harm' test.

Duration of the order

25.56 It is clear that such occupation orders may not be made after the death of either of the former spouses/civil partners and will cease to have effect on the death of one of the parties. Further, the order must be of limited specified duration not exceeding six months, but it may be extended on one or more occasions for a further specified period not exceeding six months: s. 35(9) and (10).

G   OCCUPATION ORDER WHERE APPLICANT IS A COHABITANT OR FORMER COHABITANT WITH NO EXISTING RIGHT TO OCCUPY

25.57 In these circumstances the applicant may apply for an occupation order under s. 36 provided the dwelling-house is a property in which the parties lived together at any time or intended to do so and the respondent has a right to occupy the property by virtue of a beneficial estate or interest or by virtue of any statute giving him the right to remain in occupation.

The nature of the order

An occupation order may be made containing the same provisions as under s. 35 (s. 36(3), **25.58**
(4)) (see paragraph 25.47 above).

The test for an occupation order

In addition to the matters laid down in s. 33(6), previously referred to and reproduced at **25.59**
paragraph 25.28, the court must also consider:

(a) *the nature of the relationship* and in particular the level of commitment involved in it;
(b) the length of time they have cohabited;
(c) whether there are or have been any children who are children of both parties or for
whom the parties have or have had parental responsibility;
(d) the length of time that has elapsed since the parties ceased to live together;
(e) the existence of any pending proceedings for an order for financial relief against
parents under sch. 1, CA 1989, or proceedings relating to the legal or beneficial
ownership of the dwelling-house: s. 36(6).

Regulatory orders

The position is the same as under s. 35, the relevant provisions being found at s. 36(5) (see **25.60**
paragraph 25.54 above).

The test for a regulatory order

The court is required to have regard to all the circumstances including the matters **25.61**
mentioned in s. 36(6)(a) to (d) and to consider:

(a) whether the applicant or any relevant child is likely to suffer significant harm attributable to conduct of the respondent if the regulatory provision is *not* included in the
order; and
(b) whether the *harm* likely to be suffered by the respondent or child if the provision is
included is *as great as or greater than* the harm attributable to conduct of the respondent
which is likely to be suffered by the applicant or child if the provision is not included:
s. 36(8).

The crucial difference here, however, is that the court is not required to make a regulatory
order even if the balance of harm test is fulfilled, unlike the position under ss. 33 and 35.
The balance of harm test has to be considered but it remains a matter for the court's discretion as to whether or not to make the regulatory order. See paragraph 25.31 above for case
law concerning the 'balance of harm' test.

Mental capacity

The court will need to consider whether or not the respondent has sufficient mental capacity **25.62**
to submit to the jurisdiction of the court (see paragraph 25.42 above).

Duration of the order

25.63   The order may not be made after the death of one of the parties and will cease to have effect on the death of either of them. The order must be made for a specified period not exceeding six months and may be extended on *one* occasion for a further specified period not exceeding six months: s. 36(9) and (10).

Application to be made under S. 33 or S. 36?

25.64   Section 12 of the Trusts of Land and Appointment of Trustees Act 1996 confers a general right for beneficiaries of a trust of land to occupy the land in question. Therefore, provided that a cohabitant can demonstrate that he or she has a beneficial interest in the dwelling-house, the cohabitant will be able to apply for an occupation order under s. 33 of the Family Law Act 1996. The principal benefits of being able to do so would be:

(a)   the occupation order may be of longer duration; and

(b)   the application of the 'significant harm' test may ensure that the cohabitant's application is successful.

It is important to appreciate, however, that the Trusts of Land and Appointment of Trustees Act 1996 does not assist in establishing whether an individual does have a beneficial interest and it will be necessary for the cohabitant to rely on resulting, implied, or constructive trusts in the absence of an express trust in his and/or her favour. If in doubt, therefore, the application should be made under s. 36.

H   OCCUPATION ORDER WHERE NEITHER SPOUSE OR CIVIL PARTNER IS ENTITLED TO OCCUPY

Characteristics of the order

25.65   This is dealt with in s. 37 and permits the court to make a regulatory order only. The provisions of s. 33(6) and (7) apply. Because the parties are spouses or civil partners the court is under a duty to make the order if the balance of harm test is established by the applicant. See paragraph 25.28 above for case law concerning the 'balance of harm' test.

25.66   Although neither party is entitled to occupy the property, it must be or have been either the matrimonial home or the civil partnership home. The order must be limited so as to have effect for a specified period not exceeding six months, but may be extended on one or more occasions for a further specified period not exceeding six months.

Relevance to practice

25.67   Applications of this kind will be comparatively rare since in most cases at least one of the parties will be entitled to remain in occupation of the dwelling-house. The Law Commission identified two circumstances in which an application might be made, namely in the case of squatters and of bare licensees.

It will be also be noted that it is not sufficient for the purposes of an application that the   **25.68**
parties intended to use the dwelling-house as a matrimonial home.

I   POSITION WHERE NEITHER COHABITANT NOR FORMER COHABITANT IS ENTITLED TO OCCUPY

An application may be made for a regulatory order only under the provisions of s. 38.   **25.69**

Factors to be considered

In deciding whether to exercise its powers the court must consider all the circumstances   **25.70**
including:

(a)   the housing needs and housing resources of each of the parties and of any relevant child;
(b)   the financial resources of each of the parties;
(c)   the likely effect of any order on the health, safety, or well-being of the parties and of any relevant child;
(d)   the conduct of the parties in relation to each other and otherwise and the questions mentioned in s. 38(5).

In other words, the court must consider the 'balance of harm' test, but because the applicant   **25.71**
is a non-entitled cohabitant or former cohabitant the court retains a discretion as to whether
or not to make the order sought. See paragraph 25.28 above for recent case law concerning
the 'balance of harm' test.

Duration of the order

Under s. 38(6) the order is limited for a specified period not exceeding six months but may be   **25.72**
extended on *one* occasion for a further period not exceeding six months.

J   ANCILLARY ORDERS WHERE AN OCCUPATION ORDER IS MADE UNDER SS. 33, 35, OR 36

Section 40 provides that the court, on making an occupation order under ss. 33, 35, or 36 (or   **25.73**
at any time thereafter), may make an ancillary order imposing certain obligations on either
party (e.g., as to the repair and maintenance of the dwelling-house or as to the payment of
rent, mortgage, or other relevant outgoing) or requiring the payment of rent to the party
who has been excluded. Further, the court may grant either party possession or use of furniture or other contents of the dwelling-house and impose a requirement that reasonable care
is taken of them. Such an order lasts for as long as the occupation order.

In deciding whether to exercise its powers and, if so, in what manner, the court shall have   **25.74**
regard to all the circumstances of the case including:

(a)   the financial needs and financial resources of the parties; and

(b)   the financial obligations which they have or are likely to have in the foreseeable future, including financial obligations to each other and any relevant child: s. 40(2).

The difficulty, however, with s. 40 is that there is no procedure for enforcing compliance: see *Nwogbe* v *Nwogbe* [2000] 2 FLR 744. Section 40 will only be of assistance therefore where a respondent is likely to comply without the need for enforcement.

K   NON-MOLESTATION ORDERS

Introduction

25.75   Such an order may be made under the provisions of s. 42 and may refer to molestation in general, to particular acts of molestation or to both. The order may be made for a specified period or until further order (thus ensuring considerable flexibility) and may be varied or revoked.

25.76   The order may be made on application or by the court of its own motion in 'family proceedings' where it considers that the order should be made for the benefit of any other party to the proceedings or any relevant child.

Conditions

25.77   In determining whether a client will be able to obtain a non-molestation order under the Act, the first matter to be established is whether the applicant and respondent are 'associated persons' (see paragraph 25.09 and onwards above) or the person to be protected is a 'relevant child'.

The test for a non-molestation order

25.78   In deciding whether or not to exercise its powers and, if so, in what manner, the court shall have regard to all the circumstances, including the need to secure the health, safety, and well-being:

(a)   of the applicant or the person for whose benefit the order would be made; and

(b)   of any relevant child: s. 42(5).

In practice, therefore, an applicant will have to provide evidence of molestation, that he or she (or a relevant child) needs protection and that, on the balance of probabilities, judicial intervention is required to control the respondent's behaviour (*C* v *C* (above)).

What amounts to molestation?

25.79   There is no statutory definition of 'molestation' contained in the Act and courts are guided by case law which establishes that the term includes, but is wider than, violence: see *Davis* v *Johnson* [1979] AC 264 per Viscount Dilhorne: 'Violence is a form of molestation, but molestation may take place without the threat or use of violence and still be serious and inimical to mental or physical health'. In *Vaughan* v *Vaughan* (above) the court considered a dictionary definition of molestation, namely 'to cause trouble; to vex; to annoy; to put to inconvenience'. In other cases repeated telephoning has amounted to molestation as has the positioning of embarrassing notices in public places.

Duration of non-molestation orders

Non-molestation orders are usually made for periods of six months or one year, depending on the seriousness of the molestation.   **25.80**

In *Re B–J (Power of Arrest)* [2000] 2 FLR 443 the Court of Appeal overturned previous authority and it is now clear that a non-molestation order can be set for an indefinite period (e.g., 'until further order') regardless of whether the application has arisen out of unusual or exceptional circumstances.   **25.81**

Family proceedings

Family proceedings are defined in s. 63 of the Act as any proceedings under: **25.82**

(a)   the inherent jurisdiction of the High Court in relation to children;
(b)   Part II and Part IV of the FLA 1996;
(c)   the Matrimonial Causes Act 1973 ('MCA 1973');
(d)   the Adoption Act 1976;
(e)   the Domestic Proceedings and Magistrates' Courts Act 1978;
(f)   Part III of the Matrimonial and Family Proceedings Act 1984;
(g)   Parts I, II, and IV of the CA 1989;
(h)   s. 30 of the Human Fertilisation and Embryology Act 1990;
(i)   the Adoption and Children Act 2002;
(j)   Schedules 5 to 7 of the CPA 2004.

By the operation of s. 42(3) of the Act the court may specifically make a non-molestation order in proceedings in which the court has made an emergency protection order which includes an exclusion requirement under s. 44 of the CA 1989 (see Chapter 34). That specific inclusion in the definition of 'family proceedings' is necessary because proceedings under s. 44 of the CA 1989 (for an emergency protection order) are not proceedings under Parts I, II, or IV of the CA 1989, s. 44 being contained in Part V of the CA 1989.   **25.83**

Where a non-molestation order is made in other family proceedings, the order ceases to have effect if those proceedings are withdrawn or dismissed: s. 42(8).   **25.84**

L   APPLICATIONS BY CHILDREN

Section 43(1) permits a child under the age of 16 to apply for either type of order provided he has obtained leave of a High Court judge. The court may grant leave only if satisfied that the child has sufficient understanding to make the proposed application.   **25.85**

25.86   It will be unusual for a child to seek a non-molestation order and even more unusual for a child to be entitled to apply for an occupation order since a minor child has no capacity to hold a legal estate in land and, therefore, will be unable to demonstrate an entitlement to occupy the dwelling-house (a precondition to an application under s. 33 of the Act). In exceptional cases, however, the applicant child may of course have a beneficial interest in the land under a trust and therefore have an entitlement to occupy in consequence.

'Sufficient understanding'

25.87   The issue of the sufficiency of a child's understanding was considered by the House of Lords in *Gillick* v *West Norfolk & Wisbech Area Health Authority* [1986] AC 112. It was held that the parental right to decide whether or not medical treatment could be given to a child under 16 terminated if and when the child achieved a sufficient understanding and intelligence to enable her to understand fully what was proposed. Lord Scarman used the phrase (at p. 188A): 'the attainment by a child of an age of sufficient discretion to enable him or her to exercise a wise choice in his or her own interests'.

Practice

25.88   In line with the *President's Practice Direction* of 5 March 1993 ([1993] 1 FLR 668), the application by a child for leave to apply for an occupation order or non-molestation order is to be made to the High Court: r. 3.8(2), the Family Proceedings Rules 1991 ('FPR 1991').

M   ORDERS MADE WITHOUT NOTICE

25.89   Section 45 provides for the making of both occupation and non-molestation orders without notice having first been given to the other side (in circumstances where the court considers it *just and convenient to do so*: s. 45(1)). The section goes on to prescribe the factors which the court must take into account in addition to *all the circumstances* of the case. These are set out in s. 45(2) as follows:

  (a)   any risk of *significant harm* to the applicant or a relevant child attributable to *conduct of the respondent* if the order is not made immediately;
  (b)   whether it is likely that the applicant will be deterred or prevented from pursuing the application if an order is not made immediately; and
  (c)   whether there is reason to believe that the respondent is aware of the proceedings but is *deliberately* evading service and that the applicant or a relevant child will be seriously prejudiced by the delay involved—
      (i)   where the court is a magistrates' court, in effecting service of proceedings, or
      (ii)   in any other case, in effecting substituted service.

It should be noted however that there is a fundamental difference between the granting of a without notice non-molestation order and a without notice occupation order. The former is often granted to give an applicant immediate protection and such an order does not infringe upon a respondent's legal rights, it merely prevents him from doing something that he should not be doing. The same reasoning does not apply to a without notice occupation order which would directly encroach upon a respondent's legal rights. For this reason, occupation orders are seldom granted on a without notice basis.

When the court does make an order without notice to the other side, it must give the respondent an opportunity to make representations at a full hearing as soon as just and convenient: s. 45(3). **25.90**

N   UNDERTAKINGS

Undertakings are a very useful mechanism in that if agreed they save time and the client walks away from the court without an order or findings of fact having been made against him. **25.91**

In s. 46 statutory recognition is given to this common practice of the courts of accepting undertakings. Accepting an undertaking is possible where the court has power to make an occupation order or non-molestation order or both. An undertaking is enforceable as if it were an order of the court: s. 46(4). **25.92**

However, the court is not permitted to attach a power of arrest to an undertaking nor to accept an undertaking where a power of arrest would be attached to the order: s. 46(2) and (3). In other words if the court takes the view that the grounds are made out for attaching a power of arrest to a non-molestation or occupation order, it may not in those circumstances accept an undertaking instead of making an order. This provision results in fewer undertakings because s. 47 of the Act imposes on the court an *obligation* to attach a power of arrest in all cases where it appears to the court that the respondent has used or *threatened* violence against the applicant or a relevant child *unless* it is satisfied that in all the circumstances of the case the applicant or child will be adequately protected without one: s. 47(2). **25.93**

Note that at the time of writing s. 1 and sch. 10, para. 37 of the DVCVA 2004 is not yet in force. Once it is brought into force, power of arrests are no longer attachable to non-molestation orders and breach of such an order is, itself, a criminal offence which is arrestable. Undertakings in respect of molestation will still be acceptable to the court unless a respondent has used or threatened violence against the applicant or child and, for the protection of the applicant or child, it is necessary to make a non-molestation order so that any breach is punishable under the prospective amendment to s. 42. **25.94**

O   ENFORCEMENT

Introduction

This is dealt with in s. 47 and sch. 5 with provision for remand for medical examination and reports contained in s. 48. **25.95**

At present the court *is required* to attach a power of arrest to specified provisions of either an occupation order or a non-molestation order where it appears that the respondent has used or *threatened* violence against the applicant or a relevant child, *unless* the court is satisfied **25.96** that in all the circumstances of the case the applicant or child will be adequately protected without such a power of arrest: s. 47(2). In *P* v *P* (Court of Appeal, 21 January 2000, unreported) the attaching of a power of arrest to an occupation order was not found to be justified where the last incident of physical violence had occurred more than four years previously and where the occupation order removed the most serious harm that had been found to exist. As referred to above, recent authority confirms that a non-molestation order can be set for an indefinite period without the circumstances being regarded as exceptional or unusual. Also, an attached power of arrest can be for a shorter period than that of the substantive order: *Re B–J (Power of Arrest)* (above).

25.97   If the criteria for a power of arrest is satisfied, the court is under an obligation to attach a power of arrest—it is not a matter of discretion.

25.98   Further, the court is given a discretion to attach a power of arrest to an order granted without notice having been given to the other side if it appears to the court that:

(a) the respondent has used or threatened violence against the applicant or a relevant child; and

(b) there is a risk of *significant harm* to the applicant or child attributable to conduct of the respondent if the power of arrest is not attached *immediately*: s. 47(3).

Finally, in *JH* v *RH* [2001] 1 FLR 641 the court held that a power of arrest could properly be attached to an occupation order made against a 17-year-old child if the statutory criteria were made out. The reasoning of the court indicates that the same would presently apply to non-molestation orders.

25.99   As stated above, however, s. 47 is due to be amended by sch. 10, para. 38 of the DVCVA 2004 from a date yet to be appointed. Following the change, a power of arrest can only be attached to an occupation order. Breach of a non-molestation order will automatically become an arrestable criminal offence punishable by up to five years' imprisonment following conviction on indictment or one year on summary conviction.

25.100 Once the law has changed, the decision of whether to prosecute the alleged breach of a non-molestation order will rest with the Crown Prosecution Service. Applicants are still able, however, to return the matter to the county court for a breach hearing if they do not wish the respondent to be prosecuted. In these circumstances, an applicant will have to apply to the county court on application for a committal in a notice to show cause in Form N89.

The power of arrest in practice

25.101 Where a power of arrest is attached to specific provisions of the order a constable may arrest without warrant a person whom he has reasonable cause for suspecting to be in breach of any such provision: s. 47(6).

25.102 The respondent must then be brought before the relevant judicial authority within the period of 24 hours beginning at the time of his arrest. When the 24-hour period is being calculated, no account is taken of Christmas Day, Good Friday, or any Sunday. See the *President's Practice Direction: Family Law Act 1996—Attendance of Arresting Officer* [2000] 1 FLR 270 .

The 'relevant judicial authority' depends upon the court which made the original order. For **25.103** example, if the order was made by a county court, the relevant judicial authority is a judge or district judge of that or *any* other county court. Whereas, if the order was made in a magistrates' court, the relevant judicial authority is *any* magistrates' court: s. 63(1).

All courts may now remand respondents in these circumstances if the matter is not disposed **25.104** of forthwith.

Issue of a warrant

The section goes on to deal with the position where no power of arrest is attached to the order **25.105** or is attached only to certain provisions of the order. If, at any time, the applicant considers that the respondent has failed to comply with the order, he may apply to the relevant judicial authority for the issue of a warrant substantiated on oath for the arrest of the respondent: s. 47(8), (9). This means that bail is granted on the condition that the respondent appears before the court either at the end of the period of remand or at every time and place to which the hearing may be adjourned. The court will issue the warrant if it has reasonable grounds for believing that the respondent has failed to comply with the order.

The provision in detail

Schedule 5 to the Act gives the High Court and county courts powers to remand correspond- **25.106** ing to those which apply in magistrates' courts under s. 128 and s. 129 of the Magistrates' Courts Act 1980. In county courts, the powers may be exercised by a judge or a district judge. The powers are as follows:

Remand in custody or on bail

Where a court has power to remand the respondent under s. 47 it may: **25.107**

(a) remand him in *custody*; or
(b) remand him on *bail*, either—
    (i) by taking a recognizance from him (with or without sureties), such recognizance to be 'conditioned' in accordance with sch. 5, para. 2(3), or
    (ii) by fixing the amount of the recognizances with a view to their being taken subsequently (and in the meantime committing the person to custody): sch. 5, para. 2(1).

If bail is granted, the court may require the remanded person to comply with 'such require- **25.108** ments' as appear to the court to be necessary to ensure that he does not interfere with witnesses or otherwise obstruct the course of justice: s. 47(12).

The period of remand

A period of remand may not exceed eight clear days unless: **25.109**

(a) the person is remanded on bail and both he and the applicant agree to a longer period;
(b) a case is adjourned under s. 48(1) for a medical examination and report to be made, when the court may remand for the period of adjournment (but see the limitations in s. 48, below): sch. 5, para. 2(5).

Further remand

25.110 If the court is satisfied that a remanded person is unable, because of illness or accident, to appear at the relevant time, he may be remanded in his absence (and the eight days' time limit does not apply): sch. 5, para. 3(1). Otherwise, a person may be remanded in his absence by the court's enlarging his recognizance and those of any sureties to a later date: sch. 5, para. 3(2).

25.111 For the avoidance of doubt, para. (2) of sch. 5 specifically provides that a person brought before the court after remand may be further remanded.

Remand for medical examination

25.112 Where the court has reason to consider that a medical report will be required, it may remand a person to enable a medical examination and report to be made. A remand must not exceed four weeks at a time, or three weeks if the remand is in custody: s. 48(2) and (3).

25.113 Section 48(4) gives to the civil courts powers similar to those of the Crown Court to make an order under s. 35 of the Mental Health Act 1983, remanding for a report on the mental condition of the respondent where there is reason to suspect that the person arrested is suffering from mental illness or severe mental impairment.

Extension of magistrates' courts' powers

25.114 Section 50 gives magistrates' courts the power, already available to the High Court and county courts, to suspend execution of a committal order. It must be satisfied that there has been breach of a 'relevant requirement', defined as an occupation order or non-molestation order or an exclusion requirement included in an interim care order or an emergency protection order. Section 50 allows magistrates to direct that the execution of the order of committal should be suspended for such a period or on such terms and conditions as they may specify.

25.115 The powers of magistrates' courts are further extended by s. 51. This entitles them to make a hospital order or guardianship order under s. 37 of the Mental Health Act 1983, or an interim hospital order under s. 38 of that Act in the case of a person suffering from mental illness or severe mental impairment who could otherwise be committed to custody for breach of an order.

P   VARIATION AND DISCHARGE OF ORDERS

General

25.116 Either the respondent or the applicant may apply to court to vary or discharge an occupation or non-molestation order: s. 49(1).

Court's own motion

25.117 Where a court has made a non-molestation order of its own motion under s. 42(2)(b), the court itself may vary or discharge the order, even though no separate application has been made to do so: s. 49(2).

Power of arrest

The court may of its own motion vary or discharge a power of arrest attached to an occupa- **25.118**
tion order or, at present, a non-molestation order made without notice: s. 49(4).

Q PROCEDURAL GUIDE

Where to find the rules

The county court or High Court

The procedure to be followed in the county court or High Court is to be found in the Family **25.119**
Proceedings (Amendment No. 3) Rules 1997 (SI 1997/1893) which amend the FPR 1991.

The family proceedings court

The relevant procedure is set out in the Family Proceedings Court (Matrimonial Proceed- **25.120**
ings etc.) (Amendment) Rules 1997 (SI 1997/1894) which amend the Family Proceedings
(Matrimonial Proceedings etc.) Rules 1991.

The fee

On making an application for a non-molestation order or occupation order in the county **25.121**
court or family proceedings court a fee of £60 is payable irrespective of whether or not the
applicant is publicly funded.

Only one fee is payable when an application is made for both types of order at the same time: **25.122**
the Family Proceedings Fees Order 1999 (SI 1999/690) as amended by the Family Proceedings Fees (Amendment No. 2) Order 2000 (SI 2000/938).

Where is the application to be made?

Introduction

The provisions are set out fully in the Family Law Act 1996 (Part IV) (Allocation of Proceed- **25.123**
ings) Order 1997 (SI 1997/1896). The principal features of the Order are set out below.

Choice of venue

Generally speaking, an application for an order under Part IV may be commenced in a **25.124**
county court (i.e., a designated divorce county court, a family hearing centre, or a care centre)
or a family proceedings court. For the purpose of Part IV proceedings the Principal Registry
of the Family Division of the High Court is to be treated as a county court.

However, there are some important exceptions to note: **25.125**

(a) A family proceedings court shall not be competent to entertain any application, or
    make any order, involving any disputed question as to a party's entitlement to occupy
    any property (however that might arise) unless it is unnecessary to determine the ques-
    tion in order to deal with the application or make the order. Further, the magistrate

may decline jurisdiction in any proceedings if he considers that the case can more conveniently be dealt with by another court: s. 59, FLA 1996.

(b) The family proceedings court has no jurisdiction to deal with applications for the transfer of tenancies on divorce or on the separation of cohabitants: s. 53 of and para. 1 of sch. 7 to the Act.

(c) Applications brought by an applicant who is under the age of 18 and an application for the grant of leave under s. 43 (where the applicant is a child under the age of 16) must be commenced in the High Court: Art. 4(3) of the Order.

Application to extend, vary, or discharge the order

25.126   Such an application is to be made to the court which made the original order: Art. 5.

Transfer of applications

25.127   The arrangements for transfer are set out in Arts. 6 to 14 of the Order.

25.128   As will be noted below, in the majority of cases the question of transfer will be a matter for the discretion of the court to whom the application is originally made. However, transfer of proceedings from the family proceedings court to the county court is compulsory in some instances.

25.129   **From one family proceedings court to another**   The application may be transferred from one family proceedings court to another (on application or of the court's own motion) provided that the transferring court considers that it would be appropriate for the application to be heard together with other family proceedings which are pending in the receiving court and the justices' clerk of the receiving court consents to the transfer: Art. 7.

25.130   **From the family proceedings court to the county court**   A family proceedings court *may*, on application or of its own motion, transfer the application to a county court where it considers that:

(a) it would be appropriate for those proceedings to be heard together with other family proceedings which are pending in that court; or

(b) the proceedings involve:
   (i) a conflict with the law of another jurisdiction;
   (ii) some novel and difficult point of law;
   (iii) some question of general public interest; or

(c) the proceedings are exceptionally complex: Art. 8(1).

By contrast, a family proceedings court *must* transfer proceedings to a county court where:

(a) a child under 18 is the respondent to the application or wishes to become a party to the proceedings; or

(b) a party to the proceedings is a person who, by reason of mental disorder within the meaning of the Mental Health Act 1983, is incapable of managing and administering his property and affairs: Art. 8(2).

25.131   Except where a transfer is ordered under paragraph (a) above, the proceedings shall be transferred to the nearest county court: Art. 8(3).

From family proceedings court to High Court A family proceedings court may, on application or of its own motion, transfer proceedings to the High Court where it considers that it would be appropriate for those proceedings to be heard with other family proceedings which are pending in that court: Art. 9. **25.132**

From one county court to another This is provided for in Art. 10. Transfer may arise either on application or of the court's own motion where: **25.133**

(a) the original county court considers that it would be appropriate for those proceedings to be heard together with other family proceedings which are pending in that court;

(b) the proceedings involve the determination of a question relating to entitlement to occupy and the property in question is situated in the district of another county court; or

(c) it seems necessary or expedient so to do.

From county court to family proceedings court The county court may transfer on application or of its own motion where: **25.134**

(a) it considers it would be appropriate for the proceedings to be heard together with other family proceedings which are pending in that family proceedings court; or

(b) it considers that the criterion in:

(i) Art. 8(1)(a) no longer applies because the proceedings with which the transferred proceedings were to be heard have been determined;

(ii) Art. 8(1)(b) or (c) does not apply: Art. 11.

From county court to High Court The county court may, on application or of its own motion, transfer proceedings where it considers that proceedings are appropriate for determination in the High Court: Art. 12. **25.135**

From High Court to family proceedings court Such a transfer may occur, on application or of the court's own motion, where the court considers that it would be appropriate for those proceedings to be heard together with other family proceedings pending in that court: Art. 13. **25.136**

From High Court to county court The High Court may, on application or of its own motion, transfer proceedings to the county court where it considers that: **25.137**

(a) it would be appropriate for those proceedings to be heard together with other family proceedings which are pending in that court;

(b) the proceedings are appropriate for determination in the county court; or

(c) it is appropriate for an application made by a child under the age of 18 to be heard in a county court: Art. 14 (permission to make the application having been granted by the High Court in the first place).

Disposal following arrest

Article 15 provides that where a person is brought before: **25.138**

(a) a relevant judicial authority in accordance with s. 47(7)(a); or

(b) a court by virtue of a warrant issued under s. 47(9),

and the matter is not disposed of forthwith, the matter may be transferred to be disposed of by the relevant judicial authority or court that issued the warrant or, as the case may be, that attached the power of arrest under s. 47(2) or (3), if different.

The personnel of the court

25.139 In the county court, applications will be able to be heard by circuit judges, district judges, recorders, assistant recorders, and deputy district judges. However, deputy district judges will not be able to deal with enforcement of any order which is made: the Family Proceedings (Allocation to Judiciary) Directions 1999.

R THE PROCEDURE IN DETAIL

Funding the application

The private client

25.140 Where the client is ineligible for public funding, it will be necessary to advise the client of the fee (paragraph 25.121 above) and the likely costs involved in making the application.

25.141 A payment on account should be obtained, at least to pay for the preparation of the case and to provide the court fee.

The publicly funded client

25.142 Under the Legal Services Commission's Funding Code, which governs the availability of public funding for family matters, great emphasis is placed on mediation as a means of resolving disputes. For many family matters a client must attend an assessment of suitability with a recognized mediator before an application can be made for General Family Help and for Legal Representation. However, there are a number of occasions when it will not be necessary for the client to attend an assessment appointment. These include, amongst other things, where Legal Representation should be granted as a matter of urgency and where the client has a reasonable fear of violence or significant harm from a partner or former partner. Full details are set out in para. 20.11(4) of the Funding Code—Decision Making Guidance.

25.143 A certificate authorizing Legal Representation may be applied for in emergency situations, for example, in cases where protection from domestic violence is required (see Chapter 2). This will be necessary because a certificate for General Family Help cannot cover the cost of legal representation at a final contested hearing. Where a certificate for General Family Help is already in existence, authority to provide Legal Representation may be obtained from the Commission by seeking an amendment to the existing certificate, otherwise a fresh certificate must be sought. Application to the Commission is made by completion of form CLS APP3.

25.144 Emergency Representation is only available as part of Legal Representation and it does not apply to any other level of service. Whilst a certificate for Emergency Representation should reduce the inevitable delay associated with the grant of a certificate for Legal Representation, it will be necessary not only to satisfy the standard criteria for Legal Representation but also to demonstrate that the certificate should be granted as a matter of urgency because it appears to be in the interests of justice to do so: para. 12, The Funding Code—Decision Making Guidance.

Paragraph 12 of The Funding Code—Decision Making Guidance states that the application **25.145** may be urgent if any of the following circumstances apply and there is insufficient time for an application for a substantive certificate to be made and determined:

(a) representation (or other urgent work for which Legal Representation would be needed) is justified in injunction or other emergency proceedings, including an order under Part IV of the FLA 1996;

(b) representation (or other urgent work for which Legal Representation would be needed) is justified in relation to an imminent hearing in existing proceedings; or

(c) a limitation period is about to expire.

Emergency Representation is unlikely to be granted unless:

the likely delay as a result of the failure to grant emergency representation will mean that either:

(a) there will be a risk to the life, liberty or physical safety of the client or his or her family or the roof over their heads; or

(b) the delay will cause a significant risk of miscarriage of justice, or unreasonable hardship to the client, or irretrievable problems in handling the case; and

in either case there are no other appropriate options to deal with the risk

(from para. 12.2 of The Funding Code—Decision Making Guidance).

Paragraph 19.21 of The Funding Code—Decision Making Guidance contains details of how **25.146** public funding is made available in proceedings seeking an injunction, a committal order, or other orders for the protection of a person from harm (other than public law children proceedings). Some of the principal points are as follows:

(a) The Commission will not require proceedings under Part IV of the FLA 1996 to be commenced or conducted in any particular venue.

(b) Where matrimonial proceedings are in existence or are to be commenced then any application under Part IV may be made in those proceedings. Where there is an existing certificate capable of amendment to cover proceedings under Part IV an application must be made for an amendment rather than for a fresh certificate.

(c) Any certificate covering proceedings under Part IV will cover obtaining a final order including, if appropriate, applying for a without notice order prior to that.

(d) Certificates will generally cover a non-molestation order and/or occupation order although, where appropriate, certificates will be issued covering a non-molestation order only. If cover is being sought to apply for an order, it will be necessary to consider to what extent the remedy sought is available within the provisions of Part IV and whether the application to the court is likely to succeed, having regard to the factors to be considered by the court.

(e) An occupation order may impose financial obligations. The scope of the certificate will extend to those aspects without the need for a specific amendment.

Any recovery or preservation in proceedings under Part IV is exempt from the operation of the statutory charge. It would, however, generally be reasonable to expect substantial ancillary relief issues to be adjourned for consideration in other more appropriate proceedings, e.g., ancillary relief to divorce or judicial separation.

25.147   **Non-molestation orders (Part IV)**   Where the parties are 'associated persons', Legal Representation to take non-molestation proceedings is likely to be refused:

(a)   unless a warning letter has first been sent (unless the circumstances make this inappropriate);

(b)   unless the police have been notified and have failed to provide adequate assistance;

(c)   if the conduct complained of is not of a trivial nature, took place within the last two or three weeks, and there is a likelihood of repetition.

25.148   Legal Representation to defend proceedings is likely to be refused if the matter could reasonably be dealt with by way of an undertaking. The fact that the court must consider whether to attach a power of arrest where the applicant has used or threatened violence against the applicant or a relevant child does not of itself justify the grant of representation.

25.149   **Occupation orders (Part IV)**   Legal Representation to take occupation order proceedings is likely to be refused:

(a)   unless the parties and property qualify to be covered by an order;

(b)   unless an order is likely to be considered necessary by the court in all the circumstances, including the 'greater harm' test (see paragraph 25.29 above);

(c)   unless the applicant is in a refuge or other temporary accommodation having recently been excluded from the property;

(d)   if the respondent has already left voluntarily and does not wish to return;

(e)   if the applicant has been out of occupation for some time and there are no other issues to justify the proceedings.

25.150   Legal Representation to defend proceedings is likely to be *granted* if there has been a without notice order made with no opportunity for the respondent to contest it and it would be unreasonable for the order to stand. However, Legal Representation to defend proceedings is likely to be *refused* if the respondent is already out of the property, has no good reason to return, and there are no other issues to justify the grant of representation.

Normal procedure in the county court

25.151   A free-standing application for an occupation order or a non-molestation order is to be made in Form FL401 (a copy of the form is reproduced at p. 408): r. 3.8(1). If applicants are concerned about giving their address on the application form, they may leave the form blank and complete Confidential Address Form C8.

25.152   It is recognized that the applicant may not know all the details requested on the application form and this should be stated wherever it applies.

25.153   The form should be signed by the applicant and dated.

25.154   Where the application is made in other proceedings which are pending, the application is likewise to be made in Form FL401: r. 3.9(3).

The application in Form FL401 shall be supported by a *statement* signed by the applicant and **25.155** sworn to be true: r. 3.8(4).

Procedure where the applicant is a child under the age of 16

The application is again to be made in Form FL401 but must be treated, in the first instance, **25.156** as an application to the High Court for permission to proceed. In other words there is no prescribed form for an application for leave: r. 3.8(2).

Procedure for a without notice (*ex parte*) application

The application is made in Form FL401 but the sworn statement must set out reasons why **25.157** notice was not given: r. 3.8(5).

Procedure to vary, extend, or discharge the order

The application is made in Form FL403 and the provisions as to the hearing and service of **25.158** the orders are governed by r. 3.9 (see below): r. 3.9(8).

Service of the application

On the respondent

The application on notice (together with the sworn statement and notice of proceedings **25.159** and guidance in Form FL402) shall be served by the applicant on the respondent person-ally not less than two days before the date on which the application will be heard: r. 3.8(6).

The court may abridge the period: r. 3.8(7). **25.160**

Where the applicant is acting in person, personal service of the application shall be effected **25.161** by the court if the applicant so requests. This does not affect the court's power to order substituted service: r. 3.8(8).

Service on third parties

Where an application is made for an occupation order under ss. 33, 35, or 36 a copy of the **25.162** application shall be served by the applicant by first-class post on the mortgagee or, as the case may be, the landlord of the dwelling-house with a notice in Form FL416 informing him of his right to make representations in writing or at any hearing: r. 3.8(11).

Where the application is for a transfer of a tenancy, notice of the application must be served **25.163** by the applicant on the other cohabitant or spouse and on the landlord and any person so served is entitled to be heard on the application: r. 3.8(12). Curiously, the Rules do not specify the method of service to be employed here.

Statement of service

The applicant is required to file a statement in Form FL415 after he has served the applica- **25.164** tion: r. 3.8(15). This gives details of the identity of the person served and sets out how service was effected.

Transfer to another court

25.165   The Allocation of Proceedings Order has already been considered. Rule 3.8(9) states that where an application for an occupation order or a non-molestation order is pending, the court must consider (on the application of either party or of its own motion) whether to exercise its powers to transfer the hearing of that application to another court and shall make an order for transfer in Form FL417 if it seems necessary or expedient to do so.

Investigation and requests for further information

25.166   Rule 2.62(4) to (6) of the FPR 1991 applies to applications for an occupation order under ss. 33, 35, or 36 and an application for a transfer of a tenancy as they apply to an application for ancillary relief: r. 3.8(13).

25.167   Thus an order for production and inspection of a document may be applied for.

Position of a minor in the proceedings

25.168   Rule 3.8(10) states that r. 9.2A shall not apply to an application for either type of order. It will be recalled that r. 9.2A provides for minors in certain circumstances to begin or prosecute proceedings without a next friend or Children's Guardian and for a minor to seek leave to dispense with his next friend or Children's Guardian in existing proceedings.

The hearing

25.169   Little is said in the Rules about the hearing itself save that the hearing must be in chambers unless the court otherwise directs: r. 3.9(1).

25.170   The court may direct that a further hearing be held in order to consider any representations made by a mortgagee or a landlord: r. 3.9(7).

25.171   A record of the hearing is to be issued in Form FL405 and the order made in Form FL404.

25.172   It will be noted that the Rules prescribe the wording to be used for each type of order. The precise wording of the occupation order depends, of course, on the section under which the order was made.

Service of the order

An order obtained without notice

25.173   A copy of the order obtained without notice, a copy of the application and of the sworn statement must be served by the applicant on the respondent personally: r. 3.9(2).

The order made on notice

25.174   A copy of an order made on application heard after a hearing of which both sides received notice must be served by the applicant on the respondent personally: r. 3.9(4).

25.175   Further when an occupation order is made under ss. 33, 35, or 36, a copy of the order must be served by the applicant by first-class post on the mortgagee or, as the case may be, the landlord of the dwelling-house in question: r. 3.9(3).

The applicant acting in person

In these circumstances, service of a copy of any order made *must* be effected by the court if the applicant so requests: r. 3.9(5). The method of service to be employed by the court is not indicated in the Rules. **25.176**

S ENFORCEMENT OF THE ORDER

This is dealt with in r. 3.9A. The principal features are set out below. **25.177**

Power of arrest

Where a power of arrest is attached to one or more of the provisions ('the relevant provisions') of the order: **25.178**

(a) the relevant provisions must be set out in Form FL406 and the form must not include any provisions of the order to which the power of arrest was not attached; and

(b) a copy of the form must be delivered to the officer for the time being in charge of any police station serving the area for the applicant's address or to any other police station as the court may specify: r. 3.9A(1).

The copy of the form detailing the provisions must be accompanied by a statement showing that the respondent has been served with the order or informed of its terms (whether by being present when the order was made or by telephone or otherwise): r. 3.9A(1). **25.179**

Although the Rules are silent on the point, it is assumed that it is the responsibility of the officer of the court to ensure that the police are properly informed. **25.180**

Similarly, when the relevant provisions of the order are varied or discharged the proper officer at the court must immediately inform the police officer who received the form and deliver a copy of the order to that officer: r. 3.9A(2). **25.181**

It is suggested that it would be sensible for the applicant's solicitor to ensure that the police are properly informed of the position. **25.182**

Where a power of arrest is attached to an occupation order or non-molestation order which has been granted without notice first having been given to the other side the terms of the order and the name of the party to whom it is addressed must be announced in open court on the same day as it is made, or, if there is no further business in open court on that date, then at the next listed sitting of the court: *President's Direction* [1998] 1 FLR 496. **25.183**

Issue of a warrant for arrest

This of course will arise when no power of arrest was attached to the original order but enforcement is necessary because the respondent is in breach of the terms of the order. **25.184**

25.185 An application for the issue of a warrant for the arrest of the respondent is to be made in Form FL407 and the warrant must be issued in Form FL408. The warrant will be executed by the bailiffs attached to the county court.

Hearings following arrest

25.186 The *President's Practice Direction: Family Law Act 1996—Attendance of Arresting Officer* [2000] 1 FLR 270 requires that under s. 47(7) a person arrested under a power of arrest attached to a non-molestation order or occupation order must be brought before a judge, district judge, or magistrates' court (the 'relevant judicial authority') within 24 hours beginning at the time of the arrest.

25.187 Where a person is arrested under a power of arrest but cannot be brought before the relevant judicial authority sitting in a place normally used as a court room within 24 hours after his arrest, he may be brought before the relevant judicial authority at any convenient place (*President's Direction* [1998] 1 FLR 496). However, as the liberty of the individual is involved, the press and public should be allowed access unless security requirements make this impracticable.

25.188 When an arrested person is brought before the relevant judicial authority, the attendance of the arresting officer will not be necessary unless the arrest itself is in issue. A written statement from the officer about the circumstances of the arrest should normally be sufficient. In those cases where the arresting officer was also a witness to the events leading to the arrest and his evidence about those events is required, arrangements should be made for him to attend at a subsequent hearing to give evidence.

25.189 Once the respondent has been arrested either under the power of arrest or warrant, the court may:

    (a) conduct a full hearing in open court to determine whether the facts, and the circumstances which led to the arrest, amounted to disobedience of the order; or

    (b) adjourn the proceedings, and, where such an order is made, the arrested person may be released.

The proceedings should be listed for hearing within 14 days of the date on which the respondent was arrested and he must be given not less than two business days' notice of the adjourned hearing.

25.190 If the case is adjourned the court may remand the respondent on bail or in custody. If the remand is on bail the proceedings may not be adjourned for longer than eight clear days unless both the applicant and the respondent agree to a longer adjournment. The bail may be conditional, for example that the respondent does not interfere with witnesses or obstruct justice. If the respondent is remanded in custody, the maximum duration of the remand is eight clear days at a time. Remand in custody may be for the specific purpose of obtaining medical reports on the respondent.

25.191 The court may adjourn the proceedings without considering what penalty should be imposed. Such an adjournment may be subject to conditions with which the respondent must comply. If there is a breach of the conditions, the matter may be restored for further consideration.

Committal proceedings: application of RSC and CCR

Rule 3.9A(5) provides that a number of provisions found in RSC or CCR shall apply, with **25.192** necessary modification, to the enforcement of occupation or non-molestation orders.

These include a power to suspend execution of committal order, application for leave (in **25.193** a case where an application for an order of committal is made to the High Court), committal for breach of the order, undertakings, and discharge of a person in custody.

Committal proceedings

The application for the issue of a committal order ('notice to show good reason') in Form **25.194** N78 must:

(a) specify the provisions of the order or undertaking which have been disobeyed or broken;

(b) set out the ways in which it is alleged that the order or undertaking has been disobeyed or broken;

(c) be supported by an affidavit (sworn statement) by the applicant setting out the grounds for the application. Unless the court agrees to dispense with the need for service, the notice and affidavit must be served personally on the respondent.

A fee of £80 is payable in the High Court or county court.

Committal proceedings are always important since they affect the liberty of the individual **25.195** alleged to have acted in contempt of a court order. Consequently, it is vital that such proceedings are conducted by way of a proper hearing. It is highly desirable to have written allegations of the breaches alleged placed before the judge, even if the constraints of time mean that these must be in manuscript form (*Manchester City Council* v *Worthington* [2000] Fam Law 147).

When a committal order is made otherwise than in public or a court room open to the **25.196** public, it must be announced in open court at the earliest opportunity (*President's Direction* [1998] 1 FLR 496). The announcement must include:

(a) the name of the party committed;

(b) the nature of the contempt of court (in general terms); and

(c) the length of the period of committal to prison.

Where a committal order is suspended for so long as the contemnor complies with a separate order expressed to last 'until further order' it will be valid even though its effect is to suspend a sentence of imprisonment indefinitely (*Griffin* v *Griffin* [2000] Fam Law 451). The order for suspended imprisonment must be on Form N79. It should contain as much information as possible. Failure to draw up an order on Form N79 will amount to a fundamental defect in procedure (see *Couzens* v *Couzens* [2001] 2 FLR 701—where a suspended order which had not been drawn up on Form N79 could not be activated on the wife's subsequent application following further serious breaches by the husband).

In *Begum* v *Anam* [2004] EWCA 578 the Court of Appeal set aside a committal order **25.197** following a hearing in the respondent's absence. The application had been served on the respondent while he was serving a prison sentence and he was therefore unable to obtain legal advice or obtain a production warrant so that he could be present. These failings breached the respondent's right to a fair trial under Art. 6 of the ECHR. The Court of Appeal said that in these circumstances the judge should have adjourned the hearing until a later date.

Attachment of a penal notice

25.198   Rule 3.9A(5) also provides that CCR Ord. 29, r. 1 (preserved in CPR, sch. 2) shall have effect as if for para. (3) (relating to ensuring that a copy of the injunction served on the respondent is endorsed with a penal notice informing him or her that disobedience of the order would constitute a contempt of court and render him liable to be committed to prison) were substituted the following:

> (3)   At the time when the order is drawn up, the proper officer shall
> > (i)   where the order made is (or includes) a non-molestation order; and
> > (ii)   where the order made is an occupation order and the court so directs,
> >   issue a copy of the order endorsed with or incorporating a notice in Form N77 as to the consequence of disobedience, for service in accordance with paragraph (2) [i.e., personal service on the respondent].

In other words, a penal notice *must* be attached to a non-molestation order and may be attached to an occupation order if the court so directs. The purpose of this provision is to ensure that the respondent is aware of the consequences of breach of an order even if a power of arrest has not been attached.

Penalties

25.199   Before imposing any form of penalty, a deliberate act or failure to act with knowledge of the terms of the order must be proved. The Amendment Rules are silent as to the penalties to be imposed and it is assumed that the present range of penalties (together with the making of hospital and guardianship orders under the Mental Health Act 1983) will continue to apply. County courts and the High Court therefore have power to sentence the respondent to be committed to prison for up to two years or to impose a fine, or both. There is no limit to the amount of the fine which the court may impose. If the court is considering the imposition of a prison sentence, it must take into account the effect of the sentence on the children of the family and on the financial position of the respondent.

25.200   Consideration should also be given to whether the prison sentence should be suspended (which may be for a specified period or on terms and conditions laid down by the court). In the event of a further breach the court has power to decide whether to impose the prison sentence at that point.

25.201   In any event, if a prison sentence is imposed, the length of sentence must be clearly specified. The court cannot sentence the respondent to prison for an indefinite period of time.

25.202   The general principle has been that the imposition of a prison sentence in family proceedings should only be used as a last resort: *Ansah* v *Ansah* [1977] 2 All ER 638 (CA). However, in the case of *N* v *R (Non-molestation Order: Breach)* [1998] 2 FLR 1068 the Court of Appeal clearly stated that orders must be obeyed. Here the Court substituted an immediate custodial sentence for a suspended custodial sentence where the application was to commit for a serious breach of a non-molestation order.

The jurisdiction of the court to impose an immediate custodial sentence is confirmed in **25.203** *Wilson* v *Webster* [1998] 1 FLR 1097. In *P* v *P (Contempt of Court: Mental Capacity)* [1999] 2 FLR 897, the Court of Appeal held that, provided a recalcitrant respondent understood what he was forbidden to do and that if he disobeyed the order he would be punished, the order would be enforced. In *Hale* v *Tanner* [2000] 2 FLR 879 the Court of Appeal dealt with the question of the appropriate length of a prison sentence where there had been persistent breaches of a non-molestation order. The Court recognized that there was a lack of guidance in sentencing for contempt of court and Hale LJ set out the following general guidelines:

(a) Imprisonment was not to be regarded as the automatic response to the breach of an order, although there was no principle that imprisonment was not to be imposed on the first occasion.

(b) Although alternatives to imprisonment were limited, there were a number of things the court should consider, in particular where no violence was involved.

(c) If imprisonment was appropriate, the length of the committal should be decided without reference to whether or not it was to be suspended.

(d) The seriousness of the contempt had to be judged not only for its intrinsic gravity but also in light of the court's objectives both to mark its disapproval of the disobedience to the order and to secure compliance in the future.

(e) The length of the committal should relate to the maximum available, that is, two years.

(f) Suspension was possible in a wider range of circumstances than in criminal cases, and was usually the first way of attempting to secure compliance with the order.

(g) The court had to consider whether the context was mitigating or aggravating, in particular where there was a breach of an intimate relationship and/or children were involved.

(h) The court should consider any concurrent proceedings in another court, and should explain to the contemnor the nature of the order and the consequences of breach.

The Court of Appeal held in this case that a sentence of six months' imprisonment, suspended for one year, was excessive and should be reduced to 29 days, although the period of suspension was considered to be appropriate.

In reaching its decision, the Court was influenced by the fact that there had been no **25.204** immediate threat of violence. It was rare even in more serious breaches for a sentence as long as six months to be imposed and in this case the appellant had admitted the allegation, had not been present when the order was made, had received no legal advice or warning of the penalties for breach, and was the mother of a young child.

In *H* v *O* [2005] 2 FLR 329 a father appealed against a sentence of 12 months for three **25.205** breaches of a non-molestation order. One of the breaches involved a physical attack on the person caring for the child. The other two breaches related to verbal abuse and threatening behaviour. The Court of Appeal held that the level of sentencing under the 1996 Act did not fully reflect contemporary requirements and opinion. Parliament and society now regarded domestic and other violence associated with harassment and molestation as demanding rather more condign deterrent punishment than formerly. In cases of actual or threatened violence, sentences under the 1996 Act should not be manifestly discrepant with sentences passed in the Crown Court for comparable offences, such as under the Offences Against the Person Act 1861. In this case the Court of Appeal took the view that the seriousness of the breaches was aggravated because the carer of the child had been assaulted and that the father had shown no remorse. The sentence was however reduced to nine months in view of the fact that it was a first offence.

25.206   In *Robinson* v *Murray* [2006] 1 FLR 364 the Lord Chief Justice said that where a course of domestic violence or molestation warranted a sentence towards the top of the range, it was appropriate to bring civil or criminal proceedings under the Protection from Harassment Act 1997 where a maximum of five years' imprisonment was available. He also reiterated that domestic and other violence related to harassment or molestation should be viewed rather more seriously than has previously been the case.

Applications for bail

25.207   The provisions relating to applications for bail are contained in r. 3.10 and apply where the respondent has been remanded in custody awaiting a further hearing.

25.208   An application for bail made by a person arrested under power of arrest or a warrant of arrest may be made either orally or in writing: r. 3.10(1).

25.209   Where the application for bail is made in writing, it must contain the following information:

(a)   the full name of the person making the application;

(b)   the address of the place where the person making the application is detained at the time when the application is made;

(c)   the address where the person making the application would reside if he were granted bail;

(d)   the amount of the recognizance in which he would agree to be bound; and

(e)   the grounds on which the application is made and, where a previous application has been refused, full particulars of any change in circumstances which has occurred since that refusal: r. 3.10(2).

25.210   Where the application is made in writing it must be signed by the applicant or someone duly authorized by him.

25.211   Where the applicant is a minor or for any reason is incapable of acting, a guardian ad litem should sign on his behalf.

25.212   A copy of the bail application must be served on the person who made the original application for the order: r. 3.10(3).

25.213   It should be noted that there is no prescribed form to be used in making the application for bail.

25.214   Form FL410 is to be used to record the recognizance of the applicant for bail and Form FL411 to record the recognizance of the surety. The bail notice itself is to be in Form FL412. It contains, amongst other things, details of the conditions on which bail is granted and requires the applicant for bail to attend court on the adjourned date.

A copy of the bail notice is to be given to the applicant for bail where he is remanded on bail: **25.215**
r. 3.10(6).

The person having custody of the applicant for bail is required to release the applicant: **25.216**

(a) on receipt of a certificate signed by or on behalf of the district judge stating that the recognizance of any sureties required have been taken, or on being otherwise satisfied that all recognizances have been taken; and
(b) on being satisfied that the applicant for bail has entered into his recognizance: r. 3.10(5).

T PROCEDURE IN THE FAMILY PROCEEDINGS COURT

The basic procedure

The procedure to obtain an occupation order or a non-molestation order is essentially the **25.217**
same as that described above for the county court and High Court. This means that the same
forms are to be used. However, there are some modifications to the procedure and the
principal points to note are set out below:

(a) The application for the order in Form FL401 must be supported by a statement which is signed and *declared* to be true *or* with leave of the court, by oral evidence: r. 3A(3).
(b) The application may, with leave of the justices' clerk or of the court, be made without notice, in which case the applicant must file with the justices' clerk or the court the application at the time when the application is made or as directed by the justices' clerk and the evidence in support of the application must state reasons why the application is made without notice: r. 3A(4)(a), (b).
(c) The notice period to which the respondent is entitled (unless the period has been abridged by the justices' clerk (r. 3A(6)) is two *business* days: r. 3A(5).
(d) Where an order for transfer is made, the justices' clerk must send a copy of the order for transfer in Form FL417 both to the parties and to the court to which the proceedings are transferred: r. 3A(9).

Enforcement procedure

It is important to note that the rules relating to enforcement differ considerably in the family **25.218**
proceedings court from those applying elsewhere.

The procedure is contained in r. 20 and is as follows. **25.219**

The provisions relating to the contents of the power of arrest in Form FL406, the require- **25.220**
ments for delivery to the officer in charge of the relevant police station and the notification
requirements following variation or discharge of the order are the same, as is the form to
be used for issue of the warrant for the arrest of the respondent (Forms FL407 and FL408
respectively).

However, r. 20(3) requires the justices' clerk to deliver the warrant to the officer for the time **25.221**
being in charge of the police station serving the area for the respondent's address or to such
other police station as the court may specify. See also the *President's Practice Direction: Family*

Law Act 1996—Attendance of Arresting Officer [2000] 1 FLR 270 which is discussed further in paragraph 25.186 above.

25.222 Rule 20(5) and (6) deals with enforcement of orders by committal order and r. 20(6) states that normally an order must not be enforced by way of committal order unless:

(a) a copy of the order in Form FL404 has been served personally on the respondent; and

(b) when the order requires the respondent to do an act, the copy has been so served before the expiration of the time within which he was required to do the act and was accompanied by a copy of any order, made between the date of the order and the date of service, fixing that time.

25.223 An order requiring a person to abstain from doing an act may be enforced by committal order notwithstanding that a copy of the order has not been served personally on the respondent if the court is satisfied that, pending such service, the respondent had received notice of the terms of the order because he was present when the order was made or was notified of the terms by telephone or otherwise: r. 20(11).

25.224 Rule 20(7) requires the justices' clerk to annex to the order and serve on the respondent a penal notice where the order made is (or includes) a non-molestation order and where the order made is an occupation order, provided the court so directs.

25.225 If the respondent fails to obey the order the justices' clerk must, at the request of the applicant, issue a notice in Form FL418 warning the respondent that an application will be made for him to be committed and advising him of the date he is required to attend court. Normally the notice is to be served personally on the respondent: r. 20(8).

25.226 It should be noted, however, that r. 20(12) allows the court to dispense with the need for personal service of the order in Form FL404 or the notice in Form FL418 if the court thinks it just to do so. If a committal order is made in these circumstances the court may of its own motion fix a date and time when the person to be committed is to be brought before the court: r. 20(13).

25.227 Rule 20(9) states that the notice in Form FL418 is to be treated as a complaint and must:

(a) identify the provisions of the order or undertaking which are alleged to have been disobeyed or broken;

(b) list the ways in which it is alleged that the order or undertaking has been disobeyed or broken;

(c) be supported by a statement which is signed and declared to be true and which states the grounds on which the application is made.

25.228 A copy of the statement is to be served on the respondent together with the notice in Form FL418 unless the court has dispensed with the need for service: r. 20(9). No fee is payable.

25.229 The committal order is in Form FL419. It must include provision for the issue of a warrant of committal to prison in Form FL420 and, unless the court orders otherwise:

(a) a copy of the order must be served personally on the person to be committed either before or at the time of the execution of the warrant; or

(b) the order for the issue of the warrant may be served on the person to be committed at any time within 36 hours after the execution of the warrant: r. 20(10).

The maximum period of imprisonment is two months and the period must be specified.

As for enforcement of undertakings, r. 20(14) states that the procedure set out above is to apply, but para. (6) is amended as follows: **25.230**

> A copy of Form FL422 recording the undertaking must be delivered by the justices' clerk to the person giving the undertaking:
>
> (a) by handing a copy of the document to him before he leaves the court building, or
> (b) where his place of residence is known, by posting a copy to him at his place of residence, or
> (c) through his solicitor,
>
> and where delivery cannot be effected in this way, the justices' clerk shall deliver a copy of the document to the party for whose benefit the undertaking is given and that party shall cause it to be served personally as soon as is practicable.

Magistrates are now given the power to suspend the execution of a committal order: s. 50 of the Act. The practical detail is set out in r. 20(16) and (17). Paragraph (16) confirms that the court may by order direct that the execution of the committal order be suspended for such period and on such terms or conditions as it may specify.   **25.231**

Paragraph (17) requires that in these circumstances the applicant for the order of committal must, unless the court otherwise directs, serve on the person against whom it was made a notice informing him that an order suspending committal has been made and the terms of such order.   **25.232**

The court may adjourn consideration of the penalty to be imposed for contempts found proved and such consideration may be restored if the respondent does not comply with any conditions specified by the court: r. 20(18).   **25.233**

Where a person in custody under a warrant or order desires to apply to the court for his discharge, he must make his application in writing attested by the governor of the prison showing that he has purged or is desirous of purging his contempt and the justices' clerk must, not less than one day before the application is heard, serve notice of it on the party (if any) at whose instance the warrant or order was issued: r. 20(15).   **25.234**

Application for bail

The provisions for bail are found in r. 21 and replicate those set out in r. 3.10 above.   **25.235**

Application for:	**To be completed by the court**
a non-molestation order	Date issued
an occupation order	
	Case number

Family Law Act 1996 (Part IV)

The court

Please read the accompanying notes as you complete this form.

1 About you (the applicant)

State your title (Mr, Mrs etc), full name, address, telephone number and date of birth (if under 18):

State your solicitor's name, address, reference, telephone, FAX and DX numbers:

2 About the respondent

State the respondent's name, address and date of birth (if known):

3 The Order(s) for which you are applying

This application is for:

☐   a non-molestation order

☐   an occupation order

☐   Tick this box if you wish the court to hear your application without notice being given to the respondent. The reasons relied on for an application being heard without notice must be stated in the statement in support.

4 Your relationship to the respondent (the person to be served with this application)

Your relationship to the respondent is:

(Please tick only one of the following)

1 ☐ Married

2 ☐ Civil Partners

3 ☐ Were married

4 ☐ Former civil partners

5 ☐ Cohabiting

6 ☐ Were cohabiting

7 ☐ Both of you live or have lived in the same household

8 ☐ Relative
State how related:

9 ☐ Agreed to marry.
Give the date the agreement was made.
If the agreement has ended, state when.

10 ☐ Agreed to form a civil partnership.
Give the date the agreement was made.
If the agreement has ended, state when.

11 ☐ Both of you are parents of, or have parental responsibility for, a child

12 ☐ One of you is a parent of a child and the other has parental responsibility for that child

13 ☐ One of you is the natural parent or
grandparent of a child adopted, placed or freed
for adoption, and the other is:

    (i)   the adoptive parent

or (ii) a person who has applied for an
         adoption order for the child

or (iii) a person with whom the child has
         been placed for adoption

or (iv) the child who has been adopted,
         placed or freed for adoption.

State whether (i), (ii), (iii) or (iv):

14 ☐ Both of you are the parties to the same family
proceedings (see also Section 11 below).

5   Application for a non-molestation order

If you wish to apply for a non-molestation order,
state briefly in this section the order you want.

Give full details in support of your application in
your supporting evidence.

6   Application for an occupation order

*If you do not wish to apply for an occupation order,
please go to section 9 of this form.*

(A) State the address of the dwelling-house to which
your application relates:

(B) State whether it is occupied by you or the respondent
now or in the past, or whether it was intended to be
occupied by you or the respondent:

(C) State whether you are entitled to occupy the
dwelling-house: ☐ Yes   ☐ No

If yes, explain why:

(D) State whether the respondent is entitled to occupy
the dwelling-house: ☐ Yes   ☐ No

If yes, explain why:

**On the basis of your answers to (C) and (D) above,
tick one of the boxes 1 to 6 below to show the category
into which you fit**

1 ☐ a spouse or civil partner who has home rights
in the dwelling-house, or a person who is
entitled to occupy it by virtue of a beneficial
estate or interest or contract or by virtue of
any enactment giving him or her the right to
remain in occupation.

If you tick box 1, state whether there is a
dispute or pending proceedings between you
and the respondent about your right to occupy
the dwelling-house.

2 ☐ a former spouse or former civil partner with no
existing right to occupy, where the respondent
spouse or civil partner is so entitled.

3 ☐ a cohabitant or former cohabitant with no
existing right to occupy, where the respondent
cohabitant or former cohabitant is so entitled.

4 ☐ a spouse or former spouse who is not entitled
to occupy, where the respondent spouse or
former spouse is also not entitled.

5 ☐ a civil partner or former civil partner who is not
entitled to occupy, where the respondent civil
partner or former civil partner is also not entitled.

6 ☐ a cohabitant or former cohabitant who is
not entitled to occupy, where the respondent
cohabitant or former cohabitant is also not
entitled.

Home Rights

If you do have home rights please:

State whether the title to the land is registered or unregistered (if known):

If registered, state the Land Registry title number (if known):

If you wish to apply for an occupation order, state briefly here the order you want. Give full details in support of your application in your supporting evidence:

7 Application for additional order(s) about the dwelling-house

If you want to apply for any of the orders listed in the notes to this section, state what order you would like the court to make:

8 Mortgage and rent

Is the dwelling-house subject to a mortgage?

☐ Yes   ☐ No

If yes, please provide the name and address of the mortgagee:

Is the dwelling-house rented?

☐ Yes   ☐ No

If yes, please provide the name and address of the landlord:

9   At the court

Will you need an interpreter at court?

☐ Yes   ☐ No

If yes, specify the language:

If you require an interpreter, you must notify the
court immediately so that one can be arranged.

If you have a disability for which you require special
assistance or special facilities, please state what your
needs are. The court staff will get in touch with you
about your requirements.

10 Other information

State the name and date of birth of any child living
with or staying with, or likely to live with or stay
with, you or the respondent:

State the name of any other person living in the same
household as you and the respondent, and say why
they live there:

11 Other Proceedings and Orders

If there are any other current family proceedings or
orders in force involving you and the respondent,
state the type of proceedings or orders, the court and
the case number. This includes any application for
an occupation order or non-molestation order against
you by the respondent.

This application is to be served upon the respondent

Signed: Date:

Application for non-molestation order or occupation order
Notes for guidance

Section 1

If you do not wish your address to be made known to the respondent, leave the space on the form blank and complete Confidential Address Form C8. The court can give you this form.

If you are under 18, someone over 18 must help you make this application. That person, who might be one of your parents, is called a 'next friend'.

If you are under 16, you need permission to make this application. You must apply to the High Court for permission, using this form. If the High Court gives you permission to make this application, it will then either hear the application itself or transfer it to a county court.

Section 3

An urgent order made by the court before the notice of the application is served on the respondent is called an ex-parte order. In deciding whether to make an ex-parte order the court will consider all the circumstances of the case, including:

- any risk of significant harm to the applicant or a relevant child, attributable to conduct of the respondent, if the order is not made immediately

- whether it is likely that the applicant will be deterred or prevented from pursuing the application if an order is not made immediately

- whether there is reason to believe that the respondent is aware of the proceedings but is deliberately evading service and that the applicant or a relevant child will be seriously prejudiced by the delay involved.

If the court makes an ex-parte order, it must give the respondent an opportunity to make representations about the order as soon as just and convenient at a full hearing.

'Harm' in relation to a person who has reached the age of 18 means ill-treatment or the impairment of health, and in relation to a child means ill-treatment or the impairment of health and development.

'Ill-treatment' includes forms of ill-treatment which are not physical and, in relation to a child, includes sexual abuse. The court will require evidence of any harm which you allege in support of your application.

Section 4

For you to be able to apply for an order you must be related to the respondent in one of the ways listed in this section of the form. If you are not related in one of these ways you should seek legal advice.

Cohabitants are two persons who, although not married to each other, nor civil partners of each other, are living together as husband and wife or civil partners. People who have cohabited, but have then married or formed a civil partnership will not fall within this category but will fall within the category of married people or people who are civil partners of each other.

Those who live or have lived in the same household do not include people who share the same household because one of them is the other's employee, tenant, lodger or boarder.

You will only be able to apply as a relative of the respondent if you are:

(A) the father, mother, stepfather, stepmother, son, daughter, stepson, stepdaughter, grandmother, grandfather, grandson, granddaughter of the respondent or of the respondent's spouse, former spouse, civil partner or former civil partner.

(B) the brother, sister, uncle, aunt, niece, nephew or first cousin (whether of the full blood or of the half blood or by marriage or by civil partnership) of the respondent or of the respondent's spouse, former spouse, civil partner or former civil partner.

This includes, in relation to a person who is living or has lived with another person as husband and wife or as civil partners, any person who would fall within (A) or (B) if the parties were married to, or civil partners of, each other (for example, your cohabitee's father or brother).

Agreements to marry: You will fall within this category only if you make this application within three years of the termination of the agreement. The court will require the following evidence of the agreement:

evidence in writing

or the gift of an engagement ring in contemplation of marriage

or evidence that a ceremony has been entered into in the presence of one or more other persons assembled for the purpose of witnessing it.

Agreements to form a civil partnership: You will fall within this category only if you make this application within three years of the termination of the agreement. The court will require the following evidence of the agreement:

evidence in writing

or a gift from one party to the agreement to the other as a token of the agreement

or evidence that a ceremony has been entered into in the presence of one or more other persons assembled for the purpose of witnessing it.

Section 4 continued

Parents and parental responsibility:
You will fall within this category if

> both you and the respondent are either the parents of the child or have parental responsibility for that child

or if one of you is the parent and the other has parental responsibility.

Under the Children Act 1989, parental responsibility is held automatically by a child's mother, and by the child's father if he and the mother were married to each other at the time of the child's birth or have married subsequently. Where, a child's father and mother are not married to each other at the time of the child's birth, the father may also acquire parental responsibility for that child, if he registers the birth after 1st December 2003, in accordance with section 4(1)(a) of the Children Act 1989. Where neither of these circumstances apply, the father, in accordance with the provisions of the Children Act 1989, can acquire parental responsibility.

From 30 December 2005, where a person who is not the child's parent ("the step-parent") is married to, or a civil partner of, a parent who has parental responsibility for that child, he or she may also acquire parental responsibility for the child in accordance with the provisions of the Children Act 1989.

Section 5

A non-molestation order can forbid the respondent from molesting you or a relevant child. Molestation can include, for example, violence, threats, pestering and other forms of harassment. The court can forbid particular acts of the respondent, molestation in general, or both.

Section 6

If you wish to apply for an occupation order but you are uncertain about your answer to any question in this part of the application form, you should seek legal advice.

(A) A dwelling-house includes any building or part of a building which is occupied as a dwelling; any caravan, houseboat or structure which is occupied as a dwelling; and any yard, garden, garage or outhouse belonging to it and occupied with it.

(C) & (D) The following questions give examples to help you to decide if you or the respondent, or both of you, are entitled to occupy the dwelling-house:

(a) Are you the sole legal owner of the dwelling-house?

(b) Are you and the respondent joint legal owners of the dwelling-house?

(c) Is the respondent the sole legal owner of the dwelling-house?

(d) Do you rent the dwelling-house as a sole tenant?

(e) Do you and the respondent rent the dwelling-house as joint tenants?

(f) Does the respondent rent the dwelling-house as a sole tenant?

If you answer

- **Yes** to (a), (b), (d) or (e) you are likely to be entitled to occupy the dwelling-house

- **Yes** to (c) or (f) you may not be entitled (unless, for example, you are a spouse or civil partner and have home rights – see notes under 'Home Rights' below)

- **Yes** to (b), (c), (e) or (f), the respondent is likely to be entitled to occupy the dwelling-house

- **Yes** to (a) or (d) the respondent may not be entitled (unless, for example, he or she is a spouse or civil partner and has home rights).

Box 1 For example, if you are sole owner, joint owner or if you rent the property. If you are not a spouse, former spouse, civil partner, former civil partner, cohabitant or former cohabitant of the respondent, you will only be able to apply for an occupation order if you fall within this category.

If you answer yes to this question, it will not be possible for a magistrates' court to deal with the application, unless the court decides that it is unnecessary for it to decide this question in order to deal with the application or make the order. If the court decides that it cannot deal with the application, it will transfer the application to a county court.

Box 2 For example, if the respondent is or was married to you, or if you and the respondent are or were civil partners, and he or she is sole owner or rents the property.

Box 3 For example, if the respondent is or was cohabiting with you and is sole owner or rents the property.

Home Rights
Where one spouse or civil partner "(A)" is entitled to occupy the dwelling-house by virtue of a beneficial estate or interest or contract or by virtue of any enactment giving him or her the right to remain in occupation, and the other spouse or civil partner "(B)" is not so entitled, then B (who is not entitled) has home rights.

The rights are

(a) if B is in occupation, not to be evicted or excluded from the dwelling-house except with the leave of the court; and

(b) if B is not in occupation, the right, with the leave of the court, to enter into and occupy the dwelling-house.

Note: Home Rights do not exist if the dwelling-house has never been, and was never intended to be, the matrimonial or civil partnership home of the two spouses or civil partners. If the marriage or civil partnership has come to an end, home rights will also have ceased, unless a court order has been made during the marriage or civil partnership for the rights to continue after the end of that relationship.

Section 6 (continued)

Occupation Orders

The possible orders are:

If you have ticked box 1 above, an order under section 33 of the Act may:

- enforce the applicant's entitlement to remain in occupation as against the respondent
- require the respondent to permit the applicant to enter and remain in the dwelling-house or part of it
- regulate the occupation of the dwelling-house by either or both parties
- if the respondent is also entitled to occupy, the order may prohibit, suspend or restrict the exercise by him, of that right
- restrict or terminate any home rights of the respondent
- require the respondent to leave the dwelling-house or part of it
- exclude the respondent from a defined area around the dwelling-house
- declare that the applicant is entitled to occupy the dwelling-house or has home rights in it
- provide that the home rights of the applicant are not brought to an end by the death of the other spouse or civil partner or termination of the marriage or civil partnership.

If you have ticked box 2 or box 3 above, an order under section 35 or 36 of the Act may:

- give the applicant the right not to be evicted or excluded from the dwelling-house or any part of it by the respondent for a specified period
- prohibit the respondent from evicting or excluding the applicant during that period
- give the applicant the right to enter and occupy the dwelling-house for a specified period
- require the respondent to permit the exercise of that right
- regulate the occupation of the dwelling-house by either or both of the parties
- prohibit, suspend or restrict the exercise by the respondent of his right to occupy
- require the respondent to leave the dwelling-house or part of it
- exclude the respondent from a defined area around the dwelling-house.

If you have ticked box 4 or box 5 above, an order under section 37 or 38 of the Act may:

- require the respondent to permit the applicant to enter and remain in the dwelling-house or part of it
- regulate the occupation of the dwelling-house by either or both of the parties
- require the respondent to leave the dwelling-house or part of it
- exclude the respondent from a defined area around the dwelling-house.

You should provide any evidence which you have on the following matters in your evidence in support of this application. If necessary, further statements may be submitted after the application has been issued.

If you have ticked box 1, box 4 or box 5 above, the court will need any available evidence of the following:

- the housing needs and resources of you, the respondent and any relevant child
- the financial needs of you and the respondent
- the likely effect of any order, or any decision not to make an order, on the health, safety and well-being of you, the respondent and any relevant child
- the conduct of you and the respondent in relation to each other and otherwise.

If you have ticked box 2 above, the court will need any available evidence of:

- the housing needs and resources of you, the respondent and any relevant child
- the financial resources of you and the respondent
- the likely effect of any order, or of any decision not to make an order on the health, safety and well-being of you, the respondent and any relevant child
- the conduct of you and the respondent in relation to each other and otherwise
- the length of time that has elapsed since you and the respondent ceased to live together
- where you and the respondent were married, the length of time that has elapsed since the marriage was dissolved or annulled
- where you and the respondent were civil partners, the length of time that has elapsed since the dissolution or annulment of the civil partnership

Section 6 (continued)

- the existence of any pending proceedings between you and the respondent:

    under section 23A of the Matrimonial Causes Act 1973 (property adjustment orders in connection with divorce proceedings etc.)

    or under Part 2 of Schedule 5 to the Civil Partnership Act 2004 (property adjustment on or after dissolution, nullity or separation)

    or under Schedule 1 para 1(2)(d) or (e) of the Children Act 1989 (orders for financial relief against parents)

    or relating to the legal or beneficial ownership of the dwelling-house.

If you have ticked box 3 above, the court will need any available evidence of:

- the housing needs and resources of you, the respondent and any relevant child

- the financial resources of you and the respondent

- the likely effect of any order, or of any decision not to make an order, on the health, safety and well-being of you, the respondent and any relevant child

- the conduct of you and the respondent in relation to each other and otherwise

- the nature of your and the respondent's relationship

- the length of time during which you have lived together as husband and wife or civil partners

- whether you and the respondent have had any children, or have both had parental responsibility for any children

- the length of time that has elapsed since you and the respondent ceased to live together

- the existence of any pending proceedings between you and the respondent under Schedule 1 para 1(2)(d) or (e) of the Children Act 1989 or relating to the legal or beneficial ownership of the dwelling-house.

Section 7

Under section 40 of the Act the court may make the following additional orders when making an occupation order:

- impose on either party obligations as to the repair and maintenance of the dwelling-house

- impose on either party obligations as to the payment of rent, mortgage or other outgoings affecting it

- order a party occupying the dwelling-house to make periodical payments to the other party in respect of the accommodation, if the other party would (but for the order) be entitled to occupy it

- grant either party possession or use of furniture or other contents

- order either party to take reasonable care of any furniture or other contents

- order either party to take reasonable steps to keep the dwelling-house and any furniture or other contents secure.

Section 8

If the dwelling-house is rented or subject to a mortgage, the landlord or mortgagee must be served with notice of the proceedings in Form FL416. He or she will then be able to make representations to the court regarding the rent or mortgage.

Section 10

A person living in the same household may, for example, be a member of the family or a tenant or employee of you or the respondent.

PART VI

GENERAL MATTERS CONCERNING THE HOME AND OTHER PROPERTY

26

THE HOME: PREVENTING A SALE OR MORTGAGE

A THE PROBLEM

The major asset owned by the parties to a marriage or civil partnership is usually their home. **26.01**
For each party, this represents both a roof over his or her head and a capital investment.
Whilst the marriage or civil partnership is satisfactory they are likely to discuss and agree any
step that is to be taken in relation to the home, such as selling it or mortgaging it. However,
once the relationship begins to founder, the danger arises that without consulting the other
party to the relationship, one party will engage in dealings in relation to the house which will
jeopardize either the roof over the other's head or his or her financial interest in the property.

Example 1 The parties purchase a house in 1984 with the aid of a mortgage. It is conveyed
into the husband's sole name. By 2000 the marriage is on the rocks and the wife petitions for
divorce making a comprehensive claim for ancillary relief. She is living in the house but she
goes away for two months to see her sister in Australia. Whilst she is away, the husband puts
the property on the market and sells it. By the time the wife returns the proceeds of sale have
been dissipated. She has lost both the roof over her head and any prospect of having the
home transferred to her in ancillary relief proceedings under s. 24, Matrimonial Causes Act
1973 or of receiving under s. 23 a lump sum payment of a share in the proceeds.

Example 2 Instead of selling the house, the husband grants a second mortgage of it to a bank as security for a substantial loan. Provided he keeps up the repayments on both mortgages, this does not prejudice the wife's occupation of the property but it clearly does affect her financial interest in the house. Not only the first but also the second mortgage will have to be discharged from the proceeds of sale if the house is sold before the mortgagees have been fully repaid, thus substantially reducing the equity in the house available for distribution between the parties.

If the husband falls behind with the mortgage instalments, the wife's occupation of the house may also be endangered if the mortgagees seek to enforce their rights in relation to the property.

26.02   This chapter sets out what can be done to prevent problems of this sort arising. It is assumed that the solicitor acts for a wife who wishes to prevent her husband from dealing with the property. The same principles would apply if the roles were reversed. References to spouses also include civil partners.

B   HOUSE IN JOINT NAMES

Protection against sale or mortgage by one spouse

Generally

26.03   If the house is in the joint names of both spouses the wife will automatically be protected against the husband selling the property without her consent. As she is a joint tenant of the legal estate, the property cannot be conveyed or transferred unless she joins in the conveyance or transfer.

26.04   In theory it might be possible for the husband to use the house as security for a loan without the consent of the wife. In practice, however, it would be hard for him to find anyone willing to lend on this basis because the security provided by such arrangements would be inadequate. Thus the wife is unlikely to have anything to fear from this quarter either.

Consent obtained by misrepresentation, fraud, or 'actual undue influence'

26.05   If the wife is a party to the mortgage or sale, the transaction will in most cases bind her interest. It may be, however, that her consent has been obtained by fraud, misrepresentation, or 'actual undue influence' on the part of the husband. Each will require a wife to provide cogent evidence of the deceit, particularly in the case of fraud. Where actual undue influence is alleged, the complainant must prove affirmatively that she entered into the transaction not of her own free will but as a result of the undue influence used against her.

26.06   Recent case law (see below) suggests that a categorization of forms of undue influence is confusing and it may therefore no longer be appropriate to distinguish between actual or presumed undue influence. In practice, it is likely to present considerably fewer legal hurdles if the complaint is presented as 'presumed' rather than 'actual' undue influence.

'Presumed undue influence' between husband and wife and similar relationships

26.07   The well-known case of *Barclays Bank* v *O'Brien* [1994] 1 FLR 1 set out legal principles aimed at providing protection to a wife in a situation where she had consented to the matrimonial home being used as a surety in order to support the husband's business debts. That protection took the form of presuming undue influence on the part of the husband if the wife was able to establish certain facts, and then fixing the lender with 'constructive notice' of that influence when the lender sought possession of the home. The lender was then required to satisfy the court that certain steps had been taken to ensure that the wife was not in fact the victim of such influence.

In *Royal Bank of Scotland* v *Etridge (No. 2) and other appeals* [2001] 4 All ER 449 the House of **26.08** Lords went to considerable lengths to clarify this complex area of law and to deal with practical uncertainties produced by *Barclays Bank* v *O'Brien*.

In the leading speech, Lord Nicholls confirmed that a rebuttable presumption will become **26.09** operative as a general rule depending upon the nature of the alleged undue influence, the personality of the parties, their relationship, the extent to which the transaction cannot be readily accounted for, and all the circumstances of the case. Typically, in the case of 'surety wives' the complainant must adduce sufficient evidence of the fact that she placed trust and confidence in the husband and that the transaction is not readily explicable by the relationship of the parties. This second requirement does not have to constitute 'manifest disadvantage', merely that the transaction cannot be reasonably or ordinarily accounted for.

If the evidential burden upon the wife is discharged, then the transaction is presumed to **26.10** have been procured by undue influence unless the lender can rebut the presumption. His Lordship's reasoning was that in these circumstances the lender ought to have known that the wife's agreement was not truly her own. Lord Nicholls went to considerable lengths to detail the steps that a lender must take in order to rebut the presumption and thereby enforce the mortgage against the wife.

Lenders are 'put on enquiry' in every case where the relationship between surety and debtor **26.11** is non-commercial. The lender must take reasonable steps to satisfy itself that the practical implications of the proposed transaction have been brought home to the wife, in a meaningful way, so that she enters the transaction with her eyes open so far as the basic elements are concerned. A meeting with the wife is not normally required, and, ordinarily, it will be reasonable for the lender to rely upon confirmation from a solicitor that she has been advised appropriately. In order to ensure that its position is protected, the lender should take the following steps:

(a) It should write to the wife, informing her that for its own protection it will require written confirmation from a solicitor acting for her that both the nature of the documents and the implications of the transaction have been fully explained to her. She should be informed that thereafter she will not be able to dispute that she is legally bound by the transaction.

(b) The wife should be requested to nominate a solicitor who, if she wishes, can be the same one that is acting for the husband. The bank should not proceed until it has received an appropriate response directly from the wife.

(c) Where the bank is unwilling to explain the husband's financial affairs to the wife, it should provide sufficient and adequate disclosure to the solicitor. The extent of this will depend on the facts of the case. Obviously, the consent of the husband will be required before confidential information is disclosed.

(d)   Where the bank suspects that the husband has misled the wife as to the nature of the transaction, it should inform the solicitor of this.

(e)   A letter of confirmation, as detailed below, should be obtained from the solicitor.

It is not necessary that the solicitor should act solely for the wife, as cost and familiarity of the family solicitor are important factors. The solicitor's legal and professional duties, assumed when accepting instructions to advise the wife, are owed to her alone. The solicitor should consider whether there is any conflict of duty or interest.

26.12   Lord Nicholls specified that the core duties owed to the wife by the solicitor are:

(a)   to explain the reason that the solicitor has become involved;

(b)   to explain that, if the bank decides to commence possession proceedings, the lender will rely upon the solicitor's involvement to counter any suggestion of undue influence;

(c)   to obtain instructions from the wife that she wishes the solicitor to act for her and then to advise her on the legal and practical implications of the proposed transaction.

26.13   Assuming such instructions are forthcoming, the content of that advice will typically contain:

(a)   an explanation of the nature of the documents and the practical consequences they will have for the wife if she signs them;

(b)   the seriousness of the risks involved;

(c)   the purpose of the proposed facility, its amount, and its principal terms;

(d)   whether the bank may increase the amount of the facility, or change its terms, or grant a new facility without reference to her;

(e)   the amount of the wife's liability under the guarantee;

(f)   a discussion of the wife's financial means, including her understanding of the value of the property being charged;

(g)   whether there are any other assets out of which repayment can be made if the husband's business fails;

(h)   importantly, that the wife has a choice and that the decision is hers and hers alone;

(i)   the solicitor should check whether the wife wishes to proceed and whether the wife is content that the solicitor write to the bank to confirm that the documents, the nature of the transaction, and the implications have been explained to her. Alternatively, the wife may wish the solicitor to negotiate better terms with the bank.

The solicitor's discussion with the wife should take place at a face-to-face meeting in the absence of the husband and should be presented in non-technical language. The bank ought to have provided all the information required by the solicitor. If it has not, then the solicitor ought to decline the confirmation sought by the bank.

26.14   Their Lordships noted that the decision over whether to proceed or not is the wife's and that, as a general rule, the obligation on the solicitor was not to veto the proposed transaction but merely to provide the wife with reasoned advice. Where, however, it was glaringly obvious that the transaction was procured as a result of undue influence on the part of the husband the solicitor should decline to act for her further.

26.15   Lord Nicholls confirmed that the position will be unaltered where the husband stands as surety to the wife's debts. The same will also apply in the case of unmarried couples, heterosexual or homosexual, where the lender is aware of the relationship. Importantly, cohabitation is not essential (see *Massey* v *Midland Bank plc* [1995] 1 All ER 929 at 933, per Steyn LJ).

In the subsequent case of *National Westminster Bank plc* v *Amin and Another* [2002] 1 FLR 735, **26.16** which involved the question of whether a defence of undue influence between a son and his parents who spoke only Urdu should be struck out, the House of Lords noted that the instructions received by a solicitor who had been retained by the bank raised serious questions which should be aired at trial. These included the limited extent of the instructions provided by the couple, the solicitor's communications to the lender, the fact that the lender knew that the couple did not speak English, and that they were specially vulnerable to exploitation. The case was remitted for trial.

'Presumed undue influence' and other types of relationships

In *Etridge No. 2* Lord Clyde questioned the wisdom of attempting to make classifications of **26.17** cases of undue influence. In so doing, his Lordship was seeking to move away from the well-known classification adopted by Lord Browne-Wilkinson in *O'Brien* from *Bank of Credit and Commerce International SA* v *Aboody* [1992] 4 All ER 955.

Despite this, it is apparent from *Etridge No. 2* that undue influence will be presumed in **26.18** relationships other than those described in paragraph 26.15 above. Lord Nicholls made it clear that in certain types of relationship where one party acquires influence over another who is vulnerable and dependent the law will adopt a sternly protective attitude where a gift is made by the vulnerable person which cannot be readily explained. Where the complainant can demonstrate both the existence of the relationship and the transaction, the law will presume, irrebuttably, that one party had influence over the other. The complainant need not prove that he or she actually reposed trust and confidence in the other party. Examples of the types of relationship include parent and child, guardian and ward, trustee and beneficiary, and solicitor and client. A recent example of this type of case is *Abbey National* v *Stringer and others* [2006] EWCA Civ 338.

Providing for the possibility of death before divorce

Generally

The solicitor must give some thought as to what will happen to the wife's share in the pro- **26.19** perty should she die before the parties are divorced and questions of ancillary relief resolved. If husband and wife are joint tenants in equity, the wife's interest will pass to her husband on her death by virtue of the right of survivorship. If they are tenants in common, the husband will still probably obtain the wife's share, perhaps under a will made by the wife in his favour at a time when the marriage was running smoothly, or otherwise under the statutory provisions governing intestacy (see Part IV of the Administration of Estates Act 1925, as amended). This may be perfectly acceptable to some clients; others are so embittered by the breakdown of the marriage that they wish to prevent their spouse from benefiting in any way from their death. However, the husband may be able to make a claim against the wife's estate for family provision by virtue of the Inheritance (Provision for Family and Dependants) Act 1975 (see Chapter 28, Section F). The matter must therefore be discussed with the client and, if she does not wish her property to pass to her husband, the solicitor must consider:

(a) whether there is or may be a beneficial joint tenancy, in which case he should consider serving notice of severance; *and*

(b) whether it is necessary to advise the client to make a will/a new will.

The question of a beneficial joint tenancy is dealt with below; the question of making a will is dealt with in Chapter 28.

Severance of the joint tenancy to avoid right of survivorship

26.20   The basic principles as to joint tenancies are as follows:

(a) Where property is conveyed into the names of more than one person, there is always a joint tenancy of the legal estate. The equitable interests in the property may be held on a joint tenancy or as tenants in common.

(b) If a joint tenancy exists in equity as well as in law, on the death of one joint tenant the other joint tenant will automatically become entitled to his beneficial interest in the property by virtue of the right of survivorship.

(c) If the equitable interests are held as tenants in common, there is no right of survivorship and the equitable interest of the deceased tenant in common will pass in accordance with his will or according to the intestacy provisions if he has not made one.

26.21   One of the difficulties facing the solicitor in a matrimonial case is how to determine whether or not there is a joint tenancy in equity. If:

(a) the conveyance or transfer to the parties expressly provides that they are to hold the equitable interest as tenants in common; *or*

(b) a separate declaration of trust has been made to this effect; *or*

(c) a note or memorandum of severance is endorsed on or annexed to the conveyance to the parties or an appropriate restriction entered on the proprietorship register,

this is conclusive evidence that there is an equitable tenancy in common and therefore no right of survivorship—once a tenancy in common, always a tenancy in common. In such circumstances, there is no need to serve a notice of severance but the solicitor should not forget to consider whether it is necessary to make a will/new will for the client. There is no point in going to the trouble of checking up on the right of survivorship only to overlook the fact that the client's spouse will be entitled to the property anyway under her will or by virtue of the intestacy provisions.

26.22   The solicitor will not always be in a position to find out about the equitable interest in the house (for example, a building society may hold the title deeds and may not be prepared to release them without the consent of the other party). If he is unable to find out what the position is or finds that there was originally an equitable joint tenancy which has apparently not been severed, the only safe course is to consider serving a notice of severance: see s. 36(2), Law of Property Act 1925 ('LPA 1925'). When considering whether to sever, however, it must be borne in mind that not only will severance of the joint tenancy prevent the client's share in the property passing to her spouse on her death, it will also prevent her becoming automatically entitled by survivorship to his share in the property on his death. This disadvantage must be weighed against the advantages of severance. For an interesting case of a spouse trying to hedge her bets, see *Kinch* v *Bullard* [1999] 1 FLR 66.

If the solicitor decides, in consultation with the client, that it would be appropriate to serve **26.23** notice of severance, care should be taken over the wording of the notice. Service of an unconditional notice of severance could be taken as an admission by the client that there *is* an equitable joint tenancy and that the parties are entitled to the equitable estate in equal shares. An admission of this nature could be prejudicial (for example in s. 17, Married Women's Property Act 1882 proceedings or when the operation of the Legal Services Commission's statutory charge came to be considered). Therefore, if there is any doubt at all as to whether there is an equitable joint tenancy, the notice of severance should be drafted in such a way that it is clear that no admission is made that there is a joint tenancy, but that if there is one the intention is to sever it. Again it is important that the solicitor should not stop at service of notice of severance—he must then consider whether there is any need to make a will/new will.

Note that while the issue and service of a summons and affidavit (sworn statement) under **26.24** s. 17, Married Women's Property Act 1882 will automatically sever an equitable joint tenancy (*Re Draper's Conveyance* [1969] 1 Ch 486), issue and service of a divorce petition containing a prayer for property adjustment will not: *Harris* v *Goddard* [1983] 1 WLR 1203, [1983] 3 All ER 242.

C   HOUSE IN SOLE NAME OF ONE SPOUSE

The powers of the spouse who is the legal owner to sell, mortgage, etc.

Theoretically the spouse or civil partner who is the legal owner (whom we are assuming to be **26.25** the husband) has the power to deal as he pleases with the property. However, although the husband may feel that he is sitting pretty because he is the sole legal owner, that is not, of course, the end of the story. The wife may well have rights in relation to the property; in particular:

(a)   she will have a right of occupation (known as 'home rights') by virtue of the Family Law Act 1996; *and*

(b)   she may have a beneficial interest in the property, normally arising because she has made a contribution to the purchase price.

If the appropriate steps are taken on the wife's behalf, these rights can afford her a substantial measure of protection against her husband selling or mortgaging the property. However, banks who are lending on the security of a mortgage over the matrimonial home will inevitably ask the wife to consent to the charge being granted. If the wife gives consent then she will only be able to deny the bank's priority by arguing that her consent was vitiated by virtue of undue influence or fraud in accordance with the principles set out in paragraphs 26.03 to 26.18 above.

Home rights (s. 30, Family Law Act 1996)

When the rights arise

By virtue of s. 30(1), where one spouse or civil partner is entitled to occupy a dwelling-house **26.26** by virtue of a beneficial estate or interest or contract or by virtue of any enactment giving him or her the right to remain in occupation, and the other spouse/civil partner is not so entitled, the spouse/civil partner not so entitled has 'home rights' in relation to the house.

26.27 These rights arise if the dwelling-house is, or has been, or was intended to be the family home (s. 30(7)). A spouse/civil partner has no home rights in respect of, for example, a holiday cottage owned by the other spouse/civil partner. The definition of 'dwelling-house' contained in s. 63 also includes any caravan, house-boat, or structure which is occupied as a dwelling.

26.28 Section 30(9)(a) and (b) provide that, for the purpose only of determining whether he or she has home rights under s. 30, a spouse/civil partner who has an equitable interest in a dwelling-house or in the proceeds of sale thereof, not being a spouse in whom is vested (solely or as a joint tenant) a legal estate or legal term of years absolute in the house, is to be treated as not being entitled to occupy the house by virtue of that equitable interest.

Example A dwelling-house is purchased partly from the savings of a husband, partly from his wife's savings and partly on mortgage. It is conveyed into the sole name of the husband. Both spouses move in and live in the property as their matrimonial home. The husband is entitled to occupy the house because he owns it. The wife has almost certainly got an equitable interest in the property by virtue of her initial contribution to the purchase price. Nevertheless, because she has no legal estate, s. 30(9) means that she is treated as if she is not entitled to occupy the house by virtue of her equitable interest. The situation therefore falls within s. 30(1) and she is entitled to home rights.

Meaning of 'home rights'

26.29 Where the spouse/civil partner with matrimonial home rights is in occupation of the house already, her rights of occupation amount to a right not to be evicted or excluded from the house or any part of it by the other spouse/civil partner except with leave of the court given by an order under s. 33: s. 30(2)(a).

26.30 If she is not in occupation, her home rights amount to a right with the leave of the court to enter into and occupy the house: s. 30(2)(b).

Termination of home rights

26.31 Normally home rights are brought to an end by:

(a) the death of the other spouse/civil partner; *or*
(b) the termination (other than on death) of the marriage, except to the extent that an order under s. 33(5) otherwise provides (see Chapter 25 on occupation orders).

However, where there is a matrimonial dispute or the parties are estranged, the court has power to direct that the home rights should continue despite either of these events occurring: s. 33 or s. 35. The order to this effect will be made under s. 33.

26.32 In fact, the court has a very wide power under s. 33 to deal with the question of occupation of the matrimonial home on the application of either spouse/civil partner during the marriage/civil partnership (for instance, the court can not only order the continuation of home rights post-decree, it can also terminate or suspend the right of either spouse/civil partner to occupy the house during the marriage/civil partnership). Further, under s. 35

the court may make an occupation order in favour of a former spouse with no existing right to occupy.

How do home rights protect a wife/civil partner against sale or mortgage?

It is all very well for a wife/civil partner to have the benefit of home rights under the Family **26.33** Law Act 1996 ('FLA 1996'); how do these rights protect her if her husband attempts to sell or mortgage the house over her head? The answer is, 'very little' unless her rights are registered as a charge against the property. It is therefore the solicitor's duty to take the necessary steps to register his client's home rights as soon as he is consulted in relation to her matrimonial or civil partnership problems.

The rules are as follows: **26.34**

(a) The wife/civil partner's home rights are a charge on the other party's estate or interest in the property concerned: s. 31, FLA 1996.
(b) They should be protected as follows:
    (i) in case of unregistered land, by the registration of a Class F land charge against the name of the husband in the register of land charges: s. 2, Land Charges Act 1972 ('LCA 1972');
    (ii) in the case of registered land, by the entry of a notice in the Charges Register as an agreed notice on Form HRI under Part 4 of the Land Registration Act 2002 ('LRA 1972'), FLA 1996. It is no longer possible to register a caution to protect home rights: s. 31(11), FLA 1996.

If a wife is entitled to a charge in respect of two or more dwelling-houses, only one can be **26.35** registered at any one time: sch. 4, para. 2. Note that notice of the charge is automatically provided to the registered proprietor and, no request for withholding notice to the owner will be considered. Receipt of such notice may provoke a violent reaction and clients should be fully advised of the protection available to them under the FLA 1996. The Land Registry will hold any application made for a period of one week to give the applicant wife an opportunity to consider the likely effect of her application. Where registration is by the Class F land charge, the Land Charges Department will not send out a notice. This reflects the Land Charges Department's function in administering an index of names, not of land.

It is essential to ensure that the correct form of registration is effected otherwise the charge **26.36** will be void: *Miles* v *Bull (No. 2)* [1969] 3 All ER 1585. The LRA 2002 also imposes a duty to act reasonably so that a person must not apply for entry of a notice or object to such an application without reasonable cause: s. 77(1). A duty of care is owed to any person who suffers damage in consequence of its breach.

Where the legal title to the property is vested in the sole name of the husband, it is likely that **26.37** the wife's solicitor will be denied access to the title deeds to check the position. In order to determine whether the land is registered or unregistered a search of the Index Map at the District Land Registry can be carried out using form SIM. The result of the search will indicate whether or not the land in question is registered and give the title number for identification purposes if registered. Land Registry Direct (<www.landregistry.gov.uk>) is a web-based service providing a facility to obtain official copy entries of the title and make searches on-line.

26.38 Once the wife's/civil partner rights have been properly registered, what protection is she given? Although registering her home rights will constitute actual notice of those rights to purchasers of the matrimonial or civil partnership home (see s. 198(1), LPA 1925), it does not follow that the wife will be able to continue to occupy for as long as she wishes. The purchaser may apply to the court for an order determining the wife's rights of occupation, and on such an application the court has a wide discretion, having to consider not only the circumstances of the wife (and any children residing with her) but the circumstances of the purchaser as well (now s. 33(6), FLA 1996, as explained in *Kashmir Kaur v Gill* [1988] Fam 110; [1988] 2 All ER 288).

Example (The facts of *Kashmir Kaur v Gill*.) The matrimonial home was in the husband's sole name. The wife, driven out of the house by her husband's conduct, registered her rights of occupation by way of a notice. The registration did not come to the actual notice of the purchaser, who purchased the house from the husband, until after completion. The wife then sought an order of the court under s. 1(2), Matrimonial Home Act 1983 (now s. 33(3), FLA 1996) declaring that she had the right to occupy and prohibiting the purchaser from exercising any rights over it.

The Court of Appeal held that, in hearing the wife's application, the court had to consider all of the circumstances of the case (s. 1(3), Matrimonial Home Act 1983, now s. 33(6), FLA 1996), which included the circumstances of the purchaser. The purchaser was blind and had bought the house with his special needs in mind. The judge's decision that the wife should lose her right to occupy was therefore upheld as being a proper exercise of his discretion.

26.39 However, generally the registration of home rights provides more effective protection than this. The prospective purchaser or mortgagee will carry out a search prior to completion and will uncover the wife's or civil partner rights at that stage if he has not learnt of them before. He will immediately go back to the vendor to find out how he proposes to deal with the problem. In fact a contract for the sale of a house affected by a registered charge must include a term requiring cancellation of the registration before completion: sch. 4, para. 3(1). If the wife will not agree to her charge or notice being cancelled, the vendor will be in breach of contract and the purchaser will withdraw from the deal, leaving the wife or civil partner to enjoy her home rights in peace.

The wife with a beneficial interest

26.40 It is not uncommon for a wife or civil partner to have a beneficial interest in the home even though her name is not on the property register or the title deeds. The usual reason for such a beneficial interest is that the spouse concerned has contributed to the purchase price of the house directly (for example by providing part of the deposit or making mortgage repayments). A wife with a beneficial interest in the home can register her home rights in the normal way and should be able to protect both her financial interest and her occupation of the home by thus preventing a sale/mortgage of the property except on her terms. But what if she omits to register her home rights? Has she any independent rights arising from her beneficial interest?

Overreaching provisions

26.41 Where property is held by the husband on trust for both himself and his wife (or for his wife alone), a trust of land will automatically be imposed.

Where property subject to a trust of land is sold, the purchaser, if he knows of the trust of **26.42** land, will insist that the purchase money is paid to two trustees because in this way he can ensure that the conveyance overreaches all the equitable interests under the trust of land, leaving him with the property free of obligation. Where the wife's interest is recognized on the deeds or in a separate declaration of trust, the overreaching provisions should therefore ensure that she will get the money that represents her beneficial interest (because, unless her husband has the second trustee in his pocket, her share will be paid to her by the trustees), even if she has omitted to register her home rights and thus cannot prevent the sale itself or insist on living in the property after it is sold. The overreaching provisions apply whether the property is registered or unregistered (see *City of London Building Society* v *Flegg* [1988] AC 54, [1987] 3 All ER 435).

Where a wife has a beneficial interest under an implied, resulting, or constructive trust (for **26.43** instance, where she has made substantial payments towards the acquisition of the home), a mortgagee or prospective purchaser may be unaware of this, as her rights are unlikely to appear on the register or on the title deeds. Her position is therefore vulnerable, as the mortgage money, or proceeds of sale, may be paid to the husband, who might then disappear without accounting to the wife for her share. In two situations, the wife's legal position is particularly weak:

(a)   Where the mortgagee is seeking to enforce a mortgage entered into at the date of acquisition of the property. The wife's beneficial interest will be deemed, as a matter of law, to be subject to, and bound by, the mortgage: *Abbey National Building Society* v *Cann* [1990] 1 All ER 1085.

(b)   Where the mortgagee is seeking to enforce a mortgage entered into subsequent to the date of acquisition of the property, and the wife either knew, or should have known, of the mortgage at the time it was entered into. In such circumstances, the wife is expected to inform the mortgagee of her rights, and in the event of her failure to do so, she will be estopped from later asserting a claim against the mortgagee: *Bristol & West Building Society* v *Henning* [1985] 1 WLR 778.

Subject to this, a wife whose beneficial interest is not overreached may still be protected **26.44** against a sale or mortgage quite independently of the question of registration of her matrimonial home rights. The protection she may have in these circumstances will differ according to whether the land is registered or unregistered.

Beneficial interest in registered land as an overriding interest

A sale or mortgage of registered land takes effect subject to any *overriding interest* existing at **26.45** the date of completion of the transaction in question, whether or not the purchaser or mortgagee has notice of the overriding interest. If a wife is in actual occupation of the property (i.e., physically present there), whether or not her husband is also living there, her beneficial interest can constitute an overriding interest under s. 70(1)(g), LRA 1925. This was established by the House of Lords in *Williams & Glyn's Bank Ltd* v *Boland* [1981] AC 487; [1980] 2 All ER 408. There will be no overriding interest if enquiry is made of the wife and her rights are not disclosed.

In the context of a sale or mortgage by a party whose spouse has an overriding interest **26.46** under s. 70(1)(g), as the *Williams & Glyn's* case illustrates, this means that the purchaser or mortgagee will be bound by the wife's equitable interest in the property which is not only a financial burden on the property but also gives her a right to possession.

Example (The facts of *Williams and Glyn's Bank Ltd* v *Boland*.) The husband was the registered proprietor of the matrimonial home. Both he and the wife had contributed to the purchase price of the property and they were therefore equitable tenants in common. Both spouses lived in the matrimonial home. Without the wife's knowledge, the husband mortgaged the house to the bank under a legal mortgage. The bank did not enquire of the husband or the wife before taking the mortgage whether the wife had any interest in the property. The husband defaulted on the mortgage and the bank took proceedings for a possession order which initially they obtained. The wife appealed to the Court of Appeal and the possession order was discharged on the basis that the wife, being in actual occupation of the property, had an overriding interest within s. 70(1)(g). The Court of Appeal held that the bank had taken the mortgage subject to the overriding interest and the wife was entitled to remain in possession against them. The bank's appeal to the House of Lords was dismissed.

26.47   Note that, before agreeing to lend in respect of a property, banks and building societies now tend to ask all those who are occupying or are going to occupy the property to sign a document under seal stating that any rights they have or may acquire in relation to the property are postponed to those of the bank or building society. If the wife has entered into such an agreement it may adversely affect her rights as against the bank or building society.

Beneficial interest in unregistered land and notice

26.48   The wife with a beneficial interest in unregistered land has no prospect of establishing an overriding interest since the concept is peculiar to registered land. Her rights depend instead upon the doctrine of notice. Unless the purchaser or mortgagee has actual or constructive notice of the wife's equitable interest at the time of the disposition, he will not be bound by it: *Caunce* v *Caunce* [1969] 1 WLR 286, [1969] 1 All ER 722. In *Caunce* v *Caunce* the court took the view that the mere fact that the wife is resident in the property with the husband does not fix the purchaser/mortgageee with notice. However, this view is now seriously out-moded. Whether a purchaser/mortgagee has actual or constructive notice of the wife's inter-est is a question of fact in each case: *Kingsnorth Finance Co. Ltd* v *Tizard* [1986] 1 WLR 783; [1986] 2 All ER 54. Where the purchaser/mortgagee is held to have notice, the wife may be able to enforce her rights in the property against him.

Registration of pending land action

26.49   Where proceedings are begun in relation to the matrimonial/civil partnership home (for example under s. 17, Married Women's Property Act 1882 or under s. 24, Matrimonial Causes Act 1973), a pending land action can be registered in the case of unregistered land. This protects the wife's interest in the property in much the same way as the registration of a Class F land charge save that, whereas the wife would normally have to agree to a Class F land charge being cancelled once decree absolute comes through, the registration of a pending land action will protect her until the dispute in relation to the property is settled.

26.50   Note also that a pending land action can be registered in relation to a property that was never or has never been intended to be the matrimonial home—a situation in which no

Class F land charge can be registered. In the case of registered land, the appropriate way to prevent dealings with the land where an action is pending would appear to be by lodging a caution in the Proprietorship Register.

D BANKRUPTCY AND THE MATRIMONIAL HOME

The security of the matrimonial home will be threatened in the event of either spouse (we shall assume, here, the husband) being declared bankrupt. The question will then arise whether the wife (and children) can continue to live in the home, or whether the property should be sold to pay off the landlord's creditors. **26.51**

The husband's property will vest in his 'trustee in bankruptcy'. However, his wife's home rights (under the FLA 1996) will bind the trustee and the creditors if they are duly registered, as will any rights the wife has by reason of her having a legal or beneficial interest in the home. Nevertheless, the trustee will be able to apply for an order for sale of the property (under s. 14, Trusts of Land and Appointment of Trustees Act 1996) in the bankruptcy proceedings. **26.52**

Where the order for sale is sought by the trustee in bankruptcy (as is usually the case), certain factors have to be considered by the court. These are listed in s. 25 of and sch. 3, para. 23 to the Trusts of Land and Appointment of Trustees Act 1996 which inserted a new s. 335A into the Insolvency Act 1986. On such an application the court will make such order as it thinks just and reasonable having regard to: **26.53**

(a) the interests of the bankrupt's creditors;
(b) where the application is made in respect of a dwelling-house which has been the home of the bankrupt or the bankrupt's spouse or former spouse—
   (i)   the conduct of the spouse or former spouse so far as contributing to the bankruptcy,
   (ii) the needs and financial resources of the spouse or former spouse, and
   (iii) the needs of any children;
(c) all the circumstances of the case other than the needs of the bankrupt: s. 335A(2).

Section 335A(3) states that if an application is made for an order of sale more than one year after the bankrupt's estate vested in the trustee, the court shall assume that, unless the circumstances are exceptional, the interests of the bankrupt's creditors outweigh all other considerations. In applications for sale of the matrimonial home by a trustee in bankruptcy or by a bank as chargee, the interests of the creditor will generally prevail, unless there are exceptional circumstances (*Re Citro* [1990] 3 All ER 953, *Claughton* v *Charalambous* [1999] 1 FLR 740 and *Re Bremner* [1999] 1 FLR 912). **26.54**

In *Mountney* v *Treharne* [2002] EWCA 1174, [2002] 2 FLR 930 a husband declared himself voluntarily bankrupt during the period between the granting of a property adjustment order in the wife's favour and the 14-day time limit for the transfer under the terms of the order. No transfer documents had been signed. The Court of Appeal considered the important question of whether, and at which point, title passed to the wife. In upholding the wife's appeal, the Court of Appeal held that the spouse who receives the benefit of such an order **26.55** acquires an equitable interest at the point when the order becomes effective, namely on the grant of the decree absolute of divorce ('equity considers that as done that which ought to be done'). Hence, the trustee in bankruptcy took subject to the wife's equitable interest, and, on the facts of the case, received nothing. The case demonstrates the importance of applying for the decree absolute as soon after the making of the property adjustment order as possible (unless of course the decree absolute has already been granted) in circumstances where the transferring spouse's imminent bankruptcy is anticipated.

27

KEEPING UP WITH THE MORTGAGE OR RENT

A GENERAL

The importance of keeping up with the mortgage repayments or rent on the matrimonial **27.01** home in spite of the breakdown of the marriage need hardly be stressed. If arrears are allowed to accumulate, there is a danger that the mortgagee or landlord will take action which could ultimately lead to the parties losing their home.

Example Husband and wife are joint owners of the matrimonial home. There is a mortgage in favour of a building society. Repayments are £100 per month and have always been made by the husband as the wife is not working. The marriage fails and the husband leaves to live with another woman. He ceases to pay the mortgage instalments. The wife cannot pay the instalments herself as she has no income. No payments are made for six months. The building society becomes concerned and presses for payment. It threatens to bring proceedings for possession in order to sell the property if payments are not resumed together with some payment each month off the arrears.

B STEPS THAT CAN BE TAKEN

Contacting the mortgagee/landlord

Where the client is in difficulties with mortgage instalments or rent, it is often a good idea to **27.02** contact the mortgagee/landlord straight away to explain the position and to outline what the client proposes to do to alleviate it (for example, she may be intending to make application for maintenance from her husband or to seek state benefits). Provided that it appears that the problem is capable of solution within a reasonable period of time, most building societies and banks are prepared to be patient, as are some landlords.

Seeking financial help

State benefits

27.03 It is possible for rent or the interest repayments on a mortgage to be met by state benefits (see Chapter 38). The solicitor should consider whether his client is likely to be entitled to any benefit and, if so, advise her how to go about making a claim. The claim should be made as soon as possible—the situation will be harder to deal with if arrears have been allowed to build up.

27.04 Where mortgage interest is to be covered by state benefits, arrangements will have to be made in relation to the capital repayments. The mortgagee may be prepared to agree to these being suspended temporarily; if not, the client will have to scrimp and save on other outgoings in order to be able to discharge the payments.

Maintenance

27.05 An application for maintenance from the client's spouse should be considered. If the client is to continue to discharge the mortgage payments herself, she can ask the court to take this into account in fixing the amount of her maintenance. Applications for maintenance can be made in the family proceedings court under the Domestic Proceedings and Magistrates' Courts Act 1978 (see the OUP website at <www.oup.com/uk/booksites/law> where Chapter 33 of the sixth edition of this book—where this Act is discussed—is to be found) and in the county court under the Matrimonial Causes Act 1973 ancillary to proceedings for divorce, nullity, or judicial separation or under s. 27 (see Chapters 17 and following and 35).

Submitting to a possession action

27.06 The client may, in fact, be prepared to leave her home if she can be rehoused by the local authority. If she moves out voluntarily, she will have to take her normal place in the queue. If, on the other hand, she is turned out of the house as a result of a possession order made by the court, the council is more likely to rehouse her straight away. For this reason it may be necessary for the client to allow the mortgagee/landlord to take proceedings for possession and to submit to the making of a possession order.

C   SPECIAL PROVISIONS OF THE FAMILY LAW ACT 1996

Payment of other spouse/civil partner outgoings

27.07 Where a spouse/civil partner has home rights in relation to a dwelling-house or any part of it, any payment that that spouse makes towards the other spouse's liability for the rent, rates, or mortgage payments or other outgoings affecting the house is as good as if the other spouse had made the payment himself: s. 30(3).

Example Mr Simpkins is the tenant of a flat where he lives with his wife. The marriage breaks down and Mr Simpkins walks out and stops paying the rent. His wife pays the rent instead. Her payment is as good as payment from Mr Simpkins would have been. The landlord cannot refuse Mrs Simpkins' payments and use the tenant's non-payment of rent as the ground for possession proceedings.

It is only necessary to rely on s. 30(3) where the spouse is not herself a tenant or an owner with a right to tender payment.

Where a mortgagee takes action to enforce his security

Notice of enforcement action

Where a spouse has registered a Class F land charge or notice, a mortgagee bringing an action **27.08** for enforcement of his security must serve notice of action on that spouse if she is not a party to the action: s. 56(2).

Joinder of spouse as a party

A spouse who is enabled by s. 30(3) to meet the mortgagor's liabilities under the mortgage **27.09** (see paragraph 27.07 above) can apply to the court to be made a party to an action brought by the mortgagee to enforce his security and will be entitled to be a party if:

(a) she has applied to the court before the action is finally disposed of;
(b) the court sees no special reason against her being joined and is satisfied that she may be expected to make such payments or do such other things in or towards satisfaction of the mortgagor's liabilities or obligations as might affect the outcome of the proceedings: s. 55(3).

Example Mr Michaels is the sole owner of the matrimonial home which is subject to a mortgage in favour of a building society. He leaves his wife and goes abroad where he cannot be traced. He ceases to make any mortgage repayments. Although s. 30(3) enables his wife to make the payments, Mrs Michaels cannot afford to do so immediately after the separation as she is not working. She refuses to seek state benefits on principle. The building society is informed of the position and allows the arrears to mount for six months. Thereafter it presses for payment and ultimately takes proceedings for possession to enable it to exercise its power to sell the property to recoup the mortgage debt. Mrs Michaels has registered a Class F land charge and therefore is entitled to receive notice of the proceedings by virtue of s. 56(2). She may apply to the court to be joined as a party to the action. The court orders that she should be a party as she has just obtained a sufficiently well-paid job to enable her to meet the normal mortgage repayments and pay off a small amount from the arrears each month, in which circumstances the court would be unlikely to grant immediate possession.

Security of tenure with rented property

Under the Rent Act 1977 and the Housing Acts 1985 and 1988, a tenant's security of tenure **27.10** is dependent on his remaining in possession or occupation of the property. Section 30(4),

Family Law Act 1996 ('FLA 1996') ensures that security of tenure will not be prejudiced when the tenant moves out, provided his spouse continues to live in the property. Her possession or occupation will be treated as his, thus protecting not only his rights in relation to the home but also hers (which are dependent on his).

27.11   However, if the spouse who is the tenant actually surrenders the tenancy when he leaves, the remaining spouse will lose her home rights unless she has already registered them under s. 31, FLA 1996. If there has been no such registration of rights, the remaining spouse would appear to have no defence to possession proceedings instituted by the landlord: *Sanctuary Housing Association* v *Campbell* [1999] 2 FLR 383.

27.12   Where the spouses are joint tenants of the matrimonial home and one of them terminates the joint tenancy against the will of the other, the tenancy is nevertheless brought to an end: *Bater* v *Greenwich London Borough Council* [1999] 2 FLR 993; *Newlon Housing Trust* v *Alsulaimen* [1998] 2 FLR 690.

27.13   In any situation where the unilateral act of one joint tenant is capable in law of destroying the interests of both, the vulnerable tenant who would be prejudiced by such notice should seek from the other an undertaking not to serve notice prior to the court's determination of the issue. The undertaking should be served on the landlord as well as on the departing tenant. Where the tenant concerned is unwilling or unable to give an undertaking, an application could be made for an injunction, which would also be served on the landlord as well as on the departing tenant.

28

THE QUESTION OF WILLS

A CIVIL PARTNERSHIPS

The Civil Partnership Act 2004, sch. 4, provides that the position of civil partners and **28.01** spouses will be the same in respect of each other's estate. In summary:

(a) The provisions of the Wills Act 1837 ('WA 1837') are extended to civil partnerships. This means that a will is revoked upon the testator entering into a civil partnership. The same effects will flow from dissolution or nullity of the partnership as flow from divorce and nullity in respect of a marriage. The same rules as for married couples will apply in relation to witnesses to wills and as to the priority over children in distribution of the estate.

(b) A civil partner may obtain probate or letters of administration on the intestacy of their deceased partner and has priority over the public trustee.

(c) A civil partner will have the same rights and priority upon the intestacy of their deceased partner as a surviving spouse. This means that they will be entitled to personal chattels, £200,000, plus half of the residue absolutely; or, if the deceased left issue, then the surviving partner would be entitled to personal chattels, £125,000, plus a life interest in half the residue. The surviving partner would also have the same rights as a surviving spouse to capitalize any life interest and to acquire the family home.

(d) A civil partner will have the same rights under the Inheritance (Provision for Family and Dependants) Act 1975 as a surviving spouse. The quantum of such a claim is not limited to reasonable maintenance. The court must have regard to what financial provision would have been awarded upon a dissolution of the civil partnership. Cohabitation prior to the civil partnership ceremony is likely to be taken into account in determining the length of the partnership for this purpose (*CO v CO (Ancillary Relief: Pre-marriage Cohabitation* [2004] 1 FLR 1095). Furthermore, in relation to such claims:

   (i)   Former civil partners have the same rights as former spouses, which end upon a subsequent marriage or civil partnership.

   (ii) A child of the family of a civil partnership has the same rights as a child of a marriage.

   (iii) Same sex cohabitants have the same rights as heterosexual ones, so that they no longer have to show a dependency (*Ghaidan* v *Godin-Mendoza* [2004] 2 FLR 600). It is necessary to show at least two years' cohabitation up to the time of death.

(e) The proceeds of a life insurance policy for the benefit of a civil partner or the children will not form part of the estate (s. 70). Civil partners will be presumed to have an unlimited insurable interest in the life of each other (s. 253).

28.02   For the purposes of this chapter, any reference to 'spouse' or 'partner' will include 'civil partners'; any reference to 'marriage' will include 'civil partnerships'; any reference to 'divorce' and 'nullity' will include nullity and dissolution of civil partnerships.

B   THE NEED TO CONSIDER WHAT WILL HAPPEN ON CLIENT'S DEATH

28.03   When the solicitor is consulted by a client who is experiencing matrimonial difficulties or (in the case of the unmarried client) problems with her cohabitant, or problems with their civil partner, it is most important for the solicitor to consider with her what is to happen to her property should she die.

28.04   The first matter to investigate is what the present position would be were she to die today. If the client and her spouse/partner own land (for example, the home) as joint tenants, the spouse/partner would be entitled to the whole of the property on the client's death by virtue of the right of survivorship. In the case of a married client, the chances are that her spouse would also end up with a good deal of her remaining estate by virtue of her will if she has made one and otherwise by virtue of the intestacy provisions. What would happen to the balance of the estate in the case of a cohabitant would depend on whether she had made a will benefiting her partner. If so, the partner would clearly benefit in accordance with the terms of the will; if not, property would pass in accordance with the intestacy provisions under which the partner would have no entitlement.

Having ascertained what would happen to the client's property under the present arrange-   **28.05**
ments, the solicitor should find out whether this is what the client wants. Some people are
content for their spouse/cohabitant to continue to benefit after their death despite the
breakdown of the relationship, for example, for the sake of the children or because they have
no one else to whom they wish to leave their property. Others wish to take all possible steps
to deprive their partner of any benefit, for example, because they now wish to benefit a
new girlfriend/boyfriend or child or because they are embittered over the breakdown of the
marriage/relationship.

C THE EFFECT OF MARRIAGE ON A WILL

Before considering the effect of marital breakdown on existing testamentary documents, it is   **28.06**
important to realize the effect which marriage itself may have had on an earlier will. By s. 18,
WA 1837, a will is revoked by the marriage of the testator. This rule does not apply,
however, to invalidate dispositions in the will in exercise of a power of appointment (see
s. 18(2), unless the property appointed would, in default of appointment, pass to the testator's personal representative), or (more significantly) where it appears from a will that at the
time it was made the testator was expecting to be married to a particular person *and* that he
intended that the will should not be revoked by the marriage then again the rule does not
apply: s. 18(3), as applied to wills made on or after 1 January 1983.

D THE EFFECT OF DIVORCE, JUDICIAL SEPARATION, AND NULLITY ON SUCCESSION

Certain events, such as divorce, automatically affect existing wills and entitlement on intes-   **28.07**
tacy. The rules are set out in the following paragraphs and they should be borne in mind
when considering the position with the client.

The effect of divorce or nullity on a will

Section 18A, WA 1837 (as inserted by the Administration of Justice Act 1982 and amended by   **28.08**
s. 3, Law Reform (Succession) Act 1995) provides that, unless the contrary intention appears
in the will, the granting of a decree absolute of divorce or nullity will have the following
effects on the will of either spouse:

(a) Any appointment in the will of the testator's former spouse as executor or as executor
     and trustee of the will is ignored. Similarly, a testamentary provision conferring a power
     of appointment on a spouse is revoked on divorce or annulment of the marriage.
(b) The former spouse is treated as having died at the date of dissolution or annulment
     of the marriage so that any devise or bequest to the former spouse automatically
     lapses.

The property that would have passed to the former spouse will either become part of the residue and pass to whoever is entitled to the residuary estate or, if the gift to the former spouse is a residuary gift, will pass according to the intestacy provisions. If it is intended to rely simply on s. 18A, the solicitor must be careful to check with the client that the result will fit in with her wishes. It may be, for example, that she was originally very happy for the Society for the Assistance of Beleaguered Budgerigars to benefit from her residuary estate when it was likely to be in the region of £250. She is not likely to be anxious to endow the Society with her entire estate worth £50,000.

28.09 Note that divorce and nullity have no effect on the right of survivorship. Thus any property which, at the time of her death, the deceased still holds as a joint tenant with her former spouse will pass automatically to her former spouse by survivorship despite the termination of the marriage. This underlines the necessity to consider serving a notice of severance where a joint tenancy exists or may exist (see Chapter 26, paragraph 26.20).

28.10 Note also that a decree of judicial separation has no effect on a will.

The effect of divorce or nullity on intestacy

28.11 Where a marriage is void or has been annulled or dissolved by decree absolute of nullity or divorce, on the death intestate of either party to the marriage, the other party will have no right to any part of the estate under the intestacy provisions. This is because he or she no longer qualifies as a surviving spouse. However, the former spouse (who has not married someone else) may be able to make a claim for family provision against the estate pursuant to s. 1(1)(b), Inheritance (Provision for Family and Dependants) Act 1975.

The effect of judicial separation on intestacy

28.12 Whilst a decree of judicial separation is in force and the separation is continuing, if either party dies intestate his or her real and personal estate will devolve as if the other party had been dead s.18(2), Matrimonial Causes Act 1973).

E   STEPS TO BE TAKEN

28.13 In the light of the client's instructions, either or both of the following steps may be necessary:

(a)   service of notice of severance of joint tenancy (see Chapter 26, paragraph 26.20);

(b)   drafting of will/new will.

If the will/new will is drafted before a decree of divorce or nullity is granted and contains a provision benefiting the client's spouse or appointing him executor or executor and trustee, the solicitor should take care to make it clear in the will (if it be the case) that the provisions are intended to be effective even after divorce/nullity. If this is not done, s. 18A, WA 1837 will obviously nullify the provisions relating to the spouse.

F   INHERITANCE (PROVISION FOR FAMILY AND DEPENDANTS) ACT 1975

If the client's instructions are to take steps to deprive her spouse/cohabitant of substantial   **28.14**
benefit from her estate, she should be warned that, whatever steps are taken, her spouse/
cohabitant may ultimately be able to secure a share in her estate by means of an application
under the Inheritance (Provision for Family and Dependants) Act 1975. A spouse is a
favoured class of applicant under this jurisdiction as he can claim whatever is reasonable in
all the circumstances. A cohabitant's claim is much more tightly proscribed (see further
Chapter 40, paragraph 40.08).

Applications under the Act are made on the ground that the disposition of the deceased's   **28.15**
estate effected by her will or by the intestacy rules (or by a combination of both) is not such
as to make reasonable financial provision for the applicant. In some cases, the client may be
well advised, despite her feelings, to make some limited provision for her spouse herself in
her will in an attempt to rule out the possibility of him subsequently applying to the court
under the Act for provision. At least this way she may be able to dictate her own terms rather
than leaving the matter at large for the court to sort out after her death. The procedure for
applications under the Inheritance (Provision for Family and Dependants) Act 1975 is governed by the Civil Procedure Rules 1998 and therefore reference must be made to the Woolf
reforms when pursuing such an action.

Note that a former spouse may still apply under the 1975 Act, provided that he or she has   **28.16**
not remarried. However, it is possible to preclude such an application during the course of
ancillary relief proceedings (see Chapter 19, paragraph 19.29).

G   IMPORTANCE OF CONSIDERING SUCCESSION

The importance of considering succession can be illustrated by an example.   **28.17**

Example Mr and Mrs Heap are joint tenants of the matrimonial home 'Inglefield'. Mr Heap
makes a will leaving £50,000 to his wife and the residue of his estate (which he anticipates
will be small) to his old school. Mrs Heap does not make a will. There are no children.

The marriage runs into difficulties. Mrs Heap petitions for divorce but no decree has yet
been pronounced. If Mr Heap died today, his share in Inglefield would pass to Mrs Heap by
survivorship. The balance of his estate excluding Inglefield would be worth £25,000 and this
would pass to Mrs Heap by his will.

If Mrs Heap died today, her share in Inglefield would pass to Mr Heap by survivorship and
the rest of her estate (worth £10,000) would pass to him under the intestacy provisions.

If nothing is done to alter the present position, decree absolute of divorce will automatically produce the following results:

(a) On Mr Heap predeceasing Mrs Heap:
    (i)   his share in Inglefield will still pass to Mrs Heap by survivorship;
    (ii) the gift in the will to Mrs Heap will lapse and the balance of his estate (£25,000) will
          therefore pass to his old school.
(b) On Mrs Heap predeceasing Mr Heap:

(i)   her share in Inglefield will still pass to Mr Heap by survivorship;

(ii) the balance of her estate (£10,000) would still pass under the intestacy provisions but *not* to Mr Heap who would no longer qualify as a spouse. If she has a surviving parent or parents, they would be the ones to benefit. If not, other relatives would inherit her estate.

Neither Mr nor Mrs Heap wishes the other to benefit by his/her death before or after the divorce. Mr Heap wishes to leave a slightly larger sum to his old school and the balance of his estate to his girlfriend, Miss Maybury. Mrs Heap wishes to leave her estate to her sister. The following steps should be taken by their solicitors:

(a)   The joint tenancy in relation to Inglefield should be severed with the effect that, on the death of either party, his or her interest in the property will pass with his or her estate.

(b)   A new will should be made for Mr Heap.

(c)   A will should be made for Mrs Heap.

When the new wills are being drafted, each party's solicitor should consider with him or her whether a will leaving nothing to his or her spouse would be reasonable or whether it would be a good idea to make some limited provision for the spouse in an attempt to rule out the possibility of future litigation under the Inheritance (Provision for Family and Dependants) Act 1975. This consideration is likely to be more important for Mr Heap, who has a considerably larger estate than Mrs Heap.

If either party does decide to leave money or property to his or her spouse and the will is to become effective before decree absolute, care should be taken to express in the will the intention that the provision concerning the spouse will continue after the decree is granted.

H   APPOINTING A GUARDIAN FOR CHILDREN

28.18   The solicitor should consider with the client whether it is appropriate to make provision in the will for the appointment of a guardian for her minor children. Section 5, Children Act 1989 enables parents and guardians to appoint guardians to take their place after their death. Unless the child is living under a residence order with the parent who dies, the appointment will not take effect until there is no surviving parent with parental responsibility. Such appointments will be valid if made in writing, dated, and signed at the direction of the person making the appointment and in the presence of two witnesses. This is a departure from the old rules whereby such appointments were only valid if made by deed or will. For further discussion about guardianship, see Chapter 29, paragraph 29.86.

PART VII
CHILDREN

29

THE CHILDREN ACT 1989: GENERAL PRINCIPLES, PARENTAL RESPONSIBILITY ORDERS IN FAMILY PROCEEDINGS, SECTION 8 ORDERS, GUARDIANSHIP ORDERS AND FAMILY PROCEEDINGS, FINANCIAL PROVISION AND PROPERTY ADJUSTMENT FOR CHILDREN

A INTRODUCTION

The Children Act 1989: an overview

The Children Act 1989 ('CA 1989') came into force on 14 October 1991. **29.01**

The public law (e.g., care orders, supervision orders, emergency protection orders) and the **29.02**
private law (e.g., residence orders, contact orders, prohibited steps orders, specific issue
orders) relating to children are contained in the same statute. The Act provides a clear and
consistent code for the whole of child law. It also aims to protect families from unwarranted
state interference and to promote the basic principle that parents and local authorities
should be free to work together in 'voluntary partnership' for the benefit of the children
concerned.

The Private Law Programme

The Private Law Programme commenced in 2004 and contains best practice guidance for the **29.03**
conduct of private law cases in county courts and in the High Court. It was extended to
family proceedings courts as from January 2006. See further in Chapter 30, paragraph
30.09.

B GENERAL PRINCIPLES

There are certain general principles contained in the CA 1989 which apply both to private **29.04**
law and public law proceedings alike. Those principles will be set out in this chapter.

The paramountcy of welfare

Section 1(1), CA 1989 states that **29.05**

when a court determines any question with respect to:

(a)   the upbringing of a child; or

(b)   the administration of a child's property or the application of any income arising from it,

the child's welfare shall be the court's paramount consideration.

29.06   The welfare principle will not apply to the determination of other questions which are outside the ambit of s. 1(1) even though they indirectly affect the child e.g., whether the court should make an occupation order under Part IV, Family Law Act 1996 ('FLA 1996'): see *Richards* v *Richards* [1984] AC 174, *Gibson* v *Austin* [1992] 2 FLR 437, *G* v *J (Ouster Order)* [1993] 1 FLR 1008; or whether blood tests should be taken in an attempt to ascertain paternity: *S* v *McC* [1972] AC 24. Maintenance is excluded from the definition of 'upbringing' in the Act (see s. 105(1)) and orders relating to maintenance after divorce are not subject to the welfare test in s. 1(1) but to the requirement in s. 25(1) of the Matrimonial Causes Act 1973 to give 'first consideration' to the welfare of the child.

29.07   '*Child*' is defined as anyone under the age of 18 (s. 105, CA 1989), but the court's power to make section 8 orders is restricted to children under 16 unless the case is exceptional (s. 9(7), CA 1989). Likewise, the court may not make a care or supervision order in respect of a child who has reached the age of 17 (or 16 if the child is married): s. 31(3), CA 1989.

29.08   '*Paramount*' means that 'the welfare of the child should come before and above any other consideration in deciding whether to make an order': Hansard, HL, vol. 502, col. 1167. There is no provision which indicates how the court should approach cases involving more than one child where the welfare of each conflicts. However, in *Birmingham City Council* v *H (No. 3)* [1994] 1 FLR 224 the House of Lords considered a case in which the child who was the subject of care proceedings was a baby but the mother was herself under the age of 18. They held that the question which had to be determined was as to the upbringing of the child in care and it was the welfare of that child which must be the court's paramount consideration. The fact that the parent is also a child does not mean that both the parent's and the child's welfare are paramount and that each has to be balanced against the other, since no question was to be determined as to the parent's upbringing.

29.09   '*Welfare*' is not defined by the CA 1989. However, the checklist set out in s. 1(3) indicates some of the issues which might be relevant.

29.10   Note that the Human Rights Act 1998 ('HRA 1998') came into force on 2 October 2000 and it brings with it some tension between the paramountcy of welfare principle in s. 1(1), CA 1989 and the way the interests of children are taken into account under the principles set out in the European Convention for the Protection of Human Rights and Fundamental Freedoms.

29.11   There is potential tension between the way in which the interests of the child concerned in private law or public law proceedings are treated under domestic law when compared with the way they are treated under the Convention. Section 1(1), CA 1989 states that when the court determines any question with respect to the upbringing of a child or the administration of his property 'the child's welfare shall be the court's paramount consideration'. By contrast, Art. 8 of the Convention makes it clear that the starting point when considering decisions which affect the private and family lives of individuals is that all family members have a right to respect for their private and family life; the interests of children are not said to be paramount. However, European case law indicates that the ECHR is gradually moving towards the paramountcy principle when deciding cases which affect the upbringing of children (*Hoppe* v *Germany* [2003] 1 FLR 384; *Yousef* v *The Netherlands* [2003] 1 FLR 210; *CF* v *Secretary of State for the Home Department* [2004] 2 FLR 517).

The statutory checklist

Section 1(3), CA 1989 requires the court to have regard to a 'statutory checklist' of **29.12** factors whenever it is considering the following matters:

(a) whether to make, vary, or discharge a s. 8 order, and the making, variation or discharge of the order is opposed by any party to the proceedings: s. 1(4)(a); or

(b) whether to make, vary, or discharge a special guardianship order or an order under Part IV of the CA 1989, i.e., a care or supervision order: s. 1(4)(b). (NB: the use of the list is not mandatory where the court is considering an emergency protection order.)

There would be nothing to prevent a court from referring to the statutory checklist for guidance in any other type of case. Its use is only *mandatory* for the categories of proceedings in (a) and (b) above.

The checklist consists of the following factors, which are not listed by the statute in any **29.13** order of importance:

(a) the ascertainable wishes and feelings of the child concerned (in the light of his age and understanding);

(b) his physical, emotional, and educational needs;

(c) the likely effect on him of any change in his circumstances;

(d) his age, sex, background, and any characteristics of his which the court considers relevant;

(e) any harm which he has suffered or is at risk of suffering;

(f) how capable each of his parents, and any other person in relation to whom the court considers the question to be relevant, is of meeting his needs;

(g) the range of powers available to the court under the CA 1989 in the proceedings in question.

The list aims to guide the court and to achieve consistency across the country as well as informing legal advisers and helping parties to concentrate on the issues that affect their children. In *B* v *B (Residence Order: Reasons for Decision)* [1997] 2 FLR 602, the Court of Appeal reminded judges of the importance of taking the welfare checklist fully into account, commenting that it ensured that all relevant matters were considered and that it could be useful in helping to clarify the reasons for the decision.

The wishes and feelings of the child (s. 1(3)(a))

Where a child expresses a wish to reside with a particular parent or to have contact with a **29.14** parent then the court must give due weight to that factor. The court will consider the age and maturity of the child when deciding how much weight to attach to such wishes. The court will be aware that the child is likely to be influenced, consciously or not, by the views of the parent with whom he resides. He may be afraid to voice (or even to form) his own opinion for fear of hurting one or the other parent. Even if he obviously does have strong wishes of his own, they may not be in his own interests.

29.15 The child's wishes may become known to the court in a variety of ways (for example, by the parents giving evidence of what he has said to them). The best evidence of a child's wishes is through the welfare report and from the judge's personal assessment of the child if he meets him. The children and family reporter will normally mention in his report anything that the child has said to him about his wishes; with older children, he may actually ask the child what he feels about the case.

29.16 Examples of cases in which an issue arose as to the weight to be attached to the wishes and views of the children are as follows:

   (a) In *Re S (Contact: Children's Views)* [2002] 1 FLR 1156, the court paid due regard to the clear wishes and feelings of a 16 and a 14-year-old, emphasizing that if young people are to be brought up to respect the law, the law has to respect them and their wishes, even to the extent of allowing them, as occasionally they may do, to make mistakes.

   (b) In *Re F (Minors) (Denial of Contact)* [1993] 2 FLR 677, the judge rightly took into account the views of the two boys aged 12 and 9 when deciding to refuse to make a contact order in favour of the father who had decided that he was in effect a woman in a man's body.

   (c) In *Re M (Contact: Welfare Test)* [1995] 1 FLR 274, children aged 7 and 8 expressed the clear view that they did not want to have contact with their mother. The Court of Appeal held that contact would be refused since it would be harmful if against their wishes.

   (d) In *Re S (Change of Surname)* [1999] 1 FLR 672, the two girls, now aged 15 and 16, were made subject to a care order as a result of the father's abuse of the older girl and the risk he posed to the younger girl. Both girls applied for leave to change their surname to that of their mother. The older girl was successful at first instance and the younger girl (who was assessed as *Gillick* competent) was successful after the refusal of the first instance court was overturned on appeal.

29.17 The HRA 1998 implements the European Convention for the Protection of Human Rights and Fundamental Freedoms. Article 6 of the Convention guarantees, among other things, the right to a fair hearing, including the right of access to a court. This may give scope for legal argument to the effect that children should have wider rights to representation in cases that affect them.

29.18 The ECHR has interpreted Art. 6 of the Convention as conferring an effective right of access to a court in the determination of civil rights and obligations (*Golder* v *UK* (1975) 1 EHRR 524, paras. 35 and 36). In our domestic law there are restrictions on the right of access to the court in certain circumstances, for example, where defined categories of applicants must seek permission of the court before bringing proceedings in private or public law child cases: ss. 10 and 34, CA 1989. Article 6 may serve to give children the right to be more widely represented in court proceedings which affect them than is currently the case under s. 10(8), CA 1989. Whilst there is a substantial body of opinion to the effect that it may not be a good idea to allow children to insist on being heard in court and being able to listen to the evidence, it is possible that arguments to the contrary may be made under Art. 6.

29.19 **Should the judge see the child in private?** A judge's decision whether or not personally to interview a child is entirely a matter for the exercise of his judicial discretion. Whether he will do so will depend on his own practice and, in particular, on the age of the child. It is highly unlikely that a judge will see a child of less than eight. The older the child, the more likely it is that the judge will see him and the more likely it is that his wishes will be given some weight. For example, in *Re R (A Minor)* [1993] 2 FLR 163, the Court of Appeal held that the judge could not be criticized for deciding not to interview a 10-year-old boy, particularly where the judge was aware of the strong views held by the boy as revealed in the children and family reporter's report. Where the judge does see the child it is preferable for the meeting to take place at the end of the evidence and before closing speeches, so that the judge has a clear picture of the case before seeing the child: *B v B (Minors) (Interviews and Listing Arrangements)* [1994] 2 FLR 489. It is becoming more common for judges to see children in such cases (*Mabon v Mabon* [2005] 2 FLR 1011). See also the article by DJ Crichton 'Listening to Children' [2006] Fam Law 849.

It is undesirable for the judge to give a promise to the child not to disclose anything that is **29.20** discussed between them. The judge must inform all the parties in the proceedings of any matter which a child might tell him which might influence his judgment or decision. He must give the parties the opportunity to deal with that as a matter of justice. Whatever happens, it must be made clear to the child that he is not responsible for the outcome of the case, that the court alone will decide what must be done to protect the welfare of the child and that it will not always be possible to do what the child wishes: *B v B* (above).

Should magistrates see the child in private?   The position as to whether or not it is desir- **29.21** able for magistrates to see a child privately is unclear. There is no statutory provision in the CA 1989 or the Family Proceedings Rules 1991 ('FPR 1991') or the Family Proceedings Courts (Children Act 1989) Rules 1991 ('FPC(CA 1989)R 1991') which enables any court to see children in private. In the High Court and county courts it is recognized by case law and practice that a judge may exercise his discretion to see a child in private. No such authority existed in relation to magistrates prior to the implementation of the CA 1989.

Where a children's guardian acts for the child or a children and family reporter is requested **29.22** to supply a report dealing, *inter alia*, with the wishes of the child, it should not be necessary, and it is not in general desirable for the magistrates to see the child: *Re M (A Minor) (Justices' Discretion)* [1993] 2 FLR 706; *Re W (A Minor) (Contact)* [1994] 1 FLR 843. It should only be in rare and exceptional cases where a guardian or children and family reporter is involved that the justices should themselves see the children. Where justices do see a child in private it is crucial that they should make known to the parties any matter that the child has told them which may affect their own views or which may influence the decision that they are likely to reach.

The ability of a child to participate as a party   The law in relation to the weight to be **29.23** attached to the wishes of children has been further developed in a number of interesting cases in which the court has considered whether or not children have 'sufficient understanding' to take part in family proceedings without a next friend (where the child is the plaintiff) or guardian ad litem (where the child is a defendant). The court has the ultimate right to decide whether a child has the necessary ability to instruct his solicitor: *Re S (A Minor) (Independent Representation)* [1993] 2 FLR 437; *Re CT (A Minor) (Wardship: Representation)* [1993] 2 FLR 278. In *Mabon v Mabon* [2005] 2 FLR 1011, the Court of Appeal recognized the growing acknowledgement of the autonomy and consequential rights of children to participate in decision-making processes that fundamentally affect their family life. However, the rules differ depending on whether the case involves public law or private law proceedings.

29.24 The HRA 1998 implements the European Convention for the Protection of Human Rights and Fundamental Freedoms. Article 6 of the Convention guarantees, among other things, the right to a fair hearing, including the right of access to a court. This may give scope for legal argument to the effect that children should have wider rights to representation in cases that affect them: *Re H (Contact Order) (No. 2)* [2001] 1 FLR 1028. For further discussion of this issue, see paragraph 29.14 (above).

(a) *Public law proceedings*: In public law proceedings FPR 1991, rr. 4.11 and 4.12 provide for the child to part company with his guardian in certain circumstances. In *Re H (A Minor) (Care Proceedings: Child's Wishes)* [1993] 1 FLR 440 a boy aged 15 years eight months had sufficient understanding to instruct his own solicitor in care proceedings where he disagreed with the proposals being put forward on his behalf by his guardian. Thorpe J held that in those circumstances the solicitor instructed by the guardian should have put forward the instructions given to him by the boy rather than those given to him by the children's guardian.

In *Re M (Minors) (Care Proceedings: Child's Wishes)* [1994] 1 FLR 749 the wishes of a 12-year-old boy conflicted with the views of his guardian and he was separately represented. However, the guardian had taken no steps to seek directions or the leave of the court to secure separate representation for himself. Wall J held that it was important that the guardian should inform the court where it appeared to him that the child was instructing his own solicitor direct, or that he intended to conduct or was capable of conducting the proceedings on his own behalf. The involvement of the court was important because there might be an issue about the capacity of the child to give coherent instructions which should be resolved by the court.

(b) *Private law proceedings*: In private law proceedings, FPR 1991, r. 9.2A provides for minors in certain circumstances to begin or prosecute proceedings without a next friend or guardian ad litem, and for a minor to seek leave to dispense with his next friend or guardian ad litem in existing proceedings. In *Re S (A Minor) (Independent Representation)* [1993] 2 FLR 437 an 11-year-old boy lacked sufficient understanding to participate as a party in emotionally complex and highly fraught proceedings in which his parents each sought a residence order in respect of him. In *Re CT (A Minor) (Wardship: Representation)* (above) the court held that a girl aged 13½ had sufficient understanding to apply for a residence order to enable her to live with her aunt and grandparents rather than with foster parents. In *Re H (A Minor) (Role of Official Solicitor)* [1993] 2 FLR 552 a 15-year-old boy had sufficient understanding to participate as a party in wardship proceedings in which he wished to resist an application made by his parents for him to live with them. Even where a child has sufficient understanding to instruct a solicitor independently, it is a matter of discretion for the judge as to whether or not to allow the child to become a party to proceedings: *Re H (Residence Order: Child's Application for Leave)* [2000] 1 FLR 780—where a 12-year-old boy was refused leave to become a party to residence order proceedings between his parents; his interests would be sufficiently taken into account without the need to make him a party. In *Mabon* v *Mabon* (above) three boys aged 17, 15, and 13 were granted separate representation in residence proceedings between their parents.

The FPR 1991, r. 9.5, provides for the appointment of a CAFCASS officer, the Official Solicitor, or 'some other proper person' by the court to be the children's guardian ad litem if it appears to the court that the child ought to be separately represented. See *CAFCASS and the National Assembly of Wales Practice Note (Appointment of Guardians in Private Law Proceedings)* [2006] 2 FLR 143.

The Adoption and Children Act 2002 ('ACA 2002'), s. 122 inserted into s. 41(a), CA 1989 a new sub-section (6A) so as to include within the category of proceedings which may be 'specified for the time being . . . by rules of court' (i.e., proceedings in which the court must appoint a guardian for the child unless satisfied that it is not necessary to do so in order to safeguard his interests) any proceedings for the making, varying, or discharging of an order under s. 8, CA 1989 (i.e., residence, contact, specific issue, and prohibited steps orders). This potential to widen the definition of 'specified proceedings' reflects the growing pressure for the appointment of children's guardians in certain private law children cases, for example bitterly contested residence or contact disputes, where children frequently have particular interests and standpoints which do not coincide with or cannot be adequately represented by the parents (*Re H (Contact Order) (No. 2)* [2002] 1 FLR 22). Although the court already has power (see above) to appoint a children's guardian in such cases, the new provisions would enshrine the power in statute rather than merely in statutory instrument.

The child's physical, emotional, and educational needs (s. 1(3)(b))

29.25 The fact that one parent has greater material prosperity or offers more pleasant surroundings than the other carries very little weight in a dispute as to where a child is to live. In any event, the courts are often able to go some way towards equalizing the differences between parents in this respect by making a maintenance order in favour of the carer parent or, where there is a decree of divorce, nullity, or judicial separation, by means of ancillary relief orders.

29.26 If, however, there is evidence that the accommodation offered by a parent is undesirable in some way, this will have a bearing on the decision as to where the child lives. The court needs to know if the accommodation is cramped, dirty, in a bad area, etc. This information will be provided by the welfare report although both parents are also likely to have some comments to make on the question when giving evidence. Naturally, the court will be reluctant to entrust the care of a child to a parent who is presently in unsatisfactory accommodation and has no definite plans about obtaining something better.

29.27 Another factor that will be taken into account is whether a move is proposed in the foreseeable future. Even if the accommodation presently offered is acceptable and there is no doubt that the parent will replace it with something of equal standard, the court may hesitate before transferring the care of the children to that parent if he is shortly to move areas and the children will therefore have the upheaval of changing schools, making new friends, etc. all over again. Where a move is likely in the foreseeable future, the parent concerned should do his best to provide the court with information about his proposals and should make sure that he investigates the sort of property he could afford in the new area, the schools available, etc. If he is awaiting council accommodation, he should be in a position to tell the court how he is placed on the waiting list (preferably by providing a letter from the council).

29.28   What is likely to be more important than accommodation is the standard of day-to-day care the parents offer. It is rare that one finds a parent against whom no criticism can be levelled. The court will not therefore go into all the minor grumbles that one parent has about the other's care of the children (for example, they do not go to bed until 8 o'clock and they should be in bed at 7, or they are allowed to get down from the meal-table before everyone has finished). However, if there is evidence, for example, that the children are often dirty, or hungry, or unsupervised, or that the parent does not or cannot exercise discipline, this will be relevant to the issue as to where the child is to live.

29.29   Another factor which the court will consider is the need of a child for regular medical treatment. It may be that one of the parents lives in an area where the provision of treatment is significantly better. In those circumstances the 'physical needs' of the child might be a deciding factor in determining where the child is to live. Where the child has special needs (for example, because of a physical or learning disability), the court will take this into account and will look to see who is best equipped to deal with the child in terms of accommodation, experience, patience, motivation, and so forth.

29.30   In considering the child's emotional needs the court will place weight upon the closeness of the child's ties with one or other of his parents, or with his brothers and sisters, and the trauma consequent upon a breaking of those ties. The court is reluctant to split brothers and sisters: *Re P (Custody of Children: Split Custody Order)* [1991] 1 FLR 337. However, there are, very occasionally, special cases where such an order is justified: see, for example, *B v B (Residence Order: Restricting Applications)* [1997] 1 FLR 139.

Example Gemma is 7 and her brother, Adam, is 15. The children have never been close in view of the difference in their ages and they have grown further apart since Adam went away to school two years ago. Adam has expressed the view that he wants to live with his father and Gemma has told the children and family reporter that she wants to live with her mother. The court feels that the circumstances justify making a residence order in respect of Gemma in favour of her mother and a residence order in respect of Adam in favour of his father, particularly since both parents envisage that there should be generous contact arrangements.

There is no general rule that a mother should have the children living with her (see *Re A (A Minor) (Custody)* [1991] 2 FLR 394 and *Re S (A Minor) (Custody)* [1991] 2 FLR 388). However, in practice, a mother does have a better chance than a father of obtaining a residence order, particularly in respect of young children and babies: *Re W (Residence)* [1999] 2 FLR 390; *Re W (A Minor) (Residence Order)* [1992] 2 FLR 332.

29.31   Where one parent (usually the father) is working and the other is not, the parent who can be at home full-time for the children has a considerable advantage. This is especially the case where the children are below school age. As they get older and spend time at school and with their own friends, the question of work becomes less decisive provided the arrangements proposed by the working parent for after school, school holidays, and illnesses are satisfactory.

29.32   Sometimes the father proposes to give up work or to remain unemployed in order to look after the children. The fact that he will be voluntarily unemployed and relying on the state for income is a factor to be taken into consideration in a dispute as to where the child should live. However, it is not sufficient on its own to justify the court in refusing to grant him a residence order: *B v B (Custody)* [1985] Fam Law 29.

In the past there have been few cases where the *educational* needs of the child have proved **29.33** decisive. In its widest sense 'educational needs' could cover almost anything to do with the upbringing of the child. However, education in the sense of 'schooling' may still be a significant factor, particularly if one parent is moving away from the area at a time which is especially important (for example, when the child is just about to take his GCSEs). In those circumstances the parent who will continue to live in proximity to the child's current school may well be at an advantage in any dispute over residence. The younger the child is the less weight is likely to be attached to a temporary disruption of his schooling whilst he moves from his old home to the new one. If the child needs a special school for some reason then this will be an important factor, whatever the age of the child.

The likely effect on the child of a change in circumstances (s. 1(3)(c))

The court is always very reluctant to remove a child from his present home unless there is a **29.34** strong reason to do so. It follows that the parent who is looking after the child at the time of a dispute as to where the child is to live starts with a considerable advantage over anyone else. The longer that situation continues, the greater the advantage will become. This is commonly referred to as the 'status quo' argument. For example, faced with two parents of equal merit, one of whom has been caring for the child for a considerable time already, the court will almost inevitably grant a residence order to that parent.

The child's age, sex, background, and any relevant characteristics (s. 1(3)(d))

The *age* of a child will often be an important factor in deciding what is in his best interests. **29.35** For example, a young baby's needs will usually be best satisfied by living with his mother, whereas a 15-year-old will generally be considered sufficiently mature to make up his own mind as to where he would like to live: *Re W (A Minor) (Residence Order)* (above). The age and maturity of the child will be important when the court decides what weight to attach to the child's wishes, as already discussed in paragraph 29.14 above.

The *sex* of the child is another factor to be placed in the balance. For example, importance is **29.36** often attached to the need of a teenage girl for the assistance of her mother whilst negotiating the years of puberty.

The child's *background* can cover a multitude of different factors, for example, his religious **29.37** upbringing, his family environment, and so forth.

Likewise, the child's relevant characteristics could cover a broad spectrum of matters, for **29.38** example, a disability or a severe illness. It could also cover religious, sporting, or intellectual factors.

Where the child's parents have a different culture, the court may be asked to take into **29.39** account the attitudes and habits prevalent in that culture in deciding with whom the child is to live.

Example Mother and father are both Muslims. There are two children, a boy aged 12 and a girl aged 3. The mother seeks a residence order in respect of both children and the father of the boy only. There is evidence on behalf of the mother that in the parties' Muslim community a mother is ostracized if she does not obtain the care of all her children. The court feels that the mother must have a residence order in respect of the little girl. Although, in the particular circumstances of the case, the judge is prepared to contemplate splitting the children, he takes into account that both children will be affected if their mother is ostracized and decides that both children should live with her.

Where a child is of mixed race, the court will take into account the differences between the parents' cultures and look to see how the child has been brought up so far. If he has been brought up, for example, in the mother's English way of life, the court will be reluctant to grant a residence order to the father who is now living the Indian way of life in an Indian community. However, the court will be inclined to require generous contact in such cases in order that the child should be able to maintain his links with the cultures of both parents.

29.40   Disputes over the care of children do not often centre around the child's religious upbringing these days. However, from time to time a parent is particularly concerned about the child's religious welfare and argues that it is necessary for him to have a residence order in order that he can be responsible for the child's proper religious education. Whilst the court will take into account the parent's views, it is unlikely that consideration of religion will determine the outcome of the case.

Example Mr Harris is a Catholic and his wife is an Anglican. They have two children who have been brought up in the Catholic faith. They are now three and five. The parties separate and the children live with Mrs Harris. Mr Harris does not question the fact that they are very happy with her and she cares for them satisfactorily. However, he is concerned that Mrs Harris and the children do not attend the Catholic church. On the few occasions when Mrs Harris has been to church since the separation, she and the children have attended the local Church of England. She envisages that the children should attend Sunday School there and, in due course be confirmed into the Church of England. Mr Harris seeks a residence order in order that he can bring up the children as Catholics. The court refuses his application. However, Mr Harris could ask the court to make a specific issue order as to the religious education of the children and, if the court orders that the children should receive Catholic religious instruction, Mrs Harris would have to comply with this.

If the child is old enough (see paragraph 29.14), the court can consider his wishes as to religion.

29.41   The court can use contact arrangements to ensure that the child benefits from the religions of both parents. For example, if the court grants a residence order to a parent who is a Jehovah's Witness and refuses to celebrate Christmas, it can order that the other parent (a Methodist) have contact over the Christmas period so that the child can enjoy some of the Christmas festivities and services with him.

Any harm which the child has suffered or is at risk of suffering (s. 1(3)(e))

29.42   The word 'harm' is a deliberately wide-ranging term. It covers both physical injury and psychological trauma. The ACA 2002 has extended the meaning of 'harm' in the CA 1989, s. 31(9), to include, for example, impairment suffered by hearing or seeing the ill-treatment of another.

How capable are the parents and any other relevant person of meeting the child's needs? (s. 1(3)(f))

The court will have to assess the capability for child care of the persons who apply to look **29.43** after children. If the dispute is between two parents who are equally committed and able to care for the child then the deciding factor may be that one works full-time whereas the other is available all day.

It goes without saying that if a parent has ill-treated the child in the past, this will be a very **29.44** important factor in the dispute as to with whom the child should live. His claim will also be prejudiced if he has ill-treated another child.

Other matters that may be taken into account include: **29.45**

(a) *The sexual proclivities of a parent*—the court will take into account the fact that the mother is a lesbian or the father a homosexual if this is likely to affect the children.

(b) *The criminal record/criminal conduct of a parent*—to what extent criminal conduct will affect the outcome of a dispute over the care of a child depends very much on the particular circumstances of the case. If both parents have been regularly involved in crime, it is unlikely that the application of either will be affected by this factor (although it must be remembered that the court does have power under s. 37(1), CA 1989, to order the local authority to look into the circumstances of the family to ascertain whether the local authority wishes to apply for a care or supervision order where the court feels that it is undesirable for him to be in the care of either parent or any other individual). On the other hand, if one parent is a law-abiding citizen and the other has a criminal record or is known to commit criminal offences, this will prejudice that parent's application for the care of the child. The court will be particularly reluctant to place the child in an environment where he will be subjected to bad influences in his day-to-day life (for example, where there is evidence that a parent takes drugs, regularly commits offences of dishonesty, etc.). Furthermore, the court will have to take account of the fact that a parent who commits criminal offences jeopardizes the stability of the home he offers in that he is at risk of being imprisoned, in which case other arrangements would have to be made for the care of his child.

(c) *Mental and physical illness*—the mental illness of a parent is relevant to a dispute over the care of a child. However, whether it will have any bearing on the outcome of the case depends on the nature of the mental illness. If there is evidence that the illness causes the parent concerned to behave in a way that may be harmful to the children's physical or mental state, or if the parent is likely to need regular in-patient treatment in hospital for the condition, obviously this will be an important consideration. If the question of mental illness is raised and the parent concerned feels that he or she is, in fact, perfectly well or has been treated successfully, it would be advisable to obtain medical evidence to this effect. Physical illness will only have a bearing on the case if it prevents the parent from looking after the children properly, for example because he or she is bed-ridden or disabled or has to return for prolonged stays in hospital.

(d) *Religious views*—the religious views of a parent are rarely of much importance in a case relating to the care of children. However, the court is likely to be reluctant to grant the care of a child to a parent who belongs to an extreme religious sect if there is evidence that the influence of this sect may be harmful to the child. It is worth bearing in mind that the court has wide powers to attach conditions to s. 8 orders and it may be possible in this way to ensure that the child is not exposed to harmful aspects of the parent's faith. For example, when granting a residence order to a parent who belongs to a sect that is against blood transfusions, the court may be able to impose a condition that the child should be allowed to have a transfusion if it becomes necessary for his health or life.

29.46 The court is also enjoined to consider the capability 'of any other person in relation to whom the court considers the question to be relevant'. This would include, for example, the new partner of one of the spouses, the child's grandparents or other members of the child's family, child minders, nannies, and nurseries.

29.47 Not infrequently the child will be in regular contact with someone other than the parent with care of the child. For example, either parent may be sharing accommodation with relatives for the foreseeable future, or may propose that the child is cared for by a nanny or by a relative whilst he is out at work, or may have formed a relationship with a new partner or intend to remarry. In these circumstances it is most important that the court should be informed about anyone else who will be in regular contact with the child and should hear oral evidence from anyone who will be closely involved with the care of the child as their personality, character and so on will have a bearing on the outcome of the case.

Example 1 Both parents work. The mother proposes that the child should be cared for while she is at work by her nanny who has been looking after her for six months. The father proposes that his mother should look after the child while he is at work. The court will need to hear oral evidence from both the nanny and the grandmother.

Example 2 After the parties separate, the mother returns to live with her own father and mother. She is available full-time to look after the child. However, she does not dispute that of her three brothers who also live in the family home, two are regularly in trouble with the police and one is a glue-sniffer. The father lives with his sister who has two young children and proposes that, while he is at work, his sister will look after the children. The court hears from the mother and her own father and from the father and his sister. A residence order is awarded to the father in view of the undesirable family circumstances of the mother.

The range of powers available to the court (s. 1(3)(g))

29.48 It is of particular importance for the practitioner to note the factor in s. 1(3)(g) which requires the court to have regard to the range of powers available to it in the relevant proceedings. Thus the court is able to choose the appropriate order for a case, even where nobody has made an application for that particular order. It allows the court to direct matters to a greater extent than it was able to do under the old law. For example, the court can grant *anyone* a s. 8 order, even without a formal application having been made to the court: s. 10(1)(b), CA 1989; this might happen, for example, where it becomes clear in the course of a hearing that a grandparent, rather than either of the parents, would be the most appropriate person to care for the child whose residence is in dispute: *Re J (Leave to Issue Application for Residence Order)* [2003] 1 FLR 114. Another example might arise where a parent makes an application for a residence order but during the course of the hearing the court considers that a care or supervision order may be appropriate. In that situation the court has power to adjourn the case and to direct the local authority to investigate the circumstances of the child with a view to deciding whether it would be appropriate for them to apply for an order: s. 37(1), CA 1989.

Preventing further applications under s. 91(14)

The court also has power to prevent further applications being made to the court with-**29.49** out leave for any type of order under the CA 1989, for example, for parental responsibility (s. 4), guardianship (s. 5), contact, residence, specific issue, and prohibited steps (s. 8).

Initially s. 91(14) was used mainly to deal with those cases where applications have been **29.50** made too frequently or where the previous applications were vexatious or frivolous, and the parties, including the children, are seen to be suffering or likely to suffer if such applications are allowed to continue. However, there is now emerging a new category of cases to which s. 91(14) may apply. In *C v W (Contact: Leave to Apply)* [1999] 1 FLR 916, a s. 91(14) restriction was imposed upon a parent who could not be described as a vexatious or obsessive litigant; in that case, it was the father's 'complete disregard' for the requirements of the court and for the welfare of his child which made the court conclude that the restriction was appropriate. In *Re M (Section 91(14) Order)* [1999] 2 FLR 553, the mother's children were in care with no prospect of rehabilitation to her, but due to the delay by the local authority in formulating a long-term plan for the children she had had a high level of contact with them. Once the local authority had formulated a plan then it was necessary to reduce the level of contact and the court imposed a s. 91(14) restriction for a period of 12 months in order to give the children time to settle in their new home and to give the mother time to accept the situation. Helpful guidelines dealing with the use of s. 91(14) are to be found in *Re P (S. 91(14) Guidelines) (Residence and Religious Heritage)* [1999] 2 FLR 573, as follows:

(a) Section 91(14) is to be read in conjunction with s. 1(1) (the paramountcy of the welfare of the child).

(b) The court's power under s. 91(14) is an exercise of its discretion.

(c) The use of s. 91(14) amounts to a significant statutory intrusion into a party's rights to bring proceedings before the court.

(d) The power must be used carefully and sparingly and should be the exception rather than the rule.

(e) Section 91(14) is a useful weapon of last resort in cases of repeated and unreasonable applications.

(f) In exceptional circumstances the court could use s. 91(14) in other sorts of cases to those in (e) (above) provided there is clear evidence of need and the welfare of the child demands it.

(g) In cases under (f) (above) the court must be satisfied that:
   (i) the facts go beyond the normal settling-in time and temporary hostility that can follow where a regime has been ordered by the court; and
   (ii) there is a serious risk that without a s. 91(14) restriction the child or his primary carers will be subject to strain.

(h) The court can impose a s. 91(14) restriction of its own motion, provided that the parties have been given an opportunity to be heard.

(i) A s. 91(14) restriction can be imposed without limit of time (see also *Re B (Section 91(14) Order: Duration)* [2004] 1 FLR 871).

(j)   The court should specify the extent of the restrictions and the type of application to be restrained as well as the duration of the order. The degree of restriction should be proportionate to the harm that it is intended to avoid (see also *Re G (Contempt: Committal)* [2003] 2 FLR 58).

(k)   It is undesirable to make an order without notice first having been given to the other side (i.e., *ex parte*) unless there are exceptional circumstances.

Butler-Sloss LJ also expressed the view that s. 91(14) did not infringe the HRA 1998 and Art. 6(1) of the European Convention for the Protection of Human Rights and Fundamental Freedoms since it did not deny access to the court, but merely places a preliminary hurdle in the way of a party seeking to institute proceedings. Therefore, it is unlikely that these guidelines will be successfully challenged under Art. 6 of the Convention.

Lifting the s. 91(14) bar on future applications

29.51   When the court considers an application for leave to lift a bar imposed under s. 91(14) then the test to be applied when considering whether such leave should be granted is simply:

(a)   does the application demonstrate that there is any need for renewed judicial investigation?

(b)   if 'yes', then leave should be granted.

The court considers the statements supporting the application and the contents of any court welfare officer's report and in appropriate cases the application may be determined at a directions appointment if these statements etc. indicate that the application should go no further: *Re A (Application for Leave)* [1998] 1 FLR 1. Wherever possible, all interested parties should receive notice of such hearings so that the court can consider representations from all of them when considering the application. Such orders should not be made against a litigant in person at short notice unless the circumstances are exceptional: *Re C (Prohibition on Further Applications)* [2002] 1 FLR 1136.

Presumption of no order

29.52   Section 1(5), CA 1989 provides that 'where a court is considering whether or not to make one or more orders under this Act with respect to a child, it shall not make the order or any of the orders unless it considers that doing so would be better for the child than making no order at all.'

29.53   The importance of this principle to the practitioner cannot be too greatly stressed. Increasingly, the courts are showing a tendency, where parties meet at court and reach a compromise in what was until then a dispute about their children, to make no order at all. If the court takes the view that the parties are now agreed as to what should happen then it may well decide that it would be better for the child for those agreed arrangements to prevail between the parties rather than embodying them in a court order. Such a solution may well prevent a parent from feeling bitter that he has had arrangements imposed upon him by the court (albeit in a consent order). The less bitter the parents feel about the arrangements made for the children the easier it is likely to be for them to co-operate with each other in future, with the consequence that the children will suffer less upset as a result. It is a principle running throughout the CA 1989 that wherever possible the courts should not interfere with the arrangements made by parents in respect of their children unless it is necessary in the interests of the children to do so.

Of course, it may happen that the agreed arrangements break down in any event with the **29.54** result that the case has to return to court and an order has to be made. However, at least the parties will have had every possible opportunity to achieve a solution without the interference of the court.

There will be circumstances in which an order will need to be made, despite an agreement **29.55** between the parties concerned. An example is where it is agreed that the grandmother is to care for the child. Parental responsibility may be conferred on a grandmother only as part of a residence order: s. 12, CA 1989. A residence order will therefore be necessary to ensure that the grandmother acquires *locus standi* in relation to the child and is able, for example, to give consent to medical treatment: *B v B (A Minor) (Residence Order)* [1992] 2 FLR 327. Another such example is to be found in the case of *G v F (Contact and Shared Residence: Applications for Leave)* [1998] 2 FLR 799 where two women cohabited in a lesbian relationship for five years and a child was born by artificial insemination. During their cohabitation the applicant played a full part in raising the child and continued to do so after the couple separated. It was accepted that a shared residence order was the appropriate means of conferring parental responsibility on the applicant (since she had no right to apply for parental responsibility in its own right in the way in which an unmarried father could do under s. 4 of the Act). See also *Re H (Shared Residence: Parental Responsibility)* [1995] 2 FLR 883 which concerned the conferral of parental responsibility on a stepfather by way of a shared residence order. However, there must be an element of residence in a shared residence order; it cannot be used merely as a vehicle to confer equal status on parents: *Re A (Shared Residence)* [2002] 1 FCR 177—where the child was not only not going to reside with the other parent, but was not even going to visit him, thus making a shared residence order inappropriate.

The delay principle

Section 1(2), CA 1989 requires the court 'in any proceedings in which any question with **29.56** respect to the upbringing of the child arises' to have regard 'to the general principle that any delay in determining the question is likely to prejudice the welfare of the child'.

Once again, this provision is of great importance. The practitioner must be very aware of **29.57** the court's desire to hear applications in respect of children as soon as possible. In order to put the provision into proper effect s. 11 (in relation to s. 8 orders) and s. 32 (in relation to care and supervision orders) of the CA 1989 require the court to draw up a timetable for the progress of the case with a view to eliminating undue delay in the proceedings.

The practical procedure for arranging the timing of proceedings is contained in r. 4.15, FPR **29.58** 1991 (High Court and county court) and in r. 15, FPC(CA 1989)R 1991 (family proceedings court). Experience already shows that the courts expect the timetable to be adhered to and will take steps to enforce adherence to it. This may sometimes mean, for example, that the court will proceed to hear a case without a welfare report if it decides that the advantage to the child of a speedy hearing outweighs the disadvantage to him of proceeding without a welfare report. The Private Law Programme sets down tight procedures and time limits to ensure that private law applications are resolved as speedily and effectively as possible (see further in Chapter 30, paragraph 30.08).

29.59   The procedure to be adopted once a local authority decides to apply for a care or supervision order is now governed by the public law protocol, which is discussed in detail in Chapter 33, paragraph 33.32. The main aim of the protocol is to ensure that care cases are dealt with as justly, expeditiously, and fairly as possible. It sets a guideline of 40 weeks for the conclusion of such cases. The key principles underlying the protocol are that there should be judicial continuity, active case management by the court, consistency by the standardization of steps to be taken in preparing, and a case management conference in each care case to enable the judge to identify the issues and fix the timetable for all further directions and hearings.

29.60   The HRA 1998 implements the European Convention for the Protection of Human Rights and Fundamental Freedoms. Article 6(1) of the Convention requires that cases be heard within a reasonable time and underlines the importance of rendering justice without delays which might jeopardize its effectiveness and credibility.

29.61   Time usually starts to run when the proceedings are instituted (*Darnell* v *UK* (1993) 18 EHRR 205), although it may be earlier in certain circumstances. Time ends with the final decision disposing of the matter, including any appeal. In deciding on the reasonableness of the duration the court takes into account the complexity of the case, the conduct of the applicant, the way in which the matter was dealt with by the administrative and judicial authorities and the importance of what is at stake for the applicant. In *H* v *UK* (1988) 10 EHRR 95, the court made it clear that the obligation is on the State to ensure that the systems in place for hearing cases run effectively and efficiently. In every case relating to children the Convention obligation to bring proceedings within a reasonable time must therefore be considered in addition to the existing principle in s. 1(2), CA 1989.

C   PARENTAL RESPONSIBILITY

29.62   Parental responsibility is a concept introduced by the CA 1989 and it emphasizes the importance of responsibility *for* children, rather than rights *over* children. For the rules relating to the court's jurisdiction to make parental responsibility orders, see paragraph 29.103 below.

29.63   The concept of parental responsibility is defined in s. 3(1), CA 1989 as 'all the rights, duties, powers, responsibilities and authority which by law a parent of a child has in relation to the child and his property'. However, no further definition is attempted since the Law Commission took the view that the list would be changing constantly 'to meet differing needs and circumstances' (Law Com. No. 172, 2.6). It was decided in *R* v *Tameside Metropolitan Borough Council* [2000] 1 FLR 942 that parental responsibility includes the right to decide where a child lives. In that case the local authority had care of the child by providing him with accommodation, but not by way of a care order. The local authority had no power to arrange for the child to be transferred out of a residential institution and into foster care without the permission of the child's parents.

29.64   A person with parental responsibility may not surrender or transfer any part of that responsibility: s. 2(9), CA 1989. However, he may arrange for some part, or all, of that responsibility to be met by one or more other persons, e.g., schools, local authorities, churches, etc. The exercise of parental responsibility will often be qualified in some way by agreement between the parents or by order of the court. For example, the father of a child may agree that the child should live with the mother, in which case the mother has a greater degree of day-to-day 'parental responsibility' than does the father. He agrees to his parental responsibility being curtailed and thus his ability to exercise it is subject to his agreement with the mother (or, in default of agreement, subject to the order of the court). The parent involved would not be permitted to do anything which was incompatible with the court order: s. 2(8).

In addition, the Act allows those having parental responsibility for the child to act alone and without the other (or others) in meeting that responsibility. However, if a particular statute requires the consent of another person, then this must be obtained in the manner prescribed: s. 2(7); for example, the Child Abduction Act 1984 prohibits the removal of children from the United Kingdom without the consent of all those who have parental responsibility for the child. **29.65**

Who has parental responsibility?

Under the CA 1989 there is a wide variety of people who may acquire parental responsibility for a child in different ways. The following are just some examples: **29.66**

(a) Parental responsibility is conferred automatically on the mother of a child, irrespective of her marital status: s. 2(1).
(b) If the father was married to the mother at the time of the child's birth he will automatically have parental responsibility: s. 2(3).
(c) After 1 December 2003, a father who was not married to the mother at the time of the child's birth has parental responsibility if his name is placed on the birth certificate at registration or re-registration of the birth under the Births and Deaths Registration Act 1953: s. 4(1)(a).
(d) If the father was not married to the mother at the time of the child's birth then he may acquire parental responsibility by agreement with the mother or by order of the court (s. 4), or by obtaining a residence order: s. 12(1).
(e) Guardians will acquire parental responsibility for children, so that they are equated with natural parents: s. 5(6).
(f) Local authorities may acquire parental responsibility, for example, on the making of a care order s. 33(3).
(g) A person who has been granted an emergency protection order will acquire parental responsibility for the duration of the order: s. 44(4).
(h) A person who has been granted a residence order will automatically have parental responsibility for the duration of the order: s. 12(1) and (2).
(i) When a child becomes a ward of court then the court itself will acquire parental responsibility.
(j) When a child is adopted, his adoptive parents will acquire parental responsibility (and the natural parents will lose it).
(k) A step-parent may acquire parental responsibility for a child of his spouse by agreement

between the step-parent and the parents who have parental responsibility for the child, or by order of the court: s. 4A(1).

(l)   Whilst a special guardianship order is in force the special guardian has parental responsibility for the child in respect of whom it is made and is able to exercise that responsibility to the exclusion of any other person with parental responsibility (save for another special guardian): s. 14C((1).

There is no limit on the number of people who can have parental responsibility for a child at any one time, and a person does not lose parental responsibility merely because someone else acquires it. Although on the making of a care order a local authority obtains parental responsibility for a child the parents will not lose it and it will be 'shared'.

Meaning of 'father' and 'mother'

29.67   It is to be assumed that references in the CA 1989 to 'father' and 'mother' are intended to denote the natural parents of the child. Unmarried fathers are now included within the definition of 'father'. The problem of who is the real mother of a child born as a result of *in vitro* fertilisation is resolved by s. 27(1), Human Fertilisation and Embryology Act 1990 which states that 'the woman who is carrying or has carried a child as a result of the placing in her of an embryo or of sperm and eggs, and no other woman is to be treated as the mother of the child'. Where a child is born to a married woman as a result of her having been artificially inseminated with the sperm of a man other than her husband, then the husband rather than anyone else is to be treated as the father of the child unless it is shown that he did not consent to his wife's insemination. The same rule applies where the birth of the child is the result of the placement of embryo or sperm and eggs in the married woman and the sperm donor is not the husband: s. 28, Human Fertilisation and Embryology Act 1990.

Automatic parental responsibility

29.68   Parental responsibility is conferred automatically on the mother of a child irrespective of her marital status. Whether the father also has parental responsibility depends on whether he was married to the mother at the time of the child's birth: s. 2(1). If he was so married then he will also have automatic parental responsibility. Even if the father was not lawfully married to the mother at the time of the birth he may still be treated as so married in particular circumstances (s. 2(3), importing s. 1, Family Law Reform Act 1987), e.g., if the child is subsequently legitimated. It would appear that the only way in which a parent can be divested of 'automatic' parental responsibility is upon the child being adopted.

Unmarried fathers

29.69   If the father was not married to the mother at the time of the child's birth and does not come within the extensions to this concept then on the face of it he will not have parental responsibility for the child. However, he may acquire parental responsibility in one of several ways:

(a)   After 1 December 2003, a father not married to the mother at the time of the child's birth has parental responsibility if his name is placed on the birth certificate at registration or re-registration of the birth under the Births and Deaths Registration Act 1953 (s. 4(1)(a)). However, in reality, an unmarried father will not be able to register his name without the consent of the mother. If he does acquire parental responsibility by registration of his name on the birth certificate then that responsibility can only be removed by order of the court, on application by any person with parental responsibility for the child or, with leave, on the application of the child himself (if he has sufficient understanding).

(b) By applying for and obtaining a residence order, using Form C1 to make the application (s. 12(1)), in which case parental responsibility will last for as long as the residence order is in existence (s. 12(2)).

(c) By applying to the court for a parental responsibility order, using Form C1 to make the application (s. 4(1)(a)), in which case the order will last until discharged by the court (s. 4(3)).

(d) By making a 'parental responsibility agreement' with the mother in the 'prescribed form' (s. 4(1)(b)), which will last until discharged by the court (s. 4(3)). The form which such an agreement must take is prescribed by the Parental Responsibility Agreement Regulations 1991.

(e) By being appointed the child's guardian by the court, using Form C1 to make the application: s. 5(1).

(f) By being appointed the child's guardian by the mother or by another guardian: s. 5.

The HRA 1998 implements the European Convention for the Protection of Human Rights **29.70** and Fundamental Freedoms. Article 8(1) of the Convention guarantees a right to family life but it does not place an unmarried father in the same position as a married father or an unmarried mother. The CA 1989 does not automatically give unmarried fathers parental responsibility for their children. It does, however, provide a vehicle by which unmarried fathers may acquire parental responsibility. It is likely that domestic law will be regarded, for the time being, as compatible with the Convention in the light of the change in the law from 1 December 2003 which gives parental responsibility to all unmarried fathers who register the birth of their child.

Factors to be considered in making parental responsibility order   There is now a sub- **29.71** stantial body of case law which sets out the various factors which the court must consider when deciding whether or not to make a parental responsibility order. The leading decision is *Re H (Illegitimate Children: Father: Parental Rights) (No. 2)* [1991] 1 FLR 214. The tests to be applied can be summarized as follows:

(a) The welfare of the child is the court's paramount consideration: CA 1989, s. 1(1).

(b) Was the association between the parties sufficiently enduring?

(c) Has the father by his conduct during and since the application shown sufficient commitment to the child to justify giving him a legal status equivalent to that which he would have had if the parties had been married?

(d) How great is the degree of attachment which exists between the father and the child?

(e) The court must pay due attention to the fact that a number of parental rights would, if conferred upon the father by a parental responsibility order, be unenforceable. However, although this is a relevant consideration, it is not an overriding one.

(f) What are the father's reasons for applying for the parental responsibility order?

In *Re P (A Minor) (Parental Responsibility Order)* [1994] 1 FLR 578 Wall J made some very useful **29.72** observations as to the nature of a parental responsibility order. He said (at p. 584): 'It is important to be quite clear that an order for parental responsibility to the father does not give him a right to interfere in matters within the day-to-day management of the child's life'. He went on to say (at p. 585):

> It is to be noted that on any view an order for parental responsibility gives the father no power to override the decision of the mother, who already has such responsibility: in the event of disagreement between them on a specific issue relating to the child, the court will have to resolve it. If the father were to seek to misuse the rights given him under s. 4 such misuse could, as a second to last resort, be controlled by the court under a prohibited steps order against him and/or a specific issue order. The very last resort of all would presumably be the discharge of the parental responsibility order.

29.73   The case of *C and V (Contact and Parental Responsibility Order)* [1998] 1 FLR 392, confirmed that the unmarried father's failure to obtain a contact order in his favour should not mean that his application for a parental responsibility order would also fail. The Court of Appeal reminded practitioners that a parental responsibility order was designed to enable the actual father to have the same status of fatherhood which he would have enjoyed if he had been married to the child's mother.

29.74   Even where the child of an unmarried father has already been received into the care of the local authority it may still be right to make a parental responsibility order in favour of the father, provided that he has shown commitment to the child and that his reasons for making the application are proper ones; the fact that the father is awkward, difficult, and thoroughly unresponsive to the social workers involved will not necessarily prevent the making of an order: *Re G (A Minor) (Parental Responsibility Order)* [1994] 1 FLR 504. The theme of current case law seems to show that the making of parental responsibility orders will generally be the norm rather than the exception when fathers have shown commitment to their children and their children have become attached to them: *Re J-S (Contact: Parental Responsibility)* [2003] Fam Law 65. However, the list of factors set out above is not exhaustive and each case will, of course, turn on its own facts. In *Re H (Parental Responsibility)* [1998] 1 FLR 855 Balcombe LJ emphasized that previous case law has not created a presumption that a devoted father will ordinarily be granted an order, and the court must take into account all the relevant factors in each case to decide whether the proposed order would be in the child's best interests. In that case the order was refused because the father posed a risk to his son for the future.

29.75   There are very few reported cases in which a refusal to make a parental responsibility order has been upheld. However, the following cases are examples of such refusal: in *Re T (A Minor) (Parental Responsibility: Contact)* [1993] 2 FLR 450, the father had used serious violence against the mother and had been guilty of cruel behaviour towards the child; in *Re P (Minors: Parental Responsibility Order)* [1997] 2 FLR 722, the father was serving sentences of imprisonment for robbery, had begotten one of the children concerned during a period of home leave in the course of which he committed a further offence for which he was sentenced to imprisonment. The lack of a responsible attitude towards the child or evidence that the exercise of parental responsibility will be used to interfere with or undermine the mother's care of the child may result in the court refusing to make a parental responsibility order: *Re H (Parental Responsibility)* [1998] (above); *Re P (Parental Responsibility)* [1998] 2 FLR 96.

29.76   Cases such as *Re C (A Minor) (Parental Responsibility)* [1995] 3 FLR 564 and *D v S (Parental Responsibility)* [1995] 3 FLR 783 have confirmed that the acquisition of parental responsibility by an unmarried father does not affect the day-to-day care of the child, but is formal recognition that the applicant is the father of the child in question.

Finally, it will be necessary to satisfy the court (on the balance of probabilities) that the applicant is the father of the child before an order granting him parental responsibility can be made. **29.77**

The unmarried father who does not seek parental responsibility will still remain liable to maintain his child: CA 1989, s. 3(4). However, where a father refuses to pay maintenance for his child, the court should not use the weapon of withholding a parental responsibility order to obtain from the father his financial dues: *Re H (Parental Responsibility: Maintenance)* [1996] 1 FLR 867. **29.78**

Nature of a parental responsibility agreement As already mentioned in paragraph 29.69(c), one way in which an unmarried father can obtain parental responsibility is by entering into a parental responsibility agreement with the mother, using the form prescribed in the Parental Responsibility Agreement Regulations 1991. The case of *Re X (Parental Responsibility Agreement: Children in Care)* [2000] 1 FLR 517 held that where two children were subject to care orders and the local authority wanted to place them for adoption, the local authority had no power to stop the mother from entering into a parental responsibility agreement with the unmarried father in respect of the children even though the children were subject to care orders. The court decided that to create a parental responsibility agreement both parents must act *in unison* and sign the agreement and therefore entering into the agreement was not in itself an exercise of parental responsibility; the unmarried father does not have parental responsibility when he signs the agreement and therefore the mother cannot be said to be exercising parental responsibility when she signs it either. **29.79**

Termination of parental responsibility agreements and orders A parental responsibility order or agreement will automatically end upon the child attaining the age of 18: s. 91(7) and (8), CA 1989. The order or agreement could be discharged by the court before the child attains 18 if the court is satisfied on the 'welfare' test contained in s. 1(1), CA 1989 that it would be better for the child if the court were to discharge it rather than refuse to do so: s. 4(3). Any person with parental responsibility may apply to discharge the order or agreement, as indeed may the child himself if he is of sufficient age and understanding: s. 4(3)(b) and (4), CA 1989. However, parental responsibility cannot be removed from a father in whose favour a residence order exists: s. 12(4), CA 1989. Indeed, where a residence order has been made in favour of a person who is not a parent or guardian of the child, that person must also continue to have parental responsibility while the residence order remains in force: s. 12(2), CA 1989. **29.80**

An example of a case where a parental responsibility agreement was terminated is *Re P (Terminating Parental Responsibility)* [1995] 1 FLR 1048. Here the unmarried parents entered into such an agreement shortly after the birth of the child. Later the father caused injuries to the child leaving the child physically and mentally disabled. In response to the father's application for a contact order the mother applied for termination of the agreement. Singer J indicated that the normal presumption was that once an agreement was entered into, it would remain in force until the welfare of the child warranted its termination. In order to determine whether the agreement would be terminated, the court had to consider whether it would have made a parental responsibility order in favour of the father if he did not already **29.81** have parental responsibility. On the facts, there was no aspect of parental responsibility which the unmarried father could exercise in a way which would be beneficial to the child. Accordingly, the agreement would be terminated.

Step-parents

29.82 Step-parents may acquire parental responsibility for a child of their spouse:

(a) by agreement between the step-parent and the parents with parental responsibility for the child, or by order of the court: s. 4A(1). Such an agreement will constitute a 'parental responsibility agreement' within the definition of s. 4(2), CA 1989 (see paragraph 29.79 above), and can only be terminated by the court on application by any person with parental responsibility for the child, or, with leave, on application by the child himself (provided he has sufficient understanding);

(b) by the making of a residence order in his favour, parental responsibility being retained for as long as the order remains in force: s. 12(2). However, the rights enjoyed by natural parents in relation to adoption and guardianship will not apply to him: s. 12(3);

(c) by the making of an adoption order in his favour.

A step-parent will be responsible for the maintenance of a child in so far as the step-parent is a party to the marriage (whether or not subsisting) in relation to which the child concerned is a child of the family: sch. 1, para. 16, CA 1989. (For a definition of 'child of the family' see s. 105(1), CA 1989.) This will be the case irrespective of whether the step-parent has 'parental responsibility' or not: s. 3(4)(a), CA 1989.

29.83 A step-parent who has care of a child may do what is reasonable in all the circumstances of the case for the purpose of safeguarding or promoting the child's welfare: s. 3(5).

Civil partners

29.84 By virtue of the Civil Partnership Act 2004, s. 75(2), civil partners may apply for parental responsibility for the children of their civil partners, using the same mechanism as is used for the acquisition of parental responsibility by step-parents after marriage under s. 4A(1) of the Children Act 1989 (see paragraph 29.82, above).

Person with *de facto* care of child

29.85 Where a person has *de facto* care of a child but no parental responsibility for him then that person may do whatever is reasonable to safeguard and promote the child's welfare: s. 3(5).

D   GUARDIANSHIP

29.86 Central to the role of guardians under the CA 1989 is the conferment upon them of parental responsibility for the child in question: s. 5(6), CA 1989.

Appointment of a guardian

29.87 A guardian may be appointed for a child under 18 in the following ways:

(a) by the court in family proceedings, with or without an application:
  (i) where the child has no parent with parental responsibility for him: s. 5(1)(a); or
  (ii) where a residence order has been made with respect to the child in favour of a parent or guardian of his who has died while the order was in force: s. 5(1)(b);
(b) by a parent with parental responsibility: s. 5(3);
(c) by an existing guardian: s. 5(4)

When a court decides whether or not to appoint a guardian it must apply the 'welfare' **29.88** principle set out in s. 1(1), CA 1989. As with applications for a parental responsibility order, it is not mandatory for the court to use the statutory checklist of factors in s. 1(3), CA 1989 unless it is making the decision in the course of hearing a contested application for a s. 8 order, care order, or supervision order. However, in practice the court is likely to refer to the checklist in any event, and in addition to consider the relationship between the child in question and the proposed guardian, the recorded wishes of the deceased parent, the wishes of the child's nearest relative, and other such matters.

A parent who has parental responsibility, or a guardian, may appoint a guardian to **29.89** assume parental responsibility on the death of the appointor: s. 5(3) and (4). Two or more persons may join together to make such an appointment: s. 5(10). Any such appointment need not be made by will nor by deed. It was felt that such formalities may deter people from making an appointment. Instead, it will be sufficient for the appointment to be in writing, dated, and signed at the direction of the person making the appointment in his presence and in the presence of two witnesses. Unmarried fathers will be able to make appointments if they have obtained parental responsibility or been appointed as guardians.

Revocation of guardianship

Revocation of guardianship can be achieved in the following ways: **29.90**

(a) by a later appointment of a guardian, unless it is clear that the later appointment is of an *additional* guardian: s. 6(1);
(b) by a written, signed, and dated instrument revoking the appointment: s. 6(2);
(c) by the destruction of the document in question with the intent of revoking the appointment, except in the case of a will or codicil: s. 6(3);
(d) by the revocation of the will or codicil that contains the appointment: s. 6(4).

Where the initial appointment of a guardian was by way of court order then the court **29.91** retains jurisdiction to terminate the appointment at any time in the following ways: s. 6(7):

(a) on the application of anyone with parental responsibility for the child;
(b) on the application of the child himself;
(c) by the court's own motion in the course of any family proceedings if the court considers it should be brought to an end even though no application has been made.

If the appointment is not terminated earlier it will end on the child reaching the age of 18, as will any court order made under s. 5(1): see s. 91(7) and (8).

Disclaimer of guardianship

29.92   A guardian appointed other than by way of a court order may disclaim his appointment by making an instrument in writing to this effect, provided that he does so within a reasonable time of first knowing that the appointment has taken effect: s. 6(5) and (6).

E   SPECIAL GUARDIANSHIP ORDERS

29.93   The ACA 2002, s. 115, has inserted ss. 14A–14D into the CA 1989 to introduce special guardianship orders. These orders will be particularly suitable for cases concerning older children where, although adoption is considered to be in the best interests of the child, it is important that he keeps in touch with his natural parents and that the parents are not deprived of parental responsibility.

29.94   The following categories of people may apply for a special guardianship order:

(a)   any guardian of the child;

(b)   anyone else who has a residence order for the child;

(c)   anyone who has the consent of all those who hold residence orders for the child;

(d)   a local authority foster parent with whom the child has lived for one year preceding the application;

(e)   anyone who comes within the categories set out in s. 10(5)(b) or (c), CA 1989 (see paragraph 29.109 below);

(f)   anyone else with the local authority's consent, if the child is the subject of a care order.

Applicants for a special guardianship order must give three months' notice of their intention to apply and must be vetted by the local authority. The local authority has a duty to compile a report dealing with the suitability of the applicant for the use of the court considering the order: s. 14A(8), CA 1989. Once appointed, the special guardian can exercise parental responsibility to the exclusion of all others who have parental responsibility apart from other special guardians (subject to any order of the court to the contrary): s. 14C(1)(b), CA 1989. The natural parents will retain their parental responsibility but it will be curtailed severely as a result of the order. The court will have power to vary or discharge a special guardianship order on application by defined categories of applicants: s. 14D(1), CA 1989. The first reported special guardianship order was made in the case of *A Local Authority* v *Y Z and Others* [2006] 2 FLR 41. The judge approved special guardianship orders in respect of three children who had been placed with members of their extended family. The two older children had lived with an aunt and uncle for two years and the youngest child, aged five, had lived with another aunt and her partner for almost two years. The court held that the children required the permanence, stability, and security that special guardianship provided. It was preferable to the alternatives available under the CA 1989 and adoption was neither sought nor was desirable.

F ORDERS IN FAMILY PROCEEDINGS

Introduction

The needs and circumstances of children are constantly changing and therefore it is right **29.95** that the orders that regulate the arrangements for their upbringing are sufficiently flexible to reflect those changes as and when it becomes necessary.

The orders available under the CA 1989 encourage the move away from the tendency par- **29.96** ents to feel that they have *rights over* children towards an acknowledgement by them of their *responsibilities for* their children. The principle of 'parental responsibility' under the CA 1989 has already been discussed at paragraph 29.62 and onwards.

An important aim of the CA 1989 is to ensure that wherever possible orders relating to the **29.97** upbringing of children can be made in the course of existing proceedings in respect of the same family, so as to avoid the necessity for several sets of proceedings to run concurrently. For example, where the occupation of the matrimonial home is in dispute the needs of the children are frequently an important factor in determining the relief sought. The provisions allow the court, at the same time as making an order excluding the father from the house, to make, for instance, a residence order in favour of the mother who remains there and a contact order in favour of the father.

The court is able to make a s. 8 order in the course of any 'family proceedings'. For **29.98** the purposes of the CA 1989 'family proceedings' are defined in s. 8(3) and (4) as any proceedings under:

(a) the inherent jurisdiction of the High Court in relation to children;
(b) Parts I, II, and IV of the CA 1989;
(c) the Matrimonial Causes Act 1973;
(d) the Adoption Act 1976;
(e) the Domestic Proceedings and Magistrates' Courts Act 1978;
(f) Part III of the Matrimonial and Family Proceedings Act 1984;
(g) proceedings under the FLA 1996;
(h) Schedule 5 to the Civil Partnership Act 2004;
(i) Schedule 6 to the Civil Partnership Act 2004;
(j) the Adoption and Children Act 2002;
(k) sections 11 and 12 of the Crime and Disorder Act 1998.

Jurisdiction to make s. 8 orders under the Family Law Act 1986

Meaning of 'Part I order'

The Family Law Act 1986 ('FLA 1986') (as amended by sch. 13, paras. 62 to 71 to the CA **29.99** 1989) sets out the circumstances in which a court in England and Wales will have jurisdiction to make an order under Part I of the FLA 1986 (i.e., a 'Part I order'). A court in England and Wales may make two types of Part I order:

(a) a s. 8 order, other than one varying or discharging a s. 8 order: s. 1(1)(a), FLA 1986; and

(b) an order made in the exercise of the inherent jurisdiction of the High Court with respect to children:

   (i) in so far as it gives the care of a child to any person or provides for contact with or the education of a child, but

   (ii) excluding an order varying or discharging such an order: s. 1(1)(d), FLA 1986.

The rules as to jurisdiction in relation to s. 8 orders are different for matrimonial and non-matrimonial proceedings.

Matrimonial proceedings

29.100 A court in England and Wales will only have jurisdiction to make a s. 8 order within proceedings for divorce, nullity, or judicial separation or dissolution or annulment of a civil partnership which are still continuing. If the proceedings have been dismissed then the s. 8 order must be made forthwith, or the application for the order must have been made on or before the dismissal: s. 2A(1), FLA 1986. If the court considers that it would be more appropriate for the Part I matters to be determined outside England and Wales then the court can direct that no s. 8 order be made in the matrimonial proceedings: s. 2A(4), FLA 1986.

Non-matrimonial proceedings

29.101 A court in England and Wales will only have jurisdiction to make s. 8 orders in non-matrimonial proceedings where the child is either:

(a) habitually resident in England and Wales, or

(b) present in England and Wales and not habitually resident in any part of the United Kingdom on the relevant date (i.e., on the date of the application or, if there is no application, on the date when the court is considering whether to make the orders), and

(c) in the case of either (a) or (b) above, the court's jurisdiction is not excluded.

29.102 The jurisdiction of the court will be *excluded* if, on the relevant date, matrimonial proceedings are continuing in Scotland or Northern Ireland in relation to the marriage of the child's parents, *unless* that court has made an order waiving its jurisdiction or staying proceedings so as to allow the Part I order proceedings to take place in England and Wales: s. 3, FLA 1986.

Parental responsibility orders

29.103 'Part I orders' do not include parental responsibility orders under the CA 1989. There is, therefore, no statutory limitation on the court's jurisdiction to make orders under s. 4 or s. 4A of the Act in an appropriate case, so that the court can assume jurisdiction over a child who is neither resident nor present in England or Wales. In *Re S (Parental Responsibility: Jurisdiction)* [1998] 2 FLR 921 the Court of Appeal held that the court has jurisdiction to entertain an application for an order under s. 4 whenever it is proper to do so, in respect of a child who is permanently outside the jurisdiction, notwithstanding the fact that the child was also born outside the jurisdiction.

G SECTION 8 ORDERS

Section 8 of the Children Act 1989 creates the following orders:　　　　**29.104**

(a) A residence order: this settles the arrangements to be made as to the person with whom a child is to live.
(b) A contact order: this requires the person with whom a child lives to allow the child to visit or stay with the person named in the order, or for that person and the child to otherwise have contact with each other.
(c) A prohibited steps order: this orders that no step which could be taken by a parent in meeting his parental responsibility for a child, and which is of a kind specified in the order, shall be taken by any person without the consent of the court.
(d) A specific issue order: this gives directions for the determination of a specific question which has arisen, or which may arise, in connection with any aspect of parental responsibility for a child.

Any reference to 'a s. 8 order' means any of the above orders and any order varying or discharging such an order: s. 8(2).

When a court is hearing *contested* proceedings in relation to a s. 8 order it *must* have regard to　**29.105**
the following:

(a) the principle that the child's welfare is the paramount consideration: s. 1(1);
(b) the statutory checklist of factors: s. 1(3);
(c) the principle that it must not make any order unless it considers that doing so would be better for the child than making no order at all: s. 1(5).

See paragraph 29.04 above for a detailed discussion of these principles.

Who can apply for s. 8 orders?

The court can make s. 8 orders in two ways:　　　　**29.106**

(a) in the course of existing family proceedings: s. 10(1); 'family proceedings' are defined in s. 8(3). NB: they include care proceedings and adoption proceedings;
(b) as a result of a specific self-contained application to the court for a s. 8 order: s. 10(2).

In each case certain persons are 'entitled to apply' for s. 8 orders as of right whilst anyone else may only d so with leave of the court.

Persons 'entitled to apply' for s. 8 orders

There is a distinction between those entitled to apply:　　　　**29.107**

(a) for a residence or contact order, and
(b) for a specific issue or prohibited steps order.

The class of persons entitled to apply for the orders in (a) is wider than the class of those who are entitled to apply for the orders in (b).

The following are the class of persons who can apply for *any* s. 8 order:　　　　**29.108**

(a) any parent, guardian, or special guardian of the child: s. 10(4)(a);

(b) any person who by virtue of s. 4A has parental responsibility for the child: s. 10(4)(aa);

(c) any person in whose favour a residence order is in force with respect to the child: s. 10(4)(b).

29.109   The persons who are entitled to apply to the court for a residence or contact order are *extended* by ss. 10(5) and (5A) to include:

(a) any party to the marriage (whether or not subsisting) in relation to whom a child is a child of the family (as defined in s. 105(1));

(b) any civil partner in a civil partnership (whether or not subsisting) in relation to whom the child is a child of the family: s. 10(5)(aa);

(c) any person with whom the child has lived for a period of at least three years (as defined in s. 10(10)): s. 10(5)(b);

(d) any person who (s. 10(5)(c)—

(i)   in any case where a residence order is in force with respect to the child, has the consent of each of the persons in whose favour the order was made;

(ii) in any case where the child is in the care of the local authority, has the consent of that authority; or

(iii) in any other case, has the consent of each of those (if any) who have parental responsibility for the child;

(e) a local authority foster parent is entitled to apply for a residence order with respect to a child if the child has lived with him for a period of at least one year immediately preceding the application: s. 10(5A);

(f) if a special guardianship order is in force with respect to a child, and application for a residence order may only be made with leave: s. 10(7A).

Note that this list is *in addition* to those persons set out in s. 10(4), and that it may be further extended by rules of court (s. 10(7)).

Obtaining leave of the court

29.110   Any person who does not fall within the categories set out in paragraph 29.107 above must apply to the court for leave to make a s. 8 application. If the child himself applies for leave then the court may grant leave only if it is satisfied that the child has sufficient understanding to make the proposed application: s. 10(8). If the person applying for leave is someone other than the child then the court must consider the specific matters set out in s. 10(9) when making its decision, that is to say:

(a) the nature of the proposed application for the s. 8 order;

(b) the applicant's connection with the child;

(c) any risk there might be of that proposed application disrupting the child's life to such an extent that he would be harmed by it; and

(d) where the child is being looked after by a local authority:

(i)   the authority's plans for the child's future; and

(ii) the wishes and feelings of the child's parents.

It appears that s. 1(1), CA 1989 does not apply in this context. In *Re A and W (Minors) (Residence Order: Leave to Apply)* [1992] 2 FLR 154, it was held that, since on an application for leave to apply for a residence order no question with regard to the child's upbringing is determined, and since s. 10(9) stipulates particular matters to which the court must have regard in determining such an application, s. 1(1) does not apply. However, the court may take into account additional factors where they are relevant, including the wishes of the child: *Re A (A Minor) (Residence Order: Leave to Apply)* [1993] 1 FLR 425. The court must take into account all the circumstances of the case, including the likely outcome of the substantive hearing if the application for leave is granted: *G v Kirklees MBC* [1993] 1 FLR 805. See also *North Yorkshire County Council v G* [1993] 2 FLR 732, where the judge refused to give leave for a 16-year-old boy to be made a party to care proceedings relating to his brother. In *G v F (Contact and Shared Residence: Applications for Leave)* (above) two women had cohabited in a lesbian relationship and had a child by artificial insemination, and after their separation the court granted leave to the applicant to make applications for contact and shared residence orders.

In *Re F and R (Section 8: Grandparent's Application)* [1995] 1 FLR 57, leave was granted on **29.111** appeal because the grandparent visited the children and already had close contact with them. However, there is no presumption in favour of grandparents obtaining leave. Leave will not be granted where, because of the level of disharmony between the applicant and the child's parents, the substantive application is likely to fail; nor will leave be granted if it would be harmful to the child because of the disruption which would be caused: *Re A (A Minor) (Section 8 Order: Grandparent's Application)* [1995] 2 FLR 153. See also *Re J (Leave to issue application for Residence Order)* [2003] 1 FLR 114.

In exceptional circumstances the court will entertain an oral application for leave, particu- **29.112** larly where the circumstances dictate that the application be made on an *ex parte* basis: *Re O (Minors) (Leave to Seek Residence Orders)* [1994] 1 FLR 172.

Factors in request for leave by child Where the person applying for leave is the child **29.113** himself then the application should be transferred to the High Court for hearing: *Practice Direction* [1993] 1 FLR 668; *Re AD (A Minor) (Child's Wishes)* [1993] 1 FCR 573, [1993] Fam Law 405. The factors in s. 10(9) do not specifically apply and there is no equivalent checklist which applies instead. Section 10(8) requires the court to be satisfied that the child has 'sufficient understanding' to make the application. However, even if that test is satisfied the court still has a discretion as to whether or not to allow the application: *Re SC (A Minor) (Leave to Seek Residence Order)* [1994] 1 FLR 96. The court can have regard to the likelihood of success of the proposed application. There are conflicting decisions as to whether or not the child's welfare is paramount in this type of application. In *Re C (A Minor) (Leave to Seek Section 8 Orders)* [1994] 1 FLR 26, Johnson J held that the child's welfare is paramount, but in *Re SC (A Minor) (Leave to Seek Residence Order)* (above), Booth J held that since the initial application for leave does not raise any question regarding the upbringing of a child, the child's welfare was not the court's paramount consideration when exercising its discretion. She also remarked, *obiter*, that leave should not be granted when the substantive application was bound to fail. The approach of Booth J was followed in the Family Division by Stuart-White J in *Re C (Residence: Child's Application for Leave)* [1995] 1 FLR 927, the judge remarking that 'the best interests of the child are of importance though they are not paramount in the sense in which the word is used in s. 1(1) of the Act'. This is a conflict which must await resolution by the Court of Appeal.

29.114 The meaning of 'sufficient understanding' has been considered by the courts in a number of different contexts. Caution is necessary in drawing analogies between the various categories of cases, but the case law does give some guidance as to how the courts are interpreting this phrase. The leading case is *Re S (A Minor) (Independent Representation)* (above), in which an 11-year-old boy was held (pursuant to r. 9.2A, FPR 1991) not to have sufficient understanding to participate as a party in a bitter and protracted dispute between his parents as to with which of them he should live. At p. 444H, Sir Thomas Bingham said:

> Different children have differing levels of understanding at the same age. An understanding is not absolute. It has to be assessed relatively to the issues in the proceedings. Where any sound judgement on these issues calls for insight and imagination which only maturity and experience can bring, both the court and the solicitor will be slow to conclude that the child's understanding is sufficient.

In *Re H (A Minor) (Role of Official Solicitor)* (above), a 15-year-old boy was held (pursuant to r. 9.2A of the 1991 Rules) to have sufficient understanding on the particular facts of the case to participate as a party in wardship proceedings to resist the application by his parents that he should live with them. However, in *Re H (A Minor) (Care Proceedings: Child's Wishes)* (above) (a case in which, pursuant to rr. 4.11 and 4.12 of the 1991 Rules, a 15-year-old boy had sufficient understanding to instruct his own solicitor in care proceedings), Thorpe J observed that not every child of 15 years and eight months must be taken to have sufficient understanding to instruct a solicitor. He said, at p. 449H: 'It seems to me that a child must have sufficient rationality within the understanding to instruct a solicitor. It may well be that the level of emotional disturbance is such as to remove the necessary degree of rationality that leads to coherent and consistent instruction.' In *Re CT (A Minor) (Wardship: Representation)* (above) (a case under r. 9.2A), a 13½-year-old girl had sufficient understanding to instruct a solicitor in her application for a residence order to enable her to live with her natural aunt and grandparents. However, in *Re N (Contact: Minor Seeking Leave to Defend and Removal of Guardian)* [2003] 1 FLR 652 the court held that an 11-year-old child did not have sufficient understanding to participate as a party in contact proceedings or give instructions that would be fully considered in their implications.

Foster parents

29.115 Section 9(3), CA 1989 restricts a local authority foster parent from applying for leave to apply for s. 8 orders unless:

(a) he has the consent without the consent of the local authority;

(b) he is a relative of the child; or

(c) the child has lived with him for at least one year preceding the application.

If the foster parent of a child in care has the consent of the local authority, or has cared for the child for one year, he may apply for a residence or contact order without first applying for leave (s. 10(5)(c)). However, leave will be required if he wishes to apply for a specific issue or prohibited steps order.

Duration of s. 8 orders

The main provisions which govern the duration of s. 8 orders are as follows: **29.116**

(a) As a general rule s. 8 orders will continue unless discharged by the court or otherwise, until the child reaches the age of 16: s. 91(10).

(b) The court must not make a s. 8 order which is to have effect for a period which will end after the child has reached 16, unless it is satisfied that the circumstances of the case are exceptional: s. 9(6).

(c) The court must not make a s. 8 order, other than one varying or discharging a s. 8 order, once the child has reached 16, unless it is satisfied that there are exceptional circumstances: s. 9(7).

(d) If an order is extended beyond, or made after, the child reached 16, then it comes to an end when he reaches 18: s. 91(11).

(e) The making of a care order will discharge all current s. 8 orders (s. 91(2)), as will the making of certain orders in adoption proceedings.

(f) When the court makes a residence order in favour of a person who is not a parent or guardian of the child, it has the power to direct that the order should remain in force until the child is 18: s. 12(5)

H   RESIDENCE ORDERS

Residence orders settle the arrangements to be made as to the person with whom **29.117** the child lives. They aim to cater for a wider range of situations than a custody order was able to do.

A residence order, does not have any effect on the parental responsibility of either parent; it **29.118** is intended to settle the child's living arrangements and no more.

The Court of Appeal has confirmed in *Re E (Residence: Imposition of Conditions)* [1997] 2 **29.119** FLR 638, that it is not permissible to attach to a residence order a condition that the mother live with the child at a specified address. If the mother was considered to be suitable and a residence order was made in her favour, attaching such a condition was an unjustified interference with her right to choose where to live in the United Kingdom. However, there may be exceptional circumstances which justify preventing a residential parent from moving to a different part of the United Kingdom: *Re S (A Child) (Residence Order: Condition) (No. 2)* [2003] 1 FCR 138—where the mother was prevented from moving with her nine-year-old Down's syndrome child from London to Cornwall; *Re H (Children) (Residence Order: Condition)* [2001] 2 FLR 1277, where the father was prevented from moving with the children from England to Northern Ireland; *B v B (Residence: Condition Limiting Geographical Area)* [2004] Fam 651, where the court attached to the mother's residence order a condition that she reside in a defined area of Southern England as she had no good reasons for her proposed move to Newcastle other than to be distanced further from the father.

Shared/joint residence orders

29.120   A residence order can be made in favour of more than one person. If those people are not living together then the order may specify the periods to be spent in each household (s. 11(4)); these are commonly known as 'joint' or 'shared' residence orders. When shared residence orders first became available, courts made them relatively rarely, since it was thought that giving a child two competing homes would often lead to confusion and stress. However, in *D v D (Shared Residence Orders)* [2001] 1 FLR 495, the Court of Appeal took a more relaxed approach to shared residence orders and endorsed a move away from any 'exceptional circumstances' requirement. Where the basic arrangements for the children are settled, the existence of a continuing dispute about the detail does not prevent the making of a shared order. The Court of Appeal questioned whether it is necessary to demonstrate a positive benefit, as long as the order can be shown to be in the child's interests. This approach was continued in the case of *Re F (Shared Residence)* [2003] EWCA Civ 592, [2003] 2 FLR 397, [2003] Fam 568 in which the Court of Appeal held that the fact that the parents' homes might be separated by a considerable distance did not preclude a shared residence order. The children would be based at their father's home during most school half terms and holidays and based with their mother during the term-time.

29.121   It is useful to look at examples of cases in which shared orders have been made to gain a sense of when they might or might not be appropriate.

29.122   In *G v G (Joint Residence Order)* [1993] Fam Law 615 the judge granted a joint residence order in circumstances where the father worked on a shift basis and the children had been used to dividing their time between the father's home and the mother's home for years; furthermore, the children were aged 12 and 9, they wished to continue with the joint arrangements and they were sufficiently old enough for their wishes to carry some weight. See also *Re R (Residence Order: Finance)* [1995] 2 FLR 612, where the court made a shared residence order in relation to a child aged two. In the case of *Re H (Shared Residence: Parental Responsibility)* [1995] 2 FLR 883, a shared residence order was made principally to give parental responsibility to the stepfather of a child whom the stepfather had treated as a child of the family and the court felt that it was of great therapeutic importance for the child to have this formal relationship with his stepfather. In *G v F (Contact and Shared Residence: Applications for Leave)* (above) two women had cohabited in a lesbian relationship and had a child by artificial insemination; after their separation the court granted leave to the applicant, who had been very closely involved in the upbringing of the child, to make applications for contact and shared residence orders. *In Re G (Residence: Same-Sex Partner)* [2005] 2 FLR 957, the Court of Appeal granted a joint residence order in respect of the children of former partners of the same sex, partly as a safeguard against the marginalization of the appellant from the children's lives by the biological mother.

29.123   A shared residence order should only be made if there is an element of 'residence'. In *Re A (Shared Residence)* (above) a shared residence order had been made at first instance in order to recognize the equal status of each parent. On appeal, the Court of Appeal held that where the child was not only not going to reside with the other parent, but was not even going to visit him, a residence order was not appropriate.

29.124   The decision whether or not to make such an order is in the discretion of the judge, in the light of the principles set out in the s. 1(3) checklist.

Residence orders made without notice (*ex parte*)

A residence order made without notice first having been given to the other side (i.e., an **29.125** order made on an *ex parte* basis) should be for a limited period of time and should only be made in exceptional circumstances where it is necessary for the protection of the child, for example, in a 'snatch' situation or a child abduction. There are two competing considerations: the children's long-term welfare and their short-term protection. In ordinary circumstances the court will be extremely reluctant to disturb the status quo pending a full investigation into a residence dispute. However, there may be those comparatively rare cases in which it is more important for the children to stay temporarily with the parent who has 'snatched' them, rather than that they should be returned to the parent with whom they had lived up until the 'snatch', pending the outcome of investigations into the circumstances of the 'snatch'.

In *Re G (Minors) (Ex Parte Interim Residence Order)* [1993] 1 FLR 910 the children told their **29.126** father in the course of a contact visit that their mother had been taking drugs and the Court of Appeal approved the granting to him of an *ex parte* interim residence order pending a full investigation of the allegations, but stressed that it had not been reasonable for the children to be moved from their mother without her knowledge and placed in another school before she had had an opportunity of being heard. It is clear that the court will view such applications with extreme caution. See *Re P (A Minor) (Ex Parte Interim Residence Order)* [1993] 1 FLR 915 for an example of a case in which the Court of Appeal set aside an *ex parte* interim residence order because the judge should have adjourned the matter to hear both sides. Where a party who was absent when an *ex parte* order was made wishes to challenge the order, the appropriate course is for him to apply to the judge who made it to vary or rescind the order. This should be done on short notice unless the case is wholly exceptional: *Re P (A Minor) (Ex Parte Interim Residence Order)* (above).

Restriction on change of name

Section 13(1) of the CA 1989 states that where a residence order is in force with respect to a **29.127** child then no person may cause the child to be known by a new surname without first obtaining either:

(a)   the written consent of every person with parental responsibility for the child; or
(b)   the leave of the court.

Practice Direction [1995] 1 FLR 458 sets out the relevant procedure for an application to change the surname of a child. Note that it is not only a change of name by deed poll that is prevented; the person with the residence order is equally prohibited from taking less formal steps to change the name the child is known by (for example, instructing the child's school that he should be called by a different surname).

If a person with a residence order does wish to change the child's surname then he should **29.128** first contact the other persons who have parental responsibility to see if they will consent in writing to the change. If so, the change of name can go ahead as planned. If no consent is forthcoming then the court's leave will be necessary. An application for leave should be made using the appropriate prescribed Form. In a case where a residence order is in force, an application to change a child's name is a free-standing application under s. 13, CA 1989, rather than one for a specific issue order under s. 8 of the Act.

29.129 Given the principle of non-intervention in s. 1(5), CA 1989, there will be many occasions when a residence order is not made and the provisions of s. 13(1) will not apply. In these circumstances the procedure in *Practice Direction* [1995] 1 FLR 458 requires that when a residence order is not in force an application for the enrolment of a deed poll to change the surname of a child under the age of 18 must be supported by the production of the written consent of every person with parental responsibility for the child, or by production of leave of the court (see *Re T (Change of Surname)* [1998] 2 FLR 620). The application should be made under s. 8, CA 1989. Whether the application will be for a specific issue order or a prohibited steps order will depend on the circumstances. An application under s. 13 of the 1989 Act is not appropriate in a case where no residence order is in force.

29.130 In the case of *W v A (Child: Surname)* [1981] 1 All ER 100, the Court of Appeal stressed that changing a child's name is viewed as a matter of importance and the parent seeking leave will have to show that it is in the child's best interests for his name to be changed. This view has been endorsed by the Court of Appeal in *Re F (Child) (Surname)* [1993] 2 FLR 837. Whether leave is granted is a matter for the discretion of the judge hearing the case, seeing the parents and possibly seeing the children. The judge will take into account all the circumstances of the case including, where appropriate, any embarrassment which may be caused to the child by not changing his name and, on the other hand, the long-term interests of the child, the importance of maintaining the child's links with his paternal family, and (where the mother seeks leave because she has remarried) the stability or otherwise of the mother's new marriage. In *Re B (Change of Surname)* [1996] 1 FLR 791, the court held that three children aged 16, 14, and 12 should retain their father's surname even though this ran flatly contrary to the wishes of the children.

Example (The facts of *W v A*, above.) There were two children of the marriage. The parties divorced and both remarried. They had joint custody of the children with care and control being granted to the mother and reasonable access to the father. The mother's second husband was an Australian and wished to return to Australia with her and the children. The mother wanted the children (aged 12 and 14) to use her new husband's surname and the children, who saw the judge in his room, also wanted to use his name. The judge ruled that the children were to continue to use the father's surname. He paid little regard to the children's view on the matter as he felt that it reflected that of the mother. The Court of Appeal upheld his decision.

29.131 In *Dawson v Wearmouth* [1999] 1 FLR 1167 the House of Lords reviewed the principles to be applied to a change of name application. The proper course in all cases in which a change of name is contemplated is:

(a) Consult anyone with parental responsibility, whether or not there is a residence order in force.

(b) Consult the unmarried father without parental responsibility. It is not certain the extent to which the consent of an unmarried father without parental responsibility is material to a change of name. Section 13, CA 1989 only requires the consent of those with parental responsibility and so it is possible to infer that there is no need to consult an unmarried father without parental responsibility. However, if the unmarried father finds out about the change of name and disagrees with it, he could apply to the court for a specific issue order under s. 8 of the 1989 Act. Therefore, it is probably sensible to consult the unmarried father even if he has no parental responsibility for the child: see *Re C (Change of Surname)* [1998] 2 FLR 656.

(c) If consent is obtained from the relevant people, ensure that it is put in writing.

(d) If the change of name is disputed, the matter must be referred to the court for determination as follows:

    (i) if there is a residence order in force, under s. 13;

    (ii) if there is no residence order in force, under s. 8.

Butler-Sloss LJ laid down further guidelines for cases concerning the change of a child's name in *Re W, Re A, Re B (Change of Name)* [1999] 2 FLR 930 with the warning that the guidelines do not purport to be exhaustive. Each case must be decided on its own facts with the welfare of the child the paramount consideration and all the relevant factors weighed in the balance by the court at the time of the hearing. The summary (at p. 933F) is as follows:

(a) If parents are married, they both have the power and the duty to register their child's names.

(b) If they are not married, the mother has the sole duty and power to do so.

(c) After registration of the child's names, the grant of a residence order obliges any person wishing to change the surname to obtain the leave of the court or the written consent of all those who have parental responsibility.

(d) In the absence of a residence order, the person wishing to change the surname from the registered name ought to obtain the relevant written consent or the leave of the court by making an application for a specific issue order.

(e) On any application, the welfare of the child is paramount and the judge must have regard to the s. 1(3) criteria.

(f) Among the factors to which the court should have regard is the registered surname of the child and the reasons for the registration, for instance recognition of the biological link with the child's father. Registration is always a relevant and an important consideration but it is not in itself decisive. The weight to be given to it by the court will depend upon the other relevant factors or valid countervailing reasons which may tip the balance the other way.

(g) The relevant considerations should include factors which may arise in the future as well as the present situation.

(h) Reasons given for changing or seeking to change a child's name based on the fact that the child's name is or is not the same as the parent making the application do not generally carry much weight.

(i) The reasons for an earlier unilateral decision to change a child's name may be relevant.

(j) Any changes of circumstances of the child since the original registration may be relevant.

(k) In the case of a child whose parents were married to each other, the fact of the marriage is important and there would have to be strong reasons to change the name from the father's surname if the child was so registered.

Chapter 29: The Children Act 1989

(l)   Where the child's parents were not married to each other, the mother has control over registration. Consequently, on an application to change the surname of the child, the degree of commitment of the father to the child, the quality of contact, if it occurs, between father and child, the existence or absence of parental responsibility are all relevant factors to take into account.

Use of both parents' surnames

29.132   It may be appropriate in some cases in which there is a dispute about which surname the child is to be known by for both parents' surnames to be used: *Re R (Surname: Using Both Parents')* [2001] 2 FLR 1358. In *Re R* the child of unmarried parents had been registered under the father's name, but after they separated the mother used the name of her new husband (the child's step-father) instead. It was agreed that the mother could move to Spain with her new husband, but the Court of Appeal held that the mother must retain the father's surname for the child. In Spain it is the custom to have one surname from the father and one from the mother and the Court of Appeal hoped that the mother would adopt this practice in order the ease the child's adjustment to a life in that culture. Hale LJ said (at p. 1363) 'parents and courts should be much more prepared to contemplate the use of both surnames in an appropriate case, because that is to recognize the importance of both parents'.

Change of first name

29.133   The law is more relaxed in relation to the use of first names for children than for surnames. In *Re H (A Child)* [2002] 1 FLR 973 the parents separated before the child was born and had no contact with each other. On the child's birth the father registered the birth with his choice of first names. The mother subsequently registered the birth in her choice of names, but her later registration was cancelled. The mother sought a declaration that she could use her own choice of first names for the child. It was held that no order of the court could prevent the mother from using the first name of her choice within the home. Furthermore, she was entitled to use her choice of first name in any dealings with external authorities, provided that she always recognized that the child had an immutable series of names by statutory registration.

Restriction on removal from the jurisdiction

29.134   Section 13(1), CA 1989 also dictates that where a residence order is in force with respect to a child then no person may remove him from the United Kingdom without either:

(a)   the written consent of every person with parental responsibility for the child; or
(b)   the leave of the court.

However, the person with the residence order is permitted to remove the child from the jurisdiction for a period of less than one month without having to comply with the two requirements set out above. The idea is to allow for short holiday trips. However, there is no restriction on the number of trips that may be taken.

29.135   Furthermore, the court can give a general direction at the time it makes the residence order to allow the removal of the child from the jurisdiction generally or for specified purposes. This can be in favour of the person with the residence order or any other person. This can be very useful in that it avoids repeated minor applications to the court. For instance, where the non-residential parent (say, the father) lives abroad and it is envisaged that the child will visit him regularly twice each year the court can make a direction that the father have leave to remove the child from the jurisdiction twice each year.

If a person with a residence order (say, the mother) finds that the consent of the other people **29.136** with parental responsibility is not forthcoming in respect of the proposed temporary removal from the jurisdiction then she must apply to the court for leave using the appropriate prescribed Form. In deciding whether to give leave the guiding consideration is the welfare of the children. As a general rule it should not be difficult to persuade a court to give leave unless there are grounds to suspect that the proposed holiday is really a cover for an unauthorized permanent removal of the children from the jurisdiction.

Permission to remove permanently from the jurisdiction

If it is proposed that the children should emigrate permanently but the other persons **29.137** with parental responsibility refuse to consent then the permission of the court must be sought. In considering whether to give leave to take a child out of the jurisdiction permanently, the welfare of the child is the paramount consideration. However, the current view is that permission should not be withheld unless there is a compelling reason to do so where the decision of the person with the residence order to emigrate is reasonable. The danger that must be taken into account is that there will be frustration and bitterness in the family if the court interferes with the decision of the person with the residence order and that this will rebound on the children. The leading case is *Payne* v *Payne* [2001] 1 FLR 1052, in which the Court of Appeal laid down useful guidelines in relation to such applications:

(a)   the welfare of the child is paramount;
(b)   there is no presumption created by the s. 13(1)(b), CA 1989 in favour of the applicant parent;
(c)   the reasonable proposals of the parent with a residence order wishing to live abroad carry great weight;
(d)   consequently, the proposals have to be scrutinized with care and the court needs to be satisfied that there is a genuine motivation for the move and not the intention to bring contact between the child and the other parent to an end;
(e)   the effect on the applicant parent and the new family of the child of a refusal of leave is very important;
(f)   the effect on the child of the denial of contact with the other parent, and in some cases his family, is very important;
(g)   the opportunity for continuing contact between the child and the parent left behind may be very significant.

The Court of Appeal emphasized that the implementation of the HRA 1998 has not affected the principles the courts should apply in dealing with these difficult issues. For two cases in which permission was given to remove children permanently from the jurisdiction, see *L* v *L* *(Leave to Remove Children from Jurisdiction: Effect on Children)* [2003] 1 FLR 900 and *Re C* *(Permission to Remove from Jurisdiction)* [2003] 1 FLR 1066. However, where removal from the jurisdiction will cause a significant loss to the child in relation to emotional and educational issues leave may be refused (*Re Y (Leave to Remove from Jurisdiction)* [2004] 2 FLR 330—where the child had been brought up to be bilingual in Welsh and English and the parents had shared his care since separation, the court refused the mother's application for leave to remove him from Wales to the USA).

Residence orders and parental responsibility

29.138   The granting of a residence order in favour of anyone automatically gives them parental responsibility for the child: s. 12(2). Where a father who does not have parental responsibility applies for a residence order and the court grants one in his favour, then the court must make an order under s. 4 giving the father parental responsibility: s. 12(1). The s. 4 order must last for the duration of the residence order and can only be ended by an order of the court: ss. 12(4) and 4(3). However, s. 12(3) prevents those with residence orders who are not parents or guardians from giving consent to adoption, freeing for adoption, and appointing a guardian for the child.

Restriction on local authorities applying for residence orders

29.139   A local authority may not apply for a residence order nor have one made in its favour: s. 9(2). However, a residence order may be made in favour of any child, even one subject to a care order (s. 9(1)), although in such a case the residence order will have the effect of discharging the care order (s. 91(1)).

Enforcement of residence orders

29.140   The committal of a parent to prison for failure to comply with a s. 8 order is likely to be harmful to the child and to the future relationship of the child with the parent who applied for committal. Therefore, although committal may be available as a remedy where a s. 8 order is injunctive (i.e., where it requires a person to do, within a specified time, or to abstain from doing, an act) it should be a remedy of last resort. There are other methods which should be tried first.

29.141   Where an order under s. 8, CA 1989 is enforceable by committal r. 4.21A of the FPR 1991, provides that a judge or district judge may, on the application of a person entitled to enforce such an order, direct that a penal notice be attached to it. For further details, see Chapter 30, paragraph 30.101.

29.142   Section 14, CA 1989, provides that if a person is in breach of the arrangements settled by a residence order (whether it be the person in whose favour the order has been made or some other person who is in breach), then the person with the residence order can enforce it under s. 63(3), Magistrates' Courts Act 1980, as if it were an order requiring the other person to produce the child to him. In order to enforce it he must first serve a copy of the residence order on the other person. This remedy does not prevent him from pursuing any other remedy that may be open to him.

29.143   Another way in which a residence (or indeed a contact) order may be enforced is by using s. 34 of the FLA 1986. The object of s. 34 of the FLA 1986 is to give effect to the decision of the court that a child should be given up into the care of a person in accordance with the residence order (or that a child be given up to a person for a period of contact). The FLA 1986 refers to the enforcement of 'custody' and 'access' orders. However, the CA 1989, sch. 13, para. 62 makes provision for s. 34, FLA 1986 to apply to residence and contact orders too. The effect of s. 34 is that 'the court may make an order authorising an officer of the court or a constable to take charge of the child and deliver him to the person concerned'.

Discharge of residence orders

(a) A residence order will usually end upon the child in question attaining the age of 16: **29.144**
    s. 91(10).
(b) If a residence order is made in favour of parents, each of whom have parental responsibility for the child, it will cease to have effect if they live together for a continuous period of more than six months: s. 11(5).
(c) If a care order is made in respect of a child, then any residence order (together with any other s. 8 orders) will be discharged automatically: s. 91(2). Conversely, if a child in care is made the subject of a residence order then the care order will be discharged automatically: s. 91(1).

I CONTACT ORDERS

Contact orders require the person with whom the child is living to allow the child to visit or **29.145** stay with the person named in the order, or for that person and the child otherwise to have contact with each other. Where the parties are unable to agree over the degree of contact which the non-residential parent should have with the child either party may ask the court to determine the contact arrangements. This is called making an application for 'defined contact'. Application is usually made by the non-residential parent who is not being allowed to see the child as much as he would like. However, where a defined contact order has already been made, the residential parent can apply to have contact redefined, or even stopped, if she feels that it is having a bad effect on the children. Normally applications are for definition of regular contact visits but, even where the normal contact visits are working satisfactorily, the court can be asked to resolve a particular issue over contact (for example, whether there should be contact on Christmas Day).

Reasonable contact

The usual form of order will be for 'reasonable contact', and if for some reason it is not **29.146** appropriate or practicable for the child to visit the named person then it is open to the court to order other forms of contact, e.g., telephone calls, letters, or visits by the named person *to* the child. It is a growing principle of case law that contact should not be refused between parent and child unless absolutely necessary in the child's interests: see *Re B (Minors: Access)* [1992] 1 FLR 140 and *Re H (Minors: Access)* [1992] 1 FLR 148.

Contact and human rights

29.147   The denial of contact between parent and child can amount to a breach of the parent's right to respect for family life as guaranteed by Art. 8 of the European Convention for the Protection of Human Rights and Fundamental Freedoms, which was implemented when the HRA 1998 came into force on 2 October 2000: *Hokkanen v Finland* (1995) 19 EHRR 139. Under the Convention, the parent's right to contact with his child is not an absolute right, but the public authorities (which includes the court) are under a duty to take all necessary steps to facilitate reunion as can be taken in the circumstances.

29.148   There has been a series of cases in which unmarried fathers have complained that the refusal of the court to grant them contact with their children constitutes a breach of their right to family life. These complaints were upheld in the cases of *Elsholz v Germany* [2000] 2 FLR 486, *Ciliz v The Netherlands* [2000] 2 FLR 469, *Elsholz v Italy* [2000] Fam Law 680. However, the father's complaint was rejected in *Glaser v UK* [2001] 1 FLR 153. In *S and G v Italy* [2000] 2 FLR 771 a mother's complaint that the authorities had prevented her from having contact with her children was upheld as constituting a breach of Art. 8. In *Bove v Italy* [2005] Fam Law 752, the failure of the court to enforce the father's access rights had infringed Art. 8. The key question to be asked is whether the national authority has taken all steps that are reasonable in the circumstances (*Zawadkaw v Poland* [2005] 2 FLR 897).

29.149   In public law child care cases the obligation on the authorities to promote reunification between parents and children is not absolute. The authorities must do their utmost to facilitate reunification but the rights of all parties concerned must be considered and the best interests of the child must be taken into account (*Hokkanen v Finland* [1996] 1 FLR 289; *KA v Finland* [2003] 1 FLR 696). In *Re F (Care Proceedings: Contact)* [2000] Fam Law 708, litigants were warned that where care orders have been made under, s. 31, CA 1989 together with contact orders under s. 34(4) authorizing the local authority to terminate contact with the parents of the child concerned, it would be disappointing if the Convention were to be routinely used as a makeweight ground of appeal, or if there were in every case to be extensive citation of authorities from the ECHR.

Parent's hostility to contact

29.150   However, there may be cases in which there are cogent reasons for the child to be denied the opportunity for contact with his parent (see, for example, *Re M (Contact: Welfare Test)* at paragraph 29.16 above.

29.151   Sometimes the implacable hostility of one parent towards the other means that the child might be at serious risk of major emotional harm if the reluctant parent is compelled to accept that the child must have a degree of contact with the other parent against her will: *Re D (A Minor) (Contact: Mother's Hostility)* [1993] 2 FLR 1; *Re F (Minors) (Contact: Mother's Anxiety)* [1993] 2 FLR 830; *Re J (A Minor) (Contact)* [1994] 1 FLR 729 and *Re B (A Minor) (Contact: Stepfather's Opposition)* [1997] 2 FLR 579. In *Re W (A Minor) (Contact)* [1994] 2 FLR 441 the Court of Appeal ordered contact between the children and their father to take place in spite of the mother's assertion that she would not obey such an order if it were made. (See also *Re P (Contact: Supervision)* [1996] 2 FLR 314, where contact between the father and children was ordered in spite of the adverse effect of contact on the mother's health.)

However, in *Re H (A Child) (Contact: Mother's Opposition)* [2001] 1 FCR 59 the court held that where a parent objects to contact, it should first evaluate whether that opposition is with or without objective foundation. Where it is without objective foundation the court should not give up the prospect of achieving contact at too early a stage. Rather than use its coercive powers, the court should work with local agencies for counselling and mediation to achieve contact where possible.

There have been cases in which the parent seeking contact becomes so frustrated with the **29.152** lack of co-operation of the other parent that he seeks an order transferring residence to him instead. However, the practical difficulties involved in such a transfer of residence often preclude this as a solution: *Re T (Children)* (unreported) 23 July 2002, CA; *Re K (Contact: Committal Order)* [2003] 1 FLR 277. Nevertheless, in *Re W (A Child)* (unreported) 15 May 2002, CA, a case in which the mother had refused to co-operate with numerous contact orders, the father was eventually successful in his application for a residence order in respect of the children.

Parent's extreme anxiety in relation to contact

There is a distinction between those cases where a parent is simply hostile to contact **29.153** between the other parent and the child and those where there are justified reasons for the parent's anxiety over the issue of contact. The latter tend to be cases where the mother has been so traumatized by the effect of the father's behaviour on her that the prospect of the father having any contact with the child is so stressful to her that the indirect effect of this on the child means that the child's welfare would be likely to suffer as a result of contact taking place. The leading case is *Re L; Re V; Re M; Re H* [2000] 2 FCR 404, in which the Court of Appeal considered four appeals raising the issue of the impact of domestic violence/abuse on contact decisions:

(a) Courts need a heightened awareness of the existence and consequences on children of exposure to inter-parental violence.

(b) Allegations of violence made in the course of a contact application must be adjudicated upon and determined. (Note that where a court holds a preliminary hearing focusing on the issue of domestic violence, the final hearing must be held before the same bench as the case is, effectively, part-heard: *M v A (Contact: Domestic Violence)* [2002] 2 FLR 921.)

(c) There is no prima facie barrier of no contact if violence is proved.

(d) In assessing the impact of past violence on the contact issue, the ability of the violent party to recognize his past conduct, to be aware of the need to change, and to make a genuine effort to do so are likely to be important considerations.

(e) When making an interim order, before adjudication on factual allegations, the court should ensure that the safety of the child and the residential parent is secured before and after any contact occasion.

Even in cases where the residential parent has a genuine and intense phobia of the other parent there may still be justification for ordering indirect contact instead: *Re L (Contact: Genuine Fear)* [2002] 1 FLR 621; *Re S (Violent Parent: Indirect Contact)* [2001] 1 FLR 481. For a case in which the mother's genuine fear of the father did justify the termination of contact, see *Re H (Contact Order) (No. 2)* [2002] 1 FLR 22. When considering whether to terminate contact between a father and child, the judge has to weigh more than the child's happiness in the balance; he also has to ensure that the child's needs will be satisfied not only in the present, but also in the medium and the long term, if contact were terminated: *Re J-S (A Child) (Contact: Parental Responsibility)* [2003] 3 FCR 433.

Child's objections to contact

29.154 Finally, there are also cases in which the child himself may have strong objections to the exercise of contact by his natural father, in which case the older the child is the more weight the court will attach to his wishes. In *Re S (Contact: Children's Views)* [2002] 1 FLR 1156, three children with learning difficulties, aged 16, 14, and 12, expressed views about contact which led to the court making no order regarding the elder two children, and a defined contact order in relation to the youngest child. The court held that if young people are to respect the law, the law has to respect them and their wishes, even if it sometimes means young people making mistakes. The judge so worded the preamble to the order as to underline that the court considered contact to be desirable, but to reassure the children that it would not be imposed on them against their will. Rather, the children would be free to agree to have contact with their father and their mother would not discourage this.

Indirect contact

29.155 In certain cases the court may order that a parent be allowed to maintain contact with the children indirectly, by post and/or by way of telephone calls (see for example *Re O (Contact: Imposition of Conditions)* [1995] 2 FLR 124; *A v L (Contact)* [1998] 1 FLR 361; *Re M (Contact: Family Assistance: McKenzie Friend)* [1999] 1 FLR 75; *Re P (Contact: Indirect Contact)* [1999] 2 FLR 893). However, the court should be careful to define the frequency of such contact in the order and a 'not more than' formula is often useful, for example, that the father be allowed to write to the child not more than four times in each calendar year, or, that the father be allowed to telephone the child not more than once every two weeks. In *Re M (A Minor) (Contact: Conditions)* [1994] Fam Law 252 it was decided that the court may order the mother to comply with an order for contact by post by reading messages to a child who cannot read provided that the mother agrees, but the court cannot order the mother to read to the child the contents of any letter addressed to the child, since she must be permitted to censor the contents of such letters where appropriate. The judge also held that the court cannot order the mother to write progress reports on the child to the father because it is not within the court's powers in making contact orders to order the parents to have contact with each other. Furthermore, the court does not have power to make injunctive orders dressed up as contact orders (see *D v N (Contact Order: Conditions)* [1997] 2 FLR 797, where the Court of Appeal held that the first instance court had no jurisdiction under s. 11(7) of the CA 1989 to impose conditions in the manner of injunctions in order to protect a parent from molestation by the other parent).

Contact centres

29.156 Where families need a neutral meeting place for contact to take place and are unable to find one then the Network of Access and Child Contact Centres (the 'NACCC') may be able to help. The NACCC is a loose federation of centres which each operate independently but which subscribe to a common Code of Practice. The NACCC can be contacted at the following address:

> Minerva House
> Spaniel Row
> Nottingham NG1 6EP
> Tel: 0845 4500 280
> <www.naccc.org.uk>

The NACCC has produced a Protocol for the referral of families to Child Contact Centres. It provides guidance as to which categories of cases are suitable for this service, and the practical steps to be taken in order to get in touch with an appropriate centre and has suggested wording for court orders requiring the attendance of parties and children at the centre. See also the useful article by District Judge John Mitchell 'How should contact centres be used' [2001] Fam Law 613 for guidance and a suggested draft contact order.

Relevance of blood tie in contact disputes

The relevance of a blood tie in contact disputes has been explored in *Re C* [1992] 1 FLR 306. **29.157** The applicant for access was not the child's father, although the child had believed him to be her father at one time. The mother had formed a relationship with another man (who was not the child's father either). The recorder refused the application on the basis that in the long term it would be disruptive to the child and contrary to her welfare. The Court of Appeal upheld the decision, rejecting the applicant's claim that because he had lived with the child for a period of time as her father there must be a compelling reason to justify denying him access. The Court of Appeal held that the existence of a blood tie was an important factor because children, as they grow up, are likely to want to get to know their natural parents. Thus in such a case although the short-term prognosis for contact might indicate that it would not be beneficial the long-term considerations might prevail. These long-term considerations were not present where there was no blood relationship and therefore its absence was a significant factor to be examined when assessing the course most appropriate for the welfare of the child. The observations in this case are likely to be relevant to cases concerning contact by non-parents generally. Such cases are likely to become more common as a result of the CA 1989 which makes it possible for all interested parties to seek s. 8 orders (with the leave of the court where appropriate).

What may a person with a contact order do to safeguard the welfare of the child while he is in his care?

If the child visits or stays with someone with parental responsibility for him (e.g., a parent, **29.158** guardian, or someone with a residence order) then that person may exercise his parental responsibility in so far as it is not incompatible with any order under the CA 1989: s. 2(8). If the child visits or stays with someone without parental responsibility (e.g., a grandparent) then that person may take such action as is reasonable to safeguard or promote the child's welfare: s. 3(5).

Contact order or joint residence order?

29.159 There will be occasions when it is not clear whether the appropriate order will be for a residence order in favour of one party with generous contact to the other, or for a joint residence order. For example, if a child spends each weekday with one parent and every weekend with the other then a 'joint' residence order may be more suitable. If, however, the child lives with one parent for the majority of the time and only sees the other every second or third weekend then a residence order and contact order will probably be made. See paragraph 29.120 and onwards for more detail in respect of 'joint' residence orders (also described as 'shared' residence orders).

Restrictions on the making of contact orders

29.160   (a)   The court must not make a contact order in respect of a child who has reached the age of 16 unless there are exceptional circumstances: s. 9(7).

(b)   Contact orders cannot be made in respect of children who are in local authority care by virtue of a care order, and local authorities may not apply for contact orders nor have them made in their favour: s. 9(2). However, s. 34, CA 1989 does provide a special scheme whereby orders can be made which allow or refuse contact with children in care (see Chapter 33, paragraph 33.81).

(c)   A contact order requiring one parent to allow the child to visit the other will lapse automatically if the parents live together for a continuous period of more than six months: s. 11(6).

(d)   The making of a care order will discharge a contact order (and any other s. 8 order): s. 91(2).

'No contact' orders

29.161 An order that there is to be no contact between the child and a named person falls within the general concept of contact, and it falls within the definition of 'contact order' in s. 8(1), CA 1989 (per Sir Stephen Brown P in *Nottinghamshire County Council* v *P* [1993] 2 FLR 134 at p. 143). Thus it is not appropriate to apply for a prohibited steps order when in reality the party seeks a 'no contact' order, since to do so is to use a prohibited steps order as a 'back door' method of achieving a contact order in a way which is prohibited by s. 9(5)(a), CA 1989.

Enforcement of contact orders

29.162 The enforcement of contact orders can most easily be dealt with by using s. 34, FLA 1986. This remedy is the same as that described for residence orders at paragraph 29.140 and onwards. It is a growing principle that contact should not be ended unless absolutely necessary in the interests of the child: *Re B (Minors: Access)* [1992] 1 FLR 140; *Re H (Minors: Access)* [1992] 1 FLR 148; *Re W (A Minor) (Contact)* [1994] 2 FLR 441. Contempt proceedings are not really suitable for enforcing a contact order, and should only be used as the very last resort when the parent with whom the child resides unreasonably refuses contact: *Re N (A Minor) (Access: Penal Notices)* [1992] 1 FLR 134; *F* v *F (Contact: Committal)* [1998] 2 FLR 237. However, where a parent persistently refuses to comply with a contact order the court will, in suitable cases, imprison that parent as a last resort: *A* v *N (Committal: Refusal of Contact)* [1997] 1 FLR 533; *Re M (Contact Order: Committal)* [1999] 1 FLR 810.

The Children and Adoption Bill

The Children and Adoption Bill was introduced in the House of Lords on 13 June 2005 and is **29.163** currently still going through Parliament. Some of the main changes it aims to bring about include the following:

- Where there has been a breach of a contact order, the court's powers are increased by adding:
  - a power to make enforcement orders imposing an unpaid work requirement;
  - a power to order one person to pay compensation to another for a financial loss caused by a breach.
- Improving the processes which take place before a contact order is made.
- Allowing a court, even if it does not make a contact order, to direct a party to take part in an activity ('contact activity directions') that would promote contact with a child e.g., programmes, classes, and counselling or guidance sessions which may assist with contact, including information sessions about mediation. It may make similar provision by means of a condition in a contact order (contact activity conditions). The court may ask a CAFCASS officer to monitor compliance with such directions and conditions for a period of up to a year.
- Reforming the court's existing power to make family assistance orders so that the requirement that they be made only in exceptional circumstances is removed and the maximum duration is extended from six to twelve months.

J PROHIBITED STEPS ORDERS

A prohibited steps order directs that no step which could be taken by a parent in meeting his **29.164** parental responsibility for a child, and which is of a kind specified in the order, must be taken by a person without the consent of the court. The order can be made either on its own or together with a residence or contact order. It might be used, for example, in a case where no residence order is in force, to restrain one parent from removing the child of the family from the jurisdiction without the consent of the other parent. The following are examples of circumstances in which a prohibited steps order is *not* appropriate:

(a) Where a parent wishes to apply for an order that an abducted child be returned to live with her at home, then she should apply for a residence order (possibly with conditions and directions attached), rather than a specific issue order seeking the return of the child together with a prohibited steps order to prevent further removal: see *dicta* of Butler-Sloss LJ in *Re W (A Minor) (Residence Order)* [1992] 2 FLR 332.

(b) A prohibited steps order cannot be used to prohibit the father from having contact with the mother since the act of the father in contacting the mother does not fall within the statutory definition of 'a step which could be taken by a parent in meeting his parental responsibility for a child': *Croydon LBC* v *A (No. 1)* [1992] 2 FLR 341.

(c) A local authority cannot apply for a prohibited steps order to exclude the father from the family home in circumstances in which he poses a threat to the children of the family, since that is a 'back door' method of achieving a residence order (by regulating who could live in the household) or contact order (by regulating the contact between the father and the children) and local authorities are prohibited from applying for a residence or contact order by the terms of s. 9(2), CA 1989: *Nottinghamshire County Council* v *P* [1993] 2 FLR 514; *Re S (Minors) (Inherent Jurisdiction: Ouster)* [1994] 1 FLR 623. Indeed, in *Nottinghamshire County Council* v *P* (above), Sir Stephen Brown P expressed doubt as to whether a prohibited steps order could ever be used as an 'ouster' order. This view was confirmed in *Re D (Prohibited Steps Orders)* [1996] 2 FLR 273, where the court overturned an order preventing the father from staying overnight in the matrimonial home, since in this case it operated as an 'ouster' by the 'back door' in circumstances which did not warrant it (but see Chapter 34, paragraph 34.24 for details of the court's new statutory power to include an exclusion requirement in an emergency protection order in certain circumstances).

(d) Where a court wishes to order that a named person shall have 'no contact' with a child then the order falls within the definition of a 'contact' order in s. 8(1), CA 1989, and it is not appropriate to make a prohibited steps order preventing contact *(Nottinghamshire County Council* v *P* (above); *Re H (Prohibited Steps Order)* [1995] 1 FLR 638).

Restrictions on the use of prohibited steps orders

29.165 (a) A prohibited steps order may not be made in respect of children over the age of 16, save in exceptional circumstances: s. 9(7).

(b) A prohibited steps order can only relate to an action which is within the power of a parent and does not (unlike wardship) appear to bind the child or give the court control over the decisions which the child is entitled to take for himself.

(c) A prohibited steps order cannot be made in respect of a child in the care of a local authority pursuant to a care order: s. 9(1).

(d) A prohibited steps order cannot be used as a 'back-door' method of achieving a result which could have been achieved by the making of a residence or contact order: s. 9(5)(a).

(e) A prohibited steps order cannot be used in any way which is denied to the High Court by s. 100(2) in the exercise of its inherent jurisdiction with respect to children, e.g., to commit a child to care, to require a local authority to accommodate a child or to give the local authority power to make decisions about children. The order could not be used to prevent the child's removal from care where there is no care order, but it could be used to prevent someone from visiting the child in a foster home in such circumstances: see ss. 100(2) and 9(5)(b).

(f) The making of a care order will discharge a prohibited steps order: s. 91(2).

K   SPECIFIC ISSUE ORDERS

Specific issue orders, like prohibited steps orders, are designed to be made either on their **29.166** own or together with a residence or contact order. It enables the court to give directions to determine a specific issue which has arisen, or which may arise, in connection with any aspect of parental responsibility for a child, e.g., the decision to change the child's surname, choice of schools, religious upbringing, medical treatment. However, note that where a residence order is in force an application to change a child's surname is by way of a free-standing application under s. 13, CA 1989, and not by way of a specific issue order: *Dawson* v *Wearmouth* (above); *A* v *Y (Child's Surname)* [1999] 2 FLR 5. For a more detailed discussion of the considerations involved in an application to change a child's surname, see paragraph 29.127 and onwards.

Some examples of cases in which specific issue orders were used are as follows: **29.167**

(a) *Re K (Specific Issue Order)* [1999] 2 FLR 280—where the father applied for a specific issue order that the mother tell their child of the father's existence and of his true paternity, but the order was refused since on the facts there were cogent reasons to deny the child's right to know his paternity.

(b) *Re R (A Minor) (Blood Transfusion)* [1993] 2 FLR 757—where the court held that it was appropriate for the local authority to apply for a specific issue order to authorize a blood transfusion to the 10-month-old child of parents who were Jehovah's Witnesses.

(c) *Re HG (Specific Issue Order: Sterilization)* [1993] 1 FLR 587—where it was appropriate to deal with a case concerning the sterilization of a child by way of a specific issue order. In such cases there will be a need for the child to be granted party status and to be legally represented, as to which see *CAFCASS and the National Assembly of Wales Practice Note (Appointment of Guardians in Private Law Proceedings)* [2006] 2 FLR 143 and *Practice Note 'Official Solicitor: Appointment in Family Proceedings'* [2001] 2 FLR 155, since the Official Solicitor will have a continuing role in such cases where they concern older children.

(d) *Re C (HIV Test)* [1999] 2 FLR 1004—where the court made a specific issue order authorizing blood testing of a baby girl with a view to determining whether she was infected with HIV.

(e) *Re M (Medical Treatment: Consent)* [1999] 2 FLR 1097—where a specific issue order was sought in a case in which it was proposed to carry out a heart transplant on a 15-year-old girl against her wishes.

(f) *Re P (Parental Dispute: Judicial Determination)* [2003] 1 FLR 286—where parents seek a specific issue order to determine which school the children should attend, the court must make the final decision and must not abdicate that responsibility by simply appointing one parent with absolute responsibility for the decision.

The use of specific issue orders extends to disputes involving non-parents, including some **29.168** involving local authorities, e.g., sterilization or abortion in relation to a child in care. The court could either take the relevant decision itself or direct that it should be determined by others, e.g., that a child be treated as a specified doctor deems appropriate.

Restrictions on the making of specific issue orders

29.169 The restrictions are the same as those described for prohibited steps orders at paragraph 29.165 above.

L   INTERIM ORDERS AND SUPPLEMENTARY PROVISIONS

29.170 The supplementary provisions set out in s. 11(3) and (7), CA 1989 are intended to preserve the greatest possible flexibility of the court's powers in relation to s. 8 orders so that the court can make interim orders, delay implementation of orders, or attach other special conditions to orders where the circumstances call for it. The court can, for example, direct that the order be made to have effect for a specified period, or contain provisions which are to have effect for a specified period.

When will an interim application be appropriate?

29.171 Section 11(3), CA 1989 states that where the court has power to make a s. 8 order, it may do so at any time during the course of the proceedings in question even though it is not in a position to dispose finally of those proceedings.

29.172 The solicitor should always consider applying for an interim order where the parties are unable to agree about residence or contact. The longer the period that elapses during which the client does not have residence/contact, the more damage is done to his long-term application and an interim application should therefore be made if it is felt that it will secure residence/contact for the client in advance of the full hearing. However, it should be stressed that the normal approach of the court on an interim residence hearing is to maintain the status quo unless there are strong reasons against this. (See paragraph 29.125 and onwards.) Thus where one party has in fact had the child residing with him for some time (even if not by virtue of a court order), the court is unlikely to order the child to be transferred to the other party pending the full hearing.

Example 1 Mr and Mrs Jones separate. They are in the process of a divorce. The children remain in the matrimonial home with Mrs Jones. Six months later Mr Jones manages to secure a house for himself and wishes the children to live with him. He intends to make an application for a residence order and wishes to seek an interim residence order meanwhile. His application will almost certainly fail.

Example 2 The facts are as in Example 1. Fed up with waiting, Mr Jones fails to return the children after a contact visit and keeps them at his flat. Mrs Jones makes an application for an interim residence order in respect of the children. The court takes the view that the children should be returned to Mrs Jones pending a final hearing as this was the status quo before the snatch. She is therefore granted an interim residence order.

The court is more likely to make an interim order defining contact than transferring the residence of the children. If a parent who wishes to seek a long-term order for residence or contact is being denied any, or any regular, contact with the children, application should usually be made for interim contact in order to ensure that his full application will not be prejudiced because he has lost touch with the children.

Example 3 The facts are as in Example 1 above. Mr Jones is being refused any contact with the children. Although Mr Jones is unlikely to be granted an interim residence order in respect of the children, he should apply for interim contact in an attempt to preserve close contact with the children. Depending on the reasons that Mrs Jones puts forward for her attitude, the chances are that an interim contact order will be made.

It can also be very valuable for the court hearing a final contact application if a few interim visits have taken place during the run-up to the case in order that their effect can be assessed. If there is real concern as to the children's attitude to contact, the court may order these visits to be supervised by a children and family reporter who can then report to the court.

If a parent with a residence order in respect of the children has been ordered to afford **29.173** reasonable contact or defined contact to the other parent, she should not thereafter stop contact visits of her own accord. If she does so she will be in breach of the contact order and liable to be brought before the court with a view to committal for contempt (although other methods of enforcing orders are preferred to committal proceedings except as a last resort). The proper course if she is worried about contact continuing is for her to make an application to have contact stopped and, in the meanwhile, to seek an interim order to this effect. In practice, a parent who is genuinely worried about the effect of contact on the children will normally simply refuse to let the children go, leaving it up to the other party to decide whether to take the matter back to court to obtain an order for defined contact or to enforce the existing defined contact arrangements. A parent who has stopped contact or is contemplating doing so must, however, be warned that it will weigh heavily against her in any applications concerning the children if it is found that she has done so without good reason.

Use of other supplementary provisions

Section 11(7)(a), CA 1989, allows the court to make a s. 8 order which contains directions **29.174** about how it is to be carried into effect. Section 11(7)(b) permits the court to make a s. 8 order which imposes conditions:

which must be complied with by any person:
(a)   in whose favour the order is made;
(b)   who is a parent of the child concerned;
(c)   who is not a parent of his but who has parental responsibility for him; or
(d)   with whom the child is living and to whom the conditions are expressed to apply.

There are numerous ways in which the court may make use of these provisions to give effect to s. 8 orders.

Example 1 Mr and Mrs Jones are divorcing. Mr Jones has moved to Coventry. Each of them applies for a residence order in respect of their son, Tom, aged 12. Tom is presently at school near to the former matrimonial home in Exeter where Mrs Jones still lives. The court hears the dispute in May 2004 and decides that Tom should move to live with his father. Tom is just about to take his school examinations. Therefore the court *delays implementation* of the order to allow Tom to finish the school term at his present school. The court directs that the residence order will take effect on 1 August 2004.

29.175   The court could also, for example, use the supplementary provisions to order a gradual build-up of contact in circumstances where a child had not seen the person concerned for a long time. For an example of a contact order containing conditions as to the exercise of indirect contact by the father to his child, see *Re O (Contact: Imposition of Conditions)* [1995] 2 FLR 124 and *Re P (Contact: Indirect Contact)* [1999] 2 FLR 893.

29.176   Conditions and directions under s. 11(7) may only be attached to ensure that the s. 8 order works effectively. The provisions cannot be used to impose conditions unrelated to the issue of contact, but aimed at protecting the other parent from harassment: *D v N (Contact Order: Conditions)* (above).

29.177   Note that the Children and Adoption Bill, currently still before Parliament (see further in paragraph 29.163, above), includes provisions for the court to make 'contact activity conditions' in appropriate cases and to ask a CAFCASS officer to monitor compliance of any such conditions for a period of up to one year.

M   SETTLING RESIDENCE AND CONTACT DISPUTES

29.178   It is of the utmost importance that the parties should be encouraged to resolve their differences over residence and contact. Bitter disputes between parents cause a great deal of distress to children, particularly if a full court hearing has to be held to delve into all the issues.

29.179   It should be remembered at all times that one of the fundamental principles of the CA 1989 is that the court should make no order unless it considers that to make an order would be better for the child than making no order at all (s. 1(5)). If, therefore, the parties do reach a compromise and the court takes the view that there is a realistic possibility of it working then the court may well question the necessity for embodying the agreement in any form of court order, whether by consent or otherwise.

Mediation

29.180   It is becoming more common for parents to use family mediation as a method of negotiating an agreement in relation to the issues surrounding their separation and/or divorce. This method of alternative dispute resolution is particularly suitable for disputes in relation to the arrangements as to where a child will live and how he will share time between his parents after the separation. For further discussion of this see Chapter 3.

N   VARIATION OF S. 8 ORDERS

29.181   The court has power to make new s. 8 orders from time to time and to vary or discharge existing orders. A party who seeks to vary an existing order must file the appropriate application form and apply for a hearing. Naturally the court will not make a new order if nothing has changed since the original order was made.

O   FAMILY ASSISTANCE ORDERS

The CA 1989 introduced the 'family assistance order' which is designed to involve a proba-   **29.182**
tion officer (or officer of the local authority) for a *short period* in helping a family at a time of marital breakdown.

Family assistance orders may only be made in *exceptional circumstances* and with the *agree-*   **29.183**
ment of all those involved (except the child): s. 16(3) and (7). There is no need for the court to make a s. 8 order as a prerequisite to granting a family assistance order (s. 16(1)), but the supervisor may refer the matter back to the court if there is a s. 8 order in force (s. 16(6)). However, he may only refer back issues relating to existing s. 8 orders and cannot therefore take steps for the child's committal to care. Where the case is referred back to court then the court may make any s. 8 order (s. 10(1)(b)), subject to the restrictions contained in s. 9, CA 1989; the officer would not need to make an application. When the officer is concerned about the child's well-being he should refer the case to the local authority for investigation under s. 47(1)(b), CA 1989.

Family assistance orders are still comparatively rare. In *Leeds County Council* v *C* [1993] 1 FLR   **29.184**
269 Booth J made it clear that where the court wished to make an order for supervised contact the appropriate way of achieving supervision was by way of a family assistance order; the court at first instance was wrong to purport to order contact with a condition attached to it pursuant to s. 11(7) that such contact be supervised. Furthermore, there is no power under s. 11(7), CA 1989 to make orders against a local authority in private law proceedings requiring that authority to supervise contact; instead, a family assistance order may be made: *Re E (Family Assistance Order)* [1999] 2 FLR 512.

In *Re U (Application to Free for Adoption)* [1993] 2 FLR 992 the grandparents of a child in care   **29.185**
maintained contact with their grandchild and wished in due course to adopt her. The local authority argued that the grandparents were unsuitable to be adoptive parents. The judge at first instance made a residence order in favour of the grandparents. The Court of Appeal rejected the local authority's appeal but varied the order by adding a family assistance order which required the local authority to make available one of its officers to advise and assist the grandparents over a period of six months or until the grandparents applied to adopt the child.

In *S* v *P (Contact Application: Family Assistance Order)* [1997] 2 FLR 277, Callman J in the   **29.186**
Family Division refused to grant the father's application for a family assistance order. The father was in prison and he asked the court to make a family assistance order to require the local authority to provide an escort to bring the children to prison to visit him. The Court held that it was not appropriate to make the order for this purpose.

For further comment on family assistance orders see the cases of *Re M (Contact: Supervision)*   **29.187**
[1998] 1 FLR 727, *Re M (Contact: Family Assistance: McKenzie Friend)* (above) and *Re K (Supervision Orders)* [1999] 2 FLR 303.

29.188 Note that the Children and Adoption Bill, currently still before Parliament (see further in paragraph 26.163, above), includes the removal of the requirement that family assistance orders be made only in exceptional circumstances and extends the maximum duration of such orders from six to twelve months.

P   FINANCIAL PROVISION AND PROPERTY ADJUSTMENT FOR CHILDREN

29.189 Section 15, CA 1989, together with sch. 1 of the Act, set out the provisions whereby the court can order financial provision for children. The provisions do not replace those in the Matrimonial Causes Act 1973 or the Domestic Proceedings and Magistrates' Courts Act 1978. The effect of the Child Support Act 1991 ('CSA 1991') on those provisions is set out in paragraph 29.197 and onwards.

'Financial provision' comes within definition of 'family proceedings'

29.190 An application for financial provision comes within the definition of 'family proceedings' for the purposes of the CA 1989. Therefore, a court hearing such an application may make residence or contact orders (or any other s. 8 order) if it considers such orders should be made: s. 10(1).

Who is under an obligation to pay?

29.191 The obligation to pay lies only upon parents and step-parents.

29.192 'Parents' include the child's natural mother and father and also any party to a marriage (whether or not subsisting) in relation to whom the child concerned is a child of the family and any civil partner in a civil partnership (whether or not subsisting) in relation to whom the child concerned is a child of the family (sch. 1, para. 16(2)). An order cannot be made against a person who has not been married to the applicant and is not the natural parent of the child concerned: *J v J (A Minor) (Property Transfer)* [1993] 2 FLR 56.

29.193 'Child' includes a child over 18 where an application is made under sch. 1, para. 2 or 6: sch. 1, para. 16(1).

29.194 'Child of the family' is defined in s. 105(1) as being, in relation to the parties to a marriage:

(a)   a child of both those parties;

(b)   any other child, not being a child who is placed with those parties as foster parents by a local authority or voluntary organization, who has been treated by both of those parties as a child of their family.

29.195 When deciding whether or not to exercise its powers against a person who is not the mother or father of the child, the court must have regard to:

(a)   whether that person had assumed responsibility for the maintenance of the child and, if so, the extent to which and basis on which he assumed that responsibility and the length of period during which he assumed that responsibility and the length of the period during which he met that responsibility;

(b) whether he did so knowing that the child was not his child;

(c) the liability of any other person to maintain the child.

Who can apply for payment?

Parents, including unmarried mothers, unmarried fathers without parental responsibility, **29.196** guardians, special guardians, and people with a residence order will be able to apply for a range of orders in relation to children: sch. 1, para. 1(1).

What orders are available?

As a result of the coming into force of the CSA 1991 the courts now have only limited **29.197** jurisdiction to make unsecured or secured periodical payments orders for the benefit of a child. The court retains jurisdiction to make such orders where:

(a) the child is the step-child of the prospective payer, provided that the child has been treated as a child of the family by him; or

(b) the person applying for the order is the guardian of the child; or

(c) the person applying for the order is not the parent of the child but is a person in whose favour a residence order has been made in respect of the child.

Where financial provision is sought against the natural parent of the child then in normal **29.198** circumstances it will be necessary to apply to the Child Support Agency for a maintenance assessment to be carried out. The courts no longer have jurisdiction to make periodical payments orders in these circumstances: s. 8, CSA 1991. An alternative, where the carer parent is not in receipt of state benefits, may be for the parents to enter into a maintenance agreement for the support of the child. For further details of the CSA 1991, see Chapter 20.

However, it is important to remember that the courts retain jurisdiction to make lump sum **29.199** and property settlement and property transfer orders as follows:

(a) Family proceedings court: lump sum order up to a maximum of £1,000.

(b) High Court and county court:

    (i) lump sum order of unlimited amount;

    (ii) settlement of property order for the benefit of the child;

    (iii) transfer of property order to or for the benefit of the child.

As a general rule orders for financial provision will end when the child attains the age of 17. **29.200** However, provision can be made for orders to extend until the child reaches 18 or beyond: sch. 1, paras. 2 and 3.

The court will only make a lump sum order to provide for a particular item of capital expend- **29.201** iture: lump sum orders will not be made in such a way as to provide for the regular support of the child even though the Child Support Agency had made a nil assessment and the respondent father lived in a house worth £2.6 million and had motor vehicles valued at £190,000: *Phillips* v *Peace* [1996] 2 FLR 237.

What matters will the court consider when making an order for financial provision?

29.202   The list of factors to which the court must have regard in considering whether or not to order financial provision for a child are set out in sch. 1, para. 4. The factors include the income, earning capacity, property, and other financial resources of the parents, the applicant, and any other person in whose favour the court proposes to make the order, together with their financial needs, obligations, and responsibilities; the financial needs of the child; the income, earning capacity, property, and other financial resources of the child; any physical or mental disability of the child; the manner in which the child was being, or was expected to be, educated or trained.

29.203   In a suitable case the court has power to transfer a council tenancy from the joint names of the parties into the sole name of one of them for the benefit of the children; the word 'benefit' is not limited to cases where a financial benefit is to be conferred on the child: *K v K (Minors: Property Transfer)* [1992] 2 FLR 220; *Re F (Minors) (Parental Home: Ouster)* [1994] 1 FLR 246; *B v B (Transfer of Tenancy)* [1994] Fam Law 250. However, it seems that s. 1(1), CA 1989, does not apply to applications under sch. 1: *J v C (Child: Financial Provision)* [1999] 1 FLR 152. Section 105, CA 1989, expressly excludes maintenance from the definition of the 'upbringing' of a child; it is unlikely that Parliament intended that an application for a property transfer should be governed by the principle that the child's welfare is paramount when applications for periodical payments are expressly excluded from that principle. Furthermore, in *K v H (Child Maintenance)* [1993] 2 FLR 61 Sir Stephen Brown P held that the provisions of sch. 1 deal comprehensively with financial provision and should not be confused with applications relating to the upbringing of a child or the administration of the child's own property. Nonetheless, the welfare of the child is a relevant consideration, even if not paramount or the first consideration: *J v C (Child: Financial Provision)* (above).

29.204   It is clear that property adjustment orders should not ordinarily be used to provide benefits for the child after he has attained independence: *J v C (Child: Financial Provision)* (above). Thus, the transfer of property to a child absolutely would be an exceptional order to make: *A v A (A Minor: Financial Provision)* [1994] 1 FLR 657. Furthermore, where an unmarried father is ordered to purchase a house on trust for sale for the children, with sale to be postponed until the youngest child reaches 21 or until all of the children have ceased full-time secondary or tertiary education, it is wrong to give the children beneficial interests in the proceeds of sale since this would make provision for them beyond their dependency: *T v S* [1994] 1 FCR 743 (FD).

29.205   In the case of *Re P (Child: Financial Provision)* [2003] 2 FLR 865 the father was extremely wealthy and the court made an award to the mother which drew a balance between seeking to give the child a standard of living bearing some relationship with the father's resources and lifestyle, and yet avoiding the provision of support to the mother as if it had been spousal maintenance. However, it is important for the court to guard against unreasonable claims made on behalf of the child but with a disguised element of providing for the mother's independent benefit. It is noteworthy that *Re P (Child: Financial Provision)* places more weight on the welfare of the child in sch. 1 proceedings than was the case in *J v C (Child: Financial Provision)* (above).

Variation of orders for financial relief

The provisions for variation of periodical payments are contained in sch. 1, para. 6. **29.206**

Interim orders

The court has power to make interim orders for financial provision in respect of a child and **29.207** the relevant provisions are to be found in sch. 1, para. 9. There are no time limits imposed by the statute upon interim orders and provision is made for orders to be renewed from time to time. This reflects the principle that all orders are really interim because the needs and circumstances of children are always changing. The court is given power to make further orders for periodical payments and lump sums after the original application has been determined. However, property adjustment orders remain a 'once and for all' provision.

Q   KEY DOCUMENTS

Statutes **29.208**
Adoption and Children Act 2002
Children Act 1989
Civil Partnership Act 2004
Human Rights Act 1998
Matrimonial Causes Act 1973

Statutory Instruments
Family Proceedings Rules 1991
Parental Responsibility Agreement Regulations 1991

Practice Directions/Practice Notes
Practice Note 'Official Solicitor: Appointment in Family Proceedings' [2001] 2 FLR 155
Practice Direction (Representation of Children in Family Proceedings pursuant to Family Proceedings Rules 1991, Rule 9.5) [2004] 1 FLR 1188
CAFCASS and the National Assembly for Wales Practice Note (Appointment of Guardians in Private Law Proceedings) [2006] 2 FLR 143
The President's Private Law Programme

Parliamentary Bills
Children and Adoption Bill (introduced in the House of Lords on 13 June 2005)

Websites
<www.naccc.org.uk> Network of Access and Child Contact Centres (NACCC)

Variation of orders for financial relief

The provisions for variation of periodical payments are contained in MFPA, para 6.   29.205

Interim orders

The court has power to make interim orders for financial provision in respect of a child and   29.207
the relevant provisions are to be found in section 1, para 9. There are no time limits imposed
by the statute upon an interim order and provision is made, as is usual, to be reviewed from time
to time. This reflects the principle that all orders are really interim because the needs and
circumstances of children are always changing. The court is given power to make further
orders for periodical payments and lump sums after the original application has been
determined. However, periodical adjusted orders cannot be made on death, and for all provisions.

Q KEY DOCUMENTS

29.208

Statutes
- Adoption and Children Act 2002
- Children Act 1989
- Civil Partnership Act 2004
- Human Rights Act 1998
- Matrimonial Causes Act 1973

Statutory instruments
- Family Proceeding Rules 1991
- Parental Responsibility Agreement Regulations 1991

Practice Directions and Protocols
- Practice Note (The President: Appointment of Family Experts) [2001] 2 FLR 155
- Practice Direction (Representation of Children in Family Proceedings pursuant to Family Proceedings Rules 1991 rule 9.5) [2004] 1 FLR 1188
- SFLA Code of the revised Association for the Care (Note regarding the representation of children in care credits) [2004] 1 FLR 1111
- The Pre-Action Protocol for Proceedings

Parliamentary bills
- Children and Adoption Bill Introduced in the House of Lords on 12 June 2005

Internet
- www.thecapacitypeasures of Access and Child Contact on line Comments (A&CC)

30

PROCEDURE FOR ORDERS UNDER THE CHILDREN ACT 1989

A   THE COURTS—JURISDICTION AND ALLOCATION OF PROCEEDINGS

30.01 In addition to streamlining and codifying the law relating to children, the Children Act 1989 ('CA 1989') creates a unified structure of the High Court, county courts, and family proceedings court. The structure is as follows:

(a) High Court tier: staffed by Family Division judges;
(b) county court tier: staffed by selected circuit judges sitting at designated trial centres. There are three classes of county court:
 (i) divorce county courts;
 (ii) family hearing centres;
 (iii) care centres;
(c) family proceedings court: staffed by magistrates.

The criteria that govern which court is the most appropriate venue are contained in the Children (Allocation of Proceedings) Order 1991 ('Allocation Order 1991'). After considering the important guiding principle in s. 1(2) of the CA 1989, which establishes the presumption that delay in the conduct of proceedings is prejudicial to the interests of the child, the basic factors to be taken into account (as set out in Art. 7(2) of the Allocation Order 1991), are:

(a) the length, importance, and complexity of the case;
(b) the urgency of the case;
(c) the need to consolidate the case with other proceedings that are pending.

30.02 There is some judicial guidance as to the types of cases which should generally *not* be tried in the family proceedings court. Those cases can be summarized as follows:

(a) Cases likely to last for more than two to three days: *Re H (A Minor) (Care Proceedings: Child's Wishes)* [1993] 1 FLR 440; *Essex County Council v L (Minors), The Times,* 18 December 1992.
(b) Cases in which there is complex and/or conflicting medical evidence: *Essex County Council v L (Minors)* (above); *Re H (A Minor) (Care Proceedings: Child's Wishes)* (above); *C v Solihull Metropolitan Borough Council* [1993] 1 FLR 290.
(c) Cases in which young children have sustained serious non-accidental injuries for which the parents offer no acceptable explanation: *C v Solihull Metropolitan Borough Council* (above); *S v Oxfordshire County Council* [1993] 1 FLR 452.
(d) Cases with an international element, e.g., consideration of the Hague Convention on

the Civil Aspects of International Child Abduction 1980 should be transferred to the High Court: *R v R (Residence Order: Child Abduction)* [1995] 2 FLR 625.

(e) Cases in which a party seeks leave to withhold information from another party should be transferred to the High Court: *Re C (Disclosure)* [1996] 1 FLR 797.

(f) Cases where the release of confidential information or disclosure of documentation raise difficult points of law or a sensitive exercise of discretion should be transferred to the High Court: *Re EC (Disclosure of Material)* [1996] 2 FLR 123.

However, note that the President of the Family Division has made it very clear that where points arise concerning the Human Rights Act 1998 ('HRA 1998') those points should be taken and decided in the court in which they arise and at the time they arise, whether that be in a family proceedings court, a county court, or the High Court.

Commencement of proceedings

Proceedings to be commenced in family proceedings court

Proceedings with a public law element will, generally speaking, commence in the family **30.03** proceedings court and will be governed by the public law protocol for care cases (see further in paragraph 33.32). However, there is provision for them to move horizontally within the same tier of courts or vertically up and down from one tier to another. Therefore, criteria have been created to ensure that cases are allocated to the most appropriate venue for the hearing. Those criteria are contained in the Allocation of Order 1991. Article 3 of that Order sets out those proceedings which *must* be commenced in the family proceedings court:

(a) s. 25 (use of accommodation for restricting liberty);

(b) s. 31 (care and supervision orders);

(c) s. 33(7) (leave to change name of or remove from United Kingdom child in care);

(d) s. 34 (parental contact with children in care);

(e) s. 36 (education supervision orders);

(f) s. 43 (child assessment orders);

(g) s. 44 (emergency protection orders);

(h) s. 45 (duration of emergency protection orders etc.);

(i) s. 46(7) (application for emergency protection order by police officer);

(j) s. 48 (powers to assist discovery of children etc.);

(k) s. 50 (recovery orders);

(l) s. 75 (protection of children in an emergency);

(m) s. 77(6) (appeal against steps taken under s. 77(1));

(n) s. 102 (powers of constable to assist etc.);

(o) para. 19 of sch. 2 (approval of arrangements to assist child to live abroad);

(p) para. 23 of sch. 2 (contribution orders);

(q) para. 8 of sch. 8 (certain appeals);

(r) s. 23, Adoption and Children Act 2002 ('ACA 2002') (varying placement orders);

. . .

(t) s. 20, Child Support Act 1991 (appeals) where the appeals are to be dealt with in accordance with the Child Support Appeals (Jurisdiction of Courts) Order 1993;

(u) s. 30, Human Fertilisation and Embryology Act 1990 (parental orders in favour of gamete donors).

However, the practitioner should note that there are two exceptions to the general rule that the above proceedings should commence in a family proceedings court:

(i) where proceedings within (b), (e), (f), (g), (i), or (j) above arise as a result of the High Court or county court directing that a local authority should investigate the child's circumstances, then the proceedings must be commenced in the court which directed that investigation, provided that it is the High Court or a county court 'care centre'. If it is not, then the court which directed the investigation must choose a care centre. The reason for this is that the court directing the investigation did so with a view to the possibility of the local authority instigating care or supervision proceedings;

(ii) where proceedings are of the type in (a)–(k), (n), or (o) *and* there are proceedings of the same kind pending in another court, then that *other* court is the appropriate court for *all* of the proceedings. The proceedings should be consolidated and heard together.

Extension, variation, or discharge of an order

30.04   Article 4 of the Children (Allocation of Proceedings) Order 1991 provides that, generally speaking, proceedings under the Children Act 1989 or under the ACA 2002:

(a)   to extend, vary or discharge an order, or
(b)   the determination of which may have the effect of varying or discharging an order

shall be made to the court which made the order. However, there are two exceptions to that rule:

(i)   an application for an order under ss. 8, 14A, or 14D which would have the effect of varying or discharging a s. 8 order which was made by a county court of its own motion (i.e., under s. 10(1)(b), CA 1989) must be made to a *designated county court* (Art. 4(2));

(ii)   an application to extend, vary, or discharge an interim care order or interim supervision order made by a county court under s. 38, CA 1989, or for an order which would have the effect of extending, varying or discharging of such an interim order must be made to a *care centre* (Art. 4(3)).

Transfer of proceedings

30.05   The transfer of proceedings horizontally or vertically is largely governed by the Allocation Order 1991. However, those provisions are supplemented by the Family Proceedings Rules 1991 (the 'FPR 1991'—for High Court and county court) and the Family Proceedings Courts (Children Act 1989) Rules 1991 (the 'FPC(CA 1989)R 1991'—for family proceedings courts).

30.06   There are complex provisions governing the following matters and the authors do not propose to expand upon the details here. Instead the appropriate references to the relevant provisions for each type of transfer are as follows:

(a) transfer from one family proceedings court to another—see Art. 6, Allocation Order 1991 and r. 6, FPC(CA 1989)R 1991;

(b) transfer from family proceedings court to county court by family proceedings court: see Art. 7, Allocation Order 1991 and r. 6, FPC(CA 1989)R 1991. See also Chapter 33, paragraph 33.102 and onwards;

(c) transfer from family proceedings court following refusal of family proceedings court to transfer (see Art. 9 and r. 4.6, FPR 1991);

(d) transfer from one county court to another (see Art. 10 and 14–20 of the Allocation Order 1991);

(e) transfer from county court to family proceedings court by county court (see Art. 11, Allocation Order 1991);

(f) transfer from county court to High Court by county court (see Art. 12 of the Allocation Order 1991);

(g) transfer from High Court to county court (see Art. 13, Allocation Order 1991).

Public law applications in the county court

If an application under Parts III, IV, or V of the CA 1989 (i.e., for an order with a public law   **30.07** element) is to be heard in a county court, then that county court must also be a designated *care centre* (see Art. 18 of the Allocation Order 1991). Note that as from 1 November 2003 all care cases will be regulated by the public law protocol, which is discussed in detail in paragraph 33.32.

Private law proceedings

Private law proceedings will be largely self-allocating, since they will usually arise in the   **30.08** course of divorce proceedings and so will be heard in the appropriate county court.

The Private Law Programme

The Private Law Programme commenced in 2004 and contains best practice guidance for the   **30.09** conduct of private law cases in county courts and in the High Court. It was extended to family proceedings courts as from January 2006. Where an application is made to the court under Part II of the CA 1989, the welfare of the child will be safeguarded by the application of the overriding objective of the family justice system in three respects: (1) dispute resolution at the First Hearing; (2) effective court control, including monitoring outcomes against aims; (3) flexible facilitation and referrals (matching resources to families). The First Hearing dispute resolution appointment will take place within four to six weeks of the issue of the application. It should be attended by the parents and, where appropriate court resources exist, any child concerned in the proceedings who is aged nine or over. The appointment will be held before a 'gateway' district judge with a family 'ticket' who will identify any immediate safety issues; identify the aim of the proceedings, including the timescale within which the aim can be achieved; identify the issues between the parties and the opportunities for resolution of those issues by appropriate referrals for support and assistance and any subsequent steps required. Wherever possible, a CAFCASS officer will be available to facilitate early dispute resolution rather than providing a formal report. Save in exceptional circumstances (for example, where there are safety issues), or where immediate agreement is possible, he will direct that the family be referred to local available resolution services. At the conclusion of the First Hearing dispute resolution appointment the court must identify in the order the details of what has or has not been agreed and give subsequent directions for the progress of the case, the filing of evidence, and, if necessary, the preparation of a CAFCASS report. The order may also include directions for: the facilitation of all orders, agreements, and referrals (in particular by a CAFCASS officer); the monitoring of the outcome, including any urgent relisting before the same court within 10 working days of a request by CAFCASS; enforcement.

Civil partnerships

30.10   The Civil Partnership Act 2004 ('CPA 2004') provides that any civil partner in a civil partnership is entitled to apply for a residence or contact order. This means that they do not have to seek the leave of the court before making such an application (s. 10(5), CA 1989 as inserted by s. 77, CPA 2004).

Applications within divorce proceedings

30.11   Where one or both parties to divorce proceedings decide to apply for a residence order (or any other s. 8 orders) then they should (each) make an application by using the prescribed form (Form C2). The matter will then be heard within the current divorce proceedings and dealt with by the appropriate county court judge.

30.12   If the petitioner (say, the wife) knows that the respondent will not agree to the children continuing to live with her then she should seek a residence order in the prayer of her petition. However, that will not be sufficient to put her application into effect. She must then go on to file a full application in the prescribed form. If the respondent wishes to make an application in his own right for a s. 8 order then he is quite at liberty to file a prescribed form too, setting out his alternative proposals for the child(ren).

30.13   The divorce will then be processed by the district judge, who will be relieved of the burden of considering the arrangements for the children pursuant to s. 41, Matrimonial Causes Act 1973 (see paragraph 9.83 and onwards). The contested s. 8 orders will then usually be referred to the county court judge for hearing, although there are certain matters which may be heard by a district judge (see paragraph 30.20 below).

Free-standing applications for a s. 8 order

30.14   A person who wishes to make a free-standing application for a s. 8 order should do so by completing the prescribed form. This will usually be in Form C1 unless the applicant must first obtain leave of the court to make the substantive application (see paragraph 30.31 below). The rules for service of the application will be found in r. 4.8 of the FPR 1991 and r. 8 of the FPC(CA 1989)R 1991. The application may be made to the family proceedings court, county court, or High Court. If the applicant is in receipt of public funding then his certificate will usually contain a restriction that the proceedings should be commenced in the family proceedings court since that will normally be the cheapest route (see para. 20.22(15) of The Funding Code—Decision-Making Guidance). However, if there are any other proceedings already afoot in relation to the relevant children then the new proceedings should be consolidated with them so that all matters are heard together.

The categories of persons who can apply automatically for s. 8 orders and those who may apply only with leave are set out fully in paragraph 29.106.   **30.15**

Where a question as to the child's welfare arises as part of s. 8 proceedings, a court has power to make a s. 8 order of its own motion in spite of the fact that no application has been made for such an order: s. 10(1)(b).   **30.16**

B   PROCEDURE

The procedure to be adopted in proceedings under the CA 1989 is set out in the FPR 1991 for the High Court and county court and in the FPC(CA 1989)R 1991 for the family proceedings court. The substance and order of the two sets of rules are largely the same, in accordance with the intention of Parliament to unify and streamline the law and procedure in proceedings relating to children.   **30.17**

It is noticeable that the court is encouraged to take an inquisitorial role, in an effort to play down the adversarial nature of the proceedings. The court is expected to take control of the timetable for hearings, to make directions as to the evidence to be filed, to make directions as to the conduct of the proceedings generally, and to call for welfare reports where necessary. There is now much more emphasis on written material and on disclosure by each party of its evidence in advance of the hearing so that the real issues involved in the case are clear. It is hoped that this will help to avoid the all-too-familiar scenario whereby advocates waste time during a hearing in following unproductive lines of examination and cross-examination which do not go to the heart of the issues between the parties.   **30.18**

The procedure to be adopted once a local authority decides to apply for a care or supervision order is governed by the public law protocol, which is discussed in detail in paragraph 33.32. The protocol aims to ensure that care cases are dealt with as justly, expeditiously, and fairly as possible. It sets a guideline of 40 weeks for the conclusion of such cases. The key principles underlying the protocol are that there should be judicial continuity, active case management by the court, consistency by the standardization of steps to be taken in preparing, and a case management conference in each care case to enable the judge to identify the issues and fix the timetable for all further directions and hearings.   **30.19**

Allocation of functions within the courts

Which type of case will be heard by a judge, district judge, magistrate(s), or justices' clerk? The allocation of cases to certain categories of the judiciary within the High Court and county court is governed by the Family Proceedings (Allocation to Judiciary) Directions 1999, which came into force on 1 May 1999. The schedule to the FP(AJ)D 1999 allocates specified classes of proceedings to specified classes of judge in specified circumstances.   **30.20**

County court care centres

Care centres will be staffed by: **30.21**

(a)   designated family judges;

(b) nominated care judges;

(c) nominated care district judges.

They will hear the following types of cases:

(a) transferred/issued public law cases;

(b) contested matrimonial applications;

(c) adoptions;

(d) occupation and non-molestation orders.

County court family hearing centres

30.22 Family hearing centres will be staffed by:

(a) nominated family judges;

(b) all district judges.

They will be able to hear the following cases:

(a) contested matrimonial and s. 8 applications;

(b) adoptions;

(c) occupation and non-molestation orders.

Divorce county courts

30.23 Divorce county courts will be staffed by:

(a) non-nominated circuit judges;

(b) all district judges.

They will have 'district judge jurisdiction' only.

County courts

30.24 Ordinary county courts will be staffed by:

(a) non-nominated circuit judges;

(b) all district judges.

They will have no involvement in CA 1989 proceedings save for applications for injunctions.

Family proceedings courts

30.25 Family proceedings courts hearing CA 1989 applications will be staffed by family proceedings panels of magistrates. They will hear the following types of cases:

(a) public law cases;

(b) private family proceedings (outside divorce).

There are certain types of cases in which a *single justice* may sit as the family proceedings court: see r. 2 of the FPC(CA 1989)R 1991. These are as follows:

(a) *ex parte* (i.e., without notice) applications for:
  (i)   residence orders;
  (ii) contact orders;

    (iii)   prohibited steps orders;

    (iv)   specific issue orders;

    (v)   emergency protection orders;

    (vi)   warrant under s. 48(9);

    (vii) recovery orders;

    (viii) orders under s. 75;

    (ix)   search warrant under s. 102(1);

(b) interim orders;

(c) specified provisions of the CA 1989;

(d) transfer of proceedings under the Allocation Order 1991;

(e) rr. 3–8, 10–19, 21, 22, or 27 of the FPC(CA 1989)R 1991.

There are certain functions which the justices' clerk may perform on his own, without any magistrates at all. These include the power to give, vary, or revoke directions as to:

(a) timetable;

(b) variation of time allowed by Rules;

(c) attendance of child;

(d) appointment of guardian ad litem or solicitor;

(e) service of documents;

(f) submission of evidence, including experts' reports;

(g) preparation of welfare reports;

(h) transfer from magistrates' court vertically or horizontally;

(i) consolidation of cases.

Availability of public funding

The availability of public funding under the Community Legal Service scheme for CA 1989 **30.26** proceedings is fully set out in Chapter 2. However, it is important to remember that for most private law children cases (under Parts I to III, CA 1989) the applicant will be required to attend a mediation meeting with a mediator to determine whether the case is suitable for mediation before any public funding may be made available for representation (for further discussion of mediation see Chapter 3). On the other hand, there is no such requirement to attend a meeting with a mediator for public law children cases (under Parts IV and V, CA 1989).

Where the court is considering making an order for costs against a publicly funded indi- **30.27** vidual, it must take into account the matters in s. 11, Access to Justice Act 1999. In *R v R (Costs: Child Case)* [1997] 2 FLR 95, the Court of Appeal held that the judge should adjourn the question of the father's ability to pay costs in connection with CA 1989 proceedings until after the conclusion of ancillary relief proceedings since at that stage the court would have a better idea of his resources.

Forms of application

Both r. 4.4, FPR 1991, and r. 4, FPC(CA 1989)R 1991 make provision for applications under **30.28** the CA 1989 to be made by way of a simple application. There are prescribed forms for each type of application, and the forms are to be found in Appendix 1 of the FPR 1991 and sch. 1 of the FPC(CA 1989)R 1991. The forms are designed to extract the essential information from the applicant at an early stage. They also provide litigants with essential information about the conduct of their case, for example, as to the importance of obtaining legal advice and as to the right to file an answer to an application.

Withdrawal of an application

30.29   Once an application has been made it may only be withdrawn with the leave of the court: r. 4.5(1), FPR 1991 and r. 5(1), FPC(CA 1989)R 1991. An application for leave can be made orally to the court, provided that the parties and either the children's guardian or the children and family reporter is present. Otherwise there must be a written request setting out the reasons for the request. It must be served on all parties. The court can grant the request provided that the parties consent, the guardian (if there is one) has had an opportunity to make representations and the court thinks fit. Instead of granting the request, the court may direct that a date be fixed for the hearing of the request.

30.30   The court must consider an application for leave to withdraw just as carefully as any other application in respect of a child in proceedings under the CA 1989. The court has a statutory duty to have regard to the welfare of the child, including the duty to hear expert evidence from the guardian (*Re F (A Minor) (Care Order: Withdrawal of Application)* [1993] 2 FLR 9). Although the statutory checklist in s. 1(3) of the Act does not apply to an application for leave to withdraw, it is available to the court as an *aide-mémoire (London Borough of Southwark v B* [1993] 2 FLR 559). However, the paramountcy of the child's welfare principle under s. 1(1) of the Act does apply and the court must look at each case on its facts to see if there is some 'solid advantage to the child to be derived from continuing the proceedings': *London Borough of Southwark* v B (above). For an example of the application of the test see *Re N (Leave to Withdraw Care Proceedings)* [2000] 1 FLR 134 where the court refused the local authority's application for leave to withdraw care proceedings.

Requests for leave to bring proceedings

30.31   As was explained in paragraph 29.110, in some circumstances the CA 1989 requires a person to obtain leave before commencing proceedings, e.g., applications by grandparents for s. 8 orders. Both r. 4.3, FPR 1991 and r. 3, FPC(CA 1989)R 1991 require such a person to file:

(a)   a written request for leave in Form C2 setting out the reasons for the application, and

(b)   a draft of the application in Form C1 for the making of which leave is sought.

From that point onwards the procedure for considering the request is the same as that described in paragraph 30.30 above in relation to an application for the withdrawal of an application.

Respondents

30.32   Those persons who must be made respondents to an application are set out in tabular form in Appendix 3 of the FPR 1991 and sch. 2 to the FPC(CA 1989)R 1991. They include:

(a) every person whom the applicant believes to have parental responsibility for the child;

(b) where the child is the subject of a care order, every person whom the applicant believes to have had parental responsibility immediately prior to the making of the care order;

(c) if the application is to extend, vary, or discharge an order, the parties to the proceedings leading to the original order which the applicant seeks to have extended, varied, or discharged;

(d) in certain proceedings, the child himself.

Parties

The rules concerning the joinder of parties are to be found in r. 4.7, FPR 1991 and r. 7, **30.33** FPC(CA 1989)R 1991. The respective rules provide that, in any 'relevant proceedings' (i.e., any proceedings brought under the CA 1989, under any statutory instrument made under the CA 1989 or under any amendment to the CA 1989) a person (i.e., *any* person) may make a written request that he be joined as a party or that he cease to be a party. A request for joinder *may* be granted by the court without a hearing. Otherwise the court will order that a date be fixed for a hearing to consider the request, or else it will invite the parties to make written representations, within a specific period, as to whether the request should be granted.

Where a number of different parties are putting forward essentially the same case, serious **30.34** consideration should be given to the degree of separate representation of those parties that is strictly necessary: *Birmingham City Council v H (No. 3)* [1994] 1 FLR 224.

There is no statutory guidance as to the factors which the court should take into account in **30.35** making its decision as to whether or not to give leave for a person to be joined as a party. It would appear that s. 1(1), CA 1989 does not apply in this context: *North Yorkshire County Council v G* [1993] 2 FLR 732; *G v Kirklees MBC* [1993] 1 FLR 805. However, even though the applicant does not expressly seek leave to apply for a s. 8 order it would appear that the factors in s. 10(9) nevertheless apply: *G v Kirkless MBC* (above); *North Yorkshire County Council v G* (above). The court is not precluded from considering all the circumstances of the case, including the overall merits of the case for a s. 8 order, since if the applicant has no reasonable prospects of success there is no point in joining him as a party: *North Yorkshire County Council v G* (above).

The exception to the general rule is that where a person with parental responsibility requests **30.36** that he be joined as a party, the court *must* accede to his application (r. 4.7(4), FPR 1991 and r. 7(4), FPC(CA 1989)R 1991).

Service

The applicant must serve a copy of the application in the appropriate form, together with **30.37** Form C6 which sets out the date, time, and place for a hearing or directions appointment, on each respondent at least 14 days before the hearing or appointment: r. 4.4(1), FPR 1991 and r. 4(1), FPC(CA 1989)R 1991. The rules for service will be found at r. 4.8, FPR 1991 and r. 8, FPC(CA 1989)R 1991.

30.38   Once service has been effected the applicant must lodge at court a statement of service in Form C9 confirming the date of service, method of service, documents served, and giving details of the party on whom service was effected.

Persons who must be given written notice

30.39   At the same time as effecting service of the application on the relevant respondents the applicant must give written notice of the application and of the date, time, and place of the hearing or directions appointment to those persons set out in Appendix 3 of the FPR 1991 and sch. 2 to the FPC(CA 1989)R 1991. They include:

(a)   the local authority providing accommodation for the child;

(b)   persons who are caring for the child at the time when the proceedings are commenced;

(c)   if the child is in a refuge, then the person providing the refuge;

(d)   every person whom the applicant believes:

    (i)   to be named in a current court order with respect to the child (unless the applicant believes the order is not relevant to the present application);

    (ii)   to be a party in pending proceedings in respect of the child (unless the applicant believes the pending proceedings not to be relevant to the present application);

    (iii)   to be a person with whom the child has lived for a period of at least three years prior to the application;

(e)   in special guardianship proceedings, the appropriate local authority.

Acknowledgement of application

30.40   Each respondent must file an acknowledgement in Form C7 within 14 days of being served with it: r. 4.9, FPR 1991 and r. 9, FPC(CA 1989)R 1991.

The Children and Family Court Advisory Service

30.41   In family proceedings the Children and Family Court Advisory Service ('CAFCASS') is responsible for safeguarding and promoting the welfare of children, giving advice to any court about any application made to it in such proceedings, arranging for children to be represented, and providing information, advice, and other support for children and their families (Criminal Justice and Court Services Act 2000, ss. 11, 12, 15, 16). The person responsible for preparing a CAFCASS report (formerly a 'welfare report') will usually be the 'children and family reporter' and the person appointed to represent a child in public law proceedings will usually be the 'children's guardian'. Important guidance in relation to the appointment of a children's guardian is to be found in *CAFCASS and the National Assembly of Wales Practice Note (Appointment of Guardians in Private Law Proceedings)* [2006] 2 FLR 143. The National Standards for the Children and Family Court Advisory and Support Service sets out a framework of service principles and standards, including a rigorous complaints procedure. It can be found at <www.cafcass.gov.uk>.

30.42   In October 2005 CAFCASS issued a consultation paper *'Every Day Matters: New Directions for CAFCASS'*. It aims to set out a strategy for future services, to provide early intervention in cases so as to reduce delays and backlogs and to provide a continuum of support services. In both private law and public law cases there is to be a new emphasis on dispute resolution, with less court report-based working. The consultation period ended on 31 January 2006 and the results are being collated.

CAFCASS report

A CAFCASS report will usually be ordered where there are to be contested s. 8 proceedings. **30.43** CAFCASS and local authorities are under a duty to provide reports as requested (s. 7(5)), but a local authority may delegate the task to someone who is not a member of its staff, for example a children's guardian. Usually, the CAFCASS report will be undertaken by a children and family reporter. However, where the court requests a report under s. 7(1)(b) from the local authority, the officer instructed will still be referred to as a 'welfare officer'. The court may refer the case of its own motion to a children and family reporter for investigation (s. 7(1)). Where a CAFCASS report is ordered then the report should be filed at least 14 days before the hearing for which it has been commissioned. Where any party wishes the children and family reporter to attend the hearing he must apply to the court for a direction to that effect: r. 4.11B, FPR 1991 and r. 11B, FPC(CA 1989)R 1991.

If a CAFCASS report is not ordered automatically then one of the parties should request the **30.44** district judge or justices' clerk, by way of a directions hearing, to refer the matter for a report. This must be done early on in the proceedings since it normally takes several weeks (or even months) for a report to be prepared. The party wishing for the report may find that if he delays his request for a report for too long the court may take the view that the advantages to the court of having the report for the hearing are outweighed by the disadvantages to the child of having to wait for too long for a resolution of the case; in that case the court would refuse the request for the report, in the interests of the child.

The children and family reporter will be able to inspect the court file relating to the case on **30.45** which there will, of course, be copies of all the statements filed in relation to the dispute. He will therefore be aware of what the issues between parties are. He will see both parties (often on several occasions) preferably in their homes and with and without the children present. The impression that the children and family reporter forms of a parent is vital and the client must therefore be warned to co-operate with the officer fully and make him or her welcome. The children and family reporter will also see the children on their own if they are old enough for this to be of benefit. In addition he will make whatever other enquiries seem to be appropriate in the particular case. For example, he may well visit the children's school as problems at home are often reflected in behaviour at school; he may see other relations; he will contact any social workers who have been involved with the family; he may speak to the family's general practitioner, etc. Having carried out his investigations, the children and family reporter will prepare what is usually a lengthy report for the court setting out the investigations he has made and the conclusions he has reached. The report may make a recommendation as to who should have a residence order or contact order.

It will be noted that CAFCASS reports often contain a lot of what would traditionally **30.46** be classed as hearsay evidence (for example, 'I spoke to the child's form-teacher who told me that she is often distressed at school the day after a contact visit with her father'). The court will receive such evidence in children's cases and attach to it whatever weight it thinks fit (see paragraph 30.87 below). The parties' solicitors should be fortunate enough to receive copies of the report prior to the hearing so that they can take instructions from their clients on it and review the witnesses that they were intending to call in the light of the investigations the children and family reporter has made. It may be necessary to cross-examine the officer if, for example, the officer has misreported conversations with the client or has made a clear recommendation in favour of the other party on grounds which the solicitor feels to be unsound: *Re I and H (Contact: Right to Give Evidence)* [1998] 1 FLR 876. If the children and family reporter does make recommendations which are in favour of the other party, the solicitor should consider seriously with the client whether he wishes to proceed with his application. Looking at things realistically, it is almost always an uphill battle to obtain a residence order if the children and family reporter is against you. Where the judge concludes that the children and family reporter's inquiries are inadequate because the officer has not assessed the relationship between the children and each parent individually in a natural setting (i.e., their home), the judge may order a fresh hearing with a new welfare report: *Re P (A Minor) (Inadequate Welfare Report)* [1996] 2 FLR 285, per Johnson J.

30.47 The importance of the CAFCASS report cannot be underestimated. In *Re W (Residence)* [1999] 2 FLR 390, the Court of Appeal reminded judges of the value of such reports, since the children and family reporter has the primary task of assessing factual situations and attachments. In consequence, judges should not depart from the recommendations of an experienced children and family reporter without allowing the officer an opportunity to respond to any misgivings which the judge might have about the officer's approach.

30.48 The children and family reporter is not required to attend hearings in respect of which his report has been made or in the course of which his report is due to be considered unless the court so orders: FPR 1991, r. 4.11B(3), FPC(CA 1989)R 1991, r. 11B(3). His report should be filed at least 14 days before the hearing unless the court has directed a different time limit: FPR 1991, r. 4.11B(2), FPC(CA 1989)R 1991, r. 11B(2).

30.49 If the report is not available before the hearing, it will certainly be disclosed on the day and practitioners should ensure that they ask for sufficient time to go through it thoroughly with their client before embarking on the hearing.

Appointment of children's guardian

30.50 Reference was made to the role of the children's guardian in paragraph 29.23 and onwards.

30.51 Section 41(1), CA 1989 requires the court in any 'specified proceedings' (i.e., proceedings of a public nature—care orders, supervision orders, emergency protection orders, etc.) to appoint a guardian for the child concerned *unless* it is satisfied that it is not necessary to do so in order to safeguard his interests. By s. 41(2), CA 1989 the appointment of and duties of the guardian are to be regulated by rules of court. The appropriate rules will be found in rr. 4.10, 4.11, and 4.11B, FPR 1991 and rr. 10, 11, and 11B, FPC(CA 1989)R 1991. Important guidance is to be found in *CAFCASS and the National Assembly for Wales Practice Note (Appointment of Guardians in Private Law Proceedings)* [2006] 2 FLR 143.

The ACA 2002, s. 122 has inserted into s. 41 a new sub-section (6A) so as to include within **30.52** the category of proceedings which may be 'specified for the time being ... by rules of court' (i.e., proceedings in which the court must appoint a guardian for the child unless satisfied that it is not necessary to do so in order to safeguard his interests) any proceedings for the making, varying or discharging of an order under s. 8, CA 1989 (i.e., residence, contact, specific issue, and prohibited steps orders). This reflects the growing pressure for the appointment of children's guardians in certain private law children cases, for example bitterly contested residence or contact disputes, where children frequently have particular interests and standpoints which do not coincide with or cannot be adequately represented by the parents *(Re H (Contact Order) (No. 2)* [2002] 1 FLR 22). Although the court already has power (see paragraph 29.23 and onwards) to appoint a children's guardian in such cases, it will be enshrined in statute rather than merely in statutory instrument.

Both sets of rules require that in carrying out his duties the children's guardian is to have **30.53** regard to the 'delay principle' set out in s. 1(2), CA 1989, i.e., that there is a presumption that delay in hearing a case will be prejudicial to the welfare of the child concerned. This emphasizes the need for the guardian to complete as quickly as possible any necessary inquiries and reports. Furthermore, the guardian is enjoined to have regard to the 'checklist' of 'welfare factors' set out in s. 1(3), CA 1989 when carrying out his duties.

The obligations of the children's guardian are extensive and include the following: **30.54**

(a) to appoint a solicitor to represent the child (unless this has already been done) and to instruct that solicitor, unless the child is of sufficient age and understanding to instruct a solicitor himself;

(b) to advise the court whether any person might have an interest in becoming a party to the proceedings or in making representations to the court;

(c) to attend all hearings (including directions hearings);

(d) to advise whether the child is of sufficient understanding for such purposes as the service of documents, refusal to submit to a medical or psychiatric examination or assessment, attendance at court etc.;

(e) to advise the court of the wishes of the child in respect of any relevant matter;

(f) to advise as to the appropriate forum for, and timing of, the proceedings;

(g) to advise as to the options available to the court and as to the suitability of each option;

(h) to deliver interim and final written reports as directed by the court. As a rule final reports should be served on the parties at least 14 days before the date fixed for the final hearing.

The rules provide for the inspection by the children's guardian of local authority records as allowed by s. 42, CA 1989. For example, in *Re T (A Minor) (Guardian ad Litem: Case Record)* [1994] 1 FLR 632, the guardian was entitled to see case records prepared by the local authority giving detailed information concerning prospective adopters and to include the relevant information derived from it in his report to the court. The rules also allow the guardian, either of his own motion or at the direction of the court, to obtain such professional assistance as he thinks appropriate.

It is generally expected that a children's guardian will be appointed in *most* of the cases to **30.55** which s. 41, CA 1989 applies (i.e., in 'specified proceedings' as set out in s. 41(6), CA 1989). In this context 'specified proceedings' include any proceedings:

(a)   in relation to an application for a care order or a supervision order;

(b)   in which the court has given a direction under s. 37(1), CA 1989 and has made, or is considering whether to make, an interim care order or supervision order;

(c)   on an application for the discharge of a care order or the variation or discharge of a supervision order;

(d)   in which the court is considering whether to make a residence order with respect to a child who is the subject of a care order;

(e)   with respect to contact between a child who is the subject of a care order and any other person;

(f)   in which the court is considering making an order under Part V of the CA 1989, e.g., emergency protection order, child assessment order, education supervision order etc.;

(g)   on an appeal against the orders at (a) to (f) above.

Solicitor for the child

30.56   The rules require the children's guardian to appoint a solicitor for the child unless an appointment has already been made. In that event the solicitor is required to represent the child 'in accordance with instructions received from the children's guardian': r. 4.12(1)(a), FPR 1991 and r. 12(1)(a), FPC(CA 1989)R 1991.

30.57   However, provision is made for the solicitor to receive instructions from the child personally. This will take place if the solicitor considers, having taken into account the views of the children's guardian, that:

(a)   the child wishes to give instructions which conflict with those of the guardian, and

(b)   that he is able, having regard to the degree of his understanding, to give such instructions on his own behalf.

See, for example, *Re H (A Minor) (Care Proceedings: Child's Wishes)* [1993] 1 FLR 440, where a 15-year-old boy had sufficient understanding to instruct his own solicitor in care proceedings but had been denied the opportunity to do so; his solicitor had been in error in accepting instructions from the children's guardian rather than from the boy himself. Where the child does part company with the guardian in such circumstances then the guardian will continue to participate in the proceedings to such extent as the court directs. (See also *Re M (Minors) (Care Proceedings: Child's Wishes)* [1994] 1 FLR 749.) He may well be invited to remain involved as *amicus curiae*. The role of *amicus curiae* in these circumstances has been defined in *Re H (A Minor) (Role of Official Solicitor)* [1993] 2 FLR 552 to include the authority to carry out such investigations and inquiries as the court requires, to receive all papers and reports, to be able to apply for such directions as he thinks fit. The *amicus curiae* will not become a party to the proceedings. He remains an independent adviser to the court.

30.58   See paragraph 33.97 for further discussion of the appointment of a solicitor for a child in proceedings for a care or supervision order.

Directions appointments

The provisions governing directions appointments will be found in r. 4.14, FPR 1991 and in **30.59**
r. 14, FPC(CA 1989)R 1991. They make provision for a preliminary hearing at which the
court can give directions for the subsequent conduct of the proceedings. There can be several
directions appointments. They can take place of the court's own motion or as a result of a
request made by one of the parties. The period of notice required for such hearings will
usually be two days, although in urgent cases a request for directions can (with leave) be
made orally or without notice to the other parties, or both: r. 4.14(4), FPR 1991 and r. 14(6),
FPC(CA 1989)R 1991. The matters which can be dealt with include:

(a)   timetable for the proceedings;
(b)   varying time limits;
(c)   service of documents;
(d)   joinder of parties;
(e)   preparation of welfare reports and a direction that the children and family reporter
      responsible for preparing the report is to attend the final hearing to assist the court and
      to give oral evidence, if necessary;
(f)   submission of evidence, including experts' reports;
(g)   appointment of children's guardian/solicitor;
(h)   attendance of child;
(i)   transfer of case to another court;
(j)   consolidation with other proceedings.

The aim of directions appointments is to simplify the interlocutory stages of proceedings
and to ensure that the hearings will be conducted in the most efficient and cost-effective
manner; see *Practice Direction (Family Proceedings: Court Bundles) (Universal Practice to be Applied
in All Courts Other Than the Family Proceedings Court)* [2006] 2 FLR 199 which came into force
on 2nd October 2006. See Chapter 18, paragraph 18.122 and onwards for further details of
the *Practice Direction.*

Where time estimates are given to the court in the course of directions hearings or otherwise, **30.60**
care must be taken to ensure that provision is made for judicial reading time, the length of
the opening address, the likely time to be taken in respect of the evidence of each witness,
the points of law or procedure likely to arise and the length they will take to argue, the
number and likely length of closing speeches, and the likely time it will take for the judge to
deliver an *extempore* judgment: *Re MD and TD (Minors) (Time Estimates)* [1994] 2 FLR 336.

All public law child care cases are now governed by the public law protocol which is discussed **30.61**
in paragraph 33.32 and onwards. The question of whether or not to instruct experts will be
subject to particular scrutiny and will be governed by the Code of Guidance for Expert
Witnesses in Family Proceedings contained in Appendix C of the public law protocol. The
Code is designed to draw together all the threads that have emerged through case law and
practice over the last few years. It sets out comprehensive guidance and is discussed in
greater detail in paragraph 33.113.

Although the *Code of Guidance for Expert Witnesses in Family Proceedings* (above) is contained **30.62**
in the protocol which applies to public law cases, it is likely to be adapted and applied to the

instruction of experts in private law proceedings too. Therefore, private law practitioners should be fully aware of the relevant provisions. Where pre-protocol cases containing guidance on the instruction of experts in family law proceedings conflict with the *Code*, the *Code* is likely to take precedence.

Timing

30.63   A recurring theme of the CA 1989 is the avoidance of delay in proceedings wherever possible. Thus, where the rules provide for a period of time within which, or by which, a certain act is to be performed then that period may not be extended except by direction of the court/justices' clerk: r. 4.15, FPR 1991 and r. 15(4), FPC(CA 1989)R 1991. There is also a mandatory requirement that whenever proceedings are adjourned the court *must* fix a date for reconvening: r. 4.15(2), FPR 1991 and r. 15(5), FPC(CA 1989)R 1991. The aim of these provisions is to prevent the proceedings from lying dormant through the delay of the parties or their advisers.

Attendance at hearing/directions appointment

30.64   All parties, including the child (if he is a party), *must* attend a directions appointment of which they have had notice unless the court directs otherwise: r. 4.16, FPR 1991 and r. 16, FPC(CA 1989)R 1991.

30.65   Where the child is a party then proceedings *may* take place in his absence if:

(a)   the court considers it to be in the interests of the child, having regard to the matters to be discussed or the evidence likely to be given at the hearing or directions appointment, and

(b)   the child is represented by a children's guardian or solicitor.

The court must not begin a case in the absence of a respondent unless:

(a)   it is proved that he had reasonable notice of the hearing, or

(b)   the circumstances of the case justify proceeding.

30.66   If the respondent appears but the applicant does not then the court can refuse the application, or, if it has sufficient evidence, it can proceed in the absence of the applicant.

30.67   If neither the applicant nor the respondent appear then the court may refuse the application.

30.68   In the High Court and county court most hearings and directions appointments will take place in chambers. In the family proceedings court there is provision for hearings and directions appointments to take place in private.

Documentary evidence

30.69   Great emphasis is placed upon the need for advance disclosure of evidence in proceedings under the CA 1989: see r. 4.17, FPR 1991 and r. 17, FPC(CA 1989)R 1991. Each party is required to file and serve not only written statements of the oral evidence he intends to adduce at the hearing, but also copies of documents upon which he intends to rely. The rules are very clear upon the requirement that at a hearing a party *may not adduce* evidence or seek to rely upon a document which has not been disclosed in advance to the other parties, except with the leave of the court. Statements of witnesses must be dated and signed by the person making the statement and must contain a declaration that the maker believes the statement to be true.

'In advance' means by such time as the court/justices' clerk directs, or in the absence of such a direction, before the hearing. **30.70**

The practitioner should note that in s. 8 proceedings a party must file no document other than as required or authorized by the rules without leave of the court: r. 4.17(4), FPR 1991 and r. 17(4), FPC(CA 1989)R 1991. The aim of this rule is to prevent information being set down in writing which may serve only to inflame the situation between the parties and thus prevent a sensible settlement of the matter. If it becomes clear at a later stage that the matter is not going to be settled then the court can direct that further evidence be filed in readiness for a contested hearing. **30.71**

Practice Direction (Family Proceedings: Court Bundles) (Universal Practice to be Applied in All Courts Other Than the Family Proceedings Court) [2006] 2 FLR 199 which came into force on 2nd October 2006 governs the preparation and arrangements for lodging with the court any bundles of documents for use in court proceedings. See para 18.122 for further details. **30.72**

In public law proceedings the local authority is required to file a care plan with the court and the parties (s. 31A, CA 1989). A local authority circular dated 12 August 1999 entitled *Care Plans and Care Proceedings under the Children Act 1989* (LAC(99)29) sets out the ingredients to be contained in care plans. All public law child care cases are governed by the public law protocol which is discussed in paragraph 33.32. The question of whether or not to instruct experts will be subject to particular scrutiny and will be governed by the Code of Guidance for Expert Witnesses in Family Proceedings contained in Appendix C of the public law protocol (see further in paragraph 33.113). **30.73**

Matters to be included in a statement in support of an application for a residence order

As and when it becomes necessary for further evidence to be filed then it would be advisable for the party applying for the residence (or indeed other s. 8) order to file a statement containing a declaration that the maker of the statement believes it to be true and under-stands that it may be placed before the court dealing not only with the merits of his own application but also with any matters raised by the other party in his own application/statement. **30.74**

Great care must be taken over the preparation of a party's statements. The court will read them before it hears the application and they will therefore colour the court's initial approach to the case. For this reason it is important that statements are reasonably comprehensive and read clearly. The following matters should be covered if possible: **30.75**

(a) The proposed living arrangements for the child (where he will live, who else will be living there, who will look after him when the parent is not available, etc.). If the parent proposes to move in the foreseeable future, his proposed new arrangements should also be covered. The more definite they are, the better. Indeed, if the parent can actually be installed in the new accommodation before the hearing it will be helpful as the welfare officer may then have an opportunity to visit the accommodation and report on it to the court. It is particularly important that a parent should investigate and, if possible, try to arrange alternative accommodation if his present circumstances are unsuitable for the children. If he is awaiting council accommodation he should be in a position to produce to the court a letter from the council dealing with his place on the waiting list and his prospects of obtaining housing.

(b) The proposed arrangements for school. If the parent is seeking a transfer of residence to him, he should say whether the child can stay at the same school or, if this is not possible, he should state what alternative arrangements are available. This will mean him doing some homework himself in visiting the schools in his area, checking whether they can take the child, etc. If he does make this effort, it will help to give the impression that he is a conscientious and caring parent and really does wish to have the child living with him. If the child is below school age, opportunities for nursery education, playgroups, etc. in the parent's area should be investigated.

(c) Where the parent lives with or has a close relationship with a new partner, the statement should inform the court how the child gets on with the new partner.

(d) If there are any problems over the child's health, these should be outlined in the statement and, if possible, a medical report should be exhibited.

(e) The parent's attitude to contact and also that of the child should be dealt with. For example, it will clearly help a parent's application for a residence order if he has had frequent regular contact with the child for prolonged periods and the child has enjoyed it. It will also be in his favour if he is prepared to facilitate generous contact between the child and the other parent if he obtains a residence order. The courts are disapproving of parents who try to turn the child against the other parent or to disrupt contact arrangements.

(f) Any views that the child has expressed about residence and contact. Obviously, what is said on this score will be viewed cautiously by the court, particularly if the child is young. However, it is worth mentioning in the statement if the child has made more than a throw-away remark.

(g) Any worries that the parent has about the care the other parent is giving/would give to the child. It must be emphasized that it is advisable to avoid an endless catalogue of minor grumbles about the other parent's standard of care. In particular it is not generally appropriate to go into the question of who is to blame for the breakdown of the marriage or to detail the circumstances in which the marriage broke down. Throwing mud at the other parent only encourages mudslinging in return and simply irritates the court. However, if there are *genuine* worries that really do relate to the children and not to the unfortunate situation between the parents, these must be set out fully in the statement.

(h) If the other party's statement has already been served, the statement should incorporate comments on the matters contained in it if the maker of the statement has any to make.

30.76 The most important statements in a dispute over residence or contact are obviously from the parties themselves. However, each side is free to file and serve statements from supporting witnesses if appropriate.

Expert evidence: examination of child

No person may cause a child to be medically or psychiatrically examined or otherwise **30.77** assessed for the purpose of the preparation of expert evidence for use in proceedings, *except* with the leave of the court: see r. 4.18, FPR 1991 and r. 18, FPC(CA 1989)R 1991. If such an examination or assessment is made without the leave of the court then that evidence cannot be adduced in the proceedings without the leave of the court.

All public law child care cases are governed by the public law protocol which is discussed in **30.78** Chapter 33 at paragraph 33.32. The question of whether or not to instruct experts in such cases will be subject to particular scrutiny and will be governed by the Code of Guidance for Expert Witnesses in Family Proceedings contained in Appendix C of the public law protocol. The Code is designed to draw together all the threads which have emerged through case law and practice over the last few years. It sets out comprehensive guidance and is discussed in greater detail in paragraph 33.113. Practitioners should note that although the *Code of Guidance for Expert Witnesses in Family Proceedings* (above) is contained in the protocol which applies to public law cases, it is likely to be adapted and applied to the instruction of experts in private law proceedings too. Therefore, private law practitioners should be fully aware of the relevant provisions. Where pre-protocol cases containing guidance on the instruction of experts in family law proceedings conflict with the *Code*, the *Code* is likely to take precedence.

Practitioners should take note that if a party, having obtained the leave of the court, has **30.79** commissioned an expert's report, the contents of which are relevant to the future of the child in question, then the court has power to override legal professional privilege and order that the report be disclosed even if the party who has commissioned it is unwilling to do so voluntarily: *Oxfordshire County Council* v *M* [1994] 1 FLR 175. This power stems from the principle that proceedings under the CA 1989 are not adversarial. The court's duty is to investigate and seek to achieve a result which is in the interests of the child. See also *Essex County Council* v *R* [1993] 2 FLR 826 and *Re DH (A Minor) (Child Abuse)* [1994] 1 FLR 679 which indicate that counsel has a positive duty to make voluntary disclosure of medical reports even where disclosure would be contrary to the client's interests. The House of Lords has considered the disclosure of reports in public law cases in *Re L (Police Investigation: Privilege)* [1996] 1 FLR 731 and much of the reasoning adopted in *Re L* is likely to apply to private law cases too.

Other evidence

The solicitor should consider in good time whether any evidence other than that of the party **30.80** should be obtained for the hearing. For example, where someone other than the parent (for example, a new spouse or a grandparent) is going to assist in the care of the child, there must be evidence from that person. If a parent is concerned about the standard of care that the other party would provide or about his or her lifestyle, consideration should be given to obtaining evidence from independent witnesses on these points. For example, the child's school might be approached in a case where it is alleged that the child is not properly fed, clothed, and kept clean. However, in determining whether to call further witnesses, it must be borne in mind that the children and family reporter report is likely to deal with a number of the matters that are of concern and it may be possible to rely simply on this without calling further evidence. A final decision as to this can only be taken once the CAFCASS report has been seen.

30.81   Generally speaking it is not a good tactical move to call a string of witnesses unless their evidence really does further the client's case. The solicitor will have the advantage of seeing the potential witnesses and evaluating their evidence for himself. A statement should be prepared for each of those who are to give evidence and should preferably be filed at court and served on the other side before the hearing. In addition, unless the other side indicate that they accept the evidence of the witness, the witness should be warned to attend the hearing. In particular it is vital that (whatever the attitude of the other side to the evidence) anyone who is to help in looking after the child is present at court to give oral evidence. If there is a last-minute witness, it may be possible to call oral evidence at the hearing without having filed and served a statement previously provided that the court gives leave.

30.82   Sometimes a potential witness may be reluctant to get involved. The solicitor should be wary of such witnesses—their evidence can often turn out to be less valuable than the client expects.

Amendment

30.83   If a document has been filed or served in proceedings then it cannot be amended without leave of the court: r. 4.19, FPR 1991 and r. 19, FPC (CA 1989)R 1991.

Hearing

30.84   Most hearings before the High Court or county court will be in chambers, and hearings before the family proceedings court will normally be held in private. Rule 4.21 of the FPR 1991 and r. 21 of the FPC(CA 1989)R 1991 provide that:

(a)   the court may give directions as to the order of evidence and speeches;
(b)   unless the court directs otherwise, the parties and children's guardian should usually adduce evidence in the following order:
    (i)   applicant;
    (ii)   any party with parental responsibility for the child;
    (iii) other respondents;
    (iv) children's guardian;
    (v)   the child, if he is a party and there is no children's guardian.

30.85   A question that has arisen under the HRA 1998 is the extent to which family proceedings should continue to be heard in private. As the law stands at present, hearing children cases in England and Wales in private does not breach the European Convention for the Protection of Human Rights and Fundamental Freedoms 1950, Art. 6 (*B* v *UK and P* v *UK* [2001] 2 FLR 261).

Oral evidence

30.86   The court, proper officer, or justices' clerk must keep a note of the substance of any oral evidence given at a hearing or directions appointment: r. 4.20, FPR 1991 and r. 20, FPC(CA 1989)R 1991.

Hearsay evidence

Hearsay evidence is admissible in civil proceedings before the High Court, county court, **30.87** or family proceedings court when given in connection with the upbringing, maintenance, or welfare of a child. However, the weight to be given to such evidence will be in the discretion of the judge. The Children (Admissibility of Hearsay Evidence) Order 1990 allows hearsay evidence to be admissible in respect of the following statements:

(a) statements by children;
(b) statements against interest by those with control, or concerned with the control, of the child;
(c) statements contained in reports submitted by a guardian ad litem or local authority.

The decision

After the final hearing the court must make its decision 'as soon as practicable': r. 4.21(3), **30.88** FPR 1991 and r. 21(4), FPC(CA 1989)R 1991. When making an order or refusing an application the court must state any findings of fact and the reasons for the court's decision: r. 4.21(4), FPR 1991 and r. 21(6), FPC(CA 1989)R 1991. If a s. 8 order is made, it must be recorded in the appropriate Form and as soon as possible the justices' clerk or the proper officer of the court must serve a copy of the order on the parties and on any person with whom the child is living: r. 4.21(5) and (6), FPR 1991, and r. 21(7), FPC(CA 1989)R 1991.

At present, most cases relating to children are heard in chambers and the resulting decisions **30.89** are given in private. However, there is growing pressure to allow public pronouncement of judgments in certain family cases. The court already has a discretion to sit in open court where, for example, the case decides a point of law that is of general importance or where issues of public interest arise and it considers it appropriate to give judgment in open court, providing, where desirable in the interests of the child, appropriate directions are given to avoid identification. However, the evidence relating to the welfare of a child will rarely be heard in public (*Re PB (Hearing in Open Court)* [1996] 2 FLR 765) and in many cases if judgment in a case concerning the welfare of children were to be pronounced publicly that would to a large extent frustrate the aims of holding the proceedings in chambers (*B* v *UK and P* v *UK* [2001] 2 FLR 261).

Power of court to direct investigation by local authority

If, during the course of hearing proceedings for a s. 8 order (or, indeed, in the course of **30.90** any family proceedings, as defined by s. 8(3)), it becomes apparent to the court that the circumstances of the child may merit the making of a care or supervision order, then the court has power to direct the local authority to investigate (s. 37(1)). All public law child care cases are governed by the public law protocol (see paragraph 33.32). Appendix G of the protocol sets out a standard form of 'Section 37 Request' which provides a recommended procedure within the existing rules for the timely determination of s. 37 requests by the court. On the same day as the request is made the court must (Appendix G, para. 2):

- identify the local authority that is to prepare the s. 37 report;
- fix the date for the next hearing;
- specify the date for the s. 37 report to be filed by the local authority;
- direct the court officer to give notice of the order and the Form C40 to the local authority liaison manager/lawyer by fax on the day the order is made;
- direct each party to serve upon the local authority all further documents filed with the court.

Where a s. 37 report is required in less than eight weeks, the court should make direct inquiries of the court liaison manager/local authority lawyer to agree the period within which a report can be written (Appendix G, para. 3). Within 24 hours of the order being made the court office must serve on the local authority a sealed copy of the order and such other documents as the court has directed (Appendix G, para. 4).

30.91 Within 24 hours of the receipt of the sealed order the court liaison manager/local authority lawyer must ensure that the request is allocated to a social services team manager who must (Appendix G, para. 5):

- be responsible for the preparation of the report and the allocation of a social worker/team to carry out any appropriate assessment;
- ensure that the request is treated and recorded as a formal referral by social services in respect of each child named in the order;
- notify the court and the lawyers for all parties of his/her/the team's identity and contact details;
- follow government guidance in relation to referral and assessment processes (Appendix F of protocol).

Any assessment should be completed within 35 days of the allocation above (protocol, Appendix G, para. 6). At the conclusion of the social services inquiries social services must (protocol, Appendix G, para. 7):

- consult with the family, the child, and all relevant agencies before making decisions about a plan for the child. The local authority will record the response of each person and agency consulted;
- decide whether to apply to the court for a statutory order;
- file the s. 37 report with the court and serve it upon the parties on or before the date ordered by the court.

Where social services decide not to apply for a care order or supervision order they should as part of their report set out the decisions they have made and the reasons for those decisions and any plan they have made for the child (protocol, Appendix G, para. 8) in accordance with government guidance (protocol, Appendix F).

Appeals

30.92 An appeal against the making of an order by a family proceedings court, or against the refusal of the magistrates to make an order will lie directly to the High Court (s. 94(1), CA 1989) and will usually be heard by a High Court judge of the Family Division who will normally sit in open court: *President's Direction* of 31 January 1993 ([1992] 2 FLR 140).

However, an application to withdraw such an appeal, or to have it dismissed with consent of all the parties, or to amend the grounds of appeal, may be heard by a district judge: r. 4.22(7), FPR 1991.

An appeal against the decision of a district judge will usually be made to the judge of the **30.93** court in which the decision was made: r. 8.1, FPR 1991. Note that an appeal from the district judge to the judge will *not* be conducted by way of rehearing unless it is in the interests of justice to do so: FPR 1991, r. 8.1(3)(a). Furthermore, irrespective of the nature of the hearing, fresh evidence may be admitted if it is in the interests of justice to do so: FPR 1991, r. 8.1(3)(b). Appeals against the decision of a county court or the High Court will be directly to the Court of Appeal.

Procedure

The procedure for conducting appeals is set out in r. 4.22 of the FPR 1991. The appellant **30.94** must file and serve on the parties and on the children's guardian the following documents:

(a) a written notice of appeal, setting out the grounds upon which he relies;
(b) a copy of the summons or application and of the order appealed against and any order staying its execution;
(c) a copy of any notes of evidence;
(d) a copy of any reasons given for the decision.

Note that s. 55, Access to Justice Act 1999, restricts the right to more than one appeal in most **30.95** civil cases. Section 55(1) provides that where an appeal is made to a county court or the High Court in relation to any matter, and on hearing the appeal the court makes a decision in relation to that matter, no appeal may be made to the Court of Appeal from that decision unless the Court of Appeal considers that:

(a) the appeal would raise an important point of principle or practice; or
(b) there is some other compelling reason for the Court of Appeal to hear it.

Time limits

The time limits for filing and serving notice of appeal are: **30.96**

(a) generally, within 14 days after the determination against which the appeal is brought;
(b) however, for appeals against interim care orders or interim supervision orders the time limit is seven days;
(c) otherwise, such other time as the court may direct.

Respondents to appeals

A respondent who wishes to contend: **30.97**

(a) that the decision of the court below should be varied, or
(b) that the decision of the court below should be affirmed on grounds other than those relied upon by that court, or
(c) by way of cross-appeal that the decision of the court below was wrong in whole or in part,

must, within 14 days of receipt of notice of the appeal, file and serve on all other parties to the appeal a notice in writing, setting out the grounds upon which he relies.

Procedure for interim applications

30.98 (a) Public funding: the question of costs must be sorted out before embarking on an interim application. If the matter is truly urgent, application can be made for an emergency certificate to cover the interim application. However, the solicitor may find the Legal Services Commission reluctant to grant such funding unless there are very special circumstances (e.g., where the other party has snatched the child from the care of the client and refuses to return him). If no emergency certificate is forthcoming, the solicitor will have to await the granting of a certificate for Legal Representation before taking actions.

(b) The normal method of application for an interim order will be by filing the appropriate application form and asking the court for an early hearing date before a nominated family judge. The hearing itself will be in chambers and is likely to be brief. It follows the normal pattern, but any evidence given by the parties and witnesses is likely to be short. As well as announcing its decision as to who should have a residence/contact order pending the final hearing, the court will usually order a welfare report. Other directions can be requested if they are required (e.g., a direction that the parties should file statements within a certain period).

Confidentiality of documents

30.99 Rule 10.20A of the FPR 1991 and r. 23A of the FPC(CA 1989)R 1991 set out the new rules relating to the confidentiality of documents in family proceedings heard in private and involving children. It sets out in the form of a table those parties and other specified people who may disclose certain information from the proceedings to other specified people for specific purposes without needing the permission of the court or being in contempt of court. There is a leaflet providing guidance which can be found at <www.hmcourts-service.gov.uk/docs/ex7101105.pdf> entitled *'Guidance on disclosing information about Family Proceedings involving children which are heard in private'*. The court retains its inherent power to authorize or restrict disclosure of information in any particular case (Administration of Justice Act 1960, s. 12). Any disclosure that falls outside the circumstances set out in the table requires the permission of the court.

Costs in family proceedings

30.100 It is important to note that costs in family proceedings are now governed by the Civil Procedure Rules 1998. The Family Proceedings (Miscellaneous Amendments) Rules 1999 apply the main parts of the costs rules under the Civil Procedure Rules 1998 to family proceedings. Much of the detail will be found in the related practice directions. For the purposes of the family law practitioner, the following are the important areas of the Civil Procedure Rules 1998 governing the practice and procedure relating to costs:

(a) Part 43—*Scope of Costs Rules and Definitions*.
(b) Part 44—*General Rules about Costs*.
(c) Part 47—*Procedure for Detailed Assessment of Costs etc.*
(d) Part 48—*Special Cases*.

Enforcement of a s. 8 order

The enforcement of s. 8 orders is discussed in more detail in Chapter 29, paragraphs 29.140 **30.101** (residence orders) and 29.162 (contact orders).

Section 34 of the Family Law Act 1986 empowers the High Court, county courts, or a **30.102** family proceedings court in private law proceedings to authorize an officer of the court or a constable to take charge of a child and deliver him to the person concerned. Section 34 may only be used, however, where the court is satisfied that the original order requiring the giving up of the child has been served on the relevant party and that it has been disobeyed.

Where a family proceedings court has made a residence order then this can be enforced **30.103** under s. 63(3), Magistrates' Courts Act 1980 against the party in breach of it as if the order had required the person concerned to produce the child, even though the order did not specifically say so: s. 14(1), CA 1989. This enables the enforcement of the order under s. 34(1) and (3) of the Family Law Act 1986.

The application for enforcement under s. 34, Family Law Act 1986 is made in Form C3 and it **30.104** should be made on notice unless there is an urgent need to make the order without notice. The application should be supported by evidence. The order issued by the court will be in Form C31.

It is possible to obtain an *ex parte* order under the inherent jurisdiction of the court for **30.105** the Tipstaff to seek and recover a child in appropriate cases (see further paragraph 32.22). Finally, the failure of a person to obey a court order or undertaking given to the court is a contempt which can be punished by way of imprisonment, fine, or sequestration of assets.

Best Practice Guidance

Practitioners may find it helpful in the preparation of Children Act cases to refer to the *Best* **30.106** *Practice Guidance* of June 1997 which is taken from the Children Act Advisory Committee *Handbook of Best Practice in Children Act Cases* and is set out in Part IV of *The Family Court Practice 2007* (Jordan Publishing Ltd, Family Law).

C KEY DOCUMENTS

The Children Act 1989   **30.107**
The Family Proceedings Rules 1991
The Family Proceedings Courts (Children Act 1989) Rules 1991
The Public Law Protocol: *Protocol for Judicial Case Management in Public Law Children Act Cases*
    (June 2003)
The Private Law Programme (circulated by the President of the Family Division on 10
    November 2004: set out in Family Court Practice 2006, Part IV (Jordans))
CAFCASS and the National Assembly for Wales Practice Note (Appointment of Guardians in Private
    Law Proceedings) [2006] 2 FLR 143

Websites

The National Standards for the Children and Family Court Advisory and Support Service: <www.cafcass.gov.uk>.

'Guidance on disclosing information about Family Proceedings involving children which are heard in private': <www.hmcourts-service.gov.uk/docs/ex7101105.pdf>

31

WARDSHIP AND THE INHERENT JURISDICTION

A   WHAT DOES INHERENT JURISDICTION MEAN?

31.01   The inherent jurisdiction is the exercise by the High Court of the powers of the Crown as *parens patriae*. It is based upon the duty of the Crown to protect all those subjects who owe allegiance to the Crown, and it extends to both adults and children within the areas of civil and criminal law. The inherent jurisdiction is theoretically without limit, but in practice there are far-reaching limitations on the exercise of the jurisdiction. Some examples of such limitations are:

(a)   where the welfare of the child in question is outweighed by the right of free publication: *Re X (A Minor)* [1975] Fam 47;

(b)   where the court should not supervise the exercise of a discretion within an area committed by statute to a local authority: *A v Liverpool City Council* [1982] AC 363; [1981] FLR 222;

(c)   where, although the court can authorize medical treatment, it cannot order a doctor, whether directly or indirectly, to treat a child in a manner contrary to his clinical judgement: *Re J (A Minor) (Wardship: Medical Treatment)* [1992] 2 FLR 165;

(d)   where the court cannot grant injunctions to restrain a local authority from exercising its statutory powers in relation to children, or the police from exercising their statutory or common law powers: *D v D (County Court Jurisdiction: Injunctions)* [1993] 2 FLR 82.

Where the inherent jurisdiction relates to children then the powers of the court may exceed those of the parents. Thus, the court is empowered to override both the decisions of parents and the decisions of a *Gillick*-competent child: *Re W (A Minor) (Consent to Medical Treatment)* [1993] 1 FLR 1.

31.02   The inherent jurisdiction exists independently from wardship and it can be used to protect the interests of a minor who is not a ward (*Re W (A Minor) (Consent to Medical Treatment)* (above); *Re L (An Infant)* [1968] 1 All ER 20; *Re M (Wardship: Publication of Information)* [1989] 1 FLR 443; *Re C (Detention: Medical Treatment)* [1997] 2 FLR 180. In relation to children the inherent jurisdiction is generally used to decide a specific issue, for example to authorize medical treatment, in those cases where it is not appropriate for the court to take total control over the care of the child. Wardship, on the other hand, is an exercise by the court of its inherent jurisdiction in order to assume total control over a child so that 'No important step in the child's life can be taken without the court's consent' (*Re S* [1967] 1 All ER 202). The use of wardship has been curtailed since the implementation of the Children Act 1989 ('CA 1989'). However, the inherent jurisdiction of the High Court can still be used to resolve difficult issues relating to children, particularly where the existing statutory provisions are inadequate or inappropriate for the determination of the specific issue in question.

31.03   Some examples of the exercise of the inherent jurisdiction are as follows:

(a)   To authorize a blood transfusion for a child who is seriously ill and whose parents do not consent to such treatment: *Re O (A Minor) (Medical Treatment)* [1993] 2 FLR 149.

(b)   To override the refusal of a minor to submit to assessment and medical examination and treatment, notwithstanding that she was of sufficient understanding to make an informed decision about medical examination or psychiatric examination or other assessment: *South Glamorgan County Council* v *W and B* [1993] 1 FLR 574.

(c) To grant an application of the local authority under s. 100, CA 1989 to prevent a film company and Channel Four television from continuing to film five children on the streets, some of whom were subject to care orders or interim care orders, on the basis that the filming was exploiting vulnerable children and was having a detrimental effect on their upbringing: *Nottingham City Council* v *October Films Ltd* [1999] 2 FLR 347. See paragraph 31.05 below as to the need for local authorities to apply for leave under s. 100(3) before invoking the inherent jurisdiction.

How to apply under the inherent jurisdiction

An application under the inherent jurisdiction should be commenced by originating sum- **31.04**
mons as set out in RSC Ord. 28, Appendix A, Form 8 (RSC Ord. 7, r. 2.2). If the application is to be made without notice to the other side (*ex parte*), then it should be commenced by originating summons as set out in RSC Ord. 28, Appendix A, Form 11: RSC Ord. 7, r. 2(2). Where the application is with notice, the applicant's evidence must be filed within 14 days after the respondent has acknowledged service: RSC Ord. 28, r. 1A(1). Where the application is without notice, the applicant must file his evidence at least four clear days before the hearing: RSC Ord. 28, r. 1A(2). The respondent must file his evidence within 28 days of service of the applicant's evidence, unless the court directs otherwise: RSC Ord. 28, rr. 1A(4), 2(2). The registry, on issuing the summons, should fix a date for directions before a Family Division judge on the first available date after eight weeks: RSC Ord. 28, r. 2(1). However, in the case of a without notice application, the time for the directions appointment will usually be abridged on the applicant's application. At the directions hearing, if the case appears complex and uncertain as to its outcome, the judge may give further directions, including directions for trial: *Re C* [1990] 2 FLR 527.

Application by local authority for leave to apply under the inherent jurisdiction pursuant to s. 100(3), Children Act 1989

Where a local authority wishes to apply for the leave of the court to make an application **31.05**
under the inherent jurisdiction pursuant to s. 100(3), CA 1989, this must be done *ex parte* (i.e., without notice) by filing a written request setting out the reasons for the application together with a draft of the originating summons: rr. 4.3(1)(b) and 5.1(2), Family Proceedings Rules 1991 ('FPR 1991'). The reasons given must satisfy the criteria set out in s. 100(4), CA 1989.

Although attendance at court is not necessary for such an application, where there is a **31.06**
degree of urgency about the matter it would be wise to attend before the High Court judge hearing the application with the request, a draft of the originating summons, and an affidavit in support after having given notice to all interested parties, including the Official Solicitor. This means that the court could hear all parties before giving leave, and then, if leave were given, go on to make any urgent orders that may be necessary and give any directions relevant to the substantive hearing of the matter. See paragraph 31.11 below for further details as to the use of the inherent jurisdiction by local authorities.

B   WHAT DOES WARDSHIP MEAN?

31.07   The wardship jurisdiction of the court is used to protect the interests of children. Parental responsibility for a child who is a ward vests in the court. Day-to-day care and control of the ward will be given to an individual (often one of the child's parents) or to a local authority, but no important step can be taken in the child's life without the court's consent and, if necessary, the court can give particular directions during the wardship to safeguard the welfare of the child.

31.08   Wardship proceedings are 'family proceedings' within the CA 1989 since they are part of the inherent jurisdiction of the High Court: s. 8(3)(a). Therefore, when the court is hearing wardship proceedings it may make any of the orders available to it under the CA 1989, save for those which it is prohibited from making by the Act itself. Therefore, provided that the child is not in the care of a local authority by virtue of a care order the court in wardship may make the following:

(a)   a residence order;

(b)   a contact order;

(c)   a prohibited steps order;

(d)   a specific issue order;

(e)   a special guardianship order;

(f)   it may appoint a guardian where a child has no parent with parental responsibility for him, or a parent or guardian with a residence order died while the order was in force;

(g)   a family assistance order where the circumstances of s. 16, CA 1989 are satisfied;

(h)   a care or supervision order on the application of a local authority (or other qualified applicant), provided that the statutory criteria in s. 31 are satisfied (N.B. upon the making of such a care order the child will cease to be a ward);

(i)   an order for financial provision in respect of the child whether or not any application has been made for it: see s. 15(1), CA 1989.

C   IMPACT OF THE CHILDREN ACT 1989 ON WARDSHIP

31.09   The CA 1989 has had a significant impact upon the inherent jurisdiction of the High Court. By introducing a flexible range of s. 8 orders, i.e., residence, contact, prohibited steps, and specific issue orders, the CA 1989 has incorporated the most valuable features of the wardship jurisdiction within its own proceedings. As a result, there will be very few cases in which it will still be necessary to resort to the wardship jurisdiction. The CA 1989 procedure is generally cheaper, quicker, and simpler than that for wardship proceedings.

Wardship and private law proceedings

31.10   In private law proceedings the CA 1989 makes no restriction on the use of wardship in private disputes not involving local authorities. However, the wide availability of s. 8 orders should largely obviate the need for the use of wardship in private law proceedings. It may still be useful in certain circumstances, for example, to bypass the requirement for leave to commence a s. 8 application, to gain immediate access to the High Court or to cater for the situation where there is a need for the court to have continuing control over a child's upbringing.

Wardship and local authorities

Local authorities must not use the inherent jurisdiction as a method of committing a child into their care or placing him under their supervision

The CA 1989 has severely curtailed the rights of local authorities to use the wardship juris-   **31.11**
diction. Section 100(2), CA 1989 prohibits local authorities from resorting to the inherent jurisdiction in general, and the wardship jurisdiction in particular, in order to achieve the admission of a child into their care. It also imposes substantial restrictions on the freedom of local authorities to use wardship for other purposes. As a result of the CA 1989 the only way in which a child may be committed into the care, or placed under the supervision, of a local authority is by satisfying the statutory 'threshold' criteria set out in s. 31 of the Act. This reflects one of the main principles behind the CA 1989 whereby it is intended that state interference with the upbringing of children should be kept to a minimum wherever possible. Thus, s. 100(1), CA 1989 specifically states that s. 7, Family Law Reform Act 1969 (which gave the High Court power to place a ward in the care, or under the supervision, of a local authority) ceases to have effect.

It may, however, be possible for a local authority to invoke the inherent jurisdiction of the   **31.12**
court where its powers under the CA 1989 are found to be insufficient: see *London Borough of Southwark* v *B* [1993] 2 FLR 559 and paragraph 31.16 below. Note that all public law child care cases are governed by the public law protocol which is discussed in detail in paragraph 33.32.

Inherent jurisdiction must not be used to make a child who is subject to a care order a ward of court

In pursuance of the same policy, s. 100(2)(c), CA 1989 directs that the inherent jurisdiction   **31.13**
of the High Court must not be used so as to make a child who is the subject of a care order a ward of court. The CA 1989 makes wardship and care incompatible. The current position is as follows:

(a) when a ward is committed to the care of the local authority the wardship ceases to have effect: s. 91(4);
(b) while a child is in care he cannot be made a ward of court: s. 100(2) and s. 41, Supreme Court Act 1981 as amended by sch. 13, para. 45, CA 1989.

Inherent jurisdiction may not be used to confer on a local authority power to determine any question relating to parental responsibility

Section 100(2)(d), CA 1989 prohibits the use of the High Court's inherent jurisdiction for the   **31.14**
purpose of conferring on any local authority the power to determine any question which has arisen, or which may arise, in connection with any aspect of parental responsibility for a

child. This means that, in making an order under its inherent jurisdiction the court cannot confer on the local authority any degree of parental responsibility it does not already have.

Transitional arrangements

31.15 The transitional arrangements as they affect wardship and children in the care of local authorities are contained in sch. 14, para. 15, CA 1989 (as amended by the Courts and Legal Services Act 1990, sch. 16, para. 33).

When can the local authority use the inherent jurisdiction of the High Court?

31.16 The local authority will still be able to resort to the use of the inherent jurisdiction of the High Court for limited purposes, provided that it first seeks the leave of the court to do so: s. 100(3). Leave may only be granted if the court is satisfied that:

(a) the result which the local authority wishes to achieve could not be achieved by the making of any other type of order which the local authority might be entitled to apply for under the statutory code: s. 100(4)(a) and (5); and

(b) there is reasonable cause to believe that if the court's inherent jurisdiction is not exercised with respect to the child he is likely to suffer significant harm: s. 100(4)(b).

31.17 The local authority is likely to use the inherent jurisdiction when it seeks the resolution of a specific issue concerning the future of a child in its care. Examples of this might be where it wishes to overrule the child (see *South Glamorgan County Council* v *W and B* [1993] 1 FLR 574); in sterilization cases; for injunctions which do not relate to the exercise of parental responsibility (see *Re S (Minors) (Inherent Jurisdiction: Ouster)* [1994] 1 FLR 623); to restrain publicity about the child; for wardship, if only the immediate effects of warding are required. In *Re W and X (Wardship: Relatives Rejected as Foster Carers)* [2004] 1 FLR 415, the court used its inherent jurisdiction, when the Fostering Services Regulations 2002 prevented the placement of children with their grandparents, by making the children wards of court and placing them with the grandparents in conjunction with a supervision order.

31.18 Where a child is in the care of a local authority the court is prevented from making any s. 8 order in respect of the child, save for a residence order: s. 9(1). This means that the local authority cannot apply for a prohibited steps or specific issue order in respect of a child in its care. If, however, the child is not in the local authority's care under a care order (e.g., where the child is simply being accommodated by the authority) then the authority could apply for leave to make a specific issue or prohibited steps order in respect of the child. Such an order may be available if the action which the authority wishes to take or prevent falls within the scope of parental responsibility, in which case the authority would not be able to invoke the inherent jurisdiction under s. 100.

D WHEN SHOULD WARDSHIP BE USED?

Suitable applicants

31.19 No particular relationship is required between the minor and the applicant. Wardship proceedings are therefore open not only to parents of the child concerned but also to other relatives of the child, prospective adopters, people with whom the child has had his home such as foster parents and step-parents, local authorities and their officers, etc. Even the child himself can apply, by his next friend, to be made a ward of court. However, the court will not entertain applications which are an abuse of the process of the court. The applicant is required to state his relationship to or interest in the ward in the originating summons; see paragraph 31.41 below. Once the originating summons has been issued, particulars of the originating summons will be recorded in the register of wards at the principal registry. If the recording officer is in any doubt as to whether the application is proper, the matter will be referred immediately to the appropriate district judge who, if he considers the application for wardship is an abuse of the process of the court, may dismiss the originating summons forthwith or refer the point to the judge: *Practice Direction* of 28 February 1967 [1967] 1 All ER 828, [1967] 1 WLR 623.

Example (The facts of *Re Dunhill* (1967) 111 SJ 113.) A nightclub owner made a 20-year-old model a ward, mainly for publicity purposes. The summons was struck out as being frivolous, vexatious, and an abuse of the process of the court and the nightclub owner was held liable for costs.

The child as plaintiff

The minor himself may apply for an order making him a ward. Furthermore, r. 9.2A of the FPR 1991 enables a minor, with leave of the court, to begin or prosecute any family proceedings (which includes proceedings under the inherent jurisdiction: s. 8(3), CA 1989), without a next friend provided that he has 'sufficient understanding' to do so: *Re CT (A Minor) (Wardship: Representation)* [1993] 2 FLR 278. Rule 9.2A also permits a minor, with leave, to make an application in, or defend, family proceedings without a guardian ad litem provided that he has 'sufficient understanding' to do so: *Re CT (A Minor) (Wardship: Representation)* (above); *Re H (A Minor) (Role of Official Solicitor)* [1993] 2 FLR 552. See paragraph 31.39 as to the position of a minor as defendant in wardship proceedings. See Chapter 28, paragraph 29.23 as to the ability of a child to participate generally as a party, and as to the meaning of 'sufficient understanding'.

31.20

In what type of case?

Kidnapping cases

In the past, wardship proceedings were extremely useful in cases where it was feared that a parent, or indeed some other person, was about to remove a child from England and Wales without the consent of the parent or other person with whom the child was residing. The implementation of the Child Abduction Act 1984 and the port alert system introduced in 1986 (see paragraph 32.10) has reduced the importance of wardship in this area although it is still useful in certain cases, for example, in relation to children of 16 and over. In the case of *Re KR (Abduction: Forcible Removal by Parents)* [1999] 2 FLR 542, a 17½ year-old girl was abducted from the UK to India by her parents for an arranged marriage to which she objected. The girl's sister made her a ward of court and after a series of hearings aimed at finding the whereabouts of the girl she was eventually returned to the UK and the wardship continued during her minority.

31.21

Wardship as a means of intervening in relation to proposed medical treatment

31.22   Wardship can be used as a means of influencing the medical treatment proposed for a child.

Example 1   (*Re D (A Minor) (Wardship: Sterilisation)* [1976] Fam 185, [1976] 1 All ER 326.) D was born with mental and physical handicaps. Her mother was concerned that she might, in the future, give birth to a handicapped child. When she was 11, arrangements were made for her to be sterilized. An educational psychologist attached to her local authority applied to make her a ward of court in order that the operation should be prevented. The court ordered the wardship to continue and did not consent to the operation which could therefore not be carried out (contrast *Re B (A Minor) (Wardship: Sterilisation)* [1987] 2 WLR 1213 where sterilization of Jeanette, a mentally handicapped 17-year-old, was permitted).

Example 2   (*Re B (A Minor) (Wardship: Medical Treatment)* [1981] 1 WLR 1421.) A local authority made a child suffering from Down's syndrome a ward of court in order to obtain the court's consent to an operation to save the child's life to which the child's parents were not prepared to consent. The court took the view that it was in the child's best interests for the operation to be performed and authorized it.

Example 3   (*Re C (A Baby)* [1996] 2 FLR 43.) The court made a baby a ward of court as a result of the serious brain damage which she suffered. The baby was unable to survive without artificial ventilation and, after a careful review of all the medical evidence, the court gave leave for the artificial ventilation to be discontinued.

The sterilization of a minor or a mentally incompetent adult will in virtually all cases require the prior sanction of a High Court judge. For a long time it was accepted that a court exercising wardship jurisdiction was the only authority empowered to authorize such a drastic step as sterilization: *Re B (A Minor) (Wardship: Sterilisation)* [1987] 2 FLR 314. However, in *Re HG (Specific Issue Order: Sterilisation)* [1993] 1 FLR 587, it was held that an application for leave to sterilize a child could be granted on an application under the inherent jurisdiction of the High Court or on an application for a specific issue order under s. 8, CA 1989. Where an application is made for a declaration that the proposed treatment is lawful, it is for the judge and not for the doctors to decide which treatment is in the patient's best interests: *Re S (Sterilisation: Patient's Best Interests)* [2000] 2 FLR 389. Where a child is a party to such proceedings he will be represented usually by the Official Solicitor (see *CAFCASS and the National Assembly of Wales Practice Note (Appointment of Guardians in Private Law Proceedings)* [2006] 2 FLR 143 and *Practice Note of 2 April 2001 'Official Solicitor: Appointment in Family Proceedings'* [2001] 2 FLR 155 as to the division of responsibility for such cases between CAFCASS Legal and the Official Solicitor). Where the application concerns an adult under a disability, see *Practice Note of 1 May 2001 'Official Solicitor: Declaratory Proceedings: Medical and Welfare Decisions for Adults who Lack Capacity'* [2001] 2 FLR 158.

Wardship and adoption

31.23   The court's wardship jurisdiction is not excluded by the making of an adoption order. The following paragraphs give examples of situations in which wardship jurisdiction may still be invoked. However, it will be seen that there has to be something special about the case to persuade the court to interfere with the normal course of events after the making or refusing of an adoption order. Wardship cannot be used simply to reopen old issues in relation to the adoption of the child.

Wardship application by natural parent in attempt to displace normal effect of an 31.24
adoption order The natural parent of a child who has been adopted can take wardship proceedings in an attempt to override the effects of the adoption order and to maintain contact with her child. However, the court will not necessarily be prepared to review the effects of the adoption order at a full hearing. The principles applicable are set out in *Re O (A Minor) (Wardship: Adopted Child)* [1978] Fam 196, [1978] 2 All ER 27. Whether the court will let the case proceed to a full hearing will depend on whether or not it is in the best interests of the child that there should be a full investigation or whether his interests would be better served if the wardship proceedings were dismissed at the outset so that the adoption order would take its normal course. In an ordinary case where the natural parents have parted with the child and not seen him at all and the adoptive parents have assumed the parental role, there will be a very heavy burden on a natural parent seeking to persuade the court to look into the merits of the case in wardship proceedings; the wardship proceedings would normally be dismissed in the initial stages.

There follows an example of the sort of case in which the court might be prepared to exercise 31.25
its wardship jurisdiction.

Example (The facts of *Re O* above.) When the child was adopted by Mr O'B, it was intended that the child would still be cared for by his natural mother after the adoption. The adoptive father then attempted to deny the mother contact with the child. The mother made the child a ward of court. The court held that the circumstances should be fully investigated in the wardship proceedings.

Application by prospective adopters whose application for an adoption order has 31.26
failed Wardship has been used successfully by prospective adopters whose adoption application has failed, to retain care and control of the child concerned where this was in the best interests of the child: *Re E (An Infant)* [1963] 3 All ER 874, [1964] 1 WLR 51. However, it would seem that the court will be reluctant to exercise its wardship jurisdiction to hear the merits of the case if the prospective adopters have not pursued to the full their rights of appeal against the adoption order: *Re S (A Minor)* (1978) 122 SJ 759.

Wardship can be used to obtain an order granting care and control to prospective adopters 31.27
after a failed adoption application, to maintain the status quo pending an adoption appeal: *Re C (MA) (An Infant)* [1966] 1 All ER 838, [1966] 1 WLR 646.

In *Re RJ (Fostering: Person Disqualified)* [1999] 1 FLR 605 the court discharged an interim care 31.28
order and instead made the three children concerned wards of court, granting interim care and control to their foster parents, in a case in which the foster father had been cautioned for assault occasioning actual bodily harm of another child so that under the Children (Protection from Offenders) (Miscellaneous Amendments) Regulations 1997 the placement of the children with him under a care order would not be lawful. The court felt that a s. 8 residence order was not appropriate and that wardship would enable the court to keep the case under review.

As a means of preventing undesirable associations

Wardship can be used to prevent a child forming an undesirable association. For example, 31.29
the court can grant an injunction preventing a third party from associating with the ward

where the ward proposes to make an independent marriage or has formed a relationship with an undesirable person of the same sex. The court can also intervene to prevent the ward joining an undesirable religious sect.

Where there is no subsisting residence order

31.30   Wardship can be used as a means of resolving a dispute as to who should have care and control of a child. Thus, where there is no subsisting residence order, the solicitor will (at least in theory) have the choice whether to start ordinary s. 8 proceedings or to embark on wardship proceedings.

31.31   In practice, in the vast majority of cases, ordinary s. 8 proceedings will be the appropriate choice. As a general rule, only if the case requires relief that cannot conveniently be obtained in ordinary proceedings should wardship proceedings be commenced. This is particularly so in view of the potentially high cost of wardship proceedings and also in view of the fact that an inevitable part of wardship is the continuing intervention of the court in relation to important decisions in the child's life. This can mean repeated applications to the court for directions even when the child's parents are able to reach agreement between themselves on a particular matter concerning the child and is likely to be seen by some parents as annoying interference rather than paternal protection by the court.

E   PROCEDURE

Costs

31.32   Wardship can be a very expensive procedure and the solicitor must therefore ensure that the question of cost is fully discussed with the client and, where appropriate, that an application for public funding under the Community Legal Service scheme has been made (see Chapter 2).

Jurisdiction

31.33   Jurisdiction in wardship cases depends upon the basis upon which the jurisdiction is exercised. The Family Law Act 1986 ('FLA 1986') sets out grounds upon which the wardship jurisdiction may be exercised for the purpose of making an order to which Part I of the FLA 1986 applies (for full meaning of 'Part I order' see paragraph 29.99). However, the FLA 1986 does not affect the wardship jurisdiction in so far as it is exercised otherwise than for the purpose of making a 'Part I order'.

Jurisdiction to make a Part I order under the Family Law Act 1986

31.34   A Part I order in relation to the exercise of the inherent jurisdiction, including wardship, means an order made by a court of England and Wales in the exercise of the inherent jurisdiction of the High Court with respect to children:

(a)   in so far as it gives the care of a child to any person or provides for contact with or the education of a child, but

(b)   excluding an order varying or discharging such an order: s. 1(1)(d), FLA 1986.

Furthermore, the court would only have jurisdiction to make one of the above orders if on the relevant date (i.e., the date of the application, or, if there is no application, the date on which the court is considering whether or not to make the order), the child is:

(a) habitually resident in England and Wales, or
(b) present in England and Wales and is not habitually resident in any part of the United Kingdom, or
(c) present in England and Wales on the relevant date and in need of emergency protection: s. 2(3)(b), FLA 1986.

There will be no jurisdiction in relation to (a) and (b) above if there are proceedings for divorce, nullity, or judicial separation continuing in a court in Scotland or Northern Ireland in respect of the child's parents, *unless* that court has waived its jurisdiction to deal with the Part I matters or has stayed its proceedings to enable the English court to deal with them.

Jurisdiction to make an order other than a Part I order under the Family Law Act 1986

The court has power to exercise its inherent wardship jurisdiction other than in respect of a **31.35** Part I order under the FLA 1986 over any child who is:

(a) under 18, and
(b) a British subject.

Such jurisdiction can be exercised whether or not the child is physically present within the jurisdiction and regardless of his place of birth, domicile, habitual residence, or ordinary residence. The case would have to be very exceptional, however, for the court to be persuaded to exercise its inherent jurisdiction in relation to a child who was neither born nor is resident within the jurisdiction.

The court may not, in any circumstances, exercise its wardship jurisdiction over any child **31.36** who:

(a) is in the care of the local authority by virtue of a care order, or
(b) is entitled to diplomatic immunity.

Commencing proceedings

Originating summons

Wardship proceedings are commenced in the Family Division of the High Court by originat- **31.37** ing summons issued out of the principal registry or out of a district registry: FPR 1991, r. 5.1(1).

The original originating summons will be required together with a copy for each defendant **31.38** and there is a fee to pay.

Notes on drafting originating summons

Who should be made defendant? The basic principle is that any person (or body) against **31.39** whom an order is sought should be made defendant.

Example Mr and Mrs Grant have separated. Mrs Grant is looking after their son, Peter. One day Mr Grant collects Peter from school without his wife's consent. Mrs Grant is afraid that he will take Peter out of the country to America where he has relations. Mrs Grant therefore consults her solicitor who advises that wardship proceedings should be commenced. Mr Grant should be made the defendant to the originating summons.

However, note the following points:

(a) The minor himself should not be made a defendant to the originating summons unless the district judge has given leave: r. 5.1(3), FPR 1991.

(b) Where the wardship proceedings are taken to prevent the minor from forming or continuing an undesirable association with a third party, the third party should not be made a defendant to the originating summons: *Practice Direction* of 16 June 1983 [1983] 1 WLR 790, [1983] 2 All ER 672.

(c) Sometimes there is no one other than the minor himself who is a suitable defendant (notably in cases of the kind referred to at (b) above where the minor's parents are seeking to put an end to an undesirable relationship). In such a case an application should be made to the district judge for leave to issue either an originating summons with the child as defendant or an *ex parte* originating summons: r. 5.1(3), FPR 1991. The district judge will then decide whether it is appropriate to make the minor a defendant. The minor should only be joined as a party in exceptional cases. If the minor is joined, the first port of call will be to contact CAFCASS Legal to invite them to act for him. However, CAFCASS Legal may consider that it would be better to invite the Official Solicitor to act. For the division of responsibility for such cases as between CAFCASS Legal and the Official Solicitor see *CAFCASS and the National Assembly for Wales Practice Note (Appointment of Guardians in Private Law Proceedings)* [2006] 2 FLR 143 and *Practice Note of 2 April 2001 'Official Solicitor: Appointment in Family Proceedings'* [2001] 2 FLR 155.

31.40 The practitioner will find guidance as to the meaning of 'habitual residence' in the cases of *C v S (A Minor: Abduction: Illegitimate Child)* [1990] 2 AC 562; [1990] 2 FLR 442 and *Re EW (Wardship Jurisdiction)* [1992] 2 FCR 441. In *Re S (Custody: Habitual Residence)* [1998] 1 FLR 122 (HL), the court held that although the child had been removed to Ireland, the child's habitual residence had remained in England. This meant that the court had jurisdiction to ward the child, to order interim care and control to the father, and to order that the child be returned to the jurisdiction.

31.41 **Contents of originating summons** The originating summons is in the normal form (see Form No. 8, Appendix 1 to the RSC), tailored to suit a wardship case. In particular, it must:

(a) name the minor concerned;

(b) set out the orders that the plaintiff claims (primarily, of course, an order that the minor be made a ward of court);

(c) state briefly the relationship of each party to the minor or his interest in the minor: r. 5.1(6), FPR 1991;

(d) contain a notice to the defendant informing him of his obligations under r. 5.1(8) and (9), FPR 1991 (see below at paragraph 31.52); and, unless otherwise directed,

(e) state the date of birth of the minor: FPR 1991, r. 5.1(5); and

(f) state the minor's present whereabouts (or state that the plaintiff is unaware of his whereabouts if that is the case): FPR 1991, r. 5.1(7).

Further documentation required to issue proceedings

The plaintiff's solicitor will also require: **31.42**

(a) a certified copy of the minor's birth certificate. This must be filed in the registry on issuing the originating summons or before or at the first appointment in the wardship proceedings: r. 5.1(5), FPR 1991;

(b) in publicly funded cases, a copy of the certificate. This must be filed as soon as it becomes available together with a notice of issue of the certificate and a copy notice of issue. Note that the detailed provisions of the new Community Legal Service scheme which deal with the availability of public funding for wardship cases are to be found in The Funding Code—Decision Making Guidance, para. 20.19. For a full account of the new Funding Code see Chapter 2;

(c) a certificate by the solicitor as to whether there are presently any other proceedings in relation to the minor. This must be filed when the originating summons is issued.

Issuing the originating summons

The originating summons, the fee, and the documents referred to in paragraph 31.37 above   **31.43**
should be taken to the appropriate registry to be issued. A stamped copy of the originating summons for each defendant will be returned to the plaintiff with:

(a) a slip showing the court file number allocated to the proceedings which must be endorsed on all documents filed in the registry;

(b) a notice of wardship: this is a notice stating that the minor has become a ward of court (this happens automatically on issuing the summons, see paragraph 31.46 below), that he may not marry or go outside England and Wales without leave of the court and that no material change should be made in the arrangements for his welfare, care and control, or education without leave. It also advises the ward (who may be served with a copy of the notice, see paragraph 31.44 below) that he may approach CAFCASS Legal if he is in doubt what to do;

(c) a blank form of acknowledgement of service of originating summons for each defendant.

Serving the papers

On the defendant   The solicitor must arrange to have the stamped copy of the originating   **31.44**
summons served on the defendant together with a copy of the notice of wardship. The original notice of wardship must be produced at the time of service. Although Ord. 10, RSC would seem to authorize service of the originating summons by first-class post or by insertion through the defendant's letter-box, in view of the requirement that the original notice of wardship must be produced at the time of service it would appear that strictly speaking personal service should be arranged (normally by an enquiry agent). If the minor himself is a defendant to the proceedings, he should not automatically be served with the documents himself. In such a case, CAFCASS Legal should be contacted for advice; they may be prepared to accept service on behalf of the minor even if he has not yet formally consented to act.

On other people   A copy of the notice of wardship may also be served on anyone else who   **31.45**
should be made aware that the minor has been made a ward (for example, it may be

appropriate to serve a copy of the notice of wardship on the ward himself if he is old enough to understand its meaning and the circumstances are such that he may be in need of independent advice, on a third party with whom the ward is associating and/or on the person with whom the ward is living if that person is not already a party to the proceedings). However, care must be taken that the originating summons (or indeed, in most cases, any of the other papers connected with the wardship), is not served on anyone who is not a party.

Wardship immediately effective: need to seek appointment within 21 days

31.46 The minor automatically becomes a ward as soon as the originating summons is issued: s. 41(2), Supreme Court Act 1981. He will then remain a ward for at least 21 days.

31.47 If the plaintiff wishes the minor to remain a ward for a longer period, he must make sure that he follows up the originating summons by making an application within 21 days after the issue of the originating summons for a hearing of the originating summons.

31.48 If no application is made within the 21-day period, the wardship will cease to be effective after the 21 days have elapsed. The originating summons will, however, continue to be effective and the court can be asked to order that the child become a ward again but the automatic protection enjoyed during the first 21 days will have been forfeited: r. 5.3(1)(a), FPR 1991.

31.49 On the other hand, if an application for an appointment is made during the first 21 days, unless the court orders otherwise, the minor will continue automatically to be a ward until the court hears the full wardship application and, of course, also thereafter if the court confirms the wardship at the full hearing: r. 5.3(1)(b), FPR 1991.

31.50 Note that it is not necessary for the first hearing of the originating summons actually to take place within the 21-day period, only that application should be made for an appointment for a first hearing.

Defendant's obligations when served with originating summons

To acknowledge service

31.51 The defendant must acknowledge service within 14 days of service of the originating summons. He must do this by completing the acknowledgement of service form and returning it by post or by hand to reach the registry from which the originating summons was issued before the expiry of the 14-day period: Ord. 12, RSC 1981.

To inform court and plaintiff of his own and minor's address

31.52 The defendant (other than the minor if he is the defendant) must also:

(a) lodge in the registry from which the originating summons was issued a notice stating:
   (i) his own address; *and*
   (ii) the whereabouts of the minor (or that he is unaware of the minor's whereabouts if this is the case): r. 5.1(8), FPR 1991; *and*

(b) serve a copy of this notice on the plaintiff unless the court otherwise directs: r. 5.1(8), FPR 1991; *and*

(c) if he then changes his address or becomes aware that the minor has changed his address, unless the court otherwise directs, he must lodge notice of the change in the appropriate registry and serve a copy of the notice on every other party: r. 5.1(9), FPR 1991.

The first appointment

The full hearing of the originating summons (at which it will be decided whether the minor **31.53** should remain a ward of court in the long term and, if so, what arrangements should be made for his care and control, etc.), normally takes place before a judge. Such a hearing cannot usually be arranged for several weeks. One reason for this is that the court lists are very busy and the case will therefore have to wait its turn until sufficient court time is available for a full hearing. Another reason is that all parties require time to prepare their cases. Preparation for a full wardship hearing is not unlike preparation for a contested residence dispute; there will therefore be witnesses to interview and affidavits to prepare, etc., and time will be required for a welfare report to be prepared and considered.

It is usual, therefore, for the first appointment in relation to the originating summons to be **31.54** before a district judge. This opportunity can be used to deal with a wide variety of interim matters, for example:

(a) The district judge will give directions as to the filing and giving of evidence for the final hearing.
(b) He can consider whether it is desirable that other people should be added as parties.
(c) He can consider whether CAFCASS Legal should be appointed (to look after the interests of the ward).
(d) He may (and usually will) direct that a court welfare report be prepared (i.e., an independent objective report on the child and his background prepared by a childern and family reporter after an investigation of the case).

Unless further directions are likely to be needed at a later stage, the district judge will then normally adjourn the case to the judge for a full hearing.

The full hearing

Venue

The full hearing will normally take place in front of a High Court judge sitting in chambers. **31.55** The court does, however, have power to adjourn the application to open court. It might do this, for example, in the case of a missing ward if it were felt that publicity might help in tracing the ward (see Chapter 32 and *Practice Direction* of 22 July 1979, [1980] 2 All ER 806).

Note that s. 38, Matrimonial and Family Proceedings Act 1984 (as amended by the sch. 13, **31.56** para. 51, CA 1989) gives the High Court power to transfer wardship applications to the county court, except applications that a minor be made or cease to be a ward of court. This means that the county court can deal with matters such as the appointment of a person to have day-to-day care and control of the ward, the making of maintenance orders in relation to the ward, etc. but reference should be made to the *Registrar's Direction* of 23 July 1987 and the *Practice Direction* of 5 June 1992 [1992] 2 FLR 87, for guidance as to the distribution of business between the High Court and the county courts.

The form of the hearing

31.57   The wardship hearing is likely to take much the same form as a contested residence hearing. The parties are usually represented by counsel. Evidence is given by affidavit and the court may well hear oral evidence as well. It is usual for a welfare report to be available and the children and family reporter may be asked questions about it. If CAFCASS Legal is involved in the case, the officer appointed as guardian will place before the court any evidence which he considers to be material on the ward's behalf. He will usually prepare a report based on his enquiries into the case. The report will set out his investigations (interviews with the ward, with parents and other relevant persons, reports obtained from doctors, schools, etc.), analyse the issues in the case and the courses open to the court and set out his submissions, if they can be formulated at this stage.

The court's orders

31.58   The court will decide whether or not to confirm the wardship in the long term. This will depend on whether the court feels that it is necessary for it to continue to exercise control over the arrangements for the child or whether, once the initial crisis has been resolved, it would be more appropriate to entrust the care of the child to an individual in the normal way.

31.59   If the wardship is confirmed, the court itself will have parental responsibility for the child but it will make an order as to who should have care and control. Whoever is awarded care and control, the court has power to make any of the orders set out in paragraph 31.08 above, since wardship proceedings are 'family proceedings' within s. 8(3), CA 1989.

31.60   Whether the court makes any further orders will depend on the circumstances of the case. There is power to make maintenance orders against either or both of the ward's parents (sch. 1, para. 1, CA 1989) and the court can give whatever directions are necessary as to other aspects of the ward's life such as education, religious upbringing, medical treatment, etc.

31.61   In deciding any question relating to the parental responsibility for or upbringing of a minor or to his property, s. 1, CA 1989 dictates that the court must regard the welfare of the minor as the paramount consideration. This principle applies to wardship cases just as it does to any other case concerning the upbringing of a child. As Lord Scarman pointed out giving the decision of the House of Lords in *Re E (SA) (A Minor) (Wardship)* [1984] 1 WLR 156, [1984] 1 All ER 289, the court's particular duty in a wardship case is to act in the way best suited in its judgement to serve the true interest and welfare of the ward. A fundamental feature of wardship jurisdiction is that it is not adversarial; in other words, the court's duty is not limited to the dispute between the parties. The court takes over ultimate responsibility for the child and it can look beyond the submissions of the parties and, if necessary, take a course not advocated by any party to the proceedings.

31.62   Note that it may well be appropriate for a wardship application to be coupled with an application under the CA 1989 for s. 8 orders to enable the court to deal with the question of residence, contact, prohibited steps, or specific issue orders should it decide to discontinue the wardship.

F THE FUTURE OF THE WARD

Whoever is awarded care and control of the ward should be reminded that no important step **31.63** can be taken in the ward's life without the leave of the court.

The way this restraint is most likely to be felt is in relation to trips outside the jurisdiction. **31.64** The ward cannot go or be taken outside England and Wales, even for a holiday, without leave. Clients do not always appreciate that this restriction includes holidays in Scotland. However, the court may be prepared to grant general leave for the ward to be taken for *temporary* visits outside England and Wales. In this case there is no need for the person to whom leave is granted to seek the court's approval before each proposed trip, but certain formalities must still be complied with by the person in whose favour leave has been granted, i.e., he must lodge at the registry at least seven days before the proposed departure:

(a) a written consent from the other party or parties to the ward leaving the jurisdiction for the proposed period;
(b) a written statement giving the date of departure, the period of absence, and the whereabouts of the ward during that absence; and
(c) unless otherwise directed, a written undertaking to return the ward to England and Wales at the end of the period.

Provided these formalities are complied with, a certificate for production to the immigration authorities stating that the conditions of the general leave have been complied with, may be obtained from the registry: *Practice Direction* [1973] 1 WLR 690, [1973] 2 All ER 512. If general leave is not granted, a separate application for leave will have to be made each time it is proposed to take the ward temporarily outside England and Wales and the applicant will be required to give a written undertaking to the court to return the ward after the visit.

If it is desired to take the ward out of England and Wales *permanently*, special leave must be **31.65** obtained from the court: *M v A (Wardship: Removal from Jurisdiction)* [1993] 2 FLR 715. If leave is granted, the court may or may not order that the wardship should be discontinued. If the wardship is to continue, the applicant will be asked to give an undertaking to return the child if ever ordered to do so by the court: see *Re F (A Ward) (Leave to Remove Ward Out of the Jurisdiction)* [1988] 2 FLR 116.

In considering any application for leave, the court will be concerned as to whether it is in the **31.66** child's interests to go outside England and Wales and as to whether the child will be returned to the jurisdiction at the end of his visit abroad or, if leave is given for him to leave the jurisdiction indefinitely, should the court ever order his return (see *Re F (A Ward) (Leave to Remove Ward Out of Jurisdiction)* [1988] 2 FLR 116 and *M v A (Wardship: Removal from Jurisdiction)* (above)).

Other matters which must be referred to the court for approval include medical treatment/ **31.67** examination other than normal emergency or day-to-day treatment (for example, if it is proposed that the ward should be examined by a psychiatrist with a view to a report being prepared to be put in evidence, or should have an abortion), proposals for the adoption of the ward, and any proposed marriage of the ward.

G INJUNCTIONS

General

31.68 Although the very fact that a child has been made a ward means that he will automatically be protected by the court in many respects, this is not always sufficient to ensure his welfare. Thus the court also has extensive powers to grant injunctions whenever it is necessary to safeguard the interests of the ward, for example preventing him from associating with a third party who is considered to be undesirable. (See, for example, *Re H (A Minor) (Role of Official Solicitor)* [1993] 2 FLR 552.)

31.69 The plaintiff is free to ask the court to make a long-term injunction at the full hearing of the case but in many wardship cases this will not be soon enough—the damage will already have been done by that time. In such cases it will be necessary to seek an interlocutory injunction before the full hearing. If the circumstances warrant it, such an application can be made (without notice to the other side, if necessary) even before the originating summons has been issued commencing the wardship proceedings. Indeed, it is possible to obtain an injunction within hours of first taking instructions from the client if necessary. Furthermore, the fact that the courts are closed at the relevant time is no obstacle in an emergency.

The normal procedure for seeking an interlocutory injunction (r. 1, RSC Ord. 29)

31.70 As wardship proceedings fall within the definition of 'family proceedings' for the purposes of the Civil Procedure Rules 1998, the old rules under r. 1, RSC Ord. 29, continue to apply to interlocutory injunctions made within wardship proceedings (see r. 2.1(2), Civil Procedure Rules 1998 and r. 1.3(1), FPR 1991).

(a) The normal procedure for seeking an interlocutory injunction is for the plaintiff, after the originating summons has been issued, to apply by *summons* to a judge in chambers. Notice must be given to the other party to the summons; r. 3, RSC Ord. 32 requires that the period of notice should be not less than two clear days before the day specified for the hearing in the summons.

(b) Thus the solicitor must prepare:
   (i) a summons (in the general form) with sufficient copies for service on all parties to the summons;
   (ii) an affidavit in support of the summons with sufficient copies for service;
   (iii) a draft injunction which should include a penal notice informing the defendant that disobedience to the terms of the injunction is a contempt of court and will make him liable to be committed to prison.

(c) These documents should be taken to the court office where the summons will be issued and the copies for service returned to the plaintiff's solicitor. The supporting affidavit and draft injunction should be filed with the court.

(d) The solicitor should then arrange for a copy of the summons and the supporting affidavit to be served on the other party or parties to the summons. If there is a solicitor acting for the party to be served, the documents may be served on him. If not, the documents can be posted to the party himself (see RSC Ord. 65).

(e) All parties should attend the hearing which will be before a judge in chambers. If there is time, the defendant to the summons is entitled to file an affidavit in answer to that of the plaintiff. It may be necessary for the judge to hear some oral evidence. He can be asked to grant the injunction in the terms of the draft prepared by the plaintiff's solicitor. It is not uncommon for the judge to make amendments to the draft to ensure that the injunction deals properly with the circumstances of the case as they appear at the interlocutory hearing. The injunction may be expressed to last until the full hearing of the originating summons or for a shorter period if the judge thinks fit.

(f) The injunction should be served on those parties against whom it is effective.

Ex parte (without notice) applications (r. 1, RSC Ord. 29)

In an urgent case when there is insufficient time for notice to be given or it is desirable for some reason that notice should not be given, the court can grant an injunction without notice having first been given to the other side (*ex parte*). **31.71**

The following example illustrates the sort of situation in which an injunction without notice might be appropriate and also the procedure involved in obtaining one. The procedure is more fully described in the rest of this paragraph. **31.72**

Example Mrs Smith consults her solicitor on Monday 10 February because she is concerned about a relationship her son Eric has formed with a man in his forties (Mr Jones) who has convictions for indecency with boys. Her son is at boarding school but she has received a letter from him saying that he has been in touch with the man who is coming to pick him up from school on Wednesday 12 February when half-term begins. The solicitor issues an originating summons on Monday 10 February commencing wardship proceedings. Eric is thus automatically a ward of court. However, this does not prevent Mr Jones and Eric from associating with each other. An injunction is therefore required to prevent Mr Jones from associating with Eric, visiting the school, etc. There is not time to serve Mr Jones with notice of an injunction hearing, therefore the court is asked for an appointment with the judge to request an injunction without notice to the other side. At the same time, the solicitor issues at the court office a summons for an *inter partes* injunction hearing (i.e., a hearing of which the other side *is* to be given notice). He is given a hearing date of the following Tuesday 18 February. An affidavit by Mrs Smith is sworn setting out the circumstances of the case and the reasons why it is urgent and a draft injunction is drawn up. The solicitor arranges for the summons and the supporting affidavit to be served personally on Mr Jones. On Tuesday 11 February, Mrs Smith and her solicitor attend before the judge who grants an injunction without notice in the terms requested to last until the following Tuesday (which is the date fixed for the hearing of the injunction summons). On Tuesday 18 February a hearing of which the other side *has* had notice takes place and the injunction is renewed until the full hearing of the originating summons.

The procedure for seeking an injunction without notice (*ex parte*) is as follows:

(a) Oral evidence will be sufficient in a dire emergency; the plaintiff and his solicitor should attend upon the judge to explain the position and request the injunction. This attendance may be at court or, if there is no judge sitting at court at the time, arrangements may be made for the judge to deal with the matter at his lodgings, at his home, or even over the telephone. If the solicitor is not aware of the appropriate way to trace a judge locally, he should contact the Royal Courts of Justice in London where someone is always on duty to advise.

(b) Except in an extreme emergency application should be by affidavit which should set out the full circumstances of the case and the reasons why the application is made without notice. The solicitor should prepare a draft injunction. The court should then be asked to arrange a hearing without notice to the other side in front of a judge at which the plaintiff and his solicitor should attend. Although the defendant is not entitled to notice of the hearing, there is no reason why he should not be told that it is taking place as a matter of courtesy if this is appropriate in the circumstances of the case.

(c) If the judge agrees to grant an injunction without notice, it will be an interim injunction and will be expressed to last only for a matter of days until an application can be made on notice for it to be renewed until the full hearing of the originating summons. This means that, in addition to arranging the hearing without notice, the solicitor will have to issue and serve a summons for an injunction in the normal way (see paragraph 31.70 above) giving notice of the hearing to the other side. It is not uncommon for the solicitor to issue this summons at the same time as he seeks an appointment for the hearing without notice if he has had time to prepare the papers.

(d) The injunction obtained without notice to the other side must be served personally on the defendant as soon as possible. In very urgent cases, he should be informed of the terms of the injunction over the telephone if possible.

Injunction required before originating summons issued

31.73 In practice, provided that the court office is open, it should be possible to issue an originating summons before making an application for an injunction. However, if this is not possible for any reason, the court does have power to grant an injunction (which will be without notice to the other side) even before proceedings have been commenced by the issue of an originating summons: r. 1, RSC Ord. 29.

31.74 The injunction will usually be granted on terms that the originating summons be issued as soon as possible.

Example Mr and Mrs Rose consult their solicitor on Saturday morning. They have just learnt that their 15-year-old daughter has agreed to take part in a nude modelling session for a local photographer, Mr Briggs, on the Sunday afternoon. Their attempts to dissuade her from participating have failed. They wish to seek an injunction to prevent the photographic session from taking place. No originating summons can be issued to commence wardship proceedings as the court office is closed. The solicitor contacts the Royal Courts of Justice and an appointment is arranged with the duty judge for the Saturday afternoon. There is no time to swear an affidavit. Mr and Mrs Rose and their solicitor therefore attend on the judge who hears oral evidence from Mr Rose and grants an injunction without notice first having been given to Mr Briggs forbidding Mr Briggs to hold the photographic session. The solicitor undertakes to issue an originating summons commencing wardship proceedings when the court office opens on Monday. This he does and a summons is also taken out and served on Mr Briggs giving notice of an application for an injunction to last until the full hearing of the wardship application preventing Mr Briggs from holding any photographic sessions involving Mr and Mrs Rose's daughter.

Orders restricting publicity

In wardship proceedings the court has power to make an injunction prohibiting the publica- **31.75** tion of any information which is considered to be harmful to the ward: *Re W (Wards) (Publication of Information)* [1989] 1 FLR 246; *Re X County Council* v *A* [1985] 1 All ER 53. The order is binding on every person who is potentially subject to the order but who has not been joined as a party to the proceedings. The Administration of Justice Act 1960, s. 12, provides that the publication of information relating to proceedings before any court sitting in private is not in itself a contempt. However, the exceptions to this rule include:

(a) proceedings which relate to the exercise of the inherent jurisdiction of the High Court in relation to minors;
(b) proceedings under the CA 1989; and
(c) any other proceedings which relate wholly or mainly to the maintenance or upbringing of a minor.

The court has power to allow disclosure of information the publication of which would otherwise be prohibited: *Re K (Minors) (Disclosure)* [1994] 1 FLR 377. The principles to be applied by the court on considering an application for disclosure are to be found in *Re Manda (Wardship) (Disclosure of Evidence)* [1993] 1 FLR 205, but the interests of the child concerned will always be the most important factor (see also *A* v *M (Family Proceedings Publicity)* [2000] 1 FLR 562; *Re G (Celebrities: Publicity)* [1999] 1 FLR 409). When deciding whether to allow the disclosure of wardship documents for the purpose of criminal proceedings the court must balance the importance of confidentiality in wardship proceedings against the public interest in seeing that the defendant in criminal proceedings should have available all relevant and necessary material for the proper conduct of his defence: *Re D (Minors) (Wardship: Disclosure)* [1994] 1 FLR 346.

Other useful cases which analyse the existing case law and the competing issues of the **31.76** child's rights under the European Convention for the Protection of Fundamental Freedoms 1950, Art. 8, and the rights of the press to freedom of expression under Art. 10 include *Re S (Identification: Restriction on Publication)* [2003] 2 FLR 1253; *Re Roddy (A Child)(Restriction on Publication)* [2004] 2 FLR 949; *Re B (A Child) (Disclosure)* [2004] 2 FLR 142.

H KEY DOCUMENTS

The Children Act 1989 **31.77**
The Family Proceedings Rules 1991
Rules of the Supreme Court 1965

Practice Direction (Representation of Children in Family Proceedings Pursuant to Family Proceedings Rules 1991, Rule 9.5) [2004] 1 FLR 1188

CAFCASS and the National Assembly for Wales Practice Note (Appointment of Guardians in Private Law Proceedings) [2006] 2 FLR 143

Practice Note of 1 May 2001 'Official Solicitor: Declaratory Proceedings: Medical and Welfare Decisions for Adults who Lack Capacity' [2001] 2 FLR 158

Practice Direction of 16 June 1983 'Wards of Court: Parties to the Proceedings' [1983] 1 WLR 790, [1983] 2 All ER 672

32

PREVENTING THE REMOVAL OF A CHILD FROM THE JURISDICTION AND TRACING A LOST CHILD

A   FAMILY LAW ACT 1986

The Family Law Act 1986 ('FLA 1986') considerably reduces the problems that can arise **32.01** when a child is taken out of the jurisdiction of the English courts to another part of the United Kingdom. The FLA 1986 has been amended by sch. 13, paras. 62 to 71, Children Act 1989 ('CA 1989'). The FLA 1986, in its amended form, establishes a procedure whereby a 'Part I order' made in relation to a child under 16 in one part of the United Kingdom will be recognized in any other part of the United Kingdom as having the same effect as if it had been made by a local court. It is now possible to register a 'Part I order' in the appropriate court in another part of the United Kingdom. Once this has been done, one can apply to that court for the order to be enforced as if it were one of the court's own orders (see chapter V of Part I, FLA 1986). For the meaning of 'Part I order' and for details of the other rules as to jurisdiction to make s. 8 orders under the FLA 1986, see paragraph 29.99. However, note that Part I orders include s. 8 orders (other than one varying or discharging a s. 8 order) and certain orders made in the exercise of the inherent jurisdiction of the High Court with respect to children.

B   REMOVAL FROM THE UK

Child Abduction Act 1984

32.02   Section 1(1), Child Abduction Act 1984 ('CAA 1984'), as amended by the sch. 12, para. 37, CA 1989 makes it a criminal offence for a person 'connected' with a child under 16 to take or send the child out of the United Kingdom without the appropriate consent.

32.03   The following are 'connected' with the child:

(a)   a parent of the child;

(b)   in the case of a child whose parents were not married to each other at the time of his birth, a person who there are reasonable grounds for believing to be the father of the child;

(c)   a guardian of the child;

(d)   a special guardian of the child;

(e)   a person in whose favour a residence order is in force with respect to the child;

(f)   a person who has custody of the child.

The consent that is needed is from the following:

(1)   (a)   the child's mother;

      (b)   the child's father, if he has parental responsibility for him;

      (c)   any guardian of the child;

      (d)   any special guardian of the child;

      (e)   any person in whose favour a residence order is in force with respect to the child;

      (f)   any person who has custody of the child; or

(2)   the leave of the court granted under or by virtue of any provision of Part II, CA 1989; or

(3)   if any person has custody of the child, the leave of the court which awarded custody to him.

32.04   A person does *not* commit an offence under CAA 1984 if he takes or sends a child out of the United Kingdom without the appropriate consent *if*:

(a)   he is a person in whose favour there is a residence order in respect of the child; and

(b)   he takes or sends the child out of the United Kingdom for a period of less than one month; or

(c)   he is a special guardian of the child and he takes or sends the child out of the United Kingdom for a period of less than 3 months

unless he does so in breach of the terms of an order made under Part II, CA 1989 (s. 4A, CAA 1984).

32.05   Section 1(5), CAA 1984 provides that a person does not commit an offence by doing anything without the consent of another person whose consent is technically required if:

(a) he does it in the belief that the other person:
  (i) has consented, or
  (ii) would consent if he was aware of all the relevant circumstances; or
(b) he has taken all reasonable steps to communicate with the other person but has been unable to do so; or
(c) the other person has unreasonably refused his consent.

However, (c) above does *not* apply if:

(a) the person who refused to consent is a person:
  (i) in whose favour there is a residence order in force with respect to the child; or
  (ii) who is a special guardian of the child; or
  (iii) who has custody of the child; or
(b) the person so taking or sending the child is doing so in breach of an order made by a court in the United Kingdom.

For the purposes of CAA 1984 the terms 'guardian of a child', 'special guardian', 'residence order', and 'parental responsibility' have the same meaning as in the CA 1989.

Note that there are special modifications of s. 1 for certain children, for example, those **32.06** who are in the care of local authorities, detained in a place of safety, remanded to local authority accommodation or the subject of an order relating to adoption (see s. 1(8) and the schedule to CAA 1984).

By virtue of s. 2, CAA 1984, a person who is *not* the parent, guardian, someone with a **32.07** residence order in respect of the child or someone with custody of the child commits an offence if, without lawful authority or reasonable excuse, he takes or detains a child under 16 so as:

(a) to remove him from the lawful control of any person having lawful control of him, or
(b) to keep him out of the lawful control of any person entitled to lawful control of him.

A person charged under s. 2, CAA 1984 has a defence if he can show that, at the time of the **32.08** alleged offence:

(a) he believed that the child was at least 16, or
(b) in the case of a child of unmarried parents, he had reasonable grounds for believing he was the child's father.

Although the provisions of CAA 1984 may be a psychological deterrent to anyone con- **32.09** templating abducting a child and taking him abroad, the Act itself does not establish any practical safeguards to prevent the removal of the child. What it has done, however, is to prompt the setting up of a 'port alert' system which does offer more concrete help.

The port alert system

General

The port alert system is described fully in *Practice Direction* [1986] 2 FLR 89. It is operated by **32.10** the police and replaces the former Home Office procedure for preventing the unauthorized removal of children from England and Wales.

32.11 The police provide a 24-hour service and, in conjunction with immigration officers at the ports, will attempt to prevent the unlawful removal of a child from the country. The National Ports Office can be contacted on 020 7230 4800.

Eligibility for assistance under the system

32.12 Before they will institute a port alert for a child, the police will need to be satisfied:

(a) That there is a real and imminent danger of the child being removed. 'Imminent' means within 24 to 48 hours and 'real' means that the port alert is not just being sought as an insurance.

(b) That:
   (i) the child is under 16, or
   (ii) the child is a ward (the police should be shown evidence of this, for example, confirming the wardship, an injunction or, in an urgent case, a sealed copy of the originating summons in wardship), or
   (iii) in the case of a child of 16 or over who is not a ward of court, there is in force a residence order relating to the child or an order restricting or restraining his removal from the jurisdiction.

Means of seeking police help

32.13 An application for assistance in preventing a child's removal from the jurisdiction must be made by the applicant or his legal representative to a police station. Application should normally be made to the applicant's local police station but, in urgent cases, any police station will do. The police require quite a lot of detail to be given when assistance is requested, for example, likely travel details and information about the child, the applicant and the person likely to remove the child from the jurisdiction. Reference should be made to the 1986 *Practice Direction* for a complete list of the details that should be given if possible. Where a court order has been obtained in relation to the child, it should be produced to the police even where the child is under 16 and a court order is not strictly required.

How the system works

32.14 If the police are satisfied that the port alert system should be used, the child's name will be entered on a stop list for four weeks. The ports will be notified direct, and police and immigration officers will attempt to identify the child and prevent his removal from the country. After four weeks the child's name will automatically be removed from the stop list unless a further application is made.

Passports

32.15 An interested party may give notice in writing to the Passport Department at the Home Office that passport facilities should not be provided in respect of a minor either without leave of the court or, in cases other than wardship, the consent of the other parent, guardian, or person to whom a residence order or care and control has been granted, or the consent of the mother where the child's parents are unmarried: *Practice Direction* [1986] 2 FLR 89.

32.16 If the child has not already got passport facilities, notification given to the Passport Department should be effective to prevent his unlawful removal from the country. However, it does not assist where the child already has his own passport or is mentioned on the passport of a parent who it is feared will remove him from the country. The courts can order the surrender of the child's passport or of a passport containing particulars of the child. The court informs the Passport Office if this is done, to prevent the issue of a new passport: *Practice Direction* [1983] 2 All ER 253, [1983] 1 WLR 558.

The law on the surrender of passports is statutory and found in s. 37, FLA 1986. The section **32.17** provides that where there is in force an order prohibiting or restricting the removal of a child from the United Kingdom or from any part of it, the court that made the order and appropriate courts in other parts of the United Kingdom may require any person to surrender any United Kingdom passport which has been issued to or contains particulars of the child.

C TRACING A LOST CHILD

Allowing publication of information about a child

If a child is missing, the court has power to permit the publication of information about the **32.18** child to enable him to be traced. If it is felt that publicity would help, the judge should be asked to lift reporting restrictions to enable information such as a description of the child, a photograph of him, a description of the adult thought to be accompanying him, details concerning his disappearance and anything known about where he may be to be published: *Practice Direction* of 22 July 1979 [1980] 2 All ER 806; *Re R (MJ) (A Minor) (Publication of Transcript)* [1975] Fam 89, [1975] 2 All ER 749.

Disclosure of addresses by government departments

The court can request certain government departments to provide information as to where a **32.19** missing child might be: *Practice Direction of 20 July 1995 'Disclosure of Addresses by Government Departments'* (see *Family Court Practice*, Part IV (Jordans)). The request must certify that the child cannot be traced and that the child is believed to be with the person whose address is sought. The request can be made to the Department of Social Security, the Office of Population Census and Surveys, National Health Service Central Register, the Passport Office, and the Ministry of Defence. The *Practice Direction* of 20 July 1995 (above) sets out the details which will be required by each government department before the request can be complied with.

Seeking information as to child's whereabouts: s. 33, Family Law Act 1986

Section 33, FLA 1986 (as amended by sch. 13, para. 62, CA 1989), provides that all courts **32.20** have power in proceedings for or relating to an order made under s. 8, CA 1989, to require any person whom they have reason to believe may have information relevant to where a child is to disclose that information to the court. The appropriate form to be completed is Form C4.

Recovering a child through s. 34, Family Law Act 1986

32.21 Where a person has not returned a child in accordance with a residence or contact order, the court can be asked to make a further order authorizing an officer of the court (e.g., a solicitor) or a police constable to search for, take charge of and deliver the child to him, thus giving effect to the residence or contact order (s. 34, FLA 1986). However, an order under s. 34 can be granted only once the original order to give up the child has been disobeyed. Application for such an order is made on Form C3.

Recovering a child through the inherent jurisdiction

32.22 If the applicant has good reason to believe that the person who has control of the child is likely to try to hide the child or remove him from the jurisdiction on becoming aware of the applicant's attempts to recover the child, then it may be appropriate for the applicant to apply for an order without first giving notice to the other side (i.e., *ex parte*) under the inherent jurisdiction authorising the 'Tipstaff' to 'search and find' the child (r. 5.2, FPR 1991). The Tipstaff is an officer of the High Court and has authority to arrest and bring before a court any person who obstructs him in the execution of an order of the High Court. Any such order should be carefully drafted so as to make it clear to the Tipstaff exactly what is required of him. For example, the order should specify the person, or local authority (if appropriate), to whom the Tipstaff should 'hand over' the child once he has secured his return.

Flight information

32.23 Where a person seeks an order for the return of a child who is about to arrive in England by air he will probably wish to have information to enable him to meet the aeroplane. The applicant should ask the judge to include a direction in his order that the airline operating the flight and the immigration officer at the relevant airport should supply the appropriate information to the applicant. Where the applicant already has an order for the return of the child he should apply without first giving notice to the other side (i.e., *ex parte*) to a judge for the appropriate direction to be added to the order: *Practice Direction of 18 January 1980 'Arrival of Child in England by Air'* [1980] 1 All ER 288; [1980] 1 WLR 73.

D   KEY DOCUMENTS

32.24 Child Abduction Act 1984
Family Law Act 1986
Children Act 1989
Practice Direction 20 July 1995 'Disclosure of Addresses by Government Departments' (see Family Court Practice 2006, Part IV (Jordans))
Practice Direction 14 April 1986 'Children: Removal from Jurisdiction' [1986] 2 FLR 89
Practice Direction 29 April 1983 'Children: Removal from Jurisdiction' [1983] 1 WLR 558, [1983] 2 All ER 253

Practice Direction 18 January 1980 'Arrival of Child in England by Air' [1980] 1 All ER 288, [1980] 1 WLR 73

Practice Direction 22 July 1979 'Child Abduction: Press Publicity' [1980] 2 All ER 806

33

CHILDREN IN LOCAL AUTHORITY CARE

A   INTRODUCTION—CHILDREN AND LOCAL AUTHORITIES

Only one route into care

33.01   As a result of the coming into force on 14 October 1991 of the Children Act 1989 ('CA 1989') there is now only one method of formally receiving children into the care of a local authority: that is by satisfying the statutory 'threshold' criteria set out in s. 31(2) of the Act. See also Chapter 29 for the general principles to be applied in *all* proceedings brought under the CA 1989, whether they be for private law or public law orders.

Human Rights Act 1998

33.02   The Human Rights Act 1998 ('HRA 1998') incorporated into domestic law the European Convention for the Protection of Human Rights and Fundamental Freedoms. Article 8 of the Convention guarantees the right to respect for private and family life. Article 8(2) permits interference by a public authority with an individual's private and family life only where the interference is in accordance with the law and necessary for the purposes specified in the article. There is need for proportionality between the interests of the applicant and the interests of the community. The existence of this guarantee is of crucial importance in public law child care cases in determining in what circumstances a child can properly be taken into the care of a local authority.

33.03   If such interference is justified the court must also consider whether it is proportionate to the aim of protecting the rights of the child concerned (*Re B (Care: Interference with Family Life)* [2003] 2 FLR 813). The task of the domestic court when faced with a complaint under Art. 8(1) is to review the decisions taken under the Convention by other public authorities and compare them with the case currently before it. Where the rights of parents and those of a child are at stake, the child's interests are the paramount consideration. If any balancing of interests is necessary, the child's interests must prevail (*Yousef v The Netherlands* [2003] 1 FLR 210).

33.04   When a local authority plans to take a child into care, it must ensure that the procedure at all stages is transparent and fair, both in and out of court. Article 8 requires the local authority to involve parents fully in the decision-making process, at all stages of the child protection procedure, whether before, during or after the making of a care order (*Re G (Care: Challenge to Local Authority's Decision)* [2003] 2 FLR 42). See further under paragraph 33.69 below.

The Adoption and Children Act 2002

The Adoption and Children Act 2002 ('ACA 2002') is now largely in force and has made **33.05** amendments to the CA 1989. The main changes affecting the public law relating to children (which will be referred to in more detail at appropriate points in the text) include:

(a) *Extended definition of 'harm'*—s. 120, ACA 2002 extends the definition of 'harm' in s. 31(9), CA 1989 to include, for example, impairment suffered by hearing or seeing the ill-treatment of another.

(b) *Care plans*—s. 121, ACA 2002 inserts a new s. 31A, CA 1989 which provides that in all public law cases in which a local authority seeks a care order in respect of a child it must prepare a care plan (to be known as a 'section 31A care plan'). Furthermore, the local authority is required to keep the care plan under review and make changes as and when necessary, even after a care order has been made and implemented;

(c) *Review of cases of 'looked-after' children*—s. 118, ACA 2002 amends s. 26(2)(e), CA 1989 to create a 'looked-after' children reviewing officer, so that even after the making of a care order the officer will participate in the review process and will have power to refer the case to the Children and Family Court Advisory and Support Service (CAFCASS) where appropriate. CAFCASS will have power to take proceedings on behalf of the child.

(d) *Advocacy services*—s. 119, ACA 2002 inserts a new s. 26A, CA 1989 to place a duty on local authorities to provide assistance to adults and children wishing to make representations under ss. 24D and 26, CA 1989 about the way the authority has discharged its functions.

The general duty

Local authorities are placed under a general duty to: **33.06**

(a) safeguard and promote the welfare of children within their area who are in need, and

(b) so far as it is consistent with that duty, to promote the upbringing of children by their families

by providing a range and level of services appropriate to those children's needs: s. 17(1).

Thus, the CA 1989 emphasizes that the prime responsibility for the upbringing of children **33.07** lies with their parents. The intention is that the state should be ready to help parents to discharge that responsibility, especially if it lessens the risk of family breakdown. Services to families in need of help should be arranged in voluntary partnership with parents, so far as possible. If those services include looking after the child away from home then the underlying principle is that close contact should be maintained between the child and his family and, if appropriate, the family should be reunited as soon as possible.

A child is taken to be 'in need' if he is unlikely to achieve or maintain, or to have the **33.08** opportunity of achieving or maintaining, a reasonable standard of health or development without the provision for him of services by a local authority under Part III of the CA 1989, or he is disabled: s. 17(10).

'Family', in relation to a child in need, includes any person who has parental responsibility **33.09** for the child and any other person with whom he has been living: s. 17(10).

33.10 'Development' means physical, intellectual, emotional, social, or behavioural development: s. 17(11).

33.11 'Health' means physical and mental health: s. 17(11).

33.12 The specific duties placed on local authorities are set out in the sch. 2, Part I, CA 1989 and include, for example, family centres but lack of space means that the authors do not propose to explore them in this book.

Duty to accommodate children in need

33.13 A duty is imposed on local authorities to accommodate children in need in the following circumstances:

    (a) where there is no person with parental responsibility for him;

    (b) where there is no special guardian for him;

    (c) where he is lost or has been abandoned; or

    (d) where the person who has been caring for him is prevented (whether or not permanently, and for whatever reason) from providing him with suitable accommodation or care (s. 20).

A child 'accommodated' by the local authority (but not the subject of a care order) may be removed by his parents at any time. The only way in which a local authority can assume 'parental responsibility' for a child is by applying for, and being granted, a care order. This reflects the aim of Parliament that the transfer to a local authority of the legal powers and responsibilities of caring for a child should only be done by a full court hearing following due legal process. Thus, the application of emergency powers to remove a child at serious risk (e.g., by way of an emergency protection order), which necessarily cannot be preceded by a full court hearing, should be of short duration and subject to court review.

The child's view

33.14 The CA 1989 stipulates that wherever possible the local authority should consider the wishes of the child before providing him with accommodation. It should give due consideration to such wishes as it has been able to ascertain (having regard to his age and understanding): s. 20(6).

33.15 If the child is over 16 then the CA 1989 effectively gives the child complete autonomy in that he may consent to being provided with accommodation by the local authority even though:

    (a) the person(s) with parental responsibility for him object (s. 20(11)), and

    (b) the person with parental responsibility is able to provide the child with accommodation (s. 20(4)).

Parental removal

33.16 Once a child is accommodated by a local authority, then any person with parental responsibility may *at any time* remove the child from the local authority accommodation: s. 20(8). There are only two exceptions:

(a) Where a person in whose favour a residence order has been made in respect of a child, or who has care and control of the child by virtue of an order made in the exercise of the inherent jurisdiction of the High Court (s. 20(9)) or by virtue of an existing order (sch. 14, para. 8(4)) *agrees* to the child being looked after by the local authority (s. 20(9)). If there are two such persons then *both* must agree: s. 20(10).

(b) Where the child has reached 16 and *agrees* to being so accommodated: s. 20(11).

If the local authority wishes to prevent the child from being removed from local authority **33.17** accommodation it now has only two choices:

(a) to apply to the court for a care order, by satisfying the s. 31(2) statutory grounds; or

(b) to apply to the court for an emergency protection order under s. 44(1), CA 1989; this will be suitable only where the case is urgent.

Duties of local authorities in relation to children 'looked after' by them

A child is 'looked after' by a local authority for the purposes of the CA 1989 if he is: **33.18**

(a) in local authority care by virtue of a care order; or

(b) provided with accommodation by the local authority (for a continuous period of more than 24 hours) under a voluntary arrangement: ss. 22(1) and 105(4).

General duties

When a local authority 'looks after' a child, s. 22(3), CA 1989 places upon that authority a **33.19** general duty:

(a) to safeguard and promote his welfare, including a duty to promote his educational achievement (s. 22(3A)); and

(b) to make such use of services available for children cared for by their own parents as appears to the authority reasonable in his case.

The local authority must act as a 'good parent'. *Before* making decisions about the child the authority is required by s. 22(4), CA 1989 to ascertain the wishes and feelings of the following persons:

(a) the child;

(b) the child's parents;

(c) any person who is not a parent of the child but has parental responsibility for him;

(d) any other person whose wishes and feelings the authority consider to be relevant.

Once the local authority actually engages in the process of *making* the decision, s. 22(5), **33.20** Children Act 1989 requires them to give consideration:

(a) to the wishes and feelings of those persons listed above; and

(b) to the child's religious persuasion, racial origin and cultural and linguistic background.

Provision of accommodation and maintenance

Once the local authority is 'looking after' a child it is under a duty to provide him with **33.21** accommodation and to maintain him: s. 23(1) and (2).

33.22   There is a statutory *presumption* that an authority 'looking after' a child must make arrangements enabling him to live with one of the following:

(a)   a parent;

(b)   a person who is not a parent but has parental responsibility;

(c)   a person in whose favour a residence order was in force immediately before a care order was made; or

(d)   a relative, friend, or other person connected with him,

unless those solutions would not be reasonably practicable or consistent with his welfare: s. 23(6).

33.23   Once the child is the subject of a care order that presumption is reversed.

Contact between the child and his family

33.24   Once a local authority is 'looking after' a child it must endeavour, so far as is practicable and consistent with the child's welfare, to promote contact between the child and the following persons:

(a)   his parents;

(b)   any person who is not a parent but has parental responsibility for him;

(c)   any other person connected with him: sch. 2, para. 15(1).

For further discussion of parental contact with children in care see paragraph 33.81 below.

Advice and assistance for certain children

33.25   Where a child is being 'looked after' by a local authority the authority is under a duty to 'advise, assist and befriend him' with a view to promoting his welfare when he ceases to be looked after by that authority (s. 24(1)).

Review of cases

33.26   The CA 1989 requires local authorities to conduct at regular intervals a general review of the progress of each child who is being looked after or provided with accommodation by them in accordance with the Review of Children's Cases Regulations 1991.

33.27   The CA 1989 also requires local authorities to provide a review procedure, with an independent element, to resolve disputes and complaints raised when a child, his parents, anybody with parental responsibility for him, or a local authority foster-parent is unhappy with the arrangements made for the child's care (s. 26(3)). See the Representations Procedure (Children) Regulations 1991.

33.28   The ACA 2002, s. 118, has introduced in s. 26(2)(e) of the CA 1989 (requirement to consider discharge of a care order) an amendment to create a 'looked after' children reviewing officer. The functions of the independent reviewing officer (IRO) are to participate in the process of reviewing the care plan and revising it as necessary, to monitor the local authority's functions in respect of the review and to refer the case to CAFCASS if he considers it appropriate to do so. The detailed provisions are contained in the Review of Children's Cases (Amendment)(England) Regulations 2004 (SI 2004/1419) and *Independent Reviewing Officer's*

Guidance (Department for Education and Skills, 2004)(the DfES Guidance) available at <www.dres.gov.uk/adoption>. IRO's have power to refer cases they are unable to resolve to their satisfaction to CAFCASS Legal, who may start court proceedings against the local authority seeking an order requiring it to put right its failings in relation to the care plan. It is intended that all 'looked after' children will have an IRO. CAFCASS Legal can only accept referrals from IROs and their options are to: reject the referral; attempt to resolve the matter by mediation; refer the matter to another agency; or, bring civil proceedings against the local authority. If further proceedings under CA 1989 are required, CAFCASS Legal refer the case back to the children's guardian from the care proceedings (Children and Family Court Advisory and Support Service (Reviewed Case Referral) Regulations 2004). There is an explanatory *CAFCASS Practice Note 'Cases Referred by Independent Reviewing Officers'* dated 8 June 2004 and available at <www.dca.gov.uk>. If a civil action is brought against the local authority, one of the social work practitioners in CAFCASS Legal will act as the child's litigation friend. The options for civil action are: judicial review proceedings; a compensation claim; or, a freestanding HRA 1998 application.

The second stage of the new reviewing system depends on action being taken by CAFCASS **33.29** as and when it decides that there is a need to return a case to court for further scrutiny by a judge.

The remedy available under ss. 7 and 8 of the HRA 1998. Section 7, HRA 1998, provides a **33.30** mechanism for 'victims' of an alleged breach of Convention rights to make complaints about acts of a public authority which are unlawful as being incompatible with Convention rights. There are two routes to bring such a complaint. The first route is through legal proceedings in any court or tribunal in which the proceedings are brought by or at the instigation of a public authority (s. 7(6)). The second route is by making a separate claim under s. 7(1)(a) in the High Court (or Administrative Court) for judicial review. Where the court finds that an act of a public authority is unlawful it has power to grant such relief or remedy, or make such order, within its powers as it considers just and appropriate (s. 8, HRA 1998). Damages may be awarded, but only by a court with jurisdiction to do so (s. 8(2), HRA 1998). Therefore, if a local authority conducts itself in a manner which infringes the Art. 8 rights of a parent or child, the court may grant appropriate relief on the application of a victim of the unlawful act (*Re S (Minors)(Care Order: Implementation of Care Plan); Re W (Minors) (Care Order: Adequacy of Care Plan)* [2002] 1 FLR 815).

Advocacy services

Section 119, ACA 2002 inserts a new s. 26A into the CA 1989. This places a duty on local **33.31** authorities to provide assistance to adults and children who wish to make representations under s. 24D and s. 26, CA 1989, about the way the local authority has discharged its functions. This includes arranging for that adult or child to have assistance by way of representation.

B   THE PROTOCOL FOR JUDICIAL CASE MANAGEMENT IN PUBLIC LAW CHILDREN ACT CASES

33.32   In June 2003 the Lord Chancellor and the President of the Family Division issued a Protocol for Judicial Case Management in Public Law Children Act Cases ('the public law protocol'). It has been compiled with the involvement of the many agencies and organisations that have a significant role to play in care cases and it aims to tackle delay, setting a guideline of 40 weeks for the conclusion of such cases. It sets out six steps to be followed from the time when a local authority ('LA') makes the decision to apply for a care or supervision order up to the final hearing.

33.33   The public law protocol was implemented as from 1 November 2003. It applies to all courts, including family proceedings courts, hearing applications issued by local authorities under Part IV of the CA 1989 (care and supervision orders) where:

- the application is issued on or after 1 November 2003; or
- proceedings are transferred on or after 1 November 2003 from the family proceedings court to a care centre, or from a county court to a care centre, or from a care centre to the High Court.

33.34   The *Practice Direction (Care Cases: Judicial Continuity and Judicial Case Management)* (set out at the end of the protocol, after Appendix G) intends to implement the Final Report (published in May 2003) of the Lord Chancellor's Advisory Committee on Judicial Case Management in Public Law Children Act Cases (included as the last document appended to the protocol). The *Practice Direction* sets out the overriding objective of the protocol which is to enable the courts to deal with every care case:

(a)   justly, expeditiously, fairly, and with the minimum of delay;
(b)   in ways which ensure, so far as practicable, that
    (i)   the parties are on an equal footing;
    (ii)   the welfare of the child involved is safeguarded; and
    (iii)   distress to all parties is minimized;
(c)   so far as is practicable, in ways which are proportionate
    (i)   to the gravity and complexity of the issues; and
    (ii)   to the nature and extent of the intervention proposed in the private and family life of the children and adults involved.

The *Annex to the Practice Direction* sets out the principles which govern the application of the *Practice Direction* and protocol by the courts and by the parties.

33.35   It is recommended that all practitioners undertaking public law work obtain a copy of the Protocol as the Appendices contain much essential information. Lack of space in this book restricts the authors simply to a description of what each Appendix contains. Where relevant, the appropriate Appendix is referred to at each step below.

- Appendix A/1   Standard Directions Form
- Appendix A/2   Case Management Questionnaire
- Appendix A/3   Case Management Checklist

- Appendix A/4   Witness Non-Availability Form
- Appendix A/5   PHR (Pre Hearing Review) Checklist
- Appendix B   Standard Documents
    - Case Synopsis
    - Social Work Chronology
    - Initial Social Work Statement
    - Schedule of Issues
- Appendix C   Code of Guidance for Expert Witnesses in Family Proceedings
- Appendix D   *Practice Direction (Family Proceedings: Court Bundles)* [2000] 2 FLR 199
- Appendix E/1   The Care Centre Plan
- Appendix E/2   The Family Proceedings Court Plan
- Appendix F   Social Services Assessment and Care Planning Aide-Memoire
- Appendix G   Section 37 Request
- *Practice Direction (Care Cases: Judicial Continuity and Judicial Case Management) Annex to the Practice Direction: Principles of Application*, Final Report of Lord Chancellor's Advisory Committee on Judicial Case Management in Public Law Children Act Cases (published May 2003).

Step 1: The application—days 1 to 3

When a decision is made to apply for a care or supervision order the LA must file with the court an application in Form C1 and set out in Form C13 a summary of the facts and matters relied upon to satisfy the threshold criteria (para. 1.1). On the day the application is filed the court must issue the application. It must also issue a notice in Form C6 to the LA fixing a time and date for the First Hearing, which must be not later than day 6. The court must appoint a guardian (unless it is satisfied that it is not necessary to do so to safeguard the child's interests) and must inform CAFCASS of the decision to appoint and the request to allocate a guardian (para. 1.2). **33.36**

Within two days of issue CAFCASS must inform the court of the name of the allocated guardian or the likely date upon which the allocation will be made (para. 1.3). When a guardian is allocated, the guardian must, on that day (para. 1.4): **33.37**

(a) appoint a solicitor for the child;
(b) inform the court of the name of the solicitor appointed;
(c) in the event that the guardian's allocation is delayed and the court has already appointed a solicitor, ensure that effective legal representation is maintained.

Where a guardian is not allocated within two days of issue, the court must, on day 3:

(a) consider whether a guardian will be allocated;
(b) decide whether to appoint a solicitor for the child.

In any event, on the day the appointment is made the court must notify all parties on Form C47 of the names of the guardian and/or the solicitor for the child who have been appointed.

Within two days of issue, the LA must file and serve on all parties, the solicitor for the child, and CAFCASS the following documents (para. 1.5): **33.38**

(a) Forms C1 and C13 and any supplementary forms and notices;

(b) any relevant court orders relating to the child (together with the relevant Justices Facts and Reasons in Form C22 and any relevant judgments);

(c) the initial social work statement (Appendix B/3);

(d) the social work chronology (Appendix B/2);

(e) the core or initial assessment reports (see Appendix F of protocol);

(f) any s. 37 report;

(g) any other additional evidence including specialist assessments or reports which then exist and which are relied upon by the LA.

Step 2: The First Hearing in the Family Proceedings Court—by day 6

33.39 The First Hearing must take place in the Family Proceedings Court ('FPC') on or before day 6. At every First Hearing the FPC must (step 2.1):

(a) consider who should be a party to the proceedings;

(b) make arrangements for contested interim care applications to be determined;

(c) consider whether the proceedings should be transferred to the Care Centre or to another FPC;

(d) where proceedings are not transferred, make initial case management decisions.

At the First Hearing the FPC must (step 2.2):

(a) obtain confirmation that all those who are entitled to be parties have been served;

(b) consider whether any other person should be joined as a party;

(c) give directions relating to party status and the service of documents upon parties.

If interim care orders are contested, the FPC must (step 2.3):

(a) decide whether to grant an order; or

(b) list the application for an urgent contested interim hearing in a FPC prior to the Case Management Conference ('CMC'); and

(c) give directions for the interim hearing; or

(d) transfer the proceedings to be heard at the Care Centre.

At the First Hearing the FPC must (step 2.4):

(a) hear submissions as to complexity, gravity, and urgency;

(b) consider whether to transfer to another court;

(c) give reasons for any transfer decision and record the reasons on Form C22;

(d) send the court file and transfer order in Form C49 to the receiving court within one day of the First Hearing (by day 7).

Where a decision is made to transfer to the Care Centre the FPC must take the following steps (step 2.5):

(a) In accordance with the arrangements set out in the Care Centre Plan ('CCP') and the FPC Plan ('FPCP') (Appendix E), immediately inform the court office at the Care Centre of the transfer and reasons set out on Form 22.

(b) Obtain a date and time from the court office for an Allocation Hearing/contested interim hearing (which must be between three and five days of the decision to transfer) (by day 11).

(c) Notify the parties of the Care Centre to which the proceedings have been transferred and the date and time of the Allocation Hearing/contested interim hearing.

(d) Direct the LA or the child's solicitor to prepare a case synopsis (Appendix B/1) which must be filed with the Care Centre and served within two days of the First Hearing in the FPC (by day 8).

(e) Except as to disclosure of documents, make only those case management directions upon transfer as are agreed with the Care Centre as set out in the CCP and the FPCP.

If proceedings are not transferred to the Care Centre, the FPC must at the First Hearing take the following steps (step 2.6):

(a) Consider the case management checklist (Appendix A/3).

(b) Fix a date and time for a CMC in the FPC within 54 days of the First Hearing (between days 15 and 60) unless all of the case management directions set out at step 4.8 can be taken at the First Hearing and the application can be listed for Final Hearing.

(c) Fix a date for the Final Hearing or if this is not possible fix a hearing window (not later that in the three-week period commencing in week 37).

(d) Consider whether a Pre Hearing Review (PHR) is necessary and if so fix it between two and eight weeks before the Final Hearing date/window.

(e) Give such case management directions as are necessary to ensure that all steps will have been taken prior to the CMC to enable it to be effective, in particular:

   (i) Statement of evidence from each party to be filed and served replying to the facts alleged and proposals made by the LA in the initial social work statement.

   (ii) Whether directions for disclosure of documents need to be given, and directions to ensure disclosure of relevant documents by LA occurs within 20 days of the First Hearing (by day 26).

   (iii) Whether a core assessment (Appendix F) exists or should be directed to be undertaken by the LA before the CMC.

   (iv) Record on the Standard Directions Form (SDF) (Appendix A/1) the court's case management decisions and reasons and serve the directions on the parties.

The FPC must give a direction at the First Hearing that no further documents shall be filed without the court's permission unless in support of a new application or in accordance with case management direction given at that hearing (step 2.7).

Step 3: Allocation Hearing and Directions—by day 11

Following transfer to the Care Centre or to the High Court all further hearings in the proceedings must be conducted (step 3.1): **33.40**

(a) so as to ensure judicial continuity;

(b) by one or not more than two judges (case management judges), one of whom should be (if possible) the judge who will conduct the Final Hearing.

Within two days of the transfer order (normally by day 8) the court office must (step 3.2):

(a) Allocate one and not more than two case management judges.

(b) Where possible, identify the Final Hearing judge.
(c) Attach to the FPC file Form C22, the case synopsis, and a SDF and complete the SDF only to the extent of:
  (i) the names of the allocated and identified judges;
  (ii) the proposed date of the CMC (must be between days 15 and 60).
  (iii) the proposed Final Hearing date or hearing window (not later than in the three-week period commencing in week 37);
  (iv) the proposed date of the PHR (must be between two and eight weeks before the Final Hearing).
(d) Inform the case management judge in writing:
  (i) of any urgent circumstances;
  (ii) of any contested interim hearing for an interim care order ('ICO');
  (iii) of any application for transfer to the High Court;
  (iv) of the date and time of the Allocation Hearing (by day 11); and
  (v) notify the parties of the date, time, and venue fixed for the Allocation Hearing, together with the identity of the allocated/nominated judges.

If in any family proceedings a court makes a request under s. 37 for a LA to investigate a child's circumstances, the court must follow the guidance set out in Appendix G. Where, following a s. 37 request, proceedings are transferred to the Care Centre (step 3.3):

(a) The transferring court must record the reasons for transfer on Form 22 and the court officer must send the court file, the transfer order in Form C49, and the record of reasons to the Care Centre within one day of the order.
(b) The court officer in the Care Centre must within two days take the steps set out at step 3.2 and must also:
  (i) inform the case management judge in writing of the transfer;
  (ii) request the case management judge to consider giving directions for the appointment of a guardian and/or solicitor for the child at or before the Allocation Hearing;
  (iii) notify all parties on Form C47 of the names of the guardian and/or solicitor for the child when they are appointed;
  (iv) inform the LA solicitor or the child's solicitor of the requirement that a case synopsis (Appendix B/1) be prepared and filed with the care centre and served not later that two days before the date fixed for the Allocation Hearing.

The Allocation Hearing in the Care Centre must take place by day 11. At the Allocation Hearing the case management judge must (step 3.4):

(a) Consider whether to transfer to the High Court or re-transfer to the FPC;
(b) Determine any contested interim application for care or supervision order;
(c) Where the proceedings have been transferred following a s. 37 request consider:
  (i) whether to give directions for the appointment of a guardian and/or solicitor for the child;
  (ii) whether any direction should be given for filing and service of LA documents.
(d) Consider the case management checklist (Appendix A/3).
(e) Fix a date and time for a CMC (to be between days 15 and 60).
(f) Fix a date for the Final Hearing and confirm the identity of the judge or fix a hearing window (not later than in the three-week period starting with week 37).

(g) Fix a date and time for a PHR (two to eight weeks before the Final Hearing or the window).

(h) Give case management directions to enable the CMC to be effective, in particular:
 (i) statement of evidence from each party to be filed and served replying to the facts alleged and proposals made by the LA in the initial social work statement;
 (ii) directions for disclosure and in any event directions for disclosure of relevant documents by LA by day 26;
 (iii) whether a core assessment (Appendix F) exists or should be directed to be undertaken by the LA before the CMC.

(i) Having regard to *Practice Direction (Family Proceedings: Court Bundles) (Universal Practice to be Applied in All Courts Other Than the Family Proceedings Court)* [2006] 2 FLR 199 (see further at paragraph 18.122), give directions to the LA as to which of the following case management documents in addition to the case management questionnaire (Appendix A/2) are to be filed and served for the CMC:
 (i) schedule of findings of fact which the court is invited to make;
 (ii) any update to social work chronology (Appendix B/2);
 (iii) the initial care plan (Appendix F);
 (iv) if there is a question of law, a skeleton argument with authorities;
 (v) a summary of the background (if necessary to supplement the case synopsis);
 (vi) an advocate's chronology (if necessary to supplement the social work chronology or the case synopsis).

(j) Having regard to Appendix D, give directions to the LA setting out the form of bundle or documents index that the court requires.

(k) Complete the SDF (Appendix A/1) to record the court's case management decisions and reasons.

Within one day of the Allocation Hearing (on day 12) the court officer must serve on each party (step 3.5):

(a) the completed SDF; and
(b) a case management questionnaire (Appendix A/2).

Where an application is transferred to the High Court, the court officer must within one day of the Allocation Hearing (on day 12) (step 3.6):

(a) In consultation with the Family Division Liaison Judge (or, if transferred to the Royal Courts of Justice, the Clerk of the Rules) allocate a High Court judge to be the case management judge.
(b) If necessary, allocate a second case management judge in the Care Centre, who is responsible to the allocated High Court judge for case management.
(c) Where possible, identify the Final Hearing judge.
(d) Attach to the court file Form C22, the case synopsis (Appendix B/1), and a SDF (Appendix A/1), and complete the SDF to the extent only of:
 (i) names of the allocated judges;
 (ii) date of CMC (must be between days 15 and 60);
 (iii) proposed Final Hearing date or window (no later that in the three-week period starting with week 37);
 (iv) proposed date of PHR (two to eight weeks before the Final Hearing or the window).

(e) Inform the case management judge in writing of:
  (i) any urgent circumstances;
  (ii) any contested hearing for an ICO.
(f) Within one day of receipt of the court file and completed SDF from the allocated High Court judge (by day 16), send to each party a copy of the completed SDF and a case management questionnaire (Appendix A/2).

Within three days of receipt of the court file (by day 15) the allocated case management judge must:

(a) consider the case management checklist (Appendix A/3) having regard to the matters in step 3.4;
(b) return the court file and completed SDF to the court officer.

Step 4: The Case Management Conference—between days 15 and 60

33.41 In every case the LA must, at least five days before the CMC, prepare, paginate, index, file, and serve (step 4.1):

(a) the case management documents for the CMC that were directed at the Allocation Hearing/Directions;
(b) a case management questionnaire (Appendix A/2).

At least five days before the date of the CMC, the LA must (step 4.2):

(a) for a hearing to which the *Practice Direction* on Court Bundles (Appendix D) applies, or in accordance with any directions given at a First Hearing or Allocation Hearing, file with the court a bundle;
(b) serve on each of the represented parties an index to the bundle;
(c) serve on any unrepresented party a copy indexed bundle;
(d) for hearings to which Appendix D does not apply, serve on all parties an index of the documents that have been filed.

At least two days before the date of the CMC each party other than the LA must (step 4.3):

(a) file with the court and serve on the parties the following case management documents:
  (i) a position statement—setting out that party's response to the case management documents filed by the LA indicating the issues which are agreed and those that are not;
  (ii) a completed case management questionnaire (Appendix A/2).
(b) NOT file any other case management documents without the prior direction of the court.

At least two days before the CMC the court officer must (step 4.4):

(a) place the case management documents of all parties at the front of the court file and at the front of any bundle filed by the LA;
(b) deliver the court file and bundle to the case management judge who is to conduct the CMC;
(c) ensure that any arrangements for video and telephone conferencing and with criminal and civil listing officers have been made.

Before the day of the CMC or (where not practicable to have an earlier meeting) at least one hour before the CMC, the parties and/or their lawyers must (step 4.5):

(a) meet to identify and narrow the issues in the case;

(b) consider the case management checklist (Appendix A/3);

(c) consider the case management questionnaires (Appendix A/2);

(d) consider the experts' code of guidance (Appendix C) and whether and, if so, why any application is to be made to instruct an expert;

(e) consider whether full and frank disclosure of all relevant documents has been made;

(f) draft a composite schedule of issues (Appendix B/4) which identifies:

  (i) a summary of the issues in the case;

  (ii) a summary of issues for determination at the CMC by reference to the case management questionnaires/case management checklist;

  (iii) the timetable of legal and social work steps proposed;

  (iv) the estimated length of hearing of the PHR and of the Final Hearing;

  (v) the order the Court will be invited to make at the CMC.

On the day of the CMC the parties must complete and file with the court (step 4.6):

(a) a witness non-availability form (Appendix A/4);

(b) a schedule (so far as known) of the names and contact details of:

  (i) the lead social worker and team manager;

  (ii) the guardian;

  (iii) solicitors and counsel/advocates of each party;

  (iv) unrepresented litigants;

  (v) any experts upon whose evidence it is proposed to rely.

The CMC must be conducted by one of the allocated case management judges or as directed by the FPC case management legal adviser (step 4.7). Case management through to Final Hearing must be consistently provided by the same case management judges/legal advisers/FPCs.

All advocates who are retained to have conduct of the Final Hearing must: **33.42**

(a) use their best endeavours to attend the CMC and must do so if directed by the court;

(b) bring to the CMC details of their availability for the next 12 months;

(c) attend the advocates meeting before the CMC.

At the CMC the case management judge/court must (step 4.8):

(a) consider the parties' composite schedule of issues (Appendix B/4);

(b) consider the case management checklist (Appendix A/3);

(c) consider the parties' case management questionnaires (Appendix A/2) and case management documents;

(d) fix the date of the Final Hearing (if not already done) to be no later than the three-week period starting with week 37;

(e) fix the date and time of the PHR (if not already done) to be two to eight weeks before the Final Hearing;

(f) give a time estimate for each hearing fixed;

(g)   consider whether any hearing can take place using video, telephone, or other electronic means;

(h)   consider any outstanding applications;

(i)   give all necessary case management directions to:

    (i)   timetable all remaining legal and social work steps;

    (ii)   ensure disclosure of all documents is complete;

    (iii)   ensure that a core assessment (Appendix F) or other appropriate assessment materials will be available to the court;

    (iv)   ensure that if any expert is to be instructed the expert and the parties will complete their work within the timetable and in accordance with the experts' code of guidance (Appendix C);

    (v)   provide for regular monitoring of the court's case management directions to include certification of compliance at each ICO renewal and the notification to the court by the guardian and each party of any material non-compliance;

    (vi)   permit a further Directions Hearing before the allocated case management judge if there is a change of circumstances or significant non-compliance with the court's directions;

    (vii)   update, file, and serve such of the existing case management documents as are necessary;

    (viii)   update, file, and serve a court bundle/index for the PHR and for the Final Hearing;

    (ix)   ensure that the PHR and Final Hearing will be effective.

Step 5: The Pre-Hearing Review—by week 37

33.43   The court officer must (step 5.1):

(a)   where no PHR direction has been given, send the court file/bundle to the case management judge during week 28 with a request for confirmation that no PHR is necessary or for a direction that a PHR be listed;

(b)   notify the parties of any PHR direction given by the judge;

(c)   list a PHR where directions have been given (two to eight weeks before the Final Hearing, i.e., between weeks 29 and 37);

(d)   at least two days before the PHR:

    (i)   place the updated case management documents directed at the CMC at the front of the court file and at the front of any bundle filed by the LA;

    (ii)   deliver the court file/bundle to the judge/FPC nominated to conduct the PHR;

    (iii)   ensure any arrangements for video and telephone conferencing and with criminal and civil listing officers have been made.

In the week before the PHR the advocates with conduct of the Final Hearing must (step 5.2):

(a)   communicate with each other and if necessary meet to identify and narrow the issues to be considered at the PHR and the Final Hearing;

(b)   consider the PHR checklist (Appendix A/5).

Two days before the PHR the advocates must file a composite schedule of issues (Appendix B/4) to set out:

(a)   a summary of the issues in the case;

(b)   a summary of issues for determination at the PHR;

(c)   a draft witness template;

(d)   the revised estimated length of the Final Hearing;

(e)   whether the proceedings are ready to be heard and, if not, what steps need to be taken at the PHR to ensure that they can be heard on the date fixed for Final Hearing;

(f)   the order which the court will be invited to make at the PHR.

No case management documents are to be filed for use at a PHR except (step 5.3):

(a)   any updated case management documents directed by the judge at the CMC;

(b)   the composite schedule of issues (Appendix B/4);

(c)   documents in support of a new application.

The PHR (or any FPC directions hearing which immediately precedes a Final Hearing) must be listed before the judge/FPC nominated to conduct the Final Hearing. In exceptional circumstances the court may in advance approve the release of the PHR but only to one of the allocated case management judges (step 5.4).

The advocates retained to conduct the Final Hearing must:

(a)   use their best endeavours to secure release from other professional obligations to attend the PHR;

(b)   update the case management documents as directed at the CMC;

(c)   attend the advocates' meeting.

At the PHR the court must (step 5.5):

(a)   consider the PHR checklist (Appendix A/5);

(b)   consider the parties' composite schedule of issues (Appendix B/4);

(c)   confirm or give a revised time estimate for the Final Hearing;

(d)   confirm the fixed dates, venues, and the nominated judge for the Final Hearing;

(e)   give any directions necessary to update the existing case management documents and the court bundle/index having regard to the *Practice Direction* in Appendix D;

(f)   give any directions necessary to ensure the Final Hearing will be effective.

Where the requirements of an advocates' meeting have been complied with and all parties certify (in the composite schedule of issues) that (step 5.6):

(a)   the proceedings are ready to be heard; and

(b)   the court directions have been complied with; and

(c)   all parties are agreed to all the proposed directions having regard to the PHR checklist (Appendix A/5);

the court may decide to dispense with the PHR or deal with it on paper or by electronic means, including a computer, video, or telephone conferencing.

Step 6: The Final Hearing—by week 40

The Final Hearing must be conducted by the judge or FPC identified in the allocation **33.44** directions as confirmed at the PHR (step 6.1). Where one of the allocated case management judges or an FPC has heard a substantial factual issue or there has been a 'preliminary hearing' to determine findings of fact it is necessary for the same judge/magistrates who conducted that hearing to conduct the Final Hearing.

33.45   At least two days before the Final Hearing the parties must (step 6.2):

(a)   prepare, file, and serve the case management documents for the Final Hearing as directed by the court at the PHR;

(b)   prepare, file, and serve the court bundle or index of court documents as directed by the court at the PHR.

At least two days before the Final Hearing the court officer must (step 6.3):

(a)   place any case management documents at the front of the court file and at the front of any bundle filed by the LA;

(b)   deliver the court file/bundle to the judge/FPC nominated to conduct the Final Hearing;

(c)   ensure that any arrangements for the reception of evidence by video link and telephone conferencing, interpreters, facilities for disabled persons, and special measures for vulnerable or intimidated witnesses have been made.

At the conclusion of the Final Hearing the court must (step 6.4):

(a)   set out the basis/reasons for the orders made or applications refused in a judgment and where appropriate in the form of recitals to the order or, in the case of the FPC, in Form C22;

(b)   annexe to the order the agreed or approved documents setting out the threshold criteria and the care plan for the child;

(c)   where the judgment is not in writing give consideration to whether there should be a transcript and if so who will obtain and pay for it.

In a complex case a judge (but not an FPC) may decide to reserve judgment and take time for consideration (step 6.5). In this event, the court will endeavour to fix a date for judgment to be given or handed down within 20 days (four weeks) of the conclusion of submissions. Advocates may be invited to make oral or written submissions as to consequential orders and directions at the conclusion of submissions or when the draft judgment is released.

33.46   At the end of every Final Hearing the court must consider whether to give directions for disclosure of documents, for example (step 6.6):

(a)   where it is proposed that the child should be placed for adoption and so that adoption proceedings are not delayed, to the LA adoption panel, specialist adoption agency, and/ or proposed adopters and their legal advisers for use in subsequent adoption proceedings;

(b)   for any medical or therapeutic purpose;

(c)   for a claim to be made to the CICA.

C   CARE AND SUPERVISION ORDERS

33.47   The CA 1989 has streamlined the law to the extent that there is now only one method of formally receiving a child into the care of, or placing him under the supervision of, a local authority. A summary of the main points is as follows:

(a) The court may make a care order only if it is satisfied that:
    (i) the statutory criteria in s. 31(2) have been met; and
    (ii) the child's welfare demands that a care order be made.
(b) Care orders may be made on specific application or in the course of 'family proceedings'.
(c) Wardship is no longer available to local authorities as a method of committing children into their care where they are unable to prove the statutory grounds.
(d) The family proceedings court, county court and High Court all have jurisdiction to make care orders. However, most care proceedings will commence in the family proceedings court. For further details as to the allocation of work between the courts, see paragraph 30.01.
(e) The local authority assumes parental responsibility for the child on the making of a care order and any existing s. 8 orders terminate. However, other persons having parental responsibility for the child will not be divested of it. They will 'share' parental responsibility with the local authority.
(f) There is a statutory presumption that the authority will allow the child in care to have contact with his parents and other specified persons. Section 34, CA 1989 contains the mechanisms for determining and enforcing the existence and levels of such contact.
(g) The court has power to make supervision orders in the course of care proceedings.

Who can apply for a care or supervision order?

The application for a care order may be made by: **33.48**

(a) any local authority, or
(b) an authorized person (s. 31(1)).

So far the only 'authorized person' is the NSPCC. However, there is provision for the Secretary of State to name others in due course.

Nobody else may initiate care proceedings. The court itself may not make a care or supervision **33.49** order without an application first having been made by the local authority. Where the court is concerned about a child's circumstances then the most it can do is to direct the local authority to investigate pursuant to s. 37(1), CA 1989. If the authority investigates but chooses not to make an application then the court has no power to make a care/supervision order. If a parent is unable to control his child and wishes the local authority to take care proceedings then he cannot compel a reluctant authority to do so other than by way of judicial review.

A care order may only be made where the child is under the age of 17 (or under 16 if the child **33.50** is married): s. 31(3).

What must the local authority or authorized person do before making an application?

Where a local authority or authorized person suspect that a child in their area has suffered **33.51** significant harm or is likely to do so then they must investigate fully the circumstances of the child so that they can decide whether any action should be taken to 'safeguard or promote the child's welfare': s. 47(1). *Before* making a decision the authority must (so far as is reasonably practicable) ascertain the wishes and feelings of the child, his parents, anyone else with parental responsibility (e.g., a guardian) and any other person whose wishes and feelings the authority considers to be relevant: s. 22(4). The duty to consult could be waived on the basis that it was not 'reasonably practicable' if the circumstances of the child required urgent action which might be prejudiced by such consultation. For example, where the parents are likely to run away with the child if they are informed in advance that an application for a care order is to be made.

33.52   If the authority concludes that it should take action then it must do so 'so far as it is both within [its] power and reasonably practicable for [it] to do so'.

Who are the respondents in care proceedings?

33.53   The persons who must be made respondents to an application for a care or supervision order are defined in the r. 4.7 and Appendix 3, Family Proceedings Rules 1991 ('FPR 1991') and in r. 7 and sch. 2, Family Proceedings Courts (Children Act 1989) Rules 1991 ('FPC(CA 1989)R 1991') They are as follows:

(a)   every person whom the applicant believes to have parental responsibility for the child;

(b)   where the child is the subject of a care order (i.e., in the course of an application for a supervision order), every person whom the applicant believes to have parental responsibility immediately prior to the making of the care order;

(c)   in the case of an application to extend, vary, or discharge an order, the parties to the proceedings leading to the order which it is sought to have extended, varied, or discharged;

(d)   the child.

Who may be a party to care proceedings?

33.54   Anybody can make a written request that he be joined as a party, or cease to be a party to care proceedings: r. 4.7(2), FPR 1991 and r. 7(2), FPC(CA 1989)R 1991. However, if a person with parental responsibility for the child requests to be made a party the court must grant the request: r. 4.7(4), FPR 1991 and r. 7(4), FPC(CA 1989)R 1991. In the case of anyone else making such a request the court must follow the procedure set out in FPR 1991, r. 4.7(3) and r. 7(3), FPC(CA 1989)R 1991. A request for joinder may be granted by the court without a hearing. Otherwise, the court will order that a date be fixed for a hearing to consider the request or else it will invite the parties to make written representations, within a specific period, as to whether the request should be granted. If the natural father of the child concerned wishes to participate as a party in care proceedings then he should generally be allowed to do so, even if he does not have parental responsibility, unless there are justifiable reasons for not so joining him: *Re B (Care Proceedings: Notification of Father without Parental Responsibility)* [1999] 2 FLR 408.

33.55   The court has a discretion to direct that a person who would not otherwise be a respondent be joined as a party to the proceedings or that a party to the proceedings ceases to be a party: r. 4.7(5), FPR 1991 and r. 7(5), FPC(CA 1989)R 1991. See, for example, *Re W (Discharge of Party to Proceedings)* [1997] 1 FLR 128 where the court discharged the children's natural father from the proceedings. In that case the father had been convicted of the murder of the children's half-sister, was serving a sentence of life imprisonment, had never seen the younger child and had not seen the elder child for over four years. Although it was a very serious matter to prevent a natural parent from being a party, the facts of this case justified it. An application that a person entitled to be a party should cease to be so is not governed by the principle in s. 1(1) of the Act that the welfare of the child is paramount: *Re X (Care: Notice of Proceedings)* [1996] 1 FLR 186.

The threshold criteria

Section 31, CA 1989 states that a court may make a care or supervision order *only* if it is **33.56** satisfied that:

(a)   the child is suffering, or likely to suffer, significant harm; *and*
(b)   the harm, or likelihood of harm, is attributable to:
    (i)   the care given to the child, or likely to be given to him if the order is not made, not being what it would be reasonable to expect a parent to give to him; or
    (ii) the child's being beyond parental control.

Grounds (a) and (b) are cumulative. Both must be satisfied, although (b) may be satisfied by either of its sub-paragraphs. The expression 'if [the court] is satisfied' envisages that the court must be judicially satisfied on proper material. The legal burden of establishing the relevant conditions rests on the applicant for a care order: *Re H and R (Child Sexual Abuse: Standard of Proof)* [1996] 1 FLR 80. Once the grounds have been made out then the court moves on to the second limb of its decision-making exercise. Before completing its determination of the case the court must abide by the dictates of s. 1, CA 1989, that is to say:

(a)   the child's welfare is the paramount consideration (s. 1(1)); and
(b)   in considering the welfare of the child the court must apply the statutory checklist of factors set out in s. 1(3); and
(c)   the court must bear in mind the general principle in s. 1(2) that there is a presumption that any delay in determining the matter is likely to prejudice the welfare of the child; and
(d)   the court must not make an order unless it considers that making it would be better for the child than making no order at all: s. 1(5).

Definition of terms used in s. 31(2)

For the purposes of the CA 1989 the following terms used in s. 31(2) are defined in   **33.57** s. 31(9) as follows:

'Harm' means ill-treatment or the impairment of health and development. (Note that, the meaning of harm has been extended to include, for example, impairment suffered by hearing or seeing the ill-treatment of another.)

'Development' means physical, intellectual, emotional, social, or behavioural development.

'Health' means physical or mental health.

'Ill-treatment' includes sexual abuse and forms of ill-treatment which are not physical.

'Significant' is not defined in the Children Act 1989, but it will obviously be construed by the lawyer with reference to the *de minimis* principle. The layman should be warned not to equate 'significant' with 'substantial'. Where the question of whether the harm suffered by the child is 'significant' or not turns upon the child's health or development, then his health or development is to be compared with that which could reasonably be expected of a similar child: s. 31(10). Thus, a subjective stance is to be adopted in relation to the particular characteristics and disabilities of this particular child. Thereafter, an objective test is to be applied as to whether the standard of his health and development is a standard which could reasonably be expected of a child with similar characteristics. 'Care' in s. 31(2)(b)(i) is not defined in the Act, but it has been held to go beyond physical care and to include the emotional care which a reasonable parent would give a child; in the case of a child who has been abused, that includes listening to the child and monitoring his words and actions so that a professional assessment can be carried out: *Re B (A Minor) (Care Order: Criteria)* [1993] 1 FLR 815.

Meaning of present and future harm

33.58 **Meaning of 'is suffering' significant harm** The requirement in s. 31(1)(a) that the child 'is suffering' significant harm falls to be examined on the date at which the local authority initiated the procedure for protection under the Act. In other words, the threshold criteria will be satisfied if, at the time of the local authority's decision to take the temporary measures to protect the child from immediate harm which leads to the application for the care or supervision order in due course, the child is suffering or likely to suffer significant harm: *Re M (A Minor) (Care Order: Threshold Conditions)* [1994] 3 All ER 298. However, the local authority does not have to be in possession of all the information it wishes to rely upon at the date of the application. Evidence gathering continues after proceedings have begun and later acquired information as to the state of affairs at the relevant date can be taken into account: *Re G (Care Proceedings: Threshold Conditions)* [2001] 2 FLR 1111.

33.59 **Meaning of 'likely to suffer' significant harm** The meaning of 'likely harm' was referred to by *The Law on Child Care and Family Services* (Cm. 62, 1987, para. 60) as follows:

> It is intended that 'likely harm' should cover all cases of unacceptable risk in which it may be necessary to balance the chance of harm occurring against the magnitude of that harm if it does occur . . . the court will have to judge whether there is a risk and what the nature of the risk is.

33.60 The meaning of 'likely to suffer' in s. 31(2) should not be equated with 'on the balance of probabilities'. The court is not applying a test to events which had happened in the past and then deciding on the balance of probabilities whether such events had in fact happened; instead, the court is looking to the future where all it can do is to evaluate the chance that the child will suffer significant harm in the future if the care order or supervision order is not made. The word 'likely' means a 'real possibility, a possibility that cannot sensibly be ignored having regard to the nature and gravity of the feared harm in the particular case': *Re H and R (Child Sexual Abuse: Standard of Proof)* (above). The words should not be construed unduly restrictively and a care order should be made where the evidence clearly indicates its necessity: *Newham London Borough Council v AG* [1993] 1 FLR 281; *Re A (A Minor) (Care Proceedings)* [1993] 1 FCR 824.

33.61 The relevant date for assessing the 'likelihood of harm' is the date upon which the local authority initiated protective arrangements for the relevant child, provided that those protective arrangements have been continuously in place from the time of the authority's intervention and initiation until the date when the court finally disposes of the case:

Southwark London Borough Council v *B* [1998] 2 FLR 1095; *Re M (A Minor) (Threshold Conditions)* [1994] 2 FLR 577, HL. Therefore, the relevant date is the same for both limbs of the criterion (i.e., for present and for future harm) set out in s. 31(2)(a), CA 1989.

Cause of the harm, or likely harm

Ground (b), in its alternatives, requires the court to find the cause for the harm, or likely **33.62** harm. In relation to ground (b)(i), i.e., that the care being given to the child is not that which one would expect a reasonable parent to give him, the court must look to the standard of care which the child obtains, or is likely to obtain if the care order is *not* made. It must evaluate that standard of care and then ask the following question: is that standard below that which it would be reasonable to expect the parent of *such* a child to give him? The intention is that the court should focus upon the characteristics of the particular child and that the child's *needs* be assessed subjectively. However, the standard to be applied to the care being given to that particular child is an objective one.

The phrase 'attributable to' in s. 31(2)(b) connotes a causal connection between the harm or **33.63** likelihood of harm on the one hand and the care or likely care or the child's being beyond parental control on the other hand. The connection need not be that of a sole, or dominant, or direct cause and effect; a contributory causal connection suffices. For instance, if a parent entrusts a child to a third party without taking the precautionary steps a reasonable parent would take to check the suitability of the third party, and subsequently the third party injures or sexually abuses the child, the harm suffered by the child may be regarded as attributable to the inadequate care of the parent as well as of the third party: *Lancashire County Council* v *B* [2000] 1 FLR 583, per Lord Nicholls at p. 585C–E.

To be within s. 31(2)(b)(i) the care given or likely to be given must fall below an objectively **33.64** acceptable level. That level is the care a reasonable parent would provide for the child concerned. Therefore, an absence of a reasonable standard of parental care need not imply that the parents are at fault: for example, it may be that for reasons beyond their control the parents are not able to provide a reasonable standard of care for the child: *Lancashire County Council* v *B*, above, per Lord Nicholls at p. 585F–G. In the *Lancashire* case the child was looked after by several people, including a childminder. The child suffered serious non-accidental injury causing significant harm and triggering an application by the local authority for a care order in relation to the child. The evidence was such that it was not possible to say whether the parents or the childminder was the perpetrator. The House of Lords interpreted s. 31(2)(b)(i) and stated that the phrase 'care given to the child' refers primarily to the care given to the child by a parent or parents or other primary carers. Where the care is shared and the court is unable to distinguish between the care given by the parents or primary carers and the care given by other carers then the matter stands differently. Where the care given by one or other of the carers is proved to have been deficient, with the child suffering harm in consequence, but the court is unable to identify which of the carers provided the deficient care then the 'care given to the child' embraces not just the care given by the parents or primary carers, but also the care given by *any* of the carers. This means that parents who may be wholly innocent face the possibility of losing their child. Once the threshold conditions have been crossed the court will, of course, go on to consider whether to exercise its discretionary power to make a care order or supervision order.

33.65 It was argued in the *Lancashire* case that keeping the child concerned in foster care infringed the rights of the child and her parents to respect to their right to family life as guaranteed by Art. 8(1) of the European Convention for the Protection of Human Rights and Fundamental Freedoms. The argument put forward was that once the local authority realized that it could not prove that the child was injured by either of the parents it should have withdrawn the proceedings and reinstated the child with the parents. However, the House of Lords held (at p. 591B–C) that the steps taken by the local authority were no more than the steps reasonably necessary to pursue the legitimate aim of protecting the child from further injury and that therefore the local authority in this case had acted within the exception set out in Art. 8(2) of the Convention.

33.66 In relation to ground (b)(ii) the relevant question for the court is this: is the child beyond parental control? The parent may not necessarily be at fault for this ground to be satisfied. For example, the parent may have tried to discipline the child only to find that the child will not accept it. A parent in such a position cannot force the local authority to bring proceedings in respect of the child. If he informally requests the authority to do so and it refuses then his only remedy is by way of judicial review.

Care plans

33.67 The ACA 2002, s. 124, inserted a new s. 31A into CA 1989. It places a statutory duty on the local authority to prepare a care plan (known as a 's. 31A care plan') in every case in which it seeks a care order. However, the duty does not apply where only an interim care order is sought. The local authority is required to keep the care plan under review and to make changes as and when necessary. The care plan should accord so far as possible with *The Children Act 1989 Guidance and Regulations* (HMSO), vol. 3, para. 2.62, as supplemented by the local authority circular of 12 August 1999 (LAC(99)29) *Care Plans and Care Proceedings under The Children Act 1989*. The local authority circular seeks to cover practice and policy matters and to improve the consistency between local authorities in relation to the style, format, and level of detail set out in care plans.

33.68 The care plan is of vital importance because it sets out the local authority's plans for the child's future care and gives reasons as to why a particular placement or course of action has been chosen. It should consider achievable timescales for the implementation of the plan. Where care plans are needed at an interim stage in the care proceedings they will not necessarily represent the local authority's confirmed views for the final hearing as circumstances may (and often do) change. Therefore the first page of the care plan should distinguish clearly between interim care plans for interim hearings and complete care plans for final hearings. The procedure to be adopted once a local authority decides to apply for a care or supervision order is now governed by the public law protocol, which is discussed in detail in paragraph 33.32 and onwards. Where the local authority decides to make an application to the court it will be necessary to satisfy the court that an order would be better for the child than making no order at all. An interim care plan should be prepared, filed, and served so as to be available to the court for the Case Management Conference in accordance with steps 3.4 and 4.1 of the protocol. The Social Services Assessment and Care Planning Aide-Memoire (Appendix F of the protocol), requires that the interim plan should include details of (para. 20):

(a)   the aim of the plan and a summary of the social work timetable;

(b)   a summary of the child's needs and how these are to be met;

(c)   implementation and management of the plan.

A separate plan is needed for each child who is the subject of the care proceedings, even where siblings with very similar needs are concerned in the same proceedings. See *Re J (Minors) (Care Plan)* [1994] 1 FLR 253 for useful judicial guidance as to the making of a care plan.

Duty to keep parents properly involved in planning process

It is essential that the local authority keeps the parents properly involved in the planning   **33.69**
process when care proceedings are initiated and the care plan is being formulated (*Re S (Minors)(Care Order: Implementation of Care Plan); Re W (Minors) (Care Order: Adequacy of Care Plan)* [2002] 1 FLR 815). A failure to do so may leave it open to the parents to bring an application under the ss. 6, 7, and 8, HRA 1998, for breaches of the European Convention for the Protection of Human Rights and Fundamental Freedoms 1950, Art. 6 (right to a fair trial), Art. 8 (right to respect for private and family life) (*Re C (Care Plan: Human Rights Challenge)* [2002] Fam Law 790; *Re G (Care: Challenge to Local Authority's Decision)* [2003] 2 FLR 42; *Venema* v *The Netherlands* [2003] 1 FLR 551).

Where adoption is the preferred option

If the local authority takes the view that adoption is the probable option then it needs to   **33.70**
advise the court of the likely steps and timescales required to implement the care plan. The local authority must follow the local authority circular of 28 August 1998 (LAC(98)20), *Adoption—Achieving the Right Balance*, paras. 28–33 of which were re-issued in amended form in the Chief Inspector Letter of June 1999 (CI(99)6). Paragraph 31 sets out the steps which should always have been addressed before the final care hearing in such cases.

Twin-track planning and concurrent planning

In *Re D and K (Care Plan: Twin Track Planning)* [1999] 2 FLR 872 Bracewell J highlighted the   **33.71**
problems which arise for the court in cases where the local authority recognizes from an early stage that its care plan presents options of rehabilitation within the natural family or permanency outside the family but fails to address the option of an adoptive placement until shortly before the substantive court hearing. The result is that the court is handicapped at the hearing by a lack of information as to the availability of adoptive parents; in the event that the court makes a care order and approves the care plan to place the child outside the natural family in an adoptive placement then there is a substantial delay whilst the child is considered and approved by the adoption and fostering panel and a suitable adoptive placement is identified. Where the local authority is considering two options comprising rehabilitation of the child to his natural family within a strictly limited timescale or adoption outside the family then, particularly in the case of babies or young children, the authority and children's guardian have a duty to seek to prevent delay by clearly identifying the options available to the court by twin-track planning as opposed to sequential planning. In such cases it is vital that the local authority should make it absolutely clear to the natural family as early as possible that it is considering these two options and that inquiries are proceeding on a twin track so that the court can be presented at the final care hearing with properly researched options in order to prevent delay. See *Best Practice Guidance of June 1997*, paras 7–12, which is helpfully set out in Part IV of *The Family Court Practice 2007* (Jordans, Bristol).

33.72 In appropriate cases, the authority may be able to proceed using 'concurrent planning', a form of planning which is distinct from twin-track planning. 'Concurrent planning' describes a scheme whereby the local authority chooses foster-parents who are trained and willing to foster children on the basis that they work with the natural family towards rehabilitation, but who, in the event that rehabilitation is ruled out, wish to adopt the children. The aim is to reduce the number of moves a child experiences in care, and to reduce temporary placements so that children can achieve permanence, whether rehabilitated with their family or with the foster-family, with minimum disruption. Contact between carers and birth children is encouraged and there is openness between the parties about the primary aim of rehabilitation with the alternative secondary plan of permanent placement. It is vital in such cases that the two options are clearly explained to the natural family from the outset and that they are reassured that it in no way pre-empts the outcome of the care proceedings. Not every case will be suitable for such placement. Generally it is likely to apply to babies or young children where there are some but by no means optimistic prospects of rehabilitation to the natural family. Whenever care proceedings are commenced the court should be proactive at an early directions hearing, requiring the authority to establish whether twin-track planning and/or concurrent planning is suitable and giving appropriate directions.

33.73 The procedure to be adopted once a local authority decides to apply for a care or supervision order is now governed by the public law protocol, which is discussed in detail in paragraph 33.32 and onwards. Where the local authority wishes to proceed with twin-track planning or concurrent planning, the Case Management Checklist requires the court at the First Hearing in a Family Proceedings Court, the Allocation Hearing in a Care Centre, the Allocation Directions in the High Court, and for the Case Management Conference to consider whether these have been considered. Where appropriate, directions must be given in relation to any concurrent freeing for adoption proceedings and for the filing and service of evidence relating to placement options and their feasibility (see point 57 of the checklist in Appendix A/3 of the protocol).

Effect of care orders

Local authority obtains parental responsibility under a care order

33.74 While a care order is in force with respect to a child, the local authority has parental responsibility for him: s. 33(3). However, parents do *not lose* their parental responsibility as a result of a care order being made: s. 2(5). The parents share parental responsibility with the local authority, although the authority has the power to determine, largely, the extent to which a parent, special guardian, or guardian of the child may meet his parental responsibility for the child: s. 33(3)(b). However, s. 33(4) directs that the local authority should not limit the extent to which the parent exercises his parental responsibility for the child *unless* it is satisfied that it is necessary to do so in order to safeguard or promote the child's welfare. Furthermore, s. 33(5), CA 1989 states that where a parent has *de facto* care of the child then he may do what is reasonable in all the circumstances to safeguard or promote the child's welfare (see also s. 3(5)).

33.75 However, there are certain things which the local authority has no right to do even if it has a care order in respect of a child, since those matters remain the prerogative of the parents. The authority may not:

(a) bring the child up in a different religion from that in which he would have been brought up if the order had not been made: s. 33(6)(a). However, the child could choose to practise a different religion if he was of sufficient age and understanding, since he is entitled to be consulted by the authority about such matters: s. 22(4) and (5);

(b) agree or refuse to agree to the making of an adoption order in respect of the child (s. 36(b)(ii));

(c) appoint a guardian for the child (s. 33(6)(b)(iii)).

Care order discharges all existing s. 8 orders

A care order has the effect of discharging all existing s. 8 orders (i.e., residence, con- **33.76** tact, prohibited steps, and specific issue orders). There is a separate scheme under s. 34, CA 1989 which provides for parental contact with children in care (see paragraph 33.81 below).

Restriction of change of name and removal from the jurisdiction

While a care order is in force s. 33(7), CA 1989 provides that no person may: **33.77**

(a) cause the child to be known by a new surname; or

(b) remove him from the United Kingdom,

without *either*:

(i) the written consent of every person who has parental responsibility for the child; or

(ii) the leave of the court.

However, the above consent is not necessary if the authority wishes to remove the child from the jurisdiction for periods of less than one month: s. 33(8)(a).

Local authority power to place child with his parents

Section 23(4), (5) and (6) gives the local authority power to place a child in its care with one **33.78** or both of his parents. See the Placement of Children with Parents etc. Regulations 1991. The case of *Re D (Care: Natural Parent Presumption)* [1999] 1 FLR 134 emphasizes that there is a strong presumption that where it is possible to place a child in care with his natural parent then that is the course which should be taken, unless there are compelling factors to override the presumption.

Duties of local authority towards a child in its care

The duties of local authorities in relation to children 'looked after' by them apply equally to **33.79** a child in their care by virtue of a care order. Those duties have already been discussed earlier in this chapter at paragraph 33.18.

No power to attach conditions to care order

The court has no power to attach to a care order conditions binding on a local authority **33.80** (save those under s. 34 as to contact), since Parliament has entrusted the administration of care orders to local authorities. The task of the court is to scrutinize the local authority's care plan and then to decide whether or not it is in the interests of the child to make a care order: *Re J (Minors) (Care: Care Plan)* (above). If it is, then it falls to the local authority to decide how the child's care should be managed. It is not, therefore, possible for a court to make a care order with a requirement that the local authority is to place the child with the parents: *Re T (A Minor) (Care Order: Conditions)* [1994] 2 FLR 423 (CA). See further paragraph 33.78 above.

Parental contact with children in care

33.81 Schedule 2, para. 15, CA 1989 places a duty upon local authorities to 'endeavour to promote contact' between any child they are 'looking after' (note that 'looking after' includes children being looked after by virtue of a care order) and the following persons:

(a) his parents;

(b) those who have parental responsibility for him (e.g., guardians); and

(c) any relatives, friends, or other persons connected with him.

This duty applies in all cases *unless* contact is not reasonably practicable or is not consistent with the child's welfare.

33.82 The court has no power to make a s. 8 order (other than a residence order) whilst a child is in the care of a local authority: s. 9(1). However, the CA 1989 sets out a special scheme in s. 34 which enables the court to make orders directing or refusing contact with children in care.

33.83 Where the child is the subject of a care order s. 34(1) imposes a statutory presumption that the local authority must allow the child to have reasonable contact with:

(a) his parents;

(b) any guardian or special guardian of his;

(c) any person who by virtue of s. 4A has parental responsibility for him (i.e., step-parents with parental responsibility);

(d) where there was a residence order in force with respect to the child immediately before the care order was made, the person in whose favour the residence order was made; and

(e) where, immediately before the care order was made, a person had care of the child by virtue of an order made in the exercise of the High Court's inherent jurisdiction, that person.

Section 34 of the CA 1989 makes the duty enforceable in the courts.

When may a s. 34 contact order be made?

33.84 A s. 34 contact order may be made at the same time as the care order itself or later: s. 34(10). Before making the care order the court must consider the arrangements which the authority has made, or proposes to make, for arranging contact between the child and the persons to whom s. 34 applies: s. 34(11). Therefore, in the course of care proceedings all parties should be prepared to present evidence and make submissions about contact. Indeed, the local authority is under a duty in the course of care proceedings to present to the court a care plan dealing with the matters set out in *The Children Act 1989 Guidance and Regulations*, vol. 3, ch. 2, para. 2.62, which include 'arrangements for contact and reunification': *Re J (Minors) (Care: Care Plan)* (above). See further details relating to care plans at paragraph 33.67 above.

However, where the court considers an application for contact with a child in care the **33.85** court can require the local authority to justify its long-term plans to the extent only that the plans exclude contact between the parent and the child. On the other hand, where the application for contact is, in effect, an attempt to set aside a care order then the parent must show a change of circumstances which requires further investigation and consideration of the local authority's plan, and it would be only in unusual cases that a parent would succeed with such an application: *Re B (Minors) (Care: Contact: Local Authority's Plans)* [1993] 1 FLR 543.

Who may apply for contact under s. 34?

The following persons may make an application under s. 34 that the court make such order **33.86** as it considers appropriate with respect to the contact which is to be allowed between the child and the *person named in the order*:

(a)   the local authority (s. 34(2));
(b)   the child (s. 34(2)).

The following persons may make an application under s. 34 that the court make such order as it considers appropriate with respect to the contact which is to be allowed between the child and *that person*:

(a)   any of the persons listed in paragraph 33.83(a) to (e) above: s. 34(3)(a);
(b)   anyone else who has first obtained the leave of the court to make an application (s. 34(3)(b)), for example, grandparents and siblings may well wish to retain contact with the child in care.

Power of the court to attach conditions to a s. 34 order

Section 34(7) of the CA 1989 makes provision for the court to attach to a s. 34 contact order **33.87** such conditions as it considers appropriate. It is open to the court to specify the timing, nature, and duration of the contact, if necessary, provided that such specification does not in effect constitute a review by the court of the implementation of the local authority's care plan: *Re S (A Minor) (Care: Contact Order)* [1994] 2 FLR 222. Section 34 is sufficiently wide to enable the court to make what is, in effect, an interim contact order at the same time as a care order, with a specific provision for a further hearing with a view to making further provision for contact at the subsequent hearing: *Re B (A Minor) (Care Order: Review)* [1993] 1 FLR 421.

Prohibition of contact with a child in care

If the local authority or the child wish to apply to the court to prohibit contact between **33.88** the child and the persons set out in paragraph 33.83(a) to (e) above then the appropriate section for them to use is s. 34(4), for example, to prevent contact between a child and a parent who has sexually abused him. It is not open to anyone other than the local authority or the child to apply for such a *prohibition* on contact. For example, if a mother took the view that the child's father should not have contact with the child while he is in care then she could not apply for an order under s. 34(4); she would have to rely upon the authority sharing her anxieties about contact and making the application in its own right.

33.89   The authority may refuse to allow contact that would otherwise be required by virtue of s. 34(1) or by an order under s. 34 if:

  (a)   it is satisfied that it is necessary to do so to promote the child's welfare; and
  (b)   the refusal:
     (i)   is decided upon as a matter of urgency; *and*
     (ii)   does not last for more than *seven* days: s. 34(6).

Where the authority exercises its power to refuse to allow contact with a child in care then it must adopt the procedure set out in the Contact with Children Regulations 1991. Those regulations require that the authority notify the following persons, in writing, of its decision:

  (a)   those listed in s. 34(1);
  (b)   the child, if he is of sufficient understanding; and
  (c)   any other person whose wishes and feelings the authority considers to be relevant.

In the notification the authority should give its reasons for the decision, its date, its duration, and the remedies available in case of dissatisfaction.

33.90   The same principles apply where:

  (a)   the authority decides to depart from the terms of any agreement as to contact made with the person in relation to whom the s. 34 order was made; or
  (b)   the authority intends to vary or suspend arrangements made, *other than under a s. 34 order*, with a view to affording any person contact with a child in care.

Where the authority wishes to refuse contact with a child in care for more than seven days then, after following the procedure outlined above, it must apply to the court for an order allowing it to refuse contact for a longer period. The court has a complete discretion under s. 34(4) to authorize the refusal of contact for as long as it considers it to be for the child's welfare: *West Glamorgan County Council v P (No. 1)* [1992] 2 FLR 369. However, where the child is the subject of an interim care order then contact between the child and his parents should be continued until the substantive hearing wherever possible, so that the court hearing the interim applications does not reach a firm conclusion which effectively decides the final outcome of the case: *A v M and Walsall Metropolitan Borough Council* [1993] 2 FLR 244.

33.91   Where the court has to determine an application by the local authority for the permanent cessation of contact between the child in care and his parents then the court must start with the presumption of continuing parental contact. If, on a s. 34(4) application, the judge concludes that the benefits of contact outweigh the disadvantages of disrupting any of the local authority's long-term plans which are inconsistent with such contact, then the judge must refuse the local authority's application; such action does not amount to monitoring or scrutinizing the local authority's plan, but is the discharge by the court of the duty which Parliament has placed upon the court by s. 34(4): *H v West Sussex County Council* [1998] 1 FLR 862; *Re D and H (Care: Termination of Contact)* [1997] 1 FLR 841; *Re T (Termination of Contact: Discharge of Order)* [1997] 1 FLR 517; *Re E (A Minor) (Care Order: Contact)* [1994] 1 FLR 146; *Re B (Minors) (Care: Contact: Local Authority's Plans)* (above). The Court of Appeal observed in *Re E (A Minor) (Care Order: Contact)* (above) that even where the criteria in s. 31 are satisfied, contact may still be of great importance to the long-term welfare of the child. It could give the child the security of knowing that his parents loved him and were interested in his welfare and avoid any damaging sense of loss to the child in seeing himself as abandoned by his parents. Contact could also enable a child to commit himself to a substitute family with the seal of approval of his natural parents and give the child the necessary sense of family and personal identity. Contact, if maintained, is therefore capable of reinforcing and increasing the chances of success of a permanent placement, whether on a long-term fostering basis or by adoption.

However, there will be cases in which the cessation of contact between parent and child is necessary, see for example *Birmingham City Council* v *H (No. 3)* [1994] 1 FLR 224, House of Lords. **33.92**

Once an order under s. 34(2) is in place authorizing refusal of contact there is nothing to stop the local authority from reviewing the arrangement in the future and subsequently deciding to allow contact to take place again where the local authority considers that it would be advantageous for the child: *Re W (S. 34(2) Orders)* [2000] Fam Law 235—s. 34 does not prohibit any exercise of the local authority's discretion to permit staying contact between a child and his parents. **33.93**

Variation and discharge of s. 34 contact orders

The court may vary or discharge any s. 34 order on the application of: **33.94**

(a)   the person named in the order;
(b)   the authority; or
(c)   the child concerned (s. 34(9)).

Where a person other than a local authority has made a s. 34 application and that application has been refused, then that person may not make a similar application in respect of the *same* child until at least *six months* have elapsed since the refusal, unless he has first obtained the leave of the court: s. 91(17). Before restricting or terminating contact under s. 34, the court must consider the local authority's care proposals: *Re D and H (Care: Termination of Contact)* (above).

A s. 34 contact order must be discharged if the care order to which it relates is discharged. A s. 8 contact order could be made instead in the course of the proceedings dealing with the discharge of the care order: s. 10. **33.95**

Care/supervision order procedure

The procedure to be adopted in all applications for care or supervision orders is now governed by the public law protocol, which is discussed in detail at paragraph 33.32 above. **33.96**

Representation of the child

The court is under a duty to appoint a children's guardian for a child for the purpose of 'specified proceedings' *unless* it is satisfied that it is not necessary to do so in order to safeguard the child's interests: s. 41(1). 'Specified proceedings' are defined in s. 41(6), CA 1989 and they include: **33.97**

(a)   applications for care and supervision orders;

(b)   proceedings in which the court has given a direction under s. 37(1) and has made, or is considering whether to make, an interim care order;

(c)   applications to discharge care or supervision orders;

(d)   appeals against care or supervision orders.

The above are just *some* of the relevant categories of proceedings to which the duty applies. The practitioner is referred to s. 41(6) itself for the remainder of the list.

33.98   The implementation of the HRA 1998, which incorporates the European Convention for the Protection of Human Rights and Fundamental Freedoms in our domestic law, has led to pressure for the wider representation of children in proceedings which affect them. See *CAFCASS and the National Assembly for Wales Practice Note (Appointment of Guardians in Private Law Proceedings)* [2006] 2 FLR 143 which gives guidance as to the types of cases in which separate representation for children may be appropriate.

33.99   The method of appointing a children's guardian is set out in paragraph 30.50, together with a description of his role and duties towards the child. The appropriate rules of court are rr. 4.10, 4.11, and 4.11A, FPR 1991 and rr. 10, 11, and 11A, FPC(CA 1989)R 1991.

33.100   The court may appoint a solicitor to represent the child provided that:

(a)   he is not already represented by one; and

(b)   one of the conditions in s. 41(4) is satisfied: s. 41(3). The conditions are that no children's guardian has been appointed for the child, that the child has sufficient understanding to appoint a solicitor and wishes to do so, or that it appears to be in the child's best interests for him to be represented by a solicitor.

Once appointed the solicitor must represent the child in accordance with the rules of court. The relevant rules are to be found in r. 4.12, FPR 1991 and r. 12, FPC(CA 1989)R 1991.

33.101   There is also provision for a children's guardian to appoint a solicitor for the child. This topic is further discussed in paragraph 30.56.

Jurisdiction and procedure

33.102   Proceedings with a public law element (e.g., applications for care orders, supervision orders, s. 34 contact orders, emergency protection orders) will generally commence in the family proceedings court. However, the family proceedings court, county court, and High Court all have concurrent jurisdiction, and are all capable of hearing public law cases in appropriate circumstances (note that only 'nominated care judges' may hear cases with a public law element in the county court).

33.103   Initially, the clerk to the justices (or the justices themselves) will make a decision as to the level of court at which the matter is to be tried. The criteria for transferring the proceedings upwards to the county court or High Court are set out in Art. 7, Children (Allocation of Proceedings) Order 1991 and r. 6, FPC(CA 1989)R 1991. The criteria for transferring the case include factors such as the forensic or legal complexity of the case, the number of parties involved and the involvement of a question of general public interest. For an outline on the topic of the transfer of proceedings, see paragraph 30.05.

If a party is dissatisfied with the decision reached by the family proceedings court as to the **33.104** level of court at which the matter is to be tried, then he may *apply* for a transfer before the district judge of the relevant county court: r. 4.6, FPR 1991 and r. 6(4), FPC(CA 1989)R 1991. Note that this is by way of *application* only; it is not by way of appeal from the magistrates' decision. The district judge may then make his own decision as to the level of court before which the case is to be heard.

The application

The general procedure for applications is to be found in r. 4.4, FPR 1991 and r. 4, FPC(CA **33.105** 1989)R 1991. The persons who are to be made respondents to proceedings and the persons who are to be notified of proceedings are set out in tabular form in Appendix 3, FPR 1991 and sch. 2. FPC(CA 1989)R 1991. The rules for service are set out in r. 4.8, FPR 1991 and r. 8, FPC(CA 1989)R 1991. However, the procedure to be adopted once a local authority decides to apply for a care or supervision order is now governed by the public law protocol, which is discussed in detail in paragraph 33.32 above.

Withdrawal of an application

The general rules apply. See paragraph 30.29. **33.106**

The court has given useful guidance on this type of application. In *Re N (Leave to Withdraw* **33.107** *Care Proceedings)* [2000] 1 FLR 134 the local authority, supported by the parents, sought to withdraw its application for a care order. However, the children's guardian opposed the application to withdraw on the basis that the child's welfare demanded a full hearing of the matter. The court refused the local authority's application, saying that the welfare of the child was paramount when deciding this issue. The guardian should think long and hard before opposing an agreement between the local authority and the parents, but had a duty to put his view before the court. The local authority should have consulted the guardian before taking the decision to withdraw the proceedings. The court also considered the impact of Art. 8(2) of the European Convention for the Protection of Human Rights and Fundamental Freedoms; Art. 8(2) makes it clear that interference by public authorities with the parents' right to respect for their private and family life is only justified and necessary if it fulfils a pressing social need. In this case, the guardian had shown a pressing social need for inter-vention and the court made it clear that where there is a real risk to a child the law will not allow the potential harm to actually occur before taking action.

Timetable

Section 32, CA 1989 reflects the general principle of the Act that delay in proceedings is **33.108** likely to be prejudicial to the child's welfare. It requires the court hearing applications under Part IV of the CA 1989 to draw up a timetable with a view to disposing of the application without delay. It also enables the court to give directions to ensure that the timetable is adhered to. The relevant rules of court which deal with the timing of proceedings are to be found in r. 4.15, FPR 1991 and r. 15, FPC(CA 1989)R 1991. The aim of these provisions is to prevent the proceedings from lying dormant through the delay of the parties and their advisers. However, note that the procedure to be adopted once a local authority decides to apply for a care or supervision order is now tightly governed by the public law protocol, which is discussed in detail in paragraph 33.32 above.

The hearing

33.109 A hearing before the High Court or county court will be in chambers (r. 4.16(7), FPR 1991) and a hearing before the family proceedings court may be held in private (r. 16(17), FPC(CA 1989)R 1991). However, the procedure to be adopted once a local authority decides to apply for a care or supervision order is now governed by the public law protocol, which is discussed in detail in paragraph 33.32 above.

33.110 **Attendance of parties** For the general rules as to the attendance of parties at hearings or directions appointments, see paragraph 30.64. In the course of hearing any application made under Part IV or V of the CA 1989 (e.g., for a care order, supervision order, s. 34 contact order, emergency protection order etc.), the court has a discretion to order the attendance of the child at any stage in the proceedings: s. 95(1). Where it believes that such an order will not be, or has not been, complied with the court may authorize a constable or other named person to enter and search premises in order to take charge of the child and to bring him to court: s. 95(4)(a). Furthermore, the court may order anyone whom it believes to be in a position to bring the child to court to do so, or to order a person with information as to the whereabouts of the child to disclose it to the court: s. 95(4)(b). However, in *Re C (A Minor) (Care: Child's Wishes)* [1993] 1 FLR 832, Waite J said that young children (in this case a girl aged 13) should be discouraged from attending High Court appeals from the justices in family proceedings. Where the children's guardian proposes to arrange for a young child to be present at an appeal he should give the question very careful thought beforehand and be prepared, if necessary, to explain his reasons to the judge. However, the procedure to be adopted once a local authority decides to apply for a care or supervision order is now governed by the public law protocol, which is discussed in detail in paragraph 33.32 above.

33.111 **Factors to be considered by the court** The various factors which the court must consider when hearing contested proceedings of this nature are set out fully in paragraph 29.05 onwards. In general, the court must bear in mind that the child's welfare is paramount. In doing so, it must apply the statutory checklist of factors contained in s. 1(3), and must have regard to the principle that any delay in deciding the case is likely to be prejudicial to the welfare of the child. Finally, the court must have regard to the whole range of orders available to it (and not just the one applied for), but must not make any order unless satisfied that to make an order would be better for the child than making no order at all: s. 1(5).

33.112 The 'child' to whom s. 34(3) applies is the child in care, in respect of whom an order is sought. The question to be determined relates to that child's upbringing and it is that child's welfare which must be the court's paramount consideration. The fact that the parent is also a child does not mean that both the parent's and the child's welfare are paramount and that each had to be balanced against the other, since no question is to be determined as to the parent's upbringing (*Birmingham City Council v H (No. 3)* (above)).

33.113 **Expert evidence** The question of whether or not to instruct experts will be subject to particular scrutiny and will be governed by the Code of Guidance for Expert Witnesses in Family Proceedings contained in Appendix C of the public law protocol (as to the protocol generally, see further at paragraph 33.32 above). The Code is designed to draw together all the threads which have emerged through case law and practice over the last few years. It sets out comprehensive guidance. Considerations of space allow for only a cursory overview of the Code, but practitioners are encouraged to read the Code in full.

The objective of the Code is to provide the court with early information to enable it to **33.114** determine whether it is necessary to ask an expert to assist the court:

(a) to identify, narrow, and where possible agree the issues between the parties;
(b) to provide an opinion about a question that is not within the skill and experience of the court;
(c) to encourage the early identification of questions that need to be answered by an expert;
(d) to encourage disclosure of full and frank information between the parties, the court, and any experts instructed.

The overriding duty of an expert in family proceedings is to the court and this takes precedence over any obligation to the person from whom he has received instructions or by whom he is paid (para. 1.1 of the Code). The particular duties an expert may have are set out in para. 1.2 of the Code. Provision is made for the solicitor proposing to instruct an expert to approach the expert at least 10 days before the Case Management Conference (CMC) and give him or her prescribed information about the proceedings and issues involved (Code, para. 2.1). At least five days before the CMC the solicitors must obtain the expert's response, to include confirmation that the work required is within his experience, whether or not he would be available to do the work within the suggested time scale, and the cost.

Any party who proposes to ask the court for permission to instruct an expert must at least **33.115** two days before the CMC file and serve a case management questionnaire setting out the proposal, including the prescribed details required by para. 2.3 of the Code, such as the identity and qualifications of the expert, his availability, the relevance of the evidence sought to be adduced, and whether or not the evidence can properly be obtained by the joint instruction of the expert by two or more parties.

Any party proposing to instruct an expert must in the draft order submitted at the CMC **33.116** request the court to give directions, including as to (Code, para. 2.4):

(a) the party who is to be responsible for drafting the letter of instruction and providing the documents to the expert;
(b) the issues involved and the questions about which the expert is to give an opinion;
(c) the timetable for preparation of the report;
(d) the disclosure of the report to the parties and any other expert;
(e) the conduct of an experts' discussion and the preparation of a statement of agreement and disagreement by the experts following an experts' discussion;
(f) the attendance of the expert at the Final Hearing unless agreement is reached at or before the Pre-Hearing Review about the opinions given by the expert.

The solicitor instructing the expert must within five days of the CMC prepare, file, and serve a letter of instruction to the expert which must contain the information prescribed in para. 3.1 of the Code.

The expert's report must be addressed to the court and must include the information **33.117** prescribed in para. 4.1 of the Code, for example:

(a) the details of his qualifications and experience;
(b) the substance of his instructions;
(c) details of any literature or research he has relied on;

    (d)   where there is a range of opinion on the question, summarize the range of opinion and give reasons for the opinion expressed;

    (e)   summarize his conclusions and opinions.

Any party wishing to ask supplementary questions of an expert to clarify the report must put them in writing to the parties within five days after receipt of the report (Code, para. 4.2). Only those questions that are agreed by the parties or, in default of agreement, approved by the court may be put to the expert.

33.118   The court will give directions for the experts to meet or communicate so as (Code, para. 5.1):

    (a)   to identify and narrow the issues;

    (b)   to reach agreement on the expert questions;

    (c)   to identify the reasons for any disagreement and identify what, if any, action needs to be taken to resolve it;

    (d)   to obtain clarification or amplification of relevant evidence in order to assist the court to determine the issues;

    (e)   to limit, wherever possible, the need for experts to attend court to give oral evidence.

In accordance with the directions given by the court at the CMC the solicitor so directed by the court (usually the solicitor for the child) must make arrangements for there to be a discussion between the experts within 10 days of the filing of the experts' reports (Code, para. 5.2). The following matters should be discussed:

    (a)   a global discussion of those questions that concern all or most of them;

    (b)   separate discussions where required between experts of the same or related disciplines;

    (c)   the solicitor responsible for setting up the discussion must, seven days before it, formulate an agenda. This may be in the form of a list of questions to be circulated among the parties in advance. The agenda should comprise all questions that each party wishes the expert to consider. The agenda and questions should be sent to each expert at least two days before the discussion;

    (d)   the discussion should usually be chaired by the child's solicitor;

    (e)   a minute must be taken of the questions answered by the experts and a Statement of Agreement and Disagreement must be prepared.

Where any party refuses to be bound by an agreement reached at an experts' discussion, that party must inform the court at or before the PHR of the reasons for refusing (Code, para. 5.3).

33.119   The party who is responsible for the instruction of an expert witness must ensure (Code, para. 6.1) that:

    (a)   a date and time is fixed for the court to hear the expert's evidence;

    (b)   if the expert's oral evidence is not required the expert is notified as soon as possible;

    (c)   the witness template accurately indicates how long the expert is likely to be giving evidence.

Within 10 days of the Final Hearing the solicitor instructing the expert should provide feedback to the expert as to the outcome of the case and the use made by the court of the expert's opinion (Code, para. 7.1).

Documentary evidence The general rules as to the need for the advance disclosure of **33.120**
documentary evidence are discussed in paragraph 30.69. However, the procedure to be
adopted once a local authority decides to apply for a care or supervision order is now
governed by the public law protocol, which is discussed in detail in paragraph 33.32 above.
The preparation and disclosure of documentary evidence is tightly controlled by the
court. The question of whether or not to instruct experts will be subject to particular scrutiny
and will be governed by the Code of Guidance for Expert Witnesses in Family Proceedings
contained in Appendix C of the public law protocol and discussed in paragraph 33.113
above. The court has power to override legal professional privilege and order that the report
be disclosed even if the party who has commissioned it is unwilling to do so voluntarily:
Oxfordshire County Council v *M* [1994] 1 FLR 175. This power stems from the principle
that proceedings under the CA 1989 are not adversarial. The court's duty is to investigate
and seek to achieve a result which is in the interests of the child. The cases of *Essex County
Council* v *R* [1993] 2 FLR 826 and *Re DH (A Minor) (Child Abuse)* [1994] 1 FLR 679 indicate
that counsel has a positive duty to make voluntary disclosure of medical reports even
where disclosure would be contrary to the client's interests. The House of Lords has
considered the disclosure of reports in public law cases in *Re L (Police Investigation: Privilege)*
[1996] 1 FLR 731 and this case contains useful guidance for practitioners.

Oral evidence The way in which hearings are to be conducted is now tightly governed by **33.121**
the public law protocol which is discussed in detail in paragraph 33.32 above. The court,
proper officer or justices' clerk must keep a note of the substance of any oral evidence given
at a hearing or directions appointment: r. 4.20, FPR 1991 and r. 20, FPC(CA 1989)R 1991.
In the course of any proceedings under Parts IV or V of the CA 1989 (e.g., applications for
care orders, supervision orders, s. 34 contact orders, emergency protection orders etc.) no
one is excused from giving evidence on any matter, or answering any question put to him
in the course of giving his evidence, on the ground that doing so might incriminate him
or his spouse of an offence. However, any statement or admission made in such proceedings
is not admissible in proceedings for an offence other than perjury (see ss. 98 and 48(2),
CA 1989).

Welfare reports The question of welfare reports is dealt with fully in paragraph 30.43. **33.122**

Split hearings Where there are crucial issues of disputed fact (for example, allegations **33.123**
of sexual abuse), then the court may give a direction that those issues be determined
at a preliminary hearing. Once those issues have been determined then a further substantive hearing can be fixed to consider more fully the outcome which would best
serve the child's welfare. It is imperative that those cases which are suitable for a split
hearing should be identified as early as possible by the court, with the assistance of
the local authority and the children's guardian: *Re S (Care Proceedings: Split Hearing)*
[1996] 2 FLR 773. The decision as to whether or not a preliminary hearing will be
required and, if so, how it is to be conducted, is now governed by the public law protocol
which is discussed in detail in paragraph 33.32 above. A Case Management Questionnaire
(protocol, Appendix A/2) must be filed by the local authority at least five days before
the CMC and all other parties must file one at least two days before the date fixed for
the CMC. Paragraph B of the Questionnaire requires the parties to indicate whether
or not a preliminary hearing is required. Where findings of fact are made on preliminary

issues at a split hearing there is jurisdiction to hear an appeal against them if those findings are of crucial importance to the final decision: *Re B (Split Hearings: Jurisdiction)* [2000] 1 FLR 334. Note that a decision of the court is treated as a final decision for the purpose of an appeal if it '(a) is made at the conclusion of part of a hearing or trial which has been split into parts; and (b) would, if made at the conclusion of that hearing or trial, be a final decision under para. (2)(c)' (Access to Justice Act 1999 (Destination of Appeals) Order 2000 (SI 2000/1071)). Paragraph (2)(c) of the Order defines a 'final decision' as a decision of a court that would finally determine (subject to any possible appeal or detailed assessment of costs) the entire proceedings whichever way the court decided the issues before it.

33.124 **The decision**   The way in which decisions are to be given and recorded is now governed by the public law protocol which is discussed in detail in paragraphs 33.44 and 33.45 above (see steps 6.4–6.6 of the protocol).

Interim orders

33.125 Despite the presumption that delay in proceedings is likely to prejudice the welfare of the child concerned, there will be occasions when an adjournment of care proceedings is unavoidable. For example, the parties may need time in which to prepare their cases properly, or the children's guardian may need time in which to investigate and report on the child's circumstances. It is important that in appropriate cases the court can control the case by way of interim orders until all the relevant material is before the court to enable it to make a final order: *C v Solihull Metropolitan Borough Council* [1993] 1 FLR 290; *Hounslow London Borough Council v A* [1993] 1 FLR 702; *Re J (Minors) (Care: Care Plan)* (above). The effect of an interim care order is the same as a full order (for example, the authority obtains parental responsibility and there is a presumption that it will allow reasonable contact between the child and his parents), except where express provision is made to the contrary: *A v M and Walsall Metropolitan Borough Council* (above). The two main differences between full and interim orders are in respect of their duration (see paragraph 33.131 below) and in respect of the directions which the court may make in respect of them (see paragraph 33.132 below).

33.126 The court has power under s. 38, CA 1989 to make an interim care or interim supervision order where:

(a) proceedings are adjourned on an application for a care or supervision order; or

(b) the court gives a direction under s. 37(1) (i.e., that the local authority is to investigate the child's circumstances).

33.127 The power to make an interim order must not be exercised unless the court is satisfied that there are *reasonable grounds for believing* that the statutory criteria in s. 31(2), CA 1989 are satisfied with respect to the child concerned. The court does not have to be satisfied that the s. 31(2) grounds actually *exist*, since that would defeat the purpose of an adjournment and require the authority to prove its case on the first hearing. In effect, the authority has to show a prima facie case. In addition, the court must consider the three fundamental dictates contained in s. 1, CA 1989 before making an interim order, that is to say:

(a) the child's welfare is the paramount consideration: s. 1(1);

(b) any delay in determining the proceedings is likely to prejudice the welfare of the child: s. 1(2); and

(c) the court must not make any order unless it considers that making an order would be better for the child than making no order at all: s. 1(5).

When faced with an interim hearing the matters which the court should bear in mind are set out in *Hampshire County Council* v *S* [1993] 1 FLR 559, as follows:

(a) The court should bear in mind that it will usually be required to establish no more than a holding position at the interim stage, after weighing all relevant risks, pending the final hearing.

(b) The court must ensure that the substantive hearing of the issues takes place at the earliest possible date. If the court is unable to provide the appropriate hearing time itself then it must consider transferring the case laterally to another court which does have sufficient time available.

(c) The court should rarely make findings as to disputed facts in an interim hearing.

(d) The greater the extent to which the interim order deviates from a previous order or the status quo, the more acute is the need for an early hearing date. The preferred course should be to leave the child where he is with a direction for safeguards and the earliest possible hearing date.

(e) When the court considers making an interim order which will lead to a substantial change in the child's position the court should consider permitting limited oral evidence to be led and challenged by way of cross-examination. However, the evidence must be limited to the issues which are essential at the interim stage.

(f) If possible, the court should have before it the written evidence of the children's guardian. If there are substantial issues between the parties the guardian should also be at court to give oral advice and a party who opposes the guardian's recommendations should have the opportunity to question the guardian.

(g) The court must always comply with the mandatory requirements of the rules, for example to read before the hearing all documents which have been filed (r. 21(1), FPC(CA 1989)R 1991), for the justices' clerk to make a written record of the hearing and to record the reasons for the court's decision on any findings of fact (r. 21(5), FPC(CA 1989)R 1991), and for the court when making its order or giving its decision, to state the findings of fact and reasons for the decision (r. 21(6), FPC(CA 1989)R 1991).

(h) If the justices are delayed in the preparation of their written findings of fact or reasons they should adjourn the making of the order or giving of the decision until the following day or the earliest possible court date; one of their number can be allocated to present the reasons and the orders of the court where necessary: r. 21(6), FPC(CA 1989)R 1991;

(i) When granting interim relief the justices should state their findings and reasons concisely, and summarize briefly the essential factual issues between the parties.

When a court has heard all the available evidence at a final hearing but is still considering **33.128** whether or not to make a further interim care order rather than a final care order it must approach any such decision with extreme caution. The court must be aware of the danger of using an interim care order as a means of exercising judicial supervision and of diminishing the general principle of avoiding delay. Section 38 is primarily designed to cater for the situation prior to a final hearing where a case needs to be adjourned because it is not ready for trial. In some cases the action necessary in the interests of children requires steps into the unknown. Provided that the court is satisfied that the local authority is alert to the difficulties which might arise in the execution of its care plan, then the function of the court is not to seek to oversee the plan but to entrust its execution to the local authority. If the care plan represents the only practical course of action for the children then it would be artificial for the court to make an interim order since to do so would represent an attempt to exercise a supervisory jurisdiction over matters entrusted to the local authority: *Re D (Simultaneous Applications for Care Order and Freeing Order)* [1999] 2 FLR 49; *Re J (Minors) (Care: Care Plan)* (above); *Re P (Minors) (Interim Order)* [1993] 2 FLR 742. The court cannot oversee the implementation of a care plan once a care order has been made. This can cause problems in the following cases:

(a)   where the court is left with the choice of accepting an unsatisfactory care plan or refusing to make a care order;

(b)   where the local authority make a substantial change to the care plan after the final care order has been made.

As the law stands at present the latter can only be challenged by judicial review or by an application to discharge a care order. However, see paragraph 1.6 above, 'Review of cases', which describes the role of independent reviewing officers (IROs) under s. 26(2)(e), CA 1989. Once a care order has been made, the duties of the reviewing officer will encompass a review of the care plan concerning the child and the revision of that plan as necessary in the circumstances of each particular case. The officer will have power to refer the case to the Children and Family Court Advisory and Support Service (CAFCASS) where appropriate. CAFCASS will have power to take proceedings on behalf of the child. The introduction of IROs was implemented partly to meet the criticism that the inability of the court to oversee the implementation of a care plan may well be subject to challenge under the HRA 1998.

33.129   Article 6 of the Convention, in particular, guarantees the right to a fair trial; in child care cases this would include sufficient procedural protection of parents' interests throughout the process: *W v UK* (1987) 10 EHRR 29, paras. 77 and 82. Where administrative decisions have the effect of interfering with family relationships, then Art. 8 of the Convention, which guarantees the right to respect for family life, includes the need for fair procedures to be put in place when such administrative decisions are taken: *McMichael v UK* (1995) 20 EHRR 205; *Scott v UK*, application no. 34745/97.

33.130   If the court is hearing an application for a care or supervision order but decides, instead, to make a residence order, then the court *must* make an interim supervision order as well *unless* it is satisfied that the child's welfare will be satisfactorily safeguarded without an interim supervision order: s. 38(3).

Duration of interim orders

33.131   An interim care or supervision order will last for an initial period of eight weeks: s. 38(4). The court may extend the order for a further period of four weeks (s. 38(5)), and there appears to be nothing to prevent further extensions at four-weekly intervals. The rules about extension of time are complex and the practitioner is advised to study them in detail. The important principle is that an interim care order must be used for its intended purpose and not simply extended to provide the court with continuing control over the actions of the local authority: *Re L (Sexual Abuse: Standard of Proof)* [1996] 1 FLR 116. In any event, the court must draw up a timetable with a view to disposing of the case without delay, and it is to be hoped that the duration of interim orders will thus be kept as short as possible. In fixing the period of the interim order the court can take into account whether any party opposed to the order was in a position to argue his case in full: s. 38(10).

Directions made under an interim order

When a court makes a full care order it has no jurisdiction to give directions as to the child's welfare and upbringing. In *Re B (A Minor) (Care Order: Review)* (above) the family proceedings court purported to grant a care order with the provision that the court would review the operation of the care order, progress in the care plan and contact six months after the date of the order. On appeal, Thorpe J held that the court had no power, once a care order had been made, to monitor the operation of the care order by the local authority. This approach was confirmed by the Court of Appeal in *Re T (A Minor) (Care Order: Conditions)* [1994] 2 FLR 423. However, the court did have power under s. 34 to make an interim contact order at the same time as the care order with a specific provision for a further hearing with a view to making further provision for contact at the subsequent hearing. See also *A v Liverpool City Council* [1982] AC 363; *Re B (Minors) (Care: Contact: Local Authority's Plans)* (above); and *Kent County Council v C* [1983] 1 FLR 308. However, when it makes an *interim* care or supervision order it may give directions as to the medical or psychiatric examination or other assessment of the child: s. 38(6). For example, in *Re O (Minors) (Medical Examination)* [1993] 1 FLR 860 the family proceedings court made an interim care order and directed under s. 38(6) that the children be tested to determine whether or not they were HIV positive. Furthermore, in *Berkshire County Council v C* [1993] 1 FLR 569 the family proceedings court made an interim care order, directed the local authority to arrange for the child to be assessed by a social worker and further directed that the assessment was to commence on or before a specific date. The court had power to make a mandatory direction of this type, even after being told by the local authority that such a worker would not be available for some time due to lack of resources, because the court had taken proper account of the practical consequences for the local authority of such a direction and because on the facts of the case the decision was plainly right. **33.132**

What is directed under s. 38(6) must clearly be an examination or assessment of the child, including, where appropriate, his relationship with his parents, the risk that they may present to him and the ways in which those risks may be avoided or managed. Any services which are provided for the child and his family must be ancillary to that aim. They must not be an end in themselves (*Re G (Interim Care Order: Residential Assessment)* [2006] 1 FLR 601—the court had no power to make an order the main purpose of which was to provide a continuing course of psychotherapy to the mother with a view to giving her the opportunity to change sufficiently to become a safe carer for the child). **33.133**

A direction can be to the effect that no medical or psychiatric examination or other assessment of the child is to take place: s. 38(7). If the child is of sufficient understanding to make an informed decision he may refuse to submit to such an examination or assessment: s. 38(6). **33.134**

33.135   A direction may be varied at any time on the application of a qualified applicant: s. 38(8) and r. 4.2(1), FPR 1991 and FPC(CA 1989)R 1991, r. 2(1). A direction made under s. 38(6) can be appealed: *Re O (Minors) (Medical Examination)* (above).

Exclusion requirements in interim care orders

33.136   Where the court decides to make an interim care order it may safeguard the child by including in the order a provision excluding from the home the 'relevant person' who is putting the child at risk: s. 38A.

33.137   **Meaning of 'exclusion requirement'**   An exclusion requirement is any one or more of the following provisions (s. 38A(3)):

(a)   that the relevant person must leave a dwelling-house in which he is living with the child;

(b)   that the relevant person is prohibited from entering a dwelling-house in which the child lives;

(c)   that the relevant person is excluded from a defined area in which a dwelling-house in which the child lives is situated.

33.138   **Conditions to be met for exclusion requirement**   Section 38A(1), CA 1989, provides that the court may include an exclusion requirement in an interim care order:

(a)   on being satisfied that there are reasonable grounds for believing that the circumstances with respect to a child are as mentioned in s. 31(2)(a) and (b)(i); and

(b)   the conditions in s. 38A(2) are satisfied.

It is important to note that the ground contained in s. 31(2)(b)(ii), which enables a court to make a care or supervision order where a child is beyond parental control, is not mentioned in limb (a) above, and therefore it would not be possible to include an exclusion requirement in an interim care order which was made on that ground only. Furthermore, the court must have actually decided to make an interim care order before considering the need for an exclusion requirement.

33.139   The conditions laid down in s. 38A(2), which must be met before an exclusion requirement can be made, are that:

(a)   there is reasonable cause to believe that if the relevant person is excluded from the child's home then the child will cease to suffer, or cease to be likely to suffer, significant harm, and

(b)   another person living in the same house (whether or not he or she is a parent of the child):

    (i)   is able and willing to give the child the care which it would be reasonable to expect a parent to give him, and

    (ii)   consents to the inclusion of the exclusion requirement.

33.140   **Duration of exclusion requirement**   The court can provide that the exclusion requirement itself is to have effect for a shorter period than the other provisions in the interim care order: s. 38A(4). However, the court has power on an application to vary or discharge the interim care order to extend the period specified for the exclusion requirement if it thinks fit: s. 38A(7). The exclusion requirement automatically ceases to have effect if the local authority removes the child from the home to other accommodation for a continuous period of more than 24 hours: s. 38A(10).

Power of arrest attached to exclusion requirement The court can attach a power of arrest to the exclusion requirement, and where it does so it may provide that the power of arrest is to have effect for a shorter period than the exclusion requirement: s. 38A(5), (6). Where a power of arrest is attached, a constable may arrest without warrant anyone whom he has reasonable cause to believe to be in breach of the requirement. **33.141**

The court has power on an application to vary or discharge the interim care order to extend the period so specified for the power of arrest if it thinks fit: s. 38A(7). **33.142**

The power of arrest may be varied or discharged on the application of the 'relevant person' excluded by the requirement, any person with parental responsibility for the child, the child himself, or the designated local authority: s. 39(3B). **33.143**

Discharge, extension, and variation of exclusion requirement The drafting of s. 39 does not say clearly who is entitled to apply for the discharge or variation of an exclusion requirement. The section seems to draw a distinction between (a) discharge, and (b) variation of exclusion requirements. It would appear that three categories of people may apply for discharge of the requirement: a person with parental responsibility; the child himself; the designated local authority: s. 39(1). It is not clear whether those three categories of people may also apply for the variation of the requirement. **33.144**

The 'relevant person' to whom the exclusion requirement applies specifically has the right to apply for the variation of the interim care order in so far as it imposes the exclusion requirement: s. 39(3A), CA 1989. On such an application the court has the power to vary or discharge the order in so far as it imposes the exclusion requirement. **33.145**

The application to discharge would be made to the court which made the order incorporating the exclusion requirement or to the court to which the case had been transferred. **33.146**

Procedure The procedure to be adopted in relation to cases involving exclusion requirements is to be found in r. 4.24A, FPR 1991 (for the High Court and county courts) and r. 25A, FPC(CA 1989)R 1991 (for the family proceedings court). **33.147**

The principal points to note are as follows: **33.148**

(a) Where the applicant seeks the inclusion of the exclusion requirement, she is required to prepare a separate statement of evidence in support of such application and to serve this together with a copy of the order containing the exclusion requirement on the person in respect of whom the exclusion requirement has been made: r. 2.
(b) Where the court includes the exclusion requirement in an order of its own motion, there is no requirement for the applicant to produce a statement of evidence in support: r. 4.

Final orders Exclusion requirements cannot be attached to final care orders. The expectation is that the proposed carer should in the meantime have taken steps to exclude the abuser in the long term, and if the carer has not been able to do this then she should not expect the court or the local authority to do it for her. **33.149**

Undertakings relating to interim care orders

33.150 Wherever a court has power under s. 38A, CA 1989, to include an exclusion require-ment in an interim care order the court may instead accept an undertaking from the relevant person (s. 38B). The undertaking would normally be to leave the property within a specified time, although it could contain other terms. However, the court cannot attach a power of arrest to any such undertaking: s. 38B(2). Where an undertaking is given to the court then:

(a) it will be enforceable as if it were an order of the court (s. 38B(3)(a)), and

(b) it will cease to have effect if, while it is in force, the local authority removes the child from the house from which the relevant person is excluded to other accommodation for a continuous period of more than two hours (s. 38B(3)(b)).

Discharge of care orders

33.151 A care order, other than an interim care order, will remain in force until the child reaches 18 unless determined earlier: s. 91(12). The other ways in which it might be terminated or discharged are as follows:

(a) when the court makes a residence order in respect of a child in care the care order will be discharged automatically: s. 91(1);

(b) when the court makes an adoption order the care order will be discharged automatically: s. 46(2), ACA 2002;

(c) when a successful application is made under s. 39(1) to discharge the order. Such an application may be made by:

(i) any person with parental responsibility for the child; or

(ii) the child; or

(iii) the relevant local authority.

33.152 A child does *not* require leave to make an application to discharge a care order: *Re A (Care Order: Discharge Application by Child)* [1995] 1 FLR 599. When the court considers whether or not to discharge a care order it simply applies the welfare criteria set out in s. 1, CA 1989. There are no additional criteria to be considered as there are when the court considers whether or not to *make* a care order.

33.153 Upon an application to discharge a care order the court can consider an application to substitute the care order with a supervision order (s. 39(4)). When it considers such an application the court is relieved of the exercise of deciding whether or not the s. 31(2) grounds are made out: s. 39(5).

33.154 When an unsuccessful application has been made for the discharge of a care order or for its substitution with a supervision order, then no repeat applications may be made for a period of six months following that disposal of the matter, except with the leave of the court: s. 91(15).

Supervision orders

33.155 Up until now only passing mention has been made of supervision orders. It is now proposed to examine them in more detail.

When may a supervision order be made?

The court may make an order placing a child under the supervision of a local authority or a **33.156**
probation officer pursuant to s. 31(1) provided that:

(a) the court is satisfied that the statutory grounds in s. 31(2) are made out in relation to the
     child concerned; and
(b) the making of the supervision order is for the welfare of the child: s. 1.

Many of the rules relating to care orders apply equally to supervision orders: **33.157**

(a) an application can only be made if the child is under 17 (or under 16, if married):
     s. 31(3);
(b) any delay in the determination of the application will be presumed to prejudice the
     welfare of the child, and therefore a timetable should be drawn up for the speedy disposal
     of the proceedings: s. 32;
(c) the court may take the initiative and direct the local authority to investigate the
     circumstances of the child pursuant to s. 37(1), CA 1989, in order that the authority
     might decide whether or not to make an application for a supervision (or care) order;
(d) interim supervision orders may be made on the same principles as interim care orders
     (see paragraph 33.125 above);
(e) the provisions relating to children's guardians apply equally to proceedings for a
     supervision order as they do to care order proceedings: s. 41(1);
(f) the same rules apply to the variation and discharge of supervision orders as for care
     orders (s. 39 and see paragraph 33.151 above).

When deciding whether to make a care order or a supervision order in a case where the **33.158**
balance between the two is equal, the court should take the least interventionist approach:
Re D (Care Order or Supervision Order) [2000] Fam Law 600. The court should ask itself whether:

(a) the stronger order is needed to protect the child;
(b) the risks could be met by a supervision order;
(c) there is a need for the speed of action that a care order allows the local authority;
(d) the parent could properly protect the child without sharing parental responsibility with
     the local authority;
(e) parental co-operation could only be obtained through the more draconian care order;
(f) the child's needs could be met by advising, assisting, and befriending the child rather
     than by sharing parental responsibility for him;
(g) there have been any improvements seen by objective observers during the current
     proceedings which would indicate the future; and
(h) consider the range of powers available under a supervision order, including its duration.

The choice between a care order and a supervision order has to be considered in the
context of the HRA 1998 and the European Convention for the Protection of Human Rights
and Fundamental Freedoms 1950. In each case, a court must decide whether the making
of a supervision order is a proportionate response to the risk presented: *Re O (Supervision
Order)* [2001] 1 FLR 923; *Re C (Care Order or Supervision Order)* [2001] 2 FLR 466. For a
more detailed comparison between care orders and supervision orders see paragraph 33.167
below.

Effect of supervision order

33.159 (a) The supervising officer does not acquire parental responsibility for the child.

(b) The supervisor's duties are set out in s. 35(1). His main duties are to advise, assist, and befriend the supervised child and to take such steps as are reasonably necessary to give effect to the order. Where the supervision order is not wholly complied with or the supervisor considers that it may no longer be necessary then he may consider whether or not to apply to the court for the variation or discharge of the order (s. 35(1)(c)): see *Re V (Care or Supervision Order)* [1996] 1 FLR 776).

(c) The making of a supervision order brings to an end any earlier care or supervision order made in respect of that child which would otherwise continue in force: sch. 3, para. 10, CA 1989.

Duration of supervision order

33.160 A supervision order will last for an initial period of one year, but the supervisor may apply to the court to have it extended for a period of up to three years beginning with the date on which the order was first made (sch. 3, para. 6, CA 1989). If the authority takes the view, towards the end of the three year period, that the supervision order is still necessary then it will have to apply to the court again and prove that the s. 31(2) grounds are still in existence.

Power to give directions to supervised child

33.161 A supervision order may (pursuant to sch. 3, para. 2, CA 1989) require the supervised child to comply with directions given by the supervisor to:

(a) live at a particular place for a particular period of time;

(b) present himself to specified persons at specified times and places;

(c) participate in specified activities at specified times.

Although the court has power to give directions to a supervised child, for example, that the child should comply with directions given by the supervisor as to his place of residence, the supervising authority has no way in which to enforce the order. If the child refused to comply, then the local authority would have to bring the matter back to court under s. 35, CA 1989, or apply to the court for a variation of the supervision order: *Re R and G (Minors) (Interim Care or Supervision Orders)* [1994] 1 FLR 793.

33.162 The supervisor has no power to give directions in respect of any medical or psychiatric treatment for the child: sch. 3, para. 2(3). Such directions can only be given by the court: sch. 3, para. 4 and see paragraph 33.166 below.

Imposition of obligations on responsible persons

33.163 The Children Act 1989 enables obligations to be imposed upon 'responsible persons' (sch. 3, para. 1), provided that the person concerned *consents* to those obligations.

33.164 A 'responsible person' in relation to a supervised child means:

(a) any person with parental responsibility for the child; and

(b) any other person with whom the child is living (e.g., step-parents).

The obligations can be to take all reasonable steps to:

(a)   ensure that the child complies with his supervisor's directions; and

(b)   ensure that the child complies with any requirements in the supervision order, for example, to attend for medical and psychiatric treatment.

The parent can apply to the court to have any requirement affecting him varied: s. 39(2) and (3).

Psychiatric and medical examination

A supervision order may require a child to submit to a medical or psychiatric examination, or to do so from time to time as directed by his supervisor, provided that: **33.165**

(a)   the child *consents* to it (where he is of sufficient understanding to make an informed decision): sch. 3, para. 4(4)(a); and

(b)   satisfactory arrangements have been made for the examination: sch. 3, para. 4(4)(b); and

(c)   the order must require that the examination be conducted by a specified medical practitioner at a specific place: sch. 3, para. 4(2).

In *Note: Re HIV Tests* [1994] 2 FLR 116, Singer J directed that any application to submit a child to a blood test where it appeared that the child might be HIV positive should be made only to a High Court judge in the Family Division, whether in public law or private law proceedings.

Psychiatric and medical treatment

When a court makes or varies a supervision order it may include a requirement that the child shall submit to psychiatric or medical treatment by a registered medical practitioner at a specific place: sch. 3, para. 5. Before including such a requirement the court must be satisfied: **33.166**

(a)   on the evidence of an appropriate medical practitioner that the treatment is justified; and

(b)   that the child consents to it (where he is of sufficient understanding to make an informed decision); and

(c)   that satisfactory arrangements have been made for the treatment.

The medical practitioner may seek a variation of the requirement (for example, where he feels that the treatment should continue for longer than the specified period) by submitting a written report to the supervisor to that effect. Thereupon, the supervisor must refer the report to the court and the court can make an order cancelling or varying the requirement: sch. 3, para. 5(7).

Comparison between care orders and supervision orders

A very useful summary of the differences between care orders and supervision orders is to be found in *Re S (J) (A Minor) (Care or Supervision Order)* [1993] 2 FLR 919, as follows: **33.167**

(a)   When deciding whether to make a care order or a supervision order the court needs to be clear as to what the future risks are. This requires a careful scrutiny of what has happened in the past so that a view of the future risks can be formed.

(b)   A supervision order is capable of providing a great deal of protection. It can guarantee access into the child's home, supported by a warrant under s. 102, CA 1989 if necessary.

There can be a care plan. An emergency protection order is available if there is a need to remove the child in an emergency. The child can be kept on the 'at risk' register so that the local authority is required to conduct periodic reviews.

(c) The concept of parental responsibility is at the heart of the difference between a care order and a supervision order. A care order means that a local authority can take over virtually all the parental responsibility functions if satisfied that it was necessary to do so in order to safeguard or promote the child's welfare. A supervision order does not deprive the parents of parental responsibility and does not endow the local authority with parental responsibility. Section 34 enables the local authority to control contact between the child and other people where a care order has been made.

(d) When a care order is made then a duty is imposed upon the local authority under s. 22 to safeguard the welfare of the child. A supervision order carries with it no such duty, and the obligation to keep the child safe remains with the parent who has parental responsibility.

(e) Under a supervision order the supervisor has a duty under s. 35 to advise and assist the supervised child, but not the parent.

(f) A care order places a local authority in a better position to enforce its requirements than a supervision order. For example, it has power to remove the child when it is no longer considered to be safe. Under a supervision order, information and access must be given to the supervisor, which can be enforced by a warrant under s. 102, CA 1989; that is the only part of the arrangement which is given any specific sanction. Thus, where a grave risk exists in relation to a child the court should make a care order.

(g) The court must look at the case as a whole and determine its views as to the risk of both physical and emotional harm to the child, and then decide whether, in the light of the gravity of the case, the local authority ought to have extra duties imposed on it.

33.168 In *Re D (A Minor) (Care or Supervision Order)* [1993] 2 FLR 423 there had been a history of non-accidental injury to children, culminating in the death of a child whilst in the care of the father who was subsequently imprisoned for cruelty offences. The court held that a care order rather than a supervision order should be made in relation to a child born to the father's new partner. The protection of the child was the decisive factor and it overrode the local authority's view that a supervision order would have been adequate because the child was thriving and a care order would undermine the co-operation of the parents with social services.

Care and supervision orders at the instigation of the court

33.169 It may happen that whilst the court is engaged in hearing family proceedings (for example, an application for a s. 8 order), it becomes apparent that a care or supervision order may be necessary. In those circumstances the court may direct the local authority, pursuant to s. 37(1), to investigate the circumstances of the child. Thereupon, the court will normally adjourn the matter in hand (and perhaps make an interim care or supervision order in the meantime: see paragraph 33.125 above) while the authority conducts its investigation and compiles a report.

33.170 If the authority, in due course, decides *not* to apply for a care or supervision order it must inform the court of the reasons for that decision. It must also tell the court of any services or assistance it has provided, or intends to provide, for the child and his family, and of any other action it has taken, or will take: s. 37(3). Furthermore, it must consider whether it would be appropriate to review the case at a later date: s. 37(6).

It cannot be stressed too often that the court no longer has any power to order a child to **33.171** be received into the care of, or place him under the supervision of, a local authority unless the authority concerned has made an express application (see the concern expressed about the court's lack of power in this respect in *Nottinghamshire County Council* v *P* [1993] 2 FLR 134).

D PUBLIC FUNDING

The availability of public funding for CA 1989 proceedings under the Community Legal **33.172** Service scheme is dealt with fully in paragraph 2.55. The practitioner will remember that whereas, for most private law children cases (under Parts I to III, CA 1989) the applicant will be required to attend a meeting with a mediator to determine whether the case is suitable for mediation before any public funding may be made available for representation, there is no such requirement to attend a meeting with a mediator for public law children cases (under Parts IV and V, CA 1989).

E APPEALS

The question of appeals is dealt with fully in paragraph 30.92. However, there are certain **33.173** cases relating to appeals in public law proceedings which are important.

(a) The family proceedings court has no inherent power to grant a stay of execution pending an appeal to the High Court. If an appeal is being considered against a care order and a stay is required then the proper course is immediately to apply to the High Court: *Re O (A Minor) (Care Order: Education: Procedure)* [1992] 2 FLR 7.

(b) On an appeal to the High Court from a decision of the family proceedings court dismissing an application for a care order, the High Court has no jurisdiction under s. 40(1), CA 1989, to make a care order pending the appeal, but it can make an interim care order under s. 38: *Croydon London Borough Council v A (No. 2) (Note)* [1992] 2 FLR 348.

(c) When an appeal court is considering whether or not to give leave for fresh evidence to be adduced at the appeal hearing the question to be asked is: does the evidence lead to a different conclusion from that which would otherwise prevail, i.e., does it throw a different light on the matter? The court must act cautiously in relation to the new evidence since it cannot test the evidence: *Hounslow London Borough Council v A* [1993] 1 FLR 702.

(d) Appeals in cases where an interim care order has been granted ought not to be made unless there are the very strongest grounds for interfering with the interim order: *Re M (Minors) (Interim Care Order)* [1993] 2 FLR 406.

(e)   In *Re M (A Minor) (Appeal: Interim Order) (No. 1)* [1994] 1 FLR 54 the judge refused an application for a care order. The local authority appealed and the judge made an interim care order pending the hearing of the appeal. The Court of Appeal held that it was better that the interim care order should be extended so that the child remained where she was until the appeal hearing. It was not the job of the court to prejudge what the Court of Appeal would do, other than in cases which were hopeless.

(f)   Note that s. 55, Access to Justice Act 1999, restricts the right to more than one appeal in most civil cases. Section 55(1) provides that where an appeal is made to a county court or the High Court in relation to any matter, and on hearing the appeal the court makes a decision in relation to that matter, no appeal may be made to the Court of Appeal from that decision unless the Court of Appeal considers that:

(i)   the appeal would raise an important point of principle or practice; or

(ii) there is some other compelling reason for the Court of Appeal to hear it.

F   KEY DOCUMENTS

33.174   The Children Act 1989
The Human Rights Act 1998
The Adoption and Children Act 2002
The European Convention for Human Rights and Fundamental Freedoms 1950
The Public Law Protocol
CAFCASS Practice Note 'Cases Referred by Independent Reviewing Officers' dated 8 June 2004 and
available at <www.dca.gov.uk>

34

EMERGENCY PROTECTION OF CHILDREN

A INTRODUCTION

Part V of the Children Act 1989 ('CA 1989') contains a code for the protection of children. It **34.01**
aims to ensure that proper protective action can be taken in respect of children whilst

providing proper procedures to enable parents and others connected with the child to challenge such action before the court. Whenever a local authority applies for a care or supervision order the procedure to be followed will be regulated by the public law protocol which is discussed in detail in paragraph 33.32. The main orders available under the statutory scheme are as follows:

(a) Local authorities are placed under a positive duty to investigate cases of suspected child abuse and to decide upon the appropriate action to take: s. 47 and sch. 2, para. 4.

(b) If parents refuse to co-operate with the local authority's assessment of a child whom it has reasonable cause to suspect is suffering, or is likely to suffer, significant harm then a 'child assessment order' is available to enable the authority to complete its inquiries: s. 43.

(c) The CA 1989 introduced 'emergency protection orders' to provide for the emergency protection of children. The grounds upon which they may be granted are tightly defined. Parents and others can challenge the making of an emergency protection order if they are present at the hearing; if they are not, then they can seek a discharge of the order from the court after 72 hours: ss. 44 and 45.

(d) 'Police protection': powers are available to enable the police to detain a child for the purpose of protecting him: s. 46.

(e) 'Recovery orders' are available to facilitate the recovery of children who have been abducted while the subject of a care, emergency protection, or recovery order: s. 50.

B   CHILD ASSESSMENT ORDERS

34.02   The 'halfway house' of a child assessment order is available to cover the situation where the local authority suspects that the child may be at risk of significant harm, but not at immediate risk requiring his removal or detention (e.g., in a hospital) under an emergency protection order, and his parents or others responsible for him refuse to co-operate with the authority's attempts to make an assessment of the child: s. 43. The order aims to allow the authority to complete its assessment so that it can decide whether or not to take further action in respect of the child. Where the court hears an application for a child assessment order it may, instead, make an emergency protection order if it is satisfied that the circumstances of the case warrant it: s. 43(4).

The application

34.03   Only a local authority or 'authorized person' may apply for a child assessment order. The court may only make an order if, but only if, it is satisfied that:

(a) the applicant has reasonable cause to suspect that the child is suffering, or is likely to suffer, significant harm;

(b) an assessment of the state of the child's health or development, or of the way in which he is being treated, is required to enable the applicant to establish whether or not the child is suffering, or is likely to suffer, significant harm; and

(c) it is unlikely that the assessment will be made, or be satisfactory, without a child assessment order.

Before making a child assessment order the court must also have regard to the 'welfare' and 'presumption of no order' principles set out in s. 1, CA 1989 (see paragraph 29.05 onwards).

The application should always be made on notice at a full hearing in which the parties are able to participate, so that it can be challenged at that stage. The implementation of the Human Rights Act 1998, incorporating the European Convention on Human Rights and Fundamental Freedoms 1950 into domestic law, means that certain aspects of the law and procedure relating to emergency protection orders (EPOs) may be the subject of a challenge. Article 6 of the Convention guarantees a right to a fair trial; this implies a right to give evidence. In the past applications for EPOs have frequently been made without notice to the parents of the child concerned and consequently without the right of the parents or others affected by the order to give oral evidence and without the right for them to appear in person (i.e., on an *ex parte* basis). As a result of concerns about the draconian nature of EPOs, the court has given guidance in *X Council v B (Emergency Protection Orders)* [2005] 1 FLR 341 as to the way in which such applications should be approached. The court held that there are unusual and exceptional cases (of which this was an example) in which an *ex parte* application is appropriate, but adequate evidence must be presented and a proper note of the hearing prepared by the local authority and made available to the parents. In all such cases: (1) the summary removal of a child from his parents requires exceptional justification and proof of imminent danger; (2) no EPO should be longer than absolutely necessary to protect the child; (3) supporting evidence must be full and compelling; (4) less drastic alternatives must be considered; and, (5) where an EPO is made, arrangements for reasonable contact under, s. 44(13), CA 1989 must be driven by the needs of the family and not be stunted by lack of resources. **34.04**

The court has power to prevent a further application being made by particular persons (including a local authority) without the court's leave, or to refuse to allow a further application within six months without leave: s. 91(14) and (15). **34.05**

Parties

An application can be made in respect of a child under the age of 18 (N.B. it is not subject to the age 17 limit applicable to care and supervision orders.) Those who must be respondents to child assessment order proceedings and those who must be notified of the proceedings are set out in Appendix 3, Family Proceedings Rule 1991 ('FPR 1991') and sch. 2, Family Proceedings Courts (Children Act 1989) Rules 1991 ('FPC(CA 1989)R 1991'). **34.06**

The persons who must be made respondents are: **34.07**

(a) every person the applicant believes to have parental responsibility for the child;
(b) where the child is the subject of a care order, every person the applicant believes to have had parental responsibility immediately prior to the making of the care order;
(c) where the application is to extend, vary or discharge an order, the parties to the original proceedings when the order was made;
(d) the child;
(e) any other person *may* be made a respondent, provided that he has first obtained leave of the court: r. 4.7, FPR 1991 and r. 7, FPC(CA 1989)R 1991.

Commencement and duration

34.08   The court may allow up to a maximum of seven days for the assessment, and the order must specify the date by which the assessment is to begin: s. 43(5).

Effect of child assessment order

34.09   The main effects of a child assessment order are as follows:

(a)   Parental responsibility does not vest in the applicant by virtue of an order being made.

(b)   The order requires the person in a position to do so to produce the child to the person named in the order so that the assessment may take place, and requires him to comply with any other directions contained in the order: s. 43(6).

(c)   The order authorizes the carrying out of the assessment in accordance with the terms of the order: s. 43(7).

(d)   The child to whom the order relates may refuse to consent to the assessment if he is of sufficient understanding to make an informed decision: s. 43(8).

(e)   Child assessment orders may run alongside s. 8 orders (but will not be required where a care, supervision, or emergency protection order is in force).

Directions

34.10   The court is empowered to attach directions to the child assessment order. For example, the court may wish to limit the extent of the assessment to a medical examination; it may wish to direct that a particular medical practitioner conduct the examination; it may wish to direct that specific persons be present during an examination and so forth. Furthermore, where it is necessary for the child to be kept away from home for the purposes of the assessment (e.g., in hospital), then tight conditions are imposed as to the circumstances in which this may be done and provision is made for contact between the child and persons connected with him during that time: s. 43(9) and (10).

Variation and discharge of child assessment orders

34.11   Provision is made for an application to the court for a child assessment order to be varied or discharged: see s. 43(12). Those who may apply include:

(a)   the child;

(b)   his parents;

(c)   any other person with parental responsibility for him;

(d)   any other person caring for him;

(e)   any person in whose favour a contact order is in force with respect to the child;

(f)   any person allowed to have contact with the child under a s. 34 contact order.

The circumstances in which such an application may be made, and additionally qualified applicants, are prescribed by rules of court: see rr. 4.1(2)(c), and 4.2(3); FPR 1991 r. 2(3), FPC(CA 1989)R 1991.

Appeals

The provisions for appealing from a child assessment order are the same as those for appeal- **34.12**
ing any order made under the CA 1989 (see paragraph 30.92).

C EMERGENCY PROTECTION ORDERS

Who may apply—and on what grounds?

There are three categories of applicants and different grounds apply to each category: **34.13**

(a) 'Any person' may apply for an emergency protection order under s. 44(1)(a). The court
    may only grant the order under this ground if it is satisfied that there is reasonable cause
    to believe that the child is likely to suffer significant harm if either:
    (i) he is not removed to accommodation provided by or on behalf of the applicant; or
    (ii) he does not remain in the place where he is then being accommodated.
(b) A local authority may apply on the ground set out in (a) above *or* it may, instead, rely on
    the ground set out in s. 44(1)(b), that is to say:
    (i) inquiries are being made with respect to the child under s. 47(1)(b); and
    (ii) those inquiries are being frustrated by access to the child being unreasonably
         refused to a person authorized to seek access *and* that the applicant has reasonable
         cause to believe that access to the child is required as a matter of *urgency*.
(c) An 'authorized person' (the meaning of which is the same as for the purposes of s. 31,
    i.e., at the moment only the NSPCC has this status) may apply on the ground set out in
    s. 44(1)(c) if he can show that:
    (i)   he has reasonable cause to believe that a child is suffering, or is likely to suffer,
          significant harm;
    (ii) he is making inquiries with respect to the child's welfare; and
    (iii) those inquiries are being frustrated by access to the child being unreasonably
          refused to a person authorized to seek access *and* the applicant has reasonable cause
          to believe that access to the child is required as a matter of *urgency*.

'Harm' and 'significant harm' are defined in s. 31(9) and (10) and have already been discussed in paragraph 33.57. Note that the meaning of harm has been extended to include, for
example, impairment suffered by hearing or seeing the ill-treatment of another.

A 'person authorized to seek access' is defined in s. 44(2)(b) as: **34.14**

(a) in the case of a local authority—an officer of the authority or a person authorized by it
    to act on its behalf in connection with its inquiries;
(b) in the case of an 'authorized person' that person.

Effects of an emergency protection order

The effects of an emergency protection order are as follows: **34.15**

(a) The court can direct any person who is in a position to do so to comply with any request
    to produce the child to the applicant: s. 44(4)(a).

(b) The court can authorize:

    (i) the removal of the child at any time to accommodation provided by or on behalf of the applicant; or

    (ii) the prevention of the child's removal from any hospital, or other place, in which he was being accommodated immediately before the making of the order: s. 44(4)(b).

(c) The emergency protection order gives the applicant parental responsibility for the child for the duration of the order: s. 44(4)(c). However, the applicant should only take such action in meeting his parental responsibility as is reasonably required to safeguard or promote the welfare of the child (having particular regard to the duration of the order): s. 44(5).

(d) The court has power under s. 44(6) to make directions as to:

    (i) the contact which is, or is not, to be allowed between the child and any named person; and

    (ii) the medical, psychiatric, or other assessment of the child.

Duration of emergency protection order

34.16 An EPO may have effect in the first instance for a maximum of eight days: s. 45(1). The court may extend the order once only for a period of up to seven days (s. 45(6)), but *only* if the applicant has parental responsibility for the child as a result of the emergency protection order *and* is entitled to apply for a care order with respect to the child (i.e., only local authorities and the NSPCC at the moment). The extension should only be granted if the court has reasonable cause to believe that the child is likely to suffer significant harm if the order is not extended: s. 45(4), (5), and (6).

Who should be informed?

34.17 Appendix 3, FPR 1991 and sch. 2, FPC(CA 1989)R 1991 set out those persons who should be informed of an application for an emergency protection order.

Parental contact

34.18 The court may give directions as to the contact which is, or is not, to be allowed between the child and any named person: s. 44(6)(a).

34.19 Furthermore, the applicant is under a duty, while the emergency protection order is in force, to allow the child reasonable contact (subject to any direction of the court under s. 44(6)) with the following persons (s. 44(13)):

(a) his parents;

(b) any person who is not a parent but has parental responsibility for him;

(c) any person with whom he was living immediately before the making of the order;

(d) any person in whose favour a contact order is in force with respect to him;

(e) any person who is allowed to have contact with the child by virtue of an order under s. 34; and

(f) any person acting on behalf of any of those persons.

The contact provisions may not be challenged (s. 45(10)).

Challenging an emergency protection order

An emergency protection order may be challenged by any of the following persons (s. 45(8)): **34.20**

(a) the child;

(b) any parent of his;

(c) any person who is not a parent of his but who has parental responsibility for him;

(d) any person with whom he was living immediately before the making of the order.

Any application for the order to be discharged, may only be made after a period of 72 hours **34.21** has expired. The 72 hours are calculated from the time when the order was made: s. 45(9). The right of challenge is not available where the prospective challenger was given notice of the hearing at which the order was made and was present at that hearing (or at a hearing as a result of which the period of the order was extended): s. 45(11). The reason for this is that no challenge should be allowed if it could have been made at the time of the application for the order.

There is no right to appeal against the making of, or refusal to make, an emergency protec- **34.22** tion order, or against any direction given by the court in connection with such an order: s. 45(10) and *Essex County Council* v *F* [1993] 1 FLR 847. If the magistrates act unreasonably in connection with such proceedings then the only available remedy would appear to be judicial review: *Re P (Emergency Protection Order)* [1996] 1 FLR 482. In the future it is possible that this area of the law will be the subject of challenge under the HRA 1998. See the comments made in paragraph 34.04 (above).

Returning the child

The applicant has a duty to return the child if it appears to him that it is safe for the child to **34.23** be returned or that it is safe for the child to be allowed to be removed from the place in question: s. 44(10) and (11). However, the applicant may remove the child again under the same order, provided that the order remains in force and it appears to him that a change in the circumstances of the case makes it necessary for him to do so: s. 44(10) and (12).

Exclusion requirements in emergency protection orders

The court may include an exclusion requirement in an emergency protection order in cer- **34.24** tain circumstances. To a large extent the same rules apply as when the court includes an exclusion requirement in an interim care order, including the rules relating to the attachment of a power of arrest and the acceptance by the court of undertakings. Those rules are set out in paragraph 33.136 onwards. There are, however, some differences in the conditions which must be met before the court can include an exclusion requirement in an emergency protection order. The relevant conditions are that:

(a) there is reasonable cause to believe that if a person ('the relevant person') is excluded from a dwelling-house in which the child lives—

   (i) in the case of an order based on s. 44(1)(a), the child will not be likely to suffer significant harm, even though the child is not removed or, as the case may be, does not remain, or

    (ii) in the case of an order based on s. 44(1)(b) or (c), the inquiries will cease to be frustrated; and

(b) another person living in the dwelling-house (whether or not a parent of the child)—

    (i) is able and willing to give the child the care which it would be reasonable to expect a parent to give him, and

    (ii) consents to the inclusion of the exclusion requirement.

Otherwise, ss. 44A, 44B, and 45(8A) and (8B) contain provisions identical (*mutatis mutandis*) to those set out in paragraph 33.136, in respect of exclusion requirements included in an interim care order.

D POLICE PROTECTION

34.25   The police have important powers under s. 46, CA 1989. Where a constable has reasonable cause to believe that a child would otherwise be likely to suffer significant harm, he may:

(a) remove the child to suitable accommodation and keep him there; or

(b) take reasonable steps to prevent the removal of the child from any hospital, or other place, in which he is then being accommodated.

34.26   The s. 46 power to remove a child can be exercised even where an emergency protection order (EPO) is in force in respect of the child. However, where a police officer knows that an EPO is in force he should not exercise the s. 46 power unless there are compelling reasons to do so (*Langley v Liverpool City Council* [2006] 1 FLR 342).

Duration of police protection

34.27   A child may not be kept in police protection for a period of more than 72 hours: s. 46(6). As soon as practicable after taking the child into police protection the constable must ensure that the appropriate inquiries into the case are undertaken by the police officer designated for this purpose. After completing his inquiries the designated officer must release the child unless there is still reasonable cause to believe that the child would be likely to suffer significant harm if released: s. 46(3)(e) and (5). The constable who initially took the child into police protection has a duty to inform various persons, including the local authority, the child, the child's parents, and persons with parental responsibility for the child, of, amongst other things, the steps that have been taken and the reasons for them. The full extent of those duties are set out in s. 46(3) and (4).

Parental responsibility

34.28   Neither the constable concerned nor the designated officer acquire parental responsibility for the child whilst he is in police protection. However, the designated officer must do what is reasonable to promote the child's welfare, bearing in mind the short duration of the period of police protection: s. 46(9) and s. 3(5).

Contact with the child

The designated officer must allow the following persons to have contact with the child **34.29** during the period of police protection, provided that *in his opinion* it is both reasonable and in the child's best interests:

(a) the child's parents;

(b) anyone else who has parental responsibility for the child;

(c) anyone with whom the child was living immediately before he was taken into police protection;

(d) a person who has a contact order in his favour relating to the child;

(e) anyone acting on behalf of the persons listed in (a) to (d) above: s. 46(10).

E   RECOVERY ORDERS

A court may make a 'recovery order' in respect of a child, pursuant to s. 50, CA 1989, **34.30** where:

(a) the child is in care, in police protection or is the subject of an emergency protection order: ss. 50(2) and 49(2); and

(b) there is reason to believe that the child:

   (i)   has been unlawfully taken away, or is being unlawfully kept away from the 'responsible person'; or

   (ii) has run away or is staying away from the 'responsible person'; or

   (iii) is missing.

Who can apply?

The court may make a recovery order only on the application of the following persons: **34.31**

(a) a person with parental responsibility for the child by virtue of a care order or emergency protection order; or

(b) where the child is in police protection, the designated officer: s. 50(4).

Effect of recovery order

A recovery order will have the following effects: s. 50(3): **34.32**

(a) it operates as a direction to any person who is in position to do so to produce the child on request to any authorized person;

(b) it authorizes the removal of the child by any authorized person;

(c) it requires any person who has information as to the child's whereabouts to disclose that information, if asked to do so, to a constable or an officer of the court;

(d) it authorizes a constable to enter any premises specified in the order and search for the child, using reasonable force if necessary.

F   KEY DOCUMENTS

34.33   Children Act 1989
Family Proceedings Rules 1991
Family Proceedings Court (Children Act 1989) Rules 1991

PART VIII

FINANCIAL PROVISION AND PROPERTY DURING MARRIAGE

35

SECTION 27, MATRIMONIAL CAUSES ACT 1973

A   GROUNDS FOR APPLICATION

Section 27, Matrimonial Causes Act 1973 ('MCA 1973') provides that applications may be   **35.01**
made for maintenance and/or lump sum orders by either party to a marriage (the applicant)
on the grounds that the other party (the respondent) either:

(a)   has failed to provide reasonable maintenance for the applicant; *or*

(b)   has failed to provide, or to make proper contribution towards, reasonable maintenance
   for any child of the family: s. 27(1).

B   JURISDICTION

35.02   The court has jurisdiction under s. 27 if:

(a)   the applicant or respondent is domiciled in England and Wales at the date of the application; *or*

(b)   the applicant has been habitually resident in England and Wales throughout the year ending with the date of the application; *or*

(c)   the respondent is resident in England and Wales on the date of the application: s. 27(2).

(See Chapter 6 for the meaning of domicile, habitual residence, etc.)

C   ORDERS THAT CAN BE MADE

General

35.03   The court can make one or more of the following orders:

(a)   an order that the respondent shall make periodical payments or secured periodical payments to the applicant;

(b)   an order that the respondent shall pay the applicant a lump sum;

(c)   an order that the respondent shall make periodical payments (secured or unsecured) for the benefit of a child to whom the s. 27 application relates, to the child himself or to the applicant or such other person as the court specifies (provided that the court retains jurisdiction);

(d)   an order that the respondent shall pay the child or the applicant or such other person as the court specifies a lump sum for the benefit of the child: s. 27(6).

35.04   Note that these orders are identical to the financial provision orders that can be made under s. 23, MCA 1973 after divorce, nullity, or judicial separation (see Chapter 17). Just as is the case under s. 23, the amount of any periodical payments or lump sum ordered is within the court's discretion although the court must take into account specified factors (see paragraph 35.12 and onwards below). There is no financial limit on the amount of the lump sum that can be ordered. The court has power to order that the lump sum should be paid by secured or unsecured instalments if it thinks fit: s. 27(7). The court is also able to specify the duration of any periodical payments order it makes subject to certain limitations which are set out below.

35.05   In contrast to the position on divorce, etc., the court does not have power to make property adjustment orders.

Limitations on orders relating to children and duration of orders generally

35.06   The limitations on the orders that can be made to or for the benefit of children and the duration of orders are basically the same as those applicable to financial provision orders under s. 23. In particular, it must be remembered that in most cases the court is prevented by the Child Support Act 1991 ('CSA 1991') from making orders for periodical payments for children, whether secured or unsecured. It may only make such orders in relation to children where the case falls within one of the exceptions to the general rule (see Chapter 20 for a full account of the provisions of the CSA 1991).

Limitations on orders relating to children

The restrictions imposed by s. 29(1) and (3), MCA 1973 on the making of financial provision   **35.07**
orders in favour of children who have attained the age of 18 apply also to s. 27 (see Chapter 17, paragraph 17.15 and onwards for the provisions of s. 29(1) and (3)). The restriction is disapplied by virtue of s. 29(3)(b) where there are 'special circumstances'. In *C v F (Disabled Child: Maintenance Orders)* [1998] 2 FLR 1 it was held that special circumstances may include physical or other handicap, and the expenses attributed to the child's disability should be taken into account in the broadest sense.

Duration of orders under s. 27

The provisions of s. 28 and s. 29, MCA 1973 relating to the duration of periodical payments   **35.08**
orders apply to s. 27 periodical payments orders for spouses and children. These provisions are dealt with in Chapter 16.

Note that whereas orders for periodical payments made after divorce, etc. can normally   **35.09**
date back to the date of the petition, in the case of periodical payments ordered under s. 27, back-dating can be to the date of the originating application for relief under s. 27.

The fact that there is a subsequent decree of divorce, nullity, or judicial separation has no   **35.10**
effect on the orders made under s. 27.

However, if the marriage is dissolved or annulled and the spouse in whose favour the s. 27   **35.11**
order was made remarries, the s. 27 order will automatically cease to have effect except in relation to any arrears which might have accrued up to the date of the remarriage: s. 28(2).

D   FACTORS TO BE CONSIDERED ON AN APPLICATION UNDER S. 27

The factors to be considered on a s. 27 application are virtually the same as those to be   **35.12**
considered on an application under s. 23.

In relation to orders for a spouse

In deciding whether the respondent has failed to provide reasonable maintenance for the   **35.13**
applicant and what order, if any, to make in her favour, the court shall have regard to all the circumstances of the case including the matters mentioned in s. 25(2), MCA 1973 and, where an application is also made under s. 27 in respect of a child of the family who is under 18, first consideration shall be given to the welfare of the child while a minor: s. 27(3) as substituted by s. 4, Matrimonial and Family Proceedings Act 1984. (For the matters mentioned in s. 25(2), see Chapter 19.)

Note that there are minor differences between the approach under s. 27 and that under s. 23:   **35.14**

(a) Under s. 23, first consideration must always be given to the welfare whilst a minor of any child of the family under 18 whether any application is made in respect of the child or not: s. 25(1). Under s. 27, first consideration is given to the child's welfare only if an application is made in respect of him under s. 27.

(b) Section 25(2)(c), which provides that the court must take into account the standard of living enjoyed by the family before the breakdown of the marriage is modified so that, in s. 27 cases, the court must take into account the standard of living enjoyed by the family before the failure to provide reasonable maintenance for the applicant: s. 27(3B).

(c) Section 25(2)(h) (consideration of benefits lost, such as pensions) is confined to proceedings for divorce or nullity and cannot therefore apply in s. 27 cases.

In relation to orders for a child

35.15 It must be remembered that in most cases the court is prevented by the CSA 1991 from making orders for periodical payments for children, whether secured or unsecured. It may only make such orders in relation to children where the case falls within one of the exceptions to the general rule (see Chapter 20 for a full account of the provisions of the CSA 1991).

35.16 In deciding whether the respondent has failed to provide, or to make proper contribution towards, reasonable maintenance for a child of the family in respect of whom an application under s. 27 has been made and what order, if any, to make under this section in favour of the child, the court is to have regard to all the circumstances of the case including the matters mentioned in s. 25(3)(a) to (e), MCA 1973. If the child to whom the application relates is not a child of the respondent, the court must also have regard to the matters mentioned in s. 25(4), MCA 1973 (s. 27(3A)). (For the matters mentioned in s. 25(3) and s. 25(4), reference should be made to Chapter 19, paragraph 19.107 and onwards.)

35.17 There is one minor alteration to the terms of s. 25(3) in order that it should fit the circumstances of a s. 27 application. This is to s. 25(2)(c) which deals with the standard of living enjoyed by the family before the breakdown of the marriage. This must be read as if it referred to the standard of living enjoyed by the family before the failure to provide, or to make proper contribution towards, reasonable maintenance: s. 27(3B).

Approach in practice

35.18 In practice, what the court is likely to do when faced with a s. 27 application is to decide what order it would have made had it been considering the case under s. 23 after a divorce and then to compare what it would have ordered with what the respondent has actually been paying. If his provision does not measure up, the court can be expected to make an order for periodical payments and/or lump sum payments for the application and any children of the family in substantially the same terms as the order it would have made had the application been for ancillary relief.

Expenses that can be the subject of lump sum orders

The power to order a lump sum is wide enough to enable the court to order a lump sum for **35.19** any reason whatsoever. It is specifically provided by s. 27(7) that an order may, amongst other things, be made for the payment of a lump sum to cover liabilities or expenses reasonably incurred in maintaining the applicant or any child of the family to whom the application relates before the making of the application.

E PROCEDURE

Application is to a divorce county court by originating application which must be supported **35.20** by an affidavit from the applicant. The procedure is governed by the Family Proceedings Rules 1991, r. 3.1. Public funding is available for proceedings for financial orders under s. 27, MCA 1973. The detailed provisions relating to public funding under the Community Legal Service scheme are to be found in Chapter 2. Preliminary advice may be available by way of Legal Help with the possibility of General Legal Help for the institution of proceedings. However, it will have been noted by the practitioner that proceedings under s. 27 come within the definition of 'family matters' for the purposes of public funding. This means that an applicant will be required to attend a meeting with a mediator so that an assessment may be made as to whether the case is suitable for Family Mediation before any application may be made for publicly-funded representation.

Section 27 applications are usually dealt with by a district judge and the hearing can be **35.21** expected to be much the same as the hearing of an application for ancillary relief after a divorce. See Chapter 18 for a general account of the procedure in ancillary relief cases.

F INTERIM ORDERS

Where it appears to the court that the applicant or any child of the family to whom the s. 27 **35.22** application relates is in immediate need of financial assistance but it is not yet possible to determine what order, if any, should be made on the application, the court can make an interim order for maintenance, i.e., an order requiring the respondent to make to the applicant until the determination of the application such periodical payments as the court thinks reasonable: s. 27(5). Note that there is no power to order interim periodical payments to be made to the child direct or to any person other than the applicant for the benefit of the child.

G VARIATION OF S. 27 ORDERS

It must be remembered that in most cases the court is prevented by the CSA 1991 from **35.23** making orders for periodical payments for children, whether secured or unsecured. It may only make such orders in relation to children where the case falls within one of the exceptions to the general rule (see Chapter 20 for a full account of the provisions of the CSA 1991). Subject to those matters it may be that an order for periodic payments made under s. 27 can be varied under s. 31, MCA 1973, as can the instalment element of an order for the payment of a lump sum by instalments.

H SECTION 27 COMPARED WITH DOMESTIC PROCEEDINGS AND MAGISTRATES' COURTS ACT 1978

35.24 It will have been noted that the grounds for an application under s. 27 are the same as two of the grounds for an application in the family proceedings courts for an order under s. 2, Domestic Proceedings and Magistrates' Courts Act 1978 ('DPMCA 1978') i.e., s. 1(a) (failure to provide reasonable maintenance for the applicant) and s. 1(b) (failure to provide/contribute properly towards reasonable maintenance for a child of the family).

35.25 It follows that the applicant intending to rely on failure to maintain has a choice whether to proceed in the family proceedings courts under DPMCA 1978 or in the divorce county court under s. 27, MCA 1973. In practice, by far the majority of applications appear to be made in the family proceedings courts but the solicitor must consider what is best for his particular client in each case.

35.26 The following points must be borne in mind:

(a) The grounds for an order under s. 27 relate only to failure to maintain whereas the applicant for an order under s. 2, DPMCA 1978 can rely alternatively on behaviour or desertion: s. 1(c) and (d), DPMCA 1978. If, therefore, there is doubt about proving failure to maintain but a possibility of making out one of the other grounds it may well be prudent to apply in the family proceedings court alleging, as an alternative, behaviour or desertion.

(b) The grounds for jurisdiction are more restricted under DPMCA 1978. This simply means that the solicitor must check that the family proceedings court would have jurisdiction in a particular case. If not, he may still be able to bring the case under s. 27.

(c) The orders that can be made under s. 2, DPMCA 1978, although basically the same as those available under s. 27 are, in fact, more restricted as follows:

   (i) No secured periodic payments can be ordered under s. 2, DPMCA 1978; they can under s. 27.

   (ii) There is an upper financial limit of £1,000 on a lump sum ordered under s. 2, DPMCA 1978; there is no limit under s. 27.

(d) The powers under the two Acts to make interim orders differ significantly in the following ways:

   (i) Under s. 19, DPMCA 1978 (the section dealing with interim orders), the family proceedings court has power to make an interim maintenance order requiring the respondent to make periodic payments direct to a child of the family under 18. Under s. 27, interim periodic payments can only be ordered to be made to the applicant herself. The family proceedings court has power to order interim period-ical payments for the benefit of the child to be made to his parent even if that parent is not the applicant for the order. Under s. 27, the court is limited to orders to the applicant only.

(ii) Section 27 is far more generous than s. 19, DPMCA 1978 about the duration of interim orders. Interim orders under s. 27 can go on until the determination of the s. 27 application, however long it takes for that application to be heard. Interim orders under s. 19, DPMCA 1978 can only be made for a period of up to three months in the first instance and, although they can be extended, can only be extended so that they continue for a maximum of three months more (a total of six months in all, maximum). If it takes longer than six months for the case to be heard, the applicant and child will cease to be entitled to any interim payments. It is to be hoped that this will rarely prove a problem in practice as six months should be ample time in most cases for the application to be disposed of by a final order.

In fact, the apparent choice facing the applicant may, in any event, be determined for her by the Legal Services Commission if she is reliant upon public funding. Unless good grounds can be shown for seeking an order under s. 27, it is likely that the applicant will be expected to pursue what will probably be the less expensive course of an application to the family proceedings court and that her application for funding for s. 27 will be turned down on the basis that she should seek funding by way of representation for the family proceedings courts.

36

SEPARATION AND MAINTENANCE AGREEMENTS

A THE DIFFERENCE BETWEEN SEPARATION AND MAINTENANCE AGREEMENTS

The essence of a separation agreement is that the parties agree to live apart. A separation **36.01** agreement may, however, include all manner of other terms dealing with maintenance, family property, arrangements for the children, etc.

An agreement which deals with the payment of maintenance by one spouse to or for the **36.02** benefit of the other and/or the children but not with the separation of the parties is sometimes referred to as a 'maintenance agreement'; there may or may not be other terms in the agreement as well as provision for maintenance. This general use of the term should not be confused with maintenance agreements as defined in s. 34(2), Matrimonial Causes Act 1973 ('MCA 1973').

36.03   By virtue of s. 34(2), a 'maintenance agreement' is any agreement in writing made between the parties to a marriage, being:

(a)   an agreement containing financial arrangements, whether made during the continuance or after the dissolution or annulment of the marriage; or

(b)   a separation agreement which contains no financial arrangements in a case where no other agreement in writing between the same parties contains such arrangements.

'Financial arrangements' means provisions governing the rights and liabilities towards one another when living separately from the parties to a marriage (including a marriage which has been dissolved or annulled) in respect of the making or securing of payments or the disposition or use of any property, including such rights and liabilities with respect to the maintenance or education of any child, whether or not a child of the family.

B   LIKELY CONTENTS OF SEPARATION AGREEMENTS

36.04   There are very few restrictions on the contents of a separation agreement and agreements are therefore likely to vary considerably depending on the circumstances of each case. The following are examples of matters commonly dealt with:

(a)   *Agreement to live apart*   The agreement of the parties to a marriage to live apart is central to a separation agreement. The spouses frequently also agree not to molest each other.

(b)   *Maintenance*   The spouses often agree that one spouse (usually the husband) will pay maintenance of a certain amount to or for the benefit of the other spouse and/or the children. Where the recipient is in receipt of income support the Child Support Agency will determine the level of financial support to be provided by the absent parent in respect of his natural child. On the other hand, in non-benefit cases it is possible for the parties to reach agreement on the level of support to be provided. However, such an agreement would not prevent the carer parent from subsequently requesting the Child Support Agency to carry out a maintenance assessment. Once such an assessment is made it will override the original agreement: ss. 9(2) and (3), Child Support Act 1991.

Care must be taken in drafting agreements to pay maintenance. In particular, thought must be given as to when the obligation to pay maintenance under the agreement should terminate. It is possible to draft an agreement to pay maintenance that will create an obligation that will continue irrespective of whether the parties start to live together again or get divorced and despite the remarriage or cohabitation of the payee or even the death of the payer. If such an open-ended commitment is what the parties want, all well and good. Generally, however, the payer will be anxious to limit his obligations and the relevant clauses should therefore make clear the events that will bring the duty to pay maintenance to an end.

(c)   *Property*   The spouses may also reach agreement over what is to become of the family property. This is less common than an agreement over maintenance.

(d)   *Arrangements for the children*   The agreement may provide for where, and with whom, any children of the family are to live and for any arrangements as to contact.

C   WHAT A SEPARATION AGREEMENT CANNOT DO

A separation agreement must provide for *immediate* separation. Spouses cannot enter into a   **36.05**
valid agreement to provide for their legal rights in case they should separate at any stage in
the future as this is contrary to public policy.

However, a couple who have already separated but who want to attempt a reconciliation are   **36.06**
free to negotiate a reconciliation agreement containing provisions as to what will happen
should they separate again in the future. As soon as they separate, the appropriate terms will
become effective.

D   THE FORM OF A SEPARATION OR MAINTENANCE AGREEMENT

A separation or maintenance agreement is a contract just like any other contract. It can be   **36.07**
made orally or in writing or even by conduct although if the agreement covers more than
simple separation it is prudent to record the terms of the agreement in writing so that they
are beyond dispute.

The normal contractual rules apply to determine whether a binding agreement exists, i.e.,   **36.08**
the court will look for offer and acceptance, for an intention to create legal relations, and for
consideration. However, consideration may be lacking in a maintenance agreement. An
agreement by the payee not to seek further or different provision by making application to
the court is void (*Hyman* v *Hyman* [1929] AC 601) and cannot therefore constitute good
consideration for a promise to pay maintenance. Unless there are clearly other covenants
which *are* binding on the payee, it is therefore recommended that a maintenance agreement
should be embodied in a deed to ensure that it is binding.

Note that a separation or maintenance agreement can be void for mistake or fraud and can   **36.09**
be set aside on the grounds of misrepresentation, duress or undue influence. In order to preclude future problems of this sort over the validity of the agreement, it is therefore desirable
that both parties to the agreement should receive separate legal advice.

E   EFFECT OF A SEPARATION AGREEMENT

Apart from the specific matters upon which agreement is reached, a separation agreement   **36.10**
will:

(a) release both spouses from their duty to cohabit with each other thus preventing either
     of them from alleging that the other is in desertion;
(b) provide evidence that the parties looked upon the marriage as at an end (necessary to
     prove separation for divorce and judicial separation; see *Santos* v *Santos* [1972] Fam 247,
     [1972] 2 All ER 246 and paragraph 4.33) and as to the date of their separation;
(c) if the agreement also makes provision for maintenance and the payer fulfils is obligations

in this respect, be rebuttable evidence against a claim on the basis of his failure to provide reasonable maintenance.

F   ADVANTAGES OF A SEPARATION OR MAINTENANCE AGREEMENT

36.11   The possibility of a formal separation or maintenance agreement is sometimes overlooked by solicitors who tend only to consider making an application to court for financial provision. Such an agreement does, however, have some advantages, for example:

(a)   An agreement is flexible—it can include any terms which the parties wish subject to very few limitations.

(b)   Financial matters often cause some of the most bitter disputes between couples after marriage breakdown. If its terms are observed, an agreement may serve to take the heat out of the breakdown of the marriage and will enable both parties to know where they stand. It provides a means of resolving financial and other problems formally but without the need to have recourse to court, which can be expensive and can also encourage the parties to draw up battle lines.

It should be pointed out, however, that there are disadvantages of a separation agreement in comparison with a court order, notably:

(a)   It is not so easy to enforce (for enforcement of agreements, see paragraph 36.12 below; for enforcement of court orders, see paragraph 22.02).

(b)   It cannot achieve the same degree of finality as a court order. The jurisdiction of the court to entertain future financial and property applications (for example, after divorce) cannot be ousted by an agreement.

(c)   While variation by the court can be sought if the agreement can be classed as a maintenance agreement within s. 34, MCA 1973, if the agreement falls outside the definition, it can only be varied by consent. Court orders for periodical payments are always variable by subsequent order.

G   ENFORCEMENT

36.12   A separation or maintenance agreement is enforceable in the same way as any other contract. Thus an action can be brought for damages (for example, if the breach alleged is a failure to pay maintenance, damages equal to the arrears of maintenance could be sought), and the equitable remedies of specific performance and an injunction to prevent a breach of a negative clause of the agreement are also available.

H   IMPACT OF SUBSISTING SEPARATION AGREEMENT OR MAINTENANCE AGREEMENT ON FINANCIAL ARRANGEMENTS AFTER DIVORCE, ETC.

The fact that there is a subsisting maintenance or separation agreement dealing with finance **36.13** and/or property does not preclude either party making a comprehensive application for ancillary relief in conjunction with divorce, nullity, or judicial separation even if that party undertakes in the agreement not to seek further provision from the court (an undertaking which will be void). However, the existence of the agreement will be one of the factors for the court to take into account under s. 25, MCA 1973 when it considers the application for ancillary relief (see Chapter 19).

I   KEY DOCUMENTS

The Matrimonial Causes Act 1973   **36.14**

37

SECTION 17, MARRIED WOMEN'S PROPERTY ACT 1882

A INTRODUCTION

37.01 Section 17 of the Married Women's Property Act 1882 provides a procedure for determining the property rights of spouses, of formerly engaged couples and of certain divorcees without relying on the court's powers to grant ancillary relief after divorce.

37.02 Because s. 17 proceedings are relatively rare these days, this chapter does not go into either the law or the procedure in any depth. The reader is referred to the major textbooks on family law, on property law, and on trusts for further information.

B THE BASIC PROVISION

37.03 Section 17 provides that, in any question between husband and wife as to the title to or possession of property, either party may apply in a summary way to a High Court or county court judge who may make such order with respect to the property in dispute and as to the costs of the application as he thinks fit.

C POSSIBLE APPLICANTS

37.04 The following can make application under s. 17:

(a) either party to a marriage during the marriage: s. 17;

(b) Civil partners provided that the application is made within three years of the dissolution or annulment (s. 66, Civil Partnership Act 2004);

(c) either party to a marriage within three years of the dissolution or annulment of the marriage: s. 39, Matrimonial Proceedings and Property Act 1970;

(d) engaged couples within three years of the termination of the engagement: s. 2(2), Law Reform (Miscellaneous Provisions) Act 1970. The section affords relief even where the promise to marry was not enforceable because the promisor was already married: *Shaw* v *Fitzgerald* [1992] 1 FLR 357.

Note that s. 17 does not assist cohabitants for whom no special procedure presently exists for determining property disputes. Where a dispute arises between cohabitants, therefore, the only means of resolving it is unfortunately by relying on the general jurisdiction of the county court or High Court. The exact nature of the application that should be made depends on the circumstances of the case but the following forms of relief may be sought: an order declaring and enforcing a trust; an order for sale under s. 14, Trusts of Land and Appointment of Trustees Act 1996 (see below); an order granting possession of real property;

injunctions and damages for wrongful interference with goods (where chattels are in dispute).

D   WHAT PROPERTY IS COVERED?

Application can be made under s. 17 to sort out disputes over all manner of property includ- **37.05** ing, for example, houses and land, money, shares, furniture, jewellery, and even items of very little financial value such as holiday souvenirs, garden tools, photograph albums.

Although most disputes concern property which is in the possession of one or the other **37.06** party, it is not essential for either party to have the property in his or her possession at the time of the application. By s. 7, Matrimonial Causes (Property and Maintenance) Act 1958, application can be made where it is alleged:

(a)   that the other party has had in his possession or control property to which the applicant was partly or wholly beneficially entitled even though he no longer has the property; *or*
(b)   that the other party has or has had in his possession or control money representing the proceeds of sale of property to which the applicant was wholly or partly entitled.

E   WHAT ORDERS CAN BE MADE?

Orders declaring parties' property rights

Section 17 is a procedural provision only. It empowers the court to determine in a summary **37.07** way what the parties' rights in particular property *are* as a matter of strict law and to declare them accordingly. There is no power under s. 17 to make orders *adjusting* property rights such as the court can make under s. 24, Matrimonial Causes Act 1973.

Order for sale

The court also has power under s. 17 to order a sale of the disputed property (see paragraph **37.08** 37.31 below).

F   ORDINARY TRUST PRINCIPLES GENERALLY APPLY IN DETERMINING DISPUTES

Statutory provision has been made for one or two problems that have arisen frequently in **37.09** disputes between husband and wife (see below). However, on the whole the same principles apply in determining property disputes between spouses and others under s. 17 as apply to disputes between total strangers. Thus, the courts will generally apply normal trust principles though with the assistance of numerous authorities in the reports illustrating how these principles have been interpreted in family situations (for example, in disputes between husband and wife under s. 17 or, more commonly these days, between cohabitants in a trust action).

G   DISPUTES OVER LAND

Principles to be applied

37.10   The leading cases in relation to disputes over the beneficial ownership of land are *Pettitt* v *Pettitt* [1970] AC 777, [1969] 2 All ER 385; *Gissing* v *Gissing* [1971] AC 886, [1970] 2 All ER 780, and *Lloyds Bank plc* v *Rosset* [1991] 1 AC 107; [1990] 1 All ER 1111. The principles set out in this paragraph derive largely from these decisions of the House of Lords.

Examples of the types of problem that arise

Example 1 The matrimonial home was purchased in the sole name of the husband. The wife claims to have a beneficial interest in the property because she has paid for substantial improvements to be made to the property.

Example 2 Miss James and Mr Harris are engaged. They buy a house to be their home after they are married. The house is transferred into Mr Harris's sole name but both parties contribute equally to the deposit, legal fees and mortgage instalments. The engagement is broken off. Miss James claims to have a beneficial interest in the property by virtue of her contribution to the purchase price.

Example 3 The matrimonial home was purchased in the joint names of husband and wife. The wife claims that, as she put up the deposit and her earnings have been used to pay the mortgage instalments, the whole beneficial interest in the house belongs to her.

The need to establish a trust

37.11   Where one party claims to be entitled to a greater share in the house than the legal title suggests, he or (more usually) she must establish that the legal estate in the property is held on trust for her to the extent that she alleges she is beneficially entitled. Thus, for example, in Example 2 (above), Miss James would no doubt argue that Mr Harris holds the legal estate in the house on trust for herself and himself in equal shares and in Example 3, the wife would have to establish that the parties hold the legal estate on trust for her absolutely.

Express and implied trusts

37.12   A trust may be express or implied. Implied trusts are generally subdivided into resulting and constructive trusts.

Express declaration on documents of title

37.13   In determining whether a trust exists, the first step is to examine the documents of title. The conveyance or transfer (TR1 form) will obviously stipulate who is to hold the legal estate. The beneficial interest may or may not be mentioned specifically.

If the conveyance or transfer stipulates not only who is to hold the legal estate but also who **37.14** is entitled to the beneficial interest in the property (for example, 'to Joe Bloggs and Mildred Bloggs as beneficial joint tenants' or 'to Joe Bloggs and Freda Walker as tenants in common in equal shares'), that concludes the question of beneficial ownership of the property unless it can be shown that the statement in the conveyance was the result of fraud or a mistake or that there has subsequently been a fresh agreement varying the position. The same is true where a separate deed of trust has been prepared dealing with the beneficial interest in the property (*Goodman* v *Gallant* [1986] Fam 106).

Example The matrimonial home is purchased in the joint names of husband and wife. The conveyance is expressed to be to H and W 'as joint tenants in law and equity'. Although W has never worked, and the whole of the purchase price has been provided by the husband, H cannot argue that he is entitled to the whole beneficial interest in the property, as the express declaration in the conveyance is conclusive: see *Goodman* v *Gallant* [1986] Fam 106, [1986] 1 FLR 513; and *Barclays Bank plc* v *Khaira* [1993] 1 FLR 343.

Note, however, that s. 37, Matrimonial Proceedings and Property Act 1970 can operate to entitle a spouse to a larger interest in property by virtue of improvements that he or she has effected to the property subsequently, and this provision will override the terms of the conveyance or transfer.

The implication of a trust

Where the conveyance or transfer deals with the legal estate only and is silent as to the **37.15** beneficial interests in the property, at first sight the beneficial interest goes with the legal estate. Thus where the conveyance or transfer says, for example, 'to Joe Bloggs in fee simple', Joe Bloggs is on the face of it entitled to the whole beneficial interest in the property. Where the conveyance or transfer consigns the legal estate to a husband and wife jointly, they are at first sight jointly entitled to the beneficial interest. However, these presumptions can be displaced by evidence of disparate financial contributions to the purchase of the property, or of express discussions between the spouses.

Recently, in *Carlton* v *Goodman* [2002] 2 FLR 259, Ward LJ reminded practitioners of the need **37.16** to sit purchasers down, explain the differences between a joint tenancy and a tenancy in common, find out what the purchasers want, and then expressly declare in the transfer how the beneficial interest is to be held. This is reinforced by the Land Registration Rules 1925, which require a declaration of trust where land is to vest in persons as joint proprietors whether on first registration or on registration of a dealing. Even if the parties do not go so far as an express declaration of trust or agreement, their conversations can still be taken into account as part of their conduct (see paragraph 37.20 below).

It was thought, at one time, that the provisions of s. 53, Law of Property Act 1925 would **37.17** cause difficulties for the informal creation of trusts in the family context. Section 53(1)(b) provides that a declaration of trust respecting any land or interest in land must be manifested and proved in writing signed by some person who is able to declare such a trust. Section 53(1)(c) goes further and requires that a disposition of an equitable interest or trust subsisting at the time of the disposition must be in writing signed by the person disposing of it or his agent or by will. However, the requirements of the section do not affect the creation or operation of resulting, implied or constructive trusts (s. 53(2)), thereby giving the courts a way around the strict provisions of s. 53, so that it is rare for a claimant in a family situation to fail to establish a trust simply because there is no written evidence of it (see, however, *Midland Bank plc* v *Dobson* [1986] 1 FLR 171, which makes it clear that it can still happen).

Resulting trust: direct financial contribution

37.18   It has long been recognized that a spouse who makes a financial contribution towards the acquisition of property will, in the absence of some other arrangement being intended, obtain a beneficial interest in the house commensurate to the contribution made. This is traditionally referred to as the doctrine of resulting trust (although in *Lloyds Bank plc* v *Rosset* Lord Bridge rather confusingly referred to the trust arising in such circumstances as constructive). The following count as contributions towards the purchase price:

(a)   *Outright payment of deposit/purchase price*   The most straightforward case is where a claimant has paid all or part of the initial deposit for the property, or, where the property is purchased outright without the aid of a mortgage, has paid all or part of the purchase price.

(b)   *Payment of mortgage instalment*   Where the property is purchased on mortgage (or with other borrowed finance) a share can be acquired by *direct* contribution to the mortgage instalments (at least where the claimant's contributions are substantial, not merely the odd instalment every now and then).

It is extremely doubtful whether any other form of contribution will give rise to a beneficial interest by way of *resulting* trust. Thus where W's earned income meets general household expenses, thereby freeing H's income to pay the mortgage instalments, W will be unlikely to establish a beneficial interest unless she can show that this conduct was referable to an agreement, arrangement or understanding between the spouses that she was to have an interest (in other words, that the situation gave rise to a constructive trust).

37.19   The presumption of resulting trust which arises from a contribution to the purchase price can be rebutted by evidence showing that the parties did not intend the contributor thereby to acquire a share in the equity of the house. For example, there may be evidence to show that the money was an outright gift, or was intended simply as a loan. In the past the presumption of advancement, whereby a husband who put a house which he purchased into his wife's name was presumed to intend the property to be a gift to her, was significant. However, its value was questioned in *Pettitt* v *Pettitt* [1970] AC 777, where it was thought to be anachronistic. It can therefore easily be rebutted by evidence showing that a gift to the wife was not intended.

Constructive trust: parties' common intentions

37.20   In *Lloyds Bank* v *Rosset* [1991] 1 AC 107, Lord Bridge summarized the principles for the imposition of a constructive trust as follows:

> The first and fundamental question which must always be resolved is whether, independently of any inference to be drawn from the conduct of the parties in the course of sharing the house as their home and managing their joint affairs, there has at any time prior to acquisition, or exceptionally at some later date, been any *agreement, arrangement* or *understanding* reached between them that the property is to be shared beneficially. The finding of an agreement or

arrangement to share in this sense can only, I think, be based on evidence of *express discussions* between the partners, however imperfectly remembered and however imprecise their terms may have been. Once a finding to this effect is made it will only be necessary for the partner asserting a claim to a beneficial interest against the partner entitled to the legal estate to show that he or she has acted to his or her *detriment* or significantly altered his or her position in *reliance* on the agreement in order to give rise to a constructive trust or proprietary estoppel. (Emphasis added.)

Examples of the operation of constructive trusts can be found in two decisions of the Court **37.21** of Appeal, both of which concerned unmarried cohabitants. In *Eves* v *Eves* [1975] 1 WLR 1338, the man explained that the legal estate was to be vested in his sole name because the woman was under 21, and that otherwise the house would have been put into their joint names. The woman relied on this by doing a considerable amount of building work to the house (wielding a sledge hammer and operating a cement mixer!). She thereby obtained a share in the home. In *Grant* v *Edwards* [1986] 2 All ER 426, the man told the woman that the only reason the house was not being acquired in their joint names was because to do so might prejudice the divorce proceedings to which she was then party. In the course of living with him, she made substantial, albeit largely indirect, financial contributions from her own earnings, which enabled him to meet his obligations under the mortgage. The Court of Appeal held that she thereby obtained a half share in the house. (See also *H* v *M (Property: Beneficial Interest)* [1992] 1 FLR 229.)

Improvements

Section 37, Matrimonial Proceedings and Property Act 1970 makes it clear that a share in **37.22** property can be acquired by carrying out, helping with or paying for improvements. It provides that where a husband or wife (or a partner to an engagement by virtue of s. 2(1), Law Reform (Miscellaneous Provisions) Act 1970 makes a *substantial* contribution in money or money's worth to the improvement of real or personal property in which, or in the proceeds of sale of which, either or both of them has or have a beneficial interest, the contributor shall, subject to any contrary agreement between them, be treated as having acquired a share or an enlarged share in the beneficial interest by virtue of his or her contribution. The proportion of the share/increased share acquired is dependent on the parties' agreement at the time or, in default of agreement, will be determined by the court as it thinks just in all the circumstances: see *Passee* v *Passee* [1988] 1 FLR 263, [1988] Fam Law 132, *Thomas* v *Fuller-Brown* [1988] 1 FLR 237, [1988] Fam Law 53, and *Risch* v *McFee* [1991] 1 FLR 105. It is important to note that this provision applies to spouses and engaged couples only. It does not apply to cohabitants.

Example Mr and Mrs Couch are looking for a new home. They find a row of three dilapidated cottages which are suitable for conversion and buy them. Mr Couch puts up the purchase money and the cottages are conveyed into his name. The Couches carry out much of the renovation work themselves. They re-roof the property, Mr Couch going up on the roof and Mrs Couch loading up the tiles on the conveyor at the bottom for him. They knock down several internal walls, both wielding a sledge hammer and wheeling away the stone although there are certain bits that Mr Couch has to lift as his wife is not strong enough. They install new window frames which Mrs Couch paints and glazes while Mr Couch installs central heating. Mrs Couch pays for the property to be professionally rewired. There is no doubt that Mrs Couch will acquire a beneficial interest in the property by virtue of her hard work and her payment for the rewiring.

H   THE OWNERSHIP OF CASH AND ASSETS OTHER THAN LAND

37.23   As with land, entitlement to cash and other assets generally depends on the intention of the parties. A number of matters that commonly cause difficulty are dealt with below.

Housekeeping money

37.24   Section 1 of the Married Women's Property Act 1964 provides that if any question arises as to the right of a husband or wife to money derived from any allowance made by the husband for the expenses of the matrimonial home or for similar purposes, or to any property acquired out of such money, the money or property shall, in the absence of any agreement between them to the contrary, be treated as belonging to the husband and the wife in equal shares.

Example Mr Hill pays his wife £75 housekeeping each week. She manages to save £15 a week and, at the end of the year, buys a Victorian button-back chair with the savings. Nothing is said by either party as to who the savings from the housekeeping or the chair belong to. Section 1 therefore dictates that the chair belongs to the parties equally.

Joint accounts

37.25   The ownership of a joint account and of property purchased from it depends on the intention of the parties.

37.26   In some cases, the proper inference is that the parties are pooling their resources and intend that the account and any assets acquired from it shall belong to them jointly: see, for example, *Jones* v *Maynard* [1951] 1 All ER 802. In other cases, one party provides all the funds and a joint account is only opened as a matter of convenience, in which case the funds in the account and any property bought with them belong to the spouse who put up the money unless there is specific agreement about particular items purchased: see, for example, *Heseltine* v *Heseltine* [1971] 1 WLR 342. In other cases it may be that assets bought from the joint account belong solely to the spouse making the purchase: see, for example, *Re Bishop* [1965] 1 All ER 249.

Wedding presents and other gifts

37.27   Naturally each spouse owns the items that were given to him or her personally, for example as birthday presents.

37.28   Who owns the wedding presents and other gifts to the parties jointly will depend on the intention of the donor. However, in the absence of other evidence, the court may be inclined to find that wedding presents in particular belong to the spouse whose side of the family donated them: *Samson* v *Samson* [1960] 1 All ER 653, [1960] 1 WLR 190.

Property purchased before marriage

Property purchased by one of the spouses before the marriage without a view to the marriage **37.29**
will normally belong to that spouse absolutely. It is possible, however, for that spouse subsequently to give the property or a share in it to the other spouse. Again, it is a question of
intention.

I FIXING THE SIZE OF EACH PARTY'S SHARE IN THE DISPUTED PROPERTY

If the applicant succeeds in establishing the presence of a beneficial interest, the next task **37.30**
will be to quantify that share. A declaration of trust as part of the conveyance will normally
be determinative of the share in the absence of fraud or mistake. If, however, there is no such
declaration, the court will consider all of the available evidence. If, for example, the property
is registered in joint names then that is a powerful indicator that equal shares were intended
(*Bernard* v *Josephs* [1982] Ch 391). Contributions to the running of the house can also be
considered and in these circumstances the role of the court is as follows:

> In a case where there was no evidence of any discussion between [the parties] as to the amount
> of the share which each was to have . . . each is entitled to that share which the court considers
> fair having regard to the whole course of dealing between them in relation to the property. And,
> in that context, 'the whole course of dealing between them in relation to the property' includes
> the arrangements which they make from time to time in order to meet the outgoings (for
> example, mortgage contributions, council tax and utilities, repairs, insurance and housekeep-
> ing) which have to be met if they are to live in the property as their home (*Oxley* v *Hiscock*
> [2004] 2 FLR 669 at 706 per Chadwick LJ).

Example (The facts of *Oxley* v *Hiscock*.) When the couple first cohabited Mrs Oxley purchased
property in her sole name using, in part, money from Mr Hiscock. That property was sold
and proceeds were used to buy another property, this time in Mr Hiscock's sole name. The
effective contributions to the purchase price of £126,000 were £36,000 by Mrs Oxley,
£60,000 by Mr Hiscock and the remaining £30,000 raised on a mortgage. There was no
declaration setting out the parties' respective beneficial shares and there had been no discussions between them. Both, however, worked on the house for a number of years and contributed to household expenditure. Following their separation Mrs Oxley applied under s. 14
of the Trusts of Land and Appointment of Trustees Act 1996 for a declaration that each party
held equal shares in the property. It was held that the parties' conduct was such as to justify
the implication of a beneficial interest. After examining all of the circumstances a fair
division of the proceeds of sale was 60 per cent to Mr Hiscock and 40 per cent to Mrs Oxley.

J ORDERS FOR SALE

The court has power to order a sale of the disputed property. Where there is a dispute over **37.31**
who is to have possession of a jointly owned chattel, the court can therefore order that the
item in question be sold and the proceeds divided between the parties in accordance with

their shares. The threat of sale of a cherished item (usually, of course, for considerably less than the parties feel that the garden gnomes or whatever the item is, are worth to them) is usually sufficient to introduce a more rational attitude as to who should have what.

37.32 The power is more important in relation to the matrimonial home. Where land is jointly owned, the owners of the legal title hold the land as joint tenants and trustees of land: Trusts of Land and Appointment of Trustees Act 1996. Any interested party may make an application to the court under s. 14 of the 1996 Act for an order for sale or other order concerning the land, which may include a declaration of the nature or extent of that party's interest in the land in question.

37.33 The court is not bound to order a sale. In deciding what order or orders to make the court is required to consider a number of factors, set out in s. 15 of the Act:

(a)   the intentions of the parties who established the trust;

(b)   the purposes for which the property is held;

(c)   the welfare of any minor who occupies the land as his home;

(d)   the interests of any secured creditor of any beneficiaries; and

(e)   the wishes of the owner of the equitable interest in the land.

37.34 Whether a sale will be ordered is a question for the court's discretion but basically depends on whether the underlying purpose of the trust is continuing: *Re Buchanan-Wollaston's Conveyance* [1939] Ch 738, [1939] 2 All ER 302. The court will therefore look to see why the house was bought. The normal purpose is to provide a home. In cases of this type, where there are no children (or no children living at home), the purpose of the trust will come to an end on the breakdown of the relationship and a sale will therefore normally be ordered. In contrast, where the house is still needed to provide a home for the children, the court is unlikely to order a sale.

K   PROCEDURE

37.35 Application is to the High Court or county court. In the High Court proceedings are commenced by originating summons and in the county court by originating application in Form M23. The relevant procedure is set out in the Family Proceedings Rules 1991, rr. 3.6 and 3.7.

L   PRACTICAL IMPORTANCE OF S. 17

37.36 Where one of the parties has commenced or contemplates proceedings for divorce, nullity, or judicial separation, it is generally a waste of time and money for the court to investigate their strict property rights in an application under s. 17. It is preferable to rely on the much wider powers of the court under ss. 23, 24, 24B, 25B, and 25C of the Matrimonial Causes Act 1973, which will enable the court to do broad justice between the parties.

37.37 There are, however, cases where the strict property rights of the parties have to be determined under s. 17. The following situations are examples:

(a) Where the parties have only ever been engaged.

(b) Where the spouses do not want or cannot get a decree of divorce, nullity or judicial separation.

(c) Where a claim is made on behalf of a spouse who has remarried without making ancillary relief claims and is therefore debarred from relying on the Matrimonial Causes Act 1973.

(d) Where one spouse is adjudicated bankrupt, his property vests in his trustee in bankruptcy to be administered for the benefit of his creditors. It may be necessary for the other spouse to seek a declaration of the parties' strict property rights under s. 17 in order to prevent the trustee in bankruptcy laying claim to property that is legally hers.

(In the case of (a) and (c), it is important to note the time limit in paragraph 37.04 above.)

PART IX

WELFARE BENEFITS

38

WELFARE BENEFITS

A   INTRODUCTION

38.01   This chapter deals with the following welfare benefits:

(a)   income support;
(b)   working tax credit;
(c)   child tax credit;
(d)   housing benefit;
(e)   child benefit.

The law on benefits is to be found in various statutes and regulations and is immensely detailed. It is not possible to deal with each benefit comprehensively in a book of this sort. The aim of this chapter is to give the practitioner a broad outline of the provisions, first so that he can advise his client whether it is worth his while making further enquiries of the Department for Work and Pensions ('DWP') or local authority with a view to making a claim, and secondly so that he will be aware of how maintenance and other payments to the client from his or her spouse or former spouse will affect his or her entitlement to benefit.

Should a specific problem arise over the client's benefit, the solicitor can find out more **38.02** about the rules of entitlement from specialist books on welfare benefits (e.g., the Child Poverty Action Group handbooks). The rates of benefit are raised regularly and care must be taken to find out whether the figures given in this chapter are still applicable at the time of reference. Where examples are given, the figures used are those in force from 6 April 2007 to April 2008.

The working tax credit and child tax credit (both introduced in April 2003) are in fact **38.03** administered by HM Revenue and Customs. However, details are included in this chapter since, for many, the credits will be perceived as a form of welfare benefit.

This chapter largely considers the position when a marriage has broken down. However, the **38.04** same principles apply on the breakdown of a civil partnership: s. 254 and sch. 24, Civil Partnership Act 2004.

PART 1   INCOME SUPPORT AND JOBSEEKER'S ALLOWANCE

B   INTRODUCTION

The law relating to income support is to be found in the Social Security Contributions and **38.05** Benefits Act 1992, which consolidated much of the previous legislation in the field and (among other things) the Income Support (General) Regulations 1987 (SI 1987/1967), as amended. It should be noted that in social security law the regulations are extremely important as they set out the fine detail of each benefit.

Income support is a cash benefit to help people who do not have enough money to live on. **38.06** People receiving income support will automatically be entitled to other valuable benefits, e.g., exemption from certain NHS charges, free school meals, full housing and council tax benefits. These are known as 'passport' benefits.

The Jobseeker's Act 1995 introduced, with effect from 7 October 1996, a new benefit known **38.07** as the jobseeker's allowance. It replaced unemployment benefit and also income support for claimants who are required to be available for work. Income support continues to be paid to claimants who are not required to be available for work (for example, a lone parent of a child under 16).

In order to be eligible for a jobseeker's allowance claimants are required to enter an **38.08** agreement under which they are obliged to take whatever steps are considered appropriate towards finding suitable work or retraining.

38.09 Essentially, the allowance is means-tested and payable at the same rate as personal allowances for income support, except that a higher rate of allowance will be available for a maximum period of six months to claimants who have the necessary contribution level (Class 1) and sign the agreement.

38.10 For the purpose of this chapter reference will be made to income support on the basis that the client is not required to be available for work.

C INCOME SUPPORT

Who can claim?

38.11 Claimants must:

(a) Be at least 16.

(b) Be habitually resident in the United Kingdom and present in Great Britain.

(c) Not be engaged in remunerative work for more than 16 hours per week and not have a partner who is engaged in remunerative work for more than 24 hours per week. A partner is someone to whom the claimant is married, or with whom he or she lives as if married to them.

(d) Not be receiving 'relevant education'. A child or young person is treated as receiving 'relevant education' if he is receiving full-time non-advanced education or, although not receiving such education, is treated as a child for the purposes of child benefit. In certain circumstances a young person who is in relevant education may nevertheless be entitled to income support, for example, where he is responsible for a child under the age of 16. In such cases he must also satisfy the other conditions of entitlement to income support.

(e) Have no income or an income which does not exceed the 'applicable amount'.

(f) Not have capital exceeding £16,000. Capital of less then £6,000 will be completely ignored.

Entitlement to income support

38.12 In order to be entitled to income support the claimant must satisfy a means test to ensure that his income is not above the level prescribed by law as the amount necessary for a person to live on. The income of the whole family will be taken into account in assessing entitlement. If the claimant is working for 16 hours or more each week, or has a partner who is working for 24 hours or more each week, then he or she will not normally be entitled to income support. For the purposes of this assessment the 'family' includes a married couple (who are married to each other and are members of the same household) or an unmarried couple (a man and woman who are not married to each other but are living together as husband and wife or a same sex couple).

Calculating the claimant's income

For the purposes of establishing entitlement to income support the claimant's weekly **38.13** income is calculated as follows:

(a) Take the claimant's net (not gross) weekly income—'income' includes periodical payments made to the claimant or his or her children (whether made voluntarily, under a court order or Child Support Agency calculation), lump-sum orders (whether or not payable by instalments), statutory sick pay, statutory maternity payments, and child benefit.

(b) Add to it any 'tariff income' the claimant may receive from capital. This arises if the claimant's capital exceeds £6,000; if so, then each complete £250 in excess of £6,000 (but not exceeding £16,000) is treated as a weekly income of £1.

(c) Certain sums will be disregarded in the calculation of earnings. The rules in relation to this are complex and the practitioner should refer to the appropriate regulations for full details. An example is the first £20 per week in the case of a lone parent.

(d) Child benefit is disregarded.

Amount of income support

If the claimant is entitled to income support, then the following are the amounts to which **38.14** he is entitled:

(a) if the claimant has no income, the amount of income support is the 'applicable amount';

(b) if the claimant has income, the amount of income support is the difference between the claimant's income and the 'applicable amount'.

Ordinary 'applicable amounts' fall into four categories:

(a) a 'personal allowance' for the claimant and his partner (if there is a partner), and an allowance for any child or young person that the claimant and his partner look after;

(b) a 'family premium' if the claimant is a member of a family of which at least one member is a child or young person;

(c) special 'premium payments' for groups of people with special expenses (for example, associated with disability);

(d) 'housing costs payments' to cover certain costs of accommodation not met by housing benefit.

The Social Security (Income Support and Claims and Payments) Amendment Regulations 1995 (SI 1995/1613) came into force on 2 October 1995. They amend the regulations in respect of help with housing costs in circumstances where the claimant has a mortgage. The position is as follows:

(a) If the loan was taken out *before* 2 October 1995, the claimant will receive no assistance with the payment of the mortgage for the first eight weeks of the claim, 50 per cent of the housing costs will be paid for the next 18 weeks and full housing costs after 26 weeks in receipt of income support.

(b) If the loan was taken out *after* 1 October 1995, the claimant will receive no assistance for

39 weeks of the claim but full housing costs will be paid after 39 weeks in receipt of income support.

It is important to emphasize that the 'assistance with housing costs' amounts to assistance with the payment of mortgage interest *only* and, since 10 April 1995, in respect of the first £100,000 of the loan.

38.15   Because no assistance is offered with the payment of the capital element of the mortgage nor with premiums for any linked endowment policy, it is imperative that clients are advised to inform the mortgage lender of the position as soon as a claim for income support is made. It may be possible to negotiate interest-only payments for a limited period or the conversion of an endowment mortgage into an ordinary repayment one using the surrender value (if any) of the policy to reduce the capital debt.

Current rates of benefit

38.16   The rates of benefit change regularly, and the practitioner should ascertain the appropriate rates at his time of reference.

38.17   The rates as at 7 April 2007 are as follows:

(a) *Personal allowances*

			£
(i)	Single		
	aged 18–24		46.85
	aged 25 or over		59.15
(ii)	Lone parent		
	under age 18		35.65–46.85
	aged 18 or over		59.15
(iii)	Couple		
	married or cohabiting (both aged 18 or over)		92.80
(iv)	Dependent children until day before 20th birthday		46.85

(b) *Premiums*

(i)	Family		16.43
(ii)	Lone parent		16.43
(iii)	Disability (depending on circumstances)		25.25–96.90

How to claim income support

38.18   The income support scheme is run by the DWP. Enquiries about entitlement should be made to the claimant's local benefits centre. The normal method of applying for benefits is to fill in the appropriate form which should be sent or delivered to the local office. An interview will usually be arranged to determine the claimant's circumstances unless the claimant has claimed income support before. The 'decision maker' will then determine whether the claimant is eligible for benefit and, if so, how much.

38.19   If the claimant is not required to be available for work, benefit will be paid by a book of weekly orders which can be cashed at a post office. There are provisions for certain of the claimant's expenses to be paid direct if he gets into difficulties (for example, gas and electricity bills).

Where income support includes an amount for mortgage interest, this part of the benefit is **38.20** normally sent direct to the lender.

Appeal and review

If the claimant feels he has been wrongly refused benefit or that benefit has been fixed **38.21** at too low a level, he should write to the DWP asking for a revision on the basis that the decision maker did not know about or made a mistake about some material fact, or that there has been a change in the circumstances on which the decision was based. If the outcome of the request for a revision is still not satisfactory, consideration can be given to appealing to an appeal tribunal. There is a right of appeal from any decision of the decision maker be it the original decision whether to grant benefit, or a revision decision (including a decision by the decision maker to refuse to carry out a revision at all). Written notice of appeal must be given within three months of the decision against which appeal is made. There will be a tribunal hearing and the decision will be sent to the claimant.

A further appeal by the claimant or the adjudication officer on a point of law may be possible **38.22** to the Social Security Commissioners provided permission is granted. The chairman of the tribunal should be asked for permission to appeal and, if he refuses it, an application for permission can be made to a Commissioner.

If there is a point of law involved, the claimant or the Secretary of State may then be able to **38.23** appeal from the Commissioner to the Court of Appeal. Permission to do this is required. The Commissioner can grant permission and, if he refuses, application for permission can be made to the Court of Appeal.

Statutory duty to maintain other members of the family

A 'liable relative' is under a statutory obligation to maintain certain members of his or her **38.24** family. Thus a man is liable to maintain his wife (up to, but not after, divorce) and children, whether married or not. A woman is liable to maintain her husband and all her natural children. A civil partner is obliged to maintain his civil partner until dissolution of the civil partnership.

If a liable relative fails to fulfil the obligation to maintain and the other person claims **38.25** income support, the DWP can apply for a court order obliging the liable relative to pay maintenance. They will normally contact the liable relative first to see whether a voluntary arrangement to pay can be sorted out. There is a special formula used by the DWP for calculating the appropriate amount for the liable relative to contribute. It is to be noted that there is a requirement imposed on the claimant to co-operate with the Child Support Agency in its calculation of child support and a refusal to co-operate can lead to a reduction in benefit unless there are reasonable grounds for believing that the claimant is at risk of harm or undue distress thereby.

Where a liable relative persistently refuses or neglects to maintain a person for whom he is **38.26** responsible with the result that income support has to be paid for that person, he commits a criminal offence and can be fined or imprisoned.

The diversion procedure

38.27 Where the amount that will be paid to the family by way of maintenance will not be enough to take them off income support, it can be convenient (particularly if the maintenance payments tend to be erratic) for the family to continue to receive benefit in full and for the maintenance payments to be assigned to the DWP. This is called the 'diversion procedure'.

38.28 County court maintenance orders must be registered in the family proceedings courts if the diversion procedure is to be used. The diversion procedure is not usually used where the maintenance order exceeds the income support levels and is therefore enough to take the family off benefit altogether. However, if maintenance is not paid (or not paid in full) in a particular week, the family will be able to claim income support for that week and, if it turns out over a period of time that payments are regularly not made or not made on time, the diversion procedure may prove to be the most convenient way of dealing with the problem.

38.29 It should be noted that this procedure has become much less relevant as more maintenance calculations are undertaken by the Child Support Agency and fewer maintenance orders are made through the courts.

D   THE SOCIAL FUND

38.30 The social fund was set up by s. 32 of the Social Security Act 1986. The object of payments from the social fund is to meet special needs which are not catered for by other benefits. The question of whether or not a payment will be made is decided by a social fund officer, who has a wide discretion. The most usual form of payment will be a loan. There are powers to make 'budgeting loans' which are interest-free and help to spread the cost of large one-off expenses over a longer period; 'crisis loans' which are interest-free and are for living expenses or items needed urgently (the applicant does not have to be in receipt of income support in order to qualify for one (the maximum amount of either loan is £1,500)); and 'community care grants'. Other forms of payment available include a maternity payment to help buy necessities for a baby and funeral grants. Applications for payments from the social fund should be made to the claimant's local DWP office.

PART 2   TAX CREDITS

E   INTRODUCTION

38.31 Major changes in this area came into force in April 2003 with the introduction of the child tax credit and the working tax credit, under the Tax Credits Act 2002, replacing working families tax credit.

F THE CHILD TAX CREDIT

The credit

The Child Tax Credit ('CTC') replaces the child-based elements in income support, job- **38.32**
seeker's allowance, working tax credit, disabled person's tax credit, and the current children's tax credit. CTC is designed to provide financial support for families with children. The
claimant for CTC is not required to be working.

CTC is claimed from the Inland Revenue. The claim is made in writing on Form TC 600. A **38.33**
helpline service is available on 0845 300 3909. However, child benefit remains unchanged:
the procedure for making a claim remains as previously and the benefit continues to be paid
as a separate payment.

Who can claim?

To claim CTC, the applicant must live in the United Kingdom and be responsible for at least **38.34**
one child or a 'qualifying young person' who is aged between 16 and 18 and is receiving full-
time education (up to A levels or NVQ Level 3) or has left full-time education but does not
have a job or training place and has registered with the careers service.

Responsibility for a child

To be responsible for a child means having the child living with the applicant and, if care of **38.35**
the child is shared between parties living in different households (for example, as the result
of a shared residence order), CTC will be paid to the party having 'the main responsibility'
for the child. If that cannot be agreed, the Revenue (which takes responsibility for paying
CTC) will determine the position.

Calculating child tax credit

The amount of CTC payable depends upon the applicant's income for the previous tax year **38.36**
and awards will last for 12 months. The amount may be adjusted during the year to take
account of changes in income but rises of up to £2,500 in the current tax year will be
ignored. Where the applicant is married or cohabits with another person, their incomes will
be aggregated to determine the amount of CTC payable.

Income is calculated by adding all gross earned and unearned income including benefits in **38.37**
kind and state benefits but excluding child benefit, working tax credit, housing and council
tax benefit, and student loans, etc. Maintenance from a former spouse and children's
income are ignored, so child support payments are not taken into account.

Where the applicant is in receipt of income support or income-based jobseeker's allowance, **38.38**
the maximum amount of CTC will be payable. To calculate the amount of child tax credit to
which an applicant is entitled, it is necessary to add together the appropriate 'elements',
namely 'the family element', 'the baby element', and 'the child element'.

Annual CTC rates are £545.00 for the family element and for the baby element (this is payable **38.39**
if there is a baby in the family below the age of one) and £1,845.00 for the child element.

38.40   For example, if a couple have a joint income not exceeding £10,000 per annum and one child aged four, the annual CTC payable will be £2,390 (or £45.96 per week) made up of £1,845.00 for the child element and £545 for the family element.

38.41   By contrast, once the joint income of the parties exceeds £14,495, the CTC payable is less. The child tax payable is calculated as the maximum CTC but then reduced by 37 per cent of the amount by which the applicant's income exceeds £14,495 per annum.

38.42   As the income of the applicant increases, the CTC payable is reduced.

38.43   All families receive the family element unless their income exceeds £50,000. At this point, the family element is also reduced by £1 for every £15.00 of family income exceeding £50,000. (Note: these are the present thresholds and may be subject to change in the future.)

G   THE WORKING TAX CREDIT

The credit

38.44   The Working Tax Credit ('WTC') is a payment to top up the earnings of working people on low incomes and is available to employees and the self-employed. It lasts for one year and is calculated on the basis of the applicant's income in the previous tax year. The amount payable depends upon eligibility to various elements (e.g., couple and lone parent element etc.) but the basic element is an annual rate of £1,730.00

Who can claim?

38.45   The applicant must be present in Great Britain and be working. In certain circumstances (for example, if the applicant is aged 25 or over and works for at least 30 hours per week or the applicant is aged 16 or over, works for at least 16 hours per week, and has a disability which puts the applicant at a disadvantage in obtaining employment), WTC can be claimed by the childless applicant.

38.46   WTC is paid in addition to any CTC to which the applicant may be entitled. The claimant's annual income is compared with the 'income threshold figure'. This is £5,220 for 2006–2007. If the claimant's income is below that figure the maximum amount of WTC will be payable. What is paid depends upon the claimant's circumstances. The 'basic' element of £1,730 for 2007–2008 will always be paid, as may a couple or lone parent element of £1,700 and an element if the hours worked each week amount to 30 or more in which case a further £705.00 is paid.

38.47   If the family's income exceeds £5,220 the maximum WTC is reduced by 37 per cent of the excess until it disappears.

Child care costs

38.48   As well as being entitled to WTC, an applicant may, depending on his or her income, be able to obtain extra help towards the costs of registered or approved child care—this is known as the 'child care costs element'.

The child care costs element is worth up to 80p in tax credit for every £1 per week spent on **38.49** approved child care, up to a limit of £175 per week for one child and £300 a week for two or more children. For example, if £100 per week is spent on child care, the child care element would be worth £80.00 per week and so on. The child care element is added to the amount of WTC to which the applicant is entitled.

PART 3 HOUSING BENEFIT

The law on housing benefit is to be found in the Social Security Contributions and Benefits **38.50** Act 1992 and the Housing Benefit (General) Regulations 1987, as amended. The scheme is in the form of rent rebates funded and administered by housing authorities. The benefit is non-contributory and is available to those on low income who pay rent in the public or private sector.

H WHO QUALIFIES?

In order to qualify for housing benefit the claimant must be liable to make payments in **38.51** respect of a dwelling which he occupies as his home. In general only one home is allowed.

The following people will be treated as if they are 'liable to make payments in respect of a **38.52** dwelling':

(a) the person who is liable to make those payments or his partner;

(b) a person who has to make the payments if he is to continue to live in the home, because the third party who is liable to make the payments is not doing so; in this case the claimant must have been the former partner of the defaulting third party, or some other person whom it is reasonable to treat as liable to make the payments.

I WHAT PAYMENTS WILL BE MADE?

Housing benefit is payable for rent, and the appropriate maximum housing benefit to which **38.53** the claimant is entitled is calculated by reference to the amount of the claimant's 'eligible rent'.

'Eligible rent'

The amount of the claimant's 'eligible rent' means those periodical payments which the **38.54** claimant is liable to make in respect of the dwelling which he occupies as his home. Such payments include the following: rent; payments in respect of a licence or permission to occupy the dwelling; mesne profits; payments for use and occupation of the dwelling; service charges which are a condition of the right to occupy the dwelling.

38.55 The amount of the claimant's 'eligible rent' is the total rent which the claimant is liable to pay, minus charges for water, sewerage, and certain ineligible service charges.

38.56 If the rent is registered and the rent which the claimant is liable to pay is limited to the registered rent, then the claimant's 'eligible rent' cannot exceed the amount of the registered rent.

Reduction of 'eligible rent' and maximum housing benefit

38.57 The amount of the claimant's 'eligible rent' may be reduced by an 'appropriate' amount if the assessment officer considers that:

(a) the claimant is occupying a dwelling that is too large for the requirements of the claimant and those who also occupy that dwelling; or

(b) the rent payable for the claimant's dwelling is unreasonably high for the area in which the property is situated.

In this situation the claimant's maximum housing benefit will be calculated with reference to the 'eligible rent' as reduced by the 'appropriate' amount.

J   AMOUNT OF HOUSING BENEFIT

38.58 A payment of housing benefit will be made if:

(a) the claimant has no income; or

(b) the claimant's income does not exceed the 'applicable amount'.

The applicable amount

38.59 The applicable amount appropriate for the claimant and his family includes personal allowances and premiums which are almost the same as those used for calculating income support.

Assessing the claimant's income and capital

38.60 Having ascertained the amount of a claimant's 'applicable amount', the next step is to ascertain his income and capital in order to determine whether or not his income exceeds his weekly applicable amount.

38.61 Where the claimant is a member of a family, the income and capital of any member of that family will be treated as the income and capital of that person. The capital of a child or young person who is a member of the claimant's family will not be treated as the capital of the claimant, but special rules will apply where the child or young person has capital in excess of £6,000. The practitioner is referred to the regulations for full details.

38.62 The claimant's income is assessed as follows:

(a) Calculate the claimant's weekly earnings (the sums that will be counted as part of the claimant's earnings are clearly set out in the regulations and the practitioner is referred to them. They include, for example, WTC and CTC).

(b) Adding to it any tariff income from capital—where the claimant's capital exceeds £6,000, it will be treated as equivalent to a weekly tariff income of £1 for each complete £250 in excess of £6,000 but not exceeding £16,000.

(c) Certain sums will be disregarded in assessing the claimant's income. The rules in relation to those sums are complex and the solicitor is referred to the regulations for details. However, sums to be disregarded include, among other things, child maintenance and £25.00 a week of a lone parent earnings. It should be noted that where the claimant is in receipt of income support the whole of his income will be disregarded.

Effect of capital on housing benefit

Where a claimant's capital exceeds £16,000 he will be disqualified from any entitlement to housing benefit. Certain sums will be disregarded in assessing what does and does not amount to capital.   **38.63**

Appropriate maximum housing benefit

The appropriate maximum housing benefit consists of 100 per cent of the claimant's eligible rent.   **38.64**

In each case there will be a deduction, where appropriate, in respect of a non-dependent person who resides with the claimant, ranging from £7.40 a week where the non-dependant is not working to £47.75 where the non-dependant has a gross weekly income of £353.00 or more. The rates of the relevant weekly deductions are updated regularly, and the solicitor should ascertain the appropriate rate at his time of reference.   **38.65**

Where the claimant's income exceeds the applicable amount

The amount of housing benefit to which the claimant is entitled will be reduced in certain circumstances. This will happen when the claimant's income exceeds 'the applicable amount' (i.e., the relevant income support level). The reduction is approximately 65 pence for every pound by which the claimant's income exceeds the income support level.   **38.66**

Minimum housing benefit

Housing benefit will not be payable if the amount to which the claimant is entitled is less than 50 pence per week.   **38.67**

How is the benefit paid?

Where the claimant is a tenant of the local authority (or its successor social housing landlord), housing benefit will reduce the amount of rent payable so that no money will pass through the tenant's hands. Conversely, where the claimant is a private tenant, housing benefit will usually be paid direct to the landlord.   **38.68**

K   COUNCIL TAX BENEFIT

38.69   Council tax benefit is paid by local authorities although it is a national scheme and the rules are mainly determined by DWP regulations. Details of the scheme are contained in the Council Tax Benefit (General) Regulations 1992 (SI 1992/1814, as amended). The basic conditions for eligibility are that the claimant's income is low enough and their savings and other capital do not exceed £16,000. Council tax benefit operates in a similar way to housing benefit, save that the benefit will be reduced by approximately 20 pence for each pound by which the claimant's income exceeds the relevant income support level. An income support claimant is eligible for a 100 per cent reduction in respect of the council tax; for others the council tax bill will be reduced appropriately.

38.70   Detailed guidance on the rules relating to council tax liability, valuations, reductions, discounts, and benefits may be found in CPAG's *Council Tax Handbook*.

PART 4   CHILD BENEFIT

38.71   The law on child benefit is to be found in the Social Security Contributions and Benefits Act 1992 and the various child benefit regulations.

L   CHILD BENEFIT

General

38.72   Child benefit is a standard weekly amount presently £18.10 for the only, elder, or eldest child and £12.10 for each subsequent child paid to the person (normally but not necessarily a parent) who is responsible for a child.

Definition of a child

38.73   Child benefit is payable in respect of:

(a)   all children under 16;
(b)   children of 16 to 20 who are still in full-time non-advanced (i.e., not above A level or NVQ level 3) education (amended by the Child Benefit Act 2005).

38.74   Child benefit is not paid for children at university, training for professional qualifications, apprenticed, etc., or for children in full-time employment.

38.75   When a child under 20 leaves school, child benefit will generally still be payable for him until the start of the new term after he has left, i.e., right through the school holidays, unless he gets a full-time job or a training place.

Person responsible

A person is responsible for a child if either: **38.76**

(a) he has the child living with him; *or*

(b) he contributes to the child's maintenance at a weekly rate of not less than the rate of child benefit.

More than one person may count as responsible for one child but benefit will only be paid to one person. There are rules for determining who should receive the benefit if more than one person claims it. If the child is living with both his parents (whether they are married or not), his mother will be the one entitled to claim the benefit. If the child is not living with both parents, the person with whom he is living (whether a parent or not) will have first claim to the benefit. If the household in which the child is living comprises a parent and a non-parent (for example, his mother and her boyfriend), the parent will naturally have priority over the non-parent.

Example 1 Cedric is 16 and is still at school doing A levels. He lives with his mother and father, Mr and Mrs Conn. Child benefit will be payable in respect of Cedric. As he is living with both his parents, both parents qualify as responsible for him. His mother is the one who has the prior claim to benefit, although if she wants Mr Conn to receive the benefit, he can apply enclosing her written statement that she does not wish to claim the benefit herself.

Example 2 Dennis is five. His parents, Mr and Mrs Drabble, have split up. Dennis is living with his mother who is cohabiting with Mr Eves. Mr Drabble pays voluntary maintenance for Dennis of £30 per week. Child benefit is payable in respect of Dennis. Mr Drabble, Mrs Drabble, and Mr Eves can all claim to be responsible for him (Mrs Drabble and Mr Eves because he is living with them and Mr Drabble because he contributes to Dennis's maintenance). Mrs Drabble and Mr Eves have the prior claim to the benefit over Mr Drabble because Dennis is living with them. As between Mrs Drabble and Mr Eves, Mrs Drabble has the prior claim because she is Dennis's parent.

Making a claim

A form on which to claim child benefit can be obtained from the DWP. If the claimant is   **38.77**
seeking to have the benefit transferred from someone else who has priority, he will have to provide with the claim form a statement from the person with priority that she does not want to claim the benefit herself. If he is seeking to have the benefit transferred on the basis that he now has priority, three weeks will have to elapse after the claim is made before the transfer can take place.

Payment of benefit

Child benefit is tax-free. However, it forms part of the recipient's income for the purposes of   **38.78**
income support but not for working tax credit.

PART 5   STATE BENEFITS AND MARRIAGE OR CIVIL PARTNERSHIP BREAKDOWN

M   RELEVANCE OF STATE BENEFITS IN DETERMINING APPROPRIATE MAINTENANCE

38.79   A spouse or civil partner cannot normally rely on the fact that his family will be eligible for state benefits as relieving him from his obligation to maintain them. The relevance of state benefits in an application for periodical payments after divorce is discussed in Chapter 19.

N   MAINTENANCE VERSUS STATE BENEFITS: PROS AND CONS FOR THE RECIPIENT

38.80   It quite often happens that one spouse, usually the wife, is on benefit (usually income support) and the other spouse is earning but not at a very high rate. Where it is unlikely that maintenance from the husband will be fixed at a rate significantly more than the wife would be receiving by way of state benefits, it must be remembered that if the wife is taken off benefit she may well lose not only the weekly amount of cash benefit but also the other benefits to which she is automatically entitled by virtue of the fact that she is on income support, for example, housing benefit, free school meals and prescriptions, etc. On top of this, she will lose her opportunity to claim payments from the social fund as she could have done had she remained on income support.

38.81   It follows that sometimes it may pay the wife to receive slightly less maintenance in order to stay on benefit and this possibility must be kept firmly in mind when advising on the level of maintenance which would be acceptable and in presenting applications for periodical payments to the court.

O   LUMP SUMS AND INCOME SUPPORT

38.82   A lump sum payment which is in reality a form of capitalized maintenance will be counted as income of the family for income support purposes and will prevent the family from receiving benefit for a period of time.

38.83   There does, however, seem to be some leeway over certain lump sums where what is really happening is that the recipient is realising her interest in a capital asset owned by her solely or by her and her spouse jointly and sold/divided up/retained by the other spouse on the breakdown of the marriage. Thus the following types of lump sum will be regarded as capital and will therefore only put a stop to the family's entitlement to benefit if the family has more than £16,000 capital altogether:

(a) A lump sum ordered by the court or agreed between the parties as representing the capitalization of an interest in joint property or property held by the other party solely; for example, £2,000 paid by the husband to the wife representing her interest in the family car and the furniture in the matrimonial home which he has kept.

(b) A lump sum ordered by the court or agreed between the parties representing the allocation of or division of money held in banks, building societies, or similar.

(c) A sum derived from the proceeds of sale of the matrimonial home or intended to compensate the claimant for her loss of interest in the home (such a sum will not be counted as capital for at least six months).

(d) Payments in kind. The court does not have power in ancillary relief proceedings to order one spouse to purchase any item for the other spouse so the most that could be done would be for him to give an undertaking to do so.

P WELFARE BENEFITS AND CIVIL PARTNERS

Section 254 and sch. 24, Civil Partnership Act 2004 places civil partners in the same position as spouses, and same sex cohabitants in the same position as opposite sex cohabitants, in respect of the welfare benefits discussed above. The relevant regulations have been amended accordingly. **38.84**

These provisions mark a significant change for same sex couples whether or not they are registered civil partners. Previously, such couples were not treated as a single economic unit and hence their income and capital was not aggregated. **38.85**

Guidance on what amounts to 'cohabitation' was laid down in *Kimber* v *Kimber* [2000] 1 FLR 383 and includes, for example, a shared home, stability and a degree of permanence in the relationship, a sexual relationship, and public acknowledgement of the relationship. **38.86**

Q CHAPTER SUMMARY

On the breakdown of a marriage, civil partnership, or cohabitation, one or both of the parties involved may need to claim welfare benefits. The following may be available (depending upon the precise circumstances): **38.87**

(a) income support;
(b) loans or grants from the social fund;
(c) tax credits;
(d) housing benefit;
(e) council tax benefit;
(f) child benefit.

39

THE LOCAL AUTHORITY AND HOUSING

A THE HOMELESS

Part VII of the Housing Act 1996, and the Homelessness Act 2002, deal with the provision **39.01**
of accommodation for those who are without a home. In particular the Homelessness
Act 2002 requires the local authority to formulate a homelessness strategy and to carry out
homelessness reviews. It also amends the 1996 Act at various points.

Who is homeless?

A person is 'homeless' for the purposes of the 1996 Act if he has no accommodation in the **39.02**
United Kingdom or elsewhere. He is treated as having no accommodation if:

(a) there is no accommodation which he, together with any person who normally resides
    with him as a member of his family or in circumstances in which it is reasonable for that
    person to reside with him, is entitled to occupy by virtue of an interest in it or by court
    order or by licence or statutory right; or
(b) he has accommodation but he cannot secure entry to it or it is probable that occupation
    of it will lead to domestic violence or other violence from some other person living
    there or to threats of violence from some other person with whom he is associated and
    who is likely to carry the threats out: ss. 175 and 177(1A) of the 1996 Act.

Note that the term 'domestic violence' does not include pestering or harassment but relates
to actual violence or threats of violence. The term 'associated person' has the same meaning
as found in Part IV of the Family Law Act 1996 (and as now amended) and is found in s. 178
of the 1996 Act.

39.03   However, a person must not be treated as having accommodation unless it is accommodation which it would be reasonable for that person to continue to occupy: s. 175(3), 1996 Act. Where the accommodation concerned is of a purely temporary or emergency kind, such as a women's refuge, this does not prevent the person using it from being 'homeless' under the 1996 Act (*R v Ealing London Borough Council, ex parte Sidhu* (1982) 2 HLR 45). However, in *R v Brent London Borough Council, ex parte Awua* [1996] AC 55, the House of Lords held that there was *no* requirement for the accommodation to be settled or permanent for the person to be regarded as having accommodation. The 'reasonableness' of accommodation is assessed by comparing it with the general standard of housing in that particular area (see also *R v London Borough of Brent, ex parte Sawyers* [1994] 26 HLR 44: duty of local authority under s. 23, Children Act 1989, to provide accommodation for any disabled child it is looking after which is not unsuitable to that child's particular needs).

39.04   When considering the issue of homelessness a local authority is bound to take into account matters other than the actual quality of the accommodation available; such other matters may include violence or the threat of violence from someone not residing in the available accommodation (*R v Broxbourne Borough Council, ex parte Willmoth* (1989) 22 HLR 118). Furthermore, the authority is bound to take into consideration the particular physical or mental needs or requirements of the particular applicant and his family (see *R v Broxbourne BC* (above)).

39.05   Further, a person is 'threatened with homelessness' if it is likely that he will become homeless within 28 days (s. 175(4), 1996 Act).

39.06   It is those who are homeless or threatened with homelessness who may be able to receive help under the 1996 Act. Some claimants have priority over others.

Priority need for accommodation

39.07   Under s. 189(1) of the 1996 Act, a homeless person or a person threatened with homelessness has a priority need for accommodation if:

(a)   she is a pregnant woman or he or she lives with or might reasonably be expected to live with a pregnant woman, *or*

(b)   he has dependent children who are residing with him or might reasonably be expected to reside with him; *or*

(c)   he, or any person who lives with him or might reasonably be expected to do so, is vulnerable as a result of old age, mental illness or handicap, physical disability, or other special reason; *or*

(d)   homelessness or threat of homelessness arises out of an emergency such as flood, fire, or other disaster.

39.08   The Homelessness (Priority Need for Accommodation) (England) Order 2002 (SI 2002/2051) (there are different provisions for Wales) provides that the following also have a priority need:

(a)   any child aged 16 or 17 who has not been in the care of a local authority and no duty to accommodate him is owed under s. 20, Children Act 1989;

(b)   any young person under the age of 21 who was accommodated or fostered by a local authority between the ages of 16 and 18;

(c) any person who is aged 21 or over and is vulnerable as a result of being looked after, accommodated, or fostered;

(d) any person who is vulnerable as a result of having served in the armed forces or having been in prison;

(e) any person who is vulnerable as a result of ceasing to occupy accommodation because of violence or threats of violence.

Where a woman is pregnant she qualifies as having a priority need for housing, whatever stage her pregnancy has reached. The test in paragraph (b) above is that the child must be dependent on and must reside with the applicant; this does not mean that the child must be 'wholly and exclusively dependent' on the applicant or that he must be 'wholly and exclusively residing only with the applicant' (*R v London Borough of Lambeth, ex parte Vagliviello* (1990) 22 HLR 392). It would be possible for the child, as in the case of *Vagliviello*, to live partly with one parent and partly with the other under a 'shared care' arrangement and still have a priority need for housing.

Where the dependent children are in fact living with the applicant at the time of the authority's decision then it is not relevant to apply the part of the test which requires that the child 'might reasonably be expected to reside' with him (*R v London Borough of Lambeth, ex parte Bodunrin* (1992) 24 HLR 647). Where the children are in fact residing with a parent, the grant of a residence order is irrelevant to the issue of priority need as such orders can be varied at any time (*R v Ealing London Borough Council, ex parte Sidhu* (above)). **39.09**

In *R v Port Talbot Borough Council, ex parte McCarthy* (1990) 23 HLR 207 the parents were divorced and had a joint custody order, now a residence order, in relation to the children, but with care and control having been granted to the mother. The father had visiting (but not staying) contact with the children for three days each week. The Court of Appeal held that the local authority was right to find that the father's contact did not amount to having the children to reside with him and that the children could only reasonably be expected to reside with the parent having care and control, in this case the mother. It should be remembered that children living with their parent(s) do not qualify for priority need housing in their own right (*R v Oldham Metropolitan Borough Council, ex parte Garlick* [1993] AC 509). **39.10**

For guidance on the interpretation of the term 'vulnerable' see the extensive guidance given by Auld LJ in *Osmani v Camden London Borough Council* [2005] HLR 22, followed by Jonathan Parker LJ in *Bellouti v Wandsworth London Borough Council* [2005] HLR 46. **39.11**

Duties of the housing authority

If a person applies to a housing authoity for accommodation or assistance in obtaining accommodation and the authority has reason to believe that he is homeless or threatened with homelessness the authority must make enquiries to satisfy itself whether the person is homeless or threatened with homelessness and, if so, whether he has a priority need and whether he became homeless or threatened with homelessness intentionally. If the housing authority has reason to believe that the person threatened with homelessness is eligible for assistance, has a priority need and has not become threatened by homelessness intentionally, it must take reasonable steps to secure that his accommodation does not cease to be available for his occupation (s. 195, 1996 Act). **39.12**

39.13   Once it has made its enquiries, if the housing authority is satisfied that the person *is* homeless or threatened with homelessness, it is under a duty towards him. The exact nature of the duty depends on whether he has a priority need and whether he has become homeless or threatened with homelessness intentionally (see paragraph 39.15 below):

(a)   Homeless or threatened with homelessness intentionally but with a priority need—duty to secure accommodation for his occupation and provide him with (or secure that he is provided with) advice and assistance (s. 190(2), 1996 Act), as amended. The applicant's housing needs must be assessed before advice and assistance are provided and must include information as to the likely availability in the local authority's district of accommodation appropriate to the applicant's housing needs: s 190(4) and (5).

(b)   Threatened with homelessness intentionally but with no priority need—duty to give appropriate advice and assistance to secure that accommodation becomes available for his occupation.

(c)   Homeless with a priority need, not intentionally—duty to secure that accommodation is available for his occupation—(s. 193(2), 1996 Act). This duty now lasts until one of the circumstances specified in s. 193(6), (7), and (8) applies: s. 193(3). These circumstances include, for example, the applicant ceasing to occupy as his principal home the accommodation made available for his occupation.

There are provisions enabling the housing authority to whom application has been made to pass responsibility to another housing authority if the applicant has no local connection with the area in which the application has been made (s. 198).

39.14   The accommodation provided may be in council property but applicants may be placed in private housing and temporary accommodation may be in hostels, women's refuges, bed and breakfast establishments. It amounts to 'somewhere to live': *R v London Borough of Wandsworth, ex parte Mansoor* [1996] 3 All ER 913A.

The meaning of 'intentionally homeless'

39.15   A person becomes homeless intentionally if he deliberately does or fails to do anything in consequence of which he ceases to occupy accommodation which is available for his occupation and which it would have been reasonable for him to continue to occupy: s. 191(1), 1996 Act.

39.16   A person is to be treated as becoming homeless intentionally if he deliberately enters into an arrangement the likely result of which is that he will be forced to leave accommodation which is available for his occupation and which it would have been reasonable for him to continue to occupy: s. 191(3), 1996 Act.

39.17   It would seem that people who have got into genuine financial difficulties and thus put themselves at risk of eviction will not be regarded as intentionally homeless. Thus, an act or omission in good faith on the part of a person who was (a) unaware of any relevant fact, or (b) ignorant as to his legal remedies or rights, is not to be treated as deliberate: s. 191(2), 1996 Act. On the other hand, if someone deliberately decides to sell his house or give up his tenancy or wilfully refuses to pay his rent or mortgage so that he is turned out of his house, he will probably be regarded as intentionally homeless (see, for example, *R v Oldham Metropolitan Borough Council, ex parte Garlick* [1993] AC 509). Therefore, a decision to sell a house before possession proceedings have commenced and ignoring advice not to sell may constitute intentionality (*R v Leeds City Council, ex parte Adamiec and Adamiec* (1991) 24 HLR 138).

However, it has been held that it cannot be reasonable for a person to continue to occupy accommodation when he can no longer discharge his financial obligations in respect of it (*R v Hillingdon London Borough Council, ex parte Tinn* (1988) 20 HLR 305), but it is not necessarily wrong for an authority to assert that it is reasonable for a person to continue in occupation of a property until an order for possession is made (*R v London Borough of Croydon, ex parte Jarvis* (1994) 26 HLR 194).   **39.18**

In deciding whether it is reasonable for a person to continue to occupy accommodation, a local authority may take into account violence or threats of violence by former husbands (*R v Broxbourne Borough Council, ex parte Willmoth* (above)) and other people (*R v Northampton Borough Council, ex parte Clarkson* [1992] 24 HLR 529). The authority may require the applicant in some circumstances to seek redress from the courts (see, for example, *R v Wandsworth London Borough Council, ex parte Nimako-Boateng* [1984] FLR 192), although the authority is unlikely to request this where the violence has been extreme. Therefore, battered wives who leave home because they have been subjected to violence are unlikely to be regarded as intentionally homeless.   **39.19**

B   SECURE TENANTS

Local authority tenants and other tenants classed as secure tenants under the Housing Act 1985 (see s. 79), enjoy special protection under that Act. In particular, the tenancy cannot be brought to an end by the landlord unless he obtains a court order for possession (s. 82). The grounds on which possession can be ordered are set out in the 1985 Act and include, for example, non-payment of rent.   **39.20**

C   CHAPTER SUMMARY

1. Local authorities owe a variety of duties to homeless people.   **39.21**
2. The precise duty depends upon all the circumstances leading to homelessness but where a person is unintentionally homeless and has a priority need (for example, the applicant is pregnant), the local authority will usually have to rehouse him or her.

40

COHABITANTS

A INTRODUCTION

Throughout the book reference has been made to the position of the cohabitants in contrast to the position of parties to a marriage or registered civil partners. While attempting to avoid unnecessary repetition the purpose of this chapter is to summarize the principal legal consequences of cohabitation and to refer to the various chapters where a full explanation is provided. **40.01**

This chapter concentrates on opposite sex cohabitation but reference will be made to same sex cohabitants where appropriate. **40.02**

Before going further, it may be useful to consider what the term 'cohabitation' means. **40.03**

40.04 There is no statutory definition, but a helpful and generally accepted interpretation was given by His Honour Judge Norris QC in *Churchill* v *Roach* [2003] All ER(D) 348, as follows:

> It seems to me to have elements of permanence, to involve a consideration of the frequency and intimacy of contact, to contain an element of mutual support, to require some consideration of the degree of voluntary restraint upon personal freedom which each party undertakes, and to involve an element of community of resources. None of these factors is of itself sufficient, but each may provide an indicator.

40.05 Same sex cohabitation no doubt has the same characteristics. A definition of such a relationship was offered by Baroness Hollis of Heigham during the passage of the Civil Partnership Bill through Parliament as 'two people of the same sex are to be regarded as living together as if they were civil partners if, but only if, they would be regarded as living together as husband and wife were they instead two people of the opposite sex': Hansard HL Grand Committee, col GC 490.

B PROTECTION FROM VIOLENCE

40.06 As was seen in Chapter 25, cohabitants and former cohabitants may seek occupation orders or non-molestation orders in their favour under Part IV of the Family Law Act 1996. The definition of 'cohabitant' in s. 62, Family Law Act 1996 has been extended to include same sex cohabitants who are not registered civil partners. Further, the term 'associated person' now includes a former civil partner, a same sex cohabitant, or former cohabitant, a relative of a civil partner, and a party to a civil partnership agreement.

40.07 It will be recalled that the duration of occupation orders is dependent upon the question of whether the cohabitant is entitled to occupy the dwelling-house in the first place. By contrast, non-molestation orders are not subject to a strict limit unless the court directs otherwise.

C INHERITANCE

40.08 So far as an opposite sex or same sex cohabitant is concerned there is no entitlement in the event of intestacy. It is essential therefore that the cohabitants consider whether to make appropriate provision for each other by making wills. These may need amendment on the breakdown of the relationship.

40.09 In so far as they hold property as beneficial joint tenants, the doctrine of survivorship will ensure that on the death of one, the other will obtain the property absolutely. Thus on breakdown of the relationship, severance of the joint tenancy should be considered. Where property is vested in the sole name of the deceased, it may be that as a result of the application of the principles of the law of trusts (see Chapter 28), the survivor can establish an interest enforceable against the personal representatives.

40.10 Although a cohabitant has no entitlement on intestacy, he may nevertheless benefit from the estate if the deceased leaves no relatives within the statutory list (as contained in s. 46(1), Administration of Estates Act 1925). In such circumstances, the deceased's estate will devolve to the Crown as *bona vacantia*. The Crown is empowered to provide out of the estate for 'dependants, whether kindred or not, of the intestate, and other persons for whom the intestate might reasonably have been expected to make provision'.

In the event of no will being made (and the deceased dying intestate), or a will being proved **40.11** which does not make reasonable financial provision for the surviving cohabitant, the survivor may apply to the court for financial provision pursuant to the Inheritance (Provision for Family and Dependants) Act 1975 ('IA 1975'), as amended by the Law Reform (Succession) Act 1995 and the Civil Partnership Act 2004. In these circumstances the survivor of opposite or same sex cohabition may apply to the court for financial provision from the deceased's estate. The 'financial provision' contemplated here is 'such financial provision as it would be reasonable in all the circumstances of the case for the applicant *to receive for his maintenance*': s. 1(2)(b), IA 1975 (emphasis added).

It should be noted that this is in contrast with the 'financial provision' contemplated for **40.12** spouses or civil partners which is defined as 'such financial provision as it would be reasonable in all the circumstances of the case for a husband and wife (or a civil partner) to receive, whether or not that provision is required for his or her maintenance': s. 2(a) and (aa), IA 1975, as amended. In these cases, the court is to have regard to what the survivor would have been awarded in ancillary relief proceedings.

Under previous statutory provisions, the surviving cohabitant had to satisfy the court that **40.13** immediately before the death of the deceased he or she had been wholly or partly maintained by the deceased: under the 1995 Act there is no need to prove such a dependency. However, the claiming cohabitant has to show that during the whole period of two years prior to the death of the deceased he or she was living in the same household as the deceased as the husband or wife of the deceased. The death in question must have occurred on or after 1 January 1996: s. 1(1)(ba) and s. 1(1A).

Several recent cases have interpreted the requirement for cohabitation under s. 1(1)(ba). In **40.14** *Churchill* v *Roach* [2003], for example, the applicant was found not to have lived in the same household as the deceased for the required two years because the parties had lived in separate properties for all but the final year of their relationship. Their relative independence from each other led the judge to conclude that there were 'two separate domestic economies'.

However, the claim did not fail in its entirety since the applicant had been partly maintained **40.15** by the deceased before his death and she could thus demonstrate the necessary dependency under s. 1(1)(e), IA 1975.

Occasional periods of separation will not prevent the court from holding that the couple **40.16** were 'living in the same household' provided that the separations are 'transitory' and there is evidence to suggest that, had the deceased lived, the relationship would have continued: *Gully* v *Dix* [2004] 1 WLR 1399.

What does it mean to 'live together as husband and wife'? This aspect of the requirements of **40.17** the Act was explored in *Re Watson (Deceased)* [1999] 1 FLR 878, Neuberger J recognizing 'the multifarious nature of marital relationships' so that the fact that the sexual relationship between the applicant and the deceased had ended some time ago did not mean that the application failed. It was sufficient that the parties regarded each other as important in their lives.

40.18 If the court is satisfied that the conditions under s. 1 are established, it may make an order under the terms of s. 2 of the 1975 Act.

40.19 The powers of the court are wide and include the possibility of orders for periodical payments, lump sums, transfers of property, settlements of property, and variation of settlements. Further, the court may require the acquisition of property for the benefit of the survivor using assets of the estate to fund the purchase.

40.20 When the court is deciding whether it should make an order for financial provision and, if so, the terms of the order, it must consider:

(a) the age of the applicant and the length of the period during which the applicant lived as the husband or wife of the deceased and in the same household as the deceased; and

(b) the contribution made by the applicant to the welfare of the family of the deceased, including any contribution made by looking after the home or caring for the family: s. 3(2A), IA 1975.

40.21 Where the applicant is unable to satisfy the requirements of s. 1(1)ba, IA 1975, he may still have a claim under s. 1(1)(e) of the Act for provision as a dependant of the deceased but the general view is that it is likely that he would be awarded less, the calculation being based on the values of his lost dependency.

40.22 In any event, it would seem from guidance given by Robert Walker J in *Graham* v *Graham* [1997] 1 FLR 860 that the court will be concerned to meet the applicant's reasonable future needs (in this case, for modest accommodation) rather than to match the higher standard of living enjoyed by him during the period of cohabitation.

40.23 See also Chapter 28, which deals in more detail with aspects of wills and inheritance.

D STATUS OF CHILDREN

40.24 The law relating to children is dealt with in Chapters 29 and 30. However, it is important to remember some of the distinctions which apply to a child born to married parents in comparison with one born to unmarried parents. Whereas parental responsibility is vested in both married parents, an unmarried mother has parental responsibility exclusively irrespective of the stability of her relationship with the unmarried father: s. 2(2), Children Act 1989 ('CA 1989').

40.25 However, the unmarried father may acquire parental responsibility in one of a number of ways as follows:

(a) by marrying the mother;

(b) by entering into a parental responsibility agreement with the mother. This agreement must be in writing and in a prescribed form: s. 4(1)(b) and (2), CA 1989;

(c) by obtaining a parental responsibility order. The application would normally be made to the family proceedings court but it may be made to the county court or High Court. The mother may deny that the applicant is the father of the child and the issue of paternity would then have to be dealt with as a preliminary matter. In determining the application the court must have regard to the child's welfare as its paramount consideration (s. 1(1), CA 1989), it must have regard to the principle that delay in determining the issue is likely to prejudice the welfare of the child (s. 1(2), CA 1989) and must not make an order unless it considers that doing so would be better for the child than making no order at all (s. 1(5), CA 1989). Curiously the court is not obliged to have specific regard to the so-called 'welfare checklist' in s. 1(3) but no doubt will consider these matters indirectly to seek to promote the child's welfare (see further Chapter 29).

(d) by being appointed as the guardian of the child by the court: s. 5, CA 1989. The unmarried father may appoint a testamentary guardian provided he has parental responsibility for the child in question at the date of his death. However, the appointment will only be effective if the unmarried mother is already dead;

(e) by obtaining a residence order in his favour. Section 12(1), CA 1989 provides that in these circumstances the court shall also make a s. 4 parental responsibility order in favour of the unmarried father unless he has already otherwise acquired parental responsibility.

(f) Section 111 of the Adoption and Children Act 2002 came into force on 1 December 2003 (The Adoption and Children Act 2002 (Commencement No 4) Order 2003 (SI 2003/3079)). Where a child is born to unmarried parents after this date, the father will automatically acquire parental responsibility when he is registered on the birth certificate as the father. The provision is not, however, retrospective in effect.

It should be noted also that the unmarried father is treated as a 'parent' for the purpose of applying for one or more of the s. 8 orders, irrespective of whether or not he has parental responsibility for the child in question. The significance of this is that the unmarried father need not seek the court's permission to pursue his application. **40.26**

E FINANCIAL PROVISION AND THE SIGNIFICANCE OF THE CHILD SUPPORT ACT 1991

It should be noted that, subject to the provisions of the Child Support Act 1991 ('CSA 1991'), cohabitants have no obligation to provide financial support for each other and are unable to apply for periodical payments orders for their own benefit. Further, the cohabitant may not apply for a pension sharing or pension attachment order under ss. 24B, 25B, or 25C, Matrimonial Causes Act 1973. **40.27**

Section 15 and sch. 1, CA 1989 provide a range of orders which may be sought against the parent of the child, for the benefit of the child of the unmarried family, by a parent or guardian of the child or by any person in whose favour a residence order is in force with respect to the child. **40.28**

40.29 Of particular relevance now is the availability of an order for a lump sum payment of up to £1,000 in the family proceedings court, and orders for lump sum payments of any amount and for settlement and transfer of property orders for the benefit of the child in the county court or High Court. However, note that property adjustment orders will not ordinarily be made under s. 15 and sch. 1, CA 1989, to provide benefits for the child after he has attained independence, unless there are exceptional circumstances: *A* v *A* (*A Minor: Financial Provision*) [1994] 1 FLR 657.

40.30 The position so far as financial support for the child is concerned has been affected by the coming into force of the CSA 1991.

Child Support Act 1991—the basic principles

40.31 As has been stated in previous chapters the aim of the legislation is to establish a regime to ensure that the non-resident parent (whether or not married) makes a significant contribution to the financial support of his or her natural child.

40.32 The Act empowers the Child Support Agency to trace non-resident parents, to investigate their means and calculate, collect and enforce child maintenance payments. The Act is discussed in further detail in Chapter 20.

The position of the unmarried father

40.33 The unmarried father who is a non-resident parent has a statutory obligation to maintain his natural child. This is irrespective of whether he has parental responsibility for the child or has had his parental responsibility for the child terminated by a court order: *R* v *Secretary of State for Social Security, ex parte West* [1999] 1 FLR 1233.

40.34 The man in question may, of course, deny paternity, in which case the CSA 1991 provides that a maintenance calculation may not be made against him unless the case falls into certain categories: s. 26(1).

40.35 Where one of the categories applies, a maintenance calculation will be carried out despite a denial of paternity: in other words parentage will be assumed and liability to pay will arise.

40.36 Under s. 26(2) parentage will be assumed in the following circumstances:

(a) Where the man was married to the child's mother between the conception and the birth of the child concerned and the child has not been subsequently adopted by third parties.

(b) Where the man has been registered as the father on the birth certificate.

(c) Where the man alleged to be the father of the child has refused to take a scientific test (to determine parentage) or has taken such a test but refuses to accept the result.

(d) Where the man has adopted the child—the term 'qualifying child' includes a child adopted by the prospective payer and production of an adoption order would be conclusive.

(e) Where the man alleged to be the father of the child is a parent of the child in question by virtue of an order under s. 30 of the Human Fertilisation and Embryology Act 1990

('HFEA 1990'). This arises where a married couple who have provided genetic material leading to the conception of a child apply to the court for a 'parental order' so that the child is treated in law as their child. Again the production of such an order would be conclusive.

(f)   Where the alleged parent is a parent by virtue of ss. 27 or 28, HFEA 1990. Section 28 is especially relevant here, providing that a married man will be treated as the father of a child born to his wife through AID unless he is able to demonstrate that he did not consent to the process.

(g)   Where a declaration of parentage under s. 56 of the Family Law Act 1986 is in force. (A child may use this procedure to apply to the court for a declaration that a named person is or was his parent or that he is the legitimate child of his parents.)

(h)   Where a finding of paternity has been made against the man alleged to be the father of the child in previous court proceedings (for example under s. 27, CSA 1991, discussed below or in proceedings for orders under sch. 1, CA 1989).

Where parentage is disputed and none of the above categories applies, s. 27(1) and (1A), CSA 1991 enables the Secretary of State or carer parent to apply to the family proceedings court, in the first instance, for a declaration of parentage. Such a declaration has effect only for the purposes of the CSA 1991.

The court may direct that scientific tests be undertaken to determine parentage, may draw **40.37** inferences from a refusal to undertake such tests and may consent to the carrying out of the testing on behalf of the child where the carer parent objects: s. 21(3), Family Law Reform Act 1969. The court must be satisfied that the tests are in the child's best interests.

The position of the unmarried mother

It will be recalled that where a carer parent is in receipt of income support or other specified **40.38** benefits, such a parent is treated as having applied for a maintenance calculation and the Secretary of State takes action to recover child maintenance from the non-resident parent: s. 6(1), CSA 1991.

If the carer parent requests the Child Support Agency (acting on behalf of the Secretary of **40.39** State) not to carry out a maintenance calculation, or fails to provide the Agency with information to trace and assess the liability of the non-resident parent, the carer parent's benefit may be reduced: s. 46, 1991 Act. This provision may be particularly important for the unmarried mother who may be unwilling to disclose the identity of the father of her child because of a history of violence in the relationship, or because of the risk that the father will wish to have contact with the child.

In these circumstances the carer parent is first offered an opportunity to explain her failure **40.40** to co-operate. If the child support officer considers that there are reasonable grounds for believing that the claimant or child would suffer harm or undue distress no further action will be taken. Where no reasonable grounds are established, the benefit will be reduced. The reduction may last for a period of three years.

F OWNERSHIP AND OCCUPATION OF PROPERTY

Ownership

40.41 The position relating to ownership of property and opposite sex or same sex cohabitants is discussed in Chapter 37.

40.42 Briefly, it should be recalled that there are no provisions akin to those found in s. 24, Matrimonial Causes Act 1973 to assist a cohabitant: he can only rely on the trust principles discussed in Chapter 37. The first step in advising a cohabitant on aspects of ownership is to check the title deeds to determine the extent to which ownership of legal and equitable interest in property is expressly dealt with there. In the absence of such express declaration the position is as follows. Where a cohabitant was engaged to be married, they may apply for a declaration of ownership under the terms of s. 17, Married Women's Property Act 1882.

40.43 Furthermore, where there is evidence that they made a substantial contribution to the improvement of the property, they may seek a share or enlarged share of the property because of that contribution (s. 37, Matrimonial Proceedings and Property Act 1970) provided that they were parties to an agreement to marry. Reliance on these provisions is permitted under s. 2(1) and (2), Law Reform (Miscellaneous Provisions) Act 1970.

40.44 It should be noted that a combination of ss. 66, 67, 68, and 74, Civil Partnership Act 2004 creates rights similar to those set out above for the benefit of either civil partners or parties to a civil partnership agreement.

40.45 However, where a cohabitant was neither engaged to be married nor a party to a civil partnership agreement he must apply to the court for a declaration of a resulting, implied, or constructive trust in his favour under s. 53(2), Law of Property Act 1925 and a sale under s. 14, Trusts of Land and Appointment of Trustees Act 1996.

Procedure

40.46 The procedure to pursue such an application is governed by the Civil Procedure Rules 1998.

40.47 The application is commenced by issuing a claim under Part 8 CPR (r. 8 Practice Direction 8) using the Part 8 claim form, N208. The Chancery Division of the High Court may be used or the county court for the area where the defendant lives or the property is situated.

40.48 Concise relevant details should be included on the claim form with a more detailed history set out in the supporting witness statement. The concise details should include, therefore, the declaration as to beneficial interest sought by the claimant (remembering that this may also relate to personal property and interests in endowment policies and the like), a declaration that Part 8 CPR 1998 applies to the claim and some details as to the legal basis of the claim (for example, contribution or detrimental reliance, if a declaration of a constructive trust is sought).

40.49 As for the contents of the witness statement, these should be as comprehensive as possible and separate headings are recommended in order to separate different aspects of the case and make it easier for the judge to locate relevant material.

It is suggested that the following matters should be dealt with in chronological order: **40.50**

(i) the background to the relationship;

(ii) the history of the acquisition of the asset(s);

(iii) the agreement or arrangement which the parties had as to ownership, including the reasons for a particular agreement and the words used in such discussions;

(iv) the financial arrangements between the parties both at the time of acquisition and subsequently;

(v) the contribution made both in money and money's worth as well as contribution to improvements to the property, if any;

(vi) details of acts of detriment and/or reliance on the conduct of the other party; and

(vii) concluding paragraph restating the remedies sought.

Once the claim form and witness statement have been filed at the court, the court will issue and seal the claim form and fix a date for directions.

Copies of the claim form, witness statement and notice of the directions hearing will be **40.51** served by the claimant's solicitor on the defendant who must file an acknowledgement of service in Form N210 within 14 days indicating whether he objects to the use of the Part 8 procedure, seeks a different remedy from that of the claimant or wishes to take part at any hearing. The defendant must serve any written evidence on which he wishes to rely with his acknowledgement of service. At the first directions hearing the case will be allocated to the multi-track and directions given for the future conduct of the case (for example, as to additional witness statements, valuations, and the like) with provision for a further case management conference prior to a final hearing, if necessary.

Transfer of tenancies

By virtue of sch. 7, Family Law Act 1996, as amended by sch. 9, para. 13, Civil Partnership **40.52** Act 2004, the court has power to make an order effecting the transfer of the following tenancies between opposite sex and same sex cohabitants whether or not they are joint tenants at any time after they cease to live together. The tenancies to which the Act applies are:

(a) a protected or statutory tenancy within the meaning of the Rent Act 1977;

(b) a statutory tenancy within the meaning of the Rent (Agriculture) Act 1976;

(c) a secure tenancy within the meaning of s. 79, Housing Act 1985;

(d) an assured tenancy or assured agricultural occupancy within the meaning of Part I of the Housing Act 1988.

The court may make the order in circumstances where one cohabitant is entitled to occupy the dwelling-house by virtue of a relevant tenancy and the cohabitants cease to live together. The order may be made at any time *after* the relationship comes to an end (sch. 7, para. 3).

The order may be made in respect of a dwelling-house which is or was a home in which they **40.53** cohabited (sch. 7, para. 4).

The criteria to be applied by the court in determining the application are discussed in **40.54**

Chapter 19. However, where only one cohabitant is a tenant, the court must have regard to the further matters set out in s. 36(6)(e)–(h) of the Act (see Chapter 25).

40.55   For the provisions in relation to compensation orders, see Chapter 19.

Occupation

40.56   It is crucial to appreciate that a cohabitant does not enjoy home rights such as are provided for parties to a marriage or registered civil partners under the Family Law Act 1996 with the provisions to register home rights so as to be effective against the claims of third parties.

40.57   The principal ways in which a cohabitant who is not solely and beneficially entitled to the property may remain in occupation are as follows:

(a) By obtaining an occupation order against the other party. It will be recalled that this is likely to be a temporary arrangement.

(b) By establishing a licence to occupy. It may be possible for the cohabitant to establish a contractual licence to occupy by pointing to the existence of all the elements necessary to create a valid contract the terms of which are sufficiently clear. Alternatively the court may declare the existence of a licence to occupy through application of the principles of equitable estoppel. This will arise where:

(i)   one partner has spent money or otherwise acted to his or her detriment;

(ii) there is a belief that he owned an interest in the property which justified the spending of money or that he would thereby obtain such an interest; and

(iii) the other partner actively encouraged that belief or took no steps to disabuse their partner of that belief.

(c) A beneficial interest is established in the proceeds of sale which carries with it a right to occupy: *Bull v Bull* [1955] 1 QB 234.

(d) There is a transfer of the property to the cohabitant, to be held for the benefit of a minor child, under sch. 1, CA 1989 (although note that property adjustment orders will not ordinarily be made under sch. 1 to provide benefits for the child after he has attained independence, unless there are exceptional circumstances: *A v A (A Minor: Financial Provision)* [1994] 1 FLR 657).

G   COHABITATION CONTRACTS

40.58   The proposition that cohabitants have fewer rights and less protection than parties to a marriage or civil partners is generally accepted. However, where cohabitants enter into a valid cohabitation contract they are likely to have the reassurance that the terms will be implemented. Hence, it could be argued that they enjoy more control over their financial affairs than is available to married couples or civil partners who face the court's discretion in ancillary relief proceedings. Indeed, even if matters are settled by a consent order, the terms are limited by the scope of the court's powers.

40.59   In what circumstances, therefore, will a cohabitation contract be valid and enforceable? This question was examined at length by Hart J in *Sutton* v *Mishcon de Reya and Gawor & Co* [2003] EWHC 3166.

In essence, the following principles must be observed to ensure that the contract will be **40.60** regarded as lawful and valid:

(i)   the parties must demonstrate an intention to create legal relations;

(ii) there should be no reference to the provision for payment for sexual services or relations (where there is no consideration as such, the terms should be incorporated in a deed);

(iii) the terms of the contract should be clear and unambiguous with financial terms being separated from non-financial ones; and

(iv) there must be nothing about the circumstances in which the contract was entered into which would lead to its being set aside (for example, because of evidence of duress, undue influence, or misrepresentation) arguably making essential the need for each party to receive independent legal advice before signing the document.

In its Consultation Paper (May 2006) (discussed at paragraph 40.62 and onwards), the Law **40.61** Commission has recommended that legislation should provide that cohabitation contracts dealing with property and financial matters are not contrary to public policy.

H   COHABITATION—THE FUTURE?

Following a request by the government, in May 2006 the Law Commission published its **40.62** Consultation Paper (No. 179) on cohabitation. Entitled Cohabitation: The Financial Consequences of Relationship Breakdown—A Consultation Paper, the document explores at length the options available to deal with various aspects of cohabitation breakdown, whether of opposite sex or same sex couples. The issues are also summarized in a separate Overview Consultation Paper.

A final Report containing recommendations for reform is due to be published in August **40.63** 2007.

While emphasizing that the Consultation Paper does not represent the final views of the Law **40.64** Commission, the Commission nevertheless has formed a provisional view on a number of important matters. These include, for example:

(i)   that there is a case for new remedies to be available on separation between couples who live together with children: the case is less convincing where no children are involved;

(ii) that the law governing the distribution of assets on divorce should not be extended wholesale to cohabitants (the principal reason for this view is that cohabitants have not entered into the mutual commitment which marriage—or indeed civil partnership—involves);

(iii) that any financial provision (it is expected that the court would have the same powers as in ancillary relief proceedings except that pension attachment orders would not be available) would be discretionary with no automatic entitlement even if the relationship had lasted for some time;

(iv) that any court scheme to deal with financial provision would focus on the parties' economic positions at the time of separation without conducting a lengthy examination of the history of the relationship. Emphasis would be placed on the need to identify any economic advantage which one party had retained arising from the contributions made by the other party during the relationship to be measured against the economic disadvantage which either party had suffered as a result of his or her contributions to the relationship or as a result of continuing child care responsibilities following separation;

(v) that cohabitants should not have an automatic entitlement to a share of their deceased cohabitant's estate on intestacy;

(vi) that cohabitants should be free to opt out of any statutory scheme.

40.65 Given the timescale indicated above, there will be inevitable delay before any reform in this area is in place.

PART X

YOUR PRACTICE

41

YOUR PRACTICE

A INTRODUCTION

Family law is an immense and diverse field of legal practice. Within it there are opportunities **41.01** for lawyers ranging from specialization within 'niche' fields to a more general career encompassing many, if not all, of the principal areas of family law.

This chapter is about starting a career in family law and about the resources, organizations, **41.02** and options that are available to a new practitioner.

Whatever aspect of family law you practice in you will quickly find that the work is **41.03** predominately 'people based'. Therefore a career in family law is about far more than a comprehensive knowledge of cases and statutes. The challenge lies in the application of the law to real-life situations. The good family lawyer is somebody who is able to win the confidence of his or her client through their knowledge of family law, their professional experience, and the ability to manage situations which may be fraught and emotional.

B   CAREER AVENUES

41.04   The main options for pursuing a career in family law are working as a solicitor, a legal executive, or as a barrister. This may be in either private practice, such as at a solicitors' firm or at the independent Bar, or 'in-house' as an employed lawyer working for organizations such as a local authority or within the civil service. It is difficult to generalize about each of these avenues but each certainly has its own character. As a family law solicitor you can expect to manage a large case load, have a lot of direct contact with your clients and appear frequently in court. You will however be an employee and therefore paid a monthly salary. As a barrister you will find yourself in court most days, often meeting the client for the first time shortly prior to the hearing. The challenge of court room advocacy can be very exciting but, if you are at the independent Bar, it is sometimes difficult to manage the workload and cash flow!

41.05   When considering the options open to you, there is nothing better than direct experience of what each has to offer. Therefore, approach solicitors' firms or barristers' chambers for work experience (called 'placements' or 'mini-pupillages' respectively). Only by doing this can somebody considering a career in family law gain an informed understanding of the realities of such work and which particular avenue is for you.

C   LIBRARY AND RESEARCH MATERIAL

Law reports

41.06   The two principal sets of reports are the Family Law Reports and the Family Court Reporter. Many solicitors' firms and barristers' chambers will have copies of these in their libraries. The Family Law Reports are now also available on-line.

Textbooks

41.07   There are a number of key practitioners' books which are essential in practice.

41.08   The first is the *Family Court Practice* (often known as the 'Red Book'). This is published by Family Law each year and contains all of the relevant statutes, rules, and Practice Directions with accompanying notes. It also contains a section of useful procedural guides for all of the various types of proceedings and applications within the subject.

41.09   If you are working in the field of child law, the principal practitioners' text is Hershman and McFarlane's *Children Law and Practice*. It provides a detailed commentary on all aspects of child law, both private, public, and international and is of particular use where more complex questions of law arise. This is currently a three-volume loose leaf edition and is often held in the libraries of barristers' chambers and solicitors' firms. Another very useful book in the field of child law is John Mitchell's *Children Act Private Law Proceedings: A Handbook*, which is also published by Family Law.

41.10   If your area of practice is ancillary relief, there are a number of useful text books which you may wish to use. Duckworth's *Matrimonial Property and Finance* is a one-volume loose leaf edition published by Family Law. It is a compendious and detailed reference book which is usefully aimed at day-to-day practice in this field. A simpler, shorter, and cheaper option is Roger Bird's *Ancillary Relief Handbook* (published by Family Law) which provides a clear and helpful guide. Most practitioners working in this field use *At a Glance* which is a manual, published annually, of useful tables such as mortgage costs, exchange rates, and a list of all of the leading cases. This is supplemented by 'At e-glance' which is provided on a CD-Rom format for an annual subscription. You may wish to also consider Resolution's book of precedents which is invaluable when drafting orders in ancillary relief proceedings.

The main book on divorce law is *Rayden and Jackson on Divorce*. This is an extremely detailed and thorough book which, again, is often held in practitioners' libraries. **41.11**

Practitioners' text books tend to be relatively expensive and, for a few years at least, you may find that borrowing a colleague's copy or at least sharing a book between a number of colleagues is a cost-effective way of accessing this material. It is, however, worth knowing that legal publishers often have stalls at family law conferences and tend to provide a significant reduction in the sale price of their books if you buy the book there and then! You may also be able to persuade them that a further reduction is appropriate given your junior status. **41.12**

Electronic resources

A number of the practitioners' texts (including the Red Book) are also available on CD-Rom. These are useful if your practice tends to be 'desk-based' and provides an opportunity to make searches under particular topics. **41.13**

As mentioned above, many of the law reports (including the Family Law Reports) are available on-line for an annual subscription. Another digital tool to mention is Lawtel which provides reports of many cases (both reported and unreported) as well as many other helpful resources. **41.14**

While annual subscriptions for electronic resources tend to be fairly expensive (unless you can negotiate a 'deal' involving a number of your other colleagues), there are numerous other free websites providing a great deal of useful information. Perhaps the most useful is the British and Irish Legal Information Institute (<www.bailii.org>) which provides a portal to collections of all recent statutes, statutory instruments, and case law of the Family Division of the High Court, the Court of Appeal, and the House of Lords. Other very useful sites are Delia Venables' Legal Resources (<www.venables.co.uk>) and Family Law Week (<www.familylawweek.co.uk>). **41.15**

Journals

The most helpful and widely used is Family Law. This is a monthly journal which contains recent law reports and a selection of varied articles. Many of the more general legal journals such as the New Law Journal and Law Society Gazette will often contain articles and law reports relevant to family law. **41.16**

D   FAMILY LAW ASSOCIATIONS

41.17   There are a number of well-established organizations and associations which exist in the field of family law. Resolution is the new name for the Solicitors' Family Law Association. This provides a code of practice, a database of members, publications, and events. For those in practice at the Bar, the Family Law Bar Association is well worth joining. It provides a very informative newsletter as well as a yearly conference and various training and social events.

E   CONTINUING PROFESSIONAL DEVELOPMENT (CPD)

41.18   Both the Law Society, ILEX, and the Bar Council require practitioners to undertake continuing professional development. This usually takes the form of a certain number of training hours during each year. There are numerous commercial organizations which offer such training, usually at a considerable cost. You may wish however to look out for free or modestly priced events which often take the form of lectures or talks where CPD points are available. Many of the events organized by the various family law associations are accredited with CPD points.

F   VOLUNTARY WORK

41.19   You may wish to consider undertaking some voluntary advice work (often called 'pro bono' work). This is not normally something that can be done until you are professionally qualified but, once you are, it can be very rewarding. It is sometimes possible to become involved in voluntary organizations as an assistant prior to qualification and this can help a student to develop useful practical experience. There are many voluntary organizations that provide free legal advice in family law. The largest and best known is the Citizens Advice Bureau (see <www.citizensadvice.org.uk>), but there are also many other smaller groups. Your local library is probably the best place to find out more about what is available in your area.

INDEX

Page numbers are used for copies of forms and documents and paragraph numbers for text